The Letters of Queen Victoria

A Selection From
Her Majesty's Correspondence
Between the Years 1837 and 1861
Volume 3 of 3 —1854-1861

H.M. QUEEN VICTORIA, H.R.H. THE PRINCE CONSORT, AND CHILDREN

From the picture by F. Winterhalter at Buckingham Palace

by

Queen of Great Britain Victoria

Printed on acid free ANSI archival quality paper.

Contents

INTRODUCTORY NOTE
TO CHAPTER XXIII

At the meeting of Parliament, on the 31st of January 1854, the Ministry were able triumphantly to refute the charge of illegitimate interference in State affairs which had been made by a section of the Press against Prince Albert; they were, however, severely attacked for not acting with greater vigour in Eastern affairs. In February, the Russian Ambassador left London, the Guards were despatched to the East, and the Russian Government was peremptorily called upon by Great Britain and France to evacuate the Principalities. The Peace Party, Bright, Cobden, and others, were active, but unheeded; the Society of Friends sending a pacific but futile deputation to the Czar. In March, the demand for evacuation being disregarded, war was declared, and a treaty of alliance signed between England and France; Lord Raglan and Marshal St Arnaud were appointed to command the respective armies, Vice-Admiral Sir James Dundas and Sir Charles Napier having command of the Mediterranean and Baltic Fleets respectively. The attitude of Austria was ambiguous, and, after England and France were committed to war, she contracted an offensive and defensive alliance with Prussia, each country engaging to make limited preparations for war. At home, with a view to greater efficiency, the duties of the Secretary of State for War and the Colonies, till then united in a single Secretaryship, were divided, the Duke of Newcastle assuming the former office, while Sir George Grey became Colonial Secretary; Lord John Russell also resumed office as President of the Council. The Russians were unsuccessful in their operations against the Turks, notably at Silistria and Giurgevo, while, as the summer advanced, public opinion in support of an invasion of the Crimea rose steadily, the *Times* indicated the taking of Sebastopol as indispensable, and Lord Aberdeen's hand was forced. On the 28th of June, the Cabinet sanctioned a despatch to Lord Raglan, urging (almost to the point of directing) an immediate attack upon Sebastopol; the French Emperor was in favour of the plan, though both Commanders-in-Chief entertained doubt as to whether it was immediately feasible. On the 7th of September, the allied forces (58,000 strong) sailed from Varna, a landing being effected a few days later at Old Fort, near Eupatoria; at about the same time an important interview took place at Boulogne between Prince Albert and the Emperor Napoleon. The signal victory at the Alma, on the 20th of September, was followed by the death of St Arnaud, and the appointment of Canrobert as his successor. Decisive successes were next obtained at Balaklava on the 25th of October, and at Inkerman on the 5th of November; but on the 14th a fierce gale did immense damage to life and property, both at Balaklava and on the sea. Meanwhile, indignation at home was aroused by the tidings of the breakdown of the commissariat and transport departments, and the deplorable state of the hospitals; Miss Florence Nightingale, who had sailed from England with a number of nurses, arrived at Scutari early in November, and proceeded to remedy deficiencies as far as possible; while Lord John Russell vainly urged on the Premier the substitution of Lord Palmerston for the Duke of Newcastle as Secretary for War. Sir Charles Napier, who, previously to his departure with the Baltic Fleet, had been fêted at the Reform Club, and extravagantly lauded by Cabinet Ministers, was by the month of October engaged in a recriminatory correspondence with the First Lord of the Admiralty. At about the same time the Patriotic Fund was established under the presidency of Prince Albert.

In Parliament, the last vestige of the old Navigation System, limiting the coasting trade to British ships, was repealed, and a Bill also passed for preventing corrupt practices at elections. Owing to the war, the Reform Bill was withdrawn, Lord John Russell, on announcing the fact in Parliament, being overcome, and giving way to tears. In the short session, which took place during the latter half of December, a Foreign Enlistment Act was passed, providing for a force of 10,000 foreigners, to be drilled in this country.

The Exhibition Building, which had been constructed in Hyde Park in 1851, and had been re-erected at Sydenham, was opened with great ceremony by the Queen, and was henceforth known as the Crystal Palace.

CHAPTER XXIII

1854

The Earl of Aberdeen to Queen Victoria.

London, *6th January 1854.*

Lord Aberdeen presents his humble duty to your Majesty. He cannot wonder at the indignation expressed by your Majesty at the base and infamous attacks made upon the Prince during the last two or three weeks in some of the daily papers.[1] They are chiefly to be found in those papers which represent ultra-Tory or extreme Radical opinions; but they are not sanctioned by the most respectable portion of the Press. Lord Aberdeen has received some information respecting the origin of these attacks; but it is vague and uncertain. At all events he believes that your Majesty may safely make yourself at ease upon the subject, as he is satisfied that these hostile feelings are shared by few. It is much to be desired that some notice of the subject may be taken in Parliament, when, by being treated in a proper manner, it may be effectually stopped. Lord Aberdeen has spoken to Lord John Russell, who will be quite prepared to moot it in the House of Commons.

It cannot be denied that the position of the Prince is somewhat anomalous, and has not been specially provided for by the Constitution; but the ties of Nature, and the dictates of common sense are more powerful than Constitutional fictions; and Lord Aberdeen can only say that he has always considered it an inestimable blessing that your Majesty should possess so able, so zealous, and so disinterested an adviser. It is true that your Ministers are alone responsible for the conduct of public affairs, and although there is no man in England whose opinion Lord Aberdeen would more highly respect and value, still if he had the misfortune of differing from His Royal Highness, he would not hesitate to act according to his own convictions, and a sense of what was due to your Majesty's service.

The Prince has now been so long before the eyes of the whole country, his conduct so invariably devoted to the public good, and his life so perfectly inattackable, that Lord Aberdeen has not the slightest apprehension of any serious consequences arising from these contemptible exhibitions of malevolence and faction.

Your Majesty will graciously pardon Lord Aberdeen for writing thus plainly; but there are occasions on which he almost forgets your Majesty's station, and only remembers those feelings which are common to all ranks of mankind.

Footnote 1: A section of the Press, favourable to Lord Palmerston, had insinuated that his resignation was due to "an influence behind the throne." Similar attacks were made by other journals, and not abandoned upon Lord Palmerston's re-admission to the Cabinet: the most extravagant charges of improper interference in State affairs were made against the Prince, and it was even rumoured that he had been impeached for high treason and committed to the Tower! The cartoons in *Punch* usually present a faithful reflection of current popular opinion, and in one of them the Prince was depicted as skating, in defiance of warning, over dangerous ice.

Queen Victoria to the Earl of Clarendon.

PERSIA

Windsor Castle, *9th January 1854.*

The Queen thanks Lord Clarendon for his letter just received with the enclosures.

As the proposed answer to the Emperor contains perhaps necessarily only a repetition of what the Queen wrote in her former letter,[1] she inclines to the opinion that it will be best to defer any answer for the present—the more so, as a moment might possibly arrive when it would be of advantage to be able to write and to refer to the Emperor's last letter.

With respect to the Persian Expedition[2] the Queen will not object to it—as the Cabinet appears to have fully considered the matter, but she must say that she does not much like it in a moral point of view.

---

[1] See *ante*, vol. ii

[2] Under the belief that Persia had declared war against Turkey, and that diplomatic relations between England and Persia were suspended, the Cabinet had agreed upon the occupation of the Island of Karak by a British force.

We are just putting the Emperor of Russia under the ban for trying "to bring the Sultan to his senses" by the occupation of part of his territory after a diplomatic rupture, and are now going to do exactly the same thing to the Shah of Persia!

The King of the Belgians to Queen Victoria.

Laeken, *9th January 1854.*

My dearest Victoria,—I wrote you a most abominable scrawl on Friday, and think myself justified in boring you with a few words to-day.

The plot is thickening in every direction, and we may expect a great confusion. The dear old Duke used to say "You cannot have a little war." The great politicians of the Press think differently. The Duke told me also once: "At the place where you are you will always have the power to force people to go to war." I have used that power to *avoid* complications, and I still think, blessed are the peacemakers.

How the Emperor could get himself and everybody else into this infernal scrape is quite incomprehensible; the more so as I remain convinced that he did not aim at conquest. We have very mild weather, and though you liked the cold, still for every purpose we must prefer warmth. Many hundred boats with coal are frozen up, and I am told that near two hundred ships are wanting to arrive at Antwerp....

I am much plagued also by little parliamentary nonsense of our own here, a storm in a bottle; this is the way of human kind, and in such cases it always pleases me to think that I am not bound to be always their working slave, and I cast a sly look at my beautiful villa on the Lake of Como, *quite furnished....* My beloved Victoria. Your devoted Uncle.

Leopold R.

The King of the Belgians to Queen Victoria.

THE PRESS

Laeken, *13th January 1854.*

My beloved Victoria,—I grieve to see how unjustly you are plagued, and how wonderfully untrue and passionate are the attacks of part of the Press. Abuse is somewhat the *staff of life in England*, everything, everybody is to be abused; it is a pity, as nothing more unproductive as this everlasting abuse can well be imagined. As nothing ever gave the slightest opening to this abuse, it is to be hoped that it will be soon got over—the meeting of Parliament will now do good in this respect. As far as your few continental relations are concerned, I don't think they will be able to fix anything upon your faithful servant. I have done England at all times good services, in the sense of her best interests. I hold a position of great geographical importance for England, just opposite the mouth of the Thames. Successes of vanity I am never fishing for in England, nor anywhere else. The only influence I may exercise is to prevent mischief where I can, which occasionally succeeds; if war can be avoided, and the same ends obtained, it is natural *that* that *should be tried first*. Many English superficial newspaper politicians imagine that threatening is the thing—I believe it the worst of all systems. The Emperor Nicholas and Menschikoff wanted by threatening the Turks to get certain things, and they have by that means got a very troublesome and expensive affair on their hands. I wish England too well to like to see it, but one of these days they will get into some scrape in the same way. The foolish accusation that we are doing all we can to break up the French Alliance is certainly the *most absurd of all*; if anything can be for our local advantage, it is to see England and France closely allied, and for a long period—for ever I should say....

THE FRENCH ALLIANCE

I have heard, and that from the Prussian Quarter, that great efforts are making on the part of Russia, to *gain over* Louis Napoleon. I understand, however, that though Louis Napoleon is *not* anxious for war, that his opinion is favourable to the continuation of a good understanding with England. That it should be so is, I must say, highly desirable. The poor Orleans will be grieved and hurt by all these things. The death of the child of the poor Queen of Spain will not be a favourable omen for Spain.[3]...

With my best love to Albert. Believe me ever, my beloved Victoria, your truly devoted Uncle,

Leopold R.

Queen Victoria to the Earl of Aberdeen.

THE ORLEANS FAMILY

[3] A daughter had been born to the Queen of Spain on the 5th of January, and lived only three days.

Windsor Castle, *16th January 1854.*

The Queen sends the answer she has this morning received from the Duc de Nemours, which she hopes is on the whole satisfactory as regards the reported visit of the Count de Chambord.[4] The Duke does not see in so strong a light as *we* do, the danger of even the *report* being believed—probably from living so much out of the world as he does. What would Lord Aberdeen wish her to do farther, and what does he think can be done in the way of contradiction? The Queen wishes likewise to have Lord Aberdeen's opinion and advice on the following subjects. He knows that we have invariably received the poor Orleans family (in particular our own near relations, the Nemours) from time to time *here* and in London, and that the Queen has *always* from the first year done this *openly* but *unostentatiously*. It is by *no means* her intention to change her conduct in this respect—but since the great noise caused by the "fusion" she thought it better *not* to invite the Nemours either to Osborne or here, hoping that by *this time* these tiresome rumours would have ceased. They have not, however, and we think that perhaps it would be wiser *not* to see them here, *at any rate* till after the meeting of Parliament, though it is very painful to the Queen to hurt their feelings by apparent neglect. Is Lord Aberdeen of this opinion, and does he think that it will *not* be misconstrued into an *admission* of having encouraged *intrigues* or of *submission* to the will and pleasure of Louis Napoleon?

For the Queen would never submit to such an accusation, nor would she continue (after the excitement is past) to exclude these poor exiles from occasional visits—which have been paid and received ever since *'48*, and which would be unworthy and ungenerous conduct.

Likewise does Lord Aberdeen think that a morning visit to the Duchess of Aumale to enquire after her health would be imprudent?

It goes much against the Queen's feelings of generosity and kindness to neglect the poor exiles as she has done this winter, but the present moment is one of *unparalleled* excitement and of great political importance, which requires great prudence and circumspection. There is an admirable article in the *Morning Chronicle* of to-day, taking quite the *right line* upon the infamous and *now* almost ridiculous

---

[4] Son of the Duc de Berri, and known formerly as the Duc de Bordeaux. (See *ante*, vol. i.) The Duc de Nemours denied all knowledge of the rumoured visit, and thought its importance had been exaggerated.

attacks on the *Queen* and Prince. Has Lord Aberdeen any idea who could have written it?

The Queen sends a letter she had received from her Uncle, which may amuse and interest him. To make the statement of the Queen's intercourse with the Orleans family quite clear, she should add, that when the family visit the Queen or she visits them, that it is put into the Court Circular, and this of course gets copied into country papers and foreign papers; but after consideration the Queen thought this the wiser course, for with all the spies who are no doubt about—if this were not done, and the Queen's visits and *vice versâ* were suppressed and *yet* found out—it would give them an air of *mystery* which is just what we wish to avoid.

The Earl of Aberdeen to Queen Victoria.

London, *17th January 1854.*

... With respect to your Majesty's custom of seeing the French Royal Family, Lord Aberdeen humbly thinks that there is no good reason for making any change. It has always taken place without parade or ostentation; and knowing, as Lord Aberdeen does, that no political object is in view, he would feel ashamed to advise your Majesty to do anything at variance with that sympathy which your Majesty has been careful to keep within the bounds of prudence and moderation....

Lord Aberdeen hopes that he may venture to congratulate your Majesty on the commencement of a change with respect to the newspaper attacks upon the Prince. He observed the article, to which your Majesty refers, in the *Morning Chronicle* of yesterday; and he believes he may certainly say that it was written by Mr Gladstone, although he would not wish it to be known. There was also a very sensible letter in the *Standard* of last night, signed D. C. L. This is the signature always assumed by Mr Alexander Hope,[5] in his contributions to the Press, and Lord Aberdeen does not doubt that it is written by him. It is only a wonder to find it in such a quarter; and it shows some disposition on the part of that scurrilous paper to alter its course. There is perhaps no great objection to the papers dealing with the subject as they think proper, before the meeting of Parliament, provided the *Times* takes no part at present; for as this paper is supposed to be influenced by the

[5] Mr. A. J. Hope (afterwards Beresford-Hope), at this time out of Parliament, had written over the signature "D.C.L." a series of letters to the Press on the Papal claims.

Government, this belief would injure the effect of anything that might appear in its columns.[6]...

Queen Victoria to Lord John Russell.

THE REFORM BILL

Windsor Castle, *21st January 1854.*

The Queen has received Lord John Russell's letter of the 19th, and the Bill as now agreed upon by the Cabinet, which she hopes may meet the wishes of the Country and pass into law.[7] From what she understands the chief argument used in opposition to the measure will be, that corruption and bribery is the evil which the Country really complains of, and not an unequal distribution of the representation, and that a new distribution or even extension of the franchise will not touch the evil, and may be said perhaps in some instances to tend towards increasing it. The success of the measure will therefore, she concludes, in some degree depend upon the Bribery Bills which will accompany it. How far are these advanced? and what expectation has Lord John Russell of succeeding in framing such a measure as would remove that ground of objection to the Reform Bill?

Queen Victoria to Mr Gladstone.

Windsor Castle, *7th February 1854.*

The Queen must apologise for having kept the enclosed papers so long, and in now sending them back she does so without feeling sure in her mind that she could with safety sanction Mr Gladstone's new

---

[6] On the re-assembling of Parliament, the charges against the Prince were at once refuted by the Prime Minister and Lord John Russell; and his right to assist the Queen completely established by those Ministers, with the concurrence of Lord Derby and Mr Walpole, on behalf of the Opposition, and Lord Campbell, the Chief Justice of the Queen's Bench.

[7] Notwithstanding the impending war, the Government considered itself bound in honour to bring in a Reform Bill. Lord Palmerston and his special supporters were opposed to the project, but the measure was brought forward on the 13th of February. After a chequered career it was withdrawn. The Bill for the prevention of corrupt practices at elections was introduced on the 10th of February, and after many vicissitudes and several Ministerial defeats in the Commons as well as in the Lords, it was, in a modified form, carried.

and important proposal.[8] The change it implies will be very great in principle and irretrievable, and the Queen must say that Lord John Russell's apprehensions as to the spirit it is likely to engender amongst the future civil servants of the Crown have excited a similar feeling in her mind. Where is moreover the application of the principle of public competition to stop, if once established? and must not those offices which are to be exempted from it necessarily degrade the persons appointed to them in public estimation?

Sir James Graham to Queen Victoria.

THE BALTIC COMMAND

Admiralty, *9th February 1854.*

Sir James Graham, with humble duty, begs to lay before your Majesty certain important considerations which were discussed at the Cabinet yesterday with respect to the selection of a Commander-in-Chief for the Fleet about to be appointed for Service in the Baltic.[9]...

Lord Dundonald[10] is seventy-nine years of age; and though his energies and faculties are unbroken, and though, with his accustomed courage, he volunteers for the Service, yet, on the whole, there is reason to apprehend that he might deeply commit the Force under his command in some desperate enterprise, where the chances of success would not countervail the risk of failure and of the fatal consequences, which might ensue. Age has not abated the adventurous spirit of this gallant officer, which no authority could restrain; and being uncontrollable it might lead to most unfortunate results. The Cabinet, on the most careful review of the entire question, decided that the appointment of Lord Dundonald was not expedient....

---

[8] Mr Gladstone had written on the 26th of January on the subject of competitive examinations for the Civil Service; in reply to the Queen's letter, he referred to the discontent existing in the Service with the system of appointment by favour, and of promotion by seniority alone.

[9] War had not yet been declared, but the Russian Ambassador left London on the 7th of February, and Sir Hamilton Seymour was recalled from St Petersburg on the same day.

[10] This was the Lord Cochrane who had been unjustly convicted in 1814, under the direction of Lord Ellenborough, Chief Justice, of conspiracy to defraud. His naval honours were restored to him in 1832. He is said to have stipulated, on this occasion, that he should be allowed to destroy Cronstadt by a chemical process invented by himself.

SIR CHARLES NAPIER

Sir Charles Napier is an excellent seaman, and combines boldness with discretion.[11] He has served in large squadrons, and he has commanded them. As a Second, he may not have been submissive; as a Chief, he has been successful in command. His appointment will give confidence both to officers and men; and his name is not unknown both to enemies and allies. If he has the faults of his family, he is not without their virtues; courage, genius, love of country are not wanting; and the weighty responsibilities of high command, without oppressing him, would give steadiness to his demeanour.

He behaved ill to Lord John Russell and to Sir Francis Baring; and on shore he has given just cause of complaint; but at sea and in command he is a different person; and Lord John Russell in the Cabinet yesterday, regardless of all former displeasure, pronounced an opinion favourable to the appointment of Sir Charles Napier. Lord Aberdeen, also, together with the entire Cabinet, came to the same conclusion; and Sir James Graham on their behalf, and in concurrence with his own opinion, ventures to ask the permission of your Majesty to appoint Sir Charles Napier to this important Naval command.[12]

The above is humbly submitted by your Majesty's dutiful Subject and Servant,

J. R. G. Graham.

Queen Victoria to Mr Gladstone.

Buckingham Palace, *17th February 1854.*

The Queen has received Mr Gladstone's letter and memorandum, and had heard from the Prince the further explanation of the grounds upon which he, Mr Gladstone, thinks the new regulations respecting the Civil Service necessary. The Queen, although not without considerable misgivings, sanctions the proposed plan, trusting that Mr Gladstone will do what he can, in the arrangements of the details of it,

---

[11] He had had a long naval career. In 1833 he commanded the Portuguese Fleet for Donna Maria, and won a small engagement against Dom Miguel. He was "not submissive" at Beyrout, where, having command of the land forces, and being told to retire and hand over the command, he advanced and won a victory, resulting in the evacuation of the city. He also disobeyed orders at Acre.

[12] The inadequate results of an appointment which promised so well are described in Parker's *Sir James Graham*, vol. ii. pp. 229 *et seq.*

to guard against the dangers, which she has pointed out in her former letter and through the Prince when he saw Mr Gladstone. A check, for instance, would be necessary upon the admission of candidates to compete for employment, securing that they should be otherwise eligible, besides the display of knowledge which they may exhibit under examination. Without this a young man might be very ineligible, and still after having been proclaimed to the world as first in ability, it would require very strong evidence of misconduct to justify his exclusion by the Government.

Mr Gladstone to Queen Victoria.

COMPETITIVE EXAMINATIONS

Downing Street, *17th February 1854.*

The Chancellor of the Exchequer presents his humble duty to your Majesty, and has the honour to acknowledge your Majesty's gracious letter.

He takes blame to himself for having caused your Majesty trouble by omitting to include in his short memorandum an explanation of the phrase "qualified persons."

Experience at the universities and public schools of this country has shown that in a large majority of cases the test of open examination is also an effectual test of character; as, except in very remarkable cases, the previous industry and self-denial, which proficiency evinces, are rarely separated from general habits of virtue.

But he humbly assures your Majesty that the utmost pains will be taken to provide not only for the majority but for all cases, by the strictest enquiries of which the case will admit; and he has the most confident belief that the securities for character under the system, although they cannot be unerring, will be stronger and more trustworthy than any of which the present method of appointment is susceptible.

Queen Victoria to the King of the Belgians.

Buckingham Palace, *21st February 1854.*

My dearest Uncle,— ... War is, I fear, *quite* inevitable. You will have seen that the Emperor Nicholas has not given a favourable answer to *our Brother* Napoleon (which I hear has disappointed him extremely, as he expected very great results from it); and the last proposals or attempts made by Buol[13] it is to be hoped will not be accepted by Russia, for France and England could *not* accept them; but if Austria and Prussia go with us—as we hope they will—the War will only be a local one. Our beautiful Guards sail to-morrow. Albert inspected them yesterday. George is quite delighted to have a division....

I must now conclude, with Albert's affectionate love. Believe me always, your devoted Niece,

Victoria R.

Queen Victoria to the Earl of Aberdeen.

THE BRITISH ARMY

Buckingham Palace, *24th February 1854.*

The Queen must write to Lord Aberdeen on a subject which at this moment appears to her of paramount importance—viz., the augmentation of the Army. The ten thousand men by which it has been ordered to be augmented can hardly be considered to have brought it up to more than an improved Peace *establishment*, such as we have often had during profound peace in Europe; but even these ten thousand men are not yet obtained. We have nearly pledged ourselves to sending twenty-five thousand men to the East, and this pledge will have to be redeemed. To keep even such a force up in the field will require a strong, available reserve at home, of which we shall be quite denuded. But we are going to make war upon Russia! encouraging Austria and Prussia to do so likewise, whereby we assume a moral obligation not to leave them without assistance. We engage in a War which may assume in its course a totally different character from that of its beginning. Who can say it is impossible that our own shores may be threatened by powers now in alliance with us? We are powerless for offence or defence without a *trained* Army; to obtain this will require considerable time. The Queen must, therefore, urge Lord Aberdeen to consider with the Cabinet whether it will not be essential to augment the Army at once, and by at least thirty thousand men. Considerations of home policy make this also advisable; the country is eager for War at this moment, and ready to grant men and money. It will be a great facility hereafter to have obtained what is most needed at first. If the force should finally not be wanted, retrenchments may

[13] Austrian Premier and Minister of Foreign Affairs.

very easily be made. The Crown should at least have the power of raising the men without the necessity for further application to Parliament.

The Earl of Aberdeen to Queen Victoria.

THE BRITISH ULTIMATUM

London, *26th February 1854.*

Lord Aberdeen, with his humble duty, begs to inform your Majesty that another Cabinet was held to-day, in order to consider the draft of a letter which it is proposed that Lord Clarendon should address to Count Nesselrode, and in which he should summon the Russian Government to evacuate the Principalities. The messenger will be directed to wait six days for an answer, and the British Government will consider the refusal or the silence of Count Nesselrode as equivalent to a declaration of War, and proceed to act accordingly.[14]

An assurance has been received, in general terms, of the intention of Austria to support this demand; and a telegraphic message has been sent to Vienna with a desire to know whether the Austrian Government will join in this summons, or in what manner support will be given.[15] No answer has yet been received, and Lord Aberdeen would think it right not to make the summons until Austria has declared her intention; but the Cabinet appears to desire that the letter should be sent to-morrow evening.

The period fixed for the complete evacuation of the Principalities is the 30th of April.

As it cannot be supposed that the Emperor of Russia will listen to such a demand as this, immediate hostilities must be expected, with all their consequences.

---

[14] This summons to evacuate the Principalities, and an ultimatum to a similar purport from Paris, were delivered to the Czar on the 14th of March; on their receipt the Czar intimated that he did not think it fitting (*convenable*) that he should make any reply. His decision was known in London on the 24th.

[15] The attitude of Austria caused great perplexity. Count Orloff had gone to Vienna to obtain a pledge of neutrality in the event of war, but refused to give the Emperor Francis Joseph satisfactory assurances as to the Czar's future policy, and, in particular, as to the evacuation of the Principalities at the close of the war. The Austrian Government accordingly announced its intention of acting as circumstances might dictate, but subsequently limited the assistance which it now expressed itself willing to give to England and France in insisting upon the evacuation, to diplomatic support.

Queen Victoria to the Earl of Aberdeen.

Buckingham Palace, *26th February 1854.*

The Queen has received Lord Aberdeen's letter of this day.

To be able to form a judgment on the important question to which it refers, the Queen would require to be furnished with the exact terms of "the general assurance" which Austria has given with respect to it. The Queen, however, does not doubt for a moment that the gain of a day or two in making the summons to Russia could not be compared to the advantage of being able to make the summons conjointly with Austria. She must therefore wish that the answer to the telegraphic message should be awaited before the messenger is sent off.

Queen Victoria to the King of the Belgians.

DEPARTURE OF THE GUARDS

Buckingham Palace, *28th February 1854.*

My dearest Uncle,— ... The news from Austria are quite excellent, and much more than we had any reason to expect. It will make a great difference in the nature and duration of the War. Our summons to Russia went last night *viâ* Paris, Berlin, and Vienna, and if they are received either with silence, or the Emperor refuses to evacuate the Principalities—*War* will be considered as declared. The French send a similar summons. The messenger is to wait *six* days for an answer, but no longer.

The last battalion of the Guards (Scots Fusiliers) embarked today. They passed through the courtyard here at seven o'clock this morning. We stood on the balcony to see them—the morning fine, the sun rising over the towers of old Westminster Abbey—and an immense crowd collected to see these fine men, and cheering them immensely as they with difficulty marched along. They formed line, presented arms, and then cheered us *very heartily*, and went off cheering. It was a *touching and beautiful* sight; many sorrowing friends were there, and one saw the shake of many a hand. My best wishes and prayers will be with them all....

Queen Victoria to the Earl of Aberdeen.

[*Undated.*]

The Queen was rather annoyed at the manner in which Lord Clarendon pressed the Duke of Cambridge's going to the Tuileries last night.[16] She thought it an immense boon upon her part to allow the Duke of Cambridge *to go to Paris*—and instead of its being considered as such by Lord Clarendon and Count Walewski, the Queen was told it would offend the Emperor if the Duke did not go to the Tuileries also. The Queen observed that it was unnecessary and unusual for the Duke, or any Prince almost, to live at the *Palace* of the Sovereign, unless he was a very particular friend or near relation. The Duke of Genoa had refused going there, though he had received other civilities here; in the same manner *no Prince* comes to this *Palace* unless he is a very *near relation* or particular friend. To this Lord Clarendon replied that it was "because the *Emperor wished* it," which rather shocked the Queen, and she spoke *strongly* to him upon the subject. The result was that the Queen said she would speak to the Duke of Cambridge about it, and see, as the Emperor made *so great a point of it*, and Lord Clarendon considered that the *Alliance depended upon it*, what he would do....

The Queen must and *will* protest, for she cannot mix up personal friendship with a political Alliance. The former is the *result* of the *experience* of years of mutual friendship, and cannot be *carried by storm*....

There would be nothing unusual in apartments being offered to the Duke of Cambridge, and declined by him. This was done by the King of the Belgians only last summer at Berlin and Vienna, without anybody's construing it into an affront. The Queen adds a list of the Royal personages who have been in England and never resided at the Palace. Lord Aberdeen may show this letter to Lord Clarendon.

Queen Victoria to Lord John Russell.

STABILITY OF THE GOVERNMENT

Buckingham Palace, *1st March 1854.*

The Queen has to acknowledge Lord John Russell's letter of this morning. Much as she must regret the postponement of the second reading of the Reform Bill, she must admit its wisdom under the present peculiar circumstances;[17] but she doubts the advantage of naming

---

[16] The Duke was going to the Crimea, and it was arranged that he should stop at Paris on the way.

[17] See the Queen's letter of the 4th of March, *post.*

a precise day after Easter on which it is to come on. Considering the *importance* to the country of *preserving* the present Government and of not allowing it to be beat on so vital a question, the opportunity should not be lost of ascertaining the state of feeling both in the House of Commons and in the country after the reassembling of Parliament, before the Government decide on entering upon the struggle which the carrying through of the measure might entail. It is quite impossible *now* to conjecture with certainty what that state of feeling and the general political circumstances at home and abroad may be at that time. Possibly the country may be more eager *then for* the measure—or the War may *disincline* it *altogether* towards it.

The Queen seizes this opportunity of expressing her sense of the *imperative importance* of the Cabinet being *united* and of one mind at this moment, and not to let it *appear* that there are differences of opinion within it. The knowledge that there are such is a cause of great *anxiety* to the Queen, at a time when she is to enter upon a European War, of which nobody can confidently predict the extent.

Queen Victoria to the Earl of Aberdeen.

Buckingham Palace, *2nd February (? March) 1854.*

In returning these letters to Lord Aberdeen the Queen must express to him that there are *hints* in them which give her great uneasiness. The stability of this Government is not only of *paramount importance* at the *commencement* of the War, but throughout it; the moment for negotiation may arrive much sooner than we now expect—and *then*, more than *now even*, the Government ought to be composed of the *ablest and most moderate* men which this Country can produce.

Queen Victoria to Lord John Russell.

Buckingham Palace, *4th March 1854.*

The Queen thanks Lord John Russell for his letter received this morning. She has read the proceedings in the House of Commons with much interest.[18] She was particularly pleased with Lord John's second

---

[18] Lord John Russell had announced the decision of the Government to postpone till the 27th of April the second reading of the Reform Bill, and, in reply to some sarcastic comments from Mr Disraeli, stated that he would be ashamed of himself if he preferred anything connected with his own personal

speech, in which he affirmed the principle that public men ought not to oppose the regard for personal honour or reputation to the well-understood interests of the Country. Indeed, the Queen cannot conceive the possibility of their collision, as an exclusive regard for the well-understood interests of the Country must always redound to the honour and reputation of a Statesman.

Queen Victoria to the King of the Belgians.

THE BALTIC FLEET

Osborne, *14th March 1854.*

My dearest Uncle,—Your kind letter of the 9th arrived here on Saturday just when we returned from a splendid and never-to-be-forgotten sight—the sailing of our noble Fleet for the Baltic;[19] the Navy and Nation were particularly pleased at *my leading them out*, as they call it, which in fact was the case, as, in our little *Fairy* we went on and lay to, to see them all come out, which (the wind being fair) they did, with sails set, each passing us close by, and giving us three hearty cheers, as I think none but British tars *can* give. Gloriously they bore along, followed by the prayers and good wishes of all. You should read the account in yesterday's *Times*. Another sailing squadron goes to-morrow. The Captains and Admirals all took leave on board, and seemed much impressed with the solemnity of the moment.... Ever your truly devoted Niece,

Victoria R.

Queen Victoria to the King of Prussia.

THE KING OF PRUSSIA

/Translation./

Osborne, *17th March 1854.*

Dear Sir and Brother,—General Count von der Gröben has brought me the official letter of your Majesty, as well as the confidential one,[20] and I send your kind messenger back, with these two

---

reputation to the interest of the country. He added that the security of the country depended upon its confidence in the character of public men.

[19] The Fleet, under Sir Charles Napier, had been assembled at Spithead.

[20] The Prussian Court considered itself under no obligation to engage in the impending struggle, till its own interests became directly involved; it would

answers to you. He will be able to tell you, orally, what I can express only imperfectly in writing, how deep my pain is, after our going so far, faithfully, hand in hand, to see you, at this weighty moment, separating yourself from us. My pain is still further increased by the fact that I cannot even conceive the grounds which move your Majesty to take this step.

The most recent Russian proposals came as an answer to the *last* attempt for an understanding which the Powers believed could be arrived at honourably, and they have been rejected by the Vienna Conference, not because they were not in accordance with the literal wording of the programme, but because they were contrary to the intention of it. Your Majesty's Ambassador has taken part in this Conference and its decision, and when your Majesty now says: "The task of Diplomacy ceases at the exact point where that of the Sovereigns emphatically begins"; I am unable to assent to such a definition. For what my Ambassador does, he does in my name, and I feel myself not only bound in honour thereby, but also placed under an obligation to take upon myself the *consequences* which the step which he is directed to take may lead to.

The dreadful and incalculable consequences of a War weigh upon my heart not less than on your Majesty's. I also know that the Emperor of Russia does not wish for it. He, none the less, demands from the Porte things which all the Powers of Europe—among them, yourself—have solemnly declared to be incompatible with the independence of the Porte, and the European balance of power. In view of this declaration and of the presence of the Russian Army of invasion in the Principalities, the Powers could not but be ready to confirm their word by action. If "the Turk" now goes into the background, and if the approaching War appears to you as a "War of tendency" this is the case only because the very motives which may induce the Emperor to insist on his demands—in defiance of the opposition of the whole of Europe, and with the danger of a War that may devastate the world, do betray a *distinct tendency*, and because the grave consequences of the War must appear much more momentous than the original ostensible cause of it, which at first appeared only as the request for a key to the back door of a mosque.

---

not (said Baron Manteuffel, President of the Ministry, on the 18th of March) take part, for the protection of the integrity of the Ottoman Empire, "in a conflict, the full scope of which cannot yet be apprehended, and the original subject matter of which does not affect the interests of our fatherland."

Your Majesty asks me "to examine the question in a spirit of love for peace, and even now to build a bridge for the Imperial honour." Ah, my dear Sir and Brother, all the inventive gifts, all the architecture of diplomacy and of goodwill, have been uselessly wasted during these last nine months in this bridge-building! The *Projets de Notes, de Conventions, de Protocoles*, etc., etc., have proceeded, by the dozen, from the Chancelleries of the different Powers, and one might call the ink wasted on them another Black Sea. But everything has been shipwrecked against the self-will of your honourable brother-in-law.

PRUSSIAN NEUTRALITY

If now your Majesty informs me "*that now you mean to persist in complete neutrality*," and if, on this occasion, you refer us to your Nation, who are said to exclaim with sound common sense: "Acts of violence have been done by the Turks, the Turk has good friends in large numbers, and the Emperor has done us no harm"—I do not understand you. Certainly I should understand this language if I heard it from the Kings of Hanover or of Saxony. But I have, hitherto, looked upon Prussia as one of the Great Powers which, since the peace of 1815, have been guarantors of treaties, guardians of civilisation, defenders of the right, the real arbiters of the Nations; and for my part I have felt the divine responsibility of this sacred office, without undervaluing at the same time the heavy obligation, not unconnected with danger, which it imposes on me. If you, dear Sir and Brother, abdicate these obligations, you have also abdicated that position for Prussia. And should such an example find imitators, then the civilisation of Europe would be delivered up to the play of winds; right will then no longer find a champion, the oppressed will find no longer an umpire.

Let not your Majesty believe that what has been said in this letter is aimed at persuading you to change your resolves; it flows from the affectionate heart of a sister, who could not pardon herself, were she not, at so weighty a moment, to let you see into her inmost soul. So little is it my intention to desire to win you over to our view, that nothing has grieved me more than the suspicion, expressed in your name by General von der Gröben, that England had desired to seduce you from your purpose by opening a prospect of advantages to be gained. The baselessness of such a supposition is evident from the Treaty itself which had been offered to you, and whose most important clause consisted in the promise of the contracting parties, *not to desire in any case to derive from the War any advantage for themselves*.

Your Majesty could not have given a more powerful proof of your unselfishness than by the very fact of attaching your signature to this Treaty.

WAR DECLARED

To come to a close. You suppose that War may already have been declared; you express, however, at the same time, the hope that it may not already have actually broken out. I cannot unfortunately hold out any hope that the sentence will be followed by any stay of execution. Shakespeare's words:

"Beware

Of entrance to a quarrel; but, being in,

Bear it that the opposer may beware of thee,"

are deeply engraved on the hearts of all Englishmen. Sad that they are to find an application at this crisis, in a nation with whom previously nothing prevailed but friendship and affection! And how much more melancholy must be the present emotions of your Majesty's heart and mind to see such words applied to a beloved brother-in-law, whom yet—however much you love him—your conscience cannot absolve from the crime of having brought upon the world wilfully and frivolously such awful misery!

May the Almighty take you under His protection!

With Albert's most cordial compliments, and our united greetings to the dear Queen, I remain, my much honoured Sir and Brother, your Majesty's faithful Sister and Friend,

Victoria R.[21]

Queen Victoria to the Earl of Aberdeen.

1st April 1854.

The Queen rejoices to see the Debate was favourable in the House of Lords, and that it was concluded in the House of Commons.[22]

---

[21] The King afterwards agreed to the proposed protocol for the preservation of the integrity of Turkey, which was signed at Vienna on the 7th of April.

[22] On the 27th of March the Queen announced to Parliament that the negotiations with the Czar had terminated, and that she felt bound "to afford active assistance to her ally, the Sultan." Next day the Declaration of War was issued, containing a narrative of the events which finally led to the rupture. The debates on the Address in answer to the message took place on the 31st of

She is rather startled at seeing Lord Aberdeen's answer to Lord Roden upon the subject of a day of humiliation, as he has never mentioned the subject to her, and it is one upon which she feels strongly. The only thing the Queen ever heard about it was from the Duke of Newcastle, who suggested the *possibility* of an *appropriate* prayer being introduced into the Liturgy, in which the Queen quite agreed; but he was strongly against a day of humiliation, in which the Queen also entirely agreed, as she thinks we have recourse to them far too often, and they thereby lose their effect. The Queen therefore hopes that this will be reconsidered carefully, and a *prayer* substituted for the *day of humiliation*. Were the services selected for these days of a different kind to what they are—the Queen would feel less strongly about it; but they always select chapters from the Old Testament and Psalms which are so totally inapplicable that it does away with all the effect it ought to have. Moreover, really to say (as we probably should) that the *great sinfulness of the nation* has brought about this War, when it is the selfishness and ambition of *one* man and his servants who have brought this about, while our conduct has been throughout actuated by unselfishness and honesty, would be too manifestly repulsive to the feelings of every one, and would be a mere act of hypocrisy. Let there be a prayer expressive of our great thankfulness for the benefits we have enjoyed, and for the immense prosperity of this country, and entreating God's help and protection in the coming struggle. In this the Queen would join heart and soul. If there is to be a day set apart, let it be for prayer in this sense.

Queen Victoria to Lord John Russell.

THE REFORM QUESTION

Buckingham Palace, *9th April 1854.*

The Queen is anxious to express to Lord John Russell the extreme satisfaction she experiences at the communication Lord Aberdeen yesterday evening made her of the settlement of the Reform Question, viz., of its postponement for the present Session, with the understanding that it is to be brought forward again whenever the state of affairs

March, Mr Bright, in the Commons, censuring the declaration, and being replied to by Lord Palmerston. The addresses were presented to the Queen on the 3rd of April.

will admit of its being fairly and calmly considered by Parliament.[23] The sacrifice of personal feeling which no doubt this may cost Lord John will, she is certain, be amply compensated by the conviction that he has done so for the interest and tranquillity of his Sovereign and Country, to whom a dissolution of the present Government would have been a source of immense danger and evil.

Lord John Russell to Queen Victoria.

DISSENSION IN THE CABINET

Pembroke Lodge, *9th April 1854.*

Lord John Russell presents his humble duty to your Majesty; he cannot think it consistent with fairness to conceal from your Majesty the deep feelings of mortification which affect him on reviewing the proceedings of the Cabinet yesterday.[24]

Lord Aberdeen was the only person who behaved with due regard to the honour of the Administration. The rest appeared ready to sacrifice everything in order to keep the Ministry together; and Lord John Russell feels bound to warn your Majesty that, although he was quite willing to waive the consideration of the Reform Bill for the present

---

[23] From a memorandum, made by Prince Albert, of interviews with Lord Aberdeen, it appears that before the Cabinet of the 8th of April Lord Palmerston declared that under neither present nor any future conditions could he vote for the second reading of the Reform Bill. Lord John thereupon tendered his resignation; this Lord Aberdeen asked him to suspend until after the meeting of the Cabinet.

[24] Lord John Russell's actions at this period of his career seem often incomprehensible; but his private domestic anxieties seem to have weighed him down. Having made the great sacrifice, for an ex-Premier, of taking office under an old opponent, he was now engaged in trying to regain the first place for himself. Lord Aberdeen had always contemplated retiring in his favour, but would not give up the Premiership in the face of the dangers threatening the country. Moreover, he had believed his continuance in office to be a guarantee for peace. Lord John Russell, after accepting the Foreign Office, had then insisted on being a Minister without office; later still, by displacing Mr Strutt and transferring Lord Granville to the Duchy, he himself became Lord President of the Council, an office which no commoner had held since the reign of Henry VIII. By such action, coupled with perpetual threats of resignation, he marred his prospects of succeeding Lord Aberdeen, and, as will be seen, failed in his attempt to construct an Administration when the opportunity was offered him.

Session, he is not ready to consent that it shall be entirely set aside in order to keep together a Ministry whose continuance would be dearly bought at the price of the welfare of the Country, and the consistency of public men. Lord John Russell must reflect further on this subject before he comes to a final determination.

LORD JOHN RUSSELL

Queen Victoria to Lord John Russell.

Buckingham Palace, *10th April 1854.*

The Queen received Lord John Russell's letter last night. She is much grieved that he should be "affected by deep feelings of mortification on reviewing the proceedings of the Cabinet." From all the Queen had heard of the views of the different members of the Cabinet, she believes them to have been fully convinced that the present moment would be inopportune to press the Reform Bill, but *quite* prepared to take it up again on the first fitting opportunity; she, of course, does *not* speak of Lord Palmerston.

The Queen would, no more than Lord John, wish to see "the Reform Bill set aside in order to keep together a Ministry," but does not consider the decision of the Cabinet at all to imply this, whatever Lord Palmerston's personal wishes may be, and trusts that the Country will fully understand and appreciate the motives which have guided the Government. Lord Aberdeen and Lord John will always receive every support from the Queen when they shall think it right to propose the re-introduction of the measure.

Memorandum by the Prince Albert.

LORD JOHN RUSSELL

Buckingham Palace, *10th April 1854.*

Lord Aberdeen has just left the Queen, after an interview which he had had with Sir James Graham and Lord John Russell at Lord John's request. He reported that at that interview Lord John renewed his complaint of the Cabinet, declared that he could not state to the House what was untrue, and must therefore resign. Lord Aberdeen called this "really too monstrous" after the pledge given by the Sovereign, himself as Prime Minister, and the whole Cabinet, with the exception of one man, and he would repeat his promise that whenever

Lord John said, "The Reform Bill is to come on," and Lord Palmerston opposed it, he should go.

Lord John could not be appeased, but spoke with the greatest bitterness. He had written to Lord Palmerston in the same sense; and Lord Palmerston's answer arrived during the interview. It was to the effect that if one of them was to resign, it was not Lord John, who agreed with the rest of the Cabinet upon the Bill, but himself, who was the dissentient. Lord Aberdeen asked Lord John whether Lord Palmerston's resignation would satisfy him; to which he answered, he believed it would not mend matters. Lord Aberdeen's opinion, however, is that it is what Lord John, and still more what Lady John, wants. He thinks the Country will never understand how the Government could break up, and that Lord John is cutting his own throat, and told him so. If Lord John went, he could not go on with Lord Palmerston as Leader of the House of Commons, which he called "perfectly ludicrous." Lord Palmerston would probably insist upon this, however; Lord Palmerston's retirement would be a great blow to the Government, as the Country persisted in thinking him the only able War Minister, and would cry out at "the imbecile old Head of the Government having it now all his own way." He thought, should he not be able to go on, new combinations could be formed, perhaps under the Duke of Newcastle and Mr Gladstone, as the Country liked younger men. Lord John must give his answer in the House of Commons to-morrow at half-past four. Lord Aberdeen would wish to see the Duke of Newcastle, Sir James Graham, and Mr Gladstone, as his more particular friends, this evening, to discuss the whole question with them, and would see Lord Palmerston and Lord John to-morrow, before he could make any report to the Queen.

This is all really very bad!

Albert.

Lord John Russell to Queen Victoria.

Chesham Place, *11th April 1854.*

Lord John Russell presents his humble duty to your Majesty; he has the honour to acknowledge, with gratitude, your Majesty's communication of yesterday. Lord John Russell waited to see Lord Aberdeen before he answered, and having now had a long conversation with him, Lord John Russell being assured of your Majesty's support, of Lord Aberdeen's concurrence, and of the assent of the majority of his colleagues, is willing to continue his humble services in the Cabinet, and in the House of Commons.

Lord John Russell must ask your Majesty to excuse what may have seemed intemperate in his letter of Sunday last. He is still of opinion that without public confidence in his integrity and uprightness he can be of no use to your Majesty, or to the Country.

And on that confidence must depend the continuance of his services.[25]

Memorandum by the Prince Albert.

Buckingham Palace, *11th April 1854.*

We saw Lord Aberdeen at three o'clock to-day, who reported to the Queen that the change of mind of Lord John had been the result of an hour and a half's discussion with him this morning. He must admit, however, that he found Lord John in a mood willing to let himself be convinced. The Queen's letter might have contributed to this as well as the entreaties of the Duke of Bedford and Lord Lansdowne. Lord Aberdeen could tell Lord John in truth that there was not a shadow of difference of opinion amongst any of his friends, that he would lose himself for ever, and meet with universal reprobation, if he persisted in resigning after every cause for it had been removed, and he had agreed to the course Lord Palmerston had insisted upon. Lord Palmerston had written a very clever letter to Lord John, begging him not to desert the Queen and the Country, which, if he read it to the House of Commons, would floor Lord John completely.

We asked what had been agreed upon at yesterday evening's meeting. Lord Aberdeen told us the decision, under the impression that Lord John would resign, had been for Lord Aberdeen to call upon Lord Palmerston, and to explain to him that although he had acted cordially with him as a Colleague in this Government, yet they had been political antagonists during their whole lives—the Government also was still a Reform Government; from personal, therefore, as well as

---

[25] On the same day Lord John announced in the Commons the withdrawal of the Reform Bill. He admitted that this course would expose him to the taunts and sarcasms of his opponents, and to the suspicions of his supporters. Here "his feelings overcame him, and, as he used the word 'suspicion' in reference to his motive, his utterance was choked, and the sentence he struggled to pronounce was evidently given through tears." (*Ann. Reg.*, 1854, p. 120.) Loud and sympathetic cheers followed from all parts of the House.

public, reasons it was impossible that he should be entrusted with the lead of the House of Commons, being the only anti-Reformer. And it was hoped that he would have no difficulty in letting Mr Gladstone lead the House, as Sir James Graham was the same age and political standing with Lord Palmerston, but at once cheerfully contented to waive all his claims in favour of Mr Gladstone.

Albert.

The Duke of Cambridge to Queen Victoria.[26]

THE DUKE OF CAMBRIDGE

Vienna, *28th April 1854.*

My dear Cousin,—Before leaving this place I think it right that I should once more trouble you with a letter, to informTHE EMPEROR OF AUSTRIA you that the messenger has arrived who brought your autograph letter for the Emperor, which I presented to him to-day at an audience I had for this purpose.... I had a very long and most interesting conversation with the Emperor, who opened frankly and fairly upon the great questions of the day. The impression he made upon me was an excellent one, his confidence and frankness are complete, and I have the firm conviction that he is a man of his word, and that he never would say a thing that he did not in his heart mean. The result of what he said was the following: that he naturally was most distressed at all that had occurred; that he was placed by the Emperor of Russia in a most difficult position; that he quite disapproved his acts; but that he could not but have a great disinclination to break with a very old ally; and that even still he hoped this painful step might be spared to him by the Emperor of Russia making some proposal so honourable to all parties, that it would not be rejected by the Western Powers, who would naturally not be disinclined to a peace, honourable to themselves and tranquillising for the future; that the basis of such treaty would be the position of the Christian population of the East; that this might be discussed in Conference, the Russians having *first* evacuated the Principalities, upon which the Turks would hold the right bank of

[26] The English forces destined for the East were under the command of Lord Raglan (formerly Lord Fitzroy Somerset). The Duke of Cambridge commanded one infantry division, the other three being respectively under Sir George Brown, Sir De Lacy Evans, and Sir Richard England; the cavalry division was commanded by the Earl of Lucan, General Scarlett commanding the heavy cavalry, and Lord Cardigan the Light Brigade.

the Danube, our Fleets to await events in the Bosphorus, and our armies at Constantinople, such position being highly honourable and advantageous to us in the eyes of Europe, and certainly not nearly so favourable to Russia; that he was certainly sensible that the English Government had not pressed him, feeling as they had done the extreme delicacy of his position, and the great extent of his frontier so easily attacked; that he did not wish to say now, till the moment of decision came, thinking it more honourable and straightforward not to raise false expectations, but that his interests being so completely with us, should the Emperor of Russia do nothing in the honourable direction he hoped to see him adopt, he should then consider himself called upon to express frankly to us what he proposed to do, in order that our action might become united and of advantage to one another. He further thought that the treaty with Prussia would greatly facilitate all this, as Prussia had acceded to the wishes of Austria in the event of certain eventualities, which, however, for the moment are not named, but which, as far as I understand, go to the length of leaving Austria unfettered to act as she likes at the moment when she considers her so doing essential to her position as a young Empire. It is quite evident to me that this is the general feeling here, amongst all those who have any weight in the councils of the Empire. These are *Austrian* views, and I must say I can understand them and appreciate them as such. I am confident, I am certain, they are *honest* on the part of the Emperor, and I doubt not he will carry them through to the letter, for I am confident the Emperor never would say what he did not mean. Rely upon it, this Country will never go with Russia; she knows her interests too well for that; she would like to avoid a War altogether if she could, and with that view she would be delighted to see some honourable and acceptable proposal made, but should this fail she will then take a very decided line, and that line will be in accordance with Austrian interests—which means with us. I find that most of the more prudent people, and many of those in high office, are fully alive to the advantages of the English alliance, and would wish to see this alliance confirmed *de novo*; and I think it would be very well for us to meet them half-way with this. But then it would be better to avoid all after-dinner speeches such as those at the Reform Club,[27] all Polish legions

[27] At a dinner given on the 7th of March by the Reform Club to Sir Charles Napier, Lord Palmerston, who was in the chair, and Sir James Graham, had made provocative and unbecoming speeches; on attention being called in Parliament to the proceedings, Mr Bright complained of the reckless levity

such as are talked of, and in short any of these little matters, which are painfully felt here, and which always produce an uncomfortable and distrustful effect. The Emperor expressed himself in the most grateful manner towards yourself, and I think is pleased at your having permitted me to be present on this occasion.... Hoping that you will approve of my humble endeavours here, and with sincere regards to Albert, I beg to remain, my dear Cousin, your most dutiful Cousin,

George.

Queen Victoria to the King of the Belgians.

BOMBARDMENT OF ODESSA

Buckingham Palace, *9th May 1854.*

My dearest Uncle,—Accept my best thanks for your kind letter of the 5th. I return you the Emperor's kind letter. Nothing could be more satisfactory than the reception George met with by everybody at Vienna—beginning with the Emperor. They showed him much confidence, and he obtained from them intelligence which I think no one else would. The Fleets have done their duty admirably at Odessa;[28] the town has not been touched, and all the fortifications and many ships have been destroyed....

We had a concert last night, and I saw good Sir H. Seymour, who is full of your kindness and goodness; and a most worthy, honourable and courageous little man he is.[29] If the poor Emperor Nicholas had had a few such—*nous ne serions pas où nous en sommes*. But unfortunately the Emperor does *not like* being *told* what is unpleasant and

---

displayed; Lord Palmerston made a flippant and undignified defence, the tone of which was much resented.

[28] In consequence of the Russians firing upon a flag of truce, Odessa was bombarded on the 22nd of April, and most of its batteries silenced or destroyed.

[29] The conversations of Sir Hamilton Seymour and the Emperor Nicholas in the year 1853 had now been given to the world. The Czar, believing the time ripe for the dismemberment of Turkey, had expressed himself openly to the British Ambassador, and the conversations were all reported to the British Ministry. On the 2nd of March 1854, an obviously inspired article in the *Journal de St. Pétersbourg* professed to contradict the statements of Lord John Russell in the House of Commons reflecting on the bad faith of the Russian Government, and accordingly, in their own vindication, the English Cabinet now published the conversations above referred to.

contrary to *his wishes*, and gets very violent when he hears the *real* truth—which *consequently* is not told him! There is the misery of being violent and passionate; if Princes and still more Kings and Emperors are so, *no* one will *ever* tell them the truth, and *how* dreadful that is! I think one never can be too careful in bringing up Princes to inculcate the principle of *self-control.*

We have a good deal of rain and thunder since yesterday, which I hope will revive poor parched Nature. I must now wish you good-bye, as I expect dear Victoire shortly. Nemours intends going to fetch the Queen. With Albert's love, ever your devoted Niece,

Victoria R.

The Duke of Cambridge to Queen Victoria.

THE SULTAN

Constantinople, *13th May 1854.*

My dear Cousin,—I have not as yet announced to you my safe arrival here, as I was anxious first to see the Sultan and the general state of things before giving you a report of what was really going on....

THE BRITISH FORCES

I found a great proportion of the Infantry arrived, a portion of the Artillery, but as yet no Cavalry. Lord Raglan is well and in good spirits, Lord Stratford de Redcliffe ill in bed with a bad fit of the gout—most miserable to see in every respect. The Sultan[30] received me at once on the day of arrival, and made his return visit to me yesterday. I confess I was not much impressed with either his appearance or general ability. He is, to say the truth, a wretched creature, prematurely aged, and having nothing whatever to say for himself. A few commonplace civilities was all the conversation which passed between us. I said everything I could think of to make a conversation, among other things messages of civility from yourself; but though he appeared pleased and expressed his satisfaction at our being here, I could not get him to enter into anything, and I was not sorry on both occasions when our interview was at an end. As to his Ministers, and in fact the whole population and country, with the exception of Redschid Pasha,[31] they are all a most wretched and miserable set of people, and far, far worse

[30] Abdul Medjid, born 1823, who had succeeded to the throne at the time of the Syrian War; see *ante*, vol. i.

[31] Minister of Foreign Affairs, born 1802, died 1858.

than anything I could possibly have imagined or supposed. In fact, the "sick man" is *excessively sick indeed*, dying as fast as possible; and the sooner diplomacy disposes of him the better, for no earthly power can save him, that is very evident. This is the opinion of every person out here of both armies, French and English, and you may rest assured it is the truth. The great thing is that we are here and no other Power can now step in, but diplomacy must settle what is to happen, for as to the Turks remaining in Europe that is out of the question, and the very fact of our being here now has given them their death-blow. I hope, my dear cousin, you will forgive me for being very candid on this point, but I really do not think that anybody in England had any idea of the real state of affairs here. The sooner therefore that they are put in possession of the truth unvarnished the better. The great and imperative necessity is that the four Powers of Europe should strike together, otherwise things will become much worse than they are even at present. Everybody is very civil and obliging to me, the Sultan has put me into one of his best Palaces, very nicely fitted up, and is anxious to do everything I wish. I find it inconvenient, as the troops are on the other side of the Bosphorus, and I therefore intend going over there to reside if possible. Marshal St Arnaud is here and Prince Napoleon, but no French troops. I have seen the latter once; he was very civil indeed to me, but I do not think he has made at all a good impression here, his manner being offensive and harsh. I do not think the Army like him at all. I am afraid the French Ambassador is giving much trouble. Neither St Arnaud nor the Prince like him at all, and I believe they have written to demand his recall, which would be a very good thing, as he cannot hit it off with anybody. As to our movements, I know nothing of them as yet, nor do I think that much has as yet been settled, but I fear we shall not be fit to move for some time; the difficulty of transport is very great, our Artillery only partly arrived, and no Cavalry. We require more troops, more particularly of the latter arm, in which the Russians are very strong. We ought to have at least 10,000 men more, and the sooner they are sent out the better. Even that number is not enough, for the French talk of 100,000 men, and we should be in a most dreadful minority unless we had 40,000 to 50,000. I am afraid all this will alarm people in England, but it is the truth.... I remain, my dear Cousin, your most dutiful Cousin,

George.

We never hear any news here. All that does come to us generally comes by way of Europe; another proof of what a miserable country this is.

The King of Prussia to Queen Victoria.

THE KING OF PRUSSIA

/Translation./

Sans Souci, *24th May 1854.*

Most gracious Queen,— ... My policy,[32] which has been so terribly criticised and derided as "vacillating," has been, since the beginning of this most inauspicious conflict, one and the same, and *without a hairsbreadth of deviation* either to the right or to the left. As it rests on the unshakable foundation which my conscience as a King and a Christian has laid down, and which does not admit *que je fasse la besogne ni de l'un ni de l'autre parti*, I am abused and insulted at the Winter Palace, and regarded, by way of contrast in London and Paris, as a kind of simpleton—neither of which is pleasant.

May your Majesty believe my Royal Word: I was, I am, I remain the truest and most faithful friend of Great Britain, as well in principle as from religious feeling and from true affection. I desire and practise a good and honest understanding with France; but when it comes to helping the French—to whom Prussia's geographical position between Paris and Warsaw is very inconvenient—to pull the *chestnuts from the fire* for them, for such a task I am frankly too good. If the Emperor wishes to force me to assist—as evidently he is inclined to do—it will end by becoming too difficult for him. He ought to thank God that my view of Russian policy and my fidelity to your Majesty have prevented me from making him begin this *Turkish* War on the *other side of his own frontier*. The great advantage of this result is totally forgotten in France, and, unfortunately, in England too. Those who every day fill the papers of home and foreign countries with accounts of my vacillations, nay, who represent me as leaping from my own horse on to a Russian one, are inventing lies, in a great measure, deliberately. I tell your Majesty, on my honour and conscience, that my policy is to-day *the same* as it was nine months ago. I have recognised it as my duty before God to preserve, for my people and my provinces, peace, *because I recognise Peace as a blessing and War as a curse*. I cannot

[32] In the previous portion of this long letter, here omitted, the King gives a detailed account of his position and policy.

and will not side with Russia, because Russia's arrogance and wickedness have caused this *horrible* trouble, and because duty and conscience and tradition forbid me to draw the sword against Old England. In the same degree duty and conscience forbid me to make unprovoked war against Russia, because Russia, so far, has done me no harm. So I thought, so I willed when I thought myself isolated. How then could I now suddenly abandon a steady policy, preserved in the face of many dangers, and incline to Russia at the moment when I have concluded with Austria an Alliance defensive and offensive, in which (if God grant His blessing) the whole of Germany will join in a few days, thus welding, for the entire duration of the War, the whole of Central Europe into a Unity, comprising 72,000,000 people, and easily able to put 1,000,000 men into the field? And yet, most gracious Queen, I do not take up a defiant position on the strength of this enormous power, but I trust in the Lord's help and my own sacred Right; I also believe, honestly and firmly, that the character of a so-called Great Power must justify itself, *not by swimming with the current*, but *by standing firm like a rock in the sea.*

I close this letter which, in consequence of various interruptions, is almost a week old, on the 24th of May. This is your birthday, ever dearest, most gracious Queen. On this day I lay at your Majesty's feet the expression of my wishes for every blessing. May God grant your Majesty a joyful day, and a richly blessed year of rule. May He strengthen, preserve, and invigorate your precious health, and may He give you, within the three hundred and sixty-five days of the year of your life which begins to-day, *that* one day of overabundant blessing, of unspeakable joy, for which I long, for which I pray to God—*that blissful day on which you can utter the word* Peace.

Now I beg your Majesty from the bottom of my heart not to be angry with me for my unconscionably long letter, nor to worry yourself about sending an answer, but, on the other hand, graciously to keep it secret, communicating it only to the dear Prince. It is a matter of course that the facts which it contains, and the resulting explanations, which may be of importance for your Majesty's Government, must, from their nature, no longer be kept secret, so soon as you think it right to announce them. I embrace the dear Prince tenderly, and commend myself to the grace, goodwill, and friendship of my august Royal Sister, I being your Majesty's most faithfully devoted, most attached Servant and Good Brother,

Frederic William.

Queen Victoria to the Duke of Newcastle.

MARSHAL ST ARNAUD

Osborne, *29th May 1854.*

The Queen acknowledges the receipt of the Duke of Newcastle's letter, which she received quite early this morning.

The Duke of Cambridge's letter does *not* give a flourishing account of the state of Turkey. What alarms the Queen most is the news given by the Duke of Newcastle of the pretensions of Marshal St Arnaud.[33] She does not quite understand whether he has received the supreme command over the Turkish Army, but at any rate if the Porte should be willing to allow its Army to be placed under Foreign Command, a portion of it ought to be claimed by us for Lord Raglan, which, joined to his English forces, would produce an Army capable of taking the field independently.

The Queen trusts that the Government will take this into serious consideration, and, if they should concur in this view, that no time will be lost.

Queen Victoria to the King of Prussia.

THE QUEEN'S REPLY

/Translation./

Buckingham Palace, *June 1854.*

Dearest Sir and Brother,—Your faithful Bunsen has handed me your Majesty's long explanatory letter, and has taken his leave of us,[34] with tears in his eyes, and I can assure your Majesty that I, too, see with pain the departure of one whom I have been accustomed to consider as the faithful mirror of your feelings, wishes, and views, and whose depth and warmth of heart I esteem no less highly than his high mental gifts. Sympathy with his fate is general here. I entirely recognise in your letter the expression of your friendship, which is so dear

[33] The Duke had written to say that a demand had been made by Marshal St Arnaud upon the Porte that Omar Pasha should be superseded, and the Turkish Army placed under his (St Arnaud's) orders; also that Marshal St Arnaud was desirous of assuming the supreme command of the allied forces. The incident is graphically recorded by Mr Kinglake.

[34] The influence of Russia over the King had been proved by the recall of Baron Bunsen, and the dismissal of all those Ministers who had opposed the policy of the Czar in Turkey.

to me, and which does not admit any sort of misunderstanding to exist between us, without my endeavouring at once to clear it up and remove it. How could I meet your friendship otherwise than by equally absolute frankness, allowing you to look into my inmost heart! Though you have shown me a proof of your gracious confidence in giving me, down to the smallest detail, an account of your personal and business relations with your servants, I still believe that I have no right to formulate any judgment. Only one thing my heart bids me to express, viz., that the men with whom you have broken were faithful, veracious servants, warmly devoted to you, and that just by the freedom and independence of spirit, with which they have expressed their opinions to your Majesty, *they have given an indisputable proof* of having had in view, not their own personal advantage and the favour of their Sovereign, but his true interests and welfare alone; and if just such men as these—among them even your loving brother, a thoroughly noble and chivalrous Prince, standing next to the throne—find themselves forced, in a grave crisis, to turn away from you, this is a *momentous sign*, which might well give cause to your Majesty to take counsel with yourself, and to examine with anxious care, whether perhaps the hidden cause of past and future evils may not lie in your Majesty's own views?[35] You complain, most honoured Sire and Brother, that your policy is blamed as *vacillating*, and that your own person is insulted at home and abroad (a thing which has often filled me with *deep grief and indignation*), and you asseverate that your policy rests upon a firm basis, which the conscience of "a King and a Christian has laid down for it." But should it be possible to discover in your Majesty's fundamental views something self-contradictory, then necessarily, the more consistently and conscientiously these fundamental views are revealed in their consequences, the more contradictory must your actions appear to those who are not intimately aware of your intentions, and cannot but force upon the world the impression that your views themselves were wavering.

You will not take it amiss in a true friend and sister, if she endeavours to place before you her impressions on this matter, as frankly as they appear to her.

INVASION OF THE PRINCIPALITIES

[35] The Prince of Prussia had shown his dissatisfaction with the King's policy by quitting Berlin.

Your Majesty has acknowledged in the face of the world that Russia has addressed to the Porte demands which she had no right to make. You have further acknowledged that the forcible taking possession of two Turkish provinces with the intention of enforcing the demand was a political wrong. You have, together with Austria, France, and England, several times declared in Protocols the preservation of the integrity of the Turkish empire to be a European interest. Notwithstanding all this, Russia continues to occupy the Danube principalities, penetrates further into Turkey, and, by forcing on a sanguinary and exhausting war, leads the unhappy and *suffering* empire on to the brink of the grave. What should Europe then do under these circumstances?

It could not possibly be the intention of the Powers to declare the preservation and integrity of the Porte to be a matter of European concern, solely in order to allow that empire to be destroyed before their very eyes! As to Prussia, I can conceive a line of policy, not that indeed which I should think in harmony with the generosity and chivalry of your rule, but still one possible in itself, by which she would say to herself: "The preservation of this integrity I have indeed declared to be a matter of European concern, but I wish to leave England and France to defend that policy with their wealth and blood, and reserve to myself only a *moral* co-operation." But what am I to think if, after England and France with courageous readiness have taken upon themselves alone this immense responsibility, sacrifice, and danger, your Majesty is now mainly considering the erection of a barrier of 72,000,000 of men between them and that Power, against whose encroachment the European interest is to be defended? What am I to say to the threat uttered against the *West* as well as against the *East?* and to your even asking from the West gratitude for "the enormous advantage" that you do not, into the bargain, yourself join in attacking it!! For your Majesty says expressly in your letter: "The Emperor ought to thank God that my view of Russian policy, my *fidelity* to your Majesty, have prevented me from making him begin the Turkish war on the other side of his own frontier. The enormous advantage of this abstention is totally forgotten in France, and, unfortunately, in England too!"

Dearest Sir and Brother, this language shows a contradiction in your own mind, which fills me with the greatest anxiety for possible consequences, an anxiety not diminished by your kindly adding:

"Duty, Conscience, and Tradition forbid you to draw the sword against Old England."

I shall gladly with you bless the day on which the word of Peace can be uttered. Your Majesty can, by vigorous co-operation, help to usher in that day, just as you might have—in my conviction—contributed, by vigorous co-operation to prevent the War altogether.

FRIENDLY RELATIONS

Whatever these troublous times may bring us, I harbour the firm confidence that the warmth of our friendly relations cannot be troubled by anything, and rejoice in the circumstance that the personal relations of the two Sovereigns are, in this matter, so entirely in harmony with the interests of the two nations.

Albert sends you his homage, and I remain, with most cordial remembrance to the dear Queen, and with thanks for the kind wishes expressed by both of you, ever your Majesty's faithful Sister and Friend,

Victoria R.

Minute of Interview by the Prince Albert.

THE WAR OFFICE

Buckingham Palace, *8th June 1854.*

Lord Aberdeen had an Audience to-day before the Council, and represented that what was intended was merely a division of the office of Secretary of State, and not the creation of any new power, and must be considered rather as a means of avoiding further changes.[36] Lord Grey, in hearing of this intention, called it in a letter "the worst arrangement of all," as unfavourable to his further views; the Duke of Newcastle would fill the office, and would have to prepare the changes, inherent in the arrangement, and was determined not to break down the present arrangements; Lord John Russell was agreed herewith, and Sir George Grey would take office knowing this to be Lord Aberdeen's firm decision. But there was in fact no choice. Mr Rich would this afternoon bring forward a Motion in the House of Commons for the consolidation of all military offices under one

[36] Lord John Russell had some time before proposed the separation of the War and Colonial Departments, with a view of filling the Colonial Office himself, "which, in every point of view." wrote Lord Aberdeen to the Queen, "would have been a most satisfactory arrangement."

Department and a Civil Head, and Lord John Russell, to whom Lord Aberdeen had said that the Queen still hesitated about admitting the separation of the duties of Secretary of State, declared to him angrily, if that was so, he would go down to the House and vote for Mr Rich's Motion!! The Motion would be carried without fail in the House.

So this important measure had been carried by storm (as the Queen could only give way under these circumstances), and carried without a definite plan, leaving everything to the future!!

Lord John is to be Lord President, and he insisted upon Sir George Grey taking the Colonies. Lord Aberdeen fears much dissatisfaction from Lord Canning, Mr Cardwell, and Mr Peel, and just dissatisfaction; the Cabinet are very angry at the whole proceeding. Lord Granville behaved exceedingly well, putting himself and his office entirely at Lord Aberdeen's disposal.[37]

It is supposed that in the House expressions will be dropped in favour of Lord Palmerston's taking the conduct of the War in his hands. The Duke of Newcastle, whom we saw, also states the extreme difficulty of *defining* the duties of the Secretary of State, but promises to do so, as far as possible, for the Queen's convenience.

Albert.

Queen Victoria to the Earl of Aberdeen.

Buckingham Palace, *26th June 1851.*

The Queen has not yet acknowledged Lord Aberdeen's letter of the 24th. She is very glad to hear that he will take an opportunity today of dispelling misapprehensions which have arisen in the public mind in consequence of his last speech in the House of Lords, and the effect of which has given the Queen very great uneasiness.[38] She

---

[37] Lord Fitzmaurice, in his *Life of Lord Granville*, points out that Mr Strutt was really the person who had a right to complain. He was abruptly removed from the Chancellorship of the Duchy, and replaced by Lord Granville to suit Lord John's convenience.

[38] The speech of Lord Aberdeen, to which the Queen here refers, had created a very unsatisfactory impression. On the 19th of June the venerable Lord Lyndhurst had denounced the aggressive policy and the perfidy of Russia; in the debate which followed, Lord Aberdeen spoke coldly, in a strain of semi-apology for Russia, and with an unlucky reference to the Treaty of Adrianople. Popular feeling against Russia being then at a white heat, the speech was considered indicative of apathy on behalf of the Government in the prosecu-

knows Lord Aberdeen so well that she can fully enter into his feelings and understand what he means, but the public, particularly under strong excitement of patriotic feeling, is impatient and annoyed to hear at this moment the first Minister of the Crown enter into an *impartial* examination of the Emperor of Russia's character and conduct. The qualities in Lord Aberdeen's character which the Queen values most highly, his candour and his courage in expressing opinions even if opposed to general feelings of the moment, are in this instance dangerous to him, and the Queen hopes that in the vindication of his own conduct to-day, which ought to be triumphant, as it wants in fact *no* vindication, he will not undertake the ungrateful and injurious task of vindicating the Emperor of Russia from any of the exaggerated charges brought against him and his policy at a time when there is enough in it to make us fight with all might against it.

Queen Victoria to the Earl of Clarendon.

THE RUSSIAN LOAN

Buckingham Palace, *27th June 1854.*

The Queen observes in Lord Cowley's letter a suggestion of M. Drouyn de Lhuys to stop, if possible, the Russian Loan. She thinks this of the highest importance as *cutting* the *sinews* of war of the enemy. The Queen does not know whether we have by law the power to forbid the quotation of this stock in our market, but a short Act of Parliament might be obtained for the purpose. The London and Paris markets rejecting such paper would have the greatest influence upon its issue.[39]

The Earl of Aberdeen to Queen Victoria.

INSTRUCTIONS TO LORD RAGLAN

London, *29th June 1854.*

---

tion of the war. Accordingly, by moving on a later day for a copy of his own despatch of 1829, relative to the Treaty, the Premier obtained an opportunity of dispelling some of the apprehensions which his speech had excited.

[39] Lord Clarendon replied:—"... With reference to your Majesty's note of this morning, Lord Clarendon begs to say that having laid a case fully before the Law Officers, and having ascertained from them that it would be high treason for any subject of your Majesty's to be concerned in the Russian Loan, he will give all possible circulation to the opinion, and he has this evening sent it to Vienna, Berlin, and The Hague...."

Lord Aberdeen presents his humble duty to your Majesty. The Cabinet assembled yesterday evening at Lord John Russell's, at Richmond, and continued to a very late hour.[40]

A Draft of Instructions to Lord Raglan had been prepared by the Duke of Newcastle, in which the necessity of a prompt attack upon Sebastopol and the Russian Fleet was strongly urged. The amount of force now assembled at Varna, and in the neighbourhood, appeared to be amply sufficient to justify such an enterprise, with the assistance of the English and French Fleets. But although the expedition to the Crimea was pressed very warmly, and recommended to be undertaken with the least possible delay, the final decision was left to the judgment and discretion of Lord Raglan and Marshal St Arnaud, after they should have communicated with Omar Pasha.

It was also decided to send the reserve force, now in England, of 5,000 men, to join Lord Raglan without delay. This will exhaust the whole disposable force of the country at this time, and renders it impossible to supply British troops for any undertaking in the Baltic. A communication was therefore made yesterday to the French Government to know whether they would be disposed to send 6,000 French troops, to be conveyed in English transports, to the Baltic, in order to join in an attack upon the Aland Islands,[41] which appeared to be attended with no great difficulty; although any attempt upon Helsingfors, or Cronstadt, was pronounced by Sir Charles Napier to be hopeless.

Mr Kinglake describes, in an interesting passage, the growth in the public mind of a determination that the Crimea should be invaded, and Sebastopol destroyed. The Emperor Napoleon had suggested the plan at an earlier stage, and the *Times* newspaper fanned popular en-

---

[40] The war now entered upon a new phase. Though the land forces of the Allies had hitherto not come into conflict with the enemy, the Turks under Omar Pasha had been unexpectedly successful in their resistance to the Russians, whom a little later they decisively defeated at Giurgevo. Silistria had been determinedly besieged by the Russians, and its fall was daily expected. Yet, under the leadership of three young Englishmen, Captain Butler and Lieutenants Nasmyth and Ballard, the Russians were beaten off and the siege raised. The schemes of the Czar against Turkey in Europe had miscarried.

[41] Bomarsund, a fortress on one of these islands, was taken by Sir Charles Napier, aided by a French contingent under General Baraguay d'Hilliers, on the 16th of August; but the high expectations raised as to the success of the operations in the Baltic were not realised.

thusiasm in favour of it. The improved outlook in the East warranted the attempt being made, but the plan was not regarded with unqualified approval by the commanders of the allied forces in the East. In the speech, already referred to, of Lord Lyndhurst, the project had been urged upon the Government, and Lord Raglan considered that the despatch now sanctioned by the Cabinet, which is printed in the *Invasion of the Crimea*, left him no discretion in the matter.

The scheme had previously been considered in all its aspects by the Cabinet, and Mr Kinglake gives an exaggerated importance to the fact that some of the members of the Cabinet gave way to sleep while the long draft of instructions was being read to them at the after-dinner Council at Pembroke Lodge.

The Earl of Aberdeen to Queen Victoria.

London, *30th June 1854.*

Lord Aberdeen presents his humble duty to your Majesty. He begs to call your Majesty's attention to the circumstance that, in 1842, your Majesty was graciously pleased to authorise Sir Robert Peel to declare that your Majesty had determined that the Income Tax should be charged upon the sum payable to your Majesty under the Civil List Act, and that this declaration was received with marked satisfaction. Lord Aberdeen humbly presumes that your Majesty will be disposed to follow the same course with reference to the augmentation of the Tax; and should this be the case, Lord Aberdeen begs to intimate that the time for making it known has now fully arrived....

Queen Victoria to the Duke, of Newcastle.

HOME DEFENCES

Buckingham Palace, *3rd July 1854.*

In consequence of the departure of these additional 5,000 men for the East, the Queen feels very uneasy at the very defenceless state in which the country will be left, not from any want of confidence arising from the present conjuncture of affairs, but from a strong sense of the impolicy and danger of leaving this great country in such a helpless state under any circumstances, for we never can foresee what events may not suddenly spring up at any moment (like Greece, for instance[42]) which may require a force to be in readiness for any particular purpose.

The Queen therefore wishes the Duke of Newcastle to give her detailed answers upon the various points stated in the accompanying paper; but the Queen wishes to have the "*effective* state" and not "the state upon paper only." The Duke will be able to obtain these reports from the different departments.

- What store of muskets are there *here?*
- When will the new ones be ready?
- What is the force of Artillery left in the country in men and horses?
- What amount of troops are there in the country of Infantry (deducting the 5,000 men under orders for the East), and of Cavalry, and where are they stationed?
- How much Militia has been and will be embodied?
- What is the Naval Force at home?
- How much serviceable ammunition is there both of Artillery and small arms in the country?

Queen Victoria to the Earl of Clarendon.

Buckingham Palace, *4th July 1854.*

The Queen approves the enclosed drafts, and wishes only to remark on one passage, where Lord Clarendon says, "that he acts by the unanimous desire of the Cabinet," which she thinks better altered or omitted. If left, it might weaken the authority of future instructions emanating from the Secretary of State alone; moreover, he acts constitutionally under the authority of the Queen, on his own responsibility and not that of the Cabinet.

[42] A violently hostile feeling between the Turks and Greeks had culminated earlier in the year in a formidable insurrection among the Sultan's Greek subjects. It was terminated on the 18th of June by an engagement at Kalampaka, in Thessaly.

Queen Victoria to the Earl of Aberdeen.

Buckingham Palace, *17th July 1854.*

The Queen has just received Lord Aberdeen's letter, and has fully considered the contents of it. She has finally decided to make no change in her intended departure, from a conviction that her doing so might shake confidence in the result of this night's Debate. Should anything serious occur, she would be ready to return to-morrow or at any time that her presence in town was considered of importance to the public service.

Queen Victoria to Lord John Russell.

Osborne, *19th July 1854.*

The Queen has received Lord John Russell's letter of yesterday, and was very glad to hear that both the meeting and the Debate went off so well. The party which supports the Government is certainly "a strange basis for a Government to rest upon," but such as it is we must make the best of it, and nothing will contribute more to keeping it together than to give it the impression that the Government is thoroughly united.[43]

Queen Victoria to the Marquis of Dalhousie.

INDIAN AFFAIRS

Buckingham Palace, *26th July 1854.*

It is a very long time since the Queen has had the pleasure of hearing from Lord Dalhousie, but she supposes that (fortunately) there is very little to say, everything being so quiet and prosperous. The Queen highly appreciates and values Lord Dalhousie's kind offer to remain in India while there is any prospect of difficulty being caused

---

[43] During a desultory discussion on the 13th of July, Mr Disraeli had assailed the Government and its chief in the Commons, to such purpose that Lord John Russell, stung by his sarcasms, and mortified by his own failure, asked Lord Aberdeen to relieve him of the Leadership of the House. The Queen, to whom he had also written, entreated Lord John not to let his opponent see that his object in making his attack had been successful. A meeting of the Ministerialists was held on the 17th at the Foreign Office, at which one hundred and eighty members of the House of Commons were present, and some diversity of opinion was expressed; the result of the meeting was that the Government was more satisfactorily supported.

by the present War, which will be a source of great satisfaction and tranquillity to her, as she feels that her Indian Dominions cannot be in safer hands.

The Queen wishes to tell Lord Dalhousie how much interested and pleased we have been in making the acquaintance of the young Maharajah Dhuleep Singh.[44] It is not without mixed feelings of pain and sympathy that the Queen sees this young Prince, once destined to so high and powerful a position, and now reduced to so dependent a one by her arms; his youth, amiable character, and striking good looks, as well as his being a Christian, the first of his high rank who has embraced our faith, must incline every one favourably towards him, and it will be a pleasure to us to do all we can to be of use to him, and to befriend and protect him.

It also interested us to see poor old Prince Gholam Mohammed, the last son of the once so dreaded Tippoo Sahib.

We both hope that Lord Dalhousie's health is good, and the Prince sends him his kind remembrance.

Queen Victoria to Viscount Hardinge.

MILITARY APPOINTMENTS

Osborne, *6th August 1854.*

The Queen has received Lord Hardinge's letter of the 4th.[45] She would for the future wish all papers for signature to be accompanied by a descriptive list showing at a glance the purport of the documents, as is done with papers from other Government offices.

The Queen has looked over the lists of Major-Generals made by the last brevet which Lord Hardinge submitted, and must confess that

---

[44] This young Prince was born in 1838, and was a younger son of Runjeet Singh, Chief of the Sikhs, who, after a loyal alliance with England for thirty years, died in 1839. In 1843 Dhuleep Singh was raised to the throne, which had been occupied successively by Runjeet's elder sons. After the Sikh war in 1845, the British Government gave to the boy-king the support of a British force. In 1849, after the destruction of the Sikh army at Gujerat, and the annexation of the Punjab, a pension was bestowed on the young Maharajah on condition of his remaining loyal to the British Government. He became a Christian and was at this time on a visit to England.

[45] In reply to a letter from the Queen, stating that she had inadvertently signed certain papers in the ordinary course. Her attention had not been drawn to their important features.

it does not afford a great choice; yet, leaving out the cavalry officers and those disqualified by age or infirmities, there remain some few whom she has marked with an "X," for whose exclusion no adequate reason is apparent. An exclusion of officers who have served in the Guards, *merely on that account*, the Queen would not wish to see adopted as a principle, and the selection of Colonels of the Line (because there are no Generals fit), in preference to Generals of the Guards who are perfectly so, will amount to this. General Eden,[46] moreover, has been in command of a Regiment of the Line, and General Knollys[47] has not been promoted from the Guards, and, in accepting the Governorship of Guernsey, specially begged that this might not exclude him from active service—a circumstance which he mentioned to the Prince at the time. Both these have the reputation of very good officers.

The Queen does not wish anything to be arranged prospectively now, but would recommend the subject to Lord Hardinge's future consideration.

Queen Victoria to the Earl of Aberdeen.

SPECIAL PRAYERS

Osborne, *21st August 1854.*

The Queen must repeat what she has frequently done, that she strongly objects to these *special* prayers which *are*, in fact, *not* a sign of gratitude or confidence in the Almighty—for if this is the course to be pursued, we *ought* to have one for every *illness*, and certainly in '37 the influenza was notoriously more *fatal* than the cholera had ever been, and *yet no one* would have thought of having a prayer against *that*. Our Liturgy *has* provided for these calamities, and we may have frequent returns of the cholera—and yet it would be difficult to *define* the *number* of deaths which are to *make* "a form of prayer" *necessary*. The Queen would, therefore, strongly recommend the usual prayer being used, and no other, as is the case for the prayer in time of War. What is the use of the prayers in the Liturgy, which were no doubt composed when we were subject to other equally fatal diseases, if a new one is always to be framed specially for the cholera?

---

[46] Lieut.-General John Eden, C.B., nephew of the first Lord Auckland.

[47] Sir William Knollys, K.C.B., 1797-1883, became in 1855 the organiser of the newly formed Camp at Aldershot.

The Queen would wish Lord Aberdeen to give this as her decided opinion to the Archbishop, at all events, for the present. Last year the cholera quite decimated Newcastle, and was bad in many other places, but there was *no special* prayer, and *now* the illness is in *London* but *not* in any other place, a prayer is proposed by the Archbishop. The Queen cannot see the difference between the one and the other.

The Earl of Aberdeen to Queen Victoria.

CIVIL LIST PENSIONS

London, *1st September 1854.*

Lord Aberdeen, with his humble duty, begs to lay before your Majesty the pensions proposed to be granted on the Civil List at this time. The only case requiring any special remark is that of the children of Lord Nelson's adopted daughter. There seems little doubt that the person referred to was really Lord Nelson's daughter, according to evidence recently produced, and was recommended by him to the care of the country, just before the battle of Trafalgar.[48]

A numerous party in the House of Commons wished that your Majesty's Government should propose a special vote for this person and her family; but the Cabinet thought that it would give rise to much scandal and disagreeable debate, and finally recommended Lord Aberdeen to place the three daughters on the Pension List. The circumstances of the case are, no doubt, very peculiar; and although Lord Aberdeen does not feel perfectly satisfied with the course pursued, he thinks it very desirable to avoid the sort of Parliamentary debates to which the discussion of such a subject would necessarily give rise.

[48] Horatia, daughter of Nelson and Lady Hamilton, was born on the 29th of January 1801, and married in 1822 the Rev. Philip Ward of Tenterden. She died in 1881.

The Emperor of the French to Queen Victoria.[49]

Boulogne, *le 8 Septembre 1854.*

Madame et bonne Sœur,—La présence du digne époux de votre Majesté au milieu d'un camp français est un fait d'une grande signification politique, puisqu'il prouve l'union intime des deux pays: mais j'aime mieux aujourd'hui ne pas envisager le côté politique de cette visite et vous dire sincèrement combien j'ai été heureux de me trouver pendant quelques jours avec un Prince aussi accompli, un homme doué de qualités si séduisantes et de connaissances si profondes. Il peut être convaincu d'emporter avec lui mes sentiments de haute estime et d'amitié. Mais plus il m'a été donné d'apprécier le Prince Albert, plus je dois être touché de la bienveillance qu'a eue votre Majesté de s'en séparer pour moi quelque jours.

Je remercie votre Majesté de l'admirable lettre qu'elle a bien voulu m'écrire et des choses affectueuses qu'elle contenait pour l'Impératrice. Je me suis empressé de lui en faire part et elle y a été très sensible.

Je prie votre Majesté de recevoir l'expression de mes sentiments respectueux et de me croire, de votre Majesté, le bon Frère,

Napoléon.

The Earl of Clarendon to Queen Victoria.

PRINCE ALBERT AND THE EMPEROR

Foreign Office, *22nd September 1854.*

Lord Clarendon presents his humble duty to your Majesty....

Count Walewski told Lord Clarendon to-day that the Emperor had spoken with enthusiasm of the Prince, saying that in all his experience he had never met with a person possessing such various and profound

---

[49] The French Emperor had established a camp between Boulogne and St Omer, and early in the summer had invited Prince Albert to visit him. It was reasonably conjectured at the time that one of the chief purposes of the invitation was by personal intercourse to overcome the prejudice which the Emperor believed prevailed against him. The visit lasted from the 4th till the 8th of September, and the Prince's impressions were recorded in a memorandum, "the value of which," writes Sir Theodore Martin, by way of preface to his publication of it, "cannot be overstated; nor is it less valuable for the light which it throws upon the Prince's character, by the remarkable contrasts between himself and the Emperor of the French, which were elicited in the unreserved discussions which each seems equally to have courted."

knowledge, or who communicated it with the same frankness. His Majesty added that he had never learned so much in a short time, and was grateful. He began his conversation with reproaching Count Walewski for not having written to him much oftener respecting the Prince, and endeavoured to ascertain the opinions of His Royal Highness upon all important subjects.

With respect to the invitation, the Emperor's account of it to Count Walewski was that he had apologised to the Prince for the bad reception he had given His Royal Highness, and expressed a hope that he might have an opportunity of *doing better* at Paris, if your Majesty and the Prince would honour him with a visit; and that His Royal Highness had then said, "the Queen hopes to see your Majesty at Windsor, and will be happy to make acquaintance with the Empress." The Emperor, however, had only taken this as a courteous return to his invitation, and not as intended for a positive invitation.

Lord Clarendon told Count Walewski that he believed the matter had passed inversely, and that the Prince had first communicated your Majesty's message.

Be that as it may, Count Walewski said the Emperor will be delighted to avail himself of the Queen's gracious kindness; nothing will give him so much pleasure....

Queen Victoria to the Earl of Clarendon.

THE EMPEROR'S VISIT

Balmoral, *24th September 1854.*

The Queen returns the two letters from Lord Cowley. She is very sorry to see doubts arise as to the correctness of the intelligence about the safe debarkation of our whole expeditionary force in the Crimea, but still clings to the hope of its being true.

Count Walewski's account of the Emperor's version of his conversation with the Prince explains what the Prince suspected at one time himself, that the Emperor had not understood the Prince's remark as conveying a *direct* invitation, but merely as a general term of civility. What the Prince intended to convey was something between the two, making it clear that he would be well received, and leaving it entirely open to him to come or not according to his own political views and circumstances. This appeared to the Prince the most polite and delicate, preventing all appearance as if a counter-visit for his own at Boulogne was expected. Lest the Emperor should not have rightly understood the Prince, he repeated the wish to see the Emperor in England, and the hope of the Queen to make the Empress's acquaintance also, *more directly* to Marshal Vaillant, who gave the same answer as the Emperor had done—he hoped we should come to Paris in return.

Matters stand as well as possible with regard to the visit; in the Queen's opinion, the Emperor can come if he likes, and if prevented, is bound to nothing. Should he ask when his visit would be most agreeable to the Queen, the middle of November would be the time.

Queen Victoria to the Earl of Clarendon.

Balmoral, *30th September 1854.*

The Queen returns the enclosed letters. The French show their usual vivacity in pressing so hard for decision upon what is to be done with Sebastopol when taken.[50] Surely we ought to have taken it first before we can dispose of it, and everything as to the decision about it must depend upon the state in which we receive it, and the opinion of the Military and Naval Commanders after they find themselves in possession of it. The Queen hopes, therefore, that Lord Clarendon will succeed in restraining French impatience as he has often done before.

The Earl of Aberdeen to Queen Victoria.

BATTLE OF THE ALMA

Haddo House, *1st October 1854.*

Lord Aberdeen presents his humble duty to your Majesty. He had the honour of receiving your Majesty's box this morning at nine o'clock by post; and he now sends a Messenger to Aberdeen, with

---

[50] Lord Clarendon had given the Queen the two reasons for which the French were pressing, in anticipation, the retention of the Crimea, viz. as affording suitable winter quarters, and as a guarantee in case of peace negotiations. On the 7th of September the allied forces had sailed for the Crimea; on the 21st the Queen learned by telegram that 25,000 English, 25,000 French, and 8,000 Turks had landed safely without encountering resistance, and begun the march to Sebastopol. The Queen, with her usual kindly solicitude for the health and comfort of her Ministers, had summoned Lord Aberdeen from London to have the benefit of the Scotch air; he remained at Balmoral from the 27th till the 30th, when he went to his own house at Haddo. Immediately after his departure, a telegram arrived from Lord Clarendon announcing the victory of the Alma.

Despatches received this morning from London, to meet the special conveyance to Balmoral this evening.

Lord Aberdeen humbly presumes to offer his most cordial congratulations to your Majesty on the great intelligence received by telegraph this morning. The account sent by Lord Stratford of the victory on the Alma must be correct; the report mentioned by Mr Colquhoun[51] may possibly be so too. At all events, we may fairly hope that the fall of Sebastopol cannot long be delayed.

Lord Aberdeen has written to Lord Clarendon this morning on the subject of the fortifications of Sebastopol, which although, somewhat embarrassing at the moment, is not attended with any great practical importance.

Lord Aberdeen regrets that the speedy return of the post prevents him from sending your Majesty a copy of his letter, which in substance, however, was to the following effect. Without attaching any undue importance to the decision, he was inclined to adhere to his first proposition of the immediate and entire destruction of the works. He did not see the advantage of doing the thing by halves; while the destruction of the sea defences only might give rise to erroneous impressions and would be of an equivocal character. The fall of Sebastopol would in fact be the conquest of the Crimea, and the Allies might winter there with perfect security, as, by occupying the lines of Perekop,[52] any access to the Crimea would effectually be prevented by land. Lord Aberdeen thought that with a view to peace, and the restitution of the Crimea to Russia, it would be more easy for the Emperor to accept the destruction of the fortifications when accomplished, than to agree to any stipulation having such an object.

On the whole, Lord Aberdeen was inclined to think that if the place should not be at once destroyed, it might be better to preserve it in its present state, until the matter should be further considered. The Allies would always have it in their power to act as they thought best, and the question might in some degree be affected by future events. The great objection to leaving the matter undecided for the present appeared to be from the possibility of differences hereafter between France and England upon the subject. After the astounding proposition

[51] Mr (afterwards Sir) Robert Gilmour Colquhoun (1803-1870), Agent and Consul-General at Bucharest.

[52] A district on the isthmus of Crimea, guarded by a wall and a ditch, the name meaning "Cross-ditch." The whole isthmus is now often called Perekop.

made to Lord Raglan by the French Generals when actually embarked and at sea, it would be well to leave nothing in doubt. The Turks, too, might perhaps desire to have a voice in the matter, and might become troublesome....

The Marquis of Dalhousie to Queen Victoria.

INDIAN AFFAIRS

Government House, *2nd October 1854.*

The Governor-General presents his most humble duty to your Majesty, and begs to offer his respectful thanks for the very gracious manner in which your Majesty has been pleased to acknowledge the offer he has made to retain still the Government of India during the ensuing year.

The Governor-General does not affect to say that he makes no sacrifice in so doing. Many things unite to warn him that it is time he were gone: and his family circumstances, in which your Majesty has long shown so gracious an interest, have rendered the prospect of his remaining longer absent from England a source of much anxiety and perplexity to him. But he felt that this was no time for any man, high or low, to leave his post. And as a seven-years' experience must needs have rendered him more capable of immediate usefulness than any other, though a far abler man, without such experience could possibly be, he did not hesitate to offer the continued service which your Majesty might most justly expect, and which he is proud to render cheerfully.

Your Majesty's remark on the absence of any letter from the Governor-General of late would have disquieted him with apprehensions that he had been thought neglectful, but that your Majesty at the same time ascribed the silence to its real cause. Since the announcement of the termination of the Burmese War there has, in truth, been no occurrence which, of itself, seemed worthy of being made the subject of a report to your Majesty. India has been tranquil in all her borders. And although no event could well be more gratifying than this continuous tranquillity was in itself, still the periodical report of peace and quiet on all sides seemed likely to be as uninteresting as the monotonous, though satisfactory, "All's well" of a ring of sentries.

At Christmas the Governor-General anticipated having the honour of narrating to your Majesty the events of a year which he hoped would, before its close, have been fruitful of great results....

INDIA AND RUSSIA

Very recently an interesting mission has arrived from the Khan of Kokan, a state to the north of Bokhara, reporting the capture of their fort of Ak Mussid by the Russians.

The fact was known before; but the mission is important from the certainty it imparts to us that all the Turcomans, the people of Kokan, of Khiva, and of Bokhara, all detest as much as they dread the Muscovites, with whose approach they are threatened.

The Khan asks for aid. We can render him but little. The only real bulwark which can be raised for these states of Central Asia—the only real barrier to the progress of Russia which can be set up there—must have their foundations in the Treaty, which may be framed by the Allied Powers after the present war shall have brought the spirit of Russia into temporary subjection.

The war in which your Majesty has engaged with that great Power has not been directly felt in this part of your Majesty's dominions; but its indirect influence is most sensibly apparent.

The notions entertained of Russia, and the estimate formed of her powers, by the nations of India, are exaggerated in the extreme. Although our pride must wince on hearing it, it is an unquestionable fact that the general belief in India at this moment is that Russia gravely menaces the power of England, and will be more than a match for her in the end.

This feeling cannot prudently be disregarded. The Governor-General need hardly say to your Majesty that he believes that any direct attack by Russia on these dominions at the present time is utterly impracticable; and that there is no more risk of an invasion of India by the Emperor Nicholas than of another by Mahmood of Ghuznee. Nevertheless, the uneasy feeling which now prevails among native States and among ourselves, partly of alarm, partly of indefinite expectation, ought to be guarded against; and the means of meeting any difficulties which may arise out of it should be at our command.

Earnestly desirous to contribute every possible aid to your Majesty's arms in the great contest now going on in Europe, the Governor-General has respectfully placed at the disposal of your Majesty's Ministers all the four regiments of Royal Cavalry now serving in India. The Infantry is already hardly adequate for our own necessities: and while the Governor-General will be quite ready to accept and to face any additional responsibilities which he may be called upon to bear, he has felt it to be his duty to state that, beyond the four regiments of Cavalry, European troops cannot safely be spared from India at the present time.

The Governor-General, however, feels that he is not indulging in any vain boast when he ventures to assure your Majesty that, under God's good blessing, these, your Dominions in the East, are at present absolutely safe.... Your Majesty's most obedient, most humble, and devoted Subject and Servant,

Dalhousie.

Queen Victoria to the Marquis of Dalhousie.

DEPOSED INDIAN PRINCES

Balmoral, *2nd October 1854.*

As the Queen knows that the East India Company are chiefly guided by Lord Dalhousie's advice with respect to all Indian affairs in public as well as of a more private nature, she thinks that she cannot do better than write to him upon a subject which she *feels* strongly upon, and which she is sure that Lord Dalhousie will enter into. It is the position of those unfortunate Indian Princes who have, either themselves or their fathers, been for public reasons deposed. Two instances are now before the Queen's eyes upon which she wishes to state her opinion.

The first is old Prince Gholam Mohammed, and his son Prince Feroz Shah. The Queen understands (though she is not sure of the fact) that the old man is here in order to try to obtain his pension continued to his son. This is very natural, and it strikes the Queen to be an arrangement difficult to be justified, in a moral point of view, to give these poor people—who after *all* were once so mighty—*no* security beyond their lives. Whilst we remain permanently in possession of their vast Empire, they receive a pension, which is not *even* continued to their descendants. Would it not be much the best to allow them, instead of a pension, to hold, perhaps under the Government, a property, which would enable them and their descendants to live respectably, maintaining a certain rank and position? The Queen believes that Lord Dalhousie himself suggested this principle in the case of the Ameers of Scinde.

Nothing is more painful for *any* one than the thought that their children and grandchildren have no future, and may become absolutely beggars. How much more *dreadful* must this be to proud people, who, like Prince Gholam, are the sons and grandsons of great Princes like Hyder Ali and Tippoo Sahib! Besides it strikes the Queen that the more kindly we treat Indian Princes, whom *we* have *conquered*, and the more consideration we show for their birth and former grandeur, the more we shall attach Indian Princes and Governments to us, and the more ready will they be to come under our rule.

MAHARAJAH DHULEEP SINGH

The second instance is that of the young Maharajah Dhuleep Singh (and the Queen must here observe that the favourable opinion she expressed of him, in her last letter to Lord Dalhousie, has only been confirmed and strengthened by closer acquaintance). This young Prince has the *strongest* claims upon our generosity and sympathy; deposed, for *no* fault of his, when a little boy of ten years old, he is as innocent as any private individual of the misdeeds which compelled us to depose him, and take possession of his territories. He has besides since become a Christian, whereby he is for ever cut off from his own people. His case therefore appears to the Queen still stronger than the *former* one, as he was not even a conquered enemy, but merely powerless in the hands of the Sikh soldiery.

There is something too painful in the idea of a young deposed Sovereign, once so powerful, receiving a pension, and having *no* security that his children and descendants, and these moreover Christians, should have any home or position.

The Queen hears that Lord Dalhousie himself would wish and advise his pension to be exchanged for a property on which the Maharajah might live, which he might improve (giving thereby a most valuable example) and transmit some day to his descendants, should he have any; she hopes therefore that this may be so settled, and that he may, on attaining the age of eighteen, have a comfortable and fitting position worthy his high rank.

Where such a property might be must be of course left to Lord Dalhousie to decide, but the Queen hopes that Lord Dalhousie will give it his serious attention.

Queen Victoria to the Earl of Clarendon.

THE AUSTRIAN PROPOSALS

Balmoral, *10th October 1854.*

The Queen has received Lord Clarendon's letters of the 8th.[53] She cannot consider it wise to reject the Austrian proposals *altogether*, although we may usefully amend them. The success in the Crimea ought to be followed up by strengthening the alliance of the European powers, else it may turn out a sterile victory, and the English blood will have flowed in vain; for supposing even the whole Crimea to fall into our hands, it is not likely that the war will be concluded on that account. How are England and France to bring it to a termination single-handed? Our Army in the Crimea is the only one we have....

It is true that the Austrian proposal promises little performance on her part, yet the stipulation by Treaty that she will never let the Russians pass the Pruth again is a positive advantage to us; and the other, that a defensive and offensive alliance with us is to follow the breaking out of the war by Russia against Austria, although being entirely at *our* expense, yet realises the chief condition which will make Austria hesitate less to bring it to a war with Russia. She always (and not without reason) dreaded to have to fight Russia single-handed, and the allied armies in the Crimea could not assist her. What reason could Austria put forward and justify to Prussia and Germany, for going to war at this moment? To obtain the evacuation of the Principalities was a tangible one, indeed the same *we* put forward when *we* declared war; but this is now obtained.

We must certainly not allow our policy to be mixed up with the miserable German squabbles, but we must acknowledge that Austria, as a member of the Confederation, is not and cannot be independent of them.

The Queen would accordingly advise a temperate consideration of the Austrian proposals and an amendment of them in those points which seem to require them, and which Lord Clarendon clearly points out in his letter, and the avoidance of anything which could weaken the *accord Européen*.[54]

The Emperor Napoleon's answer to Lord Cowley with reference to this visit to England renders it probable to the Queen that he was not anxious to have the general invitation changed into a special one,

---

[53] In one of which, in reference to Austria's desire for an offensive and defensive treaty with Great Britain, Lord Clarendon had described the Austrian terms as irritating, and the discussion of them a mere waste of time.

[54] The Cabinet, at its meeting on the 20th, decided to meet the Austrian proposals in the most conciliatory manner possible.

obliging him to come or to refuse. The answer is almost a refusal now, and has not improved our position. The Queen would wish that no anxiety should be shown to obtain the visit, now that it is quite clear to the Emperor that he will be *le bienvenu* at any time. His reception here ought to be a boon to him and not a boon to us.

The Queen fully enters into the feelings of exultation and joy at the glorious victory of the Alma, but this is somewhat damped by the sad loss we have sustained, and the thought of the many bereaved families of all classes who are in mourning for those near and dear to them.

Queen Victoria to the King of the Belgians.

THE ALMA

Hull, *13th October 1854.*

My dearest Uncle,—Already far away from my loved beautiful Highlands and Mountains, I find a few minutes to write and thank you for your kind letter of the 2nd, with such lively and glowing descriptions of such glorious and beautiful scenery, which I hope and trust to see *some day*. Still, with all its beauties, I would not exchange it for our northern beauties, which really they are—for a *lovelier* country with a *more beautiful* combination of wood and mountain, and river, and cultivation with the greatest wildness, at the same time close at hand, cannot, I am sure, be seen; Stockmar is in the greatest admiration of it. We left it yesterday morning, slept at Holyrood last night, and came here this evening; the good people of this large port, having since two years entreated us to come here. We shall reach Windsor to-morrow.

We are, and indeed the whole country is, *entirely* engrossed with one idea, one *anxious* thought—the *Crimea*. We have received all the *most* interesting and *gratifying* details of the *splendid* and decisive victory of the Alma; alas! it was a bloody one. Our loss was a heavy one—many have fallen and many are wounded, but my noble Troops behaved with a *courage* and *desperation* which was beautiful to behold. The Russians expected their position would hold out three weeks; their loss was immense—the whole garrison of Sebastopol was out. Since that, the Army has performed a wonderful march to Balaklava, and the bombardment of Sebastopol has begun. Lord Raglan's behaviour was worthy of the old Duke's—such coolness in the midst of the hottest fire. We have had all the details from young

Burghersh[55] (a remarkably nice young man), one of Lord Raglan's Aides-de-camp whom he sent home with the Despatches, who was in the midst of it all. I feel so *proud* of my dear noble Troops, who, they say, bear their privations, and the sad disease which still haunts them, with such courage and good humour.

George did enormously well, and was not touched. Now with Albert's love, ever your devoted Niece,

Victoria R.

Queen Victoria to the Earl of Clarendon.

FRANCE AND AUSTRIA

Windsor Castle, *5th November 1854.*

The Queen has received Lord Clarendon's letter referring to the new Draft of a Treaty with Austria proposed by the French Government, and has since attentively perused the Treaty itself.[56] Vague and inconclusive as it is as to *co-operation* (which is the main object of our desire), it is a step in advance, and has the advantage of assuring Austria of our alliance should the war between her and Russia break out. The Queen regrets to find a Clause omitted which stood in the former French project (rejected by us about three weeks ago), stipulating that Austria was to prevent the re-entry of Russia into the Principalities. Although she would of her own accord have to do this, a treaty obligation towards the *belligerents* to that effect would have made a considerable inroad into her position as a *neutral* power, and secured a co-operation in the war—*ad hoc* at least. Austria ought to be told, in the Queen's opinion, that this project of treaty contains almost nothing; and that her signing it *at once* would give a moral pledge of her sincerity towards the Western Powers, who have to pay with the lives of their best troops every day that Austria hesitates to do what in the end she must find it in her own interest to do.

---

[55] Francis, Lord Burghersh, afterwards twelfth Earl of Westmorland (1825-1891).

[56] Lord Clarendon wrote that he and Lord John Russell approved of the treaty, but that Lord Aberdeen thought that Austria would not accept it; while Lord Palmerston felt confident that Austria, even if her co-operation were not now secured, would at least not lend her support to the King of Prussia's scheme.

As to M. Olozaga's proposal,[57] the Queen thinks it ought to be treated like all the former ones, viz. met with the remark that we cannot discuss eventualities implying the dethronement of a Sovereign with whom we are on a footing of amity.

At this date only partial and misleading accounts had arrived of the battle of Balaklava, and it was believed that four English (not Turkish) redoubts had been taken; and, while the disastrous charge of the Light Brigade had been announced, the success of the heavy cavalry was not yet known. Anxiety began accordingly to be felt at home as to the adequacy of the allied forces to encounter the Russian army, augmented as it now was by the troops which had recently evacuated the Principalities. Accordingly fresh efforts were being made to engage Austria in effectual alliance with the Western Powers.

Queen Victoria to the Earl of Clarendon.

Windsor Castle, *9th November 1854.*

The Queen returns the letters from Lord Cowley and Count Walewski.[58] No consideration on earth ought to stand in the way of our sending what ships we can lay hold of to transport French reinforcements to the Crimea, as the safety of our Army and the honour of the Country are at stake. The Queen is ready to give her own yacht for a transport which could carry 1,000 men. Every account received convinces the Queen more and more that numbers alone can ensure success in this instance, and that without them we are running *serious* risks.

---

[57] The document containing this proposal does not seem to have been preserved among the papers. It was not impossibly a scheme for betrothing King Pedro to the infant Princess of the Asturias, thereby uniting the two Crowns, and bringing about the dethronement of Queen Isabella.

[58] The Count wrote that France was ready to send 20,000 men to the Crimea, if England could furnish transports. Lord Clarendon added: "We have not a single available steamer, as all must be left in the Baltic until the ice sets in, and the stores, ammunition, and clothing for the Army are going out in sailing vessels."

Queen Victoria to the King of the Belgians.

Windsor Castle, *14th November 1854.*

My dearest Uncle,—I am quite shocked to find that I missed writing my letter to-day—but really *la tête me tourne*. I am so bewildered and excited, and my mind so entirely taken up by the news from the Crimea, that I really forget, and what is worse, I get so confused about everything that I am a very unfit correspondent. My whole soul and heart are in the Crimea. The conduct of our *dear noble* Troops is *beyond praise*; it is quite heroic, and really I feel a pride to have *such Troops*, which is only equalled by my grief for their sufferings. We now know that there has been a pitched battle on the 6th, in which we have been victorious over much greater numbers, but with great loss on both sides—the greatest on the Russian. But we know *nothing* more, and now we must live in a suspense which is indeed dreadful. Then to think of the numbers of families who are living in *such* anxiety! It is terrible to think of all the wretched wives and mothers who are awaiting the fate of those nearest and dearest to them! In short, it is a time which requires courage and patience to bear as one ought.

Many thanks, dearest Uncle, for your kind letter of the 11th, which I received on Saturday. The Brabants will soon leave you; I shall write to Leo to-morrow or next day, *quand je pourrais un peu rassembler mes idées*. I must now conclude, dearest Uncle. With Albert's affectionate love, ever your devoted Niece,

Victoria R.

Queen Victoria to Lord Raglan.

INKERMAN

Windsor Castle, *18th November 1854.*

The Queen has received with pride and joy the telegraphic news of the glorious, but alas! bloody victory of the 5th.[59] These feelings of pride and satisfaction are, however, painfully alloyed by the grievous

[59] The English loss at the battle of Inkerman was over 2,500 killed and wounded; the French lost 1,800. The loss of the enemy was doubtful, but the Russian estimate (much smaller than our own) was about 12,000 killed, wounded, and prisoners. The Grand Dukes Nicholas and Michael both fought in the battle.

news of the loss of so many Generals, and in particular Sir George Cathcart—who was so distinguished and excellent an officer.[60]

We are most thankful that Lord Raglan's valuable life has been spared; and the Queen trusts that he will not expose himself more than is absolutely necessary.

The Queen cannot sufficiently express her high sense of the great services he has rendered and is rendering to her and the country, by the very able manner in which he has led the bravest troops that ever fought, and which it is a pride to her to be able to call her own. To mark the Queen's feelings of approbation she wishes to confer on Lord Raglan the Baton of Field-Marshal. It affords her the sincerest gratification to confer it on one who has so nobly earned the highest rank in the Army, which he so long served in under the immortal hero, who she laments could not witness the success of a friend he so greatly esteemed.

Both the Prince and Queen are anxious to express to Lord Raglan their unbounded admiration of the heroic conduct of the Army, and their sincere sympathy in their sufferings and privations so nobly borne.

The Queen thanks Lord Raglan for his kind letter of the 28th ultimo.

The Earl of Aberdeen to Queen Victoria.

LORD JOHN RUSSELL'S PROPOSAL

London, *23rd November 1854.*

Lord Aberdeen presents his most humble duty to your Majesty. He regrets, at a moment of such public interest and importance, to trouble your Majesty with domestic difficulties; but he thinks it his duty to lay before your Majesty the enclosed correspondence without delay.[61] Lord Aberdeen has for some time past expected a proposition

---

[60] Besides Sir George Cathcart, Brigadier-Generals Strangways and Goldie were killed. Sir George Brown was shot through the arm, Major-Generals Bentinck and Codrington, and Brigadier-General Adams were all severely wounded, but not so seriously. Sir de Lacy Evans a few days earlier, being then in shattered health, had had a fall from his horse, and was absent from the battle.

[61] Lord John Russell urged, in this correspondence, that Lord Palmerston should supersede the Duke of Newcastle at the War Office.

of this kind, and it is impossible not to see that it may be attended with very serious consequences. At first Lord Aberdeen was in doubt whether the proposition was made by Lord J. Russell in concert with Lord Palmerston; but this appears not to be the case. Much will therefore depend on the decision of Lord Palmerston. Should he join with Lord John, matters will probably be pushed to extremity; but should he decline, Lord Aberdeen does not think that Lord John will venture to act alone.

Queen Victoria to the Marquis of Dalhousie.

MAHARAJAH DHULEEP SINGH

24th November 1854.

The Queen thanks Lord Dalhousie for his long and most interesting and satisfactory letter of the 2nd of October.

It is peculiarly gratifying to hear of such quiet and prosperity in her vast Indian dominions, in which the Queen ever takes the liveliest interest, and at the present moment of intense anxiety, when England's best and noblest blood is being profusely shed to resist the encroaching spirit of Russia. The heroism of our noble Troops in the midst of herculean difficulties and great privations is unequalled, and will fill Lord Dalhousie's loyal and patriotic heart with pride and admiration. Though entirely concurring in his opinion that Russia can undertake no invasion of India, her spirit of encroachment on the north frontier must be carefully watched and, if possible, put a stop to, when peace is made.

The progress of the railroad will make an immense difference in India, and tend more than anything else to bring about civilisation, and will in the end facilitate the spread of Christianity, which hitherto has made but very slow progress.

The Queen was already aware of the idea formerly entertained by the Maharajah Dhuleep Singh of marrying the young Princess of Coorg.[62] Agreeing as she does with Lord Dalhousie in the wisdom of

[62] A few years earlier, while still holding his ancestral creed, Dhuleep Singh, had made overtures to the ex-Rajah of Coorg with a view to his betrothal to the eldest daughter of the latter; but at that time the matter was dropped. After becoming a Christian, and having also heard of the baptism of the Princess of Coorg, the Maharajah renewed his proposal, which, however, was not eventually accepted. The Princess married an English officer, and died in 1864, aged twenty-four.

advising the young man to pause before he makes his choice of a wife, she thinks such a marriage between these two most interesting young Christians most desirable; indeed, as Lord Dalhousie himself observes, the difficulty of any other marriage for either must be great. The young people have met and were pleased with each other, so that the Queen hopes that their union will, in the course of time, come to pass. Her little god-daughter has been here lately, and though still childish for her age (she is nearly fourteen) is pretty, lively, intelligent, and going on satisfactorily in her education.

Of the young Maharajah, who has now been twice our guest, we can only speak in terms of praise. He promises to be a bright example to all Indian Princes, for he is thoroughly good and amiable, and most anxious to improve himself.

Prince Edward of Saxe-Weimar[63] to Queen Victoria.

BATTLE OF INKERMAN

Camp before Sebastopol, *28th November 1854.*

Madam,—Your Majesty's very kind letter reached me by the last mail. I avail myself of your permission to write to you again, although there is not much to say since I last wrote to Prince Albert on the 7th or 8th of this month. I wrote to him soon after the battle of Inkerman, when I was still under the excitement of that fearful scene, and I am afraid that I made use of expressions that I was afterwards sorry that I had done. I believe I made some reflections on our Commanders, which are at all times wrong. By this time your Majesty will, of course, be in possession of all the details of that fearful day, on which our loss was so very great.[64] I made a mistake in stating the number of dead in the Grenadiers; it was much larger than I stated. I think we must have suffered more than any other Corps, for, on the following day, when the roll was called, two hundred and twenty-five men were absent; of these one hundred and one were killed, and the rest wounded. There cannot be any doubt that we allowed ourselves to be surprised, for the first notice we had of the Russians was receiving their heavy shot in the camp of the 2nd Division. Nearly all their tents

[63] Son of Duke Charles Bernard and Duchess Ida, the latter being a Princess of Saxe-Meiningen and sister to Queen Adelaide. The Prince was at this time Lieut.-Colonel and A.D.C. to Lord Raglan. He was afterwards A.D.C. to the Queen and ultimately Commander of the Forces in Ireland. He died in 1902.
[64] See *ante*, note 60.

were torn by round shot. It is even said that a shell lodged in an officer's portmanteau, burst, and, of course, scattered all his goods to the winds. Experience has made us wise, or rather Lord Raglan wise, for since that day the French and ourselves have been busy in entrenching our right; it is now so strong that no enemy can attack us there with the slightest chance of success; it is only a pity it was not done before. The Turks were chiefly employed making these redoubts, which is in fact the only thing they have done except burying the dead Russians. Never shall I forget the sight of the dead and dying Russians on the field. Some of these poor wretches had to lie on the field for at least sixty hours before they were removed to the hospital tents; the majority of course died. I am afraid this is one of the necessities of war, for we had to remove our own people first. I went round the hospitals next morning. It was a horrid sight to see the bodies of the men who had died during the night stretched before the tents, and to see the heaps of arms and legs, with the trousers and boots still on, that had been cut off by the surgeons.

The Russians were so near that most of the officers had to use their swords and revolvers. Many single acts of daring took place; among others, Colonel Percy,[65] of our Regiment, dashed in front of his Company, sword in hand, into a dense body of Russians who were in a battery. I was not in the thick of it, but was engaged with an outlying picquet on the left of the attack. George was in the very thick of it, and, not seeing me, kept asking some of our men where I was. They did not know. He tells me that he thought for a long time I was killed, and even fancied that he had seen me lying on the ground; it turned out later to have been poor Colonel Dawson's[66] body which he mistook for me.

On the 14th we had a terrible storm, such a one as, fortunately for mankind, does not happen but very rarely. All our tents of course were blown down, and we passed the day very uncomfortably; but at sea it was terrible. At Balaklava alone more than two hundred and sixty souls perished, and eleven ships went down. George will have been able to give you a perfect account of it, for, for many hours, the *Retribution* was in imminent danger. I went a few days after the storm to

[65] Colonel Henry Hugh Manvers Percy, 1817-1877, whose father afterwards became the fifth Duke of Northumberland. The Legion of Honour, the Medjidie, and the V.C. were all subsequently conferred on him.
[66] Hon. Thomas Vesey Dawson, brother of the third Lord Cremorne (created Earl of Dartrey).

see him on board.[67] ... He had a little fever or ague on him, but was otherwise well. He has now gone to Constantinople....

May I beg of your Majesty to remember me kindly to Prince Albert and the Duchess of Kent. I have the honour, etc.

Edward of Saxe-Weimar.

Queen Victoria to the Duke of Newcastle.

THE CRIMEAN MEDAL

Windsor Castle, *30th November 1854.*

The Queen thinks that no time should be lost in announcing the intention of the Queen to confer a *medal* on all those who have been engaged in the arduous and brilliant campaign in the Crimea.

The medal should have the word "*Crimea*" on it, with an appropriate device (for which it would be well to lose no time in having a design made) and *clasps*—like to the Peninsular Medal, with the names *Alma* and *Inkerman* inscribed on them, according to who had been in one or both battles. *Sebastopol*, should it fall, or any other name of a battle which Providence may permit our brave troops to gain, can be inscribed on other clasps hereafter to be added. The names *Alma* and *Inkerman* should likewise be borne on the colours of all the regiments who have been engaged in these bloody and glorious actions.

The Queen is sure that nothing will gratify and encourage our noble troops more than the knowledge that this is to be done.

We have just had two hours' most interesting conversation with General Bentinck,[68] whose sound good sense and energy make us

---

[67] In this terrible hurricane the *Prince*, a new and magnificent steamer, with a cargo of the value of £500,000, including powder, shot and shell, beds, blankets, warm clothing for the troops, and medical stores for the hospitals, was lost; six men only of a crew of one hundred and fifty were saved; but the soldiers of the Forty-sixth, whom she was conveying to Balaklava, had happily been landed. Thirty of our transports, as well as the French warship *Henri IV.*, were wrecked. A thousand men were lost, and many more escaped drowning, only to fall into the hands of the Cossacks and be carried to Sebastopol. One solitary source of consolation could be found in the circumstance that the tempest did not occur at an earlier period, when six hundred vessels, heavily laden and dangerously crowded together, were making their way from Varna to Old Fort.

deeply regret that he is not now on the spot; he is, however, ready to go out again next year, as Lord Raglan wishes to give him a Division. We hope that, after two or three months' rest, he may be able to go out again.

The Earl of Aberdeen to Queen Victoria.

LORD JOHN RUSSELL

London, *7th December 1854.*

Lord Aberdeen presents his humble duty to your Majesty. He would have been desirous of personally submitting to your Majesty the result of the meeting of the Cabinet last night; but he was apprehensive that his sudden journey to Windsor Castle this morning would give rise to speculations and conjectures which, in the present state of the Ministry, it is as well to avoid.

Lord Aberdeen thinks he may venture to assure your Majesty that the correspondence recently circulated is regarded by all the Members of the Cabinet precisely in the same light; and that the propositions of Lord John Russell are considered by all as quite untenable. Lord Palmerston forms no exception; and, whatever may be his views in future, it is clear that at present he contemplates no changes in the Government. Lord John was himself fully aware of this unanimity, and remained entirely silent with respect to his former suggestions. He dwelt in general terms on the absence of vigour in the prosecution of the war, and stated his conviction that the same course would be observed in future. He referred to his position in the House of Commons with much bitterness, and declared that he would never pass such another Session of Parliament as the last. He attributed the frequent defeats of the Government in the House of Commons to the Reform Bill having been withdrawn, by which it was shown that hostile attacks might be made with impunity.

It was obvious, however, that the drift of his observations tended to the substitution of himself as the Head of the Government rather than to any change of Departments; and this he did not deny, when Lord Aberdeen pointed out the inference to be drawn from his remarks.

---

[68] General (afterwards Sir Henry) Bentinck had been wounded at Inkerman; he returned to the Crimea to command a Division.

Finally, Lord John said that he had quite made up his mind. He was ready to continue in office during the short Session before Christmas, and to defend all that had been done; but that he was determined to retire after Christmas. An observation being made that it would be unconstitutional to go into Parliament with such a determination, he replied that, if such was the opinion, he would request Lord Aberdeen to convey his resignation to-morrow morning to your Majesty, which, at all events, would be perfectly constitutional.

Lord Aberdeen feels it to be his duty to state to your Majesty that, whatever may be the real cause, Lord John has made up his mind to act in the manner he has announced.

In this situation it is Lord Aberdeen's desire to come to your Majesty's assistance by any means in his power. Lord John's defection will be a great blow, from which it is very doubtful if the Government could recover; but Lord Aberdeen will come to no conclusion or form any decided opinion until he shall have had the honour of seeing your Majesty.

Memorandum by the Prince Albert.

CABINET DISSENSIONS

Windsor Castle, *9th December 1854.*

Lord Aberdeen arrived yesterday evening, leaving the Cabinet sitting, revising the Speech from the Throne.[69] He had come to no decision. Sir James Graham and Mr Gladstone had been anxious that he should accept Lord John's resignation at once. He himself felt reluctant to do anything which might be considered harsh towards Lord John, and might make him a martyr hereafter. There was no doubt, however, that they could not go on with Lord John. The universal feeling of the Cabinet seemed to be one of indignation ... at Lord John's conduct. Nobody had expressed himself stronger about it than Lord Lansdowne to Lord Clarendon, feeling it, as he said, "quite a necessity to speak out." The Chancellor said he owed his political allegiance to Lord John as well as his office; but as a man of honour he could not go with him. Lord Granville feels the same. Lord Palmerston had written a long and very able letter to Lord John, proving the impossibility of

[69] Parliament was to meet on the 12th, chiefly for the purpose of passing a Foreign Enlistment Bill, authorising the immediate enlistment of 15,000 (afterwards reduced to 10,000) foreigners, to be drilled in this country.

joining the offices of Secretary at War and Secretary of State for War. Lord John had now, however, dropped his proposal altogether, and made it quite clear that it was Lord Aberdeen he wished to have removed. He said to Lord Palmerston: "When the Cabinet was formed, I always understood that Lord Aberdeen would soon give me up my old place; it has now lasted more than two years, and he seemed to get enamoured with office, and I could not meet the House of Commons in the position I was in last Session."

In answer to Lord Palmerston's enquiry what he would do, and how he could expose the Country to such fearful risks at such a moment, he said that he would support the Government out of office. "You will support it at the head of a very virulent Opposition," was Lord Palmerston's reply; "and when you have succeeded in overthrowing the Government, which has difficulty enough to hold its ground even with your assistance, what will you say to the Country? Will you say: 'Here I am. I have triumphed, and have displaced, in the midst of most hazardous operations, all the ablest men the Country has produced; but I shall take their place with Mr Vernon Smith, Lord Seymour, Lord Minto, and others....'"

Sir Charles Wood is the only person who says it is all nothing, and he knows Lord John, and it is sure to blow over.

Lord Aberdeen said it is come to a point where this is no longer possible, as he laid his ground not only on the position that the war had been badly conducted, but that it *would* be so for the future.

At the Cabinet yesterday a significant incident occurred: Lord John asked what should become of Reform. Lord Aberdeen's answer was, that it had been set aside on account of the war, and that as the war was now raging at its height, it could not be brought on again. Later, when they came to the passage about Education, Lord John made an alteration in the Draft, adding something about strengthening the institutions of the Country. Lord Palmerston started up and asked: "Does that mean Reform?" Lord John answered: "It might or might not." "Well, then," said Lord Palmerston, with a heat of manner which struck the whole Cabinet, and was hardly justified by the occasion, "I wish it to be understood that I protest against any direct or indirect attempt to bring forward the Reform question again!" Lord John, nettled, muttered to himself, but loud enough to be heard by everybody: "Then I shall bring forward the Reform Bill at once."

It is evident to me that after this a junction between Lord Palmerston and Lord John is impossible, and that it must have been Lord

Palmerston's object to make this clear to the Cabinet. Lord Aberdeen has declared that he is quite willing to yield his post to Lord John—but that it would not suffice to have got a head—that there must be some Members also, and where are they to be found? He is certain that not one of the present Cabinet could now serve under Lord John. An attempt to solve the question how the present Government is to be maintained, naturally leads everybody to the same conclusion: that Lord Palmerston must be substituted for Lord John as the Leader of the House of Commons. Disagreeable as this must be ... to Lord Aberdeen, and dangerous as the experiment may turn out, we agreed with Lord Aberdeen that he should make the offer to him with the Queen's consent. An alternative proposed by Lord Clarendon, that Lord Aberdeen should ask Lord John what he advised him to do under the circumstances, was strongly condemned by me, as depriving Lord Aberdeen of all the advantage of the initiative with Lord Palmerston. Lord Aberdeen states his great difficulty to be not only the long antecedent and mutual opposition between him and Lord Palmerston, but also the fact that Lord Palmerston loved war for war's sake, and he peace for peace' sake.... He consoled himself, however, at last by the reflection that Lord Palmerston was not worse than Lord John in that respect, and, on the other hand, gave greater weight to the consideration of what was practicable. It remains open for the present whether Lord John is to act as the organ for the Government during the short Session, and resign afterwards, or to resign now.

Albert.

Queen Victoria to Viscount Hardinge.

LORD ROKEBY

Windsor Castle, *10th December 1854.*

The Queen is glad to hear of Lord Rokeby's readiness to go out, as she is sure that he will prove himself an efficient officer in command of that noble Brigade of Guards.[70]

The Queen must repeat again her opinion relative to General Bentinck. She thinks that he ought to go out again, and that, if a division were offered to him, he would not hesitate (when he has recruited his health) to go out. For the sake of example it would be most desirable,

[70] Lord Rokeby had on the previous evening been offered and had accepted the command.

for there evidently is an inclination to ask for leave to go home, which would be very detrimental to the Army.

The Earl of Aberdeen to Queen Victoria.

LORD JOHN RUSSELL

London, *16th December 1854.*

Lord Aberdeen presents his humble duty to your Majesty. The Cabinet met to-day, and discussed various measures, with a view to their introduction into Parliament during the course of the ensuing Session. In this discussion Lord John Russell took an active part, and must have greatly astonished his colleagues, after their knowledge of all that had recently passed. Lord Aberdeen had been previously made aware, although not by himself, of the change which had taken place in Lord John's intentions. After the meeting of the Cabinet, Lord John came to Lord Aberdeen, and spoke of the affair of Mr Kennedy,[71] but did not seem disposed to advert to any other subject. Lord Aberdeen therefore took an opportunity of referring to the correspondence which had taken place, and the notice which had been given by Lord John. Without any embarrassment, or apparent sense of inconsistency, he at once admitted that he had changed his intention, and attributed it chiefly to a conversation yesterday with Lord Panmure, who, although a great military reformer, had convinced him that the present was not a fitting time for his proposed changes.

Lord Aberdeen had not seen any member of the Cabinet this evening since the meeting terminated, and does not know how they may be affected by this change. Some, he feels sure, will be disappointed; but, on the whole, he feels disposed to be well satisfied. It is true that there can be no security for a single week; and it is impossible to escape from a sense of self-degradation by submitting to such an unprecedented state of relations amongst colleagues; but the scandal of a rupture would be so great, and the evils which might ensue so incalculable, that Lord Aberdeen is sincerely convinced it will be most advantageous for your Majesty's service, and for the public, to endeavour, by a conciliatory and prudent course of conduct, to preserve tranquillity and union as long as possible. This does not exclude the necessity of firmness; and in the present case Lord Aberdeen has

[71] Mr Kennedy (who was remotely connected by marriage with Lord John) had been removed by Mr Gladstone from an office he held. Lord John took it up as a family matter.

yielded nothing whatever, but he has received Lord John's change without resentment or displeasure.

The Duke of Newcastle to Queen Victoria.

THE SCUTARI HOSPITAL

War Department, *22nd December 1854.*

... The Duke of Newcastle assures your Majesty that the condition of the Hospital at Scutari, and the entire want of all method and arrangement in everything which concerns the comfort of the Army, are subjects of constant and most painful anxiety to him, and he wishes most earnestly that he could see his way clearly to an early and complete remedy.[72]

Nothing can be more just than are all your Majesty's comments upon the state of facts exhibited by these letters, and the Duke of Newcastle has repeatedly, during the last two months, written in the strongest terms respecting them—but hitherto without avail, and with little other result than a denial of charges, the truth of which must now be considered to be substantiated.

Your Majesty is aware that the Duke of Newcastle sent out a Commission to enquire into the whole state of the Medical Department nearly three months ago, and he expects a report very soon.

In the meantime, the Duke of Newcastle will again write in the sense of your Majesty's letter to him.

Queen Victoria to the King of the Belgians.

Windsor Castle, *30th December 1854.*

My dearest Uncle,—Once more, in this old and very *eventful* year, allow me to address you, and to ask you for the continuation of that love and affection which you have ever borne me! May God bless you and yours in this New Year—and though the old one departs in war

[72] Early in November, a band of capable and devoted nurses, under the superintendence of Miss Florence Nightingale, had arrived at Scutari, the experiment having been devised and projected by Mr Sidney Herbert, who was a personal friend of Miss Nightingale. The party was accompanied by Mr and Mrs Bracebridge, whose letters describing the condition of the hospitals had been sent by the Queen to the Duke of Newcastle.

and blood, may we hope to see this year restore peace to this troubled world, and may *we* meet again also!

With the affectionate wishes of all the children, believe me always, your most devoted Niece,

Victoria R.

INTRODUCTORY NOTE
TO CHAPTER XXIV

At the end of the year 1854, negotiations had been on foot with a view to terminating the war, on terms which were known as the "Four Points," the third of which was designed to extinguish Russian preponderance in the Black Sea; and a conference of the Powers ultimately assembled at Vienna for the purpose. Early in 1855, Sardinia, under the influence of Cavour, her Premier, joined the Western Alliance against Russia. On Parliament re-assembling in January, Mr Roebuck gave notice of a motion for the appointment of a Committee to enquire into the conduct of the war. Lord John Russell, finding himself unable to resist the motion, at once resigned, and the Ministry was overwhelmingly defeated by a majority of more than two to one. Lord Derby, as Leader of the Conservative Opposition, was summoned to form a Ministry, but failed to do so; the age of Lord Lansdowne prevented his accepting the Premiership; and Lord John Russell, whose action had largely contributed to the defeat of the coalition, then attempted the task, but found that he could not command the support even of his old Whig colleagues. The Queen accordingly desired Lord Palmerston, whom the voice of the country unmistakably indicated for the Premiership, to construct a Government; he was successful in the attempt, the Cabinet being a reconstruction of that of Lord Aberdeen, with Lord Panmure substituted for the Duke of Newcastle at the War Office, while Lord John Russell was appointed British Plenipotentiary at the Vienna Conference. The new Premier desired to prevent the actual appointment of the Committee which Mr Roebuck's motion demanded, the displacement of the late Ministry—the real objective of the attack—having been effected; but as the House of Commons manifested a determination to proceed with the appointment of the Committee, the Peelite section of the Cabinet (Sir James Graham, Mr Gladstone, and Mr Sidney Herbert) withdrew, and Lord John Russell, who was then on his way to Vienna, accepted the Secretaryship of the

Colonies. Early in March, the Czar Nicholas died suddenly of pulmonary apoplexy, and the expectation of peace increased; shortly afterwards, the Emperor and Empress of the French paid a state visit to this country, and were received with much enthusiasm, the Emperor being made a Knight of the Garter.

In February, a determined attack by the Russians upon Eupatoria was repulsed by the Turks; the defenders of Sebastopol, however, succeeded in occupying and fortifying an important position, afterwards known as the "Mamelon." The bombardment was resumed by the Allies in April, and a successful attack made upon Kertsch, from which the supplies of Sebastopol were mainly drawn; while a squadron under Captain Lyons destroyed the Russian magazines and stores in the Sea of Azov. General Canrobert was succeeded in the French command by General Pélissier, and on the 7th of June the Mamelon was taken by the French. A desperate but, as it proved, unsuccessful assault was then made by the Allies on the Redan and Malakhoff batteries; at this juncture Lord Raglan died, and was succeeded in the command by General Simpson.

The Vienna Conference proved abortive, Russia refusing to accept the third point, and though a compromise was proposed by Austria, which was favoured by the British and French Plenipotentiaries, their respective Governments did not ratify their views. The negotiations accordingly broke down, and Lord John Russell, on his return, used language in Parliament quite inconsistent with the view which it afterwards appeared he had urged at Vienna. He was loudly denounced for this, and, to avoid Parliamentary censure, again resigned office.

Among the measures which became law during the session, were those for enabling companies to be formed with limited liability, and for granting self-government to some of the Australasian Colonies. The Committee appointed by the House of Commons held its meetings in public (after a proposal to keep its investigations secret had been rejected), and, by the casting vote of the Chairman, reported that the late Cabinet, when directing the expedition to the Crimea, had had no adequate information as to the force they would have to encounter there; but a motion to "visit with severe reprehension" every member of the Cabinet was parried by carrying the "previous question."

In August, the Queen and Prince Albert paid a return visit to the French Emperor, and were received with great magnificence in Paris, while later in the year King Victor Emmanuel of Sardinia visited this country, and was made a Knight of the Garter. On the 9th of August,

Sweaborg was severely bombarded by the allied fleets in the Baltic, and a forlorn attempt to raise the siege of Sebastopol resulted in another decisive success at the Tchernaya, the Sardinian contingent fighting with great bravery. Sebastopol fell on the 8th of September, after a siege of three hundred and forty-nine days; the citadel of Kinburn was bombarded and surrendered in October, after which General Simpson retired, in favour of Sir William Codrington. On the other hand, the fortress of Kars in Armenia, which had been defended by General Fenwick Williams, had to surrender to the Russian General Mouravieff, in circumstances, however, so honourable, that the officers were allowed to retain their swords, and their General received a Baronetcy and a pension of £1000 a year.

CHAPTER XXIV
1855

Queen Victoria to the Earl of Clarendon.

THE FOUR POINTS

Osborne, *9th January 1855.*

The Queen received Lord Clarendon's box by special messenger yesterday evening. The acceptance by Russia of our interpretation of the four points[73] is a most clever, diplomatic manœuvre, and very em-

---

[73] The celebrated "Four Points" were—

1. Cessation of the Russian protectorate over Moldavia, Wallachia, and Servia: the privileges granted by the Sultan to the Principalities to be collectively guaranteed by the Powers.

2. Free navigation of the Danube.

3. Termination of the preponderance of Russia in the Black Sea.

4. Abandonment by Russia of her claim over any subjects of the Porte; the Five Powers to co-operate in obtaining from the Sultan the confirmation and observance of the religious privileges of the different Christian communities, and to turn to account in their common interest the generous intentions manifested by the Sultan, without infringing his dignity or the independence of his crown.

Towards the end of 1854, negotiations as to the Four Points had been proceeding between the Allies and Austria, and on the 28th of December the Three Powers had agreed in communicating to Russia a memorandum giving a more exact interpretation of the Four Points. This was agreed upon as the basis on which the Plenipotentiaries were to meet at Vienna to settle the Eastern Question, and to conclude the war.

Another event, productive ultimately of results of great importance, took place at the end of January. King Victor Emmanuel of Sardinia joined the Western Alliance, and despatched 15,000 men under General La Marmora to the Crimea. This act was inspired by Cavour, the Sardinian Prime Minister, who took the step that Austria hesitated to take, and thereby established strong claims both upon the Emperor Napoleon and Lord Palmerston.

barrassing for us at this moment, before Sebastopol is taken, and before Austria has been compelled to join in the war. It leaves us no alternative but to meet in conference, which, however, in the Queen's opinion, ought to be preceded by a despatch to Austria, putting on record our opinion as to the nature and object of the step taken by Russia, and the advantages she hopes to derive by it from Austria and Germany, and the disadvantages she expects to inflict on the Western Powers. As hostilities ought not to be interrupted unless the Russians give up Sebastopol and evacuate the Crimea (which would give rest and quiet to our poor soldiers), there still remains the hope of our getting the place before preliminaries of peace could be signed; and in that case a Peace on the four points would be everything we could desire, and much preferable to the chance of future convulsions of the whole state of Europe. Russia would then have yielded all our wishes for the future.

A mere moral defeat, such as Count Buol seems disposed to consider as sufficient, would soon prove to have been none at all, and Austria would be the Power which, to its cost, would find out (when too late) that the preponderance of Russia is by no means diminished.

The Queen has given her permission to Lord John to go to Paris; he will find the Emperor as little able to help himself in this stage of the business as ourselves.

The Queen is afraid that the news of the Russian acceptance may induce our commanders in the Crimea to rest on their oars, and thinks it necessary, therefore, that immediate orders should go out, pointing out that the early fall of the town is just now more important than ever.

The Queen wishes Lord Clarendon to communicate this letter to Lord Aberdeen and the Duke of Newcastle.

She returns to Windsor this afternoon.

Queen Victoria to the Earl of Aberdeen.

LORD ABERDEEN AND THE GARTER

Windsor Castle, *10th January 1855.*

Before Parliament meets for probably a very stormy Session, the Queen wishes to give a public testimony of her continued confidence in Lord Aberdeen's administration, by offering him the vacant Blue Ribbon. The Queen need not add a word on her personal feelings of regard and friendship for Lord Aberdeen, which are known to him now for a long period of years.

The Earl of Aberdeen to Queen Victoria.

London, *10th January 1855.*

Lord Aberdeen presents his most humble duty to your Majesty. He has had the honour of receiving your Majesty's most gracious letter, and humbly begs to return your Majesty his grateful acknowledgments for this mark of your Majesty's continued confidence and favour. When your Majesty mentioned the subject to Lord Aberdeen some time ago, he had not thought of any such distinction; and perhaps at his time of life, and with his present prospects, he scarcely ought to do so. There is no doubt that this unequivocal mark of gracious favour might strengthen his hands, and especially in those quarters where it would be most useful; but the power of misconstruction and malevolence is so great that the effect might possibly be more injurious than beneficial.

Perhaps your Majesty would be graciously pleased to permit Lord Aberdeen to reflect a little on the subject, and to submit his thoughts to your Majesty.

Lord Aberdeen entreats your Majesty to believe that in this, as in everything else, it is his desire to look exclusively to your Majesty's welfare. When he leaves your Majesty's service, your Majesty may be fully aware of his many imperfections as a Minister; but he trusts that your Majesty will always have reason to regard him as perfectly disinterested.

The Earl of Aberdeen to Queen Victoria.

London, *11th January 1855.*

Lord Aberdeen presents his most humble duty to your Majesty. He has maturely reflected on the subject of your Majesty's gracious letter of yesterday, and he is fully sensible of the very important advantage which, in his official position, he might derive from such a public and signal proof of your Majesty's confidence and favour.

Although this might naturally give rise to more or less of political animadversion, Lord Aberdeen would not hesitate in his decision, if the alternative were only between himself and some Peer of high rank whose claim consisted in being a supporter of the Government; but

Lord Aberdeen believes that he may venture to make a suggestion to your Majesty, the effect of which would redound to your Majesty's honour, and which might not prove altogether disadvantageous to himself.

Lord Aberdeen understands that in consequence of the regulations of the Order, Lord Cardigan could not properly receive the Grand Cross of the Bath. From his rank and station, Lord Cardigan might fairly pretend to the Garter, but his violent party politics would make it impossible for Lord Aberdeen, under ordinary circumstances, to submit his name to your Majesty for this purpose. At the same time, Lord Cardigan's great gallantry and personal sacrifices seem to afford him a just claim to your Majesty's favourable consideration; and Lord Aberdeen believes that to confer upon him the Blue Ribbon at this moment would be regarded as a very graceful act on the part of your Majesty. It is even possible that Lord Aberdeen's political opponents might give him some credit for tendering such advice.

If therefore your Majesty should be pleased to take the same view of this matter, Lord Aberdeen would communicate with Lord Cardigan on his arrival in London, and would willingly postpone all consideration of your Majesty's gracious intentions towards himself. But Lord Aberdeen will venture humbly to repeat his grateful sense of all your Majesty's kindness, and his acknowledgments for the expression of sentiments which he can never sufficiently value.[74]

Queen Victoria to the Duke of Newcastle.

WELFARE OF THE ARMY

Windsor Castle, *12th January 1855.*

The Queen returns the enclosed despatch to the Duke of Newcastle, which she has read with much pleasure, as bringing before Lord Raglan in an official manner—which will require official enquiry and *answer*—the various points so urgently requiring his attention and remedial effort. It is at the same time so delicately worded that it ought not to offend, although it cannot help, from its matter, being painful to Lord Raglan. The Queen has only one remark to make, viz. the entire omission of her name throughout the document. It speaks simply in the

[74] Subsequently Lord Aberdeen yielded to the Queen's affectionate insistence, and was installed Knight of the Garter at a Chapter held on the 7th of February.

name of the *People* of England, and of *their* sympathy, whilst the Queen feels it to be one of her highest prerogatives and dearest duties to care for the welfare and success of *her* Army. Had the despatch not gone before it was submitted to the Queen, in a few words the Duke of Newcastle would have rectified this omission.

The Duke of Newcastle might with truth have added that, making every allowance for the difficulties before Sebastopol, it is difficult to imagine how the Army could ever be *moved* in the field, if the impossibility of keeping it alive is felt in a *stationary camp* only seven miles from its harbour, with the whole British Navy and hundreds of transports at its command.

Queen Victoria to the Earl of Aberdeen.

Windsor Castle, *13th January 1855.*

The Queen has received Lord Aberdeen's letter of the 11th, and has since seen Lord John Russell's letter. It shows that the practice of the Queen's different Cabinet Ministers going to Paris, to have personal explanations with the Emperor, besides being hardly a constitutional practice, must lead to much misunderstanding. How is the Emperor to distinguish between the views of the Queen's Government and the private opinions of the different members of the Cabinet, all more or less varying, particularly in a Coalition Government?

The Queen hopes therefore that this will be the last such visit. The Ambassador is the official organ of communication, and the Foreign Secretary is responsible for his doing his duty, and has the means of controlling him by his instructions and the despatches he receives, all of which are placed on record.[75]

Lord Raglan to Queen Victoria.

LETTER FROM LORD RAGLAN

Before Sebastopol, *20th January 1855.*

Lord Raglan presents his humble duty to your Majesty, and has the honour to acknowledge with every sentiment of devotion and gratitude your Majesty's most gracious letter of 1st January, and the kind

---

[75] The cause of Lord John's visit to Paris had been the illness there of his sister-in-law, Lady Harriet Elliot; but he took the opportunity of conferring both with the Emperor and his Ministers on the conduct of the war.—Walpole's *Life of Lord John Russell*, chap. xxv.

wishes which your Majesty and the Prince are pleased to unite in offering to the Army and your Majesty's most humble servant on the occasion of the New Year.

The deep concern and anxiety felt by your Majesty and the Prince for the privations of the troops, their unceasing labours, their exposure to bad weather, and the extensive sickness which prevails among them, are invaluable proofs of the lively interest which your Majesty and His Royal Highness take in the welfare of an Army which, under no circumstances, will cease to revere the name, and apply all its best energies to the service of your Majesty.

THE COMMISSARIAT

Lord Raglan can with truth assure your Majesty that his whole time and all his thoughts are occupied in endeavouring to provide for the various wants of your Majesty's troops. It has not been in his power to lighten the burthen of their duties. Those exacted from them before Sebastopol are for the preservation of the trenches and batteries; and there are many other calls upon the men, more especially when, as at present, the roads are so bad that wheeled carriages can no longer be used, and that the horse transport is diminished by sickness and death, and that the Commissariat, having no longer any sufficient means of conveyance at its command, cannot bring up the daily supplies without their assistance, thereby adding, however inevitably, to their labour and fatigue.

Lord Raglan begs leave to submit, for your Majesty's information, that the Allied Armies have no intercourse with the country, and can derive no resources from it; and consequently all the requirements for the conveyance of stores and provisions, as well as the stores and provisions themselves, must be imported. Such a necessity forms in itself a difficulty of vast magnitude, which has been greatly felt by him, and has been productive of the most serious consequences to the comfort and welfare of the Army.

The coffee sent from Constantinople has been received and issued to the troops green, the Commissariat having no means whatever of roasting it. Very recently, however, an able officer of the Navy, Captain Heath of the *Sanspareil*, undertook to have machines made by the engineers on board his ship for roasting coffee; and in this he has succeeded, but they have not yet produced as much as is required for the daily consumption.

The Commissary-General applied to the Treasury for roasted coffee three months ago. None has as yet arrived. A very large amount of warm clothing has been distributed, and your Majesty's soldiers, habited in the cloaks of various countries, might be taken for the troops of any nation as well as those of England.

Huts have arrived in great abundance, and as much progress is made in getting them up as could be hoped for, considering that there has been a very heavy fall of snow, and that a thaw has followed it, and the extremely limited means of conveyance at command.

Much having been said, as Lord Raglan has been given to understand, in private letters, of the inefficiency of the officers of the Staff, he considers it to be due to your Majesty, and a simple act of justice to those individuals, to assure your Majesty that he has every reason to be satisfied with their exertions, their indefatigable zeal, and undeviating, close attention to their duties, and he may be permitted to add that the horse and mule transport for the carriage of provisions and stores are under the charge of the Commissariat, not of the Staff, and that the Department in question engages the men who are hired to take care of it, and has exclusive authority over them.

Lord Raglan transmitted to the Duke of Newcastle, in the month of December, the report of a Medical Board, which he caused to assemble at Constantinople for the purpose of ascertaining the state of health of the Duke of Cambridge. The report evidently showed the necessity of His Royal Highness's return to England for its re-establishment. This, Lord Raglan knows, was the opinion of the Honourable Lieutenant-Colonel Macdonald,[76] whose attention and devotion to His Royal Highness could not be surpassed, and who was himself very anxious to remain with the Army.

The Duke, however, has not gone further than Malta, where, it is said, his health has not improved.

[76] The Hon. James Bosville Macdonald [1810-1882], son of the third Baron Macdonald, A.D.C., Equerry and Private Secretary to the Duke of Cambridge.

Queen Victoria to the Earl of Aberdeen.

THE ARMY BOARD

Windsor Castle, *22nd January 1855.*

The Queen has received Lord Aberdeen's letter of yesterday, giving an account of the proceedings of the last Cabinet....

The Queen is quite prepared to sanction the proposal of constituting the Secretary of State for War, the Commander-in-Chief, the Master-General of the Ordnance, and the Secretary at War, a Board on the affairs of the Army, which promises more unity of action in these Departments, and takes notice of the fact that the powers and functions of the Commander-in-Chief are not to be changed. As these, however, rest entirely on tradition, and are in most cases ambiguous and undefined, the Queen would wish that they should be clearly defined, and this the more so as she transacts certain business directly with him, and ought to be secured against getting into any collision with the Secretary of State, who also takes her pleasure, and gives orders to the Commander-in-Chief. She would further ask to be regularly furnished with the Minutes of the proceedings of the new Board, in order to remain acquainted with what is going on.

Unless, however, the Militia be made over to the direction of the Secretary of State for *War*, our Army system will still remain very incomplete. The last experience has shown that the Militia will have to be looked upon as the chief source for recruiting the Army, and this will never be done harmoniously and well, unless they both be brought under the same control.

With reference to the Investiture of the Garter, the Queen need not assure Lord Aberdeen that there are few, if any, on whom she will confer the Blue Ribbon with greater pleasure than on so kind and valued a friend as he is to us both.

Lord John Russell to Queen Victoria.

Chesham Place, *24th January 1855.*

Lord John Russell presents his humble duty to your Majesty; he has had the honour of receiving your Majesty's gracious invitation to Windsor Castle. He would have waited upon your Majesty this day had he not been constrained by a sense of duty to write to Lord Aberdeen last night a letter of which he submits a copy.

Lord John Russell trusts your Majesty will be graciously pleased to comply at once with his request. But he feels it would be right to attend your Majesty's farther commands before he has the honour of waiting upon your Majesty.

/Enclosure in previous Letter./

Lord John Russell to the Earl of Aberdeen.

MR. ROEBUCK'S MOTION

Chesham Place, *23rd January 1855.*

My dear Lord Aberdeen,—Mr Roebuck has given notice of a Motion to enquire into the conduct of the war. I do not see how this Motion is to be resisted. But as it involves a censure of the War Departments with which some of my colleagues are connected, my only course is to tender my resignation.

I therefore have to request you will lay my humble resignation of the office, which I have the honour to hold, before the Queen, with the expression of my gratitude for Her Majesty's kindness for many years. I remain, my dear Lord Aberdeen, yours very truly,

J. Russell.

Queen Victoria to Lord John Russell.

LORD JOHN RUSSELL RESIGNS

Windsor Castle, 24th *January 1855.*

The Queen has this moment received Lord John Russell's letter and enclosure, and must express to him her surprise and concern at hearing so abruptly of his intention to desert her Government on the Motion of Mr Roebuck.

Memorandum by the Prince Albert.

Windsor Castle, *25th January 1855.*

Yesterday evening Lord Aberdeen came down here. He had heard that Lord John had written to the Queen, and she showed him the correspondence. He then reported that Lord John's letter to him had come without the slightest notice and warning, and whatever the cause for it might be, the object could only be to upset the Government. Upon receiving it, he had sent for the Duke of Newcastle and shown it to him. The Duke at once proposed, that as a sacrifice seemed to be required to appease the public for the want of success in the Crimea, he was quite ready to be that sacrifice, and entreated that Lord Aberdeen would put his office into the hands of Lord Palmerston, who possessed the confidence of the nation; Lord Aberdeen should propose this at once to the Cabinet, he himself would support the Government *out* of office like *in* office. Lord Aberdeen then went to Lord Palmerston to communicate to him what had happened, and ascertain his feelings. Lord Palmerston was disgusted at Lord John's behaviour,[77] and did not consider himself the least bound to be guided by him; he admitted that somehow or other the Public had a notion that he would manage the War Department better than anybody else; as for himself, he did not expect to do it half so well as the Duke of Newcastle, but was prepared to try it, not to let the Government be dissolved, which at this moment would be a real calamity for the country.

The Cabinet met at two o'clock, and Lord Aberdeen laid the case before it. The Duke then made his proposal, and was followed by Lord Palmerston, who stated pretty much the same as he had done in the morning, upon which Sir George Grey said it did both the Duke and Lord Palmerston the highest honour, but he saw no possibility of resisting Mr Roebuck's Motion without Lord John; Sir Charles Wood was of the same opinion. Lord Clarendon proposed that, as the Duke had given up his Department to Lord Palmerston, Lord John might be induced to remain; but this was at once rejected by Lord Aberdeen on the ground that they might be justified in sacrificing the Duke to the wishes of the Country, but they could not to Lord John, with any degree of honour. The upshot was, that the Whig Members of the Cabinet, not being inclined to carry on the Government (including Lord Lansdowne), they came to the unanimous determination to tender their resignations.

The Queen protested against this, as exposing her and the Country to the greatest peril, as it was impossible to change the Government at this moment without deranging the whole external policy in diplomacy and war, and there was nobody to whom the reins could be confided. Lord Derby and his party would never have done, but now he had allied himself with Lord Ellenborough, who was determined to have the conduct of the war....

---

[77] Lord Palmerston wrote him a most scathing letter on the subject.

Lord Aberdeen thought yet, that on him[78] devolved the responsibility of replacing what he wantonly destroyed. The Queen insisted, however, that Lord Aberdeen should make one appeal to the Cabinet to stand by her, which he promised to do to the best of his ability, but without hope of success. The Cabinet will meet at twelve o'clock today, but at five the Ministers will have to announce their determination to the Houses of Parliament, as Mr Roebuck's Motion stands for that hour.

Albert.

Lord John Russell to Queen Victoria.

LORD JOHN'S JUSTIFICATION

Chesham Place, *25th January 1855.*

Lord John Russell presents his humble duty to your Majesty. He has received with deep regret the imputations of deserting the Government.

Lord John Russell, after being at the head of the Ministry for more than five years, and being then the leader of a great party, consented to serve under Lord Aberdeen, and served for more than a year and a half without office.

After sacrificing his position and his reputation for two years, he has come to the conclusion that it would not be for the benefit of the country to resist Mr Roebuck's Motion. But it is clear that the enquiry he contemplates could not be carried on without so weakening the authority of the Government that it could not usefully go on.

In these circumstances Lord John Russell has pursued the course which he believes to be for the public benefit.

With the most sincere respect for Lord Aberdeen, he felt he could not abandon his sincere convictions in order to maintain the Administration in office.

It is the cause of much pain to him that, after sacrificing his position in order to secure your Majesty's service from interruption, he should not have obtained your Majesty's approbation.

---

[78] *I.e.*, Lord John Russell.

Queen Victoria to Lord John Russell.

Windsor Castle, *25th January 1855.*

The Queen has received Lord John Russell's letter of to-day in explanation of his resignation. She has done full justice to the high-minded and disinterested manner in which Lord John sacrificed two years ago his position as former Prime Minister and as Leader of a great party, in consenting to serve under Lord Aberdeen, and hopes she has sufficiently expressed this to him at the time. He will since have found a further proof of her desire to do anything which could be agreeable to him in his position, by cheerfully agreeing to all the various changes of offices which he has at different times wished for. If Lord John will consider, however, the moment which he has now chosen to leave her Government, and the abrupt way in which his unexpected intention of agreeing in a vote implying censure of the Government was announced to her, he cannot be surprised that she could not express her approbation.

Memorandum by Queen Victoria.

LORD JOHN'S INDIGNATION

Windsor Castle, *25th January 1855.*

Lord Aberdeen arrived at six o'clock to report the result of the meeting of the Cabinet, which was so far satisfactory that they agreed upon retaining office at present for the purpose of meeting Mr Roebuck's Motion. They expect (most of them, at least) to be beat and to have to resign, but they think it more honourable to be driven out than to run away. They will meet Parliament therefore without making any changes in the offices. Lord Aberdeen and the Duke of Newcastle fancy even that they will have a chance of defeating Mr Roebuck's Motion. Sir George Grey has declared, however, that, perfectly willing as he is not to desert his post at this moment, he will consider himself at liberty to resign even after success, as he thinks the Government has no chance of standing with Lord John in Opposition. The other Whigs would in that case very likely do the same, and the Government come to an end in this way; but it is not impossible that Sir George Grey may be prevailed upon by the Queen to stay. Much must depend upon the nature of the Debate.

Lord Aberdeen seems to have put the Queen's desire that the Cabinet should reconsider their former decision in the strongest words, which seems to have brought about the present result. He saw Lord

John this morning who, though personally civil towards himself, was very much excited and very angry at a letter which he had received from the Queen. He said he would certainly vote with Mr Roebuck. The Houses are to be adjourned to-day, and the whole discussion comes on to-morrow. Lord Aberdeen brought a copy of a letter Lord Palmerston had written to Lord John. The Peelites in the Cabinet, viz. the Dukes of Newcastle and Argyll, Sir J. Graham, Mr Gladstone, and Mr S. Herbert, seem to be very bitter against Lord John, and determined to oppose him should he form a Government, whilst they would be willing to support a Derby Government.

Victoria R.

Lord John Russell to Queen Victoria.

Chesham Place, *26th January 1855.*

Lord John Russell presents his humble duty to your Majesty, and is very grateful for your Majesty's communication of yesterday.

He confesses his resignation was very abrupt, but it is the consequence of many previous discussions in which his advice had been rejected or overruled.

Lord John Russell acknowledges the repeated instances of your Majesty's goodness in permitting him to leave the Foreign Office, and subsequently to serve without office as Leader of the House of Commons. These changes, however, were not made without due consideration. To be Leader of the House of Commons and Foreign Secretary is beyond any man's strength. To continue for a long time Leader without an office becomes absurd. Lord Aberdeen at first meant his own continuance in office to be short, which justified the arrangement.

Viscount Palmerston to Queen Victoria.[79]

MR ROEBUCK'S MOTION

144 Piccadilly, *26th January 1855.*

Viscount Palmerston presents his humble duty to your Majesty, and begs to state that Lord John Russell having made his statement, concluding with an announcement that he did not mean to vote on Mr Roebuck's Motion, and Viscount Palmerston having made a few re-

[79] His first letter to the Queen as Leader of the House of Commons.

marks on that statement, Mr Roebuck rose to make his Motion; but the paralytic affection under which he has for some time laboured soon overpowered him, and before he had proceeded far in his speech he became so unwell that he was obliged to finish abruptly, make his Motion, and sit down.

Mr Sidney Herbert, who was to reply to Mr Roebuck, rose therefore under great disadvantage, as he had to reply to a speech which had not been made; but he acquitted himself with great ability, and made an excellent statement in explanation and defence of the conduct of the Government. He was followed by Mr Henry Drummond,[80] Colonel North for the Motion, Mr Monckton Milnes against it; Lord Granby who, in supporting the Motion, praised and defended the Emperor of Russia; Mr Layard, who in a speech of much animation, gave very strong reasons to show the great impropriety of the Motion, and ended by saying he should vote for it; Sir George Grey, who made a spirited and excellent speech; Mr Walpole, who supported the Motion and endeavoured, but fruitlessly, to establish a similarity between the enquiry proposed by Mr Roebuck and the enquiry in a Committee of the whole House into the conduct of the Walcheren Expedition when the operation was over and the Army had returned to England. Mr Vernon Smith declared that his confidence in the Government had been confined to three Members—Lord Lansdowne, Lord John Russell, and Lord Palmerston—and that it was greatly diminished by the retirement of Lord John Russell. Colonel Sibthorp,[81] Sir John Fitzgerald, and Mr Knightley[82] followed, and Mr Disraeli having said that his side of the House required that the Debate should be adjourned, an adjournment to Monday was agreed to; but Viscount Palmerston, in consenting to the adjournment, expressed a strong hope that the Debate would not be protracted beyond that night.

Viscount Palmerston regrets to say that the general aspect of the House was not very encouraging.

---

[80] M.P. for West Surrey.

[81] Sibthorp, whose name is almost forgotten, earned some fame as an opponent of the Exhibition of 1851, and remained faithful to Protection, after Lord Derby and his party had dropped it. His beard, his eye-glass, and his clothes were a constant subject for the pencil of Leech.

[82] Mr (afterwards Sir) Reginald Knightley, M.P. for South Northamptonshire, 1852-1892. In the latter year he was created Lord Knightley of Fawsley.

The Earl of Aberdeen to Queen Victoria.

THE DEBATE

London, *27th January 1855.*

Lord Aberdeen presents his humble duty to your Majesty. It is probable that your Majesty may have heard from Lord Palmerston some account of the debate in the House of Commons last night; but perhaps your Majesty may not object to learn the impressions which Lord Aberdeen has received on the present state of affairs both in and out of the House.

There can be no doubt that Lord John Russell has injured his position by the course which he has pursued. His own friends having remained in the Cabinet, is his practical condemnation. He made a very elaborate and dexterous statement; but which, although very plausible, did not produce a good effect. It had been decided that he should be followed by Mr Gladstone, who was in full possession of the subject; but at the Cabinet yesterday held before the meeting of the House, it was decided that Lord Palmerston should follow Lord John, in order to prevent the appearance of a division in the Cabinet between the Whig and Peelite Members. As Lord Palmerston was to act as Leader of the House, the substitution of Mr Gladstone would have appeared strange. But the decision was unfortunate, for by all accounts the speech of Lord Palmerston was singularly unsuccessful.

In the debate which followed, the impression in the House was strongly against the War Department; and the indications which occasionally appeared of the possibility of Lord Palmerston filling that office were received with great cordiality. Sir George Grey made an excellent speech, and his censure must have been deeply felt by Lord John.

Lord Aberdeen has waited until the Cabinet had met to-day before he had the honour of writing to your Majesty, in order that he might learn the impressions and opinions of the Members, especially of those who are in the House of Commons. All agree that if the division had taken place last night, Mr Roebuck's Motion would have been carried by a large majority. This still seems to be the prevailing opinion, but there is considerable difference. The Motion is so objectionable and so unconstitutional that delay is likely to be favourable to those who oppose it. A little reflection must produce considerable effect. Lord Aberdeen sees that Mr Gladstone is preparing for a great effort, and he will do whatever can be effected by reason and eloquence.

It is said that Lord Derby shows some reluctance to accept the responsibility of overthrowing the Government; but the part taken last night by Mr Walpole, and the notice of a Motion in the House of Lords by Lord Lyndhurst, would appear to denote a different policy. The result of the Division on Monday will depend on the course adopted by his friends, *as a party*. It is said that Mr Disraeli has signified a difference of opinion from Mr Walpole.

Viscount Palmerston to Queen Victoria.

DEFEAT OF THE MINISTRY

144 Piccadilly, *30th January 1855.*

(2 a.m.)

Viscount Palmerston presents his humble duty to your Majesty, and begs to state that Mr Roebuck's Motion has been carried by 305 to 148, being a majority of 157 against the Government, a great number of the Liberal party voting in the majority.

The debate was begun by Mr Stafford,[83] who gave a very interesting but painful account of the mismanagement which he had witnessed in the Hospitals at Scutari and Sebastopol, while he gave due praise to the conduct of His Royal Highness the Duke of Cambridge toward the men under his command, and related the cheering effect produced by your Majesty's kind letter, when read by him to the invalids in Hospital. He was followed by Mr Bernal Osborne,[84] who found fault with all the military arrangements at home, and with the system under which Commissions in the Army are bought and sold, but who declared that he should vote against the Motion.

Mr Henley then supported the Motion, directing his attack chiefly against the management of the Transport Service.

Admiral Berkeley,[85] in reply, defended the conduct of the Admiralty. Major Beresford supported the Motion, but defended Lord Raglan against the attacks of the newspapers. Mr. Rice, Member for

---

[83] Augustus Stafford (formerly Stafford O'Brien), Secretary of the Admiralty in the Derby Ministry of 1852.

[84] Secretary of the Admiralty, who, contrary to modern practice, criticised on this occasion the action of his own colleagues.

[85] Maurice Frederick Fitzhardinge Berkeley, 1788-1867, M.P. for Gloucester 1831-1857.

Dover, opposed the Motion. Mr Miles[86] found fault with the Commissariat, and supported the Motion, saying that the proposed enquiry would apply a remedy to the evils acknowledged to exist in the Army in the Crimea; and Sir Francis Baring, after ably pointing out the inconveniences of the proposed Committee, said he should vote against it, as tending to prevent those evils from being remedied. Mr Rich criticised the composition of the Ministry, and the conduct of the war, and supported the Motion as a means of satisfying public opinion. Sir Edward Lytton Bulwer supported the Motion in a speech of considerable ability, and was replied to by Mr Gladstone in a masterly speech, which exhausted the subject, and would have convinced hearers who had not made up their minds beforehand.

He was followed by Mr Disraeli, who in the course of his speech made use of some expressions in regard to Lord John Russell, which drew from Lord John some short explanations as to the course which he had pursued. Viscount Palmerston then made some observations on the Motion, and, after a few words from Mr Muntz,[87] Mr Thomas Duncombe[88] asked Mr Roebuck whether, if he carried his Motion, he really meant to name and appoint the Committee and prosecute the enquiry, saying that he hoped and trusted that such was Mr Roebuck's intention. Mr Roebuck declared that he fully meant to do so, and after a short speech from Mr Roebuck, who lost the thread of his argument in one part of what he said, the House proceeded to a division.

The Conservative Party abstained, by order from their Chiefs, from giving the cheer of triumph which usually issues from a majority after a vote upon an important occasion....

Memorandum by Queen Victoria.

LORD ABERDEEN RESIGNS

Windsor Castle, *30th January 1855.*

Lord Aberdeen arrived here at three. He came from the Cabinet, and tendered their unanimous resignation. Nothing could have been better, he said, than the feeling of the members towards each other. Had it not been for the incessant attempts of Lord John Russell to keep up Party differences, it must be confessed that the experiment of a coa-

---

[86] M.P. for Bristol.

[87] M.P. for Birmingham.

[88] M.P. for Finsbury.

lition has succeeded admirably. We discussed future possibilities, and agreed that there remained nothing to be done but to offer the Government to Lord Derby, whose Party was numerically the strongest, and had carried the Motion. He supposed Lord Derby would be prepared for it, although he must have great difficulties, unless he took in men from other Parties, about which, however, nothing could be known at present.

Lord Aberdeen means to behave more generously to Lord Derby than he had done to him, and felt sure that his colleagues would feel a desire to support the Queen's new Government.

He said Lord Grey's plan[89] had not met with the approbation of the House of Lords. The indignation at Lord John's conduct on all sides was strongly on the increase.

Lord Aberdeen was much affected at having to take leave of us.

Victoria R.

Queen Victoria to the Earl of Derby.

LORD DERBY SUMMONED

Windsor Castle, *30th January 1855.*

The Queen would wish to see Lord Derby at Buckingham Palace (whither she is going for a few hours) to-morrow at half-past eleven.

Queen Victoria to the Duke of Newcastle.

Buckingham Palace, *31st January 1855.*

The Queen has just received the Duke of Newcastle's letter.

She readily grants him the permission he asks,[90] and seizes this opportunity of telling him how much she feels for him during this trying time, and what a high sense she shall ever entertain of his loyal, high-minded, and patriotic conduct, as well as of his unremitting exertions to serve his Sovereign and Country.

---

[89] For concentrating in a single department the business connected with the administration of the Army.

[90] The Duke, in order to refute Lord John Russell, asked leave to state what had passed in the Cabinet.

Memorandum by Queen Victoria.

INTERVIEW WITH LORD DERBY

Windsor Castle, *31st January 1855.*

We went up to Buckingham Palace and saw Lord Derby at half-past eleven. The Queen informed him of the resignation of the Government, and of her desire that he should try to form a new one. She addressed herself to him as the head of the largest Party in the House of Commons, and which had by its vote chiefly contributed to the overthrow of the Government. Lord Derby threw off this responsibility, saying that there had been no communication with Mr Roebuck, but that his followers could not help voting when Lord John Russell told them on authority that there was the most ample cause for enquiry, and the whole country cried out for it. Moreover, the Government, in meeting the Motion, laid its chief stress upon its implying a want of confidence in the Government—a confidence which they certainly did not enjoy. He ownedTHE LEADERSHIP that his Party was the most compact—mustering about two hundred and eighty men—but he had no men capable of governing the House of Commons, and he should not be able to present an Administration that would be accepted by the country unless it was strengthened by other combinations; he knew that the whole country cried out for Lord Palmerston as the only man fit for carrying on the war with success, and he owned the necessity of having him in the Government, were it even only to satisfy the French Government, the confidence of which was at this moment of the greatest importance; but he must say, speaking without reserve, that whatever the ignorant public might think, Lord Palmerston was totally unfit for the task. He had become very deaf as well as very blind, was seventy-one years old, and ... in fact, though he still kept up his sprightly manners of youth, it was evident that his day had gone by.[91] ... Lord Derby thought, however, he might have the Lead of the House of Commons, which Mr Disraeli was ready to give up to him. For the War Department there were but two men—both very able, but both liable to objections: the first was Lord Grey, who would do it admirably, but with whom he disagreed in general politics, and in this instance on the propriety of the war, which he

[91] Lord Derby's judgment was not borne out by subsequent events. Lord Palmerston was Prime Minister when he died on the 18th of October 1865, ten years later. "The half-opened cabinet-box on his table, and the unfinished letter on his desk, testified that he was at his post to the last,"—Ashley's *Life of Lord Palmerston*, vol. ii. p. 273.

himself was determined to carry on with the utmost vigour; then came his peculiar views about the Amalgamation of Offices, in which he did not at all agree. The other was Lord Ellenborough, who was very able, and would certainly be very popular with the Army, but was very unmanageable; yet he hoped he could keep him in order. It might be doubtful whether Lord Hardinge could go on with him at the Horse Guards. We agreed in the danger of Lord Grey's Army proposal, and had to pronounce the opinion that Lord Ellenborough was almost mad. This led us to a long discussion upon the merits of the conduct of the war, upon which he seemed to share the general prejudices, but on being told some of the real facts and difficulties of the case, owned that these, from obvious reasons, could not be stated by the Government in their defence, and said that he was aware that the chief fault lay at headquarters in the Crimea. Lord Raglan ought to be recalled, as well as his whole staff, and perhaps he could render this less painful to him by asking him to join the Cabinet, where his military advice would be of great value.

To be able to meet the House of Commons, however, Lord Derby said he required the assistance of men like Mr Gladstone and Mr S. Herbert, and he was anxious to know whether the Queen could tell him upon what support he could reckon in that quarter. We told him we had reason to believe the Peelites would oppose a Government of Lord John Russell, but were inclined to support one of Lord Derby's; whether they were inclined to join in office, however, appeared very doubtful. The Queen having laid great stress on a good selection for the office of Foreign Affairs, Lord Derby said he would have to return to Lord Malmesbury, who, he thought, had done well before, and had now additional experience.

Should he not be able to obtain strength from the Peelites, he could not be able to form a creditable Government; he must give up the task, and thought the Queen might try some other combinations with Lord John Russell or Lord Lansdowne, etc.

He did not think a reconstruction of the old Government would be accepted by the country; however, whatever Government was formed to carry on the war, should not only not be opposed by him, but have his cordial support, provided it raised no question of general constitutional importance.

Should all attempts fail, he would be ready to come forward to the rescue of the country with such materials as he had, but it would be "a desperate attempt."

Lord Derby returned a little before two from Lord Palmerston, to whom he had gone in the first instance. Lord Palmerston was ready to accept the Lead of the House of Commons, and acknowledged that the man who undertook this could not manage the War Department besides. He undertook to sound Mr Gladstone and Mr S. Herbert, but had, evidently much to Lord Derby's surprise, said that it must be a coalition, and not only the taking in of one or two persons, which does not seem to suit Lord Derby at all—nor was he pleased at Lord Palmerston's suggestion that he ought to try, by all means, to retain Lord Clarendon at the Foreign Office. Lord Palmerston was to sound the Peelites in the afternoon, and Lord Derby is to report the result to the Queen this evening.

Victoria R.

The Earl of Derby to Queen Victoria.

LORD CLARENDON

St James' Square, *31st January 1855.*

(9:30 p.m.)

Lord Derby, with his humble duty, hastens to submit to your Majesty the answer which he has this moment received from Viscount Palmerston to the communication which he made to him this morning by your Majesty's command. Lord Derby has not yet received from Mr Sidney Herbert and Mr Gladstone the answers referred to in Lord Palmerston's letter; but, from the tenor of the latter, he fears there can be no doubt as to their purport. With respect to Lord Clarendon, Lord Derby is fully sensible of the advantage which might accrue to your Majesty's service from the continuance in office of a Minister of great ability, who is personally cognizant of all the intricate negotiations and correspondence which have taken place for the last two years; and neither personally nor politically would he anticipate on the part of his friends, certainly not on his own part, any difficulty under existing circumstances, in co-operating with Lord Clarendon; but the present political relations between Lord Clarendon and Lord Derby's friends are such that, except upon a special injunction from your Majesty, and under your Majesty's immediate sanction, he would not be justified in making any overtures in that direction.[92] Should Lord Derby receive

[92] Although opposed to the ordinary procedure of party government, there were recent precedents for such overtures being made. When the Whigs dis-

any communication from Mr Gladstone or Mr. Sidney Herbert before morning, he will send it down to your Majesty by the earliest opportunity in the morning. Lord Derby trusts that your Majesty will forgive the haste in which he writes, having actually, at the moment of receiving Lord Palmerston's answer, written a letter to say that he could not longer detain your Majesty's messenger. Lord Derby will take no farther step until he shall have been honoured by your Majesty's farther commands.

The above is humbly submitted by your Majesty's most dutiful Servant and Subject,

Derby.

Memorandum by the Prince Albert.

LORD DERBY'S REFUSAL

1st February 1855.

Lord Derby came down here at eleven o'clock, and brought with him two letters he had received from Mr Gladstone and Mr Sidney Herbert, who both declared their willingness to give Lord Derby's Government an independent support, but on mature consideration their impossibility to take office in his Administration. Lord Derby said, as to the independent support, it reminded him of the definition of an independent Member of Parliament, viz. one that could not be depended upon. Under the circumstances, he would not be able to form such an Administration as could effectively carry on the Government.

He thought that Lord Palmerston had at first been willing to join, but it was now evident that the three letters had been written in concert.[93]

He was anxious to carry any message to any other statesman with which the Queen might wish to entrust him. This the Queen declined,

---

placed Peel in 1846, Lord John Russell attempted to include three of the outgoing Ministers in his Cabinet, and on the formation of the Coalition Ministry, negotiations were on foot to retain Lord St. Leonards on the woolsack.

[93] Lord Palmerston wrote that, upon reflection, he had come to the conclusion that he would not, by joining the Government, give to it that stability which Lord Derby anticipated. He, however, gave the promise of his support to any Government which would carry on the war with energy and vigour, and maintain the alliances which had been formed.

with her best thanks. He then wanted to know what statement Lord Aberdeen would make to-night in the House, stating it to be very important that it should not appear that the Administration had gone from Lord Aberdeen through any other hands than the ones which should finally accept it.

It would be well known that he had been *consulted* by the Queen, but there was no necessity for making it appear that he had undertaken to form an Administration. The fact was, that he had consulted none of his Party except Mr Disraeli, and that his followers would have reason to complain if they thought that he had put them altogether out of the question. We told him that we did not know what Lord Aberdeen meant to say, but the best thing would be on all accounts to state exactly the truth as it passed.

After he had taken leave of the Queen with reiterated assurances of gratitude and loyalty, I had a further long conversation with him, pointing out to him facts with which he could not be familiar, concerning our Army in the Crimea, our relations with our Ally, negotiations with the German Courts, the state of public men and the Press in this country, which convinced me that this country was in a crisis of the greatest magnitude, and the Crown in the greatest difficulties, which could not be successfully overcome unless political parties would show a little more patriotism than hitherto. They behaved a good deal like his independent Member of Parliament, and tried to aggravate every little mishap in order to get Party advantages out of it. I attacked him personally upon his ... opposition to the Foreign Enlistment Bill, and pointed to the fact that the French were now obtaining the services of that very Swiss Legion we stood so much in need of. His defence was a mere Parliamentary dialectic, accusing the clumsy way in which Ministers had introduced their Bill, but he promised to do what he could to relieve the difficulties of the country. In conclusion I showed him, under injunctions of secrecy, the letter I had received from Count Walewski, which showed to what a state of degradation the British Crown had been reduced by the efforts on all sides for Party objects to exalt the Emperor Napoleon, and make his will and use the sole standard for the English Government.[94]

[94] This curious letter of the Count stated in effect that the alliance of England and France, and the critical circumstances of the day, made Lords Palmerston and Clarendon indispensable members of any Ministry that might be formed.

Lord Derby called it the most audacious thing he had ever seen, adding that he had heard that Count Walewski had stated to somebody with reference to the Vienna Conferences: "What influence can a country like England pretend to exercise, which has no Army and no Government?"

I told him he was right, as every one here took pains to prove that we had no Army, and to bring about that the Queen should have no Government.

Memorandum by the Prince Albert.

LORD LANSDOWNE CONSULTED

Windsor Castle, *2nd February 1855.*

Lord Lansdowne arrived late yesterday evening. The Queen, after having stated that Lord Derby had given up the task of forming a Government, asked his advice under the present circumstances, to which he replied that he had little advice to give. I interrupted that at least he could impart knowledge to the Queen, upon which she could form a decision. The first and chief question was, What was Lord JohnLORD JOHN RUSSELL SUGGESTED Russell's position? Lord Lansdowne declared this to be the most difficult question of all to answer. He believed Lord John was not at all dissatisfied with the position he had assumed, and was under the belief that he could form an Administration capable of standing, even without the support of the Peelites. He (Lord Lansdowne) would certainly decline to have anything to do with it, as it could receive its support only from the extreme Radical side, which was not favourable to Lord John, but shrewd enough to perceive that to obtain a Government that would have to rest entirely upon themselves would be the surest mode of pushing their own views. Lord John, although not intending it, would blindly follow this bias, excusing himself with the consideration that he must look for support somewhere. He himself doubted, however, even the possibility of Lord John succeeding; but till he was brought to see this no strong Government was possible. We asked about the Peelites, Lord Palmerston, etc. He did not know whether the Peelites would serve with Lord John Russell—they certainly would not under him. There was a strong belief, however, particularly on the part of Lord Clarendon, and even shared by Lord Palmerston, that without Lord John a stable Government could not be formed. The Queen asked whether they could unite under him (Lord Lansdowne). He replied he had neither youth nor strength to make an efficient Prime Minister, and although Lord John had often told him "If you had been in Aberdeen's place my position would have been quite different," he felt sure Lord John would soon be tired of him and impatient to see him gone. He thought an arrangement might be possible by which Lord Clarendon might be Prime Minister, Lord John go to the House of Lords and take the Foreign Office, and Lord Palmerston the Lead in the House of Commons. We told him that would spoil two efficient men. Lord Clarendon had no courage for Prime Minister, and Lord John had decidedly failed at the Foreign Office.

Lord Lansdowne had had Lord Palmerston with him during the Derby negotiation, and clearly seen that at first he was not unwilling to join, but had more and more cooled upon it when he went further into the matter. Lord Derby and Lord Palmerston had had a full discussion upon Lord Grey, and discarded him as quite impracticable.... After much farther discussion it was agreed that Lord Lansdowne should go up to Town this day, see first Lord Palmerston, then the Peelites, and lastly Lord John, and come to Buckingham Palace at two o'clock, prepared to give answers upon the question what was feasible and what not. He inclines to the belief that we shall have to go through the ceremony at least of entrusting Lord John with the formation of an Administration.

Lord John was not without large following amongst the Whigs, and whatever was said about his late conduct in the higher circles, he believed that it is well looked upon by the lower classes. His expression was, that it would be found that the first and second class carriages in the railway train held opposite opinions.

Memorandum by Queen Victoria.

Buckingham Palace, *2nd February 1855.*

Lord Lansdowne arrived at two o'clock, and reported that he had seen all the persons intended, but he could not say that he saw his way more clearly. They all gave pledges generally to support any Government, but were full of difficulties as to their participation in one.

Mr Gladstone would clearly not serve under Lord John—might possibly with him—if much pressed by Lord Aberdeen to do so. He would probably serve under Lord Palmerston. Mr S. Herbert expressed apprehension at the effect upon the prospects of peace which would be produced by Lord Palmerston's being at the head of the Government.

Lord John Russell would not serve under Lord Palmerston, and fancies he might form a Whig Administration himself, of which Lord Palmerston, however, must be the chief member. Lord Palmerston would not like to serve under Lord John Russell—would be ready to form an Administration, which could not have duration, however, in his opinion, if Lord John Russell held aloof!

He found Lord John fully impressed with the fact of his having brought the Queen into all these difficulties, and of owing her what reparation he could make. Lord Palmerston also felt that he had some amends to make to the Queen for former offences. We asked Lord Lansdowne whether they could not be combined under a third person. He felt embarrassed about the answer, having to speak of himself. Both expressed their willingness to serve under him—but then he was seventy-five years old, and crippled with the gout, and could not possibly undertake such a task except for a few months, when the whole Administration would break down—of which he did not wish to be the cause. In such a case, Lord John had stated to him that the man to be Leader of the House of Commons was Lord Palmerston, meaning himself to be transferred to the House of Lords, in his former office as President of the Council.

Without presuming to give advice, Lord Lansdowne thought that under all circumstances it would do good if the Queen was to see Lord John Russell, and hear from himself what he could do. She could perfectly keep it in her power to commission whom she pleased hereafter, even if Lord John should declare himself willing to form a Government.

Victoria R.

Queen Victoria to Lord John Russell.

LORD JOHN RUSSELL SUMMONED

Buckingham Palace, *2nd February 1855.*

The Queen has just seen Lord Lansdowne. As what he could tell her has not enabled her to see her way out of the difficulties in which the late proceedings in Parliament have placed her, she wishes to see Lord John Russell in order to confer with him on the subject.

Memorandum by Queen Victoria[95]

INTERVIEW WITH LORD JOHN

Buckingham Palace, *2nd February 1855.*

Lord John Russell came at five o'clock.

The Queen said she wished to consult him on the present crisis, and hear from him how the position of Parties stood at this moment. He said that immediately at the meeting of Parliament a general desire became manifest for a modification of the Government; that the Protectionists were as hostile to the Peelites as they had been in the year '46; that the old Whigs had with difficulty been made to support the late Government; that the dissatisfaction with the conduct of the war was general, and the country cried out for Lord Palmerston at the War Department; that he considered it of the greatest importance that Lord Clarendon should remain at the Foreign Office, where he had gained great reputation, and nobody could replace him. On the question whether Lord Palmerston would be supported if he formed an Administration, he said everybody would give a general support, but he doubted the Whigs joining him. He did not know what the Peelites would do, but they would be an essential element in the Government, particularly Mr Gladstone; the best thing would be if Lord Palmerston took the lead of the House of Commons. A Government formed by Lord Lansdowne or Lord Clarendon would ensure general support, but Lord Lansdowne had declared that he would not undertake it for more than three months, and then the Government would break down again; and we objected that Lord Clarendon ought, as he had said, not to be moved from the Foreign Office, to which he agreed. He himself would prefer to sit on the Fourth Bench and support the Government. The Queen asked him whether he thought he could form a Government. After having taken some time for reflection, he said he thought he could,[96] but he thought it difficult without the Peelites, and next to im-

[95] This Memorandum, though signed by the Queen, was written by the Prince.

[96] Colonel Phipps thus describes Lord Aberdeen's comment on Lord John Russell's words:—"I told Lord Aberdeen that Lord John had said that he thought that he could form a Government. He laughed very much, and said: 'I am not at all surprised at that, but whom will he get to serve under him? Has he at present any idea of the extent of the feeling that exists against him?' I replied that I thought not, that it was difficult for anybody to tell him, but that I thought that it was right that he should know what the feeling was, and that he would soon discover it when he began to ask people to join his Government. Lord Aberdeen said that was very true...."

possible without Lord Palmerston;NEGOTIATIONS he did not know whether both or either would serve with or under him; he would offer Lord Palmerston the choice between the Lead of the House of Commons and the War Department—and in case he should choose the former, ask himself to be removed to the House of Lords; he had been Leader of the House of Commons since '34, and as far as being able to support his title, he was enabled to do so, as his brother, the Duke of Bedford, intended to leave an estate of £5000 a year to his son. The Queen asked him whether he would do the same under the Administration of Lord Lansdowne, for instance; he begged to be allowed time to consider that. He acknowledged to the Queen—on her remark that he had contributed to bring her into the present difficulties—that he was bound to do what he could to help her out of them; and on the Queen's question what he could do, he answered that depended very much on what the Queen would wish him to do.

She commissioned him finally to meet Lord Lansdowne and Lord Palmerston, to consult together, and to let Lord Lansdowne bring her the result of their deliberation this evening, so that she might see a little more clearly where the prospect of a strong Government lay.

We had some further discussion upon Mr Roebuck's Committee, which he thinks will not be as inconvenient as all his friends suppose. It would meet with great difficulties, and might be precluded from drawing up a report. On Lord Grey's Motion[97] and the Army question he declared that he held to his Memorandum of the 22nd January which the Duke of Newcastle had read to the House of Lords, and acknowledged the necessity of maintaining the office of the Commander-in-Chief, although subordinate to the Secretary of State, and retaining the Army Patronage distinct from the Political Patronage of the Government.

I omitted to mention that Lord John, in answer to the question whether Lord Clarendon would serve under Lord Palmerston, answered that he could not at all say whether he would; he had mentioned to him the possibility, when Lord Clarendon drew up and made a long face.

Victoria R.

---

[97] See *ante*, note 17.

Queen Victoria to Lord John Russell.

Buckingham Palace, *2nd February 1855.*

The Queen has just seen Lord Lansdowne after his return from his conference with Lord John Russell and Lord Palmerston. As moments are precious, and the time is rolling on without the various consultations which Lord Lansdowne has had the kindness and patience to hold with the various persons composing the Queen's late Government having led to any positive result, she feels that she ought to entrust some one of them with the distinct commission to attempt the formation of a Government. The Queen addresses herself in this instance to Lord John Russell, as the person who may be considered to have contributed to the vote of the House of Commons, which displaced her late Government, and hopes that he will be able to present her such a Government as will give a fair promise successfully to overcome the great difficulties in which the country is placed. It would give her particular satisfaction if Lord Palmerston could join in this formation.

Lord John Russell to Queen Victoria.

LORD JOHN RUSSELL'S ATTEMPT

Chesham Place, *2nd February 1855.*

Lord John Russell presents his humble duty to your Majesty. He acknowledges that having contributed to the vote of the House of Commons, which displaced your Majesty's late Government (although the decision would in any case have probably been unfavourable), he is bound to attempt the formation of a Government.

As your Majesty has now entrusted him with this honourable task, and desired that Lord Palmerston should join in it, Lord John Russell will immediately communicate with Lord Palmerston, and do his utmost to form a Government which will give a fair promise to overcome the difficulties by which the country is surrounded.

Lord John Russell considers Lord Clarendon's co-operation in this task as absolutely essential.

Memorandum by the Prince Albert.

Buckingham Palace, *3rd February 1855.*

Lord John Russell arrived at half-past one o'clock, and stated that he had to report some progress and some obstacles. He had been to Lord Palmerston, and had a long and very free discussion with him.

He (Lord Palmerston) told him although the general voice of the public had pointed him out as the person who ought to form a Government, he had no pretensions himself or personal views, and was quite ready to accept the lead of the House of Commons under Lord John in the House of Lords; but that he thought that, if the Queen would see him, now that she had seen Lord Derby, Lord John, and Lord Lansdowne, it would remove any impression that there were personal objections to him entertained by the Queen, which would much facilitate the position of the new Government. They then discussed the whole question of offices, agreed that Lord Panmure would be the best person for the War Department; that Lord Grey could not be asked to join, as his views on the Foreign Policy differed so much from theirs, and he had always been an intractable colleague; that if Mr Gladstone could not be prevailed upon to join, Mr Labouchere,[98] although an infinitely weaker appointment, might be Chancellor of the Exchequer, and Sir F. Baring replace Sir J. Graham, if he could not be got to stay.

Lord John then saw Mr S. Herbert, who declared to him that it was impossible for any of the Peelites to join his Government, connected as they were with Lord Aberdeen and the Duke of Newcastle, but that they would infinitely prefer a Government of Lord John's to one of Lord Palmerston, whose views on Foreign Policy, uncontrolled by Lord Aberdeen, they sincerely dreaded.

Lord John then went to Lord Clarendon, and was surprised to find that he could not make up his mind to remain at the Foreign Office under his Government. Lord John thought that the expression of a wish on the part of the Queen would go a great way to reconcile him. His objections were that he had always received the handsomest support from the Peelites, and thought the Government too weak without their administrative ability.

Lord John had seen none of his own friends, such as Sir G. Grey, Sir C. Wood, Lord Lansdowne, and Lord Granville, but had not the smallest doubt that they would cordially co-operate with him.

Lord John is to come again at a quarter before six o'clock. The Queen has appointed Lord Palmerston for three o'clock, and Lord Clarendon at four.

---

[98] He had been President of the Board of Trade in the former administration of Lord John Russell.

Memorandum by Queen Victoria.[99]

ATTITUDE OF THE PEELITES

Buckingham Palace, *3rd February 1855.*

In the Audience which the Queen has just granted to Lord Palmerston, he thanked her for the message which she had sent him through Lord John Russell, and declared his readiness to serve her in any way he could under the present difficulties. He had preferred the lead of the House of Commons to the War Department, having to make a choice between two duties which no man could perform together.

THE FOREIGN OFFICE

In answer to a question from the Queen, he said he hoped that the present irritation in the Whig party would subside, and that he would be able to complete a Government. He regretted that the Peelites thought it impossible for them to join, which would make it very difficult for Lord John. He had just heard from Count Walewski that Lord Clarendon was very much disinclined to remain at the Foreign Office under Lord John. They were to have a meeting at Lord John's at five, where he hoped to find that he had waived his objections; but he must say that if Lord Clarendon persisted he must himself withdraw, as he had indeed made it a condition with Lord John. The Queen asked him whether, if this attempt failed, she could reckon upon his services in any other combination. His answer was that it was better not to answer for more than one question at a time; we must now suppose that this will succeed.

What he stated with reference to the Army question and the Committee of the House of Commons was perfectly satisfactory.

LORD CLARENDON

Lord Clarendon, whom we saw at four o'clock, complained very much of the unfairness of Lord John in making him personally answerable for impeding the progress of Lord John's Government. The fact was that his opinion was only that of every other member of the late Government, and of the public at large; which could be heard and seen by anybody who chose to listen or to read. So impossible had it appeared to the public that Lord John should be blind enough to consider his being able to form a Government feasible, that it was generally supposed that he had been urged to do so by the Queen, in order to escape the necessity of Lord Palmerston. He acknowledged

[99] This Memorandum, though signed by the Queen, was written by the Prince.

that the Queen's decision in that respect had been the perfectly correct and constitutional one, and perhaps necessary to clear the way; but he hoped that for her own sake, and to prevent false impressions taking root in the public mind, the Queen would give afterwards Lord Palmerston his fair turn also, though he could not say that he would be able to form an Administration. The Queen said that this was her intention, that she never had expected that Lord John would be able to form one, but that it was necessary that his eyes should be opened; Lord Clarendon only regretted the precious time that was lost.

He must really say that he thought he could do no good in joining Lord John; his Government would be "a stillborn Government," which "the country would tread under foot the first day," composed as it would be of the same men who had been bankrupt in 1852, minus the two best men in it, viz. Lord Lansdowne and Lord Grey, and the head of it ruined in public opinion. If he were even to stay at the Foreign Office, his language to foreign countries would lose all its weight from being known not to rest upon the public opinion of England, and all this would become much worse when it became known that from the first day of Lord John's entering into Lord Aberdeen's Government, he had only had one idea, viz. that of tripping him up, expel the Peelites, and place himself at the head of an exclusive Whig Ministry. Besides, he felt that the conduct of all his colleagues had been most straightforward and honourable towards him, and he was not prepared "to step over their dead bodies to the man who had killed them." The attempt of Lord John ought *not* to succeed if public morality were to be upheld in this country. He had avoided Lord John ever since his retirement, but he would have now to speak out to him, as when he was asked to embark his honour he had a right to count the cost.

Lord Lansdowne had no intention to go to Lord John's meeting, as he had originally taken leave of public life, and had only entered the Coalition Government in order to facilitate its cohesion; among a Government of pure Whigs he was not wanted, for there was no danger of their not *cohering*. Sir C. Wood declared he had no business to be where Lord Lansdowne refused to go in.

He thought Lord Palmerston would have equal difficulty in forming an administration, but when that had failed some solid combination would become possible.

Lord Lansdowne had declared that he could not place himself at the head for more than three months, but that was a long time in these days.

Victoria R.

Memorandum by Queen Victoria.

FRESH DIFFICULTIES

Lord John Russell returned at six o'clock from his meeting, much put out and disturbed. He said he had nothing good to report. Mr Gladstone, whom he had seen, had declined to act with him, saying that the country did not wish for Coalitions at this moment. Sir J. Graham, whom he had visited, had informed him that the feeling against him was very strong just now, precluding support in Parliament; he gave him credit for good intentions, but said the whole difficulty was owing to what he termed his (Lord John's) *rashness*. He felt he could not separate from Lord Aberdeen, and had no confidence in the views of Foreign Affairs of Lord Palmerston.

He had then seen Sir George Grey, who told him he had no idea that a Government of Lord John's could stand at this moment; the country wanted Lord Palmerston either as War Minister or as Prime Minister. He must hesitate to engage himself in Lord John's Government, which, separated from the Peelites, would find no favour. Lord Clarendon had reiterated his objections, saying always that this must be gone through, and something new would come up at the end, when all these attempts had failed. He could not understand what this should be. Did Lord Clarendon think of himself as the head of the new combination? I asked what Lord Lansdowne had said. He answered he had a letter from him, which was not very agreeable either. He read it to us. It was to the purport—that as Lord John had been commissioned to form an Administration, and he did not intend to join it, he thought it better not to come to his house in order to avoid misconstruction. Lord John wound up, saying that he had asked Lord Clarendon and Sir G. Grey to reflect further, and to give their final answer to-morrow morning. The loss of the Peelites would be a great blow to him, which might be overcome, however; but if his own particular friends, like Lord Clarendon and Sir G. Grey, deserted him, he felt that he could go on no farther, and he hoped the Queen would feel that he had done all he could.

Victoria R.

Memorandum by Queen Victoria.[28]

LORD JOHN'S FAILURE

Buckingham Palace, *3rd February 1855.*

Footnote 28: This Memorandum, though signed by the Queen, was written by the Prince.

Lord Lansdowne arrived at half-past nine in the evening, and met our question whether he had anything satisfactory to report, with the remark that he saw his way less than ever, and that matters had rather gone backward since he had been here in the morning. He had been in the afternoon at Sir James Graham's bedside, who had had a consultation with Mr Gladstone, and declared to him that the country was tired of Coalitions, and wanted a united Cabinet; that they (the Peelites) could not possibly serve under Lord John or even with him after what had happened; that he felt the strongest objections to serving under Lord Palmerston. They were one and all for the vigorous prosecution of the war, but in order to attain a speedy peace. Lord Palmerston was known to entertain ulterior views, on which he was secretly agreed with the Emperor of the French; and when it came to the question of negotiations, the Government was sure to break up on a ground most dangerous to the country. Lord Lansdowne could but agree in all this, and added he had been tempted to feel his pulse to know how much it had gone down since he had been with Sir James.

The meeting between Lord Palmerston and Lord John had just taken place in his presence. They had discussed everything most openly, but being both very guarded to say nothing which could lead the other to believe that the one would serve under the other. He confessed everything was darker now than before. They both seemed to wish to form a Government, but he could really not advise the Queen what to do under the circumstances.

I summed up that the Queen appeared to me reduced to the necessity of now entrusting one of the two with a *positive* commission. It was very important that it should not appear that the Queen had any personal objection to Lord Palmerston; on the other hand, under such doubtful circumstances, it would be safest for the Queen to follow that course which was clearly the most constitutional, and this was, after having failed with Lord Derby, to go to Lord John, who was the other party to the destruction of the late Government. The Queen might write such a letter to Lord John as would record the political reasons which led to her determination. Lord Lansdowne highly approved of this, and suggested the addition of an expression of the Queen's hope of seeing Lord Palmerston associated in that formation.

I drew up the annexed draft which Lord Lansdowne read over and entirely approved.

He has no idea that Lord John will succeed in his task, but thinks it a necessary course to go through, and most wholesome to Lord John to have his eyes opened to his own position, of which he verily believed he was not the least aware.

Victoria R.

Queen Victoria to the Earl of Aberdeen.

Windsor Castle, *4th February 1855.*

The Queen quite approves of the pension to Sir G. Grey, which he has fully earned, but would wish Lord Aberdeen well to consider the exact moment at which to offer it to him, as Sir George is so very delicate in his feelings of honour. Lord John Russell will probably have to give up the task of forming an Administration on account of Sir George's declining to join him. If the pension were offered to him by Lord Aberdeen during the progress of negotiations, he could not help feeling, she thinks, exceedingly embarrassed.

Lord John Russell to Queen Victoria.

Chesham Place, *4th February 1855.*

Lord John Russell presents his humble duty to your Majesty. He saw last night Sir George Grey, who is extremely averse to the formation of a purely Whig Government at this time. Since that time he has received the two notes enclosed: one from Lord Palmerston, the other early this morning from Lord Clarendon.[100]

---

[100] Lord Palmerston wrote:—

"144 Piccadilly, *3rd February 1855.*

"My dear John Russell,—I certainly inferred from what Clarendon said this afternoon at your house, that he had pretty well made up his mind to a negative answer, and I could only say to you that which I said to Derby when he asked me to join him, that I should be very unwilling, in the present state of our Foreign relations, to belong to any Government in which the management of our Foreign Affairs did not remain in Clarendon's hands.

"George Grey, by your account, seems to tend to the same conclusion as Clarendon, and I think, from what fell from Molesworth, whom I sat next to at the Speaker's dinner this evening, that he would not be disposed to accept any offer that you might make him.

—Yours sincerely, Palmerston."

Lord Clarendon wrote:—

"Grosvenor Crescent, *3rd February 1855.*

It only remains for him to acknowledge your Majesty's great kindness, and to resign into your Majesty's hands the task your Majesty was pleased to confide to him.

Queen Victoria to Viscount Palmerston.

LORD PALMERSTON PREMIER

Windsor Castle, *4th February 1855.*

Lord John Russell having just informed the Queen that he was obliged to resign the task which the Queen confided to him, she addresses herself to Lord Palmerston to ask him whether he can undertake to form an Administration which will command the confidence of Parliament and efficiently conduct public affairs in this momentous crisis? Should he think that he is able to do so, the Queen commissions him to undertake the task. She does not send for him, having fully discussed with him yesterday the state of public affairs, and in order to save time. The Queen hopes to receive an answer from Lord Palmerston as soon as possible, as upon this her own movements will depend.

Viscount Palmerston to Queen Victoria.

144 Piccadilly, *4th February 1855.*

Viscount Palmerston presents his humble duty to your Majesty, and with a deep sense of the importance of the commission which your Majesty asks whether he will undertake, he hastens to acknowledge the gracious communication which he has just had the honour to receive from your Majesty.

Viscount Palmerston has reason to think that he can undertake with a fair prospect of success to form an Administration which will

---

"My dear Lord John,—The more I reflect upon the subject, the more I feel convinced that such a Government as you propose to form would not satisfy the public nor command the confidence of the Country.

"To yourself personally I am sure it would be most injurious if you attempted to carry on the Government with inadequate means at this moment of national danger.

"On public and on private grounds, therefore, I should wish to take no part in an Administration that cannot in my opinion be either strong or permanent. Yours sincerely,
Clarendon."

command the confidence of Parliament and effectually conduct public affairs in the present momentous crisis, and as your Majesty has been graciously pleased to say that if such is his opinion, your Majesty authorises him to proceed immediately to the accomplishment of the task, he will at once take steps for the purpose; and he trusts that he may be able in the course of to-morrow to report to your Majesty whether his present expectations are in the way to be realised.

Viscount Palmerston to Queen Victoria.

WHIG SUPPORT

Piccadilly, *5th February 1855.*

(5 p.m.)

Viscount Palmerston presents his humble duty to your Majesty, and has had the honour to receive your Majesty's communication of to-day; and in accordance with your Majesty's desire, he begs to report the result of his proceedings up to the present time.

The Marquis of Lansdowne, the Lord Chancellor, the Earl of Clarendon, the Earl Granville, Sir George Grey, Sir Charles Wood, have expressed their willingness to be members of the Administration which Viscount Palmerston is endeavouring to form, provided it can be constructed upon a basis sufficiently broad to give a fair prospect of duration.

Mr Gladstone, Mr Sidney Herbert, and the Duke of Argyll have declined chiefly on the ground of personal and political attachment to the Earl of Aberdeen, against whom, as well as against the Duke of Newcastle, they say they consider the vote of the House of Commons of last week as having been levelled. Viscount Palmerston has not yet been able to ascertain the decision of Sir James Graham, but it will probably be the same as that of his three colleagues.

Viscount Palmerston hopes, nevertheless, to be able to submit for your Majesty's consideration such a list as may meet with your Majesty's approval, and he will have the honour of reporting further to your Majesty to-morrow.

Memorandum by Queen Victoria.

THE PEELITES

Buckingham Palace, *6th February 1855.*

We came to Town to hear the result of negotiations, and saw Lord Palmerston at one o'clock. He said there were circumstances which prevented him from submitting a List of the Cabinet, but would at all events be able to do so in the afternoon.

Lords Lansdowne, Clarendon, Granville, Sir G. Grey, Sir C. Wood, Sir William Molesworth, and the Chancellor had consented to serve—unconditionally—having withdrawn their former conditions in consequence of the very general opinion expressed out of doors that the country could not much longer be left without a Government. He heard this had also made an impression upon the Peelites, who had refused to join. He submitted their letters (declining) to the Queen, of which copies are here annexed. They had been written after consultation with Sir J. Graham, but Lord Aberdeen and the Duke of Newcastle having heard of it, have since exerted themselves strongly to prevail upon them to change their opinion, and it was still possible that they would do so. Lord Clarendon had suggested that if Lord Aberdeen himself was invited to join the Government, and could be induced to do so, this would obviate all difficulty. He had in consequence asked Lord Lansdowne to see Lord Aberdeen on the subject, as his joining could only be agreeable to him. Many of the Peelites not in the late Cabinet had strongly disapproved of the decision taken by Mr Gladstone and friends, and offered their services, amongst others Lord Canning, Lord Elcho,[101] and Mr Cardwell.

Lord Palmerston had been with Lord John Russell yesterday, and had had a very long conversation with him in a most friendly tone; he asked Lord John whether he would follow out the proposal which he had lately made himself, and take the lead in the House of Lords as President of the Council. He declined, however, saying he preferred to stay out of office and to remain in the House of Commons, which Lord Palmerston obviously much regretted. They went, however, together all over the offices and their best distribution. He would recommend Lord Panmure for the War Department and Mr Layard as Under Secretary.... Lord Palmerston was appointed to report further progress at five o'clock.

Victoria R.

---

[101] Now Earl of Wemyss.

The Prince Albert to the Earl of Aberdeen.

Buckingham Palace, *6th February 1855.*

My dear Lord Aberdeen,—It would be a great relief to the Queen if you were to agree to a proposal which we understand is being made to you to join the new Government, and by so doing to induce also Mr Gladstone, Mr S. Herbert, and Sir James Graham to do the same.

Ever yours truly, Albert.

The Earl of Aberdeen to the Prince Albert.

LORD ABERDEEN INTERVENES

London, *6th February 1855.*

Sir,—I am sanguine in believing that the great object of the union of my friends with the new Government may be attained without the painful sacrifice to which your Royal Highness refers. Contrary to my advice, they yesterday declined to remain in the Cabinet, but I have renewed the subject to-day, and they have finally decided to place themselves in my hands. This rendered other explanations necessary, before I could undertake so great a responsibility. When I shall have the honour of seeing your Royal Highness, I will, with your Royal Highness's permission, communicate what has passed, so far as I am concerned.

I venture to enclose the copy of a letter which I addressed to Mr Herbert this morning, in answer to one received from him late last night, in which he expressed his doubts of the propriety of the first decision at which they had arrived. I have the honour to be, Sir, your Royal Highness's most humble and devoted Servant,

Aberdeen.

/Enclosure—Copy./

The Earl of Aberdeen to Mr S. Herbert.

MR SIDNEY HERBERT

Argyll House, *6th February 1855.*

My dear Herbert,—I received your letter too late to answer it last night. In fact, I had gone to bed.

You say that you are in a great difficulty as to the course you ought to take. I am in none whatever.

I gave you my decided opinion yesterday that you ought to continue in Palmerston's Administration; and I endeavoured to support this opinion by the very arguments which you repeat in your letter to me. Surely this letter ought to have been addressed to Gladstone and Graham, and not to me. I fully concur in thinking that you came to a wrong conclusion yesterday, and I would fain hope that it would still be reversed.

When you sent to me yesterday to attend your meeting, I certainly hoped it was with the intention of following my advice.

Your reluctance to continue in Palmerston's Cabinet is chiefly founded on the apprehension that he will pursue a warlike policy beyond reasonable bounds. I have already told you that I have had some explanations with him on the terms of peace, with which I am satisfied. But whatever may be his inclinations, you ought to rely on the weight of your own character and opinions in the Cabinet. I am persuaded that the sentiments of the great majority of the Members of the Cabinet are similar to your own, and that you may fairly expect reason and sound policy to prevail in the question of peace and war.

But above all I have recently had some very full conversations with Clarendon on the subject, and I am entirely satisfied with his disposition and intentions. I am sanguine in the belief that he will give effect to his present views.

A perseverance in the refusal to join Palmerston will produce very serious effects, and will never be attributed to its true cause. The public feeling will be strongly pronounced against you, and you will greatly suffer in reputation, if you persevere at such a moment as this in refusing to continue in the Cabinet.

In addition to the public necessity, I think you owe much to our late Whig colleagues, who behaved so nobly and generously towards us after Lord John's resignation. They have some right to expect this sacrifice.

Although your arguments do not apply to me, for I yesterday adopted them all, you conclude your letter by pressing me to enter the Cabinet. Now there is really no sense in this, and I cannot imagine how you can seriously propose it. You would expose me to a gratuitous indignity, to which no one ought to expect me to submit. I say *gratuitous*, because I could not be of the slightest use in such a situation for the purpose you require.

I can retire with perfect equanimity from the Government in consequence of the vote of the House of Commons; but to be stigmatised as the Head and tolerated as the subordinate member I cannot endure.

If at any future time my presence should be required in a Cabinet, I should feel no objection to accept any office, or to enter it without office. But to be the Head of a Cabinet to-day, and to become a subordinate member of the very same Cabinet to-morrow, would be a degradation to which I could never submit, that I would rather die than do so—and indeed the sense of it would go far to kill me.

If you tell me that your retaining your present offices, without the slightest sacrifice, but on the contrary with the approbation of all, is in any degree to depend on my taking such a course, I can only say that, as friends, I cannot believe it possible that you should be guilty of such wanton cruelty without any national object.

I must, then, again earnestly exhort you to reconsider the decision of yesterday, and to continue to form part of the Government. I will do anything in my power to facilitate this. If you like, I will go to Palmerston and promote any explanation between him and Gladstone on the subject of peace and war. Or I will tell him that you have yielded to my strong recommendation. In short, I am ready to do anything in my power.

I wish you to show this letter to Gladstone and to Graham, to whom, as you will see, it is addressed as much as to yourself.

I hope to meet you this morning, and Gladstone will also come to the Admiralty. Yours, etc.

Aberdeen.

The Prince Albert to the Earl of Aberdeen.

ADHESION OF THE PEELITES

Buckingham Palace, *6th February 1855.*

My dear Lord Aberdeen,—We are just returning to Windsor. Lord Palmerston kissed hands after having announced that his Peelite colleagues also have agreed to keep their offices. The Queen is thus relieved from great anxiety and difficulty, and feels that she owes much to your kind and disinterested assistance. I can quite understand what you say in the letter which I return. You must make allowances also, however, for the wishes of your friends not to be separated from you. You will not be annoyed by further proposals from here.

To-morrow we shall have an opportunity of further conversation with you upon the state of affairs. Believe me always, yours, etc.,

Albert

Queen Victoria to the King of the Belgians.

Buckingham Palace, *6th February 1855.*

My dearest Uncle,—We are here again for a few hours in order to try and facilitate the formation of a Government, which seemed almost hopeless.

Van de Weyer will have informed you of the successive failures of Lord Derby and *Lord John* ... and of Lord Palmerston being now charged with the formation of a Government! I had *no* other alternative. The Whigs *will* join with him, and I have got hopes, *also* the Peelites, which would be very important, and would tend to allay the *alarm* which his name will, I fear, produce abroad.

I will leave this letter open to the last moment in the hope of giving you some decisive news before we return to Windsor....

I am a good deal worried and knocked up by all that has passed; my nerves, which have suffered very severely this last year, have not been improved by what has passed during this trying fortnight—for it *will* be a *fortnight* to-morrow that the beginning of the mischief began....

Six o'clock p.m.—One word to say that *Lord Palmerston* has just *kissed* hands as *Prime* Minister. All the *Peelites* except poor dear Aberdeen (whom I am deeply grieved to lose) and the Duke of Newcastle, remain. It is *entirely* Aberdeen's *doing*, and very patriotic and handsome of him. In haste, ever your devoted Niece,

Victoria R.

Queen Victoria to the Earl of Aberdeen.

A FAREWELL LETTER

Windsor Castle, *7th February 1855* .

Though the Queen hopes to see Lord Aberdeen at six, she seizes the opportunity of approving the appointment of the Hon. and Rev. A.

Douglas[102] to the living of St Olave's, Southwark, to say what she hardly dares to do verbally without fearing to give way to her feelings; she wishes to say what a pang it is for her to separate from so kind and dear and valued a friend as Lord Aberdeen has ever been to her since she has known him. The day he became Prime Minister was a very happy one for her; and throughout his Ministry he has ever been the kindest and wisest adviser—one to whom she could apply on all and trifling occasions even. This she is sure he will still ever be. But the thought of losing him as her First Adviser in her Government is very painful. The pain is to a certain extent lessened by the knowledge of all he has done to further the formation of this Government, in so noble, loyal, and disinterested a manner, and by his friends retaining their posts, which is a great security against possible dangers. The Queen is sure that the Prince and herself may ever rely on his valuable support and advice in all times of difficulty, and she now concludes with the expression of her warmest thanks for all his kindness and devotion, as well as of her unalterable friendship and esteem for him, and with every wish for his health and happiness.

Viscount Palmerston to Queen Victoria.

LEADERSHIP OF THE LORDS

Piccadilly, *7th February 1855.*

Viscount Palmerston presents his humble duty to your Majesty, and begs to state that a difficulty has arisen in regard to the reconstruction of the Administration, which your Majesty might perhaps be able to assist in removing. It is considered by the Members of the proposed Cabinet to be a matter of great importance that Lord Lansdowne should not only be a Member of the Cabinet, but that he should also be the Organ of the Government in the House of Lords.

Viscount Palmerston pressed this upon Lord Lansdowne yesterday afternoon, and was under the impression that Lord Lansdowne had consented to be so acknowledged, with the understanding that Lord Granville, as President of the Council, should relieve him from the pressure of the daily business of the House, while Lord Clarendon would take the burthen of Foreign Office discussions, and that thus the ordinary duties of Leader of the House of Lords would be performed by others, while Lord Lansdowne would still be the directing chief,

[102] The Hon. Arthur Gascoigne Douglas (1827-1905), son of the nineteenth Earl of Morton; Bishop of Aberdeen and Orkney, 1883-1905.

who would give a character and tone to the body. But Viscount Palmerston learns this morning from Lord Granville and Lord Bessborough that Lord Lansdowne does not so understand the matter, and is unwilling to assume the ostensible Leadership, even upon the above-mentioned arrangement, and that he wishes Lord Granville to be the Leader in the House of Lords.

Lord Granville, however, with reason urges that there are many members of the House of Lords who would show to Lord Lansdowne, from his long standing and high political position, a deference which they would not show towards Lord Granville, so much younger a man. If Lord Lansdowne were in Town, Viscount Palmerston would have gone to him strongly to entreat him to be the person to announce in the House of Lords the formation of a Ministry, and to continue to be the organ of the Government in that House, at least till Easter, and upon such matters and occasions as might require the weight of his authority; but if your Majesty were to view the matter in the same light in which it has presented itself to Viscount Palmerston, to the Chancellor, to Lord Clarendon, to Lord Granville and others, and if your Majesty should think fit to express an opinion upon it to Lord Lansdowne, such an opinion would no doubt have great weight with Lord Lansdowne.

Viscount Palmerston submits a list of the proposed Cabinet. Until Sir George Grey returns to Town this afternoon from Portsmouth, whither he went yesterday evening to take leave of his son, who has a commission in the Rifles,[103] and was to embark this morning for the Crimea, Viscount Palmerston will not know whether he prefers the Colonial Office or the Home Office. Whichever of the two he chooses, Mr Herbert will take the other. Viscount Palmerston does not submit to your Majesty the name of any person for the office of Secretary at War, as he proposes that that office shall merge in the office of Secretary of State for the War Department, and Viscount Palmerston suspends for the present any recommendation to your Majesty for the office of Chancellor of the Duchy of Lancaster, as that office may be made available for giving strength either in the House of Lords or in the House of Commons according to circumstances.

THE NEW CABINET

---

[103] George Henry Grey, afterwards Lieut.-Colonel of the Northumberland Militia, and Captain in the Grenadier Guards; father of the present Sir Edward Grey, M.P. He predeceased his father in 1874.

Proposed Cabinet.

First Lord of Treasury	Viscount Palmerston.
Organ of the Government or Leader of the House of Lords	Marquis of Lansdowne.
Lord Chancellor	Lord Cranworth.
President of the Council	Earl Granville.
Privy Seal	Duke of Argyll.
Foreign Affairs	Earl of Clarendon.
War Department	Lord Panmure.
Home Office	Mr Sidney Herbert or Sir George Grey.
Colonial Department	Sir George Grey or Mr Sidney Herbert.
Admiralty	Sir James Graham.
Chancellor of Exchequer	Mr Gladstone.
India Board	Sir Charles Wood.
Board of Works	Sir William Molesworth.
Post Office	Viscount Canning.

Queen Victoria to Viscount Palmerston.

Windsor Castle, *7th February 1855.*

The Queen has just received Lord Palmerston's letter with the List of the Government, which she approves. She entirely agrees with him in the view he takes with respect to Lord Lansdowne's position in the House of Lords, and will write to him on the subject. From what he said, however, the Queen would hope that he would not be disinclined to make the announcement of the Government as well as to take the lead on all occasions of great importance.[104]

---

[104] Lord Lansdowne consented, on particular occasions only, to represent the Government, but claimed to be himself the judge of the expediency or necessity of his doing so. The ministerial life of this *doyen* of the Whig Party

The Queen approves that the office of Secretary at War should remain open at present; but as regards the question itself of these two offices, she reserves her judgment till the subject is submitted to her in a definite form.

The Earl of Clarendon to Queen Victoria.

THE VIENNA CONFERENCE

10th February 1855.

Lord Clarendon presents his humble duty to your Majesty, and humbly begs to say that, with the permission of Lord Palmerston, and at the urgent recommendation of Lord Aberdeen and Lord Lansdowne, he has made to Lord John Russell the proposal to act as our negotiator at Vienna, which your Majesty was pleased to sanction on Wednesday night.[105]

Lord Clarendon thinks, that whether the negotiations end in peace or are suddenly to be broken off, no man is so likely as Lord John to be approved by the Country for whichever course of proceeding he may adopt, and it will be a great advantage that the negotiator himself should be able to vindicate his own conduct in Parliament.

Lord Clarendon has this evening received a very kind and friendly answer from Lord John, who is disposed to accept, but desires another day to consider the proposal.

As our relations with the United States are of the utmost importance at this moment, and as they have rather improved of late, Lord Clarendon humbly hopes he may be excused if he ventures to suggest to your Majesty the expediency of inviting Mr Buchanan[106] to Windsor.

---

spanned half a century, for he had, as Lord Henry Petty, been Chancellor of the Exchequer in the ministry of "All the Talents" in 1806-1807. Lord Granville now assumed the Liberal leadership in the Lords, which, as Lord Fitzmaurice points out, he held, with a brief exception of three years, till his death in 1891.

[105] In pursuance of the negotiations referred to (*ante*), a conference of the Powers was held at Vienna. Lord John's view of the attitude which he hoped Great Britain would take up is clearly stated in his letter of the 11th to Lord Clarendon, printed in Walpole's *Life of Lord John Russell*, vol. ii. p. 242. He favoured the admission of Prussia to the Conference.

[106] American Minister to Great Britain, afterwards President of the United States.

Viscount Palmerston to Queen Victoria.

Piccadilly, *10th February 1855.*

Viscount Palmerston presents his humble duty to your Majesty, and begs to state that having been very kindly received at Paris by the Emperor of the French, he thought it would be useful to write to the Emperor on the formation of the present Government, and he submits a copy of the letter which he addressed to the Emperor.

The Emperor, when Viscount Palmerston took leave of him, signified his intention of writing occasionally to Viscount Palmerston, and that is the reason why Viscount Palmerston adverts to such communications in his letter.

Viscount Palmerston has just had the honour to receive your Majesty's communication of this day, and will not fail to bear in mind the suggestions which it contains.

Viscount Palmerston to the Emperor of the French.

Londres, *8 Février 1855.*

Sire,—Appelé par la Reine ma Souveraine au poste que maintenant j'occupe, je m'empresse de satisfaire au besoin que je sens d'exprimer à votre Majesté la grande satisfaction que j'éprouve à me trouver en rapport plus direct avec le Gouvernement de votre Majesté.

L'Alliance qui unit si heureusement la France et l'Angleterre et qui promet des résultats si avantageux pour toute l'Europe, prend son origine dans la loyauté, la franchise, et la sagacité de votre Majesté; et votre Majesté pourra toujours compter sur la loyauté et la franchise du Gouvernement Anglais. Et si votre Majesté avait jamais une communication à nous faire sur des idées non encore assez mûries pour être le sujet de Dépêches Officielles, je m'estimerais très honoré en recevant une telle communication de la part de votre Majesté.

Nous allons mettre un peu d'ordre à notre Camp devant Sevastopol, et en cela nous tâcherons d'imiter le bel exemple qui nous est montré par le Camp Français. A quelque chose cependant malheur est bon, et le mauvais état de l'Armée Anglaise a donné aux braves et généreux Français l'occasion de prodiguer à leurs frères d'armes des soins, qui ont excité la plus vive reconnaissance tant en Angleterre qu'à Balaclava. J'ai l'honneur d'être, Sire, etc. etc.,

Palmerston.

Memorandum by the Prince Albert.

PALMERSTON AND THE EMPEROR

Windsor Castle, *11th February 1855.*

This letter gave us great uneasiness.... The sort of private correspondence which Lord Palmerston means to establish with the Emperor Napoleon is a novel and unconstitutional practice. If carried on behind the back of the Sovereign, it makes her Minister the Privy Councillor of a foreign Sovereign at the head of her affairs. How can the Foreign Secretary and Ambassador at Paris, the legitimate organs of communication, carry on their business, if everything has been privately preconcerted between the Emperor and the English Prime Minister? What control can the Cabinet hope to exercise on the Foreign Affairs under these circumstances?...

Queen Victoria to Viscount Palmerston.

Windsor Castle, *11th February 1855.*

The Queen thanks Lord Palmerston for his letter of the 10th, and for communicating to her the letter which he had addressed upon the 8th to the Emperor of the French on the formation of the present Government, the copy of which the Queen herewith returns.

Viscount Palmerston to Queen Victoria.

THE ROEBUCK COMMITTEE

Piccadilly, *16th February 1855.*

(*Friday night.*)

Viscount Palmerston presents his humble duty to your Majesty, and begs to state that after he had made his statement this afternoon, a conversation of some length took place, in which Mr Disraeli, Mr Roebuck, Mr Thomas Duncombe, and several other Members took part, the subject of discussion being whether Mr Roebuck's Committee should or should not be appointed.

Viscount Palmerston is concerned to say that it was not only his own impression but the opinion of a great number of persons with whom he communicated in the course of the evening, including the Speaker, that the appointment of the Committee will be carried by a very great majority, perhaps scarcely less great than that by which the original Motion was affirmed; and it was also the opinion of good judges that a refusal to grant an enquiry would not be a good ground on which to dissolve Parliament and appeal to the Country. The general opinion was that the best way of meeting the Motion for naming the Committee which Mr Roebuck has fixed for next Thursday, would be to move some instruction to the Committee directing or limiting the range of its enquiry. This is a matter, however, which will be well considered at the meeting of the Cabinet to-morrow....

The reason alleged for the determination of Members to vote for Mr Roebuck's Committee is the general desire throughout the Country that an enquiry should be instituted to ascertain the causes of the sufferings of your Majesty's troops in the Crimea.

Queen Victoria to the King of Prussia.

/Translation./

Buckingham Palace, *20th February 1855.*

Dearest Brother,—I must not let Lord John Russell visit Berlin without personally recommending him to your Majesty—an honour which he deserves in a high degree, as a statesman of wide outlook, well-informed, and moderate. At the same time I may be allowed to repeat my conviction, which I have expressed several times already, that it appears to me impossible to obtain peace so long as Prussia continues indisposed to maintain, in case of necessity by force of arms, the principles publicly expressed in concert with the belligerent Powers and Austria.

Much blood, very much blood, has already been shed. Honour and justice force the belligerent Powers to make every sacrifice in continually defending those principles to the utmost. Whether diplomacy will succeed in saving Prussia from taking an active share in this defence—that remains the secret of the future, which the King of kings alone possesses!

Albert presents his homage to your Majesty, and I beg to be most cordially remembered, and remain as ever, my dear Brother, your Majesty's faithful Servant and Friend,

Victoria R.

Memorandum by the Prince Albert.

MR GLADSTONE

Buckingham Palace, *21st February 1855.*

I have just seen Mr Gladstone, who received my box so late that I did not wish to detain him more than a few minutes, as the Cabinet was waiting for him. I told him, however, the substance of Lord Palmerston's letter, and of the Queen's answer, the wisdom of which, he said, nobody could doubt for a moment, and added that the choice lying only between many evils, I hoped he and his friends would not strive to obtain an absolute good, and thereby lose the Queen the services of an efficient Government. He begged that I should rest assured that the first and primary consideration which would guide their determination would be the position of the Crown in these critical circumstances. He had had no opportunity of consulting these last days either Mr S. Herbert or Sir James Graham. But for himself he felt the greatest difficulty in letting the House of Commons succeed in what he must consider a most unconstitutional, most presumptuous, and most dangerous course, after which it would be impossible for the Executive ever to oppose again the most absurd and preposterous demands for enquiry.[107]

I asked, "But can you stop it?"

He answered: I believe Lord Palmerston made a mistake in not grappling with it from the first, and using all the power the Crown had entrusted to him, even ostentatiously, for the purpose. Now it might be most difficult—but it ought not to pass without a solemn protest on the part of the men who were not connected with the Government, and should not be supposed to have any other than the interests of the Country at heart. A Government was powerless in resisting such an encroachment of the House, where the whole Opposition, from personal motives, and the supporters of Government from fear of their constituents, were bent upon carrying it. Such a protest, however, might form a rallying-point upon which future resistance might be based, and the Country, now intoxicated by agitation, might come to its senses.

As to the strength of the Government, he believed it had very little at this moment in the House, and that such would be the case with any Government Lord Palmerston could form, he had foretold him, when

---

[107] See *post*, note 38.

Lord Derby had made him the offer to join an Administration of his forming. At this moment the secession of the Peelites would rather strengthen the Government than otherwise, as, from their connection with Lord Aberdeen, they had been decried in the Country with him, and the Whigs looked upon them with all the personal feelings of men deprived of their offices by them.

He agreed with me that in the present disruption of Parties, the difficulty of obtaining any strong Government consists, not in the paucity of men, but in the over-supply of Right Honourable gentlemen produced by the many attempts to form a Government on a more extended base. There were now at least three Ministers for each office, from which the two excluded were always cried up as superior to the one in power. He said this could not be amended until we got back to two Parties—each of them capable of presenting to the Queen an efficient Administration. Now the one Party did not support its Chief from personal rivalry—and the other, from the very feeling of its own incapacity, became reckless as to the course of its political actions.

He concluded by saying he felt it right to reserve his final determination till the last moment at which it would become necessary.

Albert.

Viscount Palmerston to Queen Victoria.

RESIGNATION OF THE PEELITES

Downing Street, *21st February 1855.*

Viscount Palmerston presents his humble duty to your Majesty, and feels extreme regret in having to state to your Majesty that Sir James Graham, Mr Gladstone, and Mr Sidney Herbert announced at the Cabinet Meeting to-day their determination to retire from the Government in consequence of their inability to consent to the nomination of Mr Roebuck's Committee.[108] *No other* Member of the Government has as yet intimated any intention to retire. Viscount Palmerston will assemble the remaining Members of the Government to-morrow at

[108] The retirement of the Peelites in a body from Lord Palmerston's Ministry is a curious instance of the tenacity of Party ties, since the prosecution of the enquiry into the conduct of the war affected the Whig as much as the Peelite section of the Aberdeen Cabinet. In reference to their reason for resignation (*viz.* that the investigation was a dangerous breach of a great constitutional principle, and that similar enquiries could never thenceforward be refused), see Parker's *Sir James Graham*, vol. ii. pp. 268-272.

twelve to take into consideration the steps to be taken for supplying the places of the retiring Members.[109]

An endeavour has been made to induce Mr Roebuck to postpone the appointment of the Committee till Monday, but he will not consent to delay it beyond to-morrow, and he will insert in the votes to-night, to be printed to-morrow morning (in accordance with the rules of the House), the proposed list of names which have been settled between the Government and Mr Roebuck, and which seem to be unobjectionable, all things considered....

The secession of the Peelites, however, did not make the Ministry a Whig Government. The last Whig Administration was that which left office early in 1852. Had Lord John Russell succeeded in his attempt on the present occasion, the Whig party might have endured *co nomine*; but Palmerston had, notwithstanding Cobden's distrust, been popular with the Radicals, and henceforward his supporters must be known as the Liberal Party.

Queen Victoria to the King of the Belgians.

CRIMEAN HEROES

Buckingham Palace, *27th February 1855.*

My dearest Uncle,—Since I last wrote to you, we have again had much trouble, as Van de Weyer will have informed you. We have lost our *three* best men—certainly from the purest and best of motives—but the result is *unfortunate*. Altogether, affairs are very unsettled and very unsatisfactory. The good people here are really a little *mad*, but I am certain it *will* right itself; one must only *not* give way to the nonsense and absurdity one hears.

Lord John's return to office *under* Lord Palmerston is very extraordinary![110] I hope he may do good in his mission; he is most anxious for it.

---

[109] Sir Charles Wood became First Lord of the Admiralty (Mr. Vernon Smith succeeding him at the Board of Control), Sir George Lewis succeeded Mr Gladstone at the Exchequer, and the Colonial Office was offered to and accepted by Lord John Russell, who was at the moment in Paris on his way to attend the Vienna Conference.

[110] For twenty years Lord John Russell had been Leader of the Whig Party in the House, and Lord Palmerston subordinate to him.

Many thanks for your kind letter of the 23rd. The frost has left us, which personally I regret, as it agrees so well with me; but I believe it was very necessary on account of the great distress which was prevalent, so many people being thrown out of employment.

The Emperor's meditated voyage[111]—though natural in him to wish—I think most alarming; in fact, I don't know how things are to go on without him, independent of the great danger he exposes himself to besides. I own it makes one tremble, for *his life* is of such *immense importance*. I still hope that he may be deterred from it, but Walewski was in a great state about it.

On Thursday we saw twenty-six of the wounded Coldstream Guards, and on Friday thirty-four of the Scotch Fusileers. A most interesting and touching sight—*such* fine men, and so brave and patient! *so ready* to go back and "*be at them again.*" A great many of them, I am glad to say, will be able to remain in the Service. Those who have lost their limbs cannot, of course. There were two poor boys of nineteen and twenty—the one had lost his leg, quite high up, by the bursting of a shell in the trenches, and the other his poor arm so shot that it is perfectly useless. Both had smooth girls' faces; these were in the Coldstream, who certainly look the worst. In the Scotch Fusileers, there were also two very young men—the one shot through the cheek, the other through the *skull*—but both recovered! Among the Grenadiers there is one very sad object, shot *dreadfully*, a ball having gone in through the cheek and behind the nose and eye and out through the other side! He is shockingly disfigured, but is recovered. I feel so much for them, and am *so fond* of my dear soldiers—so *proud* of them! We could not have avoided sending the Guards; it would have been their ruin if they had not gone....

---

[111] The Emperor had announced his intention of going to the Crimea, and assuming the conduct of the war. The project was most unfavourably regarded by the Queen and the Prince, by Lord Palmerston, and by the Emperor's own advisers. But the intention, which had been carefully matured, was arrived at in full loyalty to the Alliance with this country, and had to be tactfully met. Accordingly, it was arranged that when Napoleon was at the Camp in Boulogne in March, Lord Clarendon should visit him there, and discuss the question with him. Eventually, the Foreign Secretary persuaded the Emperor to relinquish, or at any rate defer, his expedition; a memorandum of what passed on the occasion was drawn up by the Prince from the narration of Lord Clarendon, and printed by Sir Theodore Martin. (*Life of the Prince Consort*, vol. iii. p. 231.)

I must now conclude. Ever your devoted Niece,

Victoria R.

Queen Victoria to the Earl of Clarendon.

Buckingham Palace, *1st March 1855.*

The Queen thanks Lord Clarendon for his letter received this evening, and will return the enclosures to-morrow.

The Queen gathers from what she has read that the Emperor is bent upon going, and that nothing in the shape of remonstrance or argument will turn him from his purpose.

Should the Emperor's journey take place, Lord Cowley's accompanying him appears to the Queen in all respects a most useful step, and the Queen gives accordingly her permission for him to go.

The Emperor's taking the management of the whole Campaign, as well as the command of our Forces, entirely into his own hands, involves so many considerations that it may be worth considering whether we ought not previously to come to a more direct and comprehensive understanding with him, such as full and verbal discussion would alone afford—to which, in some shape or other, his present stay at Boulogne might afford some facilities.

From Sir Ralph Abercromby[112]

DEATH OF THE CZAR

The Hague. *2nd March 1855.*

(Received 3.45 p.m.)

The Emperor Nicholas died this morning at 1 A.M. of Pulmonic Apoplexy, after an attack of Influenza.[113]

---

[112] Who had married the sister of Lady John Russell.

[113] Nothing had been known publicly of the Czar's illness, and the startling news of his death caused a sensation in England of tragedy rather than of joy. Mr Kinglake has vividly depicted the feelings of agony and mortification with which the news of the earlier Russian reverses had been received by Nicholas. On the 1st of March, he received the full account of the disaster at Eupatoria, after which he became delirious, and died on the following day. He had stated, in referring to the horrors of that Crimean winter, that Russia had still two Generals on whom she could rely: Generals Janvier and Février; and Leech, with matchless art, now made his famous cartoon—"General Février

Viscount Palmerston to Queen Victoria.

THE COMMITTEE OF ENQUIRY

House of Commons, *2nd March 1855.*

Viscount Palmerston presents his humble duty to your Majesty....

The death of the Emperor of Russia may or may not produce important changes in the state of affairs. It is probable that the Grand Duke Hereditary will succeed quietly, notwithstanding the notion that a doubt would be started whether he, as son of the Grand Duke Nicholas, would not be superseded by his younger brother born son of the Czar.[114] It is possible that the new Emperor may revert to that peaceful policy which he was understood to advocate in the beginning of these transactions, but it is possible, on the other hand, that he may feel bound to follow out the policy of his father, and may be impelled by the headstrong ambition of his brother Constantine. At all events, this change at Petersburg should not for the present slacken the proceedings and the arrangements of the Allies.

The House of Commons has been engaged in discussing Mr Roebuck's proposal that the Committee of Enquiry should be a secret one. This proposal was made by the majority of the Committee on the ground that they anticipated a difficulty in conducting their enquiries without trenching on the delicate and dangerous ground of questioning the proceedings of the French. The proposal was objected to by Lord Seymour[115] and Mr Ellice, members of the Committee, by Sir James Graham as unjust towards the Duke of Newcastle, and others whose conduct ought to be enquired into with all the safeguards which publicity secures for justice, and not before a Secret Tribunal in the nature of an Inquisition. The general sense of the House was against secrecy, and Viscount Palmerston expressed an opinion adverse to it, on the ground that it could not be enforced because the Committee could not gag the witnesses, and that the character of secrecy would excite suspicion and disappoint public expectation. Sir John Pakington, a

---

turned traitor," depicting Death, in the uniform of a Russian officer, laying his bony hand on the Emperor's heart.

[114] The eldest son, the Grand Duke Alexander (1818-1881), succeeded as Czar Alexander II.

[115] Lord Seymour (afterwards Duke of Somerset) drafted the Report of the Committee.

member of the Committee, was for secrecy, Mr Disraeli spoke against it, and the Motion has been withdrawn.

Queen Victoria to the Princess of Prussia.

[Translation.]

Buckingham Palace, *4th March 1855.*

Dear Augusta,—The astounding news of the death of your poor uncle the Emperor Nicholas reached us the day before yesterday at four o'clock. A few hours previously we had learnt that his condition was hopeless. The news is sudden and most unexpected, and we are naturally very anxious to learn details. His departure from life at the present moment cannot but make a particularly strong impression, and what the consequences of it may be the All-knowing One alone can foresee. Although the poor Emperor has died as our enemy, I have not forgotten former and more happy times, and no one has more than I regretted that he himself evoked this sad war.[116] To you I must address my request to express to the poor Empress, as well as to the family, my heartfelt condolence. I cannot do it officially, but you, my beloved friend, you will surely be able to convey it to your sister-in-law as well as to the present young Emperor in a manner which shall not compromise me. I have a deep, heartfelt desire to express this. To your dear, honoured mother convey, pray, my condolence on the death of her brother....

Queen Victoria to Lord Panmure.

THE HOSPITAL QUESTION

Buckingham Palace, *5th March 1855.*

The Queen is very anxious to bring before Lord Panmure the subject which she mentioned to him the other night, viz. that of Hospitals for our sick and wounded soldiers. This is absolutely necessary, and *now* is the moment to have them built, for no doubt there would be no difficulty in obtaining the money requisite for this purpose, from the strong feeling now existing in the public mind for improvements of all kinds connected with the Army and the well-being and comfort of the soldier.

[116] The Queen records, in the *Life of the Prince Consort*, that she entertained a sincere respect for the Emperor personally, and received the news of his death with regret (vol. iii. p. 225, note).

Nothing can exceed the attention paid to these poor men in the Barracks at Chatham (or rather more Fort Pitt and Brompton), and they are in that respect very comfortable; but the buildings are bad—the wards more like prisons than hospitals, with the windows so high that no one can look out of them; and the generality of the wards are small rooms, with hardly space for you to walk between the beds. There is no dining-room or hall, so that the poor men must have their dinners in the same room in which they sleep, and in which some may be dying, and at any rate many suffering, while others are at their meals. The proposition of having hulks prepared for their reception will do very well at first, but it would not, the Queen thinks, do for any length of time. A hulk is a very gloomy place, and these poor men require their spirits to be cheered as much as their physical sufferings to be attended to. The Queen is particularly anxious on this subject, which is, he may truly say, constantly in her thoughts, as is everything connected with her beloved troops, who have fought so bravely and borne so heroically all their sufferings and privations.

The Queen hopes before long to visit all the Hospitals at Portsmouth, and to see in what state they are.

When will the medals be ready for distribution?

The Marquis of Dalhousie to Queen Victoria.

LORD DALHOUSIE RESIGNS

Ootacamund, *14th March 1855.*

The Governor-General presents his most humble duty to your Majesty; and in obedience to the command, which your Majesty was pleased to lay upon him, that he should keep your Majesty acquainted with the course of public events in India, he has the honour to inform your Majesty that he has now felt it to be his duty to request the President of the Board of Control to solicit for him your Majesty's permission to retire from the office of Governor-General of India about the close of the present year.

The Governor-General begs permission respectfully to represent, that in January next, he will have held his present office for eight years; that his health during the last few months has seriously failed him; and that although he believes that the invigorating air of these hills will enable him to discharge all his duties efficiently during this season, yet he is conscious that the effects of an Indian climate have laid such a hold upon him that by the close of the present year he will be wholly unfit any longer to serve your Majesty.

Lord Dalhousie, therefore, humbly trusts that your Majesty will graciously permit him to resign the great office which he holds before he ceases to command the strength which is needed to sustain it. He has the honour to subscribe himself, your Majesty's most obedient, most humble and devoted Subject and Servant,

Dalhousie.

Queen Victoria to the Earl of Clarendon.

Buckingham Palace, *14th March 1855.*

The Queen returns the letter and Despatches from Vienna. They don't alter her opinion as to our demands. Every concession in form and wording ought to be made which could save Russian *amour-propre*; but this ought in no way to trench upon the *substance* of our demands, to which Austria must feel herself bound.[117]

Queen Victoria to the Earl of Clarendon.

THE VIENNA CONFERENCE

Osborne, *19th March 1855.*

The Queen has read with the greatest interest Lord Cowley's three reports. The changeableness of the French views are most perplexing, although they have hitherto not prevented a steady course from being followed in the end. Lord Cowley seems to have been a little off his guard when he took the proposal of our taking Sinope as a second Malta or Gibraltar, for a mere act of generosity and confidence towards us. We must be careful not to break down ourselves the barrier of the "abnegation clause" of our original treaty.[118] The Austrian proposal can hardly be serious, for to require 1,200,000 men before going to war is almost ridiculous.

[117] As has already been stated, the "Four Points" were the basis of the negotiations at Vienna; the third alone, which the Allies and Austria had defined as intended to terminate Russian preponderance in the Black Sea, caused difficulty.

[118] *I.e.* the formal renunciation by the Allies of any scheme of territorial acquisition.

The Queen read with much concern the two simultaneous proposals from the King of Prussia's simultaneous Plenipotentiaries—both inadmissible, in her opinion. A very civil answer would appear to the Queen as the best, to the effect that, as Prussia was evidently not now in a mood to resume her position amongst the great Powers with the responsibilities attaching to it, we could not hope to arrive at any satisfactory result by the present negotiations, but shall be ready to treat Prussia with the same regard with which we have always done, when she shall have something tangible to propose.

Queen Victoria to Viscount Palmerston.

THE BALTIC EXPEDITION

Osborne, *19th March 1855.*

With regard to the Expedition to the Baltic[119] the Queen concurs in believing it probable that we shall have to confine ourselves to a blockade, but this should be with the *certainty* of its being done effectually and free from any danger to the squadron, from a sudden start of the Russian fleet. Twenty sail of the Line (to which add five French) would be a sufficient force if supported by the necessary complement of frigates, corvettes, and gunboats, etc., etc.; alone, they would be useless from their draught of water, and if twenty ships only are meant (not sail of the Line), the force would seem wholly inadequate. The Queen would therefore wish, before giving her sanction to the proposed plan of campaign, to have a complete list submitted to her of what it is intended to constitute the Baltic Fleet.[120] We ought likewise not to leave ourselves destitute of any Reserve at home, which the uncertain contingencies of another year's war may call upon at any moment.

The Queen regrets Lord Shaftesbury's declining office, and approves of Lord Elgin's selection in his place.[121]

She thanks Lord Palmerston for the clear and comprehensive explanation of Sir George Lewis's Stamp Duties Bill,[122] and approves of

[119] The expedition was commanded by Rear-Admiral Richard Dundas. About the same time Vice-Admiral Sir James Dundas retired from the Mediterranean Command, in favour of Sir Edmund Lyons.

[120] The allied fleet comprised 23 line-of-battle ships, 31 frigates and corvettes, 29 smaller steamers and gunboats, and 18 other craft.

[121] As Chancellor of the Duchy of Lancaster; Mr Matthew Talbot Baines was ultimately appointed.

Lord Palmerston's proposal for the adjournment of Parliament for the Easter holidays.

Queen Victoria to Lord Panmure.

Osborne, *22nd March 1855.*

The other day, when the Queen spoke to Lord Panmure on the subject of the distribution of the *Medal* for the *Crimean* Campaign amongst the Officers, and those who *are* in *this* country, no decision was come to as to how this should be done. The Queen has since thought that the value of this Medal would be greatly enhanced if *she*, were *personally* to deliver it to the officers and a certain number of men (selected for that purpose). The valour displayed by our troops, as well as the sufferings they have endured, have never been surpassed—perhaps hardly equalled; and as the Queen has been a witness of *what* they have gone through, having visited them in their hospitals, she would *like* to be able *personally* to give them the reward they have earned so well, and will value so much. It will likewise have a very beneficial effect, the Queen doubts not, on the recruiting. The manner in which it should be done, and the details connected with the execution of this intention of hers, the Queen will settle with Lord Panmure, when she sees him in Town.

Will the Medals now be soon ready?

Queen Victoria to the King of the Belgians.

THE IMPERIAL VISIT

Windsor Castle, *17th April 1855.*

Dearest Uncle,—Your kindness will, I know, excuse any description of all that has passed, and *is* passing, and I leave it to Charles. The impression is very favourable.[123] There is great fascination in the quiet, frank manner of the Emperor, and *she* is very pleasing, very graceful,

---

[122] Imposing a penny stamp upon bankers' cheques, if drawn within fifteen miles of the place where they were payable.

[123] The Emperor and Empress of the French arrived on the 16th of April, on a visit to England. They were enthusiastically received both at Dover (notwithstanding a dense fog, which endangered the safety of the Imperial yacht) and on their progress from the South-Eastern terminus to Paddington. In passing King Street, the Emperor was observed to indicate his former residence to the Empress.

and very unaffected, but very delicate. She *is* certainly very pretty and very uncommon-looking. The Emperor spoke very amiably of you. The reception by the public was *immensely* enthusiastic. I must end here. Ever your devoted Niece,

Victoria R.

Queen Victoria to the King of the Belgians.

Buckingham Palace, *19th April 1855.*

Dearest Uncle, ... I have not a moment to myself, being of course entirely occupied with our Imperial guests, with whom I am much pleased, and who behave really with the greatest tact.[124] The Investiture went off very well, and to-day (we came from Windsor) the enthusiasm of the thousands who received him in the City was immense. He is much pleased. Since the time of my Coronation, with the exception of the opening of the great Exhibition, I don't remember anything like it. To-night we go in state to the Opera. In haste, ever your devoted Niece,

Victoria R.

Queen Victoria to the King of the Belgians.

Buckingham Palace, *24th April 1855.*

My dearest Uncle,—Many thanks for your kind letter of the 19th and 20th, by which I am glad to see that you were well. Our great visit is past, like a brilliant and most successful dream, but I think the effect on the visitors will be a good and lasting one; they saw in our reception, and in that of the whole Nation, nothing *put on*, but a warm, hearty welcome to a faithful and steady Ally. I think also that for Bel-

---

[124] A review of the Household troops in Windsor Park was held on the 17th, and a ball was given at the Castle in the evening. A Council of War on the 18th was attended by the Prince, the Emperor, and some of their Ministers; in the afternoon the Queen invested the Emperor with the Garter. On the following day the Emperor received an address at Windsor from the Corporation of London, and lunched at the Guildhall; the Queen and Prince and their guests paid a State visit to Her Majesty's Theatre in the evening to hear *Fidelio.* On the 20th the party, with brilliant ceremonial, visited the Crystal Palace at Sydenham, and were enthusiastically received by an immense multitude; another important Council, relative to the future conduct of the war, was held in the evening.

gium this visit will be very useful, for it will increase the friendly feelings of the Emperor towards my dear Uncle, and towards a country in which England takes so deep an interest.

The negotiations are broken off, and Austria has been called upon to act according to the Treaty of the 2nd December. She intends, I believe, to make some proposal, but we know nothing positive as yet. In the meantime I fear the Emperor (I mean Napoleon) *will* go to the Crimea, which makes one anxious.... Ever your devoted Niece,

Victoria R.

Queen Victoria to Viscount Palmerston.

Buckingham Palace, *25th April 1855.*

The Queen has read the letter of Lady —— to Lady Palmerston, and now returns it to Lord Palmerston.

She has to observe that it has been with her an invariable rule never to take upon herself the office of sitting in judgment upon accusations or reports against private character. No person therefore can have any reason to suppose that she will by marked neglect or manner appear to pronounce a verdict upon matters in which she is not the proper Court of Appeal.

The Emperor of the French to Queen Victoria.

THE EMPEROR'S LETTER

Palais des Tuileries, *le 25 Avril 1855.*

Madame et bonne Sœur,—A Paris depuis trois jours, je suis encore auprès de votre Majesté par la pensée, et mon premier besoin est de Lui redire combien est profonde l'impression que m'a laissée son accueil si plein de grâce et d'affectueuse bonté. La politique nous a rapprochés d'abord, mais aujourd'hui qu'il m'a été permis de connaître personnellement votre Majesté c'est une vive et respectueuse sympathie qui forme désormais le véritable lien qui m'attache à elle. Il est impossible en effet de vivre quelques jours dans votre intimité sans subir le charme qui s'attache à l'image de la grandeur et du bonheur de la famille la plus unie. Votre Majesté m'a aussi bien touché par ses prévenances délicates envers l'Impératrice; car rien ne fait plus de plaisir que de voir la personne qu'on aime devenir l'objet d'aussi flatteuses attentions.

Je prie votre Majesté d'exprimer au Prince Albert les sentiments sincères que m'inspirent sa franche amitié, son esprit élevé et la droiture de son jugement.

J'ai rencontré à mon retour à Paris bien des difficultés diplomatiques et bien d'autres intervenants au sujet de mon voyage en Crimée. Je dirai en confidence à votre Majesté que ma résolution de voyage s'en trouve presque ébranlée. En France tous ceux qui possèdent sont bien peu courageux!

Votre Majesté voudra bien me rappeler au souvenir de sa charmante famille et me permettre de Lui renouveler l'assurance de ma respectueuse amitié et de mon tendre attachement. De votre Majesté, le bon Frère,

Napoléon.

Queen Victoria to the Emperor of the French.

THE QUEEN'S REPLY

Buckingham Palace, *le 27 Avril 1855.*

Sire et mon cher Frère,—Votre Majesté vient de m'écrire une bien bonne et affectueuse lettre que j'ai reçue hier et qui m'a vivement touchée. Vous dites, Sire, que vos pensées sont encore auprès de nous; je puis Vous assurer que c'est bien réciproque de notre part et que nous ne cessons de repasser en revue et de parler de ces beaux jours que nous avons eu le bonheur de passer avec Vous et l'Impératrice et qui se sont malheureusement écoulés si vite. Nous sommes profondément touchés de la manière dont votre Majesté parle de nous et de notre famille, et je me plais à voir dans les sentiments que vous nous témoignez un gage précieux de plus pour la continuation de ces relations si heureusement et si fermement établies entre nos deux pays.

Permettez que j'ajoute encore, Sire, combien de prix j'attache à l'entière franchise avec laquelle Vous ne manquez d'agir envers nous en toute occasion et à laquelle Vous nous trouverez toujours prêts à répondre, bien convaincus que c'est le moyen le plus sûr pour éloigner tout sujet de complication et de mésentendu entre nos deux Gouvernements vis-à-vis des graves difficultés que nous avons à surmonter ensemble.

Depuis le départ de votre Majesté les complications diplomatiques ont augmenté bien péniblement et la position est assurément devenue bien difficile mais le Ciel n'abandonnera pas ceux qui n'ont d'autre but que le bien du genre humain.

J'avoue que la nouvelle de la possibilité de l'abandon de votre voyage en Crimée m'a bien tranquillisée parce qu'il y avait bien des causes d'alarmes en vous voyant partir si loin et exposé à tant de dangers. Mais bien que l'absence de votre Majesté en Crimée soit toujours une grande perte pour les opérations vigoureuses dont nous sommes convenus, j'espère que leur exécution n'en sera pas moins vivement poussée par nos deux Gouvernements.

Le Prince me charge de vous offrir ses plus affectueux hommages et nos enfants qui sont bien flattés de votre gracieux souvenir, et qui parlent beaucoup de votre visite, se mettent à vos pieds.

Avec tous les sentiments de sincère amitié et de haute estime, je me dis, Sire et cher Frère, de V.M.I. la bien bonne Sœur,

Victoria R.

H.M. Eugénie, Empress of the French.
From a miniature by Sir W. K. Ross at Windsor Castle

Viscount Palmerston to Queen Victoria.[125]

RUSSIA AND THE BLACK SEA

Piccadilly, *26th April 1855.*

Viscount Palmerston presents his humble duty to your Majesty, and begs to state that the Members of the Cabinet who met yesterday evening at the Chancellor's were of opinion that the Austrian proposal adopted by M. Drouyn de Lhuys,AUSTRIAN PROPOSALS even with his pretended modification, could not be described more accurately than in the concise terms of H.R.H. the Prince Albert, namely, that instead of making to cease the preponderance of Russia in the Black Sea, it would perpetuate and legalise that preponderance, and that instead of establishing a secure and permanent Peace, it would only establish a prospective case for war. Such a proposal therefore your Majesty's Advisers could not recommend your Majesty to adopt; but as the step to be taken seems rather to be to make such a proposal to Austria than to answer such a proposal which Austria has not formally made, and as M. Drouyn's telegraphic despatch stated that he thought that Lord John Russell would recommend such an arrangement to his colleagues, the Cabinet were of opinion that the best course would be simply to take no step at all until Lord John Russell's return, which may be expected to-morrow or next day, especially as Lord Clarendon

[125] It had long become evident that Russia would refuse assent to the Third Point, terminating her preponderance in the Black Sea, but Austria now came forward with a proposal to limit the Russian force there to the number of ships authorised before the war. This was rejected by Russia, whereupon the representatives of England and France withdrew from the negotiations. Count Buol, representing Austria, then came forward again with a scheme the salient features of which were that, if Russia increased her Black Sea fleet beyond its existing strength, Turkey might maintain a force equal to it, and England and France might each have a naval force in the Black Sea equal to half the Russian force, while the increase of the Russian fleet beyond its strength in 1853 would be regarded by Austria as a *casus belli*. These terms were satisfactory neither to the British Government nor to the French Emperor, so that it was learned with some surprise that Lord John Russell and M. Drouyn de Lhuys (the French Plenipotentiary) had approved of them. Upon the Emperor definitely rejecting the proposals, M. Drouyn de Lhuys resigned; he was succeeded as Foreign Minister by Count Walewski, M. de Persigny becoming Ambassador in London. Lord John Russell tendered his resignation, but, at Lord Palmerston's solicitation, and most unfortunately for himself, he withdrew it.

had already, by telegraphic message of yesterday, intimated to the French Government that such an arrangement as that proposed by M. Drouyn, and which would sanction a Russian Fleet in the Black Sea to any amount short by one ship of the number existing in 1853, could not be agreed to by the British Government. Such an arrangement would, in the opinion of Viscount Palmerston, be alike dangerous and dishonourable; and as to the accompanying alliance with Austria for the future defence of Turkey and for making war with Russia, if she were to raise her Black Sea Fleet up to the amount of 1853, what reason is there to believe that Austria, who shrinks from war with Russia now that the Army of Russia has been much reduced by the losses of the last twelve months—now that her Forces are divided and occupied elsewhere than on the Austrian frontier, and now that England and France are actually in the field with great Armies, supported by great Fleets, what reason is there to believe that this same Austria would be more ready to make war four or five years hence, when the Army of Russia shall have repaired its losses and shall be more concentrated to attack Austria, when the Austrian Army shall have been reduced to its Peace Establishment, and when the Peace Establishments of England and France, withdrawn within their home stations, shall be less ready to co-operate with Austria in war? What reason, moreover, is there for supposing that Austria, who has recently declared that though prepared for war she will not make war for ten sail of the Line more or less in the Russian Black Sea Fleet, will some few years hence, when unprepared for war, draw the sword on account of the addition of one ship of war to the Russian Fleet in the Black Sea?

Such proposals are really a mockery.

Queen Victoria to the Earl of Clarendon.

Buckingham Palace, *28th April 1855.*

The Queen returns these very important letters. She thinks that it will be of great use to ask the Emperor to send M. Drouyn de Lhuys over here after having discussed the plans of peace with him, in order that he should hear our arguments also, and give us his reasons for thinking the terms acceptable. The influence of distance and difference of locality upon the resolves of men has often appeared to the Queen quite marvellous.

Queen Victoria to the King of the Belgians.

THE IMPERIAL VISIT

Buckingham Palace, *1st May 1855*.

My dearest Uncle,—On this day, the fifth birthday of our darling little Arthur—the anniversary of the opening of the Great Exhibition—the *once* great day at Paris, viz. the poor King's name-day—and also the birthday of the dear old Duke—I write to thank you for your kind and affectionate letter of the 27th. The *attentat*[126] on the Emperor will have shocked you, as it did us; it shocked me *the more* as we had *watched over* him with such anxiety while he was with us.

It has produced an immense sensation in France, we hear, and many of *his* political *enemies*, he says, cheered him loudly as he returned to the Tuileries. As you say, he is *very personal*, and *therefore* kindness *shown* him *personally* will make a *lasting* effect on his mind, peculiarly susceptible to *kindness*. Another feature in his character is that *il ne fait pas de phrases*—and *what* is said is the result of deep reflection. I therefore send you (in *strict confidence*) a copy of the really very kind letter he wrote me, and which I am sure is *quite sincere*. He felt the simple and kind treatment of him and her *more* than *all* the outward homage and display.

Please kindly to return it when you have done with it.

I am sure you would be charmed with the Empress; it is not such great beauty, but such grace, elegance, sweetness, and *nature*. Her manners are charming; the *profile* and figure beautiful and particularly *distingués*.

You will be pleased (as I was) at the abandonment of the journey to the Crimea, though I think, as regarded the Campaign, it would have been a good thing....

Lord John is returned. I can't say more to-day, but remain, ever your devoted Niece,

Victoria R.

We have a Childs' *Ball* to-night.

---

[126] An Italian, Giacomo Pianori, fired twice at the Emperor, while he was riding in the Champs Elysées, on the 29th of April; the Emperor was uninjured.

Memorandum by Queen Victoria.

THE QUEEN'S IMPRESSIONS

Buckingham Palace, *2nd May 1855.*

The recent visit of the Emperor Napoleon III. to this country is a most curious page of history, and gives rise to many reflections. A remarkable combination of circumstances has brought about the very intimate alliance which now unites England and France, for so many centuries the bitterest enemies and rivals, and this, under the reign of the present Emperor, the nephew of our greatest foe, and bearing his name, and brought about by the policy of the late Emperor of Russia, who considered himself as the head of the European Alliance against France!

In reflecting on the character of the present Emperor Napoleon, and the impression I have conceived of it, the following thoughts present themselves to my mind:

That he *is* a very *extraordinary* man, with great qualities there can be *no* doubt—I might almost say a mysterious man. He is evidently possessed of *indomitable courage*, *unflinching firmness of purpose*, *self-reliance*, *perseverance*, and *great secrecy*; to this should be added, a great reliance on what he calls his *Star*, and a belief in omens and incidents as connected with his future destiny, which is almost romantic—and at the same time he is endowed with wonderful *self-control*, great *calmness*, even *gentleness*, and with a *power* of *fascination*, the effect of which upon all those who become more intimately acquainted with him is *most sensibly* felt.

How far he is actuated by a strong *moral* sense of *right* and *wrong* is difficult to say. On the one hand, his attempts at Strasbourg and Boulogne, and this last after having given a solemn promise never to return or make a similar attempt—in which he openly called on the subjects of the then King of the French to follow him as the successor of Napoleon, the *Coup d'État* of December 1851, followed by great ... severity and the confiscation of the property of the unfortunate Orleans family, would lead one to believe that he is not. On the other hand, his kindness and gratitude towards all those, whether high or low, who have befriended him or stood by him through life, and his straightforward and steady conduct towards us throughout the very difficult and anxious contest in which we have been engaged for a year and a half, show that he is possessed of noble and right feelings.

My impression is, that in all these apparently inexcusable acts, he has invariably been guided by the belief that he is *fulfilling a destiny* which God has *imposed* upon him, and that, though cruel or harsh in themselves, they were *necessary* to obtain the result which he considered *himself* as *chosen* to carry out, and *not* acts of *wanton* cruelty or injustice; for it is impossible to know him and not to see that there is much that is truly amiable, kind, and honest in his character. Another remarkable and important feature in his composition is, that everything he says or expresses is the *result* of deep reflection and of settled purpose, and not merely *des phrases de politesse*, consequently when we read words used in his speech made in the City, we may feel sure that he *means* what he says; and therefore I would rely with confidence on his behaving honestly and faithfully towards us. I am not able to say whether he is deeply versed in History—I should rather think not, as regards it *generally*, though he may be, and probably is, well informed in the history of his own country, certainly fully so in that of the *Empire*, he having made it his special study to contemplate and reflect upon all the acts and designs of his great uncle. He is very well read in German literature, to which he seems to be very partial. It is said, and I am inclined to think with truth, that he reads but little, even as regards despatches from his own foreign Ministers, he having expressed his surprise at my reading them daily. He seems to be singularly ignorant in matters not connected with the branch of his *special* studies, and to be ill informed upon them by those who surround him.

LOUIS PHILIPPE AND NAPOLEON III

If we compare him with poor King Louis Philippe, I should say that the latter (Louis Philippe) was possessed of vast knowledge upon all and every subject, of immense experience in public affairs, and of great activity of mind; whereas the Emperor possesses greater judgment and much greater firmness of purpose, but no experience of public affairs, nor mental application; he is endowed, as was the late King, with much fertility of imagination.

Another great difference between King Louis Philippe and the Emperor is, that the poor King was *thoroughly French* in character, possessing all the liveliness and talkativeness of that people, whereas the Emperor is as *unlike* a *Frenchman* as possible, being much more *German* than French in character.... How could it be expected that the Emperor *should* have any *experience* in *public affairs*, considering that till six years ago he lived as a poor exile, for some years even in prison, and never having taken the slightest part in the *public* affairs of *any* country?

It is therefore the more astounding, indeed almost incomprehensible, that he should show all those powers of Government, and all that wonderful tact in his conduct and manners which he evinces, and which many a King's son, nurtured in palaces and educated in the midst of affairs, never succeeds in attaining. I likewise believe that he would be incapable of such tricks and over-reachings as practised by poor King Louis Philippe (for whose memory, as the old and kind friend of my father, and of whose kindness and amiable qualities I shall ever retain a lively sense), who in great as well as in small things took a pleasure in being cleverer and more cunning than others, often when there was no advantage to be gained by it, and which was, unfortunately, strikingly displayed in the transactions connected with the Spanish marriages, which led to the King's downfall and ruined him in the eyes of all Europe. On the other hand, I believe that the Emperor Napoleon would not hesitate to do a thing by main force, even if in itself unjust and tyrannical, should he consider that the *accomplishment of his destiny* demanded it.

ISOLATION OF THE EMPEROR

The *great advantage* to be derived for the permanent alliance of England and France, which is of such vital importance to both countries, by the Emperor's recent visit, I take to be this: that, with his peculiar character and views, which are very personal, a kind, unaffected, and hearty reception by us *personally* in our own family will make a lasting impression upon his mind; he will see that he can rely upon our friendship and honesty towards him and his country so long as he remains faithful towards us; naturally frank, he will see the advantage to be derived from continuing so; and if he reflects on the downfall of the former dynasty, he will see that it arose *chiefly* from a *breach* of pledges,... and will be sure, if I be not very much mistaken in his character, to *avoid* such a course. It must likewise not be overlooked that this kindly feeling towards us, and consequently towards England (the interests of which are *inseparable* from us), must be increased when it is remembered that *we* are almost the only people in *his* own position with whom he has been able to be on any terms of intimacy, consequently almost the only ones to whom he could talk easily and unreservedly, which he cannot do naturally with his inferiors. He and the Empress are in a most isolated position, unable to trust the only relations who are near them in France, and surrounded by courtiers and servants, who from fear or interest do not tell them the truth. It is, therefore, natural to believe that he will not willingly separate from those who, like us, do not scruple to put him in possession of the real facts, and whose conduct is guided by justice and honesty, and this the more readily as he is supposed to have always been a searcher after truth. I would go still further, and think that it is in our power to *keep* him in the right course, and to protect him against the extreme flightiness, changeableness, and to a certain extent want of honesty of his own servants and nation. We should never lose the opportunity of checking in the bud any attempt on the part of his agents or ministers to play us false, frankly informing him of the facts, and encouraging him to bring forward in an equally frank manner whatever he has to complain of. This is the course which we have hitherto pursued, and as he is France in his own sole person, it becomes of the utmost importance to encourage by every means in our power that very open intercourse which I must say has existed between him and Lord Cowley for the last year and a half, and now, since our personal acquaintance, between ourselves.

THE FRENCH ALLIANCE

As I said before, the words which fall from his lips are the result of deep reflection, and part of the deep plan which he has staked out for himself, and which he intends to carry out. I would therefore lay stress on the following words which he pronounced to me immediately after the investiture of the Order of the Garter: "*C'est un lien de plus entre nous, j'ai prêté serment de fidélité à votre Majesté et je le garderai soigneusement. C'est un grand événement pour moi, et j'espère pouvoir prouver ma reconnaissance envers votre Majesté et son Pays.*" In a letter said to be written by him to Mr F. Campbell, the translator of M. Thiers's *History of the Consulate and Empire*, when returning the proof-sheets in 1847, he says "Let us hope the day may yet come when I shall carry out the intentions of my Uncle by uniting the policy and interests of England and France in an indissoluble alliance. That hope cheers and encourages me. It forbids my repining at the altered fortunes of my family."

If these be truly his words, he certainly has acted up to them, since he has swayed with an iron hand the destinies of that most versatile nation, the French. That he should have written this at a moment when Louis Philippe had succeeded in all his wishes, and seemed securer than ever in the possession of his Throne, shows a calm reliance in his destiny and in the realisation of hopes entertained from his very childhood which borders on the supernatural.

These are a few of the many reflections caused by the observation and acquaintance with the character of this most extraordinary man, in whose fate not only the interests of this country, but the whole of Europe are intimately bound up. I shall be curious to see if, after the lapse of time, my opinion and estimate of it has been the right one.

Victoria R.

Queen Victoria to the Earl of Clarendon.

Buckingham Palace, *10th May 1855.*

The Queen returns these interesting letters to Lord Clarendon. When the Emperor expresses a wish that positive instructions should be sent to Lord Raglan to join in a general forward movement about to take place, he should be made aware that Lord Raglan has been ready and most anxious for the assault taking place on the 26th, and that he only consented to postpone it for a few days at General Canrobert's earnest desire, who wished to wait for the army of Reserve. It should be kept in mind, however, that the English cannot proceed farther as long as the Mamelon has not been taken, and that as long as the French refuse to do this they must not complain of Lord Raglan's not advancing. The refusal to undertake this has, the Queen is sorry to say, produced a bad feeling amongst many of our officers and men, which she owns alarms her.[127]

Queen Victoria to the King of the Belgians.

THE CRIMEAN MEDAL

Buckingham Palace, *22nd May 1855.*

---

[127] General Canrobert was deficient in dash and initiative; he knew his defects, and was relieved of his command at his own request, being succeeded by General Pélissier.

On the 24th of May (the Queen's Birthday) a successful expedition was made against Kertsch, the granary of Sebastopol, and vast quantities of coal, corn, and flour were either seized by the Allies, or destroyed in anticipation of their seizure by the Russians.

On the 7th of June, the Mamelon (a knoll crowned by a redoubt and protected by the Rifle Pits) was taken by the French, and the Gravel Pits, an outwork in front of the Redan, by the English.

My dearest, kindest Uncle,— ... The state of affairs is uncomfortable and complicated just now, but our course is *straight*; we *cannot* come to any peace unless we have such guarantees by *decided* limitation of the Fleet, which would secure us against Russian preponderance for the future.[128]

Ernest will have told you what a *beautiful* and *touching* sight and ceremony (the first of the kind ever witnessed in England) the distribution of the Medals was. From the highest Prince of the Blood to the lowest Private, all received the same distinction for the bravest conduct in the severest actions, and the rough hand of the brave and honest private soldier came for the first time in contact with that of their Sovereign and their Queen! Noble fellows! I own I feel as if they were *my own children*; my heart beats for *them* as for my *nearest and dearest*. They were so touched, so pleased; many, I hear, cried—and they won't hear of giving up their Medals, to have their names engraved upon them, for fear they should *not* receive the *identical one* put into *their hands by me*, which is quite touching. Several came by in a sadly mutilated state. None created more interest or is more gallant than young Sir Thomas Troubridge, who had, at Inkerman, *one leg* and the *other foot* carried away by a round shot, and continued commanding his battery till the battle was won, refusing to be carried away, only desiring his shattered limbs to be raised in order to prevent too great a hemorrhage! He was dragged by in a bath chair, and when I gave him his medal I told him I should make him one of my Aides-de-camp for his very gallant conduct, to which he replied: "I am amply repaid for everything!"[129]

One must revere and love such soldiers as those! The account in the *Times* of Saturday is very correct and good.

I must, however, conclude now, hoping soon to hear from you again. Could you kindly tell me if you could in a few days forward some letters and papers with *safety* to good Stockmar. Ever your devoted Niece,

Victoria R.

---

[128] Prince Albert, in a Memorandum dated the 25th of May, emphasised the difficulties in the way of peace caused by the attitude of Austria, and the possibility of her passing from the one alliance to the other.

[129] He was made a C.B. and a Brevet-Colonel; and also received the Legion of Honour.

Queen Victoria to Mr Vernon Smith.

SUCCESSOR TO LORD DALHOUSIE

Buckingham Palace, *19th June 1855.*

The Queen has received Mr Vernon Smith's letter on the subject of Lord Dalhousie's resignation and the appointment of a successor. She was somewhat astonished that the name of a successor to that most important appointment should for the first time be brought before her after all official steps for carrying it out had been completed. If the selection should now not receive the Queen's approval, it is evident that great awkwardness must arise.[130]

Queen Victoria to Mr Vernon Smith.

Buckingham Palace, *20th June 1855.*

The Queen received Mr V. Smith's letter yesterday evening after her return from Chatham. She readily acquits him of any *intentional* want of respect towards her, or of any neglect in going through the prescribed forms with regard to the appointment in question, neither of which she meant to insinuate by her letter. But she does not look upon the question as one of form. She takes a deep and natural interest in the welfare of her Indian Empire, and must consider the selection of the fittest person for the post of Governor-General as of paramount importance. She had frequently discussed this point with Lord Palmerston, but the name of Lord Canning never occurred amongst the candidates alluded to. The Queen is even now quite ignorant as to the reasons and motives which led to his selection in preference to those other names, and Mr V. Smith will see at once that, were the Queen inclined to object to it, she could not *now* do so without inflicting a deep, personal injury on a public man, for whose personal qualities and talents the Queen has a high regard.

She accordingly approves the recommendation, but must repeat her regret that no opportunity had been given to her to discuss the propriety of it with her Ministers previous to the intention of the recommendation becoming known to all concerned in it.

---

[130] Mr Vernon Smith, in reply, referred to the statutory power then existing of the Directors of the East India Company to nominate a Governor-General, subject to the approbation of the Crown.

General Simpson to Lord Panmure.[131]

/Telegram./

DEATH OF LORD RAGLAN

29th June 1855.

(8.30 A.M.)

Lord Raglan had been going on favourably until four in the afternoon yesterday, when very serious symptoms made their appearance. Difficulty of breathing was experienced, which gradually increased. Up to five o'clock he was conscious, and from this time his strength declined almost imperceptibly until twenty-five minutes before nine, when he died. I have assumed the command, as Sir George Brown is too ill on board ship.

Queen Victoria to General Simpson.

Buckingham Palace, *30th June 1855.*

Not being aware whether Sir George Brown is well enough by this time to assume the command of the Army, the Queen writes to General Simpson, as the Chief of his Staff, to express to him, and *through* him to the Army, her deep and *heartfelt grief* at the irreparable loss of their gallant and excellent Commander, Lord Raglan, which has cast a gloom over us all, as it must do over the whole Army.

But, at the same time, the Queen wishes to express her earnest hope and confident trust that every one will more than ever now do their duty, as they have hitherto so nobly done, and that she may continue to be as proud of her beloved Army as she has been, though their brave Chief who led them so often to victory and to glory, has been taken from them.

Most grievous and most truly melancholy it is that poor Lord Raglan should die *thus*—from sickness—on the eve, as we have every reason to hope, of the glorious result of so much labour, and so much anxiety, and not be allowed to witness it.

---

[131] On the 18th of June, the fortieth anniversary of Waterloo, a combined attack by the English on the Redan, and the French on the Malakhoff, was repulsed with heavy losses. The scheme was that of Pélissier, and Lord Raglan acquiesced against his better judgment. The result depressed him greatly; he was attacked with cholera, and died on the 28th.

The Queen's prayers will be more than ever with her Army, and most fervently do we trust that General Simpson's health, as well as that of the other Generals, may be preserved to them unimpaired!

Queen Victoria to Lady Raglan.

Buckingham Palace, *30th June 1855.*

Dear Lady Raglan,—Words *cannot* convey *all* I feel at the irreparable loss you have sustained, and I and the Country have, in your noble, gallant, and excellent husband, whose loyalty and devotion to his Sovereign and Country were unbounded. We both feel *most deeply* for you and your daughters, to whom this blow must be most severe and sudden. He was so strong, and his health had borne the bad climate, great fatigues, and anxieties so well, ever since he left England, that, though we were much alarmed at hearing of his illness, we were full of hopes of his speedy recovery.

We must bow to the will of God; but to be taken away thus, on the eve of the successful result of so much labour, so much suffering, and so much anxiety, is cruel indeed!

We feel much, too, for the brave Army, whom he was so proud of, who will be sadly cast down at losing their gallant Commander, who had led them so often to victory and glory.

If sympathy can be any consolation, you have it, for *we all* have *alike* to mourn, and no one more than I, who have lost a faithful and devoted Servant, in whom I had the greatest confidence.

We both most anxiously hope that your health, and that of your daughters, may not materially suffer from this dreadful shock. Believe me always, my dear Lady Raglan, yours very sincerely,

Victoria R.

Queen Victoria to General Simpson.

GENERAL SIMPSON TAKES COMMAND

Buckingham Palace, *7th July 1855.*

When the Queen last wrote to General Simpson to express to him, and through him to her Army in the Crimea, her *deep* grief at the loss of their noble, gallant, and excellent Commander, it was not yet known that Sir George Brown would return home, and that the command of the Army would devolve upon General Simpson. She writes to him, therefore, to-day, for the *first* time as the Commander-in-Chief of her heroic Army in the East, to assure him of her confidence and support. It is as proud a command as any soldier could desire, but its difficulties and responsibilities are also very great.

General Simpson knows well how admirably his lamented predecessor conducted all the communications with our Allies the French, and he cannot do better than follow in the same course. While showing the greatest readiness to act with perfect cordiality towards them, he will, the Queen trusts, never allow her Army to be unduly pressed upon, which would only injure both Armies.

The Queen feels very anxious lest the fearful heat which the Army is exposed to should increase cholera and fever. Both the Prince and herself, the Queen can only repeat, have their minds *constantly* occupied with the Army, and count the days and hours between the mails, and it would be a relief to the Queen to hear herself directly from General Simpson from time to time when he has leisure to write.

The Prince wishes to be most kindly named to General Simpson, and joins with the Queen in every possible good wish for himself and her brave and beloved troops.

Viscount Palmerston to Queen Victoria.

LORD JOHN RUSSELL'S UNPOPULARITY

Piccadilly, *12th July 1855.*

Viscount Palmerston presents his humble duty to your Majesty....

Viscount Palmerston very much regrets to have to say that the adverse feeling in regard to Lord John Russell grows stronger and spreads wider every day, and there is a general desire that he should resign.[132] This desire is expressed by the great bulk of the steadiest

---

[132] Lord John Russell had, as stated above, favoured the proposals of Count Buol at Vienna, compromising the Third Point to the advantage of Russia. The Ministry had disavowed this view, but Lord John had remained in office. On the 24th of May, Mr Disraeli moved a vote of censure on the Government for its conduct of the war, fiercely assailing Lord John for his proceedings both at Vienna and as Minister. In repelling the charge, Lord John made a vigorous speech disclosing no disposition to modify the British attitude towards Russian preponderance in the Black Sea, and Mr Disraeli's Motion was lost by a majority of 100. On a subsequent night he made a further speech strongly antagonistic to Russia, his attitude as to the Austrian proposals being still undisclosed to the public. But these speeches caused Count Buol to reveal the favourable view taken of his proposals by the English and French

supporters of the Government, and was conveyed to Lord John this evening in the House of Commons by Mr Bouverie on behalf of those members of the Government who are not in the Cabinet. Lord John has himself come to the same conclusion, and informed Viscount Palmerston this evening in the House of Commons that he has finally determined to resign, and will to-morrow or next day write a letter to that effect to be laid before your Majesty. Viscount Palmerston told him that however great would be the loss of the Government by his resignation, yet as this is a question which more peculiarly regards Lord John personally, his course must be decided by his own judgment and feelings; but that if he did not think necessary to resign, Viscount Palmerston would face Sir Edward Bulwer's Motion with the Government as it is.[133] He asked Lord John, however, whether, if he determined to resign, there was any arrangement which he would wish to have submitted for your Majesty's consideration, and especially whether, if your Majesty should be graciously pleased to raise him to the Peerage, such an Honour would be agreeable to him. He said that perhaps in the autumn such an act of favour on the part of your Majesty might fall in with his views and would be gratefully received, but it would not do at present, and should not be mentioned....

Viscount Palmerston to Queen Victoria.

LORD JOHN RUSSELL RESIGNS

Piccadilly, *13th July 1855.*

Viscount Palmerston presents his humble duty to your Majesty, and submits for your Majesty's gracious acceptance the resignation of Lord John Russell's office, which Viscount Palmerston trusts your Majesty will think is expressed in terms highly honourable to Lord John Russell's feelings as a man and as a Minister.

The step, Viscount Palmerston regrets to say, has become unavoidable. The storm of public opinion, however much it may exceed any just or reasonable cause, is too overbearing to be resisted, and Lord John Russell has no doubt best consulted his own personal inter-

---

Plenipotentiaries, and Lord John Russell's inconsistency aroused widespread indignation.

[133] This Motion was one of censure on Lord John Russell for his conduct at Vienna, and it was deeply galling to be informed by subordinate members of the Government that, unless he resigned, they would support the vote of censure. Lord John bowed before the storm and retired from office.

ests in yielding to it. After a time there will be a reaction and justice will be done; but resistance at present would be ineffectual, and would only increase irritation.

Viscount Palmerston is not as yet prepared to submit for your Majesty's consideration the arrangement which will become necessary for filling up the gap thus made in the Government....

Queen Victoria to Viscount Palmerston.

Osborne, *13th July 1855.*

The Queen is much concerned by what Lord Palmerston writes respecting the feeling of the House of Commons. Lord John's resignation, although a severe loss, may possibly assuage the storm which he had chiefly produced. But she finds that Sir E. Lytton's Motion will be equally applicable to the Government after this event as it would have been before it. She trusts that no stone will be left unturned to defeat the success of that Motion, which would plunge the Queen and the executive Government of the Country into new and most dangerous complications. These are really not times to play with the existence of Governments for personal feeling or interests!

Queen Victoria to Viscount Palmerston.

Osborne, *14th July 1855.*

The Queen has received Lord Palmerston's letter of yesterday, and returns Lord John Russell's letter,[134] which reflects the greatest credit on him. The resignation had become unavoidable, and Lord Palmerston will do well to let the Debate go by before proposing a successor, whom it will be difficult to find under any circumstances. Having expressed her feelings on the position of affairs in her letter of yesterday, she will not repeat them here.

She grants her permission to Lord Palmerston to state in Parliament what he may think necessary for the defence of the Cabinet. She could have the Council here on Wednesday, which day will probably be the least inconvenient to the Members of the Government.

---

[134] Stating that his continuance in office would embarrass and endanger the Ministry.

The Queen has just received Lord Palmerston's letter of last night, which gives a more cheering prospect.[135]

Queen Victoria to the King of the Belgians.

Osborne, *24th July 1855.*

My dearest Uncle,—I feel *quite* grieved that it must again be *by letter* that I express to you all my feelings of love and affection, which yesterday morning I could still do *de vive voix*. It was indeed a *happy* time; I only fear that I was a dull companion—silent, absent, stupid, which I feel I have become since the War; and the constant anxiety and preoccupation which that odious Sebastopol causes me and my dear, brave Army, added to which the last week, or indeed the *whole fortnight* since we arrived here, was one of such uncertainty about this tiresome scarlatina, that it made me still more *préoccupée*.

The *only* thing that at all lessened my sorrow at seeing you depart was my thankfulness that you got safe *out* of our *Hospital*.... Ever your devoted Niece and Child,

Victoria R.

Queen Victoria to the Earl of Clarendon.

AFFAIRS OF SWEDEN

Osborne, *27th July 1855.*

The Queen has delayed answering Lord Clarendon's letter respecting Sweden till she received the first letter from Mr Magenis,[136] omitted in Lord Clarendon's box. Now, having read the whole of these documents, she confesses that she requires some explanation as to the advantages which are to arise to England from the proposed Treaty, before she can come to any decision about it. When a Treaty with Sweden was last in contemplation, she was to have joined in the war against Russia and to have received a guarantee of the integrity of her

---

[135] In consequence of Lord John's resignation, the motion of censure was withdrawn.

[136] Mr (afterwards Sir) Arthur Charles Magenis, Minister at Stockholm (and afterwards at Lisbon), had written to say that an attempt was being made to change the partial guarantee of Finmark into a general guarantee on behalf of Sweden and Norway. An important Treaty was concluded between Sweden and Norway, and the Western Powers, in the following November, which secured the integrity of Sweden and Norway.

dominions by England and France in return; yet this clause was found so onerous to this Country, and opening so entirely a new field of questions and considerations, that the Cabinet would not entertain it. Now the same guarantee is to be given by us without the counterbalancing advantage of Sweden giving us her assistance in the war.

Queen Victoria to Lord Panmure.

GENERAL SIMPSON'S DIFFICULTIES

Osborne, *30th July 1855.*

The Queen has received Lord Panmure's letter of yesterday evening, and has signed the dormant Commission for Sir W. Codrington. A similar course was pursued with regard to Sir George Cathcart. The Queen hopes that General Simpson may still rally. He must be in a great state of helplessness at this moment, knowing that he wants, as everybody out there, the advantages which Lord Raglan's name, experience, position, rank, prestige, etc., etc., gave him, having his Military Secretary ill on board, the head of the Intelligence Department dead, and no means left him whereby to gather information or to keep up secret correspondence with the Tartars—Colonel Vico[137] dead, who, as Prince Edward told the Queen, had become a *most important* element in the good understanding with the French Army and its new Commander, and not possessing military rank enough to make the Sardinian General[138] consider him as his Chief. If all these difficulties are added to those inherent to the task imposed upon him, one cannot be surprised at his low tone of hopefulness. As most of these will, however, meet every Commander whom we now can appoint, the Queen trusts that means will be devised to assist him as much as possible in relieving him from too much writing, and in the diplomatic correspondence he has to carry on. The Queen repeats her opinion that a *Chef de Chancellerie Diplomatique*, such as is customary in the Russian Army, ought to be placed at his command, and she wishes Lord Panmure to show this letter to Lords Palmerston and Clarendon, and to consult with them on the subject. Neither the Chief of the Staff nor the Military Secretary can supply that want, and the General himself must feel unequal to it without any experience on the subject, and so will his successor.

---

[137] Colonel Vico, the French Commissioner attached to Lord Raglan's staff, had died on the 10th.

[138] General La Marmora.

Prince Edward told the Queen *in strict confidence* that General Simpson's position in Lord Raglan's Headquarters had been anything but pleasant, that the Staff had been barely civil to him; he was generally treated as an interloper, so that the Sardinian and French Officers attached to our Headquarters observed upon it as a strange thing which would not be tolerated in their Armies, and that General Simpson showed himself grateful to them for the civility which they showed to a General Officer of rank *aux cheveux blancs*. These little details, considered together with the General's extreme modesty, enable one to conceive what his present feelings must be.[139]

Queen Victoria to Viscount Palmerston.

[Osborne, *7th August 1855*.]

The Queen has read Sir B. Hall's[140] letter, and must say that she quite concurs in the advantage resulting from the playing of a band in Kensington Gardens on Sunday afternoon, a practice which has been maintained on the Terrace at Windsor through good and evil report, and she accordingly sanctions this proposal.[141] [She would wish Lord Palmerston, however, to notice to Sir B. Hall that Hyde Park, although under the management of the Board of Works, is still a Royal Park, and that all the Regulations for opening and shutting gates, the protection of the grounds and police regulations, etc., etc., stand under the Ranger, who alone could give the order Sir B. Hall proposes to issue....][142]

---

[139] The Russian resources for the defence of Sebastopol, both as to ammunition and provisions, were becoming exhausted, and a supreme effort was to be made, by massing more Russian troops in the Crimea, to inflict a decisive blow on the besieging forces of the Allies. Early on the morning of the 16th of August Prince Gortschakoff attacked the French and Piedmontese at the River Tchernaya. The attack on the left was repulsed by the French with the utmost spirit and with very little loss; while the Russian loss, both in killed and wounded, was severe. The Sardinian army, under General La Marmora, were no less successful on the right. The news of this victory did not reach England until the Queen and Prince had left for their visit to Paris.

[140] First Commissioner of Public Works; afterwards Lord Llanover.

[141] The Government granted permission for the Band to play, but the practice was discontinued in 1856. See *post*, note 31.

[142] The portion of the letter within brackets was struck out of the draft by the Queen.

Queen Victoria to the King of the Belgians.

VISIT TO PARIS

St Cloud[143] *23rd August 1855.*

My dearest Uncle,—I do not intend to attempt any description, for I have no time for anything of the sort; besides, I have no doubt you will read the papers, and I know good Van de Weyer has written *au long* to you about it all. I will therefore only give in a few words my impressions.

ENTHUSIASTIC RECEPTION

I am *delighted*, *enchanted*, *amused*, and *interested*, and think I never saw anything more *beautiful* and gay than Paris—or more splendid than all the Palaces. Our reception is *most* gratifying—for it is enthusiastic and really kind in the highest degree; and Maréchal Magnan[144] (whom you know well) says that such a reception as I have received *every day here* is much greater and much more enthusiastic even than Napoleon on his return from his victories had received! Our entrance into Paris was a scene which was *quite feenhaft*, and which could hardly be seen anywhere else; was quite *overpowering*—splendidly decorated—illuminated—immensely crowded—and 60,000 troops out—from the Gare de Strasbourg to St Cloud, of which 20,000 Gardes Nationales, who had come great distances to see me.

The Emperor has done wonders for Paris, and for the Bois de Boulogne. Everything is beautifully *monté* at Court—*very* quiet, and in excellent order; I must say we are both much struck with the difference between this and the poor King's time, when the noise, confusion, and bustle were great. We have been to the Exposition, to Versailles—which is most splendid and magnificent—to the Grand Opéra, where the reception and the way in which "God save the Queen" was sung were *most magnificent*. Yesterday we went to the Tuileries; in the evening *Théâtre ici*; to-night an immense ball at the Hôtel de Ville. They have asked to call a new street, which we opened, *after me!*

---

[143] The Queen and Prince left Osborne early on the 18th in their new yacht, *Victoria and Albert*, for Boulogne, and the visit to France, which lasted nine days, was brilliantly successful. The Queen, in her Journal, recorded with great minuteness the details of this interesting time, and some extracts are printed by Sir Theodore Martin in *The Life of the Prince Consort*.

[144] Marshal Magnan had repressed an insurrection in Lyons in 1849, and aided in the *Coup d'État* of 1851.

The heat is very great, but the weather splendid, and though the sun may be hotter, the air is certainly *lighter* than ours—and I have no headache.

The *Zouaves* are on guard here, and you can't see finer men; the Cent Gardes are splendid too.

We drove to look at poor Neuilly on Sunday, the Emperor and Empress proposing it themselves; and it was a most *melancholy sight*, all in ruins. At *le grand Trianon* we saw the pretty chapel in which poor Marie was married; at the Tuileries the Cabinet where the poor King signed his fatal abdication. I wish *you* would take an opportunity of telling the poor Queen that we had thought much of her and the family here, had visited those spots which were connected with them in particular, and that we had greatly admired the King's great works at Versailles, which have been left *quite intact*. Indeed, the Emperor (as in everything) has shown *great* tact and good feeling about all this, and spoke without any bitterness of the King.

I still mean to visit (and this was *his* proposition) the Chapelle de St Ferdinand, which I hope you will likewise mention to the Queen....

The children are so fond of the Emperor, who is so very kind to them. He *is* very *fascinating*, with that great quiet and gentleness. He has certainly excellent manners, and both he and the dear and *very* charming Empress (whom Albert likes particularly) do the *honneurs extremely* well and *very* gracefully, and are full of *every kind* attention....

Instead of my short letter I have written you a very long one, and must end. Many thanks for your kind letter of the 17th.

How beautiful and how enjoyable is this place! Ever your devoted Niece,

Victoria R.

Queen Victoria to the Emperor of the French.

LETTER TO THE EMPEROR

Osborne, *le 29 Août 1855*.

Sire et mon cher Frère,—Une de mes premières occupations en arrivant ici est d'écrire à votre Majesté et d'exprimer du fond de mon cœur combien nous sommes pénétrés et touchés de l'accueil qui nous a été fait en France d'abord par votre Majesté et l'Impératrice ainsi que par toute la Nation. Le souvenir ne s'effacera jamais de notre mémoire, et j'aime à y voir un gage précieux pour le futur de la cordialité qui unit nos deux Gouvernements ainsi que nos deux peuples. Puisse cette heureuse union, que nous devons surtout aux qualités personnelles de votre Majesté, se consolider de plus en plus pour le bien-être de nos deux nations ainsi que de toute l'Europe.

C'était avec le cœur bien gros j'ai pris congé de vous, Sire, après les beaux et heureux jours que nous avons passés avec vous et que vous avez su nous rendre si agréables. Hélas! comme toute chose ici-bas, ils se sont écoulés trop vite et ces dix jours de fêtes paraissent comme un beau rêve, mais ils nous restent gravés dans notre mémoire et nous aimons à passer en revue tout ce qui s'est présenté à nos yeux d'intéressant et de beau en éprouvant en même temps le désir de les voir se renouveler un jour.

Je ne saurais vous dire assez, Sire, combien je suis touchée de toutes vos bontés et de votre amitié pour le Prince et aussi de l'affection et de la bienveillance dont vous avez comblé nos enfants. Leur séjour en France a été la plus heureuse époque de leur vie, et ils ne cessent d'en parler.

Nous avons trouvé tous les autres enfants en bonne santé, et le petit Arthur se promène avec son bonnet de police qui fait son bonheur et dont il ne veut pas se séparer. Que Dieu veille sur votre Majesté et la chère Impératrice pour laquelle je forme bien des vœux.

Vous m'avez dit encore du bateau "au revoir," c'est de tout mon cœur que je le répète aussi!

Permettez que j'exprime ici tous les sentiments de tendre amitié et d'affection avec lesquelles je me dis, Sire et cher Frère, de votre Majesté Impériale, la bien bonne et affectionnée Sœur et Amie,

Victoria R.

Je viens à l'instant même de recevoir la si aimable dépêche télégraphique de votre Majesté. Recevez-en tous mes remercîments les plus affectueux.

Queen Victoria to the King of the Belgians.

AN *ENTENTE CORDIALE*

Osborne, *29th August 1855.*

My dearest Uncle,—Here we are again, after the *pleasantest* and *most interesting* and triumphant ten days that I think I ever passed. So complete a success, so very hearty and kind a reception with and from so *difficile* a people as the French is indeed *most* gratifying and *most* promising for the future. The Army were most friendly and amicable towards us also.

In short, the *complete* Union of the two countries is stamped and sealed in the most satisfactory and solid manner, for it is not *only* a Union of the two Governments—the two Sovereigns—it is that of the *two Nations!* Albert has told you of all the very extraordinary combinations of circumstances which helped to make all so interesting, so satisfactory. Of the splendour of the *Fête* at Versailles I can really give *no* faint impression, for it exceeded all imagination! I have formed a *great* affection for the Emperor, and I believe it is very reciprocal, for he showed us a confidence which we must feel as very gratifying, and spoke to us on all subjects, even the *most delicate*. I find *no* great personal rancour towards the Orleans. He has destroyed nothing that the King did, even to the Gymnastics of the children at St Cloud, and showed much kind and good feeling in taking us to see poor Chartres' monument, which is beautiful. Nothing could exceed his tact and kindness. I find I must end in a great hurry, and will say more another day. Ever your devoted Niece,

Victoria R.

Queen Victoria to Baron Stockmar.

PERSONAL FRIENDSHIP

Osborne, *1st September 1855.*

You continue to refuse to answer me, but I am *not* discouraged by it; but on the contrary *must* write to you to give *vent* to my *delight* at our triumphant, most interesting, and most enjoyable visit to Paris! The Prince has written to you, and given you some general accounts, which will please you, and the *Times* has some descriptions ... of the wonderful beauty and magnificence of *every*thing. I never enjoyed myself more, or was more delighted or more interested, *and I can think* and talk of nothing else. I am *deeply* touched by the extraordinary warmth, heartiness, and enthusiasm with which we have been received by *all* ranks, and the kindness shown to every one has brought us all back—beginning with ourselves and ending with the lowest of our servants—full of gratitude, pleasure, admiration, regret at its being over, and a great desire to see such a visit renewed! It was touching and pleasing in the extreme to see the alliance sealed so completely, and without lowering *either* Country's pride, and to see old enmities and rivalries *wiped out* over the tomb of Napoleon I., before whose coffin I stood (by torchlight) at the arm of Napoleon III., now my nearest and dearest ally! We have come back with feelings of *real* affection for and interest in *France*—and indeed how could it be otherwise when one saw *how* much was done to *please* and delight us? The Army too (such a fine one!) I feel a real affection for, as the companions of my beloved troops!

For the Emperor *personally* I have conceived a *real* affection and friendship, and so I may truly say of the Prince. You know what *I felt* the moment I saw him and became acquainted with him, what I wrote down about him, etc. Well, we have now seen him for full *ten days*, from twelve to fourteen hours every day—often alone; and I cannot say *how* pleasant and easy it is to live with him, or how attached one becomes to him. I know *no* one who puts me more at my ease, or to whom I felt more inclined to talk unreservedly, or in whom involuntarily I should be more inclined to confide, than the Emperor! He was entirely at his ease with us—spoke most openly and frankly with us on all subjects—EVEN the *most* delicate, viz. the Orleans Family (this was with *me*, for I was driving alone with him), and I am happy to *feel* that there is nothing now between us which could *mar* our personal good *entente* and friendly and intimate footing. He is so simple, so *naïf*, never making *des phrases*, or paying compliments—so full of tact, good taste, high breeding; his attentions and respect towards us were so simple and unaffected, his kindness and friendship for the Prince so natural and so gratifying, *because* it is *not* forced, not *pour faire des compliments*. He is quite *The Emperor*, and yet in *no* way playing it; the Court and whole house infinitely more *regal* and better managed than in poor Louis Philippe's time, when all was in great noise and confusion, and there was *no* Court. We parted with *mutual* sorrow, and the Emperor expressed his hope that we shall frequently meet and "pas avec de si grandes cérémonies"!

What I write here is my feeling and conviction: wonderful it is that this *man*—whom certainly we were *not* over well-disposed to—should by *force* of *circumstances* be drawn into such close connection with us, and become *personally* our friend, and *this* entirely by his *own personal* qualities, in spite of so much that *was and could* be said against him! To the children (who behaved beautifully, and had the most extraordinary success) his kindness, and judicious kindness, was *great*, and they are *excessively* fond of him. In short, without *attempting* to do anything particular to *make* one like him, or ANY personal attraction in outward appearance, he *has* the power of *attaching* those to him who come near him and know him, which is *quite incredible.* He is excessively kind in private, and so very quiet. I shall always look back on the time passed not only in France, but with *him* personally, as *most* agreeable. The Prince, though less enthusiastic than I am, I can see well, shares this feeling, and I think it is very reciprocal on the Emperor's part; he is very fond of the Prince and truly appreciates him. With respect to the War, nothing can be more frank and fair and honest than he is about it, but it makes him unhappy and anxious.

The dear Empress, who was all kindness and goodness, whom we are all very fond of, we saw comparatively but little of, as for *really* and *certainly very* good reasons she must take great care of herself....

Victoria R.

Queen Victoria to the Earl of Clarendon.

MISGOVERNMENT AT NAPLES

Osborne, *3rd September 1855.*

The Queen has read the enclosed papers, and must express her strongest objection to a Naval Demonstration (which to be effectual must be prepared to pass on to measures of hostility), in order to obtain changes in the *internal system of Government* of the Kingdom of Naples.[145] England would thereby undertake a responsibility which she is in no way capable of bearing, unless she took the Government permanently into her own hands. The plea on which the interference is to be based, viz. that the misgovernment at Naples brings Monarchical institutions into disrepute, and might place weapons in the hands of the democracy (as put forth by Sir W. Temple),[146] would be wholly *insufficient* to justify the proceeding. Whether such an armed interference in favour of the people of Naples against their Government would lead to a Revolution or not, as apprehended by the French Government and disbelieved by Lord Palmerston, must be so entirely a matter of chance that it would be idle to predict the exact consequences. If 99 out of every 100 Neapolitans, however, are dissatisfied with their Govern-

---

[145] Lord Palmerston had suggested co-operation by England and France in obtaining the dismissal of the Neapolitan Minister of Police as an *amende* for an affront offered to this country, to be enforced by a naval demonstration, coupled with a demand for the liberation of political prisoners.

[146] The Hon. Sir William Temple, K.C.B. [*d.* 1856], only brother of Lord Palmerston, Minister Plenipotentiary to the Court of Naples.

ment (as Lord Palmerston states), it is not unreasonable to expect that our demonstration may give them confidence enough to rise, and if beat down by the King's troops in presence of our ships, our position would become exceedingly humiliating.

Any insult offered to the British Government, on the other hand, it has a perfect right to resent, and to ask reparation for. The case, however, is a very unpleasant one. The Neapolitan Government deny having intended any slight on the British Legation by the order respecting the Box of the "Intendant du Théâtre," which they state to have been general, and deny any intention to interfere with the free intercourse of the members of our Legation with Neapolitans, to which Sir W. Temple merely replies that notwithstanding the denial such an intention is believed by the public to exist.

The case becomes therefore a very delicate one, requiring the greatest care on our part not to put ourselves in the wrong.

CO-OPERATION OF THE POWERS

It will be of the greatest importance to come to a thorough understanding with France, and if possible also with Austria, on the subject.

Lord Panmure to Earl Granville.[147]

/Telegram./

10th September 1855.

Telegram from General Simpson, dated Crimea, nine September, one eight five five, ten nine a.m. "Sebastopol is in the possession of the Allies. The enemy during the night and this morning have evacuated the south side after exploding their Magazines and setting fire to the whole of the Town. All the men-of-war were burnt during the night with the exception of three Steamers, which are plying about the Harbour. The Bridge communicating with the North side is broken."

War Department, tenth September, one eight five five, four forty-five p.m....

---

[147] Minister in attendance at Balmoral. The Queen and Prince occupied their new home for the first time on the 7th of September; it was not yet completed, but, the Queen wrote, "the house is charming, the rooms delightful, the furniture, papers, everything, perfection."

Queen Victoria to the King of the Belgians.

FALL OF SEBASTOPOL

Balmoral Castle, *11th September 1855.*

My dearest Uncle,—The great event has at length taken place—*Sebastopol has fallen!* We received the news here last night when we were sitting quietly round our table after dinner. We did what we could to celebrate it; but that was but little, for to my grief we have not *one* soldier, no band, nothing here to make any sort of demonstration. What we did do was in Highland fashion to light a *bonfire* on the top of a hill opposite the house, which had been built last year when the premature news of the fall of Sebastopol deceived every one, and which we had to leave *unlit*, and found here on our return!

On Saturday evening we heard of one Russian vessel having been destroyed, on Sunday morning of the destruction of another, yesterday morning of the fall of the Malakhoff Tower —and *then* of *Sebastopol!* We were not successful against the Redan on the 8th, and I fear our loss was considerable. Still the *daily* loss in the trenches was becoming so serious that no loss in achieving such a result is to be compared to that. This event will delight my brother and faithful ally—and *friend*, Napoleon III.—I may add, for we really are *great friends*; this attempt,[148] though that of a madman, is very distressing and makes one *tremble*....

We expect the young Prince Fritz Wilhelm[149] of Prussia on a little visit here on Friday.

I must now conclude. With Albert's love, ever your devoted Niece,

Victoria R.

---

[148] As he was about to enter the Opera House on the evening of the 7th, the Emperor was fired at without effect by one Bellegarde, who had been previously convicted of fraud, on which occasion his punishment had been mitigated by the Emperor's clemency; he was now sentenced to two years' imprisonment.

[149] Only son of the Prince of Prussia, and afterwards the Emperor Frederick.

Lord Panmure to General Simpson.

/Telegram./

THE MALAKHOFF

12th September 1855.

The Queen has received, with deep emotion, the welcome intelligence of the fall of Sebastopol.

Penetrated with profound gratitude to the Almighty, who has vouchsafed this triumph to the Allied Armies, Her Majesty has commanded me to express to yourself, and through you to the Army, the pride with which she regards this fresh instance of its heroism.

The Queen congratulates her Troops on the triumphant issue of this protracted siege, and thanks them for the cheerfulness and fortitude with which they have encountered its toils, and the valour which has led to its termination.

The Queen deeply laments that this success in not without its alloy in the heavy losses which have been sustained; and while she rejoices in the victory, Her Majesty deeply sympathises with the noble sufferers in their country's cause.

You will be pleased to congratulate General Pélissier in Her Majesty's name upon the brilliant result of the assault on the Malakhoff, which proves the irresistible force as well as indomitable courage of her brave Allies.

Queen Victoria to General Simpson.

Balmoral, *14th September 1855.*

With a heart full of gratitude and pride, as well as of sorrow for the many valuable lives that have been lost, the Queen writes to General Simpson to congratulate him, as well on her own part as on that of the Prince, on the glorious news of the *Fall of Sebastopol!* General Simpson must indeed *feel proud* to have commanded the Queen's noble Army on *such* an occasion.

She wishes him to express to that gallant Army her high sense of their gallantry, and her joy and satisfaction at their labours, anxieties, and cruel sufferings, for nearly a year, having *at length* been crowned with such success.

To General Pélissier[150] also, and his gallant Army, whom the Queen ever unites in her thoughts and wishes with her own beloved troops, she would wish General Simpson to convey the expression of her personal warm congratulations, as well as of her sympathy for their losses.

The Queen intends to mark her sense of General Simpson's services by conferring upon him the Grand Cross of the Bath.

We are *now* most anxious that not a moment should be lost in following up this great victory, and in driving the Russians, while still under the depressing effect of their failure, from the Crimea!

Earl Granville to the Earl of Clarendon.

ATTITUDE OF AUSTRIA

Balmoral, *14th September 1855.*

My dear Clarendon,—I was sent for after breakfast. The Queen and the Prince are much pleased with the draft of your Despatch to Naples; they think it good and dignified. With respect to the draft to Lord Stratford, instructing him to recommend to the Porte an application to the Austrian Government for the withdrawal or diminution of the Austrian troops in the Principalities, I have been commanded to write what the Queen has not time this morning to put on paper. Her Majesty does not feel that the objects of this proposed Despatch have been sufficiently explained. It does not appear to Her Majesty that, in a military point of view, the plans of the Allies are sufficiently matured to make it clear whether the withdrawal of the Austrian Army would be an advantage or a disadvantage. If the Allies intend to march through the Principalities, and attack Russia on that side, the presence of the Austrians might be an inconvenience. If, on the other hand, they advance from the East, it is a positive advantage to have the Russians contained on the other flank, by the Austrians in their present position. Looking at the political bearing of this move, Her Majesty thinks that it will not fail to have an unfavourable effect on Austria, who will be hurt at the Allies urging the Porte to endeavour to put an end to an arrangement entered into at the suggestion, or at all events with the approval, of the Allies. It cannot be an object at this moment, when extraneous circumstances have probably acted favourably for us on the minds of the Emperor of Austria and his Government, to check that

---

[150] He now became Duke of Malakhoff, and a Marshal of the French Army.

disposition, make them distrust us, and incline them to throw themselves towards Russia, who now will spare no efforts to gain them. Her Majesty sees by your proposed Despatch you do not expect the Austrians to comply with this demand. Even if they consented to diminish the numbers of their Troops, they would do so only to suit their own convenience, and such diminution would in no ways decrease the evils of the occupation. Lastly, the Queen is of opinion that if such a proposal is to be made, it ought not to be done through Lord Stratford and the Porte, but that the subject should be broached at Vienna and the Austrian Government asked what their intentions are; that this would be the more friendly, more open, and more dignified course, and more likely than the other plan of being successful. Her Majesty, however, doubts that any such demand will be acceded to by the Austrians, and believes that their refusal will put the Allies in an awkward position.

This is, I believe, the pith of Her Majesty's opinions—there appears to me to be much sense in them—and they are well deserving of your and Palmerston's consideration. Yours sincerely,

Granville.

Queen Victoria to Viscount Palmerston.

LIFE PEERAGES

Balmoral, *19th September 1855.*

The Queen has to thank Lord Palmerston for his letter of the 16th. The want of Law Lords in the Upper House has often been complained of, and the Queen has long been of opinion that in order to remedy the same without adding permanently to the Peerage, the Crown ought to use its prerogative in creating Peers for life only. Lord Lansdowne coincided with this view, and Lord John Russell actually proposed a "Life Peerage" to Dr. Lushington, who declined it, however, from a dislike to become the first of the kind. Mr Pemberton Leigh has *twice* declined a Peerage, but the Queen can have no objection to its being offered to him again.[151]...

[151] See *ante*, vol. ii.

Viscount Palmerston to Queen Victoria.

Piccadilly, *20th September 1855.*

Viscount Palmerston presents his humble duty to your Majesty....

A Blue Ribbon has become vacant by the death of the late Duke of Somerset, and Viscount Palmerston having communicated with Lord Lansdowne and Lord Clarendon on the subject, would beg to submit for your Majesty's gracious consideration that this honour might be well conferred upon the Duke of Newcastle, who has been the object of much undeserved attack, though certainly from inexperience not altogether exempt from criticism, and who since his retirement from office has shaped his public course in a manner honourable to himself, and advantageously contrasting with the aberrations of some of his former colleagues.[152]

Your Majesty must no doubt have been struck with the vast accumulation of warlike stores found at Sebastopol. That there should have remained there four thousand cannon, after the wear and tear of the Siege, proves the great importance attached by the Russian Government to that Arsenal over which your Majesty's Flag is now triumphantly flying.

Queen Victoria to Viscount Palmerston.

DISTRIBUTION OF HONOURS

Balmoral, *21st September 1855.*

The Queen is anxious to mark her sense of the services of the Army and Military Departments at home by conferring the rank of Field-Marshal on Lord Hardinge, who, from his position as Commander-in-Chief, and his long, distinguished services, has a strong claim to such an honour. Moreover, Marshal Vaillant receiving the G.C.B., whilst it has been thought more prudent not to accept the *Légion d'Honneur* for Lord Hardinge, makes it the more desirable. The Prince is now again the only Field-Marshal in the Army, which has always had several. The Queen thinks that Lord Combermere, being the second senior officer of the whole Army, a full General of 1825, might expect not to be passed over when Lord Hardinge is made. The only other General of distinction and seniority might be Lord Straf-

---

[152] He had gone out to the Crimea, and entered Sebastopol with General Simpson. The Duke did not at this time accept the Garter, which was bestowed on Earl Fortescue. See *post*, note 98.

ford, but he is only a full General of 1841. On this point Lord Palmerston might consult Lord Hardinge himself. If he and Lord Combermere alone are made, the honour is the greater for him.[153]

The Queen thinks likewise that Lord Panmure ought to receive a mark of favour and approval of his conduct on the occasion of the Fall of Sebastopol; either the Civil G.C.B. or a step in the Peerage—that of Viscount.[154]

Lord Palmerston would perhaps, without delay, give his opinion on these subjects to the Queen; the honours she would wish then *personally* to bestow upon the recipients, and she thinks the arrival of the official Despatches the right moment for doing so.

The Prince Albert to the Earl of Clarendon.

Balmoral, *21st September 1855.*

My dear Lord Clarendon,—The Queen wishes me to send you the enclosed letters, with the request that they may be sent by messengers to Coblentz.[155]

I may tell you in the strictest confidence that Prince Frederic William has yesterday laid before us his wish for an alliance with the Princess Royal with the full concurrence of his parents, as well as of the King of Prussia. We have accepted his proposal as far as we are personally concerned, but have asked that the child should not be made acquainted with it until after her confirmation, which is to take place next Spring, when he might make it to her himself, and receive from her own lips the answer which is only valuable when flowing from those of the person chiefly concerned. A marriage would not be possible before the completion of the Princess's seventeenth year, which is in two years from this time. The Queen empowers me to say that you may communicate this event to Lord Palmerston, but we beg that under present circumstances it may be kept a strict secret. What the world may say we cannot help. Ever yours, etc.,

Albert.

---

[153] Lord Hardinge, Lord Strafford, and Lord Combermere were all made Field-Marshals.

[154] He received the G.C.B.

[155] The Prince and Princess of Prussia were then at Coblentz.

Queen Victoria to the King of the Belgians.

PRINCE FREDERICH WILLIAM

Balmoral, *22nd September 1855.*

My dearest Uncle,—I profit by your own messenger to confide to *you*, and to *you alone*, begging you not to mention it to your children, that *our* wishes on the subject of a future marriage for Vicky *have* been realised in the *most gratifying* and *satisfactory* manner.

On Thursday (20th) after breakfast, Fritz Wilhelm said he was anxious to speak of a subject which *he* knew his parents had never broached to us—which *was to belong to our* Family; that this had long been his wish, that he had the entire concurrence and *approval* not only of his parents but of the King —and that finding Vicky *so allerliebst*, he could delay *no* longer in making this proposal. I need *not* tell you with *what* joy *we* accepted him *for* our part; but the child herself is to know nothing till *after* her confirmation, which is to take place next Easter, when he probably will come over, and, as he wishes himself, make her the proposal, which, however, I have little—indeed no—doubt she will gladly *accept*. He is a dear, excellent, charming young man, whom we shall give our dear child to with perfect confidence. What pleases us greatly is to see that he is really delighted with Vicky.

Now, with Albert's affectionate love, and with the prayer that *you* will give *your* blessing to this alliance, as you have done to ours, ever your devoted Niece and Child,

Victoria R.

Viscount Palmerston to Queen Victoria.

Piccadilly, *22nd September 1855.*

Viscount Palmerston presents his humble duty to your Majesty, and begs, in the first place, to be allowed to offer to your Majesty his most sincere congratulations upon the prospective arrangement which His Royal Highness the Prince Albert announced in his letter to Lord Clarendon, but which, for obvious reasons, should be left to public conjecture for the present. Viscount Palmerston trusts that the event, when, it takes place, will contribute as much to the happiness of those more immediately concerned, and to the comfort of your Majesty and of the Royal Family, as it undoubtedly will to the interests of the two countries, and of Europe in general....

Viscount Palmerston begs to state that the Professorship of Greek at the University of Oxford, which was held by the late Dean of Christchurch,[156] is still vacant, Viscount Palmerston having doubts as to the best person to be appointed. The present Dean of Christchurch admitted that the Professorship ought to be separated from the Deanery; he has now recommended for the Professorship the Rev. B. Jowett, Fellow and Tutor of Balliol College, who is an eminent Greek scholar and won the Hertford Scholarship; and Viscount Palmerston submits, for your Majesty's gracious approval, that Mr Jowett may be appointed.

Viscount Palmerston to Queen Victoria.

THE COLONIAL OFFICE

Piccadilly, *31st October 1855.*

Viscount Palmerston presents his humble duty to your Majesty, and begs to state that he has this morning seen Lord Stanley, and offered to him the post of Secretary of State for the Colonies.[157] Lord Stanley expressed himself as highly gratified personally by an offer which he said he was wholly unprepared to receive, and which was above his expectations and pretensions; but he said that as he owed to his father Lord Derby whatever position he may have gained in public life, he could not give an answer without first consulting Lord Derby. Viscount Palmerston said that of course in making the proposal, he had taken for granted that Lord Stanley would consult Lord Derby first, because a son would not take a decision on such a subject without consulting his father, even if that father were merely in private life; and next because such a course would be still more natural in this case, considering Lord Derby's political position with reference to those with whom Lord Stanley has more or less been generally acting. Lord

---

[156] The Very Rev. Thomas Gaisford, D.D., who was appointed Regius Professor of Greek in 1811, and Dean of Christchurch in 1831.

[157] Sir William Molesworth, who had represented Radicalism in the Cabinets of Lord Aberdeen and Lord Palmerston, died on the 22nd, at the age of forty-five. The Premier thereupon offered the vacant place to Lord Stanley, one of his political opponents, then only twenty-eight, who was the son of the leader of the Conservative Opposition, and had already held office under his father. Lord Stanley's temperament was, in fact, more inclined to Liberalism than that of Lord Palmerston himself, and, twenty-seven years later, he took the office in a Liberal Government which he now declined.

Stanley said that he should go down to Knowsley by the five o'clock train this afternoon, and that he would at an early moment communicate his answer to Viscount Palmerston; but he said that if he was to state now his anticipation of what Lord Derby would recommend and wish him to do, it would rather be to decline the offer.

Viscount Palmerston to Queen Victoria.

MR SIDNEY HERBERT

Piccadilly, *10th November 1855.*

Viscount Palmerston presents his humble duty to your Majesty, and begs to state that in consequence of some things that passed in conversation at Sir Charles Wood's two days ago, when Mr and Mrs Sidney Herbert dined there, Sir Charles Wood is under a strong impression that Mr Herbert would be willing to separate himself from Mr Gladstone and Sir James Graham, and the Peace Party, and to join the present Government. Viscount Palmerston having well considered the matter in concert with Sir Charles Wood and Sir George Grey, is of opinion that it would be advantageous not only for the present, but also with a view to the future, to detach Mr Herbert from the clique with which accidental circumstances have for the moment apparently associated him, and to fix him to better principles of action than those by which Mr Gladstone and Sir James Graham appear to be guided. For this purpose Viscount Palmerston proposes with your Majesty's sanction to offer to Mr Herbert to return to the Colonial Office, which he held on the formation of the present Government.

Mr Herbert is the most promising man of his standing in the House of Commons, and is personally very popular in that House; he is a good and an improving speaker, and his accession to the Government would add a good speaker to the Treasury Bench, and take away a good speaker from ranks that may become hostile.

He would also supply the place of Lord Canning as a kind of link between the Government and some well-disposed members of both Houses who belonged more or less to what is called the Peel Party. It would be necessary, of course, to ascertain clearly that Mr Herbert's views about the war and about conditions of peace are the same as they were when he was a Member of the Government, and not such as those which Mr Gladstone and Sir James Graham have of late adopted.

If Mr Herbert were to accept, Sir George Grey, who has a strong disinclination for the Colonies, would remain at the Home Office; and if Lord Harrowby would take the Post Office, which must be held by a Peer, the Duchy of Lancaster, which may be held by a Commoner, might be offered to Mr Baines[158] with a seat in the Cabinet, and Mr Baines might perhaps, with reference to his health, prefer an office not attended with much departmental business of detail, while he would be thus more free to make himself master of general questions. Such an arrangement would leave the Cabinet, as stated in the accompanying paper, seven and seven; and if afterwards Lord Stanley of Alderley were added in the Lords, and Sir Benjamin Hall in the Commons, which, however, would be a matter entirely for future consideration, the equality of division would still be preserved.[159]

Viscount Palmerston finds that Mr Herbert is gone down to Wilton, and as Viscount Palmerston is going this afternoon to Broadlands to remain there till Tuesday morning, he proposes during the interval to communicate with Mr Herbert, Wilton being not much more than an hour's distance from Broadlands by the Salisbury railway.

Viscount Palmerston to Queen Victoria.

MR HERBERT DECLINES OFFICE

Broadlands, *11th November 1855.*

Viscount Palmerston presents his humble duty to your Majesty, and begs to state that he has seen Mr Sidney Herbert, who declines joining the Government, because he thinks that his doing so would expose both him and the Government to the suspicion of having altered their opinions. The difference between him and the Government is not as to the necessity of prosecuting the war with vigour, but as to the conditions of peace with which he would be satisfied. He would consent to accept conditions which he is aware that the country would not approve, and to which he does not expect that the Government would agree. Viscount Palmerston will have to consider with his Colleagues on Tuesday what arrangement it will be best for him to submit for the sanction of your Majesty.

---

[158] Mr. Matthew Talbot Baines died prematurely in 1860. His abilities were of a solid rather than a brilliant kind.

[159] Mr. Labouchere became Colonial Secretary. See List of Cabinet as it stood in 1858, *post*, p. 272.

Queen Victoria to the Earl of Clarendon.

PEACE NEGOTIATIONS

Windsor Castle, *13th November 1855.*

The Queen returns the enclosed most important letters. She has read them with much interest, but not without a very anxious feeling that great changes are taking place in the whole position of the Eastern Question and the War, without our having the power to direct them or even a complete knowledge of them.[160] Should Austria really be sincere,—if the Emperor Napoleon is really determined not to carry on the war on a large scale without her joining, we shall be obliged by common prudence to follow him in his negotiations. He may mistrust our secrecy and diplomacy, and wish to obtain by his personal exertions a continental league against Russia. The missions to Stockholm and Copenhagen, the language to Baron Beust and M. von der Pfordten and M. de Bourqueney's single-handed negotiation, seem to point to this. Can Russia have secretly declared her readiness to accept the "Neutralisation"? It is hardly possible, and if so it would be a concession we cannot refuse to close upon. Whatever may be the case, the Queen thinks it the wisest course not to disturb the Emperor's plans, or to show suspicion of them, but merely to insist upon the importance of the Army in the Crimea being kept so imposing that Russia cannot safely arrange her plans on the supposition of a change of policy on the part of the Western Powers.

Had the Queen known of Lord Cowley's letter a few hours earlier, she could have spoken to the Duke of Cambridge, who was here; as it was, both she and the Prince were very cautious and reserved in what they told him.

---

160 The Emperor was now bent on the termination of hostilities, and the French and Austrian Governments had concerted proposals for peace to be submitted to Russia, with which they somewhat peremptorily demanded that England should concur. Lord Palmerston announced that, rather than make an unsatisfactory peace, he would continue the war without the aid of France. States such as Saxony and Bavaria favoured Russia, and Baron Beust and M. von der Pfordten, their respective Prime Ministers, had interviews with the Emperor, who was anxious for peace on the basis of the Third Point, on which, since the fall of Sebastopol, the Allies were in a better position to insist.

The Queen thought it right to let Sir Hamilton Seymour, who is staying here, see the letters, as his thorough acquaintance with the present position of affairs is most important.

Queen Victoria to Sir Charles Wood.

Windsor Castle, *16th November 1855.*

The Queen wishes to draw Sir Charles Wood's attention to a subject which may become of much importance for the future. It is the absence of any Dockyard for building and repairing out of the Channel, with the exception of Pembroke. Should we ever be threatened by a combination of Russia and France, the absence of a Government establishment in the north would be very serious. It strikes the Queen that the present moment, when our yards hardly supply the demands made upon them, and when attention is directed to the Baltic, is a particularly favourable one to add an establishment in the Firth of Forth, for which the Queen believes the Government possess the ground at Leith. Such a measure would at the same time be very popular in Scotland, and by making the Queen's Navy known there, which it hardly is at present, would open a new field for recruiting our Marine.

Whether Cork in Ireland should not also be made more available is very well worth consideration.

The Queen would ask Sir Charles to communicate this letter to Lord Palmerston, who has always had the state of our powers of defence so much at heart.

Queen Victoria to the Earl of Clarendon.

THE AUSTRIAN ULTIMATUM

Windsor Castle, *19th November 1855.*

The Queen has attentively perused the voluminous papers, which she now returns according to Lord Clarendon's wish.

An anxious consideration of their contents has convinced her that it would be the height of impolicy if we were not to enter fairly and unreservedly into the French proposal, and she wishes Lord Clarendon to express this her opinion to the Cabinet.

The terms of the Austrian Ultimatum are clear and complete and very favourable to us, if accepted by Russia.[161] If refused, which they almost must be, rupture of diplomatic relations between Austria and Russia is a decided step gained by us, and will produce a state of things which can scarcely fail to lead them to war.

A refusal to entertain the proposal may induce and perhaps justify the Emperor of the French in backing out of the War, which would leave us in a miserable position.

If we are to agree to the Emperor's wishes, it must be politic not to risk the advantage of the whole measure by a discussion with Austria upon minor points of detail, which will cost time, and may lead to differences.

Queen Victoria to Viscount Hardinge.

Windsor Castle, *22nd November 1855.*

The Queen informs Lord Hardinge that on speaking to Sir Colin Campbell yesterday, and informing him how much she wished that his valuable services should not be lost to her Army in the Crimea, he replied in the handsomest manner, that he would return immediately—"for that, if the Queen wished it, he was ready to serve under a Corporal"! Conduct like this is very gratifying, and will only add to Sir Colin Campbell's high name; but, as by Lord Hardinge's and Lord Panmure's advice, the Queen has obtained from him this *sacrifice* of *his own* feelings to *her* wishes, *she* feels personally bound *not* to *permit* him to be passed over a *second* time should the Command again become vacant.

The Queen has had a good deal of conversation with him, and from what he told her, as well as from what she has heard from others, there seems to be a good deal of laxity of discipline—particularly as regards the officers—in the Army in the Crimea; and she thinks Lord Hardinge should give an order to prevent so many officers coming home on leave except when *really ill.* The effect of this on the French is very bad, and the Prince had a letter only two days ago from the

---

[161] The Queen and her Ministers, however, insisted that the neutralisation clause (the Third Point) should be made effective, not left illusory, and incorporated in the principal and not in a supplementary treaty. Modified in this and other particulars, an ultimatum embodying the Austrian proposals, which stipulated, *inter alia,* for the cession of a portion of Bessarabia, was despatched to St Petersburg on the 15th of December, and the 18th of January was fixed as the last day on which a reply would be accepted.

Prince of Prussia, saying that every one was shocked at the manner in which our officers came home, and that it lowered our Army very much in the eyes of foreign Armies, and generally decreased the sympathy for our troops. We deeply regret the death of poor General Markham.[162]

Queen Victoria to the Earl of Clarendon.

FRANCE AND AUSTRIA

Windsor Castle, *23rd November 1855.*

The Queen has received Lord Clarendon's letter, and returns the very satisfactory enclosures from Lord Cowley. Count Walewski remains true to himself; yet the admission that the Neutralisation Clause ought to be part of the European treaty, and not an annex, which *he makes*, is the most important concession which we could desire. That the Sea of Azov is to be dropped the Queen is glad of, as it would appear so humiliating to Russia that Austria would probably decline proposing it. What the Queen is most afraid of, and what she believes actuates the Emperor also, is the consideration that Austria, made aware of the intense feeling for Peace *à tout prix* in France, might get frightened at the good terms for us she meant to propose to Russia, and might long for an opportunity given by us, in any unreasonable demand for modification, to back out of her proposal altogether. Lord A. Loftus in his last letter states that Baron Manteuffel[163] even was afraid of having admitted as proper, terms too hard upon Russia, since peace is wanted at Paris.

The course intended to be pursued by Lord Clarendon in summing up the whole question in a public Despatch seems quite the right one, as it would never do, on the other hand, to let England be considered as merely *à la remorque* of France, an impression unfortunately very prevalent on the Continent at this moment.[164]

---

[162] He commanded the 2nd Division of the Army at the attack on the Redan, and after the fall of Sebastopol, his health, already shattered, broke down completely; he returned home, and died on the 21st of November.

[163] President of the Prussian Ministry.

[164] Lord Clarendon, in the letter to which this was a reply, observed that he had asked Lord Cowley to inform Count Walewski that he would have to learn that England was a principal in the matter, and "not a political and diplomatic Contingent."

As to Marshal Pélissier, the best thing the Emperor could do would be to recall him, and to put a younger and more enterprising man in his place. As we have got our hero coming home, his French colleague might be recalled also.

The Duke of Newcastle's letter is very interesting; the Queen will return it this evening. It confirms the truth of the axiom that a *settled policy* ought to precede a military plan of campaign, for which the Prince is always contending.

We have been much pleased with old Sir Colin Campbell, who is a thorough soldier, and appears not at all wanting in good sense. On asking him about our rising men, and the officer whom *he* would point out as the one of most promise, he said that Colonel Mansfield[165] was without comparison the man from whom great services could be expected both in the Field and as an Administrator. Lord Clarendon will be pleased to hear this, but will also not be surprised if the Queen should look out for an opportunity to reclaim him for the Army from the Foreign Office.

Queen Victoria to the Earl of Clarendon.

THE NEUTRALISATION CLAUSE

Windsor Castle, *24th November 1855.*

The Queen returns Lord Cowley's letter and General Pélissier's telegram. Lord Cowley is quite right in insisting upon a clear understanding between England and France before negotiations are entered into with Austria. To come to a speedy agreement, it will be wise to drop the minor points and *insist* upon the most important. These the Queen takes to be the incorporation of the *Neutralisation* Clause in the general Treaty, and the promise on the part of Austria not to accept and communicate to us counter-proposals from Russia. If France agreed to this, we might agree to the rest of the arrangement. General Pélissier's plan has the advantage of setting us free, but deprives us of the Sardinians in the field, an object the French have kept steadily in view. The Duke of Cambridge will come down here to-night, and we may then hear more on the subject.

The Queen of the French has been taken dangerously ill at Genoa; the Duc d'Aumale and Prince de Joinville have been summoned by

---

[165] He had distinguished himself in the first Sikh War, and was in 1855 Military Adviser to the British Ambassador at Constantinople.

telegraph. The Queen has asked the Foreign Office to telegraph to enquire after the Queen's state.

Queen Victoria to Sir William Codrington.[166]

SIR WILLIAM CODRINGTON

Windsor Castle, *26th November 1855.*

The first Despatches of Sir William Codrington, acknowledging his appointment to the Command of the Queen's gallant Army in the East, having arrived, she will no longer delay writing herself to Sir William, to assure him of her support and confidence in his new, proud, and important, though at the same time difficult position. She wishes to assure him of her confidence and support. It is with pleasure that she sees the son of her old friend and devoted servant, himself so distinguished in the sister Service, raised by his own merits to so exalted a position. Sir William knows the Queen's pride in her beloved Troops, as well as her unceasing solicitude for their welfare and glory, and she trusts he will on all occasions express these feelings from herself personally.

The Queen feels certain that Sir William Codrington will learn, with great satisfaction, that that distinguished and gallant officer, Sir Colin Campbell, has most readily and handsomely complied with the Queen's wishes that he should return to the Crimea and take command of the First Corps d'Armée. His presence and his assistance will be of essential service to Sir William Codrington, who, the Queen knows, entertains so high an opinion of him.

The Prince wishes his sincere congratulations and kind remembrance to be conveyed to Sir William Codrington.

The Queen would be glad if Sir William could—when he has leisure to do so—from time to time write to her himself, informing her of the state of her Army, and of affairs in the Crimea.

She concludes with every wish for his welfare and success.

---

[166] Considerable difficulty had been found in appointing a successor to General Simpson, who had resigned a task which he found overtaxed his powers. Sir William Codrington was junior to three other Generals, who might have felt aggrieved by being passed over. The sagacity of the Prince found a way out of the difficulty by appointing two of the three to the commands of the two *corps d'armée* into which the Army had, at his instance, been subdivided. See *ante.* p. 153.

Queen Victoria to the King of the Belgians.

VISIT OF KING OF SARDINIA

Windsor Castle, *5th December 1855.*

My dearest Uncle,—I must make many excuses for not writing to you yesterday, to thank you for your kind letter of the 30th, as on Friday and Saturday my time was entirely taken up with my *Royal* brother, the King of Sardinia,[167] and I had to make up for loss of time these last days. He leaves us to-morrow at an extraordinary hour—four o'clock in the morning (which you did once or twice)—wishing to be at Compiègne to-morrow night, and at Turin on Tuesday. He is *eine ganz besondere, abenteuerliche Erscheinung*, startling in the extreme in appearance and manner when you *first* see him, but, just as Aumale says, *il faut l'aimer quand on le connaît bien.* He is so frank, open, just, straightforward, liberal and tolerant, with much sound good sense. He never breaks his word, and you may rely on him, but wild and extravagant, courting adventures and dangers, and with a very strange, short, rough manner, an exaggeration of that short manner of speaking which his poor brother had. He is shy in society, which makes him still more brusque, and he does not know (never having been out of his own country or even out in Society) what to say to the number of people who are presented to him here, and which is, I know from experience, a most odious thing. He is truly attached to the Orleans family, particularly to Aumale, and will be a friend and adviser to them. To-day he will be invested with the Order of the Garter. He is more like a Knight or King of the Middle Ages than anything one knows nowadays.

On Monday we go to Osborne till the 21st.

One word about Vicky. I must say that she has a quick discernment of character, and I have never seen her take *any* predilection for a person which was *not motivé* by personal amiability, goodness, or distinction of some kind or other. You need be under no apprehension whatever on this subject; and she has, moreover, great tact and *esprit de conduite*. It is quite extraordinary how popular she is in Society—

---

[167] King Victor Emmanuel was received with great cordiality by the English people, grateful for his co-operation and for the gallantry of his soldiers at the Tchernaya. Count Cavour accompanied him, and drafted the reply read by the King at Guildhall to the address of the Corporation.

and again now, all these Foreigners are so struck with her sense and *conversation* for her age.

Hoping soon to hear from you again, and wishing that naughty Stockmar may yet be brought to come, believe me ever your devoted Niece,

Victoria R.

Viscount Palmerston to Queen Victoria.

GARTER FEES

Downing Street, *11th December 1855.*

Viscount Palmerston presents his humble duty to your Majesty and submits a letter which he received a few days ago from the Duke of Newcastle declining the Garter. Viscount Palmerston on his return from Woburn, where he was for two days, saw the Duke of Newcastle, but found that the enclosed letter expressed the intention which he had formed. Viscount Palmerston would propose to your Majesty the Earl of Fortescue as a deserving object of your Majesty's gracious favour; Lord Fortescue held the high office of Lord-Lieutenant of Ireland, and is a person highly and universally respected.[168]

Viscount Palmerston cannot refrain from saying on this occasion that he is not without a misgiving that the high amount of fees which he understands is paid by persons who are made Knights of the Garter may have some effect in rendering those whose incomes are not very large less anxious than they would otherwise be to receive this distinction; and he cannot but think that it is unseemly in general that persons upon whom your Majesty may be disposed to confer dignities and honours, either as a mark of your Majesty's favour or as a reward for their public services, should on that account be subject to a heavy pecuniary fine; and he intends to collect information with a view to consider whether all such fees might not be abolished, the officers to whom they are now paid receiving compensation in the shape of adequate fixed salary.[169] ...

[168] Earl Fortescue received the Garter; he died in 1861.
[169] This reform was effected in 1905.

Queen Victoria to Lord Panmure.

Windsor Castle, *22nd December 1855*.

The Queen has received Lord Panmure's answer to her letter from Osborne, and is glad to see from it that he is quite agreed with the Queen on the subject of the Land Transport Corps. She would *most strongly* urge Lord Panmure to give at once *carte blanche* to Sir W. Codrington to organise it as he thinks best, and to make him personally responsible for it. We have only eight weeks left to the beginning of spring; a few references home and their answers would consume the whole of that time! The Army has now to carry their huts on their backs up to the Camp; if it had been fighting, it would have perished for want of them, like the last winter. If each Division, Brigade, and Battalion has not got within itself what it requires for its daily existence in the field, a movement will be quite impossible.

The Queen approves the intended increase of Artillery and Sappers and Miners; but hopes that these will be taken from the *nominal* and *not* the existing strength of the Army.

INTRODUCTORY NOTE
TO CHAPTER XXV

After two years' duration, the Crimean War was terminated in March 1856, at a Conference of the Powers assembled at Paris, by a treaty the principal terms of which provided for the integrity of Turkey, and her due participation in the public law and system of Europe, the neutralisation of the Black Sea, and the opening of its waters to commerce (with the interdiction, except in a limited degree, of the flag of war of any nation, and of the erection by either Russia or Turkey of arsenals), free navigation of the Danube, cession of a portion of Bessarabia by Russia, and the reciprocal evacuation of invaded territories; the Principalities to be continued in their existing privileges under the suzerainty of the Porte and a guarantee of the Contracting Powers. No European protectorate was to be established over the Sultan's Christian subjects. Certain general principles of International Law were also agreed upon. In the course of the summer, the Guards made a public re-entry into London; and the Crimea was finally evacuated; great reviews of the returned troops taking place at Aldershot. The thanks of Parliament were accorded to the soldiers and sailors engaged, and peace-rejoicings celebrated on a great scale.

The Commissioners who had been sent out, nearly a year before, to the Crimea, to investigate the causes of the breakdown in various military departments, presented a Report, censuring several high officials; a Military Commission was accordingly appointed to investigate the Report, and after sitting for some months at Chelsea, completely exonerated the officials in question.

The Government having resolved to strengthen the administration of the appellate jurisdiction of the House of Lords, Letters Patent were made out purporting to create Sir James Parke, an ex-Judge, a Baron for his life, under the title of Lord Wensleydale. After frequent and protracted debates on this question, the Peers decided that such a patent conferred no right to sit and vote in Parliament. The Government gave up the contest by creating Sir James (who had no son) a hereditary peer.

The Czar Alexander was crowned at Moscow in September with great ceremonial, the Sultan being duly represented, while Lord Granville was present as special Ambassador for the Queen. The discovery of the cruelty with which political offenders were being treated in Neapolitan prisons led to the rupture of diplomatic relations between England in union with France on the one hand, and King Ferdinand on the other; while a dispute as to the enlistment of recruits for the English Army in the United States led to the dismissal of the British Minister at Washington, and to temporary friction between the two countries.

The provisions of the Treaty of Paris were not carried out without considerable procrastination on the part of Russia, which, by its method of evacuating Kars and surrendering Ismail and Reni, and by laying claim to Serpent's Island at the mouth of the Danube, compelled England to send a fleet to the Black Sea, to enforce strict observance of the Treaty. By the end of the year the matter was arranged, though in the meantime the possibility of Great Britain being represented at the Czar's coronation had been imperilled.

The abuses which had long existed in the Government of Oudh induced the Governor-General of India, early in the year, to issue a proclamation placing that kingdom permanently under the authority of the British Crown. Lord Dalhousie at this time retired from the office (which he had held for eight years) of Governor-General, and was succeeded by Lord Canning. It fell to the lot of the latter to announce the commencement of hostilities between this country and Persia, on the ground that the latter was endeavouring, in defiance of Treaties, to subvert the independence of Herat. The Shah had laid siege to the town, when, in December, the English fleet, under Admiral Sir Henry Leeke, attacked and captured Bushire on the Persian Gulf. Soon afterwards, Sir James Outram arrived on the scene from Bombay, and assumed the command.

CHAPTER XXV

1856

Queen Victoria to Lord Panmure.

Windsor Castle, *5th January 1856.*

The Queen returns the drawings for the "Victoria Cross." She has marked the one she approves with an X; she thinks, however, that it might be a trifle smaller. The motto would be better "For Valour" than "For the Brave," as this would lead to the inference that only those are deemed brave who have got the Victoria Cross.

Queen Victoria to the Earl of Clarendon.

Windsor Castle, *7th January 1856.*

The Queen has received Lord Clarendon's letter, and in answer to his question expresses her opinion that Lord Cowley's presence at the Council of War will be absolutely necessary.[170] She believes Lord Clarendon to be agreed with her, that the value of a plan of military campaign is entirely dependent upon the *general policy* which the Government intends to pursue. As none of our Commissioners at the Council of War are in the least acquainted with the latter, they might be drawn into plans which would not at all agree with it. Lord Cowley would take that part of the question into his own hands, in which it will be quite safe. The Queen thinks that it is of secondary importance

---

[170] A satisfactory and speedy conclusion of hostilities appearing at this time far from probable, a Council of War to settle the course of operations was, at the Emperor's suggestion, summoned to meet at Paris. Lord Cowley, Count Walewski, Prince Jérôme Bonaparte, and others, were present, besides Naval and Military representatives of the Allies, among whom was the Duke of Cambridge.

whether Count Walewski attends or not, but that the Emperor cannot have the same need of his presence which we have of that of our Ambassador.

Queen Victoria to the Earl of Clarendon.

POLICY OF CAVOUR

Windsor Castle, *9th January 1856.*

The Queen has read Sir J. Hudson's[171] letter with much interest. There is much truth in what Count Cavour says, and it must ever be our object and our interest to see Sardinia independent and strong; as a Liberal constitutional country, opposing a barrier alike to unenlightened and absolute as well as revolutionary principles—and this she has a right to expect us to support her in.

But *what* she wants to obtain from Austria is not clear. She has no right, however, to expect further assurances from us on wishes which she seems even to be afraid to state distinctly.

It is clearly impossible to ask Austria to give up a portion of Italy to her, if nothing has occurred to make this necessary to Austria. At any rate Sardinia can have lost nothing, but on the contrary must have gained by the position which she is placed in as an ally of the Western Powers.

Queen Victoria to the Earl of Clarendon.

Windsor Castle, *11th January 1856.*

The Queen now returns the draft[172] to Lord Bloomfield, which she could only write about in haste yesterday, as being of a nature not to be sanctioned by her. It is quite natural and excusable that our patience

---

[171] British Minister at Turin, and an enthusiastic sympathiser with Cavour. The latter had complained to him that if the Austrian proposals were accepted, and peace were made, Sardinia could expect no realisation of her cherished hopes, viz. Anglo-French support against Austria and against Papal aggression, increased political consideration in Europe, and the development of Constitutional Government.

[172] The draft expressed disapproval of the silence maintained by the Prussian Government towards England with regard to the Austrian proposals, of the active measures adopted to induce the German Powers not to take part with Austria, as well as of the extended facilities afforded by Prussia to Russia for carrying on the war.

should at last be worn out by the miserable policy which Prussia is pursuing, but it can never be our interest openly to quarrel with her. This would be simply playing the game of Russia, who would thus be relieved from all attacks upon her and see the theatre of the war transferred to Germany; all other complications (which would arise therefrom)—ruinous to the best interests of the Western Powers as they would be—the Queen need not refer to. But when the draft concludes with a declaration to Prussia that England "*considers her neutrality as now at an end*," this is tantamount to a declaration of *war!* The late articles in our newspapers, and the language of Count Walewski to Lord Cowley, make the Queen doubly anxious to warn the Government not to let themselves be drawn on to such a policy.

The Emperor of the French to Queen Victoria.

LETTER FROM NAPOLEON III

Tuileries, *le 14 Janvier 1856.*

Madame et chère Sœur,—Votre Majesté m'ayant permis de lui parler à cœur ouvert toutes les fois que des circonstances graves se présenteraient, je viens aujourd'hui profiter de la faveur qu'elle a bien voulu m'accorder.

Je viens de recevoir aujourd'hui la nouvelle de la réponse de la Russie à l'Ultimatum de Vienne, et avant d'avoir manifesté mon impression à qui que ce soit, pas même à Walewski, je viens la communiquer à votre Majesté pour avoir son avis.

Je résume la question: La Russie accepte tout l'Ultimatum autrichien sauf la rectification de frontière de la Bessarabie, et sauf le paragraphe relatif aux conditions *particulières* qu'elle déclare ne pas connaître. De plus, profitant du succès de Kars, elle s'engage à rendre cette forteresse et le territoire occupé en échange des points que nous possédons en Crimée et ailleurs.

Dans quelle position allons-nous nous trouver? D'après la convention, l'Autriche est obligée de retirer son ambassadeur, et nous, nous poursuivons la guerre! Mais dans quel but allons-nous demander à nos deux pays de nouveaux sacrifices d'hommes et d'argent? Pour un intérêt purement autrichien et pour une question qui ne consolide en rien l'empire ottoman.

Cependant nous y sommes obligés et nous ne devons pas avoir l'air de manquer à nos engagements. Nous serions donc placés dans une alternative bien triste si l'Autriche elle-même ne semblait pas déjà nous inviter de ne point rompre toute négociation. Or en réfléchissant aujourd'hui à cette situation, je me disais: ne pourrait-on pas répondre à l'Autriche ceci: La prise de Kars a tant soit peu changé nos situations; puisque la Russie consent à évacuer toute l'Asie Mineure nous nous bornons à demander pour la Turquie, au lieu de la rectification de frontière, les places fortes formant *tête de pont* sur le Danube, tels que Ismail et Kilia. Pour nous, nous demandons en fait de conditions particulières, l'engagement de ne point rétablir les forts des îles d'Aland et une amnistie pour les Tartares. Mon sentiment est qu'à ces conditions-là la paix serait très désirable; car sans cela je ne puis pas m'empêcher de redouter l'opinion publique quand elle me dira: "Vous aviez obtenu le but réel de la guerre, Aland était tombé et ne pouvait plus se relever, Sebastopol avait eu le même sort, la flotte Russe était anéantie, et la Russie promettait non seulement de ne plus la faire reparaître dans la Mer Noire, mais même de ne plus avoir d'arsenaux maritimes sur toutes ses rives; la Russie abandonnait ses conquêtes dans l'Asie Mineure, elle abandonnait son protectorat dans les principautés, son action sur le cours du Danube, son influence sur ces correligionnaires sujets du Sultan, etc., etc. Vous aviez obtenu tout cela non sans d'immenses sacrifices et cependant vous allez les continuer, compromettre les finances de la France, répandre ses trésors et son sang et pourquoi: pour obtenir quelques landes de la Bessarabie!!!"

THE EMPEROR AND PEACE

Voilà, Madame, les réflexions qui me préoccupent; car autant je me sens de force quand je crois être dans le vrai pour inculquer mes idées à mon pays et pour lui faire partager ma persuasion, autant je me sentirais faible si je n'étais pas sûr d'avoir raison ni de faire mon devoir.

Mais ainsi que je l'ai dit en commençant à votre Majesté je n'ai communiqué ma première impression qu'au Duc de Cambridge, et autour de moi au contraire j'ai dit qu'il fallait continuer la guerre. J'espère que votre Majesté accueillera avec bonté cette lettre écrite à la hâte et qu'elle y verra une nouvelle preuve de mon désir de m'entendre toujours avec elle avant de prendre une résolution. En remerciant votre Majesté de l'aimable lettre que S.A.R. le Duc de Cambridge m'a remise de sa part, je la prie de recevoir la nouvelle assurance de mes sentiments de tendre et respectueux attachement avec lesquels je suis de votre Majesté, le bon frère et ami,

Napoleon.

Je remercie bien le Prince Arthur de son bon souvenir.

Queen Victoria to the Earl of Clarendon.

Windsor Castle, *15th January 1856.*

... The Queen will send her letter to the Emperor this evening for transmission to Paris. She will enclose it *open* to Lord Clarendon, who will seal and send it after having read it.

The Queen cannot conceal from Lord Clarendon what *her own* feelings and wishes at this moment are. They *cannot* be for peace *now*, for she is *convinced* that this country would *not* stand in the eyes of Europe as she *ought*, and as the Queen is convinced she *would* after *this* year's campaign. The honour and glory of her dear Army is as *near* her heart as almost anything, and she cannot *bear* the thought that "the failure on the Redan" should be our *last fait d'Armes*, and it would cost her more than words can express to conclude a peace with *this* as the end. However, what is best and wisest must be done.

The Queen cannot yet bring herself to believe that the Russians are at all sincere, or that it will *now* end in peace.

Queen Victoria to the Emperor of the French.

THE QUEEN'S REPLY

Windsor Castle, *le 15 Janvier 1856.*

Sire et cher Frère,—La bonne et aimable lettre que je viens de recevoir de la main de votre Majesté m'a causé un très-vif plaisir. J'y vois une preuve bien satisfaisante pour moi que vous avez apprécié tous les avantages de ces épanchements sans réserve, et que votre Majesté en sent comme moi le besoin dans les circonstances graves où nous sommes. Je sens aussi toute la responsabilité que votre confiance m'impose, et c'est dans la crainte qu'une opinion formée et exprimée par moi trop à la hâte pourrait nuire à la décision finale à prendre que je me vois obligée de différer pour le moment la réponse plus détaillée sur les considérations que vous avez si clairement et si consciencieusement développées. Cependant, je ne veux point tarder de vous remercier de votre lettre, et de vous soumettre de mon côté les réflexions qui me sont venues en la lisant. La Réponse Russe ne nous est pas encore arrivée; nous n'en connaissons pas exactement les termes; par conséquent, il serait imprudent de former une opinion définitive sur la manière d'y répondre, surtout comme le Prince Gortschakoff paraît avoir demandé un nouveau délai du Gouvernement Autrichien et de nouvelles instructions de St Pétersbourg, et comme M. de Bourqueney paraît penser que la Russie n'a pas dit son dernier mot. Nous pourrions donc perdre une chance d'avoir de meilleures conditions, en montrant trop d'empressement à accueillir celles offertes dans ce moment. Celles-ci arriveront peut-être dans le courant de la journée, ou demain, quand mon Cabinet sera réuni pour les examiner. Nous sommes au 15; le 18 les relations diplomatiques entre l'Autriche et la Russie doivent être rompues; je crois que notre position vis-à-vis de la Russie sera meilleure en discutant ses propositions après la rupture et après en avoir vu les effets. En attendant, rien ne sera plus utile à la cause de la paix que la résolution que vous avez si sagement prise de dire à tous ceux qui vous approchent qu'il faut continuer la guerre. Soyez bien sûr que dans l'opinion finale que je me formerai, votre position et votre persuasion personnelle seront toujours présentes à mon esprit et auront le plus grand poids.

Queen Victoria to the Earl of Clarendon.

THE BRITISH ARMY

Windsor Castle, *17th January 1856.*

The Queen returns the Duke of Cambridge's and Lord Cowley's letters, which together with the account which Lord Clarendon gives of his interview with M. de Persigny causes the Queen no little anxiety. If negotiations on a vague basis are allowed to be begun, the Russian negotiator is sure to find out that the French are ready to grant anything....

However, whatever happens, one consolation the Queen ever will have, which is—that with the one exception of that failure on the *Redan*, her noble Army—in spite of every possible disadvantage which any army could labour under, *has* invariably been victorious, and the Russians have always and everywhere been beaten excepting at Kars, where *famine* alone enabled them to succeed.

Let us therefore not be (as alas! we have often been) its detractors by our croaking.

Viscount Palmerston to Queen Victoria.

POSITION OF THE EMPEROR

Piccadilly, *17th January 1856.*

Viscount Palmerston presents his humble duty to your Majesty, and concludes that Lord Lansdowne informed your Majesty that the Cabinet, after hearing from Lord Clarendon a statement of the course of the recent negotiations as explained by the despatches which Lord

Clarendon read, came to the decision that no further step should be taken, and no further communication should be made to the Government of France on the matters at issue, until the final decision of the Russian Government on the pure and simple adoption of the Austrian ultimatum[173] should be known. Viscount Palmerston begs to congratulate your Majesty upon the telegraphic message received this morning from Sir Hamilton Seymour, announcing that the Russian Government has adopted that Austrian ultimatum. So far so well, and the success which has attended firmness and steadiness of purpose in regard to those conditions may be looked upon as a tolerably sure indication that a perseverance in the same course will bring the Russian Government to consent to those remaining conditions which the Austrian Government has not yet (as it says) made known to the Cabinet of Petersburg.

With regard to the letter of the Emperor of the French to your Majesty, and the statements made to Lord Clarendon by the Count de Persigny as to the difficulties of the Emperor's internal position with respect to finance, and a general desire for peace throughout the Nation, Viscount Palmerston expressed his opinion to the Cabinet yesterday that all those representations were greatly exaggerated. He is convinced that the Emperor of the French is perfectly master of his own position, and that he can as to peace or war take the course which he may determine to adopt.

The cabal of stock-jobbing politicians, by whom he is surrounded, *must* give way to him if he is firm. They have no standing place in the confidence and respect of their fellow-countrymen, they represent nothing but the Stock Exchange speculations in which they are engaged, and the Emperor's throne would probably be stronger, rather than weaker, if they were swept away, and better men put in their places. And it is a very remarkable circumstance that at the very moment when your Majesty and your Majesty's Government were being told that the Emperor would be unable to go on with the war on account of the difficulty of finding money, the French Government was putting forth in the *Moniteur* an official statement showing that they have a reserve surplus of twenty-one millions sterling for defraying the expenses of a campaign in the ensuing spring, without the necessity of raising any fresh loan.

Viscount Palmerston fully concurs in the sentiment of regret expressed by your Majesty to Lord Clarendon that the last action of the

---

[173] See *ante*, p. 152.

war in which your Majesty's troops have been engaged, should, if peace be now concluded, have been the repulse at the Redan; but however it may suit national jealousy, which will always be found to exist on the other side of the Channel, to dwell upon that check, yet your Majesty may rely upon it that the Alma and Inkerman have left recollections which will dwell in the memory of the living and not be forgotten in the page of history; and although it would no doubt have been gratifying to your Majesty and to the Nation that another summer should have witnessed the destruction of Cronstadt by your Majesty's gallant Navy, and the expulsion of the Russians from the countries south of the Caucasus by your Majesty's brave Army, yet if peace *can* now be concluded on conditions honourable and secure, it would, as your Majesty justly observes, not be right to continue the war for the mere purpose of prospective victories. It will, however, be obviously necessary to continue active preparations for war up to the moment when a definite Treaty of Peace is signed, in order that the Russians may not find it for their interest to break off negotiations when the season for operations shall approach, emboldened by any relaxation on the part of the Allies induced by too ready confidence in the good faith of their adversary....

The Duke of Cambridge to Queen Victoria.

DUKE OF CAMBRIDGE AT PARIS

Tuileries, *20th January 1856.*

My dear Cousin,—Your letters of the 14th and 18th have reached me, and I am happy to find by them that you approve in conjunction with the Government with what has been done by me and my colleagues whilst at Paris.[174] I have given all the messages and carried out all the instructions as contained in your letters, and I trust as far as possible I have been enabled to do some good. On the other hand, I cannot deny that the feelings universally expressed here as to the prospects of a speedy peace are so different from those felt in England, that it is extremely difficult to produce any impression in the sense that we could wish it. France wishes for peace more than anything else on earth, and this feeling does not confine itself to Walewski or the Ministers—it extends itself to all classes. The Emperor alone is reasonable and sensible in this respect, but his position is a most painful one, and he feels it very much. The fact is that public opinion is much more felt

[174] At the Council of War. See *ante*, p. 160.

and more loudly expressed in this country than anybody in England at all imagines. No doubt the Emperor can do much that he wishes, but still he cannot go altogether against a feeling which so loudly expresses itself on all occasions, without thereby injuring his own position most seriously. I have written to Clarendon very fully on this subject, and have explained to him my reasons for wishing to return to England as soon as possible, now that our military mission is concluded. It is essential that I should see the members of the Government, and that I should communicate to them the exact state of feeling here and the views of the Emperor as to the mode of smoothing down all difficulties. This can only be done by a personal interview on the part of somebody thoroughly aware of the present position of affairs. Probably at this moment I am in a better position to do this than anybody else, from the peculiar circumstances in which I have been placed while here, and it is this feeling which makes me desirous to return to England with the least possible delay. It is my intention therefore to start with my colleagues to-morrow, Monday night, for England, to which arrangement the Emperor has given his sanction, and by which time he will be prepared to tell me what he thinks had best be done, from his view of the question. I think it my duty to communicate this to you, and hope that you will give my resolution your sanction. I beg to remain, my dear Cousin, your most dutiful Cousin,

George.

Queen Victoria to the Earl of Clarendon.

ENGLAND AND FRANCE

Windsor Castle, *28th January 1856.*

The Queen sends a letter which she wishes Lord Clarendon to give to General La Marmora.[175] We have been extremely pleased with him (indeed he is a universal favourite) and found him so sensible, mild, and right-minded, in all he says—and a valuable adviser to the King. The Queen wishes *just* to mention to Lord Clarendon that the Duke of Cambridge told her that the Emperor had spoken to *him* about what the King of Sardinia had said relative to *Austria and France*, asking the Duke whether such a thing had been said.[176] The Duke seems

[175] The Sardinian Commander had been attending the Council of War at Paris.

[176] The King of Sardinia was reported to have told the Emperor that the latter's loyalty to the Alliance was questioned by Great Britain, and that it was

to have answered as we could wish, and the Queen pretended *never* to have *heard* the report, merely saying that as the proposed ultimatum was then much talked of, it was very possible the King might unintentionally have mistaken the observations of the Ministers and ourselves as to our being *unable* to *agree*, without great caution, to what appeared to be *agreed* on beforehand between *France* and *Austria*, and possibly *might* have in his blunt way stated something which alarmed the Emperor—but that she could not imagine it could be anything else. There seems, however, really no *end* to *cancans* at *Paris*; for the Duke of Cambridge seems to have shared the same fate. The two atmospheres of France and England, as well as the Society, are so different that people get to talk differently. It seems also that the King got frightened lest he should at Paris be thought too liberal in his *religious* views (having been complimented for it) which he was very proud of—and thought it necessary to tell the *Emperor* he was a *good Catholic*. This is not unnatural in his peculiar position. When Lord Clarendon goes to Paris, he will be able to *silence* any further allusion to these idle stories which only lead to mischief, and which even Lord Cowley seems to have made more of (as to his own feelings upon them) than was necessary, but that is equally natural. Speaking of his King—General La Marmora said: "Il ne dira jamais ce qu'il ne pense pas, mais il dit quelquefois ce qui serait mieux qu'il ne dit pas." He more than any other regrets the King's not having seen more of the world, and says his journey had done him a *great* deal of good.

Queen Victoria to Viscount Palmerston.

THE SPEECH FROM THE THRONE

28th January 1856.

The Queen returns to Lord Palmerston the draft of the speech, which she thinks *extremely well* worded, and which she therefore trusts will be (with the exception of those passages marked) as little altered as possible. Lord John Russell used to say that as soon as a speech was discussed in the Cabinet, it was so much *pruned* and altered as to lose all its force. The Queen must own that she is *much* alarmed at hearing that the *papers* of the War Council were to be printed and circulated amongst the Cabinet, as she fears that the secrecy, which is so necessary, upon which the Emperor laid so *much*

---

conjectured in London that he was in favour of co-operation with Austria instead.

stress, will be very difficult to be maintained. The Emperor's opinion at least, the Queen hopes, will *not* be printed or generally circulated?

The Queen must again press for a very early decision on the subject. If this is allowed to *drag*, it will appear, particularly to the *Emperor*, as if we were not really in earnest, though we stickled so much for our additional conditions, which might lessen the hopes of peace. Of course the Government must not give any answer on this subject—should Parliament be so indiscreet as to ask *what* the result of the deliberations of the Council of War has been.

Queen Victoria to the King of the Belgians.

Windsor Castle, *29th January 1856.*

My dearest Uncle,—You will kindly forgive my letter being short, but we are going to be present this morning at the wedding of Phipps's daughter[177] with that handsome lame young officer whom you remember at Osborne. It is quite an event at Windsor, and takes place in St George's Chapel, which is very seldom the case.

Many thanks for your kind letter of the 25th, by which I am glad to see that dear good Philip has arrived safe and well and brought back *de bons souvenirs*. We shall always be *happy* to see him.

The *peace negotiations* occupy every one; *if* Russia is *sincere*, they will end most probably in peace; but *if* she is *not*, the war will be *carried* on with *renewed vigour*. The recollection of last year makes one *very distrustful*.

England's policy throughout has been the *same*, *singularly unselfish*, and *solely* actuated by the *desire* of *seeing Europe saved* from the *arrogant* and *dangerous pretensions* of that *barbarous power* Russia—and of having *such safeguards* established for the *future*, which may ensure us against a *repetition* of similar *untoward events*.

I repeat now, what we have said from the beginning, and what I have *repeated* a *hundred* times, *if Prussia* and *Austria* had held *strong and decided* language to *Russia in* '53, we should *never* have had *this war!*

Now I must conclude. With Albert's best love, ever your devoted Niece,

Victoria R.

---

[177] Maria Henrietta Sophia, daughter of Sir Charles Beaumont Phipps, K.C.B., Keeper of the Privy Purse, married Captain Frederick Sayer, 23rd Royal Welsh Fusiliers.

Queen Victoria to Miss Florence Nightingale.

MISS NIGHTINGALE

Windsor Castle, *[January] 1856.*

Dear Miss Nightingale,—You are, I know, well aware of the high sense I entertain of the Christian devotion which you have displayed during this great and bloody war, and I need hardly repeat to you how warm my admiration is for your services, which are fully equal to those of my dear and brave soldiers, whose sufferings you have had the *privilege* of alleviating in so merciful a manner. I am, however, anxious of marking my feelings in a manner which I trust will be agreeable to you, and therefore send you with this letter a brooch, the form and emblems of which commemorate your great and blessed work, and which, I hope, you will wear as a mark of the high approbation of your Sovereign![178]

It will be a very great satisfaction to me, when you return at last to these shores, to make the acquaintance of one who has set so bright an example to our sex. And with every prayer for the preservation of your valuable health, believe me, always, yours sincerely,

Victoria R.

Queen Victoria to the Earl of Clarendon.

Windsor Castle, *7th February 1856.*

With respect to Lord Clarendon's observation that he hopes that the Queen "will approve of his upholding the Sardinians in the Conference and in all other respects," she can only assure him that she is *most sincerely* anxious that he should do so, as the Queen has the greatest respect for that noble little country, which, since it has possessed an honest, straightforward as well as courageous King, has been a bright example to all Continental States.

The Queen rejoices to hear that Count Cavour is coming to Paris. The Queen hopes that the determination not to admit Prussia will be

[178] The presentation took place on the 29th of January. The jewel resembled a badge rather than a brooch, bearing a St George's Cross in red enamel, and the Royal cypher surmounted by a crown in diamonds. The inscription "Blessed are the Merciful" encircled the badge which also bore the word "Crimea."

adhered to.[179] She hears that Baron Beust[180] means to go to Paris to represent the German Confederation; this should be prevented by all means.

Queen Victoria to the King of the Belgians.

BELGIAN NEUTRALITY

Buckingham Palace, *13th February 1856.*

My dearest Uncle,—I had the happiness of receiving your kind letter of the 8th on Saturday, and thank you much for it. I gave your kind message to Colonel Phipps, who was much gratified by it. We came here in wretched weather yesterday, leaving Mamma *still* at Frogmore.

The Conferences will begin very shortly; Lord Clarendon starts for Paris on Friday. *No* one but him could undertake these difficult negotiations. *No* one can tell *what* the result will be—and I will say nothing, for I have *too strong* personal feelings to speak upon the subject.

With respect to your answer respecting your *neutrality*, and the possibility of your being obliged to break it, I must repeat that I see *no possibility* or *eventuality* that *could oblige* you to do so. *Belgium* of its own accord bound itself to remain neutral, and its very existence is *based* upon that neutrality, which the other Powers have guaranteed and are bound to maintain *if Belgium keeps* her engagements. I cannot at all see HOW you could *even* entertain the question, for, as I just said, the *basis* of the *existence* of Belgium is her *neutrality*.

The weather is so mild that we should almost hope Stockmar would start soon. If *he* can't come himself, he should send his son for a few days, who could bring us any confidential communication from his father, and could be the bearer of any from us. Something of this kind is most necessary, for it is overwhelming to write to one another upon so many details which require immediate answer....

With Albert's love, and ours to your young people, believe me, always, your devoted Niece,

Victoria R.

---

[179] Prussia was not admitted to the sitting of the Conference until a later stage.

[180] Prime Minister of Saxony.

Queen Victoria to Viscount Palmerston.

14th February 1856.

The Queen has seen in the reports of the House of Commons that a return has been moved for of all the decorations of the Bath given since the war. The Queen hopes the Government will not allow the House of Commons so much further to trespass upon the prerogatives of the Crown as now *virtually* to take also the control over the distribution of honours and rewards into their hands.

The King of the Belgians to Queen Victoria.

TERMS OF PEACE

Laeken, *15th February 1856.*

My dearest Victoria,—I have to thank you for your dear kind letter of the 12th. Madame de Sévigné says, with great truth, that a letter to be a good letter ought to be as if one heard the person speak; your dear letters are always so, and you would therefore be praised by Madame de Sévigné, and that very deservedly. Lord Clarendon is, Heaven be praised, well calculated to bring matters to a happy conclusion. I will try to make some impression on the mind of the Emperor Alexander, his best policy will be the most honest. By all I can learn they wish most sincerely the conclusion of this war. If on the side of the Allies only the things which really protect the territories of the present Turkish Empire are asked, the Russians ought not to manœuvre, but grant it, and the Allies also ought to be moderate. You are very properly never to be contradicted, but there are a few things to be remarked. This neutrality was in the real interest of this country, but our good Congress here did *not* wish it, and even opposed it; it was *imposé* upon them. A neutrality to be respected must be *protected.* France at all time in cases of general war can put an end to it, by declaring to us *Vous devez être avec nous ou contre nous*. If we answer *Nous sommes neutres*, they will certainly try to occupy us; then the case of self-defence arises and the claim to be protected by the other powers....

My beloved Victoria, your devoted Uncle,

Leopold R.

Queen Victoria to the Emperor of the French.

THE CONFERENCE

Buckingham Palace, *le 15 Février 1856.*

Sire et cher Frère,—Mes Commissaires pour le Conseil de Guerre sont à peine revenus de Paris et notre plan de campagne est à peine arrêté, que mes Plénipotentiaires pour la Conférence de paix se mettent en route pour assister sous les yeux de V.M. à l'œuvre de la pacification. Je n'ai pas besoin de vous recommander Lord Clarendon, mais je ne veux pas le laisser partir sans le rendre porteur de quelques mots de ma part.

Quoique bien convaincue qu'il ne pourra dans les discussions prochaines s'élever de questions sur lesquelles il y aurait divergence d'opinions entre nos deux Gouvernements, j'attache toutefois le plus haut prix à ce que l'accord le plus parfait soit établi avant que les conférences ne soient ouvertes; et c'est dans ce but que j'ai chargé Lord Clarendon de se rendre à Paris quelques jours avant, afin qu'il pût rendre un compte exact des opinions de mon Gouvernement, et jouir de l'avantage de connaître *à fond* la pensée de V.M.

J'éprouverai un sentiment d'intime satisfaction dans ce moment critique, et je le regarderai comme une preuve toute particulière de votre amitié, si vous voulez permettre à Lord Clarendon de vous exposer personnellement mes vues et d'entendre les Vôtres de Votre proper bouche.

Les opérations de nos armées et de nos flottes combinées, sous un commandement divisé, ont été sujettes à d'énormes difficultés; mais ces difficultés ont été heureusement vaincues. Dans la Diplomatie comme à la guerre, les Russes auront sur Nous le grand avantage de l'unité de plan et d'action, et je les crois plus forts sur ce terrain que sur le champ de bataille; mais à coup sûr, nous y resterons également victorieux, si nous réussissons à empêcher l'ennemi de diviser nos forces et de nous battre en détail.

Sans vouloir jeter un doute sur la sincérité de la Russie en acceptant nos propositions, il est impossible d'avoir à ce sujet une conviction pleine et entière. J'ai tout lieu de croire cependant que nul effort et nul stratagème ne seront negligés pour rompre, s'il était possible, ou au moins pour affaiblir notre alliance. Mais je repose à cet égard dans la fermeté de V.M. la même confiance qui saura détruire toutes ces espérances, que j'ai dans la mienne et dans celle de mes Ministres. Cependant, on ne saurait attacher trop d'importance à ce que cette commune fermeté soit reconnue et appréciée dès le commencement des négociations, car de là dépendra, j'en ai la conviction, la solution, si nous devons obtenir une paix dont les termes pourront être considérés comme satisfaisants pour l'honneur de la France et de l'Angleterre, et comme donnant une juste compensation pour les énormes sacrifices que les deux pays ont faits. Une autre considération encore me porte à attacher le plus haut prix à cet accord parfait, c'est que si, par son absence, nous étions entraînés dans une paix qui ne satisferait point la juste attente de nos peuples, cela donnerait lieu à des plaintes et à des récriminations qui ne pourraient manquer de fausser les relations amicales des deux pays au lieu de les cimenter davantage comme mon cœur le désire ardemment.

D'ailleurs, je ne doute pas un moment qu'une paix telle que la France et l'Angleterre ont le droit de la demander sera bien certainement obtenue par une détermination inébranlable de ne point rabaisser les demandes modérées que nous avons faites.

Vous excuserez, Sire, la longueur de cette lettre, mais il m'est si doux de pouvoir épancher mes sentiments sur toutes ces questions si importantes et si difficiles, avec une personne que je considère non seulement comme un Allié fidèle, mais comme un ami sur lequel je puis compter en toute occasion, et qui, j'en suis sûre, est animé envers nous des mêmes sentiments.

Le Prince me charge de vous offrir ses hommages les plus affectueux, et moi je me dis pour toujours, Sire et cher Frère, de V.M.I., la très affectionnée Sœur et Amie,

Victoria R.

Queen Victoria to Viscount Palmerston.

THE CRIMEAN ENQUIRY

Buckingham Palace, *16th February 1856.*

The subject to which Lord Palmerston refers in his letter of last night, and upon which the Cabinet is going to deliberate to-day, has also caused the Queen much anxiety.

A Civil Commission is sent out by the Government to enquire into the conduct of the officers in command in the Crimea; this is done without any consultation with the Commander-in-Chief. They report to the Government, inculpating several general officers and others in high command; this report is not communicated to the military authorities, nor to the persons affected by it, but is laid on the table of both Houses of Parliament.[181] These officers then for the first time find themselves accused under the authority of Government, and that accusation communicated to the Legislature without ever having been heard in answer or allowed an opportunity to defend themselves. It is stated in both Houses by the Government that the officers may send papers in reply if they choose! But who is to be the Judge on the trial? The Press, of course, and the *Times* at the head, have already judged and condemned, and the House of Commons is now moving *in default of another Judge* to constitute its tribunal by a Committee of Enquiry.

It is quite evident if matters are left so, and military officers of the Queen's Army are to be judged as to the manner in which they have discharged their military duties before an enemy by a Committee of the House of Commons, the command of the Army is at once transferred from the Crown to that Assembly.

This result is quite inevitable if the Government appear as accusers, as they do by the report of their Commission, and then submit the accusation for Parliament to deal with, without taking any steps of their own!

The course suggested by Sir James Graham and alluded to by Lord Palmerston, of following the precedent of the enquiry into the Convention of Cintra,[182] appears therefore to the Queen to be the only prudent one.

---

[181] Sir John MacNeill and Colonel Tulloch had been sent out to the Crimea early in 1855 to investigate the breakdown of various military departments. They had issued a preliminary report in the summer of 1855, and a final one in January 1856, which was presented to Parliament. The officers specially censured were Lord Lucan (who had been given the command of a Regiment), Lord Cardigan, Inspector of Cavalry, Sir Richard Airey, Quartermaster-General, and Colonel Gordon, Deputy Quartermaster-General. Lord Panmure wrote on the 17th of February that the Government recommended the appointment of a Commission of Enquiry, consisting of General Sir Howard Douglas and six other high military officers. The Commission sat at Chelsea, and made its report in July, exonerating the officers censured.

[182] The Convention of Cintra was concluded on the 30th of August 1808. It was founded on the basis of an armistice agreed upon between Sir Arthur Wellesley and General Kellerman, on the day after the battle of Vimiera, and some of its provisions were considered too favourable to the French. A Board of Enquiry, under the presidency of Sir David Dundas, in the first instance exculpated the British officers; but the Government having instructed the

The Queen thinks it most unfair to the officers to publish their statements beforehand, as these will not go before judges feeling the weight of their responsibility, but before the newspapers who are their sworn enemies and determined to effect their ruin, for which they possess unlimited means.

The Queen wishes Lord Palmerston to read this letter to the Cabinet.

The Earl of Clarendon to Queen Victoria.

THE EMPEROR'S CORDIALITY

Paris, *18th February 1856.*

Lord Clarendon presents his humble duty to your Majesty, and humbly begs to say that he dined last night at the Tuileries, and had a conversation of two hours with the Emperor, which was in all respects satisfactory. On no occasion has Lord Clarendon heard the Emperor express himself more warmly or with greater determination in favour of the Alliance, and H.M. entirely concurred with Lord Clarendon, that upon the perfect understanding between the two Governments, and the conviction on the part of others that the Alliance was not to be shaken, depended the facility with which negotiations might be conducted, and the terms on which peace would be made. Lord Clarendon spoke with the utmost frankness about the flattery that had been and would continue to be addressed to His Majesty, and the contrast perpetually drawn between England and France, to the disparagement of the former, for the purpose of disturbing the relations between them; but that your Majesty and your Majesty's Government had always treated these tricks with contempt, because the confidence in the Emperor's honour and loyalty was complete. Lord Clarendon dwelt particularly upon the feelings of your Majesty and of the Prince on this subject, and the pleasure it gave the Emperor was evident; and he desired Lord Clarendon to say that your Majesty should never find such confidence misplaced.

He promised Lord Clarendon that he would give Baron Brunnow and Count Buol to understand that if they thought the Alliance could be disturbed by them they would find themselves grievously mistaken,

---

members of the Board to give their opinions individually, four were found to approve and three to disapprove the armistice and convention.

and that it would be waste of time to try and alter any conditions upon which he had agreed with the English Government.

The Emperor appeared to be much gratified by your Majesty's letter, for the first thing he said to Lord Clarendon on coming into the room before dinner was "*quelle charmante lettre vous m'avez apportée de la Reine*," and then began upon the extraordinary clearness with which your Majesty treated all matters of business, and the pleasure he derived from every discussion of them with your Majesty....

The Empress was looking in great health and beauty. She was in the highest spirits, and full of affectionate enquiry for your Majesty.

The Marquis of Dalhousie to Queen Victoria.

OUDH

Calcutta, *19th February 1856.*

The Governor-General presents his most humble duty to your Majesty, and has the honour of submitting to your Majesty a copy of a Proclamation, whereby the Kingdom of Oudh has been placed exclusively and permanently under the authority of your Majesty's Government.[183]

The various considerations, and the course of public events, which led to this necessity, have long since been laid before your Majesty's Government in great detail.

The Governor-General during the past summer communicated to the Home Authorities his readiness to remain in India as long as he dared, namely, for one additional month, until the 1st of March, for the purpose of carrying into effect the proposed policy regarding Oudh—if it was desired that he should do so.

The orders from the Home Government reached the Governor-General only upon the 2nd of January, leaving barely two months for the assembling of the military force which was necessary to provide against all risks—for the negotiations with the King—and for the organisation of the future Civil and Military Administration of Oudh.

Every preparation having been completed, the Resident at Lucknow waited upon the King in person—communicated to him the

---

[183] In a letter of the 13th, Mr Vernon Smith had told the Queen that the Press rumours of "annexation" were premature, and that the use of the word itself had been avoided in Lord Canning's correspondence with the Court of Directors.

resolution which the British Government had taken—and tendered for his acceptance a new Treaty, whereby the transfer of the Government of Oudh would have been made a matter of amicable agreement.

The King wholly refused to sign any Treaty. He declared himself ready to submit to the will of the British Government in all things. He bade the Resident observe that every mark of power had already been laid down by His Majesty's own orders—the guns at the palace gates were dismounted, the guards bore no arms, and, though drawn up as usual in the Court, they saluted the Resident with their hands only; while not a weapon was worn by any officer in the Palace.

THE KING'S APPEAL

The King gave way to passionate bursts of grief and anger—implored the intercession of the Resident in his behalf—and finally, uncovering his head, he placed his turban in the Resident's hands. This act—the deepest mark of humiliation and helplessness which a native of the East can exhibit—became doubly touching and significant when the head thus bared in supplication was one that had worn a royal crown.

The Government, however, had already borne too long with the wrongs inflicted by the sovereigns of Oudh upon their unhappy subjects. The clamorous grief of the King could not be allowed to shut out the cry of his people's misery. The King's appeal, therefore, could not be listened to; and as His Majesty, at the end of the three days' space which was allowed him for deliberation, still resolutely refused to sign a Treaty, the territory of Oudh was taken possession of, by the issue of the Proclamation which has now been respectfully submitted to your Majesty.

It is the fourth kingdom in India which has passed under your Majesty's sceptre during the last eight years.[184]

Perfect tranquillity has prevailed in Oudh since the event which has just been narrated. General Outram writes that the populace of Lucknow, more interested than any other community in the maintenance of the native dynasty, already "appear to have forgotten they ever had a King." In the districts the Proclamation has been heartily welcomed by the middle and lower classes; while even the higher or-

[184] The earlier annexations were those of the Punjab (1849), Pegu (1852), and Nagpur (1853); some minor additions were also made under what was called the "doctrine of lapse."

ders, who of course lose much in a native state by the cessation of corruption and tyranny, have shown no symptoms of dissatisfaction.

There seems every reason to hope and expect that the same complete tranquillity will attend the further progress of our arrangements for the future administration of Oudh....

The Governor-General has only further to report to your Majesty that Lord Canning arrived at Madras on the 14th inst., and that he will assume the Government of India on the last day of this month.

The Governor-General will report hereafter Lord Canning's arrival at Fort William; and he has now the honour to subscribe himself, your Majesty's most obedient, most humble and devoted Subject and Servant,

Dalhousie.

Queen Victoria to Viscount Palmerston.

PRELIMINARIES OF PEACE

Buckingham Palace, *27th February 1856.*

The Queen returns Lord Clarendon's letter.

The matter becomes very serious, and it would be a bad position for us to be left quite alone in the Conference, which the Russians, the Queen has every reason to believe, are anxiously striving to bring about. In fact, well-informed persons pretend that this was the main aim of Russia in accepting the Austrian ultimatum and going to Paris.

Would it not answer to take this line: to say to Russia, "You have accepted the ultimatum, *pur et simple*, and have now again recognised its stipulations as preliminaries of peace. You will, therefore, first of all, have to execute them; you may then come to the question of Kars and say you mean to keep it—then you will see that Europe, bound to maintain the integrity of Turkey, will be obliged to go on with the war, and it will be for you to consider whether you mean to go on fighting for Kars; but at present this is not in question, as you are only called upon to fulfil the engagements to which you have solemnly pledged yourself"?

Perhaps Lord Palmerston will discuss this suggestion with his colleagues to-night.

Viscount Palmerston to Queen Victoria.

Piccadilly, *27th February 1856.*

Viscount Palmerston presents his humble duty to your Majesty, and begs to state that as the result of the deliberations of the Cabinet this evening, the accompanying telegraphic message is proposed to be sent to-morrow morning to Lord Clarendon. It is founded upon the substance of your Majesty's memorandum of this afternoon. Viscount Palmerston has taken another copy of this draft.

Telegram to the Earl of Clarendon.

28th February 1856.

[*Enclosure.*]

Your letter has been considered by the Cabinet.

Russia should be told that she cannot recede from the conditions which she deliberately agreed to by a *pur et simple* acceptance at Petersburg, which she afterwards formally recorded in a protocol at Vienna, and which she has within a few days solemnly converted into preliminaries of peace.

Those engagements must be fulfilled, and those conditions must be carried into execution.

As to Kars, Austria, France, and Great Britain have undertaken to maintain the integrity of the Turkish Empire, and that integrity must be maintained.

Russia received no equivalent for giving up the principalities which she had occupied as a material pledge. She can receive none for giving up Kars.

If Russia determines to carry on the war, rather than give up Kars, things must take their course.

The Marquis of Dalhousie to Queen Victoria.

TRANQUILLITY OF INDIA

Government House, *29th February 1856.*

Lord Dalhousie presents his most humble duty to your Majesty.

The guns are announcing from the ramparts of Fort William that Lord Canning has arrived. In an hour's time he will have assumed the Government of India. Lord Dalhousie will transfer it to him in a state of perfect tranquillity. There is peace, within and without. And although no prudent man will ever venture to predict the certainty of continued peace in India, yet Lord Dalhousie is able to declare, within reservation, that he knows of no quarter in which it is probable that trouble will arise.[185]

Lord Dalhousie desires that his very last act, as Governor-General, should be to submit to your Majesty a respectful expression of the deep sense he entertains of your Majesty's constant approbation of his public conduct while he has held the office of Governor-General of India; together with a humble assurance of the heartfelt gratitude with which he shall ever remember your Majesty's gracious favour towards him through the eight long years during which he has borne the ponderous burden he lays down to-day.

Lord Dalhousie begs permission to take leave of your Majesty, and has the honour to subscribe himself, with deep devotion, your Majesty's most obedient, most humble and faithful Subject and Servant,

Dalhousie.

Queen Victoria to Viscount Palmerston.

LORD CLARENDON'S INSTRUCTIONS

Buckingham Palace, [*? March*] *1856.*

The Queen returns these letters to Lord Palmerston. She entirely concurs in Lord Palmerston's general views of the question, but at the same time she thinks—as circumstances, which are beyond our control, may so vary from day to day or even from hour to hour—that Lord Clarendon should receive full powers to act according to what may appear to him to be best and wisest at the time, even if it should not be in strict accordance with what we originally contemplated and must naturally wish. Such a power would certainly not be misplaced in Lord Clarendon's hands; his firmness, and his sense of what this country expects, are too well known to lead us to doubt of his permitting anything but what would *really* be for the best of this country, and for the maintenance of the Alliance.

---

[185] It has been, however, freely alleged that the failure to repress acts of insubordination in the administration of Lord Dalhousie was a contributory, if not the direct, cause of the events of 1857. See *post*, p. 223, and Walpole's *History of England from the Conclusion of the Great War in 1815*, ch. xxvii., and authorities there referred to.

Queen Victoria to Viscount Palmerston.

THE PEACE NEGOTIATIONS

Buckingham Palace, *6th March 1856.*

With reference to Lord Clarendon's letter, the Queen must say that she, though *very reluctantly*, shares his opinion, that we have no choice *now* but to accept the peace, even if it is not all we could desire, and if another campaign might have got us better terms. She feels certain that the bad accounts of the French Army in the Crimea, which appears to suffer *now* all the misery which ours suffered last year at the worst time of the siege, will more than ever indispose the Emperor from risking a renewal of hostilities. It is affirmed that the French have beyond 20,000 men in hospital!

If we are to have this peace, however, the Queen must again agree with Lord Clarendon that we ought not *ourselves* to depreciate it, as our Press has done the deeds of our Army.

With regard to the principalities, it is the Queen's opinion that nothing will oppose a barrier to Russia and her intrigues but the arrangement which will satisfy the people themselves, viz. an *hereditary monarchy*. The example of Egypt might perfectly well be followed in Wallachia and Moldavia.

The subject of Poland would, in the Queen's opinion, be much better left unintroduced into the present negotiations; we have no claim arising out of this war to ask Russia to make concessions on that head, which, moreover, would be treated by her as an internal question not admitting of foreign interference.

The clause in the Treaty of Vienna about the Bonapartes is a dead letter, as this very Treaty, now to be signed, will prove, and the Emperor would act very unwisely to call for an alteration in which all Powers who signed the original Treaty would claim to be consulted. We have every interest not to bring about a European Congress *pour la Révision des Traités*, which many people suspect the Emperor wishes to turn the present Conference into.

The Queen wishes only to add that, should Prussia be asked to join in the final Treaty on the ground of her having been a party to the July Treaty, we should take care that it does not appear that this was an act of courtesy of all the other Powers towards Prussia except England, who need not be made to take additional unpopularity in Germany upon herself.

The Earl of Clarendon to Queen Victoria.

Paris, *18th March 1856.*

Lord Clarendon presents his humble duty to your Majesty, and humbly begs to say that the Emperor gave him to-day the most satisfactory report of the Empress and the young Prince.[186] There appears to be little or no fever now, and a great power of sleeping. The Emperor's eyes filled with tears when he described the tortures of the Empress and his own sensations. He said he hardly knew how to express his gratitude for the interest which your Majesty had manifested for the Empress, and for the letters which he had received from your Majesty and the Prince.

The Prussian Plenipotentiaries[187] were admitted at the close of the Conference this afternoon—all important matters under negotiation having been concluded.

Count Walewski made an ineffectual attempt to make it appear by a doubtful form of expression that Prussia had taken part throughout in the negotiations. Lord Cowley and Lord Clarendon said that they wished to show all courtesy to Prussia, but could not consent to sign what was manifestly untrue....

Extract of a Letter from Mr Cobden to a Friend.[188]

THE PRINCESS ROYAL

Midhurst, *20th March 1856.*

... It is generally thought that the young Prince Frederic William of Prussia is to be married to our Princess Royal. I was dining *tête-à-tête* with Mr Buchanan, the American Minister, a few days ago, who had dined the day before at the Queen's table, and sat next to the Princess Royal. He was in raptures about her, and said she was the most charming girl he had ever met: "All life and spirit, full of frolic and fun, with an excellent head, and a *heart as big as a mountain*"—those were his words. Another friend of mine, Colonel Fitzmayer, dined with the Queen last week, and in writing to me a description of the company, he says, that when the Princess Royal smiles, "it makes one

---

[186] The Prince Imperial, Napoléon Eugène Louis Jean Joseph, was born on the 16th of March.

[187] Baron Manteuffel and Count Hatzfeldt.

[188] Submitted to the Queen.

feel as if additional light were thrown upon the scene." So I should judge that this said Prince is a lucky fellow, and I trust he will make a good husband. If not, although a man of peace, I shall consider it a *casus belli....*

The Earl of Clarendon to Queen Victoria.

Paris, *29th March 1856.*

Lord Clarendon presents his humble duty to your Majesty, and humbly begs to say that the Emperor sent General Ney to him this morning to request that Lord Clarendon would convey the cordial thanks of the Emperor to your Majesty for the *feu de joie* fired by your Majesty's troops in the Crimea upon the announcement of the birth of the Prince Imperial.

Lord Clarendon was much embarrassed by a letter this morning from Lord Palmerston, desiring that the signature of the Treaty should be postponed till Monday, in case the Cabinet should have any amendments to propose; and Lord Clarendon humbly hopes that your Majesty may not be displeased at his not having acted upon this injunction, because he had promised to sign the Treaty to-morrow in accordance with the general wish of the Congress, notwithstanding that it was Sunday, and he could not therefore go back from his engagement—every preparation is made for illuminations, not alone at Paris, but throughout France, as all the Prefects have been informed of the signature—the odium that would have fallen [on] us all would have been extreme throughout Europe it may be said, and it would have been regarded as a last proof of our unwillingness to make peace. The friendly feeling of the Congress towards the English P.P.'s[189] would have changed, and they probably would have agreed to no amendments, requiring that all the seven copies of the Treaty should be recopied. In short, Lord Clarendon felt that he had no choice but to take upon himself the responsibility of signing to-morrow; but he has suggested that Lord Palmerston's private letter should be converted into a despatch, in order that the sole and entire blame should rest with Lord Clarendon....[190]

---

[189] *I.e.*, Plenipotentiaries.

[190] For the chief stipulations of the Treaty, see Introductory Note, *ante*, p. 158. In addition to the actual Treaty, an important declaration was made as to the rules of international maritime law, to be binding only on the signatory powers, dealing with the following points:—

Viscount Palmerston to Queen Victoria.

TERMS ARRIVED AT

Piccadilly, *30th March 1856.*

Viscount Palmerston presents his humble duty to your Majesty, and in submitting the accompanying letter from Lord Clarendon, he begs to state that he informed Lord Clarendon by the messenger yesterday evening that all he had done and agreed to was approved, and that he might sign the Treaty to-day. It was to be signed at half-past twelve this day.

Viscount Palmerston begs to congratulate your Majesty upon an arrangement which effects a settlement that is satisfactory for the present, and which will probably last for many years to come, of questions full of danger to the best interests of Europe. Greater and more brilliant successes by land and sea might probably have been accomplished by the Allies if the war had continued, but any great and important additional security against future aggressions by Russia could only have been obtained by severing from Russia large portions of her frontier territory, such as Finland, Poland, and Georgia; and although by great military and financial efforts and sacrifices those territories might for a time have been occupied, Russia must have been reduced to the lowest state of internal distress, before her Emperor could have been brought to put his name to a Treaty of Peace finally surrendering his sovereignty over those extensive countries; and to have continued the war long enough for these purposes would have required greater endurance than was possessed by your Majesty's Allies, and might possibly have exhausted the good-will of your Majesty's own subjects....

(*a*) Abolition of Privateering.

(*b*) Neutral flag to cover enemy's goods, other than contraband of war.

(*c*) Neutral goods, other than contraband of war, under enemy's flag, to be exempt from seizure.

(*d*) Blockades to be binding must be effective, *i.e.* maintained by adequate marine force.

The Earl of Clarendon to Queen Victoria.

THE TREATY OF PARIS

Paris, *30th March 1856.*

Lord Clarendon presents his humble duty to your Majesty, and humbly begs to congratulate your Majesty upon the signature of peace this afternoon. It is not to be doubted that another campaign must have brought glory to your Majesty's arms, and would have enabled England to impose different terms upon Russia, but setting aside the cost and the horrors of war, in themselves evils of the greatest magnitude, we cannot feel sure that victory might not have been purchased too dearly—a continuation of the war would hardly have been possible either with or without France—if we had dragged her on with us it would have been most reluctantly on her part, her finances would have suffered still more, she would have borne us ill-will, would have acted feebly with us, and would on the first favourable occasion have left us in the lurch. If we had continued the war single-handed, France would feel that she had behaved shabbily to us, and would *therefore* have hated us all the more, and become our enemy sooner than under any other circumstances; a coalition of Europe might then have taken place against England, to which the United States would but too gladly have adhered, and the consequence might have been most serious.

Lord Clarendon would not make such an assertion lightly, but he feels convinced that your Majesty may feel satisfied with the position now occupied by England—six weeks ago it was a painful position here, everybody was against us, our motives were suspected, and our policy was denounced; but the universal feeling now is that we are the only country able and ready, and willing, if necessary, to continue the war; that we might have prevented peace, but that having announced our readiness to make peace on honourable terms we have honestly and unselfishly acted up to our word. It is well known, too, that the conditions on which peace is made would have been different if England had not been firm, and everybody is, of course, glad *even here* that peace should not have brought dishonour to France.

Lord Clarendon, therefore, ventures to hope that the language in England with respect to the peace will not be apologetic or dissatisfied. It would be unwise and undignified, and would invite criticism if such language were held before the conditions are publicly known.

Queen Victoria to the Earl of Clarendon.

END OF THE WAR

Windsor Castle, *31st March 1856.*

The Queen thanks Lord Clarendon much for his two letters of Saturday and yesterday; and we congratulate *him* on the success of his *efforts* in obtaining the Peace, for to him *alone* it is due, and also *to him alone* is due the dignified position which the Queen's beloved country holds, and which she owes to a straightforward, steady, and unselfish policy throughout.

Much as the Queen disliked the idea of *Peace*, she has become reconciled to it, by the conviction that France would either not have continued the war, or continued it in such a manner that *no* glory could have been hoped for for us.

We have a striking proof of this in Pélissier not having obeyed the Emperor's orders and never having thought of occupying Sak.[191] *This really might* be hinted to the Emperor....

The Queen finds Lord Palmerston very well pleased with the Peace, though he struggled as long as he could for better conditions....

Queen Victoria to the King of the Belgians.

Windsor Castle, *1st April 1856.*

My dearest Uncle,— ... *Peace is signed!* But till the ratifications have taken place its terms cannot be known. That so *good* a Peace *has* been obtained, and that this country stands in the high position she now does by *having* made peace, but *not* yielding to *unworthy* and dishonourable terms, is *all* owing to Lord Clarendon, whose difficulties were immense, and who cannot be too highly praised.

May I beg to remind you to make enquiries, *quietly*, about the young Prince of Orange[192]—as to his education, *entourage*, and disposition? Pray also don't forget to try and let us have a *new* Russian; it would be infinitely *better*.[193]

[191] The word is so written in the original draft. There was a place of the name near Old Fort in the Crimea, but this is more probably an abbreviation for Sakatal in Caucasia.

[192] Prince William Nicholas, born 1840, elder son of King William III. of Holland.

[193] The new Russian Ambassador was Count Creptowitch.

We were much grieved to hear the day before yesterday from Sommer that poor Stockmar had had a relapse, but the illness is clearly of a spasmodic nature and therefore *not* at all dangerous, and the pain had speedily left him, but of course left him again weaker, which is most distressing.

Now with Albert's affectionate love and our reiterated *warmest* thanks, in which Vicky is included, for your having so VERY kindly come over for her Confirmation, believe me, ever, your devoted Niece and Child,

Victoria R.

Queen Victoria to the Emperor of the French.

Palais de Buckingham, *le 3 Avril 1856.*

Sire et mon cher Frère,—V.M. me permettra de lui offrir toutes mes félicitations à l'occasion de la paix qui a été conclue sous vos auspices, et peu de jours seulement après l'heureux événement qui vous a donné un fils. Quoique partageant le sentiment de la pluspart de mon peuple qui trouve que cette paix est peut-être un peu précoce, j'éprouve le besoin de vous dire que j'approuve hautement les termes dans lesquels elle a été conçue, comme un résultat qui n'est pas indigne des sacrifices que nous avons faits mutuellement pendant cette juste guerre, et comme assurant autant que cela se peut, la stabilité de l'équilibre Européen....

Le Prince me charge de vous offrir ses hommages les plus affectueux, et je me dis pour toujours, Sire et cher Frère, de V.M.I., la bien affectionnée Sœur et Amie,

Victoria R.

The Earl of Clarendon to Queen Victoria.

HONOURS GRATEFULLY DECLINED

Paris, *6th April 1856.*

Lord Clarendon presents his humble duty to your Majesty....

Lord Clarendon humbly begs in Lord Cowley's name and his own most gratefully to acknowledge the kind and gracious intention of your Majesty to raise each of them a step in the Peerage, and they venture to hope that your Majesty will not have been displeased at their having respectfully declined this great distinction. Lord Cowley's reason was his extreme poverty, and the feeling that an accession of rank would only aggravate the inconvenience he already experiences from being a Peer....

Lord Clarendon felt that courtesy titles to his younger sons would be a positive injury to them in working for their bread, and he relied upon your Majesty's unvarying kindness for appreciating his reluctance to prefer himself to his children. He may, with entire truth, add that the knowledge that your Majesty has approved of their conduct is ample and abundant reward for Lord Cowley and himself. Lord Clarendon hopes it is not presumptuous in him to say that he would not exchange your Majesty's letters of approval for any public mark of your Majesty's favour....

Queen Victoria to Viscount Palmerston.

LORD PALMERSTON AND THE GARTER

Buckingham Palace, *11th April 1856.*

Now that the moment for the ratification of the Treaty of Peace is near at hand, the Queen wishes to delay no longer the expression of her satisfaction as to the manner in which both the War has been brought to a conclusion, and the honour and interests of this country have been maintained by the Treaty of Peace, under the zealous and able guidance of Lord Palmerston. She wishes as a public token of her approval to bestow the Order of the Garter upon him. Should the two vacant Ribbons already have been promised to the Peers whose names Lord Palmerston has on a former occasion submitted to the Queen, there could be no difficulty in his being named an extra Knight, not filling up the next vacancy which may occur; this course was followed when Lord Grey received the Garter from the hands of King William.

Viscount Palmerston to Queen Victoria.

Piccadilly, *11th April 1856.*

Viscount Palmerston presents his humble duty to your Majesty, and is unable to express in words the gratification and thankfulness which he feels upon the receipt of your Majesty's most gracious and unexpected communication of this morning. The utmost of his ambition has been so to perform the duties of the high position in which your Majesty has been pleased to place him, as to prove himself not unworthy of the confidence with which your Majesty has honoured him; and the knowledge that your Majesty has found no reason to be dissatisfied with your choice; and that his endeavour properly to discharge his duties to your Majesty and the country have met with your Majesty's approval would of itself be an ample reward for any labour or anxiety with which the performance of those duties may have been attended, and, therefore, the gracious communication which he has this morning received from your Majesty will be preserved by him as in his eyes still more valuable even than the high honour which it announces your Majesty's intention to confer upon him.

That high and distinguished honour Viscount Palmerston will receive with the greatest pride as a public mark of your Majesty's gracious approbation, but he begs to be allowed to say that the task which he and his colleagues have had to perform has been rendered comparatively easy by the enlightened views which your Majesty has taken of all the great affairs in which your Majesty's Empire has been engaged, and by the firm and steady support which *in* all these important transactions your Majesty's servants have received from the Crown.

Queen Victoria to Viscount Palmerston.

SERVICE RETRENCHMENTS

Buckingham Palace, *12th April 1856*.

The Queen returns the draft of Treaty, which she approves, and of which she would wish to have a copy.

The Queen believes that the Cabinet are going to consider to-day the amount of retrenchments which may be necessary in the Army and Navy.

She trusts and *expects* that this will be done with great *moderation* and very *gradually*; and that the difficulties we have had, and the sufferings which we have endured, may not be forgotten, for to the miserable reductions of the last thirty years are entirely owing our state of *helplessness* when the War began; and it would be unpardonable if we were to be found in a similar condition, when another War—and *who* can tell *how* soon there may be one?—breaks out.

We must *never* for a moment forget the very peculiar state of France, and *how entirely all there* depends upon *one* man's life.

We *ought* and *must* be prepared for every *eventuality*, and we have splendid material in that magnificent little Army in the Crimea.

The Queen wishes Lord Palmerston to show this letter to the Cabinet.

The Emperor of the French to Queen Victoria.

LETTER FROM THE EMPEROR

Paris, *le 12 Avril 1856.*

Madame et très chère Sœur,—Votre Majesté m'a fait grand plaisir en me disant qu'elle était satisfaite de la conclusion de la paix, car ma constante préoccupation a été, tout en désirant la fin d'une guerre ruineuse, de n'agir que de concert avec le Gouvernement de votre Majesté. Certes je conçois bien qu'il ait été désirable d'obtenir encore de meilleurs résultats, mais était-ce raisonnable d'en attendre de la manière dont la guerre avait été engagée? J'avoue que je ne le crois pas. La guerre avait été trop lentement conduite par nos généraux et nos amiraux et nous avions laissé le temps aux Russes de se rendre presque imprenables à Cronstadt comme en Crimée. Je crois donc que nous aurions payé trop chèrement sous tous les rapports les avantages que nous eussions pu obtenir. Je suis pour cette raison heureux de la paix, mais je suis heureux surtout que notre Alliance sorte intacte des conférences et qu'elle se montre à l'Europe aussi solide que le premier jour de *notre union.* (Je prie le Prince Albert de ne pas être jaloux de cette expression.)

Nous avons appris avec la plus vive satisfaction que les projets que votre Majesté avait conçus pour le bonheur de la Princesse Royale allaient bientôt se réaliser. On dit tant de bien du jeune Prince Frédéric Guillaume que je ne doute pas que votre charmante fille ne soit heureuse. L'Impératrice, qui attend avec impatience le moment de pouvoir écrire à votre Majesté, a été bien touchée de votre aimable lettre. Vers le commencement de Mai nous irons à St Cloud où votre souvenir nous y accompagne toujours, car ces lieux nous rappellent le séjour de votre Majesté et nous faisons des vœux pour qu'un si heureux événement puisse se renouveler.

Je prie votre Majesté de me rappeler au souvenir du Prince Albert et de recevoir avec bonté l'assurance des sentiments de respectueuse amitié avec lesquels je suis, de votre Majesté, le dévoué Frère et Ami,

Napoléon.

Queen Victoria to Viscount Hardinge.

Buckingham Palace, *21st April 1856.*

The Queen has heard from Colonel Phipps that Lord Hardinge is most anxious for her sanction to the paper submitted yesterday, if even as merely a temporary measure, before the mail goes this evening, as all the shipping at Balaklava is waiting for it. She hopes Lord Hardinge will see how inconvenient and unpleasant it must be to the Queen to have important matters submitted at such short notice that they cannot even be discussed by her without detriment to the public service, and trusts that she may not again be placed in a similar position. She has now signed the paper, but *only* as a temporary measure, and upon the understanding that Lord Hardinge will submit to her, between this and the next mail, the arrangements which are now wanting.

She has also signed the proposal about Canada, but must express her conviction that General Le Marchant,[194] as Civil Governor of the Colony, cannot possibly attend to the command of the Brigade, which ought to have a distinct Commander. There may be Artillery in Canada, but is it horsed? and in Batteries?

We are rapidly falling back into the old ways!

Queen Victoria to the King of the Belgians.

Buckingham Palace, *6th May 1856.*

My dearest Uncle,—Having returned late from a drive, I have but little time to spare to thank you for your kind letter of the 2nd. Last Thursday (1st) was our darling Arthur's sixth birthday, which he enjoyed duly. On the 3rd we received Brunnow[195]—who was so nervous and humble, and so *ému* that he could hardly speak. He dines with us to-night, and the dinner is given for him, being a *funny collection of antagonistic elements*—Granville, Clarendon, Lansdowne, Aberdeen, Graham, John Russell, Derby, and Malmesbury! "The Happy Family," I call it.

The Opposition have taken the line of disapproving the Peace and showing great hostility to Russia.

To-morrow we have a Levée, and on Thursday a ball in our fine new room, which we open on that day; and on Friday there is a *Peace*

[194] Sir John Gaspard Le Marchant, 1803-1874, Lieutenant-Governor of Nova Scotia from 1852 to 1857.

[195] He had come to England, charged with a special mission.

Fête at the Crystal Palace. On Saturday we go out of town; and now I must end, begging to be forgiven for so hurried a scrawl, but I had to write a long letter and to *sit* to Winterhalter. Ever your devoted Niece,

Victoria R.

Queen Victoria to Mr Labouchere.

COLONIAL GOVERNORSHIPS

Osborne, *14th May 1856.*

The Queen has received Mr Labouchere's letter, and hastens to express her opinion that Mr Wilson[196] would not be at all a proper person to be Governor of so large and important a Colony as Victoria. It ought to be a man of higher position and standing, and who could represent his Sovereign adequately....

She wishes further to observe that Mr Labouchere should in future take care that, while he tries to ascertain the feelings of people as to their accepting the offer of a Colonial appointment, before he submits them to the Queen, that these enquiries should be made in such a manner as not to lead these persons to *expect* the appointment, else, if the *Queen* does not approve of them, the whole odium of the refusal will fall upon her. The best way, and the way in which similar appointments are conducted in the other Offices, would be to mention the names first to the Queen, and if she approves of them, to ascertain the feelings of the respective candidates. This would avoid all difficulties on the subject.

Queen Victoria to Mr Labouchere.

14th May 1856.

The Queen would quite approve of the selection of Sir H. Bulwer, Lord Lyttelton, or Sir H. Barkly for Victoria. She is decidedly of opinion that the Governor should be an Englishman and not a Colonist. Now that self-Government has been established in the Colonies, the person of the Governor is the only connection remaining with the Mother Country; and if the Government were once filled from among the public men in the Colonies, this would become a precedent most

[196] James Wilson, the founder of *The Economist*, was at this time Financial Secretary to the Treasury. In 1859 he accepted the new office of Financial Member of the Council of India, but died in the following year.

difficult to break through again, and possibly paving the way for total separation.[197]

Queen Victoria to Sir Charles Wood.

NAVAL POLICY

Osborne, *18th May 1856.*

The Queen has to thank Sir C. Wood for his long and clear statement as to the present position of the Naval Force, which she quite understands. She attaches the greatest importance to perfect faith being kept with the sailors, and on that account was distressed to hear of the misapprehension at Portsmouth the other day.

A good system for a Naval Reserve would be most important. The Queen thinks a Commission, composed chiefly of *younger officers* still conversant with the *present* feelings of our sailors, would best be able to advise on the subject; the old Admirals are always and not unnaturally somewhat behind their time.

With respect to the policy of not too rapidly reducing our naval armaments, Sir C. Wood only anticipates the Queen's most anxious wish on this subject, for we cannot tell what may not happen anywhere at any moment; our relations with America are very unsettled, and our Alliance with France *depends* upon the life of one man. And it is best to be prepared, for else you excite suspicion if you have suddenly to make preparations without being *able* to state for what they are intended.

With regard to the Sailors' Homes, the Queen concurs in the advantage of leaving them to private management; but the Government, having so large a stake in the sailors' welfare, would act wisely and justly to make a handsome donation to all of them at the present moment, taking care that this should be used by the different establishments for their permanent extension. Five thousand pounds amongst them would be by no means an unreasonable sum to give as a token of the interest taken in the well-being of these brave men when no immediate return in shape of service was expected for it.

---

[197] Sir Henry Bulwer declined. Sir Henry Barkly was appointed.

Queen Victoria to Viscount Palmerston.

Osborne, *21st May 1856.*

The Queen is very anxious about the fixing of our Peace establishment both for the Army and Navy. Although Lord Hardinge's proposals are before the Government already for some time, no proposal has yet been submitted to the Queen; and on enquiry from Sir C. Wood, he stated but two days ago that no reduction of the Navy was yet settled. On the other hand, the Queen sees from the Chancellor of the Exchequer's speech that he specifies the sums by which both Army and Navy estimates are to be reduced. This *prejudges* the whole question, and will deprive the Government of all power freely to consider these important questions. The Queen was, moreover, sorry to find Mr Disraeli, Mr Gladstone, and Sir Francis Baring agreeing with the doctrine of the *Times* and Lord Grey that we ought *not* to improve our state of preparation for war; and if we had been better prepared for the late war, we should have been still more disappointed.[198]

Memorandum by Queen Victoria.

TITLE OF PRINCE CONSORT

Windsor Castle, *May 1856.*

It is a strange omission in our Constitution that while *the wife* of a *King* has the highest rank and dignity in the realm after her husband assigned to her by law, the *husband* of a *Queen regnant* is entirely ignored by the law. This is the more extraordinary, as a husband has in this country such particular rights and such great power over his wife, and as the Queen is married just as any other woman is, and swears to obey her lord and master, as such, while by law he has no rank or defined position. This is a strange anomaly. No doubt, as is the case *now*—the Queen *can* give her husband the highest *place* by *placing* him *always near her person*, and the Nation would give it him as a *matter of course*. Still, when I first married, we had much difficulty on this subject; much bad feeling was shown, and several members of the Royal Family showed bad grace in giving precedence to the Prince, and the late King of Hanover positively resisted doing so. I gave the

[198] In the course of an elaborate reply, Lord Palmerston stated that the country had never been in a better condition of defence than at the present time, but he insisted that the Militia, which from 1815 to 1832 had been allowed to become extinct, must be maintained in an efficient state—120,000 strong.

Prince precedence by issuing Letters Patent, but these give no rank in Parliament—or at the Council Board—and it would be far better to put this question beyond all doubt, and to secure its settlement for *all future Consorts of Queens*, and thus have this omission in the Constitution rectified. Naturally my own feeling would be to give the Prince the same title and rank as I have, but a Titular King is a complete novelty in this country, and might be productive of more inconveniences than advantages to the individual who bears it. Therefore, upon mature reflection, and after considering the question for nearly *sixteen years*, I have come to the conclusion that the title which is now by universal consent given him of "Prince Consort," with the highest rank in and out of ParliamentPRECEDENCE OF PRINCE ALBERT immediately after the Queen, and before every other Prince of the Royal Family, should be the one assigned to the husband of the Queen regnant *once and for all*. This ought to be done before our children grow up, and it seems peculiarly easy to do so *now* that none of the old branches of the Royal Family are still alive.

The present position is this: that while every British subject, down to the Knight, Bachelor, Doctor, and Esquire, has a rank and position by *Law*, the Queen's husband alone has one by *favour*—and by his wife's favour, who may grant it or not! When granted as in the present case, it does not extend to Parliament and the Council, and the children may deny the position which their mother has given to their father as a usurpation over them, having the law on their side; or if they waive their rights in his favour, he will hold a position granted by the forbearance of his children. In both cases this is a position most derogatory to the Queen as well as to her husband, and most dangerous to the peace and well-being of her family. If the children resist, the Queen will have her husband pushed away from her side by her children, and they will take precedence over the man whom she is bound to obey; if they are dutiful, she will owe her peace of mind to their continued generosity.

With relation to Foreign Courts, the Queen's position is equally humiliating in this respect. *Some* Sovereigns (crowned heads) address her husband as "Brother," some as "Brother and Cousin," some merely as "Cousin." When the Queen has been abroad, her husband's position has always been a subject of negotiation and vexation; the position which has been accorded to him the Queen has always had to acknowledge as a grace and favour bestowed on her by the Sovereign whom she visited. While last year the Emperor of the French treated the Prince as a Royal personage, his uncle declined to come to Paris avowedly because he would not give precedence to the Prince; and on the Rhine in 1845 the King of Prussia could not give the place to the Queen's husband which common civility required, because of the presence of an Archduke, the third son of an uncle of the then reigning Emperor of Austria, who would not give the *pas*, and whom the King would not offend.

The only legal position in Europe, according to international law, which the husband of the Queen of England enjoys, is that of a younger brother of the Duke of Saxe-Coburg, and this merely because the English law does not know of him. This is derogatory to the dignity of the Crown of England.

But *nationally* also it is an injury to the position of the Crown that the Queen's husband should have no other title than that of Prince of Saxe-Coburg, and thus be perpetually represented to the country as a foreigner. "The Queen and her foreign husband, the Prince Albert of Saxe-Coburg and Gotha!"

The Queen has a right to claim that her husband should be an Englishman, bearing an English title, and enjoying a legal position which she has not to defend with a wife's anxiety as a usurpation against her own children, her subjects, and Foreign Courts.

The question has often been discussed by me with different Prime Ministers and Lord Chancellors, who have invariably entirely agreed with me; but the wish to wait for a good moment to bring the matter before Parliament has caused one year after another to elapse without anything being done. If I become *now* more anxious to have it settled, it is in order that it should be so before our children are grown up, that it might not appear to be done in order to guard their father's position against them personally, which could not fail to produce a painful impression upon their minds.

If properly explained to Parliament and the country, I cannot foresee the slightest difficulty in getting such a necessary measure passed, particularly if it be made quite clear to the House of Commons that it is in no way connected with a desire to obtain an increased grant for the Prince.[199]

Victoria R.

---

[199] See *post*, p. 197.

Queen Victoria to Viscount Hardinge.

SABBATARIANISM

Buckingham Palace, *1st June 1856.*

The Queen understands that there is an attempt to be made to prevent the military bands from playing when the Troops march to church on a Sunday.

She is anxious to express to Lord Hardinge her very strong feeling on this subject, and her wish that he should on *no* account give way to such a proposal. *Whatever* has been the custom should be firmly adhered to, and Lord Hardinge is perfectly at liberty to make use of the Queen's name, and say he could not bring such a proposal before her, as he knew she would not consent to it.[200]

Queen Victoria to the King of the Belgians.

WELLINGTON COLLEGE

Buckingham Palace, *3rd June 1856.*

My dearest Uncle,—I hasten to thank you for your very kind letter of yesterday, just received. Your kind *question* puts me into considerable perplexity, and I think I cannot do better than by putting you in full possession of the state of the case.

Our house is very full—and it is *possible* that we may have very shortly the visit of Prince Oscar of Sweden. These Princes have very large *suites*, and I should therefore in such a case be totally unable to lodge you and *them*. But there is another reason. While Fritz Wilhelm is here, *every* spare moment Vicky has (and *I* have, for I must chaperon this loving couple—which takes away so much of my precious time) is devoted to her bridegroom, who is *so* much in love, that, even if he is out driving and walking with her, he is not satisfied, and says he has not seen her, unless he can have her for an hour to himself, when I am naturally bound to be acting as chaperon. Under these circumstances I may truly say that dear Charlotte would have very little enjoyment; she would see very little of Vicky, *I could not* take care of

[200] The custom of bands playing in the public parks on Sundays had been objected to by various religious bodies, and in April a letter on the subject was written to Lord Palmerston by the Archbishop of Canterbury, after which the performances were discontinued, the Government giving way before the threat of a vote of censure. A similar movement was made in opposition to the playing of regimental bands. See *ante*, p. 135, note 71.

her, and I fear it would be anything but agreeable for her. Fritz Wilhelm would besides be miserable if I took Vicky more away from him than I already do, and therefore *while he* is here, it would *not*, I think, be advisable that *Charlotte* should come. Could you *not* come a little in August when the Prince and Princess of Prussia have left us? Or would you prefer coming in October, when we return from Scotland? You will easily believe, dearest Uncle, *what* pleasure it gives me to see you; but I know you will understand the reasons I here give for begging you to delay this dear visit either to August or October....

I had a little hope that the Archduke and Charlotte *might* take a mutual liking; it would be such a good *parti*.

We had an interesting ceremony yesterday, the laying of the first stone of the Wellington College—which is the monument to the memory of the dear old Duke. Dear little Arthur appeared for the first time in public, and I hope you will approve my answer.[201]

Now, dearest Uncle, ever your truly devoted Niece,

Victoria R.

Queen Victoria to Lord Panmure.

Windsor Castle, *12th June 1856*.

The Queen and Prince had intended to take their visitors down to the Camp on Monday next—the *only day* which we shall have for a fortnight free from other engagements—and hears, to her *utter astonishment*, that *all* the troops are gone—not only the Militia, but the 3rd Battalion of the Rifles!—and this without the Queen's hearing *one* word of it! The Queen is the more astonished and annoyed, as Lord Panmure had promised that the Militia regiments should *not* be disembodied until there were other troops to replace them, which will not be the case for some little time. *What* is the cause of this, sudden determination? The Queen is much vexed, as her visitors will not stay long, and are very anxious to visit the Camp; and it is of much importance that Foreign Princes should see what we have, and in what state of efficiency our troops are.

[201] The Queen's reply to an address presented to her, on behalf of the College, by Lord Derby.

Queen Victoria to Viscount Palmerston.

THE NATIONAL GALLERY

Buckingham Palace, *26th June 1856.*

The Queen hopes Lord Palmerston will make it quite clear to the subordinate Members of the Government that they cannot be allowed to vote against the Government proposal about the National Gallery to-morrow, as she hears that several fancy themselves at liberty to do so.

The Earl of Derby to Queen Victoria.[202]

TITLE OF PRINCE CONSORT

St James's Square, *28th June 1856.*

Lord Derby, with his humble duty ... will be prepared, as well as Lord Lyndhurst, to give his cordial support to such a Bill as that sketched out by the Lord Chancellor; but using that freedom which is invited by and due to the gracious confidence reposed in him by your Majesty, he hopes he may be pardoned for earnestly submitting to your Majesty's serious consideration the question whether it may be expedient to raise a discussion on such a subject during the short remainder of the present Session of Parliament. Measures of public importance already in progress are now beginning to be abandoned in consequence of the advanced period of the Session, and Lord Lyndhurst concurs very strongly in Lord Derby's apprehensions as to the result on public feeling of the introduction of such a measure at the present moment. If it could be stated that your Majesty contemplated a foreign visit in the course of the summer, which rendered it desirable that a measure should be passed to obviate the embarrassment which had been created on previous occasions of the same sort, some case might be made out for immediate legislation, though even then the question would arise why it was not thought of sooner; but in the absence of any change of circumstances, and in the present unfortunate

---

[202] The Queen had sent to Lord Derby a copy of her Memorandum, *ante*, p. 194, a letter from Lord Palmerston to herself on the same subject, and the sketch of a Bill drawn up by the Lord Chancellor to give effect to her wishes. On the 25th of June 1857, the title of "Prince Consort" was conferred on Prince Albert by Royal Letters Patent. "I should have preferred," wrote the Queen, "its being done by Act of Parliament, and so it may still be at some future period; but it was thought better upon the whole to do it *now* in this simple way."

temper of the House of Commons, of which a proof was given last night, such a course would probably lead to suspicions and remarks of the most painful character. It would be said, and with some justice, that the greater the constitutional importance of a settlement, the greater was also the necessity of ample opportunity for consideration being given to Parliament; and the hurry of passing the Bill would be cited as a proof that it covered some unavowed and objectionable design. If such suspicions should lead to the postponement of the measure, not only would the Crown have been subjected to a mortifying defeat, but the Bill would be open to the hostile criticisms of the Press during the whole summer and autumn, the effect of which might even endanger its ultimate success....

Should your Majesty be otherwise advised, Lord Derby will be ready to give the Bill his personal support, but he would be wanting in candour if he did not frankly state to your Majesty the serious apprehensions which he should entertain as to the result. Such an unreserved expression of his opinions is the only and very inadequate return which he can make to your Majesty for the gracious confidence with which your Majesty has honoured him, and for which he feels most deeply grateful.

The above is humbly submitted by your Majesty's most dutiful Servant and Subject,

Derby.

Viscount Hardinge to Queen Victoria.

RETIREMENT OF LORD HARDINGE

15 Great Stanhope Street, *10th July 1856.*

Field-Marshal Viscount Hardinge,[203] with his most humble duty to your Majesty, is conscious that his power of serving your Majesty in

[203] A great review of the troops lately returned from the Crimea was held in most unfavourable weather at Aldershot, on the 8th of July, King Leopold among others being present; Lord Hardinge, who had brought with him the Report of the Military Commission which had been sitting at Chelsea, was struck by paralysis during an Audience with the Queen; the next day Lord Panmure wrote: "His leg is entirely useless, and his right arm visibly affected. I spoke to him for a moment as he got into his carriage, and his head is quite clear, but his public career is closed; and knowing his high mind as I do, I would not be surprised to learn that he made a communication to that effect to the Queen very shortly."

the high position of General Commanding-in-Chief has ceased in consequence of the state of his health, which leaves him no other course to pursue than that of placing in your Majesty's hands the resignation of his office, the duties of which his sudden and severe illness has rendered him incapable of performing.

Lord Hardinge cannot take this step without thanking your Majesty for the great consideration and support which he has at all times received at a period of no ordinary difficulty, and which have impressed him with such sentiments of gratitude as can only cease with his life.

All of which is most humbly submitted to your Majesty by your Majesty's dutiful and devoted Servant,

Hardinge.

Queen Victoria to Viscount Palmerston.

Buckingham Palace, *10th July 1856.*

The Queen has received the enclosed letter from Lord Hardinge, conveying his resignation, for which she was prepared. She asks Lord Palmerston to enable her, by the assistance of his advice, soon to appoint a successor to the important office of Commander-in-Chief. She has again considered the question, and is confirmed in her opinion that the Duke of Cambridge stands almost without a competitor.

Queen Victoria to Viscount Hardinge.

Buckingham Palace, *11th July 1856.*

The Queen received yesterday evening Field-Marshal Lord Hardinge's letter resigning his office of Commander-in-Chief. She cannot sufficiently express how deeply grieved she is to feel that from Lord Hardinge's state of health she must accept his resignation. The loss of his services will be immense to the Queen, the country, and the Army—and she trusts that he is well assured of her high sense of the very valuable services he has long rendered. She hopes, however, that she may still reckon on his advice and assistance on matters of importance, though he will no longer command her noble Army.

She cannot conclude without expressing the Prince's and her fervent wishes that he may rapidly recover, and his valuable life be long preserved to all his friends, amongst whom we shall ever consider ourselves.

Viscount Palmerston to Queen Victoria.

THE COMMANDERSHIP-IN-CHIEF

Downing Street, *12th July 1856.*

Viscount Palmerston presents his humble duty to your Majesty, and begs to state that he has consulted with his colleagues as to the advice to be tendered to your Majesty in regard to the appointment of a successor to Lord Hardinge as General Commanding-in-Chief; and upon a full consideration of the subject, the Cabinet are of opinion that your Majesty's choice could not fall upon any General Officer better suited to that important position than His Royal Highness the Duke of Cambridge, and Lord Panmure will have the honour of taking your Majesty's pleasure upon the matter officially.

It seems quite clear that there is no General Officer senior to His Royal Highness the Duke of Cambridge to whom it would in all respects be desirable to intrust the duties of the command of the Army, and there is no General Officer below him in seniority who has claim sufficiently strong to justify his being preferred to His Royal Highness....

Queen Victoria to the Earl of Clarendon.

Buckingham Palace, *13th July 1856.*

The Queen wishes to ask, before she sanctions this draft, whether the Cabinet have fully considered the consequences of this declaration to the Persians, which may be war;[204] and if so, whether they are prepared to go to war with Persia, and have provided the means of carrying it on? The draft itself the Queen approves.

Queen Victoria to the King of the Belgians.

THE DUKE OF CAMBRIDGE

Osborne, *21st July 1856.*

My dearest Uncle,— ... We had a delightful little *séjour* at Aldershot—much favoured by fine weather. The first day, Wednesday, the wind was too high for *me* to ride, but the second (Thursday) we had one of the prettiest and *most* interesting field days I ever remember. I

[204] The Shah, availing himself of the departure of the British Minister from Teheran, laid siege to Herat, in direct violation of a treaty of 1853.

rode about everywhere and enjoyed it so much. On Thursday and Friday morning we visited the Camp. The new Troops from the Crimea which we saw were the 34th, 41st, and 49th, particularly fine Regiments; the 93rd Highlanders, the 2nd Rifle Battalion, and three Companies of splendid Sappers and Miners, all very fine; and the Scots Greys and Enniskillen Dragoons. The Prussians[205] were *émerveillés* at the looks of our Troops on returning from the Crimea! We came here on the 18th, and have really *hot* weather.

George has been appointed Commander-in-Chief. There was really *no one* who could have been put over him; though in some respects it may be a weakness for the Crown, it is a great strength for the Army....

I fear I must end here for to-day. Ever your devoted Niece,

Victoria R.

Viscount Palmerston to Queen Victoria.

Piccadilly, *24th July 1856.*

Viscount Palmerston presents his humble duty to your Majesty, and will give directions for the Council at Osborne at one o'clock on Monday, according to your Majesty's desire; and he would beg to submit for your Majesty's gracious consideration that the General Commanding-in-Chief has usually been a Privy Councillor, and that His Royal Highness the Duke of Cambridge might, if your Majesty thought fit, be sworn in on Monday.

Viscount Palmerston will communicate with Dr. Goodford, but he finds that he was misled by the Headmaster and one of the Governors of Harrow at the Speech Day; he understood from them that an additional week's holiday would at his request be given to the boys at this vacation in commemoration of the Peace. He has now received a letter from the Governors to say that the school had an additional week on the occasion of the Peace at Easter, and that an additional week will be given, not now, but at Christmas, in commemoration of the laying the first stone of the new Chapel. If, therefore, the Eton boys had an additional week at Easter in honour of the Peace, as the Harrow boys had, there will be no reason for any addition to the Eton holidays now....

---

[205] The Prince and Princess of Prussia were on a visit to the Queen and Prince.

Mr Labouchere to Queen Victoria.

SOUTH AFRICA

26th July 1856.

With Mr Labouchere's humble duty to Her Majesty. Mr Labouchere begs to submit the following observations in reply to Her Majesty's enquiries respecting the Free States in the vicinity of the British Colonies in South Africa.

There are two independent States there:—

(1.) The Transvaal Republic, founded by Boers who left the Colony for the most part from ten to fifteen years ago. The territory on which they are established never was British. The Government of the day, thinking it useless and impolitic to pursue them there, entered into a capitulation with them and recognised their independent existence. They inhabit the plains north of the Vaal or Yellow River.

(2.) The Orange River Free State. This occupies the territory between the Vaal River to the north and the Orange River to the south. This territory, like the former, was occupied originally by emigrant Boers, and was beyond the boundaries of the Colony of the Cape of Good Hope. But Sir Harry Smith, in 1849, after a severe military struggle with the Boers, thought proper without authority from home to annex it to British Dominion.[206] This annexation was ratified by Lord Grey, and the country remained for three or four years under British rule. Afterwards it was resolved to abandon it, during the administration of the Duke of Newcastle, as a result of the general revision of our affairs which took place at the conclusion of the Kaffir War. The Orange River Territory was recognised as a separate Republic in 1854.

It is certainly true that the existence of these Free States may complicate our relations with the Kaffirs, and possibly be a source of danger to the security of British dominion in South Africa. But the latter danger seems very remote. They possess *no* portion of the sea coast, and are altogether a pastoral people, and are engaged in a constant struggle with the barbarous tribes in their neighbourhood.

To retain and protect these territories would have involved an immense expenditure, and been attended with great difficulties. Besides, the same question would have speedily recurred, as these emigrant Boers would have soon gone further into the interior, and

[206] See *ante*, vol. ii. pp. 142 and 200.

again have asserted their independence. Our present relations with both these States are very amicable. When Governor Sir George Grey went to the Cape all these questions had been finally disposed of.[207]

There seems to be good reason to hope that the apprehensions of a Kaffir War will not be realised. The Colony is very prosperous, and is beginning to export wool in large quantities. The new legislature appears to be disposed to act harmoniously with the Governor, and to be actuated by a spirit of loyalty and attachment to this country. What they most want is a supply of European settlers, which it is to be hoped that the soldiers of the German and Swiss Legions will give them.

Queen Victoria to the King of the Belgians.

FOREIGN ORDERS

Osborne, *30th July 1856.*

My dearest Uncle,—I am much grieved to have to retract the permission which in my letter of yesterday I said I would give to Lord Westmorland.[208] When I said so, I had *not* received the opinion of the Ministers, which I have since done, and this is, I am sorry to say, conclusive *against* it. I quite overlooked *one* very important case of very late date, viz. the Plenipotentiary at Paris—on whom the Emperor pressed very hard to confer his order in commemoration of the Peace; but it was refused, and the Emperor was a good *deal hurt*. If *now* Lord Westmorland received the permission, the Emperor might with *right* complain. I am much grieved, dearest Uncle, at all this, but it was quite unavoidable, and I was at the time much distressed at your giving the order to Lord Westmorland as I foresaw nothing but difficulties. Ever your devoted Niece,

Victoria R.

---

[207] Sir George Grey had been sent out by the Duke of Newcastle in 1854. He had previously been Governor of South Australia and New Zealand successively. He returned to New Zealand as Governor in 1861, and was Premier of the Colony, 1877-1884. He died in 1898, and was buried in St Paul's Cathedral.

[208] King Leopold had proposed to bestow a decoration on Lord Westmorland.

The King of the Belgians to Queen Victoria.

Laeken, *1st August 1856.*

My dearest Victoria,— ... When your excellent Ministers will consider things coolly, which is not to be expected in this hot weather, I am sure they will come to other conclusions. The rule is a *very wise one*, and has been kept up even at the time of those great congresses of Paris, Vienna, and ditto Paris in 1815. But in cases of particular affection and feeling *not* connected with politics, there have been during the reigns of George IV. and William IV. exceptions. The Duke of Devonshire was sent to the Coronation, I think, of the Emperor Nicholas, because one knew the Emperor liked him. And he has worn ever since that diamond star of the St Andrew of the largest dimensions.

Our Napoleon is too wise not to understand that a treaty has a direct political character. And, during the next fifty years of your glorious reign, there will be most probably a great many more treaties and congresses. You may get all sorts of things during that time, but you cannot either by the power of heaven or of earth get a new uncle, who has kept his word twenty-five years; rather an undertaking considering circumstances.... I remain, my dearest Victoria, your devoted Uncle,

Leopold R.

Queen Victoria to the King of the Belgians.

On Board the *Victoria and Albert*,

14th August 1856.

Dearest Uncle,—You will be surprised to get a letter so soon again from me, and still more on *so* trivial a subject, but I come as a petitioner for a supply of the cakes or *Oblaten* which you kindly always send me, but which have come to a dead *stop*, having been too rapidly consumed; *all* the children having taken to eat them. As I am not a very good breakfast eater, they are often the *only* things I *can* take at that time, and consequently I miss them much. May I therefore beg them to be sent?

We are still here; profiting by the *bad* sea, to visit many beautiful *points de vue* in this really beautiful country. We saw yesterday one of the loveliest places possible—*Endsleigh*—the Duke of Bedford's, about twenty miles from here.

The weather is so bad, and it blows so hard, that we shall go back to Southampton to-morrow by railroad—a beautiful line which we have never seen. I must close in haste. Ever your devoted Niece,

Victoria R.

We went to Saltram, Lord Morley's, this afternoon.

Earl Granville to Queen Victoria.[209]

LORD GRANVILLE'S MISSION

Moscow, *30th August 1856.*

Lord Granville presents his humble duty to your Majesty, and begs, according to your Majesty's desire, to submit to your Majesty the impressions which he has received during the short time of his stay in this country.

THE CZAR ALEXANDER

Lord Granville's conversation with the Emperor of Russia, and what he has heard from various reliable sources, have led him to the following conclusions respecting His Imperial Majesty.

He is handsome, but thinner and graver than when he was in England. When speaking with energy to Lord Granville his manner seemed to be rather an imitation of some one else than his own, and he did not look Lord Granville in the face. His usual manner is singularly gentle and pleasing. He does not give the idea of having much strength either of intellect or of character, but looks intelligent and amiable. Although the education of a Cæsarwitch must be subject to pernicious influences, the present Emperor has had advantages which those in his position have not usually had. The Emperor Nicholas came to the throne without having had the confidences of his predecessor. He initiated his son into everything that was going on, while others who knew the good-nature of the Grand Duke Alexander's character, told him that which they did not tell his father. He was supposed to have different tastes from the late Emperor, but, since the death of the latter, he has liked the late Emperor's favourite residence which he himself had formerly disliked, he has taken to all the military pursuits of his father, and is said to have shown undignified haste in issuing regulations about, and in appearing in, new uniforms. He is liked by those who surround him, but is blamed for not having those habits of punctuality

[209] Lord Granville was appointed head of a special mission, with the temporary rank of Ambassador, to attend the Coronation of the Czar Alexander.

and of quick decision in business which characterised the late Emperor.

There is still much talk of stimulants to be applied by His Imperial Majesty to commerce and to the development of the resources of the country.... There are persons, however, here well qualified to judge, who doubt whether much more will be performed than has formerly been done, after brilliant promises at the beginning of a reign. His Imperial Majesty is not supposed to have that power of will which will enable him to deal with the mass of corruption which pervades every class in this country. The Empress,[210] a woman of sense and ability, is believed to have great influence with her husband when he is with her, but he is generally guided by the person who speaks last to him before he acts—and His Imperial Majesty has not the talent of surrounding himself with able men. His Ministers certainly do not appear to be men of that remarkable intellect as have been usually supposed to be employed by the Court of St Petersburg. Count Orloff is stated to have but little influence, and to have lost his former activity. Prince Gortschakoff is clever in society, of easy conversation and some smartness in repartee. He is vain, a great talker, and indiscreet. It is difficult to keep him to the point. He flies about from one thing to another, and he is so loose in his talk, that the repetition of isolated phrases might lead to impressions of his meaning, which would not be correct....

The Serf Question is admitted by all to be of a very difficult character, and will become more so as the wealth of the country increases. Indeed when that state of things occurs, it is more than likely that popular movements will take place, and it is frightful to consider the immediate results of a revolution in a country organised as this is at present. No country in Europe will furnish so fair a chance of success to Socialism. The reins of Government were held so tight during the last reign, that even the relaxation which now exists is not altogether without danger.

CORONATION OF THE CZAR

The preparations for the Coronation are on an immense scale. The present estimate of the expenses is £1,000,000; the last Coronation cost half that sum; the Coronation of Alexander, £150,000; while that of the Emperor Paul did not exceed £50,000. The military household

---

[210] Marie Alexandrovna, formerly the Princess Marie of Hesse, daughter of the Grand Duke Louis II.

of the present Emperor consists of one hundred and twenty generals—that of Nicholas, at the beginning of his reign, consisted of twenty.

Your Majesty is spoken of by the Emperor and by the Society here with the greatest respect. Lord and Lady Granville have met with nothing but remarkable civility from all classes.

Lord Granville has had great pleasure in seeing His Royal Highness Prince Frederick William of Prussia in such good health and spirits. His only anxiety was an interval of fourteen days during which His Royal Highness did not hear from England. That anxiety has been relieved by a letter received to-day. Lord Granville ventures to request your Majesty to present his respectful remembrances to the Princess Royal with his congratulations at Her Royal Highness's complete recovery. Lord Granville begs to advise Her Royal Highness, when residing abroad, not to engage a Russian maid. Lady Wodehouse found hers eating the contents of a pot on her dressing-table—it happened to be castor oil pomatum for the hair.

Lord Granville has been requested to convey to your Majesty and to His Royal Highness Prince Albert the Prince of Nassau's expressions of devotion and respect. The atmosphere in which His Highness at present resides does not appear to have had much influence on His Highness's opinions.

Viscount Palmerston to Queen Victoria.

CHURCH APPOINTMENTS

St Leonards, *6th September 1856.*

Viscount Palmerston presents his humble duty to your Majesty, and begs to submit for your Majesty's gracious approval that Dr Tait, Dean of Carlisle, should be appointed Bishop of London with a clear explanation to him that the Diocese will probably be divided into two—one of London and one of Westminster.

That the Bishop of Ripon[211] should be appointed Bishop of Durham, with a like explanation that the Diocese of Durham may possibly be divided into two—one for Durham and one for Northumberland.

That the Dean of Hereford[212] should be appointed Bishop of Ripon; and that Dr Trench[213] be appointed Dean of Westminster with

[211] Charles Thomas Longley (1774-1868) became Bishop of Durham 1856, Archbishop of York 1860, and Archbishop of Canterbury 1862.

the condition that he is not to receive any fees or emoluments arising out of appointments of Knights of the Bath.

Dr Trench is a man of the world and of literature, and would in those respects be well suited to be Dean of Westminster, and if his tendencies are, as some persons suppose, rather towards High Church opinions, his position as Dean would not afford him any particular means of making those opinions prevail; while his appointment would show that the patronage of the Crown was not flowing exclusively in one direction.

Viscount Palmerston will, on another occasion, submit to your Majesty the names of persons for the Deaneries of Hereford and Carlisle.[214]

The Duke of Cambridge to Queen Victoria.

St James's Palace, *17th September 1856.*

My dear Cousin,—This morning the reply from Baden reached me, and I hasten to inform you at once of the purport of it, embodied in a very excellent letter written by my sister Mary, who *declines* the proposal made to her on the part of the King of Sardinia, for some very excellent and weighty reasons.[215]

---

[212] Richard Dawes, who became Dean in 1850, and restored the Cathedral. He did not become Bishop of Ripon; Robert Bickersteth, a Canon of Salisbury, being eventually appointed. See *post*, p. 217, note 60.

[213] Richard Chenevix Trench (1807-1886), Archbishop of Dublin from 1864-1884.

[214] Francis Close (1797-1882), Rector of Cheltenham, succeeded Dr Tait as Dean of Carlisle.

[215] The King had, in January 1855, lost his consort, Queen Marie Adélaïde, daughter of the Archduke Rénier of Austria. Lord Clarendon wrote to Baron Marochetti:—...

"The Queen's first care was for the happiness of Princess Mary, and it was the wish of Her Majesty and of Her Majesty's Government that the decision should be left to the unbiassed judgment of Her Royal Highness.

"Princess Mary, having maturely weighed the matter in all its different bearings, has come to the conclusion that it is her duty as regards both the King of Sardinia and herself to decline the offer, which you were empowered to make on the part of His Majesty.

"Princess Mary fully appreciates the many excellent and noble qualities of the King. She does not doubt that in him individually she would be happy,

I must confess that I fully agree with her in the view she has taken, and, I can say with truth, that I think her decision is a very judicious and very correct one, and I am not at all sorry she has come to it. As I know that Clarendon was very anxious to have an early reply, I have in the first instance sent Mary's letter on to him, and have requested him, after perusing it, to send it on to you, and I hope you will not think that I have been wanting in respect to you in so doing. With many thanks to you for your great kindness in having left the decision of this weighty matter entirely in our hands, I beg to remain, my dear Cousin, your most dutiful Cousin,

George.

Queen Victoria to the King of the Belgians.

THE KING OF PORTUGAL

Balmoral, *19th September 1856.*

My dearest Uncle,—I cannot have your kind and confidential letter of the 15th answered, and therefore write to-day to thank you for it.

---

and she thinks that the alliance would be popular in England; but Her Royal Highness feels that as the Protestant Queen of Sardinia she must be in a false position, and that a wife can never find herself thus placed without injury to her husband.

"Princess Mary is deeply attached to her religion, which is the first consideration in this world, and in the free and undisturbed exercise of that religion, however much it might be sanctioned by the King, and supported by His Majesty's Government, she feels that she would be the object of constant suspicion, that her motives would be liable to misconstruction, and that the King would be exposed to grave embarrassments, which time would only serve to increase.

"I am not surprised at this decision, which, from my knowledge of Princess Mary's profound religious feeling, I rather led you to anticipate; but I am bound to say that with reference to her religion, and with reference to that alone, Her Royal Highness has, in my opinion, decided with wisdom and foresight.

"I am convinced, however, that in renouncing upon conscientious grounds the brilliant position which has been offered to her, of which she fully appreciated the advantages, Princess Mary can only have added to the respect which the King already feels for the noble and elevated character of Her Royal Highness."

You may rely on our divulging nothing. We are, however, both very anxious that dear Pedro should be preferred.[216] He is out and out *the* most distinguished young Prince there is, and besides that, good, excellent, and steady according to one's heart's desire, and as one could wish for an *only and beloved daughter.* For Portugal, too, an *amiable*, well-educated Queen would be an immense blessing, for there *never* has been one. I am sure you would be more likely to secure Charlotte's happiness if you gave her to Pedro than to one of those innumerable Archdukes, or to Prince George of Saxony. Pedro should, however, be written to, if you were favourably inclined towards him.

I must end now, hoping soon to hear from you again. Pedro is *just* nineteen; he can therefore well wait till he has completed his twentieth year. Ever your devoted Niece,

Victoria R.

Queen Victoria to the Empress of the French.

RUSSIAN PROCRASTINATION

[*Draft.*][217]

Septembre 1856.

Je regrette autant que V.M.I. les divergences existantes entre les vues de nos deux Gouvernements au sujet du Traité de Paris.[218] [Il est impossible pour nous cependant de céder aux Russes les demandes qu'ils mettent en avant, seulement parcequ'elles sont soutenues par la France. Le fait est que] Ma manière d'envisager la situation actuelle est

---

216 Both the Queen and King Leopold were desirous of arranging a marriage between King Pedro and the Princess Charlotte, which, however, did not take place. See *post* pp. 211, 234, note 19, and 332, note 35.

217 This is the original draft, which appears to have been modified later by the omission of the sentences in brackets.

218 The Treaty had involved the restitution of the fortress and district of Kars to Turkey. The Russians, however, delayed the stipulated evacuation in an unwarrantable manner. Ismail also was included within the portion of Bessarabia to be ceded to Turkey, but, instead of surrendering it intact, the Russians destroyed its fortifications; they also laid claim to Serpent's Island at the mouth of the Danube, which was within the ceded portion, and of Bolgrad, the future ownership of which was, owing to the inaccuracies of maps, in dispute. The English Government sent a fleet to the Black Sea to enforce the obligations of the Treaty, while the French Government seemed to make unnecessary concessions to Russia.

celle-ci: les Russes ne cessent de suivre la même politique dès le commencement de la complication Orientale jusqu'à présent. Ils cèdent où la force majeure les y contraint, mais tâchent de se réserver par des chicanes ou subterfuges les moyens de reprendre à un temps plus opportun leurs attaques sur l'indépendance et l'intégrité de cette pauvre Turquie. [Nous au contraire sommes déterminés.] La France et l'Angleterre au contraire ont manifesté leur détermination de la sauver et de l'assurer contre ces attaques. C'était là la cause de la guerre; c'était là le but de la paix; mon Gouvernement n'oserait le sacrifier vis-à-vis de mon peuple par complaisance envers l'Empereur de Russie. Un coup d'oeil sur la Carte, par exemple, démontre qu'en détruisant Ismail, Kilia, etc., etc. [(acte auquel nous ne venons qu'à présent d'apprendre que la France avait donné son assentiment à notre insu)] la Russie a privé l'aile droite de la nouvelle ligne de frontière de toute défense; tandis qu'en substituant le nouveau Bolgrad à celui connu au Congrès elle pousserait un point stratégique au centre, couperait la partie cédée de la Bessarabie du reste de l'Empire Ottoman, et se mettrait à même de devenir de nouveau maîtresse de la rive gauche du Danube, quand elle le voudra. Comme dans ce cas [nous] nos deux pays sont tenus par Traité à reprendre les armes, il me paraît de notre devoir à prévenir de tels dangers. Ces dangers seront écartés à l'instant que la France s'unira à nous pour tenir un langage ferme à la Russie, qui tâche de nous désunir et il ne faut pas qu'elle y réussisse.

Je vous exprime là toute ma pensée, sachant que l'Empereur attend une franchise entière de son amie, convaincue aussi, que si son opinion diffère de la mienne, c'est dû au moins d'importance qu'il attache peut-être aux points en dispute avec la Russie, et à un sentiment de générosité envers un ennemi vaincu, auquel il me serait doux de m'abandonner avec lui, si je pouvais le faire de manière à concilier les intérêts de la Turquie et de l'Europe.

The Earl of Clarendon to Queen Victoria.

ALTERATIONS SUGGESTED

Taymouth, *21st September 1856.*

Lord Clarendon presents his humble duty to your Majesty, and humbly ventures to express his opinion that the Empress might think the tone of your Majesty's letter rather too severe. It is by no means severe, but perfectly just and true as regards the conduct of Russia and

France, and on that very account it might wound the *amour-propre* of the Emperor.

Lord Clarendon ventures to suggest the omission of the second sentence beginning by "*il est impossible*," and of the parenthesis at the bottom of the second page.[219] In the concluding sentence it might perhaps be better to say "*la France et l'Angleterre*" instead of "*nous*," which would possibly be taken as an announcement of separate action. Your Majesty might perhaps think it right to add after the last words "*tels dangers*"—"*ces dangers seront écartés à l'instant que la France s'unira à nous pour tenir un langage ferme à la Russie qui tâche de nous désunir et il ne faut pas qu'elle y réussisse.*"[220]

Queen Victoria to the Duke of Cambridge.

Balmoral, *22nd September 1856.*

My dear George,—I waited to thank you for your letter of the 17th till I had received Mary's from Lord Clarendon, which I did yesterday morning, and which I now return to you. It is admirably written, and does dear Mary the greatest credit; she puts it on the *right* ground, viz. that of the *Protestant feeling* which should *always* actuate our family, and to this we *now must* keep. It *effectually* closes, however, the door to *all Catholic* proposals—whether from Kings or Princes, which makes matters easier.

I must say, however, that I think it very wrong of *certain* ladies to have spoken of Mary's feelings and wishes on the subject, which has no doubt encouraged the idea when they had no reason for doing so.

I am very glad that the decision has been so entirely dear Mary's own, and that *she is* convinced of my anxious wish for her happiness and welfare—which I have as much at heart as if she were my own sister.

It is very necessary, however, that *not* a word should be breathed of this whole affair, and I trust that you will caution your mother and sisters and their relations to be very silent on the subject, as it would be otherwise very offensive to the King.

With Albert's love, ever your very affectionate Cousin,

Victoria R.

---

[219] *I.e.* the passage from "acte auquel" to "notre insu."

[220] The Prince wrote in reply to this letter: "The draft of letter to the Empress of the French has been altered in every particular as you suggest, and I will send you a corrected copy of it by to-morrow." See *post*, p. 213, note 54.

Queen Victoria to Viscountess Hardinge.

DEATH OF LORD HARDINGE

Balmoral, *26th September 1856.*

My dear Lady Hardinge,—Where can I find words to express to you our *deep heartfelt* sorrow at the sad and totally unexpected news conveyed to us by telegraph yesterday.[221]

My first thought was for you, dear Lady Hardinge, whose whole existence was so completely bound up in *his*, that this blow must be awful indeed. We feel *truly* and sincerely what we, and the country, have lost in your dear, high-minded, noble husband, whose *only* thought was *his duty*. A more loyal, devoted, fearless public servant the Crown never possessed. His loss to *me* is one of those which in our times is quite *irreparable*. Added to all this we have ever had *such* a true affection and personal friendship for dear Lord Hardinge, and know how warmly these feelings were requited. *All* who had the pleasure of knowing him must ever remember his benevolent smile and kind eye.

But I speak of ourselves and of what we have lost, when I *ought* only to express *our* sympathy with *you*, in your present overwhelming loss, but I could not restrain my pen, and the expression of our feelings may perhaps be soothing to your bleeding heart.

Most truly also do we sympathise with your children.

Pray do not think of answering this yourself, but let us hear through your son or daughter how you are. Ever, dear Lady Hardinge, with the sincerest regard and truest sympathy, yours affectionately,

Victoria R.

The King of the Belgians to Queen Victoria.

THE ARCHDUKE MAXIMILIAN

Laeken, *10th October 1856.*

My dearest Victoria,—Since your kind letter of the 2nd I have not had any communications from you. I can well understand that it grieves you to leave the Highlands. It is not a great proof of the happiness of human kind, that all love to be elsewhere than at the place

[221] Lord Hardinge, who had only temporarily rallied from the stroke he had received at Aldershot, died on the 24th.

where their real residence is, notwithstanding all songs of home sweet home, etc. I plead quite guilty to this, though I used to be much attached to my old home at Coburg and to Claremont. That the weather should have been unfavourable is a great pity; here we have had a most beautiful and mild weather till the 8th, when a severe thunderstorm put an end to it.

Poor Lord Hardinge! I believe after all, though all these people pretend *not* to mind it, that the Press killed him. I once told Lady Maryborough and the late Duchess of Wellington that it was fortunate the Duke cared so little for the Press. "Care little," they said, "why, nothing annoys and irritates him more." I find it natural; doing one's best, working with all one's nerves, and to be abused for it, is not pleasant.

To explain the real state of dear Charlotte's affair I enclose the only copy of my letter which exists, and pray you kindly to send it me back. My object is and was that Charlotte should decide as *she* likes it, and uninfluenced by what I might prefer. *I* should *prefer* Pedro, that I confess, but the Archduke[222] has made a favourable impression on Charlotte; I saw that long before any question of engagement had taken place. The Archduke is out at sea, and nothing can well be heard before the 25th of this month. If the thing takes place the Emperor ought to put him at the head of Venice; he is well calculated for it.

I am going on the 15th to Ardenne for a week. I have been since that revolution of 1848 kept away from it almost entirely, compared to former days. And now, with my best love to Albert, I must end, remaining ever, my dearest Victoria, your truly devoted and only Uncle,

Leopold R.

Queen Victoria to the King of the Belgians.

Balmoral, *13th October 1856.*

My dearest Uncle,—I am truly thankful for your kind letter and the very confidential enclosure which I return, and which has interested us both very much, and is truly kind and paternal. I *still hope* by your letter that Charlotte has not finally made up her mind—as we both feel so strongly convinced of the immense superiority of Pedro over any other young Prince even *dans les relations journalistes*, be-

[222] The Archduke Ferdinand Maximilian Joseph of Austria, afterwards Emperor of Mexico.

sides which the position is so infinitely preferable. The Austrian society is *médisante* and profligate and worthless—and the Italian possessions very shaky. Pedro is full of resource—fond of music, fond of drawing, of languages, of natural history, and literature, in all of which Charlotte would suit him, and would be a *real* benefit to the country. If Charlotte asked *me*, I should not hesitate a moment, as I would give any of my own daughters to him were he not a Catholic; and if Charlotte consulted her friend Vicky I know what *her* answer would be as she is so very fond of Pedro.

14th.—I could not finish last night, and so continue to-day. I shall be most anxious to hear from you about Charlotte, when a *final* decision has been taken.

Since the 6th we have the *most beautiful weather*—with the country in the *most* brilliant beauty—but *not* the bracing weather which did one so much good; yesterday and to-day it is *quite* warm and relaxing. Albert has continued to have wonderful sport; not only has he killed seven more stags since I wrote, but the finest, largest stags in the whole neighbourhood—or indeed killed in almost any forest!...

Ever your devoted Niece,

Victoria R.

Queen Victoria to Lord Panmure.

MILITARY EFFICIENCY

Windsor Castle, *9th November 1856.*

The Queen has received Lord Panmure's two boxes of the 4th. She is glad to hear that the Military and the Defence Committees of the Cabinet are to be reassembled. The absence of all plans for our defences is a great evil, and hardly credible. There should exist a well-considered general scheme for each place supported by a detailed argument; this when approved by the Government, should be sanctioned and signed by the Sovereign, and not deviated from except upon re-submission and full explanation of the causes which render such deviation necessary; no special work should be undertaken which does not realise part of this general scheme. The Queen trusts that Lord Panmure will succeed in effecting this.

It is very much to be regretted that so few of the soldiers of the German Legion should have accepted the liberal terms of the Government. Those should, however, be made to sail soon.

The returns of the different Departments for the last quarter show a lamentable deficiency in small arms. Fifty-two thousand three hundred and twenty-two for the whole of the United Kingdom is a sadly small reserve to have in store; we should never be short of 500,000. The Queen was struck also with the little work done at Enfield. It appears that during the whole quarter this new and extensive establishment has completed only three muskets!

With regard to some of the barracks, the tenders have not even yet been accepted, although the year is nearly drawing to a close. The Queen hopes soon to receive the returns for the Fortification Department, which is fully two months in arrear....

With respect to the list for the Bath, the Queen is somewhat startled by the large number. Before sanctioning it, she thinks it right to ask for an explanation of the services of the officers, and the reasons for which they are selected for the honour. She returns the list for that purpose to Lord Panmure, who will perhaps cause the statement to be attached to each name. This, of course, does not apply to the foreigners. Amongst the Sardinians, however, the Queen observes the absence of the names of the Military Commissioners attached first to Lord Raglan and afterwards to General Simpson. The first was a Count Revel, who has frequently applied for the honour, and the Queen thinks ought to have it.

The Earl of Clarendon to Queen Victoria.

FRANCE AND RUSSIA

Foreign Office, *10th November 1856.*

Lord Clarendon presents his humble duty, and humbly begs to transmit a letter from the Empress which was left here this afternoon by M. de Persigny, who also left a despatch from Count Walewski, of which Lord Clarendon begs to transmit a copy.[223] It is a most unsatis-

[223] Count Walewski had written to Count Persigny: "The communications which I have received give us cause to fear that Her Majesty's Government may persist in declining the proposal to reassemble the Conference.... We only know of five Powers which have had an opportunity to express an opinion on the point at issue.... It appears that Sardinia has not yet formed her decision. We cannot therefore foresee in what sense the majority will pronounce, and it is evident to us that the reunion will realise the object desired, that of bringing on a decision which cannot be questioned by any one, seeing

factory result of all the tripotage that has been going on, as it is an invitation *pur et simple* to reassemble the conference with Prussia, and to abide by the decision of the majority.

Lord Clarendon is to see M. de Persigny to-morrow morning.

The Empress of the French to Queen Victoria.

NEUCHÂTEL

Compiègne, *le 7 Novembre 1856.*

Madame et très chère Sœur,—Je viens après plus de deux mois m'excuser près de votre Majesté d'une faute bien involontaire; par quelques mots que Persigny m'a dit j'ai cru comprendre que votre Majesté s'étonnait que je ne lui eusse pas écrit en réponse à sa lettre. La seule crainte d'ennuyer votre Majesté m'a empêché de le faire, je croyais d'ailleurs que vous n'aviez pas besoin d'assurances sur la bonne foi et surtout sur la bonne volonté de l'Empereur.

J'espère que grâce à Dieu tous les petits différens qui ont surgi dans ces derniers temps s'aplaniront, car c'est l'intérêt des deux pays, et le vœu le plus cher que nous puissions former.[224]

L'Empereur a été bien peiné d'apprendre les fausses suppositions auxquelles out donné lieu un désaccord momentaire; il n'aurait jamais supposé que le désir de maintenir un engagement pris peut-être même trop à la hâte, mais dont un honnête homme ne peut se départir ait pu faire croire que l'alliance avec votre Majesté ne lui était pas tout aussi chère et tout aussi précieuse qu'auparavant; il est heureux de penser que la réunion de la conférence sera un moyen de tout arranger, puisque l'opinion de la Sardaigne n'était pas encore connue; elle créera par sa voix une majorité, et le Gouvernement français ne faisant rien pour influencer l'opinion du Piémont, le cabinet de votre Majesté peut

---

that it will have been obtained by the concurrence of the Representatives of all the Powers."

[224] Besides the complications arising out of the procrastination of Russia, in carrying out the Treaty of Paris, an international difficulty had lately arisen in Switzerland. A rising, professedly in defence of the hereditary interests of the King of Prussia, took place in the Canton of Neuchâtel, but was suppressed, and some of the insurgents taken prisoners by the Republican Government. The King of Prussia virtually expressed his approval of the movement by claiming the liberation of the prisoners, and his action was, to some extent, countenanced by the French Emperor. The matter was finally adjusted in 1857.

sans concession accepter cette combinaison. Je ne saurais assez dire combien pour ma part je suis tourmentée, car je voudrais partout et en tout voir nos deux pays marcher d'accord et surtout quand ils ont le même but. Nous sommes à Compiègne depuis trois semaines, l'Empereur chasse souvent, ce qui l'amuse beaucoup et lui fait beaucoup de bien...

L'Empereur me charge de le mettre aux pieds de votre Majesté. Je la prie en même temps de ne point nous oublier auprès du Prince Albert, et vous, Madame, croyez au tendre attachement que [je] vous ai voué et avec lequel je suis, Madame et très chère Sœur, de votre Majesté la toute dévouée Sœur,

Eugénie.

The Earl of Clarendon to Queen Victoria.

M. DE PERSIGNY

Foreign Office, *11th November 1856.*

Lord Clarendon presents his humble duty to your Majesty, and humbly begs to transmit the letters which arrived yesterday together with a copy of Count Walewski's despatch.

Lord Clarendon begs to return his thanks to your Majesty for allowing him to see the Empress's letter.... The letter does not seem to require an answer at present.

Lord Clarendon had a conversation of two hours this morning with M. de Persigny, who fought all his battles o'er again, but did not say much beyond what Lord Cowley had reported. He is quite sure that the Emperor is as staunch as ever to the Alliance, and that he believes all his own personal interests as well as those of France are bound up with England. He said, too, that the Empress was not the least taken in by the flatteries of Russia, which she estimates at their *juste valeur*.

M. de Persigny seems to have performed an act of painful duty and rather of true devotion, by giving the Empress some advice about her own conduct and the fate she was preparing for herself if she was not more properly mindful of her position and the obligations it entails. Lord Clarendon has seldom heard anything more eloquent or more touching than the language of M. de Persigny in describing what he said to the Empress, who appears to have taken it in the best part, and to have begun acting upon the advice the next day. M. de Persigny has no doubt that Count Walewski will soon be removed from his present office, and will be *promoted to St. Petersburg*, but Lord Clarendon will wait to believe this until it is a *fait accompli*, as it is more likely than not that when M. de Persigny is no longer on the spot to urge the Emperor, Count Walewski will resume his influence.

Count Walewski's despatch made a very unfavourable impression upon the Cabinet, who were of opinion that upon such an invitation and such slender assurances respecting the course that Sardinia might take, we ought not to give up our solid and often repeated objections to reassembling the Congress—at all events it was considered that we ought to have a positive answer from Turin before we gave a final answer....

Viscount Palmerston to Queen Victoria.

SIR ALEXANDER COCKBURN

Piccadilly, *13th November 1856.*

Viscount Palmerston presents his humble duty to your Majesty, and begs to state that Sir Alexander Cockburn[225] accepts the office of Chief Justice of the Common Pleas, but expresses a strong wish not altogether to be shut out from Parliamentary functions. His health, which has frequently interfered with his attendance in the House of Commons, makes him feel uncertain as to the future, and he is not desirous of being immediately placed in the House of Lords, but he would be glad to be allowed to look forward to such a favour from your Majesty at some future time if he should find his health stand sufficiently good to give him a fair prospect of being useful in the House of Lords. He says that with the Baronetcy of an uncle he will succeed to an estate of £5,000 a year, independent of what he has realised by his own professional exertions; and that consequently there would be a provision for a Peerage. Viscount Palmerston begs to submit for your Majesty's gracious approval that such a prospect might be held out to Sir Alexander Cockburn. The Chancellor and Lord Lansdowne and Lord Granville concur with Viscount Palmerston in

[225] Sir Alexander Cockburn's parliamentary success dated from his speech in the Don Pacifico debate; see *ante*, vol. ii, p. 252, note 23. He was made Solicitor-General shortly after, and then Attorney-General, being reappointed to the latter office in the end of 1852. He had defended both McNaghten and Pate for attacks on the Queen's person. The uncle whom he soon afterwards succeeded as baronet was now Dean of York.

thinking that much public advantage would arise from the presence of both Sir Alexander Cockburn, and of the Master of the Rolls,[226] in the House of Lords, and there are numerous precedents for the Chief Justice of the Common Pleas, and for the Master of the Rolls being Peers of Parliament.[227] Their judicial duties would no doubt prevent them from sitting in the morning on appeal cases, but their presence in the evening in debates in which the opinions and learning of men holding high positions in the legal profession would be required, could not fail to be of great public advantage. Of course any expectation to be held out to Sir Alexander Cockburn would for the present be a confidential and private communication to himself....

The King of the Belgians to Queen Victoria.

PRINCE CHARLES OF LEININGEN

Laeken, *21st November 1856.*

My dearest Victoria,—On Vicky's sixteenth birthday I cannot write on black-edged paper, it looks too gloomy, and I begin by wishing you joy on this day, with the sincere hope that it will also *dans l'avenir* prove to you one of satisfaction and happiness. I must now turn to your kind and affectionate letter of the 19th. I was sure that your warm heart would feel deeply the loss we have sustained.[228] You must, however, remember that you were ever a most affectionate sister, and that Charles was fully aware and most grateful for these your kind and sisterly sentiments. The real blow was last year; if that could have been mitigated, life might have been preserved under tolerable circumstances. As things, however, proceeded, if the present attack could have been warded off, Charles's existence would have been one of the most awful suffering, particularly for one whose mental disposition was quick and lively. Your sentiments on this occasion do you honour; it is by feelings like those you express that evidently *der Anknüpfungspunkt* with a future life must be looked for, and that alone with such sentiments we can show ourselves fit for such an existence.

For your precious health we must now claim that you will not permit your imagination to dwell too much on the very melancholy

[226] Sir John Romilly, created a peer in 1866.

[227] *E.g.*, Lord Eldon in the former office; Lord Langdale in the latter.

[228] The Queen's half-brother, Prince Charles of Leiningen, had died on the 13th.

picture of the last moments of one whom you loved, however natural it may be, and however difficult it is to dismiss such ideas.

Feo feels all this in a most beautiful and truly pious way. It is strange that November should be so full of sad anniversaries. I can well understand what Vicky must have suffered, as it could not be expected that Fritz Wilhelm could quite understand her grief....

Now I must leave you, remaining ever, my beloved Victoria, your truly devoted Uncle,

Leopold R.

My best love to Albert.

Queen Victoria to Viscount Palmerston.

Windsor Castle, *24th November 1856.*

The Queen approves the recommendation of Mr Bickersteth[229] for the vacant Bishopric of Ripon, but she cannot disguise from herself that however excellent a man Mr Bickersteth may be, his appointment will be looked upon as a strong party one, as he is one of the leaders of the Low Church Party; but perhaps Lord Palmerston may be able in the case of possible future appointments to remove any impression of the Church patronage running unduly towards party extremes.

Queen Victoria to the King of the Belgians.

THE QUEEN'S GRIEF

Windsor Castle, *26th November 1856.*

My dearest Uncle,—I was again prevented from writing to you yesterday as I intended, by multitudinous letters, etc. I therefore come only to-day with my warmest thanks for your most kind, feeling, and sympathising letter of the 23rd, which I *felt deeply.*

Poor dear Charles, I loved him *tenderly* and *dearly*, and feel every day *more* how impossible it is that the great blank caused by his loss should *ever* be filled up, and how *impossible it is to realise* the dreadful thought that I shall never see his dear, dear face again in this world! All the accounts of his peaceful death, of his fine and touching funeral,

---

[229] Mr Bickersteth (a nephew of Lord Langdale, a former Master of the Rolls) was then Rector of St Giles'. Lord Palmerston had written that he thought him well qualified for a diocese "full of manufacturers, clothier-workmen, Methodists, and Dissenters."

seem to me to be the descriptions of *another person's* death and burial—not poor dear Charles's.

Don't fear for my health, it is particularly good—and *grief* never seems to affect it; little worries and annoyances fret and irritate me, but *not great* or sad events. And I *derive* benefit and *relief* both in my body and soul in *dwelling* on the sad object which is *the* one which fills my heart! The having to think and talk of other and indifferent things (I mean *not* business so much) is very trying to my nerves, and does me harm.

Vicky is well again, and the young couple seem really very fond of each other. We have from living [together] for twelve days—as we did entirely alone with him and Vicky in our own apartments—got to know him much more intimately, and to be much more *à notre aise* with him than we could be in the London season, and he is now quite *l'enfant de la maison!* He is excellent and very sensible. I hope that you may be equally pleased and satisfied with *your* future son-in-law.

I must now conclude in great haste; excellent Stockmar is particularly well and brisk. Ever your devoted Niece,

Victoria R.

Queen Victoria to Viscount Palmerston.

Osborne, *8th December 1856.*

Lord Palmerston's explanation of Lord Panmure's object in proposing the appointment of a Director-General of Education of the Army in the Civil Department of its Government has but confirmed the Queen's apprehensions as to the effect of that step, if sanctioned. The Queen has for some time been expecting the proposal of a well-digested and considered plan for the education of the officers of the Army, and knows that the Duke of Cambridge has had such a one elaborated. Surely, in the absence of any fixed and approved system of education, it would be most imprudent to establish an Office for the discharge of certain important functions which are not yet defined. The Queen must therefore ask that the system of education to be in future adopted should first be submitted to her, and afterwards only the plan for the machinery which is to carry this out, the fitness of which can only be properly judged of with reference to the object in view.

Queen Victoria to the Earl of Clarendon.

Osborne, *12th December 1856.*

The Queen returns the enclosed letters. Sir H. Bulwer's is a clever composition, showing his wit and powers of writing.

The Queen has never, however, seen anything from him producing the impression that great and important affairs would be safe in his hands.

The mission to Washington will be difficult to fill.[230] Is it necessary to be in a hurry about it? Lord Elgin is sure to perform the duties very well, but is his former position as Governor-General of Canada not too high for him to go to Washington as Minister?...

Memorandum by Queen Victoria.

THE MAHARAJAH DHULEEP SINGH

Osborne, *15th December 1856.*

The Queen has seen the Memorandum which the Maharajah Dhuleep Singh has sent to the East India Company; she thinks all he asks very fair and reasonable, and she trusts that the East India Company will be able to comply with them. As we are in complete possession since 1849 of the Maharajah's enormous and splendid Kingdom, the Queen thinks we ought to do *everything* (which does not interfere with the safety of her Indian dominions) to render the position of this interesting and peculiarly good and amiable Prince as agreeable as possible, and not to let him have the feeling that he is *a prisoner*.

His being a Christian and completely European (or rather more English) in his habits and feelings, renders this much more necessary, and at the same time more easy.

The Queen has a very strong feeling that everything should be done to show respect and kindness towards these poor fallen Indian Princes, whose Kingdoms we have taken from them, and who are naturally very sensitive to attention and kindness.

---

[230] A complaint had been made by the Government of the United States of the unlawful enlistment in that country of recruits for the English army, and Mr Crampton, the British Minister at Washington, had been dismissed. Diplomatic relations were resumed after a suspension of some months; and Lord Napier was appointed British Minister in March 1857.

Amongst all these, however, the Maharajah stands to a certain degree alone, from his civilisation, and likewise from his having lost his kingdom when he was a child entirely by the faults and misdeeds of others.[231]

Queen Victoria to Viscount Palmerston.

MILITARY EDUCATION

Osborne, *18th December 1856.*

In answer to Lord Palmerston's explanation with regard to Colonel Lefroy's[232] appointment, the Queen has to say, that if he is to be made Inspector of Regimental Schools, she has no objection; but she must protest against his being made *Director* of Education for the Army generally. We want a Director-General of Education very much, but he ought to be immediately under the Commander-in-Chief, if possible a General Officer of weight, assisted by a Board of Officers of the different Arms.

Education ought to be made one of the essential requisites of an officer, and the reports on his proficiency ought to go direct through the proper superior from the bottom to the top, particularly if selection by merit is to receive a greater application for the future. If for his military proficiency and moral discipline, an officer is to be responsible to his Military chief, but for his mental acquirements to a Civil department, the unity of the system will be broken and the Army ruined; and this *must* be the case if the superintendence of the education is separated from the Military command.

The subject of Military Education has, as Lord Palmerston says, often been discussed in Parliament, which expects that some sufficient arrangement shall be made for it. But the mere creation of a place for an officer, however meritorious, to find him an equivalent for one which has to be reduced, can hardly be so called, and may even defeat the object itself. This subject is a most important one, and ought to be thoroughly examined before acting. The Queen understands that the Duke of Cambridge has transmitted to Lord Panmure a complete scheme, which must be now before him. If Lord Palmerston, Lord

---

[231] In reply, Mr Vernon Smith stated that he had brought all the Queen's wishes before the Company.

[232] John Henry Lefroy, who now became Inspector-General of Army Schools, was an artillery officer of considerable scientific attainments. Many years later he was K.C.M.G. and Governor of Tasmania.

Panmure, the Duke of Cambridge, and the Prince were to meet to consider this scheme, and the whole question in connection with it, the Queen would feel every confidence that a satisfactory decision would be arrived at.

The Emperor of the French to Queen Victoria.

BESSARABIA

[*Undated.*]

Madame et très chère Sœur,—Le Prince Frédéric Guillaume m'a remis la lettre que votre Majesté a bien voulu lui donner pour moi. Les expressions si amicales employées par votre Majesté m'ont vivement touché et quoique je fusse persuadé que la diversité d'opinion de nos deux Gouvernements ne pouvait en rien altérer vos sentiments à mon égard, j'ai été heureux d'en recevoir la douce confirmation. Le Prince de Prusse nous a beaucoup plu et je ne doute pas qu'il ne fasse le bonheur de la Princesse Royale, car il me semble avoir toutes les qualités de son âge et de son rang. Nous avons tâché de lui rendre le séjour de Paris aussi agréable que possible, mais je crois que ses pensées étaient toujours à Osborne ou à Windsor.

Il me tarde bien que toutes les discussions relatives au Traité de Paix aient un terme, car les partis en France en profitent pour tenter d'affaiblir l'intimité de l'alliance.[233] Je ne doute pas néanmoins que le bon sens populaire en fasse promptement justice de toutes les faussetés qu'on a répandues.

Votre Majesté, je l'espère, ne doutera jamais de mon désir de marcher d'accord avec son Gouvernement et du regret que j'éprouve quand momentairement cet accord n'existe pas.

En la priant de présenter mes hommages à S.A.R. la Duchesse de Kent et mes tendres amitiés au Prince, je lui renouvelle l'assurance de la sincère amitié et de l'entier dévouement avec lesquels je suis, de votre Majesté, le bon Frère et Ami,

Napoléon.

---

[233] A settlement with Russia of the disputed Bessarabian frontier was at length decided upon, on lines suggested by the Emperor to the British Government.

The Earl of Clarendon to Queen Victoria.

The Grove, *22nd December 1856.*

Lord Clarendon presents his humble duty to your Majesty, and humbly begs to transmit a letter from Lord Cowley, which contains the report of a curious conversation with the Emperor, and which might make a despatch not very unlike Sir H. Seymour's when he reported the partitioning views of the Emperor Nicholas.[234]

It is curious that in both cases the bribe to England should be Egypt. The Emperor of the French said nothing about the share of the spoils that France would look for, but His Majesty means Morocco, and Marshal Vaillant[235] talked to Lord Clarendon of Morocco as necessary to France, just as the Americans declare that the United States are not safe without Cuba....

Queen Victoria to the Emperor of the French.

THE DISPUTE ADJUSTED

Château de Windsor, *le 31 Décembre 1856.*

Sire et cher Frère,—Je saisis avec empressement l'occasion de la nouvelle année pour remercier votre Majesté de son aimable lettre, en vous priant d'agréer mes bons vœux autant pour le bonheur de V.M. que pour celui de l'Impératrice et de votre fils.

La nouvelle année commence encore avec le bruit des préparatifs de guerre, mais j'espère qu'on restera aux préparatifs et après le rapprochement qui a eu lieu entre vous, Sire, et la Prusse, j'ai toute confiance qu'il vous sera possible d'assurer une solution pacifique de cette question Suisse,[236] malheureusement envenimée par l'amour-propre froissé de tous côtés.

Je suis bien heureuse que nos difficultés survenues à l'exécution du Traité de Paris soient maintenant entièrement aplanies et que ce que V.M. signalait dans votre lettre comme une espérance soit à présent une réalité. Rien ne viendra désormais, je l'espère, troubler notre bonne entente qui donne une garantie si importante au bien-être de l'Europe. Nous avons été bien contents d'apprendre que notre futur gendre vous ait tant plu; il nous a écrit plein de reconnaissance de

---

[234] See *ante* p. 27, note 30. The Queen does not appear to have preserved a copy of Lord Cowley's letter.

[235] Minister of War.

[236] See *ante*, p. 214, note 55.

l'aimable accueil que vous lui avez donné et plein d'admiration de tout ce qu'il a vu à Paris.

Ma mère se remet peu à peu de la terrible secousse qu'elle a éprouvée, et me charge ainsi que le Prince de leurs félicitations pour le jour de l'an.

J'embrasse l'Impératrice et me dis pour toujours, Sire et cher Frère, de V.M.I., la bien affectionnée Sœur, et fidèle Amie,

Victoria R.

INTRODUCTORY NOTE

TO CHAPTER XXVI

The closing months of 1856 had witnessed the beginning of a dispute with China, a party of Chinese having boarded the lorcha *Arrow*, a vessel registered under a recent ordinance of Hong Kong, arrested the crew as pirates, and torn down the British flag. The Captain's right to fly the flag was questionable, for the term of registry, even if valid in the first instance, which was disputed, had expired (though the circumstance was unknown to the Chinese authorities), and the ship's earlier history under the Chinese flag had been an evil one. But Sir John Bowring, British Plenipotentiary at Hong Kong, took punitive measures to enforce treaty obligations; Admiral Seymour destroyed the forts on the river, and occupied the island and fort of Dutch Folly. In retaliation, the Chinese Governor Yeh put a price on Bowring's head, and his assassination, and that of other residents, by poison, was attempted. The British Government's action, however, was stigmatised as highhanded, and a resolution censuring them was carried in the Commons, being moved by Mr Cobden and supported by a coalition of Conservatives, Peelites, and the Peace Party,—Lord John Russell also opposing the Government. In consequence of this vote, Parliament was dissolved, and at the ensuing election the Peace Party was scattered to the winds; Bright, Milner Gibson, and Cobden all losing their seats. Lord Palmerston obtained a triumphant majority in the new House of Commons, of which Mr J. E. Denison was elected Speaker in succession to Mr Shaw-Lefevre, now created Viscount Eversley. At the end of the year an ultimatum was sent to Governor Yeh, requiring observance of the Treaty of Nankin, Canton was bombarded, and subsequently occupied by the English and French troops.

Hostilities with Persia were terminated by a treaty signed at Paris; the Shah engaging to abstain from interference in Afghanistan, and to recognise the independence of Herat.

A century had passed since the victory of Clive at Plassey, but the Afghan disasters and the more recent war with Russia had caused doubts to arise as to British stability in India, where the native forces were very large in comparison with the European. Other causes, among which may be mentioned the legalising of the remarriage of Hindoo widows, and a supposed intention to coerce the natives into Christianity, were operating to foment dissatisfaction, while recent acts of insubordination and symptoms of mutiny had been inadequately repressed; but the immediate visible provocation to mutiny among the Bengal troops was the use of cartridges said to be treated with a preparation of the fat of pigs and cows, the use of which was abhorrent, on religious grounds, both to Hindoos and Mohammedans. The Governor-General assured the Sepoys by proclamation that no offence to their religion or injury to their caste was intended; but on the 10th of May the native portion of the garrison at Meerut broke out in revolt. The Mutineers proceeded to Delhi, and were joined by the native troops there; they established as Emperor the octogenarian King, a man of unscrupulous character, who had been living under British protection.

Great cruelties were practised on the European population of all ages and both sexes, at Lucknow, Allahabad, and especially Cawnpore; by the end of June, the Sepoys had mutinied at twenty-two stations—the districts chiefly affected being Bengal, the North-West Provinces, and Oudh. To cope with this state of things, a large body of British soldiers on their way to China were diverted by Lord Elgin to India, and a force of 40,000 men was despatched from England round the Cape; while Sir Colin Campbell was sent out as Commander-in-Chief. Meanwhile reinforcements had been drawn from the Punjab, which had remained loyal. Lucknow was for a long time besieged by the rebels, and Sir Henry Lawrence, its gallant defender, killed. The garrison was reinforced on the 25th of September by General Havelock; but the non-combatants could not be extricated from their perilous position till November, when the Garrison was relieved by Sir Colin Campbell. Delhi was taken in the course of September, but a considerable period elapsed before the rebellion was finally suppressed. Summary vengeance was inflicted on the Sepoy rebels, which gave rise to some criticism of our troops for inhumanity; but Lord Canning, the Governor-General, was no less severely blamed for his clemency; and the general verdict was in favour of the measures adopted by the military and civilian officers, whose zeal and capacity suppressed the Mutiny.

Before the Dissolution of Parliament, Mr Gladstone and Mr Disraeli had joined in an attack on the budget of Sir George Lewis, and the Peelite ex-Chancellor of the Exchequer seemed for the moment disposed definitely to return to the Conservative party. To the Divorce Bill, the chief legislative result of the second Session, Mr Gladstone gave a persistent and unyielding opposition: but it passed the Commons by large majorities; a Bill for the removal of Jewish disabilities was much debated, but not carried. In August, another visit, this time of a private character, was paid by the Emperor and Empress of the French to the Queen at Osborne. In the middle of November a series of commercial disasters of great magnitude took place. The Government, as in 1847, authorised the infringement for a time of the Bank Charter Act, and a third session was held to pass an Act of Indemnity.

CHAPTER XXVI

1857

Queen Victoria to Mr Labouchere.

Windsor Castle, *8th January 1857.*

The despatches from Sir George Grey[237] which the Queen returns are most interesting. The two chief objects to accomplish appear to be the bringing the Kaffirs in British Kaffraria within the pale of the law, so that they may know the blessings of it—and the re-absorption, if possible, of the Orange River Free State. To both these objects the efforts of the Government should be steadily directed.

Viscount Palmerston to Queen Victoria.

HOME AND FOREIGN POLICY

Broadlands, *13th January 1857.*

Viscount Palmerston presents his humble duty to your Majesty, and he and Lady Palmerston will have the honour of waiting upon your Majesty as soon as he is able to move. He is, however, at present on crutches, and can hardly expect to be in marching order for some few days to come. With regard to the matters that are likely to be discussed when Parliament meets, Viscount Palmerston would beg to submit that the one which has for some months past occupied the attention of all Europe, namely, the execution of the Treaty of Paris, has been settled in a manner satisfactory to all parties; and this is not only a great relief to the Government, but is also a security for the continuance of the Anglo-French Alliance, which would have been greatly

---

[237] See *ante*, pp. 200-1. The task of dealing with the Hottentots and Kaffirs, and coming to an understanding with the recalcitrant Boers, was a difficult one.

endangered by the discussions and explanations that might otherwise have been forced on.

The various questions of difference between your Majesty's Government, and that of the United States, have also been settled, and the diplomatic relations between the two countries are about to be replaced upon their usual footing. This result will have given great satisfaction to the commercial and manufacturing interests.

Some discussion will take place as to the Expedition to the coast of Persia, and some persons will, of course, find fault with the whole policy pursued on that matter; but people in general will understand that Herat is an advanced post of attack against British India, and that whatever belongs nominally to Persia must be considered as belonging practically to Russia, whenever Russia may want to use it for her own purposes.

The outbreak of hostilities at Canton[238] was the result of the decision of your Majesty's officers on the spot, and not the consequence of orders from home. The first responsibility must therefore rest with the local authorities, but Viscount Palmerston cannot doubt that the Government will be deemed to have acted right in advising your Majesty to approve the proceedings, and to direct measures for obtaining from the Chinese Government concessions which are indispensable for the maintenance of friendly relations between China and the Governments of Europe.

Of domestic questions, that which will probably be the most agitated will be a large and immediate diminution of the Income Tax; but any such diminution would disturb the financial arrangements of the country, and it is to be hoped that Parliament will adopt the scheme which will be proposed by Sir G. C. Lewis, by which the Income Tax would be made equal in each of the next three years, the amount now fixed by Law for 1857 being diminished, but the amount now fixed by Law for 1858 and 1859 being increased....

Viscount Palmerston hears from persons likely to know, that the Conservative Party are not more united than they were last Session.

---

[238] *See* Introductory Note, *ante*, p. 223. The difficulty with China had arisen out of her refusal to throw open the city of Canton to European trade in conformity with the Treaty of Nankin, *ante*, vol. i. p. 441. Sir John Bowring, Chief Superintendent of Trade (and, in effect, British Plenipotentiary) at Hong-Kong, had resented this, and the feeling thus engendered had come to a crisis on the occasion of the seizure of the crew of the *Arrow*.

That Mr Disraeli and the great bulk of his nominal followers are far from being on good terms together, and that there is no immediate junction to be expected between Mr Disraeli and Mr Gladstone.[239]

Mr Cobden has given it to be understood that he wishes at the next General Election to retire from the West Riding of Yorkshire. The real fact being that the line he took about the late war has made him so unpopular with his constituents that he would probably not be returned again.[240]

Viscount Palmerston has heard privately and confidentially that Lord John Russell wrote some little time ago to the Duke of Bedford to say that it had been intimated to him that an offer would be made to him if he were disposed to accept it, to go to the House of Lords and to become there the Leader of the Government. In case your Majesty may have heard this report, Viscount Palmerston thinks it right to say that no such communication to Lord John Russell was ever authorised by him, nor has been, so far as he is aware, ever made, and in truth Viscount Palmerston must candidly say that in the present state of public opinion about the course which Lord John has on several occasions pursued, he is not inclined to think that his accession to the Government would give the Government any additional strength.

Queen Victoria to Viscount Palmerston.

CHURCH APPOINTMENTS

Buckingham Palace, *25th February 1857.*

The Queen would wish to know before she approves of the appointment of Mr Alford, of Quebec Chapel, to the head Deanery of Canterbury, whether he is a very Low Churchman, as Lord Palmerston will remember that he agreed in her observation after the appointment of several of the Bishops, that it would be advisable to choose those who were of moderate opinions—not leaning too much to either side. Extreme opinions lead to mischief in the end, and produce much discord in the Church, which it would be advisable to avoid.[241]

---

[239] The probability of this combination was now being perpetually mooted, and, in fact, the two ex-Chancellors combined in attacking the Budget.

[240] He stood instead for Huddersfleld, and was defeated by an untried politician; one Liberal (the present Lord Ripon) and one Conservative were returned unopposed in the West Riding.

[241] The Deanery was offered to and accepted by Mr Alford.

With respect to the Garter, which the Duke of Norfolk has declined, she approves of its being offered to the Duke of Portland.[242] She thinks that the one now vacant by the death of poor Lord Ellesmere[243] might most properly be bestowed on Lord Granville—he is Lord President and Leader of the House of Lords, and acquitted himself admirably in his difficult mission as Ambassador to the Emperor of Russia's Coronation.

Should Lord Palmerston agree in this view he might at once mention it to Lord Granville.

Viscount Palmerston to Queen Victoria.

DEBATE ON CHINESE AFFAIRS

Piccadilly, *28th February 1857.*

Viscount Palmerston presents his humble duty to your Majesty, and has seen Mr Hayter[244] this morning, and finds from him that the disposition of the House of Commons is improving, and that many of the supporters of the Government who had at first thought of voting with Mr Cobden[245] are changing their minds. It has been suggested to Viscount Palmerston that it would be useful to have a meeting of the Party in Downing Street on Monday, and that many wavering members only want to have something said to them which they could quote as a reason for changing their intended course; and Viscount Palmerston has given directions for summoning such a meeting.

Lord Derby has had meetings of his followers, and has told them that unless they will support him in a body he will cease to be their

---

[242] William John Cavendish Bentinck-Scott, fifth Duke (1800-1879). He did not accept the honour, which was conferred on the Marquis of Westminster.

[243] Lord Francis Egerton had inherited a vast property from the third and last Duke of Bridgewater (the projector of English inland navigation), and was created Earl of Ellesmere in 1846. The Garter was accepted by Lord Granville.

[244] Mr (afterwards Sir) William Hayter, Liberal Whip, the father of Lord Haversham.

[245] See Introductory Note, *ante*, p. 223. Mr Cobden's motion of censure affirmed that the papers laid on the table of the House did not justify the violent measures resorted to by the Government at Canton in the affair of the *Arrow*. He was supported by Lord John Russell, Mr Roebuck, Mr Gladstone, and Mr Disraeli, the latter emphatically challenging the Premier to appeal to the country.

leader, as he will not be the head of a divided Party. Viscount Palmerston can scarcely bring himself to believe that the House of Commons will be so fickle as suddenly and without reason to turn round upon the Government, and after having given them last Session and this Session large majorities on important questions, put them in a minority on what Mr Disraeli last night in a few words said on the motion for adjournment described as a Vote of Censure. With regard, however, to the question put by your Majesty as to what would be the course pursued by the Government in the event of a defeat, Viscount Palmerston could hardly answer it without deliberation with his colleagues. His own firm belief is that the present Government has the confidence of the country in a greater degree than any other Government that could now be formed would have, and that consequently upon a Dissolution of Parliament, a House of Commons would be returned more favourable to the Government than the present. Whether the state of business as connected with votes of supply and the Mutiny Act would admit of a Dissolution, supposing such a measure to be sanctioned by your Majesty, would remain to be enquired into; but Viscount Palmerston believes that there would be no insurmountable difficulty on that score. He will have the honour of waiting upon your Majesty at a little before three to-morrow.

The Prince Albert to Viscount Palmerston.

Buckingham Palace, *3rd March 1857.*

My dear Lord Palmerston,—The Queen has this moment received your letter giving so unfavourable an account of the prospects of to-night's division. She is sorry that her health imperatively requires her going into the country for a few days, and having put off her going to Windsor on account of the Debate which was expected to close yesterday, she cannot now do so again to-day. She feels, however, the inconvenience of her absence should the division turn out as ill as is now anticipated. The Queen could not possibly come to a decision on so important a point as a Dissolution without a personal discussion and conference with you, and therefore hopes that you might be able to go down to-morrow perhaps for dinner and to stay over the night.

The Queen feels herself physically quite unable to go through the anxiety of a Ministerial Crisis and the fruitless attempt to form a new Government out of the heterogeneous elements out of which the present Opposition is composed, should the Government feel it necessary to offer their resignation, and would on that account *prefer any other alternative*.... Ever, etc.,

Albert.

Viscount Palmerston to Queen Victoria.[246]

DEFEAT OF THE GOVERNMENT

House of Commons, *5th March 1857.*

(*Quarter to Eight.*)

Viscount Palmerston presents his humble duty to your Majesty, and begs to state that his communication to the House of an intention to give the constituencies of the country an opportunity of judging between the present Government and any other administration which might be formed, has been on the whole well received, and, with the exception of Mr Gladstone, most of the persons who spoke intimated a willingness to allow without interruption the completion of such business as may be necessary before the Dissolution. Mr Disraeli said that he and those who act with him would give all fair assistance consistent with their opinions, but hoped nothing would be proposed to which they could reasonably object. Mr Gladstone, with great vehemence, repelled the charge of combination, evidently meaning to answer attacks made out of the House....

The result of what passed seems to be that no serious difficulty will be thrown in the way of an early Dissolution.

Earl Granville to Queen Victoria.

[*Undated. ? 16th March 1857.*]

Lord Granville presents his humble duty to your Majesty, and begs to submit that Lord Derby made a speech of two hours, in which he glanced at the present state of affairs.[247] He made a personal attack on Lord Palmerston, and described his colleagues as cyphers and appendages. The rest of his speech was of a singularly apologetic and

[246] Mr Cobden's motion was carried by 263 to 247, and Lord Palmerston promptly accepted Mr Disraeli's challenge to dissolve Parliament.

[247] Lord Derby's resolutions in the Lords, which were to the same effect as Mr Cobden's motion, were rejected by 146 to 110. On the 16th of March Lord Derby took the opportunity of announcing the views of his chief supporters in reference to the General Election.

defensive character. He was quite successful in clearing himself from an understanding—not from political conversations with Mr Gladstone.

Lord Granville, in his reply, was thought very discourteous by Lord Malmesbury and Lord Hardwicke, who closed the conversation.

Viscount Palmerston to Queen Victoria.[248]

RETIREMENT OF THE SPEAKER

Piccadilly, *18th March 1857.*

... Viscount Palmerston begs to state that the Speaker has chosen the title of Eversley, the name of a small place near his residence[249] in Hampshire, all the large towns in the county having already been adopted as titles for Peers. The ordinary course would be that your Majesty should make him a Baron, and that is the course which was followed in the cases of Mr Abbot made Lord Colchester, and Mr Abercromby made Lord Dunfermline; but in the case of Mr Manners Sutton a different course was pursued, and he was made Viscount Canterbury. The present Speaker is very anxious that his services, which, in fact, have been more meritorious and useful than those of Mr Manners Sutton, should not appear to be considered by your Majesty as less deserving of your Majesty's Royal favour, and as the present Speaker may justly be said to have been the best who ever filled the chair, Viscount Palmerston would beg to submit for your Majesty's gracious approval that he may be created Viscount Eversley. It will be well at the same time if your Majesty should sanction this arrangement that a Record should be entered at the Home Office stating that this act of grace and favour of your Majesty being founded on the peculiar circumstances of the case, is not to [be] deemed a precedent for the cases of future Speakers.

Lord Canterbury was also made a Grand Cross of the Civil Order of the Bath; it will be for your Majesty to consider whether it might not be gracious to follow in all respects on the present occasion the course which was pursued in the case of Mr Manners Sutton.

---

[248] On the 9th, Mr Speaker Shaw-Lefevre had announced in the House of Commons his intended retirement from the Chair, which he had occupied since 1839, when his election had been made a trial of strength between parties. He was voted an annuity of £4,000 a year, and created Viscount Eversley, receiving also the G.C.B.

[249] Heckfield Place, near Winchfield.

Queen Victoria to the King of the Belgians.

THE GENERAL ELECTION

Buckingham Palace, *24th March 1857.*

My dearest Uncle,— ... The Opposition have played their game most foolishly, and the result is that *all* the old Tories say they will certainly *not* support them; they very truly say Lord Derby's party—that is those who want to get into office *coûte que coûte*—whether the country suffers for it or not, wanted to get in under *false colours*, and that they won't support or abide—which they are *quite* right in. There is reason to hope that a better class of men will be returned, and returned to support the Government, not a particular cry of this or that.... Ever your devoted Niece,

Victoria R.[250]

Earl Granville to Queen Victoria.

[*Undated. ? 19th May 1857.*]

Lord Granville presents his humble duty to your Majesty, and begs to submit that the Lord Chancellor made the best statement he has yet done, introducing his Divorce Bill.[251]... Lord Lyndhurst made a

---

[250] In his address to the electors of Tiverton, the Premier declared that "an insolent barbarian, wielding authority at Canton, had violated the British flag, broken the engagements of treaties, offered rewards for the heads of British subjects in that part of China, and planned their destruction by murder, assassination, and poison." The courage and good temper displayed by Lord Palmerston, and the energy with which he had carried the country through the Crimean struggle, had won him widespread popularity, and the Peace party were generally routed, the prominent members all losing their seats. The Peelite ranks were also thinned, but Lord John Russell, contrary to general expectation, held his seat in the City. There were one hundred and eighty-nine new members returned, and the Ministry found themselves in command of a handsome majority.

[251] Before this date a divorce could only be obtained in England by Act of Parliament, after sentence in the ecclesiastical Court, and (in the case of a husband's application) a verdict in *crim. con.* against the adulterer. The present English law was established by the Bill of 1857, the chief amendment made in Committee being the provision exempting the clergy from the obligation to marry divorced persons. Bishop Wilberforce opposed the Bill strenuously, while Archbishop Sumner and Bishop Tait of London supported

most able speech in favour of the Bill, but wished it to go further, and give permission to a woman to sue for a divorce if she was "maliciously deserted" by her husband.... The Bishop of Oxford pretended that he was not going to speak at all, in order to secure his following instead of preceding the Bishop of London; but upon a division being called he was obliged to speak, and did so with considerable force and eloquence, but betraying the greatest possible preparation. The Bishop of London, after showing that the Bishop of Oxford's speech was a repetition of Mr Keble's speech, made an excellent answer. The Debate was finished by the Duke of Argyll.

For the Bill, 47. Against it, 18.

Vicount Palmerston, K.G.

From the drawing by Sir Geo. Richmond, R.A., in the possession of the Earl of Carnwath.

---

it. Sir Richard Bethell, the Attorney-General, piloted the measure most skilfully through the Commons, in the teeth of the eloquent and persistent opposition of Mr Gladstone, who, to quote a letter from Lord Palmerston to the Queen, opposed the second reading "in a speech of two hours and a half, fluent, eloquent, brilliant, full of theological learning and scriptural research, but fallacious in argument, and with parts inconsistent with each other."

The Earl of Clarendon to the Prince Albert.

THE FRENCH *ENTENTE*

20th May 1857.

Sir,—I have the honour to inform your Royal Highness that I have had a very long and interesting conversation with M. de Persigny to-day. He told me of the different *Utopias* which the Emperor had in his head, of His Majesty's conviction that England, France, and Russia ought between them to *régler les affaires de l'Europe*, of the *peu de cas* which he made of Austria or any other Power, and of the various little complaints which His Majesty thought he had against Her Majesty's Government, and which had been magnified into importance by the malevolence or the stupidity of the persons who had more or less the ear of the Emperor.[252]

M. de Persigny told me also that in a conversation with the Emperor at which he had taken care that Count Walewski should be present, he had solemnly warned the Emperor of the danger he would incur if he swerved the least from the path of his true interest which was the English Alliance, that all the Sovereigns who were flattering and cajoling him for their own purposes looked down upon him as an adventurer, and no more believed in the stability of his throne, or the duration of his dynasty, than they did in any other events of which extreme improbability was the character; whereas the English, who never condescended to flatter or cajole anybody, but who looked to the interests of England, were attached to the French Alliance and to the Sovereign of France because peaceful relations with that country were of the utmost importance to England. France was the only country in Europe that could do England harm, and on the other hand England was the only country that could injure France—the late war with Russia had not the slightest effect upon France except costing her money, but a war with England would set every party in France into activity each with its own peculiar objects, but all of them against the existing order of things—*l'ordre social serait bouleversé* and the Empire might perish in the convulsion.

THE EMPEROR'S VISIT

---

[252] A difference had arisen as to the future of the Principalities—France, Sardinia, and Russia favouring their union, while England, Austria, and Turkey held that a single state, so formed, might become too Russian in its sympathies.

The result of this and other conversations appears to be an earnest desire of the Emperor to come to England on a private visit to the Queen, if possible at Osborne, and at any time that might be convenient to Her Majesty. M. de Persigny describes him as being intent upon this project, and as attaching the utmost importance to it in order to *éclairer* his own ideas, to guide his policy, and to prevent by personal communication with the Queen, your Royal Highness, and Her Majesty's Government the dissidences and *mésintelligences* which the Emperor thinks will arise from the want of such communications.

I fear that such a visit would not be very agreeable to Her Majesty, but in the Emperor's present frame of mind, and his evident alarm lest it should be thought that the Alliance has been in any way *ébranlée*, I cannot entertain a doubt that much good might be done, or, at all events, that much mischief might be averted by the Emperor being allowed to pay his respects to Her Majesty in the manner he proposes.

I have discussed the matter after the Cabinet this evening with Lord Palmerston, who takes entirely the same view of the matter as I have taken the liberty of expressing to your Royal Highness. I have the honour to be, with the greatest respect, Sir, your Royal Highness's most faithful and devoted Servant,

Clarendon.

The Prince Albert to the Earl of Clarendon.

Osborne, *21st May 1857*.

My dear Lord Clarendon,—I have shown your letter to the Queen, who wishes me to say in answer to it that she will, of course, be ready to do what may appear best for the public interest. We shall, therefore, be ready to receive the Emperor, with or without the Empress, here at Osborne in the quiet way which he proposes. The present moment would, however, hardly do, Drawing-rooms and parties being announced in London, Parliament sitting, and the Season going on and the Queen having only a few days from the Grand Duke's visit to her return to Town. The latter half of July, the time at which the Queen would naturally be here and the best yachting season, might appear to the Emperor the most eligible, as being the least *forcé*.

Till then a cottage which is rebuilding will, we hope, be ready to accommodate some of the suite, whom we could otherwise not properly house.

I have no doubt that good will arise from a renewed intercourse with the Emperor; the only thing one may perhaps be afraid of is the possibility of his wishing to gain us over to his views with regard to a redistribution of Europe, and may be disappointed at our not being able to assent to his plans and aspirations.

Albert.[253]

Queen Victoria to the King of the Belgians.

Buckingham Palace, *16th June 1857.*

My dearest Uncle,—The christening of little Beatrice[254] is just over—and was very brilliant and nice. We had the luncheon in the fine ball-room, which looked very handsome. The Archduke Maximilian (who is here since Sunday evening) led me to the chapel, and at the luncheon I sat between him and Fritz. I cannot say how much we like the Archduke; he is charming, so clever, natural, kind and amiable, so *English* in his feelings and likings, and so anxious for the best understanding between Austria and England. With the exception of his mouth and chin, he is good-looking; and I think one does not the least care for that, as he is so very kind and clever and pleasant. I wish you really joy, dearest Uncle, at having got *such* a husband for dear Charlotte, as I am sure he will make her happy, and is quite worthy of her. He may, and will do a great deal for Italy.[255]...

I must conclude for to-day, hoping soon to hear from you again. Ever your devoted Niece,

Victoria R.

Viscount Palmerston to Queen Victoria.

THE INDIAN MUTINY

Piccadilly, *26th June 1857.*

---

[253] See *post*, p. 242, note 30.

[254] Princess Beatrice (now Princess Henry of Battenberg) was born on the 14th of April.

[255] The tragic end of a union which promised so brightly came in 1867, when the Archduke Maximilian, having accepted the Imperial crown of Mexico, offered to him by the Provisional Government, was shot by order of President Juarez. The Empress Charlotte had come to Europe a year earlier to seek help for her husband from the French Emperor. In consequence of the shock caused by the failure of her mission, her health entirely gave way.

... Viscount Palmerston is sorry to have received the accompanying account of the extension of the Mutiny among the native troops in India, but he has no fear of its results.[256] The bulk of the European force is stationed on the North-West Frontier, and is, therefore, within comparatively easy reach of Delhi, and about six thousand European troops will have returned to Bombay from Persia. It will, however, seem to be advisable to send off at once the force amounting to nearly eight thousand men, now under orders for embarkation for India; and when the despatches arrive, which will be about the middle of next week, it will be seen whether any further reinforcements will be required.

The extent of the Mutiny appears to indicate some deeper cause than that which was ascribed to the first insubordination. That cause may be, as some allege, the apprehension of the Hindoo priests that their religion is in danger by the progress of civilisation in India, or it may be some hostile foreign agency.

Queen Victoria to Lord Panmure.

THE VICTORIA CROSS

[*Undated, ? June 1857.*]

The Queen thinks that the persons decorated with the Victoria Cross might very properly be allowed to bear some distinctive mark after their name.[257] The warrant instituting the decoration does not style it "an Order," but merely "a Naval and Military Decoration" and a distinction; nor is it properly speaking an order, being not *constituted*. V.C. would not do. K.G. means a *Knight* of the Garter, C.B. a *Companion* of the Bath, M.P. a *Member* of Parliament, M.D. a *Doctor* of Medicine, etc., etc., in all cases designating a person. No one could be called a Victoria Cross. V.C. moreover means Vice-Chancellor at

---

[256] Alarming accounts of disturbances in India had been received for some weeks past, but Lord Palmerston failed to grasp the gravity of the situation. Even after the intelligence reached England of the mutiny of the native regiments at Meerut, on the 10th of May, and of the horrible massacres of women and children, the Ministry did not fully realise the peril threatening our Indian possessions.

[257] The Victoria Cross had just been instituted by Royal Warrant, and the Queen had, with her own hand, decorated those who had won the distinction, in Hyde Park, on the 26th of June.

present. D.V.C. (decorated with the Victoria Cross) or B.V.C. (Bearer of the Victoria Cross) might do. The Queen thinks the last the best.

Queen Victoria to Lord Panmure.

REINFORCEMENTS FOR INDIA

Buckingham Palace, *29th June 1857.*

The Queen has to acknowledge the receipt of Lord Panmure's letter of yesterday. She had long been of opinion that reinforcements waiting to go to India ought not to be delayed. The moment is certainly a very critical one, and the additional reinforcements now proposed will be much wanted. The Queen entirely agrees with Lord Panmure that it will be good policy to oblige the East India Company to keep permanently a larger portion of the Royal Army in India than heretofore. The Empire has nearly doubled itself within the last twenty years, and the Queen's troops have been kept at the old establishment. They are the body on whom the maintenance of that Empire depends, and the Company ought not to sacrifice the highest interests to love of patronage. The Queen hopes that the new reinforcements will be sent out in their Brigade organisation, and not as detached regiments; good Commanding Officers knowing their troops will be of the highest importance next to the troops themselves.

The Queen must ask that the troops by whom we shall be diminished at home by the transfer of so many regiments to the Company should be forthwith replaced by an increase of the establishment up to the number voted by Parliament, and for which the estimates have been taken, else we denude ourselves altogether to a degree dangerous to our own safety at home, and incapable of meeting a sudden emergency, which, as the present example shows, may come upon us at any moment. If we had not reduced in such a hurry this spring, we should now have all the men wanted!

The Queen wishes Lord Panmure to communicate this letter to Lord Palmerston. The accounts in to-day's papers from India are most distressing.

Queen Victoria to Lord Panmure.

Buckingham Palace, *3rd July 1857.*

The Queen has received Lord Panmure's letter of yesterday. She has sanctioned the going of four Regiments to the East Indies. With regard to the reduction of the garrison of Malta to four Regiments, she hopes the Government will well consider whether this will not reduce this valuable and exposed spot to a state of insecurity.

The Queen is sorry to find Lord Panmure still objecting to a proper Brigade system, without which no army in the world can be efficient. We want General Officers, and cannot train them unless we employ them on military duty, not on clerks' duty in district or colony, but in the command of troops. The detachment of Regiments is no reason for having no system, and the country will not pay for General Officers whose employment is not part of a system; our Army is then deprived of its efficiency by the refusal to adopt a system on the part of the Government.

Viscount Canning to Queen Victoria.

DELHI

Calcutta, *4th July 1857.*

Lord Canning presents his humble duty to your Majesty, and although unable to give to your Majesty the complete details of the capture of Delhi, and of the defeat of the rebels in that city,[258] as he has long desired to do, he can at least announce to your Majesty that the city is in the possession of the British troops, under Major-General Sir Henry Barnard; and that nothing remains in the hands of the insurgents except the Palace or Fort, in which they have all taken refuge. This was the state of things on the 13th and 14th of June, the latest day of which any certain accounts have been received from Delhi; but nothing was likely to interfere with the completion of the capture within forty-eight hours.

This event has been long and anxiously awaited, and the time which has elapsed has cost England and India very dear. Many precious lives have been lost, and much heartrending suffering has been endured, for which there can be no compensation. The reputation of England's power, too, has had a rude shake; and nothing but a long-continued manifestation of her might before the eyes of the whole Indian Empire, evinced by the presence of such an English force as shall

[258] After the outbreak at Meerut in May, the fugitive Sepoys fled to Delhi, and endeavoured to capture the magazine, which, however, was exploded by British soldiers. Delhi was not captured until September (see *post*, p. 249). On the 11th of July, the Government received intelligence of the spread of the Mutiny throughout Bengal, and the resulting diminution of the Indian Army.

make the thought of oppositon hopeless, will re-establish confidence in her strength.

Lord Canning much fears that there are parts of India where, until this is done, a complete return to peace and order will not be effected. Wherever the little band of English soldiers—little when compared with the stretch of country over which they have to operate—which Lord Canning has at his disposal has shown itself, the effect has been instantaneous.

Except at Delhi, there has scarcely been an attempt at resistance to an European soldier, and the march of the smallest detachments has preserved order right and left of the roads. The same has been the case in large cities, such as Benares, Patna, and others; all going to prove that little more than the presence of English troops is needed to ensure peace. On the other hand, where such troops are known not to be within reach, anarchy and violence, when once let loose, continue unrestrained; and, until further additions are made to the English regiments in the disturbed districts, this state of things will not only continue, but extend itself. The fall of Delhi will act to some degree as a check; but where rapine and outrage have raged uncontrolled, even for a few hours, it is to be feared that nothing but the actual presence of force will bring the country into order.

Lord Canning rejoices to say that to-day the first Regiment of your Majesty's Forces destined for China has entered the Hooghly. Lord Canning did not scruple, knowing how much was at stake, earnestly to press Lord Elgin to allow those forces to be turned aside to India before proceeding to the support of your Majesty's Plenipotentiary in China;[259] and to this, so far as regards the first two Regiments, Lord Elgin readily assented. From what Lord Canning has ventured to state above, your Majesty will easily understand the satisfaction with which each new arrival of an English transport in Calcutta is regarded by him.

As yet no military operations south of Delhi have been undertaken. Next week, however, a column composed of your Majesty's 64th and 78th (Highland) Regiments will reach Cawnpore[260] and

---

[259] For Sir George Grey's action at Cape Town, in reference to the troops destined for China, see his Memoir, in the *Dictionary of National Biography*.

[260] On the 4th of June, two native regiments had mutinied at Cawnpore, and the English residents, under General Sir Hugh Wheeler, were besieged. After many deaths and much privation, the garrison were induced by the perfidy of

Lucknow, in the neighbourhood of which it is probable that an opportunity will offer of striking a decisive blow at the band of rebels which, after that in Delhi, is the strongest and most compact. But Lord Canning greatly doubts whether they will await the onset. Unfortunately, they may run away from the English troops, and yet prove very formidable to any who are weaker than themselves—whether Indians or unarmed Europeans.

GRAVE ANXIETY

Your Majesty is aware that in the critical condition of affairs which now exists, Lord Canning has felt himself compelled to adopt the measure of placing the King of Oudh in confinement in Fort William, in consequence of the use made of his name by those who have been busy tampering with the Sepoys; and of the intrigues which there is good reason to believe that the Minister of the King, who is also in the Fort, has carried on in his master's name.[261] The King has been, and will continue to be, treated with every mark of respect and indulgence which is compatible with his position, so long as it may be necessary that he should be retained in the Fort.

Lord Canning earnestly hopes that your Majesty and the Prince are in the enjoyment of good health, and prays your Majesty to be graciously pleased to accept the expression of his sincere devotion and dutiful attachment.

Viscount Palmerston to Queen Victoria.

DEBATE ON INDIAN AFFAIRS

Piccadilly, *27th July 1857.*

Viscount Palmerston presents his humble duty to your Majesty, and begs to state that Mr Disraeli this afternoon, in a speech of three hours, made his Motion on the state of India. His Motion was ostensibly for two papers, one of which does not exist, at least in the

---

Nana Sahib, who had caused the Cawnpore rising, to surrender, on condition of their lives being spared. On the 27th of June, not suspecting their impending fate, the enfeebled garrison, or what was left of it, gave themselves up. The men were killed, the women and children being first enslaved and afterwards massacred. On the 16th of July, General Havelock defeated Nana Sahib at Cawnpore, the city was occupied by the English, and a sanguinary, but well-merited, retribution exacted.

[261] The ex-King had been living under the protection of the Indian Government. The arrest took place early in June at his residence at Garden Beach.

possession of the Government, and the other of which ought not to be made public, as it relates to the arrangements for defending India against external attack. He represented the disturbances in India as a national revolt, and not as a mere military mutiny; and he enumerated various causes which in his opinion accounted, for and justified this general revolt. Some of these causes were various measures of improved civilisation which from time to time during the last ten years the Indian Government had been urged by Parliament to take. Mr Vernon Smith followed, and in a very able speech answered in great detail Mr Disraeli's allegations. Sir Erskine Perry,[262] who evidently had furnished Mr Disraeli with much of his mistaken assertions, supported his views. Mr Campbell, Member for Weymouth, who had been many years in India, showed the fallacy of Mr Disraeli's arguments, and the groundlessness of many of his assertions. Mr Whiteside supported the Motion. Lord John Russell, who had after Mr Disraeli's speech communicated with the Government, expressed his disapprobation of Mr Disraeli's speech, and moved as an Amendment an Address to your Majesty expressing the assurance of the support of the House for measures to suppress the present disturbances, and their co-operation with your Majesty in measures for the permanent establishment of tranquillity and contentment in India.[263] Mr Mangles, the Chairman of the Directors, replied at much length, and very conclusively to Mr Disraeli's speech. Mr Liddell, with much simplicity, asked the Speaker to tell him how he should vote, but approved entirely of Lord John Russell's address. Mr Ayrton moved an adjournment of the Debate, which was negatived by 203 to 79. Mr Hadfield then shortly stated in his provincial dialect that "we can never keep our 'old upon Hindia by the Force of Harms." Mr Disraeli then made an animated reply to the speeches against him, but in a manner almost too animated for the occasion. Mr Thomas Baring set Mr Disraeli right, but in rather strong terms, about some proceedings of the Committee on Indian Affairs in 1853, with regard to which Mr Disraeli's memory had proved untrustworthy. Viscount Palmerston shortly made some observations on the Motion and the speech which had in-

[262] Chief Justice of Bombay 1847-1852, and M.P. for Devonport 1854-1859.

[263] "One of those dry constitutional platitudes," said Mr Disraeli in reply, "which in a moment of difficulty the noble lord pulls out of the dusty pigeon-holes of his mind, and shakes in the perplexed face of the baffled House of Commons." Mr Disraeli was admittedly much annoyed by the statesmanlike intervention of Lord John.

troduced it; and the Motion was then negatived without a division, and the Address was unanimously carried.

Queen Victoria to the King of the Belgians..

MARRIAGE OF PRINCESS CHARLOTTE

Osborne, *27th July 1857.*

My dearest Uncle,—At *this* very *moment* the marriage[264] is going on—the *Knot* is being tied which binds your lovely sweet child to a thoroughly worthy husband—and I am sure you will be much moved. May every blessing attend her! I wish *I* could be present—but my dearest *Half* being there makes me feel as I were there myself. I try to picture to myself how *all* will be. I could not give you a greater proof of my love for you all, and my anxiety to give you and dearest Charlotte pleasure, than in urging my dearest Albert to go over—for I encouraged and *urged* him to go though you cannot think *combien cela me coûte* or how completely *déroutée* I am and *feel* when he is away, or how I count the hours till he returns. *All* the numerous children are as *nothing* to me when *he is away*; it seems as if the whole life of the house and home were gone, when he is away!

We do all we can to *fêter* in our very *quiet* way this dear day. We are all out of mourning; the younger children are to have a half-holiday, Alice is to *dine* for the first time in the evening with us; we shall drink *the Archduke and Archduchess's* healths; and I have ordered *wine* for our servants, and *grog* for our sailors to do the same.

Vicky (who is painting in the Alcove near me) wishes me to say everything to you and the *dear young couple*, and pray tell dear Charlotte *all* that we have been doing....

Here we are in anxious (and I fear many people in very *cruel*) suspense, for news from India. They *ought* to have arrived the day before yesterday.

On Thursday, then, we are to have Prince Napoleon, and on the following Thursday the Emperor and Empress; and after them for *one* night, the Queen of Holland,[265] whose activity is astounding—and she sees everything and everybody and goes everywhere; she is certainly clever and amiable....

---

[264] Of the Princess Charlotte to the Archduke Ferdinand Maximilian at Brussels.

[265] Sophia Frederica, born 1818, daughter of King William I. of Würtemberg.

Now, with our children's affectionate love, ever your devoted Niece,

Victoria R.

Pray offer my kind regards to *all* your visitors, even to those whom I do *not* know. I only hope my dearest husband will tell me *all* about everything. Vicky is constantly talking and thinking of Charlotte.

Queen Victoria to Viscount Palmerston.

THE MILITIA

Osborne, *2nd August 1857*.

The Queen has to thank Lord Palmerston for his letter of the 27th July.

The embodying of the Militia will be a most necessary measure, as well for the defence of our own country, and for keeping up on the Continent of Europe the knowledge that we are not in a defenceless state, as for the purpose of obtaining a sufficient number of volunteers for the Army.

The Queen hopes, therefore, that the Militia to be embodied will be on a proper and sufficient scale. She must say, that the last accounts from India show so formidable a state of things that the military measures hitherto taken by the Home Government, on whom the salvation of India must mainly depend, appear to the Queen as by no means adequate to the emergency. We have nearly gone to the full extent of our available means, just as we did in the Crimean War, and may be able to obtain successes; but we have not laid in a store of troops, nor formed Reserves which could carry us over a long struggle, or meet unforeseen new calls. Herein we are always most shortsighted, and have finally to suffer either in power and reputation, or to pay enormous sums for small advantages in the end—generally both.

The Queen hopes that the Cabinet will look the question boldly in the face; nothing could be better than the Resolutions passed in the House of Commons, insuring to the Government every possible support in the adoption of vigorous measures. It is generally the Government, and not the House of Commons, who hang back. The Queen wishes Lord Palmerston to communicate this letter to his Colleagues.

Queen Victoria to Viscount Palmerston.

THE NAVY

Osborne, *4th August 1857.*

The defenceless state of our shores, now that the Army has been reduced to eighteen effective Battalions, and the evident inclinations of the Continental Powers, chiefly France and Russia, to dictate to us with regard to the Oriental Question, makes the Queen naturally turn her attention to the state of our naval preparations and force.

To render it possible to salute the Emperor[266] when he comes here, the old *St Vincent* has been brought out of the harbour, but has been manned chiefly by the men of the *Excellent* gunnery ship; and we have been warned by the Admiralty not to visit the *Excellent* in consequence. This does not show a very brilliant condition! But what is still more worthy of consideration is, that our new fleet, which had been completed at the end of the Russian War, was *a steam* fleet; when it was broken up at the Peace the dockyard expenses were also cut down, and men discharged at the very moment when totally new and extensive arrangements became necessary to repair and keep in a state of efficiency the valuable steam machinery, and to house our gunboat flotilla on shore. To render any of these steamships fit for sea, now that they are dismantled, with our *small* means as to basins and docks, must necessarily cost much time.

The Queen wishes accordingly to have a report sent to her as to the force of screw-ships of the Line and of other classes which can be got ready at the different dockyards, and the time required to get them to sea for actual service; and also the time required to launch and get ready the gunboats. She does not wish for a mere general answer from the Lords of the Admiralty, but for detailed reports from the Admirals commanding at the different ports, and particularly the Captains in command of the Steam Reserve. She would only add that she wishes no unnecessary time to be lost in the preparation of these reports. She requests Lord Palmerston to have these, her wishes, carried out.

---

[266] The Emperor and Empress of the French arrived at Osborne on the 6th of August on a visit to the Queen and Prince, lasting for four days, during which time much discussion took place between the Prince and Emperor on affairs in Eastern Europe.

Queen Victoria to Viscount Palmerston.

DEATH OF SIR HENRY LAWRENCE

Osborne, *22nd August 1857.*

The Queen is afraid from the telegram of this morning that affairs in India have not yet taken a favourable turn. Delhi seems still to hold out, and the death of Sir H. Lawrence[267] is a great loss. The Queen must repeat to Lord Palmerston that the measures hitherto taken by the Government are not commensurate with the magnitude of the crisis.

We have given nearly all we have in reinforcements, and if new efforts should become necessary, by the joining of the Madras and Bombay Armies in the Revolt, for instance, it will take months to prepare Reserves which ought now to be ready. Ten Battalions of Militia to be called out is quite inadequate; forty, at least, ought to be the number, for these also exist only on paper. The augmentation of the Cavalry and the Guards has not yet been ordered.

Financial difficulties don't exist; the 14,000 men sent to India are taken over by the Indian Government, and their expense saved to us; and this appears hardly the moment to make savings on the Army estimates.

Viscount Palmerston to Queen Victoria.

RECRUITING

Downing Street, *22nd August 1857.*

Viscount Palmerston presents his humble duty to your Majesty.... Viscount Palmerston has had the honour of receiving your Majesty's communication of this morning. It is, no doubt, true that the telegraphic account received yesterday evening does not show, that at the dates mentioned from India, any improvement had taken place in the state of affairs, and the loss of Sir Henry Lawrence and of General Barnard,[268] but especially of the former, is deeply to be lamented.

---

[267] On the previous day, the Queen and Prince had returned from a visit to Cherbourg, and found very disquieting news from India. Sir Henry Lawrence was the Military Administrator and Chief Commissioner of Oudh; on the 30th of May, the 71st N.I. mutinied at Lucknow, but Sir Henry drove them from their position and fortified the Residency. Some weeks later, on sallying out to reconnoitre, the English were driven back and besieged in the Residency; Sir Henry dying from the effects of a wound caused by a shell.

[268] He died of cholera at Delhi, on the 5th of July.

With regard, however, to the measures now taking to raise a force to supply the place of the troops sent to India, and to enlist recruits to fill up vacancies in the Regiments in India, Viscount Palmerston would beg to submit that the steps now taking seem to be well calculated for their purpose. The recruiting for the Army has gone on more rapidly than could have been expected at this particular time of year, and in a fortnight or three weeks from this time will proceed still more rapidly; the ten thousand Militia to be immediately embodied will be as much as could probably be got together at the present moment without much local inconvenience; but if that number should be found insufficient, it would be easy afterwards to embody more. But, if the recruiting should go on successfully, that number of Militiamen in addition to the Regulars may be found sufficient. Viscount Palmerston begs to assure your Majesty that there is no wish to make savings on the amount voted for Army Services, but, on the other hand, it would be very inconvenient and embarrassing to exceed that amount without some urgent and adequate necessity....

Queen Victoria to Viscount Palmerston.

Osborne, *22nd August 1857.*

In answer to Lord Palmerston's observations on our Military preparations, the Queen must reply that, although Lord Palmerston disclaims, on the part of the Government, the intention of making a saving on the Army estimates out of the fearful exigencies caused by the Indian Revolt, the facts still remain. The Government have sent fourteen Battalions out of the country and transferred them to the East India Company, and they mean to replace them only by ten new ones, whose organisation has been ordered; but even in these, they mean for the present to save four Companies out of every twelve. The Queen, the House of Lords, the House of Commons, and the Press, all call out for vigorous exertion, and the Government alone take an apologetic line, anxious to do as little as possible, to wait for further news, to reduce as low as possible even what they do grant, and reason as if we had at most *only* to replace what was sent out; whilst if new demands should come upon us, the Reserves which ought now to be decided upon and organised, are only then to be discussed. The Queen can the less reconcile herself to the system, of "letting out a little sail at a time," as Lord Palmerston called it the other day, as she feels convinced that, if vigour and determination to get what will be eventually wanted is shown by the Cabinet, it will pervade the whole Government machinery and attain its object; but that if, on the other hand, people don't see what the Government really require, and find them satisfied with a little at a time, even that little will not be got, as the subordinates naturally take the tone from their superiors. Ten Militia Regiments would not even represent the 10,000 men whom Parliament has voted the supplies for. A Battalion will probably not reach 600 for a time, and from these we hope to draw volunteers again!

The Queen hopes the Cabinet will yet look the whole question in the face, and decide while there is time what they must know will become necessary, and what must in the hurry at the end be done less well and at, probably, double the cost. The Queen can speak by very recent experience, having seen exactly the same course followed in the late War.

Queen Victoria to Viscount Palmerston.

Osborne, *23rd August 1857.*

The Queen approves of Lord Fife[269] and Lord R. Grosvenor being made Peers, and of an offer being made to Mr Macaulay, although she believes he will decline the honour....

Queen Victoria to Viscount Palmerston.

THE ARMY RESERVES

Osborne, *25th August 1857.*

The Queen has received Lord Palmerston's letter of yesterday, and must say that she is deeply grieved at her want of success in impressing upon him the importance of meeting the present dangers by agreeing on, and maturing a general plan by which to replace *in kind* the troops sent out of the country, and for which the money *has* been voted by Parliament.[270] To the formation of the full number of Battal-

---

[269] James, fifth Viscount Macduff and Earl of Fife in the peerage of Ireland, was, on the 1st of October, created a Baron of the United Kingdom; he was the father of the present Duke of Fife. Lord Robert Grosvenor became Lord Ebury, and Mr Macaulay Lord Macaulay of Rothley Temple (his birthplace), in the county of Leicester.

[270] After referring to the necessity for supplying by fresh drafts the gaps created in the regiments in India, Lord Palmerston had written:—

ions, and their full strength in Companies, Lord Palmerston objects that the men will not be found to fill them, and therefore it is left undone; to the calling-out of more Militia, he objects that they ought not to be used as Recruiting Depôts, and if many were called out the speed with which the recruiting for the Army went on, would oblige them to be disbanded again. The War Office pride themselves upon having got 1,000 men since the recruiting began; this is equal to 1,000 a month or 12,000 a year, the ordinary wear and tear of the Army!! Where will the Reserves for India be to be found? It does not suffice merely to get *recruits*, as Lord Palmerston says; they will not become *soldiers* for six months when got, and in the meantime a sufficient number of Militia Regiments ought to be drilled, and made efficient to relieve the Line Regiments already sent, or yet to be sent, for these also are at present necessarily good for nothing.

The Queen must say that the Government incur a fearful responsibility towards their country by their apparent indifference. God grant that no unforeseen European complication fall upon this country—but we are really tempting Providence.

The Queen hopes Lord Palmerston has communicated to the Cabinet her views on the subject.

"If the Militia officers were to find that they were considered merely as drill sergeants for the Line, they would grow careless and indifferent, and many whom it is desirable to keep in the Service would leave it.

"With regard to the number of Militiamen to be embodied, the question seems to be, What is the number which will be wanted for the whole period to the 31st of March, because it would be undesirable to call out and embody now Militia Regiments which would become unnecessary during the winter by the progress of recruiting, and which, from there being no funds applicable to their maintenance, it would become necessary to disembody. The men would be now taken from industrial employment at a time when labour is wanted, and would be turned adrift in the winter when there is less demand for labour.

"With respect to recruiting for the Army, every practicable means has been adopted to hasten its success. Recruiting parties have been scattered over the whole of the United Kingdom, and the permanent staff of the disembodied Militia have been furnished with Beating Warrants enabling them to enlist recruits for the Line; and the recruiting has been hitherto very successful. The only thing to be done is to raise men as fast as possible, and to post them as they are raised to the Regiments and Battalions for which they engage. The standard, moreover, has been lowered...."

Viscount Palmerston to Queen Victoria.

LORD LANSDOWNE

Piccadilly, *31st August 1857.*

... Viscount Palmerston would beg to submit for your Majesty's consideration whether he might be authorised by your Majesty to offer to Lord Lansdowne promotion to the title of Duke. Your Majesty may possibly not have in the course of your Majesty's reign, long as it is to be hoped that reign will be, any subject whose private and public character will during so long a course of years as those which have been the period of Lord Lansdowne's career, have more entitled him to the esteem and respect of his fellow-countrymen, and to the approbation of his Sovereign.

Lord Lansdowne has now for several years given your Majesty's Government the great and valuable support of his advice in council, his assistance in debate, and the weight of his character in the country, without any office. His health and strength, Viscount Palmerston cannot disguise from himself, have not been this year such as they had been; and if your Majesty should contemplate marking at any time your Majesty's sense of Lord Lansdowne's public services, there could not be a better moment for doing so than the present; and Viscount Palmerston has reason to believe that such an act of grace would be very gratifying to the Liberal Party, and would be deemed well bestowed even by those who are of opposite politics.[271]

Mr Macaulay accepts the Peerage with much gratitude to your Majesty.

Queen Victoria to the King of the Belgians.

THE INDIAN MUTINY

Balmoral Castle, *2nd September 1857.*

Dearest Uncle,—... We are in sad anxiety about India, which engrosses all our attention.[272] Troops cannot be raised fast or largely enough. And the horrors committed on the poor ladies—women and children—are unknown in these ages, and make one's blood run cold.

---

[271] Lord Lansdowne declined the honour.

[272] At Balmoral the Queen learned in greater detail of the atrocities which had been committed upon the garrison at Cawnpore.

Altogether, the whole is so much more distressing than the Crimea—where there was *glory* and honourable warfare, and where the poor women and children were safe. Then the distance and the difficulty of communication is such an additional suffering to us all. I know you will feel much for us all. There is not a family hardly who is not in sorrow and anxiety about their children, and in all ranks—India being *the* place where every one was anxious to place a son!

We hear from *our* people (not Fritz) from Berlin, that the King is in a very unsatisfactory state. *What* have you heard?...

Now, with Albert's love, ever your devoted Niece,

Victoria R.

Viscount Palmerston to Queen Victoria.

Brocket, *10th September 1857.*

Viscount Palmerston presents his humble duty to your Majesty and begs to submit that an impression is beginning to prevail that it would be a proper thing that a day should be set apart for National Prayer and Humiliation with reference to the present calamitous state of affairs in India, upon the same principle on which a similar step was taken during the Crimean War; and if your Majesty should approve, Viscount Palmerston would communicate on the subject with the Archbishop of Canterbury.... It is usual on such occasions that the Archbishop of Canterbury should attend,[273] but in consideration of the distance his attendance might well be dispensed with on the present occasion.

Queen Victoria to Viscount Palmerston.

A DAY OF INTERCESSION

Balmoral, *11th September 1857.*

Lord Palmerston knows what the Queen's feelings are with regard to Fast-days, which she thinks do not produce the desired effect—from the manner in which they are appointed, and the selections made for the Service—but she will not oppose the natural feeling which any one must partake in, of a desire to pray for our fellow-countrymen and women who are exposed to such imminent danger, and therefore sanctions his consulting the Archbishop on the subject. She would,

[273] *I.e.* at the meeting of the Council which was to be summoned.

however, suggest its being more appropriately called a day of prayer and intercession for our suffering countrymen, than of fast and humiliation, and of its being on a *Sunday*, and not on a week-day: on the last Fast-day, the Queen heard it generally remarked, that it produced more harm than good, and that, if it were on a Sunday, it would be much more generally observed. However, she will sanction whatever is proper, but thinks it ought to be as soon as possible[274] (in a fortnight or three weeks) if it is to be done at all.

She will hold a Council whenever it is wished.[275]

Queen Victoria to the Earl of Clarendon.

Balmoral Castle, *23rd September 1857.*

The Queen hopes that the arrival of troops and ships with Lord Elgin will be of material assistance, but still it does not alter the state of affairs described by the Queen in her letter, which she wrote to Lord Palmerston, and which she is glad to see Lord Clarendon agrees in. Though we might have perhaps wished the Maharajah[276] to express his feelings on the subject of the late atrocities in India, it was hardly to be expected that he (naturally of a negative, though gentle and very amiable disposition) should pronounce an opinion on so painful a subject, attached as he is to his country, and naturally *still* possessing, with all his amiability and goodness, an *Eastern nature*; he can also hardly, a deposed Indian Sovereign, *not very* fond of the British rule as represented by the East India Company, and, above all, impatient of Sir John Login's[277] tutorship, be expected to *like* to hear his country-people called *fiends* and *monsters*, and to see them brought in hundreds, if not thousands, to be executed.

His best course is to say nothing, she must think.

It is a great mercy he, poor boy, is not there.

---

[274] It was kept on the 7th of October (a Wednesday).

[275] Shortly after the date of this letter came the intelligence from India that Delhi had not fallen, and that the Lucknow garrison was not yet relieved. This news, coupled with the tidings of fresh outbreaks, and the details of the horrors of Cawnpore, generated deep feelings of resentment in the country.

[276] Lord Clarendon had written that he was "sorry to learn that the Maharajah (Dhuleep Singh) had shown little or no regret for the atrocities which have been committed, or sympathy with the sufferers."

[277] Sir John Spencer Login, formerly surgeon at the British Residency, Lucknow, guardian of the Maharajah Dhuleep Singh, 1849-1858.

Viscount Canning to Queen Victoria.

LETTER FROM LORD CANNING

Calcutta, *25th September 1857.*

Lord Canning presents his humble duty to your Majesty, and asks leave again to address your Majesty, although the desire which he has felt that his next letter should announce to your Majesty the fall of Delhi, and the first steps towards a restoration of your Majesty's Authority throughout the revolted Districts, cannot as yet be accomplished. But although it is not in Lord Canning's power to report any very marked success over the Rebels, he can confidently assure your Majesty that a change in the aspect of affairs is gradually taking place, which gives hope that the contest is drawing to a close, and the day of punishment at hand....

Another ground for good hopes is the appearance of things at Lucknow. News just received from Sir James Outram announces that he has joined General Havelock's force at Cawnpore, and that the Troops crossed the Ganges into Oudh on the 19th, with hardly any opposition. The European force now advancing on Lucknow is about [ ][278] strong, well provided with Artillery. The beleaguered Garrison was in good spirits on the 16th of September, and had provisions enough to last to the end of the month. They had lately inflicted severe losses on their assailants, and some of the latter had dispersed. The influential proprietors and chiefs of the country had begun to show symptoms of siding with us.

This is a very different state of things from that which existed when General Havelock's force retired across the Ganges in July; and Lord Canning prays and believes that your Majesty will be spared the pain and horror of hearing that the atrocities of Cawnpore have been re-enacted upon the brave and enduring garrison of Lucknow. Every English soldier who could be made to reach Cawnpore has been pushed on to General Outram, even to the denuding of some points of danger in the intervening country, and General Outram's instructions are to consider the rescue of the garrison as the one paramount object to which everything else is to give way. The garrison (which, after all, is nothing more than the House of the Resident, with defences hastily thrown up) contains about three hundred and fifty European men, four

[278] Word omitted in the original.

hundred and fifty women and children, and one hundred and twenty sick, besides three hundred natives, hitherto faithful. The city, and even the province, may be abandoned and recovered again, but these lives must be saved now or never; and to escape the sorrow and humiliation of such barbarities as have already been endured elsewhere is worth any sacrifice. It is in consideration of the state of things at these two most critical points, Delhi and Lucknow, that Lord Canning ventures to ask your Majesty to look hopefully to the events of the next few weeks; notwithstanding that he is unable to announce any signal success....

SIR COLIN CAMPBELL

Sir Colin Campbell has been in a state of delight ever since his favourite 93rd landed five days ago.[279] He went to see them on board their transport before they disembarked, and when Lord Canning asked how he found them, replied that the only thing amiss was that they had become too fat on the voyage, and could not button their coats. But, indeed, all the troops of the China force have been landed in the highest possible condition of health and vigour. The 23rd, from its large proportion of young soldiers, is perhaps the one most likely to suffer from the climate and the hardships of the Service—for, although no care or cost will be spared to keep them in health and comfort, Lord Canning fears that hardships there must be, seeing how vast an extent of usually productive country will be barren for a time, and that the districts from which some of our most valuable supplies, especially the supply of carriage animals, are drawn, have been stripped bare, or are still in revolt. As it is, the Commander-in-Chief has most wisely reduced the amount of tent accommodation for officers and men far below the ordinary luxurious Indian allowance.

The presence of the ships of the Royal Navy has been of the greatest service. At least eleven thousand seamen and marines have been contributed by them for duty on shore, and the broadsides of the *Sanspareil*, *Shannon*, and *Pearl*, as they lie along the esplanade, have had a very reassuring effect upon the inhabitants of Calcutta, who, un-

[279] At the battle of the Alma, Sir Colin Campbell, in command of the 2nd or Highland Brigade of the 1st Division, had, with his Highlanders in line, routed the last compact column of the Russians. On the 11th of July 1857, he was appointed Commander-in-Chief in India, and started literally at one day's notice, reaching Calcutta on the 14th of August.

til lately, have insisted pertinaciously that their lives and property were in hourly danger.[280]

No line-of-battle ship has been seen in the Hooghly since Admiral Watson sailed up to Chandernagore just a hundred years ago;[281] and certainly nothing in his fleet was equal to the *Sanspareil.* The natives stare at her, and call her "the four-storied boat."

INDIA

For the future, if Delhi should fall and Lucknow be secured, the work of pacification will go forward steadily. Many points will have to be watched, and there may be occasional resistance; but nothing like an organised contest against authority is probable. The greatest difficulties will be in the civil work of re-settlement. The recent death of Mr Colvin,[282] the Lieutenant-Governor of the North-Western Provinces, has removed an officer whose experience would there have been most valuable. He has died, fairly exhausted; and is the fourth officer of high trust whose life has given way in the last four months.

One of the greatest difficulties which lie ahead—and Lord Canning grieves to say so to your Majesty—will be the violent rancour of a very large proportion of the English community against every native Indian of every class. There is a rabid and indiscriminate vindictiveness abroad, even amongst many who ought to set a better example, which it is impossible to contemplate without something like a feeling of shame for one's fellow-countrymen. Not one man in ten seems to think that the hanging and shooting of forty or fifty thousand mutineers, besides other Rebels, can be otherwise than practicable and right; nor does it occur to those who talk and write most upon the matter that for the Sovereign of England to hold and govern India without employing, and, to a great degree, trusting natives, both in civil and military service, is simply impossible. It is no exaggeration to say that a vast number of the European community would hear with pleasure and approval that every Hindoo and Mohammedan had been proscribed, and that none would be admitted to serve the Government

[280] The services of the Naval Brigade, at the relief of Lucknow, were warmly recognised by Sir Colin Campbell, and especially the gallantry of Captain Peel of the *Shannon.*

[281] In retribution for the atrocity of the Black Hole of Calcutta, Watson, under instructions from Clive, reduced Chandernagore on the 23rd of March 1757; the battle of Plassey was fought on the 23rd of June.

[282] John Russell Colvin, formerly Private Secretary to Lord Auckland, had been Lieutenant-Governor since 1853.

except in a menial office. That which they desire is to see a broad line of separation, and of declared distrust drawn between us Englishmen and every subject of your Majesty who is not a Christian, and who has a dark skin; and there are some who entirely refuse to believe in the fidelity or goodwill of any native towards any European; although many instances of the kindness and generosity of both Hindoos and Mohammedans have come upon record during these troubles.

THE POLICY OF CLEMENCY

To those whose hearts have been torn by the foul barbarities inflicted upon those dear to them any degree of bitterness against the natives may be excused. No man will dare to judge them for it. But the cry is raised loudest by those who have been sitting quietly in their homes from the beginning and have suffered little from the convulsions around them unless it be in pocket. It is to be feared that this feeling of exasperation will be a great impediment in the way of restoring tranquillity and good order, even after signal retribution shall have been deliberately measured out to all chief offenders.[283]

Lord Canning is ashamed of having trespassed upon your Majesty's indulgence at such length. He will only add that he has taken the liberty of sending to your Majesty by this mail a map which has just been finished, showing the distribution of the Army throughout India at the time of the outbreak of the Mutiny. It also shows the Regiments of the Bengal Army which have mutinied, and those which have been disarmed, the number of European troops arrived in Calcutta up to the 19th of September, and whence they came; with some few other points of information.

There may be some slight inaccuracies, as the first copies of the map have only just been struck off, and have not been corrected; but Lord Canning believes that it will be interesting to your Majesty at the present moment.

Lord Canning begs to be allowed to express his earnest wishes for the health of your Majesty, and of His Royal Highness Prince Albert, and to offer to your Majesty the humble assurance of his sincere and dutiful devotion.

---

[283] Lord Canning having promulgated a Proclamation in July, enjoining the Civil Servants of the East India Company to refrain from unnecessary severity, had earned the *sobriquet* of "Clemency Canning."

Queen Victoria to the Earl of Clarendon.

Balmoral, *28th September 1857.*

The Queen is much surprised at Lord Clarendon's observing that "from what he hears the Maharajah was either from nature or early education cruel."[284] He must have changed very suddenly if this be true, for if there was a thing for which he was remarkable, it was his extreme gentleness and kindness of disposition. We have known him for three years (our two boys intimately), and he always shuddered at hurting anything, and was peculiarly gentle and kind towards children and animals, and if anything rather timid; so that all who knew him said he never could have had a chance in his own country. His valet, who is a very respectable Englishman, and has been with him ever since his twelfth year, says that he never knew a kinder or more amiable disposition. The Queen fears that people who do not know him well have been led away by their present very natural feelings of hatred and distrust of all Indians to slander him. What he might turn out, if left in the hands of unscrupulous Indians in his own country, of course no one can foresee.

Queen Victoria to Viscount Palmerston.

Windsor Castle, *17th October 1857.*

The Queen has received yesterday evening the box with the Dockyard Returns. It will take her some time to peruse and study them; she wishes, however, to remark upon two points, and to have them pointed out also to Sir Charles Wood,[285] viz. first, that they are dated some as early as the 27th August, and none later than the 10th September, and that she received them, only on the *17th October*; and then that there is not one original Return amongst them, but they are all copies! When the Queen asks for Returns, to which she attaches great importance, she expects at least to see them in original.

Queen Victoria to the Earl of Clarendon.

MARRIAGE OF THE PRINCESS ROYAL

Windsor Castle, *25th October 1857.*

---

[284] See *ante*, p. 248, note 40.

[285] First Lord of the Admiralty.

The Queen returns these letters. It would be well if Lord Clarendon would tell Lord Bloomfield not to *entertain* the *possibility* of such a question as the Princess Royal's marriage taking place at Berlin.[286] The Queen *never* could consent to it, both for public and private reasons, and the assumption of its being *too much* for a Prince Royal of Prussia to *come* over to marry *the Princess Royal of Great Britain* IN England is too *absurd*, to say the least. The Queen must say that there never was even the *shadow* of a *doubt* on *Prince Frederick William's* part as to *where* the marriage should take place, and she suspects this to be the mere gossip of the Berliners. Whatever may be the usual practice of Prussian Princes, it is not *every* day that one marries the eldest daughter of the Queen of England. The question therefore must be considered as settled and closed....

Queen Victoria to the Earl of Clarendon.

DEATH OF THE DUCHESS DE NEMOURS

Windsor Castle, *12th November 1857.*

The Queen thanks Lord Clarendon much for his kind and sympathising letter, and is much gratified at Count Persigny's kind note. He *is* a good, honest, warm-hearted man, for whom we have sincere esteem. The news from India was a great relief and a *ray* of sunshine in our great affliction.[287] The Queen had the happiness of informing poor Sir George Couper of the relief of Lucknow, in which for four months his son, daughter-in-law, and grandchildren were shut up. The loss of two such distinguished officers as Generals Nicholson and Neill, and alas! of many inferior ones, is, however, very sad.

We visited the house of mourning yesterday, and *no words can* describe the scene of woe.[288] There was the venerable Queen with the

---

[286] The marriage took place at the Chapel Royal, St James's.

[287] Havelock, in consequence of the strength of the rebels in Oudh, had been unable to march to the assistance of Lucknow immediately after the relief of Cawnpore. He joined hands with Outram on the 10th of September, and reinforced the Lucknow garrison on the 25th.

[288] In a pathetic letter, just received, the Duc de Nemours (second son of Louis Philippe) had announced the death of his wife, Queen Victoria's beloved cousin and friend. She was only thirty-five years of age, and had been married at eighteen. She had seemed to make a good recovery after the birth of a child on the 28th of October, but died quite suddenly on the 10th of November, while at her toilette.

motherless children, admirable in her deep grief, and her pious resignation to the Will of God! yet even now the support, the comfort of all, thinking but of others and ready to devote her last remaining strength and her declining years to her children and grandchildren. There was the broken-hearted, almost distracted widower—*her son*—and lastly, there was in one room the lifeless, but oh! even in its ghostliness, most beautiful form of his young, lovely, and angelic wife, lying in her bed with her splendid hair covering her shoulders, and a heavenly expression of peace; and in the next room, the dear little pink infant sleeping in its cradle.

The Queen leaves to Lord Clarendon's kind heart to imagine what this spectacle of woe must be, and how *deeply* afflicted and impressed *we must be*—who have only so lately had a child born to us and have been so fortunate! The Prince has been *completely* upset by this; and she was besides like a dear sister to us. God's will be done! But it seems *too* dreadful almost to believe it—too hard to bear. The dear Duchess's death must have been caused by some affection of the heart, for she was perfectly well, having her hair combed, suddenly exclaimed to the Nurse, "Oh! mon Dieu, Madame"—her head fell on one side—and before the Duke could run upstairs her hand was cold! The Queen had visited her on Saturday—looking well—and *yesterday* saw her lifeless form in the very same spot!

If Lord Clarendon could give a slight hint to the *Times* to say a few words of sympathy on the awful and unparalleled misfortune of these poor exiles, she is sure it would be very soothing to their bleeding hearts.... The sad event at Claremont took place just five days later than the death of poor Princess Charlotte under very similar circumstances forty years ago; and the poor Duchess was the niece of Princess Charlotte's husband.

Viscount Palmerston to Queen Victoria.

CRISIS IN THE CITY

Downing Street, *12th November 1857.*

Viscount Palmerston presents his humble duty to your Majesty, and begs to state that the condition of financial affairs became worse to-day than it was yesterday.[289] The Governor of the bank represented

[289] The financial crisis had originated in numerous stoppages of banks in the United States, where premature schemes of railway extension had involved

that almost all private firms have ceased to discount bills, and that the Reserve Fund of the Bank of England, out of which discounts are made and liabilities satisfied, had been reduced last night to £1,400,000, and that if that fund should become exhausted the bank would have to suspend its operations. Under these circumstances it appeared to Viscount Palmerston, and to the Chancellor of the Exchequer, that a case had arisen for doing the same thing which was done under somewhat similar circumstances in 1847—that is to say, that a letter should be written by the first Lord of the Treasury and the Chancellor of the Exchequer to the Governor of the Bank of England, saying that if under the pressure of the emergency the bank should deem it necessary to issue more notes than the amount to which they are at present confined by law, the Government would apply to Parliament to grant them an indemnity.

This Measure, in 1847, had the effect of stopping the then existing panic, and the necessity for making such an issue did not arise; on the present occasion this announcement will, no doubt, have a salutary effect in allaying the present panic, but as the bank had to discount to-day bills to the amount of £2,000,000, which they could not have done out of a fund of £1,400,000, unless deposits and payments in, to a considerable amount, had been made, the probability is that the issue thus authorised will actually be made. The Governor and Deputy-Governor of the bank represented that the communication, in order to be effectual and to save from ruin firms which were in imminent danger, ought to be made forthwith, so that they might be enabled to announce it on the Stock Exchange before the closing of business at four o'clock. Viscount Palmerston and Sir George Lewis therefore signed at once, and gave to the Governor of the bank the letter of which the accompanying paper is a copy, the pressure of the matter not allowing time to take your Majesty's pleasure beforehand.

SUSPENSION OF BANK CHARTER ACT

The state of things now is more urgent than that which existed in 1847, when the similar step was taken; at that time the Reserve Fund was about £1,900,000, last night it was only £1,400,000; at that time the bullion in the bank was above £8,000,000, it is now somewhat less

---

countless investors in ruin; in consequence, the pressure on firms and financial houses became even more acute than in 1847; see *ante*, vol. ii. pp. 130, 131. The bank rate now rose to 10 per cent. as against 9 per cent. in that year, and the bank reserve of bullion was alarmingly depleted.

than £8,000,000; at that time things were mending, they are now getting worse.

But however necessary this Measure has been considered, and however useful it may be expected to be, it inevitably entails one very inconvenient consequence. The Government have authorised the bank to break the law, and whether the law shall actually be broken or not, it would be highly unconstitutional for the Government not to take the earliest opportunity of submitting the matter to the knowledge of Parliament. This course was pursued in 1847. The letter from Lord John Russell and Sir Charles Wood to the Governor of the bank was dated on the 25th October, Parliament then stood prorogued in the usual way to the 11th November, but a council was held on the 31st October, at which your Majesty summoned Parliament to meet for the despatch of business on the 18th November; and on that day the session was opened in the usual way by a Speech from the Throne. It would be impossible under present circumstances to put off till the beginning of February a communication to Parliament of the step taken to-day.

Viscount Palmerston therefore would beg to submit for your Majesty's approval that a Council might be held at Windsor on Monday next, and that Parliament might then be summoned to meet in fourteen days. This would bring Parliament together in the first days of December, and after sitting ten days, or a fortnight, if necessary, it might be adjourned till the first week in February.[290]

Viscount Palmerston submits an explanatory Memorandum which he has just received for your Majesty's information from the Chancellor of the Exchequer....

Queen Victoria to Lord Panmure.

ARMY ESTABLISHMENT

Osborne, *18th December 1857.*

The Queen has had some correspondence with Lord Panmure upon the Establishment of the Army for the next financial year.[291] She

[290] Parliament accordingly met on the 3rd of December, and the Session was opened by the Queen in person. The Act of Indemnity was passed without serious opposition, and a select committee re-appointed to enquire into the operation of the Bank Charter Act.

[291] On the 14th of December, the Queen had pressed the immediate formation of two new Cavalry Regiments.

wishes now to lay down the principle which she thinks ought to guide our decision, and asks Lord Palmerston to consider it with his colleagues in Cabinet. Last year we reduced our Army suddenly to a low peace establishment to meet the demand for reduction of taxation raised in the House of Commons. With this peace establishment we had to meet the extraordinary demands of India, we have sent almost every available regiment, battalion, and battery, and are forced to contemplate the certainty of a large increase of our force in India as a permanent necessity. What the Queen requires is, that a well-considered and digested estimate should be made of the additional regiments, etc., etc., so required, and that after deducting this number from our establishment of 1857-1858, that for the next year should be brought up again to the same condition as if the Indian demand, which is foreign to our ordinary consideration, had not arisen. If this be done it will still leave us militarily weaker than we were at the beginning of the year, for the larger English Army maintained in India will require proportionally more reliefs and larger depôts.

As the Indian finances pay for the troops employed in India, the Force at home and in the colonies will, when raised to its old strength, not cost a shilling more than the peace establishment of 1857 settled under a pressure of financial reduction.

Anything less than this will not leave this country in a safe condition. The Queen does not ask only for the same number of men as in 1857-1858, but particularly for Regiments of Cavalry, Battalions of Infantry and Batteries of Artillery, which alone would enable us in case of a war to effect the increase to a war establishment.

The Queen encloses her answer to Lord Panmure's last letter.

Queen Victoria to Viscount Palmerston.

GOVERNMENT OF INDIA

Windsor Castle, *24th December 1857.*

The Queen only now returns to Lord Palmerston the Memorandum containing the Heads of an arrangement for the future Government of India, which the Committee of Cabinet have agreed to recommend. She will have an opportunity of seeing Lord Palmerston before the Cabinet meet again, and to hear a little more in detail the reasons which influenced the Committee in their several decisions. She wishes only to recommend two points to Lord Palmerston's consideration: 1st, the mode of communication between the Queen and the new Government which it is intended to establish. As long as the Government was that of the Company, the Sovereign was generally left quite ignorant of decisions and despatches; now that the Government is to be that of the Sovereign, and the direction will, she presumes, be given in her name, a direct official responsibility to her will have to be established. She doubts whether any one but a Secretary of State could speak in the Queen's name, like the Foreign Secretary to Foreign Courts, the Colonial Secretary to the Governors of the Colonies, and the Home Secretary to the Lord-Lieutenant of Ireland and the Lieutenants of the Counties of Great Britain, the Judges, Convocations, Mayors, etc., etc. On the other hand, would the position of a Secretary of State be compatible with his being President of a Council? The Treasury and Admiralty act as "My Lords," but they only administer special departments, and do not direct the policy of a country in the Queen's name. The mixture of supreme direction, and also of the conduct of the administration of the department to be directed, has in practice been found as inconvenient in the War Department as it is wrong in principle.

The other point is the importance of having only *one* Army, whether native, local, or general, with one discipline and one command, that of the Commander-in-Chief. This is quite compatible with first appointments to the native Army, being vested as a point of patronage in the members of the Council, but it ought to be distinctly recognised in order to do away with those miserable jealousies between the different military services, which have done more harm to us in India than, perhaps, any other circumstance.

Perhaps Lord Palmerston would circulate this letter amongst the members of the Committee who agreed upon the proposed scheme?

Viscount Canning to Queen Victoria.

DEATH OF HAVELOCK

Government House, Calcutta, *24th December 1857.*

Lord Canning presents his humble duty to your Majesty, and begs permission to express to your Majesty at the earliest opportunity the respectful gratitude with which he has received your Majesty's most gracious letter of the 9th of November.

However certain Lord Canning might have been as to the sentiments with which your Majesty would view the spirit of bitter and unreasoning vengeance against your Majesty's Indian subjects with which too many minds are imbued in England as well as in this country, it has been an indescribable pleasure to him to read what your Majesty has condescended to write to him upon this painful topic. Your Majesty's gracious kindness in the reference made by your Majesty to what is said by the newspapers is also deeply felt by Lord Canning. He can truly and conscientiously assure your Majesty of his indifference to all such attacks—an indifference so complete indeed as to surprise himself.

Lord Canning fears that the satisfaction which your Majesty will have experienced very shortly after the date of your Majesty's letter, upon receiving the news of Sir Henry Havelock's entry into Lucknow, will have been painfully checked by the long and apparently blank interval which followed, and during which your Majesty's anxieties for the ultimate safety of the garrison, largely increased by many precious lives, must have become more intense than ever. Happily, this suspense is over; and the real rescue effected by a glorious combination of skill and intrepidity on the part of Sir Colin Campbell and his troops must have been truly gratifying to your Majesty.[292] The defence of Lucknow and the relief of the defenders are two exploits which, each in their kind, will stand out brightly in the history of these terrible times.

... Lord Canning has not failed to transmit your Majesty's gracious message to Sir Colin Campbell, and has taken the liberty to add your Majesty's words respecting his favourite 93rd, which will not be less grateful to the brave old soldier than the expression of your Majesty's consideration for himself.

Your Majesty has lost two most valuable officers in Sir Henry Havelock and Brigadier-General Neill. They were very different, however. The first was quite of the old school—severe and precise with his men, and very cautious in his movements and plans—but in action bold as well as skilful. The second very open and impetuous, but full of resources; and to his soldiers as kind and thoughtful of their comfort as if they had been his children.

---

[292] Sir Colin Campbell had relieved Lucknow on the 17th of November, but Sir Henry Havelock (as he had now become) died from illness and exhaustion. General Neill had been killed on the occasion of the reinforcement in September, *ante*, p. 254.

With earnest wishes for the health and happiness of your Majesty and the Prince, Lord Canning begs permission to lay at your Majesty's feet the assurance of his most dutiful and devoted attachment.

Queen Victoria to Lord Panmure.

ARMY ORGANISATION

Windsor Castle, *29th December 1857.*

The Queen has received Lord Panmure's letter and Memorandum of the 24th. She must say that she still adheres to her views as formerly expressed. Lord Panmure admits that the two plans don't differ materially in expense. It becomes, then, a mere question of organisation and of policy. As to the first, all military authorities of all countries and times agree upon the point that numerous *cadres* with fewer men give the readiest means of increasing an army on short notice, the main point to be attended to in a constitutional and democratic country like England. As to the second, a system of organisation will always be easier defended than mere numbers arbitrarily fixed, and Parliament ought to have the possibility of voting more or voting fewer men, according to their views of the exigencies of the country, or the pressure of finance at different times, and to be able to do so without deranging the organisation.

The Queen hopes Lord Panmure will look at our position, as if the Indian demands had not arisen, and he will find that to come to Parliament with the Cavalry borne on the estimates reduced by three regiments (as will be the case even after two shall have returned from India, and the two new ones shall have been formed), will certainly not prove *too little* anxiety on the part of the Government to cut down our military establishments.

INTRODUCTORY NOTE
TO CHAPTER XXVII

On the 25th of January of the new year (1858) Prince Frederick William of Prussia (afterwards the Emperor Frederick) was married, with brilliant ceremonial, to the Princess Royal, at the Chapel Royal, St James's, an event marked by general national rejoicings; another event in the private life of the Queen, but one of a melancholy character, was the death of the Duchess of Orleans at the age of forty-four.

A determined attempt was made by Orsini, Pierri, and others, members of the Carbonari Society, to assassinate the Emperor and Empress of the French by throwing grenades filled with detonating powder under their carriage. The Emperor was only slightly hurt, but several bystanders were killed, and very many more wounded. The plot had been conceived, and the grenades manufactured in England, and a violently hostile feeling was engendered in France against this country, owing to the prescriptive right of asylum enjoyed by foreign refugees. The French *militaires* were particularly vehement in their language, and Lord Palmerston so far bowed to the demands of the French Foreign Minister as to introduce a Bill to make the offence of conspiracy to murder, a felony instead of, as it had previously been, a misdemeanour. The Conservative Party supported the introduction of the Bill, but, on the second reading, joined with eighty-four Liberals and four Peelites in supporting an Amendment by Mr Milner Gibson, postponing the reform of the Criminal Law till the peremptory demands of Count Walewski had been formally answered. The Ministry was defeated and resigned, and Lord Derby and Mr Disraeli returned to Office. Orsini and Pierri were executed in Paris, but the state trial in London of a Dr Bernard, a resident of Bayswater, for complicity, ended, mainly owing to the menacing attitude of France over the whole question, in an acquittal. The Italian nationality of the chief conspirators endangered, but only temporarily, the important *entente* between France and Sardinia.

Before the resignation of the Ministry, the thanks of both Houses of Parliament were voted to the civil and military officers of India for their exertions in suppressing the Mutiny; the Opposition endeavoured to obtain the omission of the name of Lord Canning from the address, till his conduct of affairs had been discussed. The difficulties in India were not at an end, for Sir Colin Campbell had been unable to hold Lucknow, and had transferred the rescued garrison to Cawnpore, which he re-occupied. It was not till the end of March that Lucknow was captured by the Commander-in-Chief, who was raised to the peerage as Lord Clyde, after the taking of Jhansi and of Gwalior in Central India, by Sir Hugh Rose, had virtually terminated the revolt.

In anticipation of the capture of Lucknow, the Governor-General had prepared a proclamation for promulgation in Oudh, announcing that, except in the case of certain loyal Rajahs, proprietary rights in the soil of the province would be confiscated. One copy of the draft was sent home, and another shown to Sir James Outram, Chief Commissioner of Oudh, and, in consequence of the latter's protest against its severity, as making confiscation the rule and not the exception, an exemption was inserted in favour of such landowners as should actively co-operate in restoring order. On receiving the draft in its unaltered form, Lord Ellenborough, the new President of the Board of Control, forwarded a despatch to Lord Canning, strongly condemning his action, and, on the publication of this despatch, the Ministry narrowly escaped Parliamentary censure. Lord Ellenborough himself resigned, and was succeeded by Lord Stanley. Attempts had been made by both Lord Palmerston and Lord Derby to pass measures for the better government of India. After two Bills had been introduced and withdrawn, the procedure by resolution was resorted to, and a measure was ultimately passed transferring the Government of India to the Crown.

The China War terminated on the 26th of June, by the treaty of Tien-tsin, which renewed the treaty of 1842, and further opened up China to British commerce. A dispute with Japan led to a treaty signed at Yeddo by Lord Elgin and the representatives of the Tycoon, enlarging British diplomatic and trade privileges in that country.

The Budget of Mr Disraeli imposed for the first time a penny stamp on bankers' cheques; a compromise was arrived at on the Oaths question, the words "on the true faith of a Christian" having hitherto prevented Jews from sitting in Parliament. They were now enabled to take the oath with the omission of these words, and Baron Rothschild took his seat for the City of London accordingly.

Among the other events of importance in the year were the satisfactory termination of a dispute with the Neapolitan Government arising out of the seizure of the *Cagliari*; a modified union, under a central Commission, of Moldavia and Wallachia; the despatch of Mr Gladstone by the Conservative Government as High Commissioner to the Ionian Islands; and the selection of Ottawa, formerly known as Bytown, for the capital of the Dominion of Canada.

CHAPTER XXVII
1858

Queen Victoria to the King of the Belgians.

Windsor Castle, *12th January 1858.*

My dearest Uncle,—Accept my warmest thanks for your kind and affectionate letter of the 8th. I hope and trust to hear that your cold has left you, and that on Monday I shall have the immense happiness of embracing you.

It is a time of immense bustle and agitation; I *feel* it is terrible to give up one's poor child, and *feel* very nervous for the coming time, and for the departure. But I am glad to see Vicky is quite well again and *unberufen* has got over her cold and is very well. But she has had ever since January '57 a succession of emotions and leave-takings—most trying to any one, but particularly to so young a girl with such *very* powerful feelings. She is so much improved in self-control and is so clever (I may say wonderfully so), and so sensible that we can talk to her of anything—and therefore shall miss her sadly. But we try *not* to dwell on or to think of *that*, as I am sure it is much better *not* to do so and not get ourselves *émus* beforehand, or she will break down as well as we, and that never would do.

To-day arrive (on a visit *here*) *her* Court—which is a very good thing, so that she will get acquainted with them....

The affection for her, and the loyalty shown by the country at large on this occasion is *most* truly gratifying—and for so young a child really *very, very* pleasing to our feelings. The Nation look upon her, as Cobden said, as "*England's* daughter," and as if they married a child of their own, which is *very* satisfactory, and shows, in spite of a few newspaper follies and absurdities, how really *sound* and *monarchical* everything is in this country. Now, with Albert's love, ever your devoted Niece,

Victoria R.

Queen Victoria to the King of the Belgians.

MARRIAGE OF THE PRINCESS ROYAL

Buckingham Palace, *9th February 1858.*

My dearest Uncle,—Accept my warmest thanks for your very kind and affectionate letter of the 4th, with such kind accounts of our dear child, who was so thankful for your kindness and affection, and of whose immense and universal success and admirable behaviour—natural yet dignified—we have the most charming accounts. I send you a letter from Augusta[293] (Mecklenburg), which will give you an idea of the impression produced, begging you to let me have it back soon. She is quite well and *not* tired. But the separation was *awful*, and the poor child was *quite* broken-hearted, particularly at parting from her dearest beloved papa, whom she *idolises*. *How* we miss her, I can't say, and never having been separated from her since thirteen years above a fortnight, I am in a constant fidget and impatience to know everything about *every*thing. It is a *great, great* trial for a *Mother* who has watched over her child with such anxiety day after day, to see her far away—dependent on herself! But I have great confidence in her good sense, clever head, kind and good heart, in Fritz's excellent character and devotion to her, and in faithful E. Stockmar, who possesses her *entire* confidence.

The blank she has left behind is *very great* indeed....

To-morrow is the eighteenth anniversary of my blessed marriage, which has brought such universal blessings on this country and Europe! For *what* has not my beloved and perfect Albert done? Raised monarchy to the *highest* pinnacle of *respect*, and rendered it *popular* beyond what it *ever* was in this country!

The Bill proposed by the Government to improve the law respecting conspiracy and assassination will pass, and Lord Derby has been most useful about it.[294] But people are very indignant here at the conduct of the French officers, and at the offensive insinuations against this country.[295]....

---

[293] Elder daughter of Adolphus, Duke of Cambridge, and now Grand Duchess-Dowager of Mecklenburg-Strelitz.

[294] Lord Derby and his party, however, changed their attitude in the next few days, and succeeded in putting the Government in a minority.

[295] On the 14th of January, the assassination of the French Emperor, which had been planned in England by Felice Orsini and other refugees, was attempted. On the arrival of the Imperial carriage at the Opera House in the Rue

Hoping to hear that you are quite well, and begging to thank Leopold very much for his very kind letter, believe me, your devoted Niece,

Victoria R.

Viscount Palmerston to Queen Victoria.

DEFEAT OF THE GOVERNMENT

Piccadilly, *19th February 1858.*

Viscount Palmerston presents his humble duty to your Majesty, and is sorry to have to inform your Majesty that the Government were beat this evening on Mr Milner Gibson's[296] Amendment by a majority of 19,[297] the numbers being for his Amendment, 234, and against it 215.

Mr Milner Gibson began the Debate by moving his Amendment in a speech of considerable ability, but abounding in misrepresentation, which nevertheless produced a marked effect upon the House. Mr Baines followed, but only argued the Bill without replying to Mr Gibson's speech. This was remarked upon by Mr Walpole, who followed

---

Lepelletier, explosive hand-grenades were thrown at it, and though the Emperor and Empress were unhurt, ten people were either killed outright or died of their wounds, and over one hundred and fifty were injured. Notwithstanding the scene of carnage, their Majesties maintained their composure and sat through the performance of the Opera. In the addresses of congratulation to the Emperor on his escape (published, some of them inadvertently, in the official *Moniteur*), officers commanding French regiments used language of the most insulting character to England, and Count Walewski, the French Foreign Minister, in a despatch, recommended the British Government to take steps to prevent the right of asylum being abused.

296 Mr Milner Gibson had found a seat at Ashton-under-Lyne.

297 The Conspiracy Bill aimed at making conspiracy to murder a felony, instead of, as it had previously been, a misdemeanour, and leave had been given by a large majority to introduce it; but when Count Walewski's despatch to Count de Persigny came to be published, the feeling gained ground that the Government had shown undue subservience in meeting the representations of the French Ambassador. The despatch had not actually been answered, although verbal communications had taken place. The opposition to the Bill was concerted by Lord John Russell and Sir James Graham; see Parker's *Sir James Graham*, vol. ii. p. 236, and the observation of the Prince, *post*, p. 268. The purport of the Amendment was to postpone any reform in the criminal law till the French despatch had been replied to.

him, and who said that though he approved of the Bill he could not vote for reading it a second time until Count Walewski's despatch had been answered. Mr MacMahon supported the Amendment, as did Mr Byng. Sir George Grey, who followed Mr Walpole, defended the Bill and the course pursued by the Government in not having answered Count Walewski's despatch until after the House of Commons should have affirmed the Bill by a Second Reading. Mr Spooner remained steady to his purpose, and would vote against the Amendment, though in doing so he should differ from his friends. Lord Harry Vane opposed the Amendment, as interfering with the passing of the Bill, and Mr Bentinck took the same line, and replied to some of the arguments of Mr Milner Gibson. Mr Henley said he should vote for the Amendment. The Lord Advocate made a good speech against it. Mr Gladstone spoke with his usual talent in favour of the Amendment, and was answered by the Attorney-General in a speech which would have convinced men who had not taken a previous determination. He was followed by Mr Disraeli, who seemed confident of success, and he was replied to by Viscount Palmerston, and the House then divided.

It seems that Lord Derby had caught at an opportunity of putting the Government in a minority. He saw that there were ninety-nine Members who were chiefly of the Liberal Party, who had voted against the Bill when it was first proposed, and who were determined to oppose it in all its stages. He calculated that if his own followers were to join those ninety-nine, the Government might be run hard, or perhaps be beaten, and he desired all his friends[298] to support Mr Milner Gibson; on the other hand, many of the supporters of the Government, relying upon the majority of 200, by which the leave to bring the Bill in had been carried, and upon the majority of 145 of last night, had gone out of town for a few days, not anticipating any danger to the Government from Mr Gibson's Motion, and thus an adverse division was obtained. Moreover, Count Walewski's despatch, the tone and tenor of which had been much misrepresented, had produced a very unfavourable effect on the mind of members in general, and there was a prevailing feeling very difficult to overcome, that the proposed Bill was somehow or other a concession to the demand of a Foreign Government. The Cabinet will have to consider at its meeting at three o'clock to-morrow what course the Government will have to pursue.

[298] See Ashley's *Life of Lord Palmerston*, vol. ii. p. 146.

Memorandum by the Prince Albert.

RESIGNATION OF THE GOVERNMENT

Buckingham Palace, *21st February 1858.*

Lord Palmerston came at five o'clock from the Cabinet, and tendered his resignation in his own name, and that of his Colleagues. The Cabinet had well considered their position and found that, as the vote passed by the House, although the result of an accidental combination of parties, was virtually a vote of censure upon their conduct, they could not with honour or with any advantage to the public service carry on the Government.

The combination was the whole of the Conservative Party (Lord Derby's followers), Lord John Russell, the Peelites, with Mr Gladstone and the whole of the Radicals; but the Liberal Party generally is just now very angry with Lord Palmerston personally, chiefly on account of his apparent submission to French dictation, and the late appointment of Lord Clanricarde as Privy Seal, who is looked upon as a reprobate.[299] Lord Clanricarde's presence in the House of Commons during the Debate, and in a conspicuous place, enraged many supporters of Lord Palmerston to that degree that they voted at once with the Opposition.

LORD DERBY SUMMONED

The Queen wrote to Lord Derby the letter here following;[300] he came a little after six o'clock. He stated that nobody was more surprised in his life than he had been at the result of the Debate, after the Government had only a few days before had a majority of more than 100 on the introduction of their Bill. He did not know how it came about, but thought it was the work of Lord John Russell and Sir James Graham in the interest of the Radicals; Mr Gladstone's junction must have been accidental. As to his own people, they had, owing to his own personal exertions, as the Queen was aware, though many very

---

[299] Since his triumph at the polls in 1857, Lord Palmerston had been somewhat arbitrary in his demeanour, and had defied public opinion by taking Lord Clanricarde into the Government, after some unpleasant disclosures in the Irish Courts. While walking home on the 18th, after obtaining an immense majority on the India Bill, he was told by Sir Joseph Bethell that he ought, like the Roman Consuls in a triumph, to have some one to remind him that he was, as a minister, not immortal. Next day he was defeated.

[300] Summoning him to advise her.

unwillingly, supported the Bill; but the amendment of Mr Milner Gibson was so skilfully worded, that it was difficult for them not to vote for it; he had to admit this when they came to him to ask what they should do, merely warning them to save the Measure itself, which the Amendment did. He then blamed the Government very much for leaving Count Walewski's despatch unanswered before coming before Parliament, which he could hardly understand.

OFFER TO LORD DERBY

On the Queen telling him that the Government had resigned, and that she commissioned him to form a new Administration, he begged that this offer might not be made to him without further consideration, and would state clearly his own position. After what had happened in 1851 and 1855, if the Queen made the offer he *must* accept it, for if he refused, the Conservative Party would be broken up for ever. Yet he would find a majority of two to one against him in the House of Commons, would have difficulty in well filling the important offices, found the external and internal relations of the country in a most delicate and complicated position, war in India and in China, difficulties with France, the Indian Bill introduced and a Reform Bill promised; nothing but the forbearance and support of some of his opponents would make it possible for him to carry on any Government. The person who was asked first by the Sovereign had always a great disadvantage; perhaps other combinations were possible, which, if found not to answer, would make him more readily accepted by the country. The position of Lord Palmerston was a most curious one, the House of Commons had been returned chiefly for the purpose of supporting him *personally*, and he had obtained a working majority of 100 (unheard of since the Reform Bill), yet his supporters had no principles in common and they generally suspected him; the question of the Reform Bill had made him and Lord John run a race for popularity which might lead to disastrous consequences. Lord Derby did not at all know what support he would be able to obtain in Parliament.

The Queen agreed to deferring her offer, and to take further time for consideration on the understanding that if she made it it would at once be accepted. Lord Derby expressed, however, his fear that the resignation of the Palmerston Cabinet might only be for the purpose of going through a crisis in order to come back again with new strength, for there existed different kinds of resignations, some for this purpose, others really for abandoning office.

A conversation which I had with Lord Clarendon after dinner, convinced me that the Cabinet had sent in their resignations from the real conviction of the impossibility to go on with honour and success; all offers of the friends of the Government to pass a vote of confidence, etc., etc., had been rejected. Lord Derby was the only man who could form a Government; Mr Gladstone would probably join him. The whole move had been planned, and most dexterously, by Sir James Graham.

Albert.

Queen Victoria to the Earl of Derby.

Buckingham Palace, *21st February 1858.*

The Queen has reconsidered the question of the formation of a new Government as she had settled with Lord Derby yesterday, and now writes to him to tell him that further reflection has only confirmed her in her former resolution to offer the task to Lord Derby. The resignation of the present Government is the result of a conscientious conviction on their part, that, damaged by the censure passed upon them in the House of Commons, they cannot with honour to themselves, or usefulness to the country, carry on public affairs, and Lord Derby is at the head of the only Party which affords the materials of forming a new Government, is sufficiently organised to secure a certain support, and which the country would accept as an alternative for that hitherto in power. Before actually offering any specific office to anybody, Lord Derby would perhaps have another interview with the Queen; but it would be right that he should have satisfied himself a little as to his chances of strengthening his hands before she sees him. With regard to the position of the India Bill, the Queen must also have a further conversation with him.

The Earl of Derby to Queen Victoria.

LORD DERBY'S VIEW

St James's Square, *21st February 1858.*

Lord Derby, with his humble duty, begs your Majesty to accept his grateful acknowledgment of the signal mark of your Majesty's favour, with which he has this morning been honoured. Encouraged by your Majesty's gracious confidence, he does not hesitate to submit himself to your Majesty's pleasure, and will address himself at once to the difficult task which your Majesty has been pleased to entrust to him. He fears that he can hardly hope, in the formation of a Government, for much extrinsic aid; as almost all the men of eminence in either House of Parliament are more or less associated with other parties, whose co-operation it would be impossible to obtain. Lord Derby will not, however, hesitate to make the attempt in any quarters, in which he may think he has any chance of success. With regard to the filling up of particular offices, Lord Derby would humbly beg your Majesty to bear in mind that, although among his own personal friends there will be every desire to make individual convenience subservient to the public interest, yet among those who are not now politically connected with him, there may be some, whose co-operation or refusal might be greatly influenced by the office which it was proposed that they should hold; and, in such cases, Lord Derby must venture to bespeak your Majesty's indulgence should he make a definite offer, subject, of course, to your Majesty's ultimate approval.

As soon as Lord Derby has made any progress in his proposed arrangements, he will avail himself of your Majesty's gracious permission to solicit another Audience.

Queen Victoria to the Earl of Derby.

Buckingham Palace, *21st February 1858.*

The Queen has just received Lord Derby's letter, and would wish under all circumstances to see him at six this evening, in order to hear what progress he has made in his plans. The two offices the Queen is most anxious should not be prejudged in any way, before the Queen has seen Lord Derby again, are the Foreign and the War Departments.

The Earl of Derby to Queen Victoria.

MR GLADSTONE AND LORD GREY

St James's Square, *21st February 1858.*

Lord Derby, with his humble duty, submits to your Majesty the two letters which he has this evening received from Lord Grey and Mr Gladstone.[301] The reasons contained in the latter do not appear to Lord

[301] Lord Grey wrote—"I am much obliged to you for the manner in which you have asked my assistance in performing the task confided to you by Her Majesty.

"I am not insensible to the danger of the present crisis, or to the duty it imposes on public men, of giving any aid in their power towards forming an Administration which may command respect. I am also aware that the settlement of the important political questions, on which we have differed, has removed many of the obstacles which would formerly have rendered my acting with you impracticable. Upon the other hand, upon carefully considering the present state of affairs and the materials at your disposal (especially in the House of Commons) for forming an Administration, and that all the political friends with whom I have been connected, would probably be opposed to it, I do not think it would be either useful to you or honourable to myself that I should singly join your Government."

Mr Gladstone wrote—"I am very sensible of the importance of the vote taken on Friday, and I should deeply lament to see the House of Commons trampled on in consequence of that vote. The honour of the House is materially involved in giving it full effect. It would therefore be my first wish to aid, if possible, in such a task; and remembering the years when we were colleagues, I may be permitted to say that there is nothing in the fact of your being the Head of a Ministry, which would avail to deter me from forming part of it.

"Among the first questions I have had to put to myself in consequence of the offer, which you have conveyed to me in such friendly and flattering terms, has been the question, whether it would be in my power by accepting it, either alone, or in concert with others, to render you material service.

"After the long years, during which we have been separated, there would be various matters of public interest requiring to be noticed between us; but the question I have mentioned is a needful preliminary.

"Upon the best consideration which the moment allows, I think it plain that alone, as I must be, I could not render you service worth your having.

"The dissolution of last year excluded from Parliament men with whom I had sympathies, and it in some degree affected the position of those political friends with whom I have now for many years been united, through evil and (much more rarely) good report.

"Those who lament the rupture of old traditions may well desire the reconstruction of a Party; but the reconstitution of a Party can only be effected, if at all, by the return of the old influences to their places, and not by the junction of one isolated person.

"The difficulty is now enhanced in my case by the fact that in your party, reduced as it is at the present moment in numbers, there is a small but active and not unimportant section, who avowedly regard me as the representative of the most dangerous ideas. I should thus, unfortunately, be to you a source of weakness in the heart of your own adherents, while I should bring you no Party or group of friends to make up for their defection or discontent.

Derby to be very conclusive; but he fears the result must be that he cannot look, in the attempt to form a Cabinet, to much extraneous assistance. With deep regret Lord Derby is compelled to add that he finds he cannot rely with certainty on the support of his son as a member of his proposed Cabinet.[302] Still, having undertaken the task he has in obedience to your Majesty's commands, Lord Derby will not relax in his efforts to frame such a Government as may be honoured with your Majesty's gracious approval, and prove itself equal to the emergency which calls it together.

While in the very act of putting up this letter, Lord Derby has received one, which he also presumes to enclose to your Majesty, from Lord St Leonards, alleging his advanced age as a reason for not accepting the Great Seal which he formerly held. This reply has been wholly unexpected; and it is yet possible that Lord St Leonards may be induced, at least temporarily, to withdraw his resignation. Should it, however, prove otherwise, and Lord Derby should succeed in making his other arrangements, he would humbly ask your Majesty's permission to endeavour to persuade Mr Pemberton Leigh to accept that high office, of course accompanied by the honour of the Peerage, which he is aware has been already on more than one occasion offered to him. Lord Derby begs to add that he has not had the slightest communication with Mr Pemberton Leigh on the subject, nor has the least idea as to his feelings upon it.

Queen Victoria to the Earl of Derby.

THE CHANCELLORSHIP

Buckingham Palace, *22nd February 1858.*

The Queen acknowledges Lord Derby's letter of yesterday, and returns him these three letters. She much regrets that he cannot reckon on the support and assistance in the Government, which he is about to

---

"For the reasons which I have thus stated or glanced at, my reply to your letter must be in the negative.

"I must, however, add that a Government formed by you at this time will in my opinion have strong claims upon me, and upon any one situated as I am, for favourable presumptions, and in the absence of conscientious difference on important questions, for support.

"I have had an opportunity of seeing Lord Aberdeen and Sidney Herbert, and they fully concur in the sentiment I have just expressed."

[302] See *ante*, p. 148, note 87

form, of such able men. The Queen authorises Lord Derby to offer the office of Lord Chancellor with a Peerage to Mr Pemberton Leigh; but she fears from what passed on previous occasions that he is not likely to accept it.[303]

Queen Victoria to the Earl of Derby.

Buckingham Palace, *22nd February 1858.*

The Queen has had a long conversation with the Duke of Newcastle, which however ended, as Lord Derby will have expected from what the Duke must have told him, in his declaring his conviction that he could be of no use to the new Government by joining it, or in persuading his friends to change their minds as to joining. The Duke was evidently much pleased by the offer, but from all he said of his position, the Queen could gather that it was in vain to press him further.

The Earl of Derby to Queen Victoria.

THE NEW CABINET

St James's Square, *25th February 1858.*

Lord Derby presents his humble duty to your Majesty, and fears that after your Majesty's most gracious acceptance of the propositions which he has made, he may appear to your Majesty very vacillating, in having at the last moment to submit to your Majesty another change.... But he finds that Lord John Manners, though he consented to take the Colonial Department, would infinitely prefer resuming his seat at the Board of Works; and on the urgent representation of his Colleagues that the Government would be strengthened by such a step, Lord Stanley has consented to accept office; and the arrangement which he would now venture humbly to submit to your Majesty would be the appointment of Lord Stanley to the Colonial Secretaryship, and Lord John Manners to the Board of Works....

---

[303] He declined the office, and the Great Seal was offered to and accepted by Sir Frederick Thesiger, who was created Lord Chelmsford.

The Ministry as it stood on the 1st of January 1858.		The Ministry as formed by the Earl of Derby in February 1858.
Viscount Palmerston	*First Lord of the Treasury*	Earl of Derby.
Marquis of Lansdowne	(*Without Office*).	
Lord Cranworth	*Lord Chancellor*	Lord Chelmsford.
Earl Granville	*President of the Council*	Marquis of Salisbury.
Marquis of Clanricarde	*Lord Privy Seal*	Earl of Hardwicke.
Sir George Grey	*Home Secretary*	Mr Walpole.
Earl of Clarendon	*Foreign Secretary*	Earl of Malmesbury.
Mr Labouchere (afterwards Lord Taunton) }	*Colonial Secretary*	{ Lord Stanley (afterwards Earl of Derby).
Lord Panmure (afterwards Earl of Dalhousie) }	*War Secretary*	General Peel.
Sir G. C. Lewis	*Chancellor of the Exchequer*	{ Mr Disraeli (afterwards Earl of Beaconsfield)
Sir Charles Wood (afterwards Viscount Halifax) }	*First Lord of the Admiralty*	{ Sir John Pakington (afterwards Lord Hampton).
Mr Vernon Smith (afterwards Lord Lyveden) }	*President of the Board of Control*	Earl of Ellenborough.
Lord Stanley of Alderley	*President of the Board of Trade*	Mr Henley.
Mr M. T. Baines	*Chancellor of the*	(*Not in the Cabinet.*)

	Duchy of Lancaster	
Duke of Argyll	*Postmaster-General*	(*Not in the Cabinet.*)
(*Not in the Cabinet*)	*First Commissioner of Works and Public Buildings*	{ Lord John Manners (afterwards Duke of Rutland).

The Earl of Malmesbury to Queen Victoria.

THE ORSINI PLOT

Whitehall, *7th March 1858.*

The Earl of Malmesbury presents his humble duty to the Queen, and has the honour to thank your Majesty for the interesting letter[304] sent to him by your Majesty, and which he returns to your Majesty by this messenger. Lord Malmesbury hopes and believes that much of the excitement that prevailed on the *other* side the water is subsiding. All his letters from *private* sources, and the account of Colonel Claremont, agree on this point. In this country, if our differences with France are settled, it is probable that the popular jealousy of foreign interference will be killed; but at least for some time it will show foreign Courts how dangerous it is *even to criticise* our *domestic* Institutions. Lord Malmesbury has carefully abstained from giving Lord Cowley or M. de Persigny the slightest hope that we could alter the law, but has confined himself to saying that the law was itself as much on its trial as the prisoners Bernard and Truelove.[305] If, therefore, the law should

[304] This was a letter from the Prince de Chimay to the King of the Belgians in reference to the Orsini plot.

[305] Before Lord Palmerston's Government had retired, Simon Bernard, a resident of Bayswater, was committed for trial for complicity in the Orsini *attentat*. He was committed for conspiracy only, but, at the instance of the new Government, the charge was altered to one of feloniously slaying one of the persons killed by the explosion. As this constructive murder was actually committed on French soil, Bernard's trial had, under the existing law, to be held before a Special Commission, over which Lord Campbell presided. The evidence overwhelmingly established the prisoner's guilt, but, carried away by the eloquent, if irrelevant, speech of Mr Edwin James for the defence, the jury acquitted him. Truelove was charged with criminal libel, for openly approving, in a published pamphlet, Orsini's attempt, and regretting its failure.

prove to be a phantom of justice, or anomalous in its action, whatever measures your Majesty's Government may hereafter take to reform it, it will be received by France as an unexpected boon and a proof of good faith and amity.

THE EMPEROR AND THE CARBONARI

In attending to the idea referred to by your Majesty that the Emperor took the oath of the Assassins' Society, Lord Malmesbury can almost assure your Majesty that such is not the case.[306] Lord Malmesbury first made His Majesty's acquaintance in Italy when they were both very young men (twenty years of age). They were *both* under the influence of those romantic feelings which the former history and the present degradation of Italy may naturally inspire even at a more advanced time of life—and the Prince Louis Napoleon, to the knowledge of Lord Malmesbury, certainly engaged himself in the conspiracies of the time—but it was with the higher class of the Carbonari, men like General Sercognani and General Pépé. The Prince used to talk to Lord Malmesbury upon these men and their ideas and plans with all the openness that exists between two youths, and Lord Malmesbury has many times heard him condemn with disgust the societies of villains which hung on the flank of the conspirators, and which deterred many of the best families and ablest gentlemen in Romagna from joining them. Lord Malmesbury believes the report therefore to be a fable, and at some future period will, if it should interest your Majesty, relate to your Majesty some details respecting the Emperor's share in the conspiracies of 1828-1829....

The Government threw up the prosecution, pusillanimously in the judgment of Lord Campbell, who records that he carefuly studied, with a view to his own hearing of the case, the proceedings against Lord George Gordon for libelling Marie Antoinette, against Vint for libelling the Emperor Paul, and against Peltier for libelling Napoleon I.

[306] The Queen had written:—"There are people who pretend that the Emperor, who was once a member of the Carbonari Club of Italy, and who is supposed to be condemned to death by the rules of that Secret Society for having violated his oath to them, has offered them to pardon Orsini, if they would release him from his oath, but that the Society refused the offer. The fact that all the attempts have been made by Italians, Orsini's letter, and the almost mad state of fear in which the Emperor seems to be now, would give colour to that story." Orsini had written two letters to the Emperor, one read aloud at his trial by his counsel, Jules Favre, the other while lying under sentence of death. He entreated the Emperor to secure Italian independence.

Mr Disraeli to Queen Victoria.

House of Commons, *12th March 1858.*

(*Friday.*)

The Chancellor of the Exchequer with his humble duty to your Majesty.

The Opposition benches very full; the temper not kind.

The French announcement,[307] which was quite unexpected, elicited cheers, but only from the Ministerial side, which, he confesses, for a moment almost daunted him.

Then came a question about the *Cagliari* affair,[308] on which the Government had agreed to take a temperate course, in deference to their predecessors—but it was not successful. The ill-humour of the House, diverted for a moment by the French news, vented itself on this head.

What struck the Chancellor of the Exchequer in the course of the evening most was the absence of all those symptoms of "fair trial," etc., which have abounded of late in journals and in Society.

Lord John said something; Mr Gladstone said something; but it was not encouraging.

Nevertheless, in 1852 "fair trial" observations abounded, and the result was not satisfactory; now it may be the reverse.

The House is wild and capricious at this moment.

Your Majesty once deigned to say that your Majesty wished in these remarks to have the temper of the House placed before your Majesty, and to find what your Majesty could not meet in newspapers. This is the Chancellor of the Exchequer's excuse for these rough notes, written on the field of battle, which he humbly offers to your Majesty.

---

[307] Parliament reassembled on the 12th of March, and Mr Disraeli then stated that the "painful misconceptions" which had for some time existed between England and France had been "terminated in a spirit entirely friendly and honourable."

[308] Two English engineers, Watt and Park, had been on the Sardinian steamer *Cagliari* when she was seized by the Neapolitan Government, and her crew, including the engineers, imprisoned at Naples. At the instance of the Conservative Government, who acted more vigorously than their predecessors had done, the engineers were released, and £3,000 paid to them as compensation.

Queen Victoria to the Earl of Derby.

THE NAVY

Osborne, *15th March 1858.*

The Queen sends to Lord Derby a Memorandum on the state of preparation of our Navy in case of a war, the importance of attending to which she has again strongly felt when the late vote of the House of Commons endangered the continuance of the good understanding with France. The whole tone of the Debate on the first night of the reassembly of Parliament has shown again that there exists a great disposition to boast and provoke foreign Powers without any sincere desire to investigate our means of making good our words, and providing for those means which are missing.

The Queen wishes Lord Derby to read this Memorandum to the Cabinet, and to take the subject of which it treats into their anxious consideration.

The two appendices, stating facts, the one with regard to the manning of the Navy by volunteers with the aid of bounties, the other with regard to impressment, have become unfortunately more lengthy than the Queen had wished, but the facts appeared to her so important that she did not like to have any left out.

Mr Disraeli to Queen Victoria.

House of Commons, *22nd March 1858.*
(*Monday, half-past eight o'clock.*)

The Chancellor of the Exchequer with his humble duty to your Majesty.

This evening was a great contrast to Friday. House very full on both sides....

Mr B. Osborne commenced the general attack, of which he had given notice; but, after five years' silence, his weapons were not as bright as of yore. He was answered by the Government, and the House, which was very full, became much excited. The Ministerial benches were in high spirit.

The Debate that ensued, most interesting and sustained.

Mr Horsman, with considerable effect, expressed the opinions of that portion of the Liberal Party, which does not wish to disturb the Government.

Lord John Russell vindicated the Reform Bill of 1832 from the attacks of the Chancellor of the Exchequer, and with great dignity and earnestness.

He was followed by Mr Drummond on the same subject in a telling epigram. Then Lord Palmerston, in reply to the charges of Mr Horsman, mild and graceful, with a sarcastic touch. The general impression of the House was very favourable to the Ministry; all seemed changed; the Debate had cleared the political atmosphere, and, compared with our previous state, we felt as if the eclipse was over.

Queen Victoria to the King of the Belgians.

RESIGNATION OF PERSIGNY

Buckingham Palace, *23rd March 1858.*

My dearest Uncle,—You will, I trust, forgive my letter being short, but we have only just returned from Aldershot, where we went this morning, and really have been quite baked by a sun which was hardly hotter in August, and without a breath of wind....

Good Marie[309] has not answered me, will you remind her? I *did* tell her I hoped for her child's[310] sake she would give up the nursing, as we Princesses had other duties to perform. I hope she was not shocked, but I felt I only did what was right in telling her so.

I grieve to say we lose poor Persigny, which is a real loss—but he would resign. Walewski behaved ill to him. The Emperor has, however, named a successor which is *really* a compliment to the Army and the Alliance—and besides a distinguished and independent man, viz. the Duc de Malakhoff.[311] This is very gratifying.

In all this business, Pélissier has, I hear, behaved extremely well. I must now conclude. Ever your devoted Niece,

Victoria R.

Mr Disraeli to Queen Victoria.

THE HOUSE OF COMMONS

House of Commons, *23rd March 1858.*

---

[309] Marie Henriette, Duchess of Brabant, afterwards Queen of the Belgians; died 1902.

[310] Princess Louise of Belgium was born on the 4th of February.

[311] Formerly General Pélissier; see *ante*, p. 143, note 80.

(*Tuesday.*)

The Chancellor of the Exchequer with his humble duty to your Majesty.

The discussion on the Passport Question, this evening, was not without animation; the new Under-Secretary, Mr Fitzgerald,[312] makes way with the House. He is very acute and quick in his points, but does not speak loud enough. His tone is conversational, which is the best for the House of Commons, and the most difficult; but then the conversation should be heard. The general effect of the discussion was favourable to the French Government.

In a thin House afterwards, the Wife's Sister Bill was brought in after a division. Your Majesty's Government had decided among themselves to permit the introduction, but a too zealous member of the Opposition forced an inopportune division.

Mr Disraeli to Queen Victoria.

House of Commons, *25th March 1858.*

(*Thursday.*)

The Chancellor of the Exchequer with his humble duty to your Majesty.

The Lease of the Lord-Lieutenancy was certainly renewed tonight—and for some years. The majority was very great against change at present, and the future, which would justify it, it was agreed, should be the very decided opinion of the Irish members. It was left in short to Ireland.

The Debate was not very animated, but had two features—a most admirable speech by Lord Naas[313] quite the model of an official statement, clear, calm, courteous, persuasive, and full of knowledge; it received the praises of both sides.

The other incident noticeable was Mr Roebuck's reply, which was one of the most apt, terse, and telling I well remember, and not bitter.

---

[312] William Robert Seymour Vesey Fitzgerald, M.P. for Horsham 1852-1865. He was Governor of Bombay 1867-1872.

[313] Chief Secretary to the Lord-Lieutenant, afterwards (as Earl of Mayo) Viceroy of India, assassinated in the Andaman Islands, 1872.

Mr Disraeli to Queen Victoria.

CAPTURE OF LUCKNOW

House of Commons, *13th April.*

(*Tuesday night.*)

The Chancellor of the Exchequer with his humble duty to your Majesty.

The night tranquil and interesting—Lord Bury, with much intelligence, introduced the subject of the Straits Settlements;[314] the speech of Sir J. Elphinstone,[315] master of the subject, and full of striking details, produced a great effect. His vindication of the convict population of Singapore, as the moral element of that strange society, might have been considered as the richest humour, had it not been for its unmistakable simplicity.

His inquiry of the Governor's lady, who never hired any servant but a convict, whether she employed in her nursery "Thieves or Murderers?"—and the answer, "Always murderers," was very effective....

The Secretary of State having sent down to the Chancellor of the Exchequer the telegram of the fall of Lucknow,[316] the Chancellor of the Exchequer read it to the House, having previously in private shown it to Lord Palmerston and others of the late Government.

After this a spirited Debate on the conduct of Members of Parliament corruptly exercising their influence, in which the view recommended by the Government, through Mr Secretary Walpole, was adopted by the House.

Queen Victoria to the King of the Belgians.

Windsor Castle, *2nd April 1858.*

My dear Uncle,—I am sure you will kindly be interested in knowing that the Examination and Confirmation of Bertie have gone off extremely well.[317] Everything was conducted as at Vicky's, and I

---

[314] These detached provinces were at this time under the control of the Governor-General of India; but in 1867 they were formed into a Crown Colony.

[315] Sir J. D. H. Elphinstone, Conservative member for Portsmouth, afterwards a Lord of the Treasury.

[316] Sir Colin Campbell had at length obtained entire possession of the city, which had been in the hands of the rebels for nine months.

[317] See the Prince Consort's letter to Stockmar, *Life of the Prince Consort*, vol. iv. p. 205.

thought *much* of you, and wished we could have had the happiness of having you there. I enclose a Programme. The examination before the Archbishop and ourselves by the Dean on Wednesday was long and difficult, but Bertie answered extremely well, and his whole manner and *Gemüthsstimmung* yesterday, and again to-day, at the Sacrament to which we took him, was gentle, good, and proper.... Now, good-bye, dear Uncle. Ever your devoted Niece,

Victoria R.

Queen Victoria to Sir John Pakington.

NAVAL PREPARATIONS

Windsor Castle, *12th April 1858.*

The Queen has received Sir John Pakington's letter of the 10th, and thanks him for the transmission of the printed copy of his confidential Memorandum.

The object of the paper which the Queen sent from Osborne to Lord Derby was to lead by a thorough investigation to an exact knowledge of the state of our Naval preparations in the event of a war, with the view to the discovery and suggestion of such remedies as our deficiencies imperatively demand. This investigation and thorough consideration the Queen expects from her Board of Admiralty, chosen with great care, and composed of the most competent Naval Authorities. She does not wish for the opinion of this or that person, given without any responsibility attaching to it, nor for mere returns prepared in the Office for the First Lord, but for the collective opinion of Sir John Pakington and his Board with the responsibility attaching to such an opinion given to the Sovereign upon a subject upon which the safety of the Empire depends. The Queen has full confidence in the honour of the gentlemen composing the Board, that they will respect the *confidential* character of the Queen's communication, and pay due regard to the importance of the subject referred to them.

Mr Disraeli to Queen Victoria.

PROCEDURE BY RESOLUTION

House of Commons, *12th April 1858.*

(*Monday night.*)

The Chancellor of the Exchequer with his humble duty to your Majesty.

House reassembled—full. Chancellor of Exchequer much embarrassed with impending statement, on the part of your Majesty's servants, that they intended to propose Resolutions on the Government of India, instead of at once proceeding with their Bill.[318]

Received, five minutes before he took his seat, confidential information, that Lord John Russell, wishing to defeat the prospects of Lord Palmerston, and himself to occupy a great mediatory position, intended, himself, to propose the mezzotermine of resolutions!

Chancellor of Exchequer felt it was impossible, after having himself introduced a Bill, to interfere with the Resolutions of an independent member, and one so weighty and distinguished: therefore, confined his announcement to the Budget on Monday week, and consequent postponement of India Bill.

Soon after, Lord John rose, and opened the case, in a spirit most calm and conciliatory to the House, and to your Majesty's Government.

The Chancellor of Exchequer responded, but with delicacy, not wishing rudely to deprive Lord John of his position in the matter; deeming it arrogant—but the real opposition, extremely annoyed at all that was occurring, wishing, at the same time, to deprive Lord John of the mediatory position, and to embarrass your Majesty's Government with the task and responsibility of preparing and introducing the resolutions, *insisted* upon Government undertaking the task. As the Chancellor of Exchequer read the sketch of the Resolutions in his box, this was amusing; he undertook the responsibility, thus urged, and almost menaced; Lord John, though greatly mortified at not bringing in the Resolutions himself, for it is since known they were prepared, entirely and justly acquits Chancellor of Exchequer of any arrogance and intrusion, and the affair concludes in a manner dignified and more than promising. It is now generally supposed that after the various Resolutions have been discussed, and passed, the Bill of your Majesty's servants, modified and reconstructed, will pass into a law.

[318] Lord Palmerston had obtained leave, by a large majority, to introduce an India Bill, vesting the Government of India in a Council nominated by the Crown. On his accession to office, Mr Disraeli proposed that the Council should be half nominative and half elective, and in particular that London, Manchester, Liverpool, Glasgow, and Belfast should each be entitled to elect one member. These proposals were widely condemned, and especially by Mr Bright.

The Chancellor of Exchequer will have a copy of the Resolutions, though at present in a crude form, made and forwarded to your Majesty, that they may be considered by your Majesty and His Royal Highness. Chancellor of Exchequer will mention this to Lord Derby, through whom they ought to reach your Majesty.

After this unexpected and interesting scene, because it showed, in its progress, a marked discordance between Lord John and Lord Palmerston, not concealed by the latter chief, and strongly evinced by some of his principal followers, for example, Sir C. Wood, Mr Hall, Mr Bouverie, the House went into Committee on the Navy Estimates which Sir J. Pakington introduced in a speech, lucid, spirited, and comprehensive. The feeling of the House as to the maintenance of the Navy was good.

Queen Victoria to the Earl of Malmesbury.

Buckingham Palace, *1st May 1858.*

The Queen has received a draft to Lord Cowley on the Danish Question,[319] which she cannot sanction as submitted to her. The question is a most important one, and a false step on our part may produce a war between France and Germany. The Queen would wish Lord Malmesbury to call here in the course of to-morrow, when the Prince could discuss the matter with him more fully.

Mr Disraeli to Queen Victoria.

House of Commons, *7th May 1858.*

The Chancellor of the Exchequer with his humble duty to your Majesty.

At half-past four o'clock, before the Chancellor of the Exchequer could reach the House, the Secretary of the Board of Control had already presented the Proclamation of Lord Canning, and the despatch

---

[319] The dispute as to the Duchies of Schleswig and Holstein. The German Diet had refused to ratify the Danish proposal that Commissioners should be appointed by Germany and Denmark to negotiate an arrangement of their differences. Lord Malmesbury had written that the Governments (including England) which had hitherto abstained from interference, should now take measures to guard against any interference with the integrity of the Danish Monarchy. The Queen and Prince considered that the attitude of the British Government was unnecessarily pro-Danish.

thereon of Lord Ellenborough, without the omission of the Oudh passages.[320]

The Chancellor of the Exchequer has employed every means to recall the papers, and make the necessary omissions, and more than once thought he had succeeded, but unhappily the despatch had been read by Mr Bright, and a considerable number of members, and, had papers once in the possession of the House by the presentation of a Minister been surreptitiously recalled and garbled, the matter would have been brought before the House, and the production of the complete documents would have been ordered.

In this difficult and distressing position the Chancellor of the Exchequer, after consultation with his colleagues in the House of Commons, thought it best, and, indeed, inevitable, to submit to circumstances, the occurrence of which he deeply regrets, and humbly places before your Majesty.

Queen Victoria to the Earl of Derby.

Buckingham Palace, *9th May 1858.*

The Queen has received Lord Derby's letter of last night, and was glad to see that he entirely concurs with her in the advantage and necessity of appointing a Commission to consider the question of the organisation of the future Army of India.[321] She only hopes that no time will be lost by the reference to the different bodies whom Lord Derby wishes previously to consult, and she trusts that he will not let

---

[320] See Introductory Note, *ante*, p. 262. The draft proclamation (differing from the ultimate form in which it was issued), with a covering despatch, were sent home to the Board of Control by Lord Canning, who at the same time wrote an unofficial letter to Mr Vernon Smith, then President of the Board, stating that he had not been able to find time before the mail left to explain his reasons for adopting what appeared a somewhat merciless scheme of confiscation. Lord Ellenborough thereupon wrote a despatch, dated the 19th of April, reprobating the Governor-General for abandoning the accustomed policy of generous conquerors, and for inflicting on the mass of the population what they would feel as the severest of punishments. This despatch was made public in England, as will be seen from the dates, before it could possibly have reached Lord Canning.

[321] The Queen had written that she thought the Commission should be composed of officers of the Home and the Indian Armies, some politicians, the Commander-in-Chief, the President of the Board of Control, with the Secretary-for-War as President.

himself be overruled by Lord Ellenborough, who may very likely consider the opinion and result of the labours of a Committee as entirely valueless as compared with his own opinions.

The Queen has not the same confidence in them, and is, therefore, doubly anxious to be advised by a body of the most competent persons after most careful enquiry.

Queen Victoria to the Earl of Derby.

Buckingham Palace, *9th May 1858.*

The Queen has received Lord Derby's letter of yesterday. She is very sorry for the further complication likely to arise out of the communication to the House of Commons of the despatch in full, which is most unfortunate, not less so than the communication of it previously to Mr Bright and his friends. The Queen is anxious not to add to Lord Derby's difficulties, but she must not leave unnoticed the fact that the despatch in question ought never to have been written without having been submitted to the Queen. She hopes Lord Derby will take care that Lord Ellenborough will not repeat this, which must place her in a most embarrassing position.

The Earl of Ellenborough to Queen Victoria.

ELLENBOROUGH'S RESIGNATION

Eaton Square, *10th May 1858.*

Lord Ellenborough presents his most humble duty to your Majesty, and regarding the present difficult position of your Majesty's Government as mainly occasioned by the presentation to Parliament of the letter to the Governor-General with reference to the Proclamation in Oudh, for which step he considers himself to be solely responsible, he deems it to be his duty to lay his resignation at your Majesty's feet.

Lord Ellenborough had no other object than that of making it unmistakably evident to the Governor as well as to the governed in India that your Majesty was resolved to temper Justice with Clemency, and would not sanction any measure which did not seem to conduce to the establishment of permanent peace.[322]

---

[322] On the same day Lord Shaftesbury in the Lords and Mr Cardwell in the Commons gave notice of Motions censuring the Government for Lord Ellenborough's despatch. The debates commenced on the 14th.

Memorandum by the Prince Albert.

A CRISIS

Buckingham Palace, *11th May 1858.*

Lord Derby had an Audience at twelve o'clock. He said he had received a copy of Lord Ellenborough's letter, and had told him that should the Queen consult him (Lord Derby) he should advise her to accept the resignation, Lord Ellenborough had behaved in the handsomest manner, and expressed his belief that he had brought bad luck to the Government, for this was now the second difficulty into which they had got by his instrumentality, the first having been the Election Clause in the India Bill. Lord Derby hoped that this resignation would stop the vote of censure in the House of Commons, as the House could not hold responsible and punish the Cabinet for that with which they had had no concern. If the House persisted, it was clear that the motives were factious, and he hoped the Queen would allow him to threaten a Dissolution of Parliament, which he was certain would stop it. The Queen refused to give that permission; she said he might leave it quite undecided whether the Queen would grant a Dissolution or not, and take the benefit of the doubt in talking to others on the subject; but she must be left quite free to act as she thought the good of the country might require at the time when the Government should have been beat; there had been a Dissolution within the year, and if a Reform Bill was passed there must be another immediately upon it; in the meantime most violent pledges would be taken as to Reform if a general election were to take place now. Lord Derby concurred in all this, and said he advised the threat particularly in order to render the reality unnecessary; when she persisted in her refusal, however, on the ground that she could not threaten what she was not prepared to do, he appeared very much disappointed and mortified.

We then discussed the state of the question itself, and urged the necessity of something being done to do away with the injurious impression which the publication of the despatch must produce in India, as the resignation of Lord Ellenborough left this quite untouched, and Parliament might with justice demand this. He agreed, after much difficulty, to send a telegraphic despatch, which might overtake and mitigate the other. On my remark that the public were under the impression that there had been collusion, and that Mr Bright had seen the despatch before he asked his question for its production, he denied this stoutly, but let us understand that Mr Bright had known of the existence of such a despatch, and had wished to put his question before, but had been asked to defer it until Lord Canning's Proclamation should have appeared in the newspapers! (This is nearly as bad!!) The Queen could not have pledged herself to dissolve Parliament in order to support such tricks!

Albert.

It was arranged that Lord Derby should accept Lord Ellenborough's resignation in the Queen's name.

Queen Victoria to the Earl of Ellenborough.

Buckingham Palace, *11th May 1858.*

The Queen has to acknowledge Lord Ellenborough's letter, which she did not wish to do before she had seen Lord Derby.

The latter has just left the Queen, and will communicate to Lord Ellenborough the Queen's acceptance of his resignation, which he has thought it right to tender to her from a sense of public duty.

The Earl of Derby to Queen Victoria.

ELLENBOROUGH'S STATEMENT

St James's Square [*11th May*].
(9 P.M., *Tuesday.*)

Lord Derby, with his humble duty, submits to your Majesty the expression of his hope that the discussion, or rather conversation, which has taken place in the House of Lords this evening, may have been not only advantageous to the Government, but beneficial in its results to the public service....

After the discussion, Lord Ellenborough made his statement; and it is only doing bare justice to him to say that he made it in a manner and spirit which was most highly honourable to himself, and was fully appreciated by the House.

Public sympathy was entirely with him, especially when he vindicated the policy which he had asserted, but took upon himself the whole and sole responsibility of having authorised the publication of the despatch—which he vindicated—and announced his own resignation rather than embarrass his colleagues. Lord Grey shortly entered his protest against bringing into discussion the policy of the Proclamation and of the consequent despatch, into which Lord Ellenborough had certainly entered too largely, opposing, very broadly, the principle of confiscation against that of clemency. Lord Derby followed Lord Grey, and after an interruption on a point of form, vindicated the policy advocated in Lord Ellenborough's despatch, at the same time that he expressed not only his hope, but his belief, that in practice the Governor-General would be found (and more especially judging from the alterations inserted in the last Proclamation of which an unofficial copy has been received) acting on the principles laid down in Lord Ellenborough's despatch. In the tribute which he felt it his duty to pay to the personal, as well as political, character of Lord Ellenborough, the House concurred with entire unanimity and all did honour to the spirit which induced him to sacrifice his own position to the public service; and to atone, and more than atone, for an act of indiscretion by the frank avowal that he alone was responsible for it. Lord Derby thinks that the step which has been taken may, even probably, prevent the Motions intended to be made on Friday; and if made, will, almost certainly, result in a majority for the Government.

LORD DERBY'S DESPATCH

Lord Derby believes that he may possibly be in time to telegraph to Malta early to-morrow, to Lord Canning. In that case he will do himself the honour of submitting to your Majesty a copy of the message[323] sent, though he fears it will be impossible to do so before its despatch. He proposes in substance to say that the publication has been

---

[323] *The Earl of Derby to Lord Lyons.*

12th May 1858.

Send on the following message to Lord Canning by the Indian mail.

The publication of the Secret Despatch of 19th April has been disapproved. Lord Ellenborough has resigned office. His successor has not been appointed. Nevertheless the policy indicated in the above despatch is approved by Her Majesty's Government. Confiscation of property of private individuals (Talookdars and others) ought to be the exception and not the rule. It ought to be held out as a penalty on those who do not come in by a given day. From your amended Proclamation it is hoped that such is your intention. Let it be clearly understood that it is so. You were quite right in issuing no Proclamation till after a signal success. That once obtained, the more generous the terms, the better. A broad distinction must be drawn between the Talookdars of Oudh and the Sepoys who have been in our service. Confidence is felt in your judgment. You will not err if you lean to the side of humanity, especially as to nations of Oudh.

No private letters have been received from you since the change of Government.

disapproved—that Lord Ellenborough has resigned in consequence—but that your Majesty's Government adhere in principle to the policy laid down in the despatch of 19th April, and entertain an earnest hope that the Governor-General, judging from the modifications introduced into the amended Proclamation, has, in fact, the intention of acting in the same spirit; but that your Majesty's Government are still of opinion that confiscation of private property ought to be made the exception, and not the rule, and to be enforced only against those who may stand out after a certain day, or who may be proved to have been guilty of more than ordinary crimes.

Lord Derby hopes that your Majesty will excuse a very hasty sketch of a very large subject.

Queen Victoria to the Earl of Derby.

14th May 1858.

The Queen returns the extracts Lord Derby has sent to her. Lord Ellenborough's despatch,[324] now before her for the first time, is very good and just in principle. But the Queen would be much surprised if it did not entirely coincide with the views of Lord Canning, at least as far as he has hitherto expressed any in his letters. So are also the sentiments written by Sir J. Lawrence; they contain almost the very expressions frequently used by Lord Canning.

Sir J. Login,[325] who holds the same opinion, and has great Indian experience, does not find any fault with the Proclamation, however seemingly it may sound at variance with these opinions, and this on account of the peculiar position of affairs in Oudh. It is a great pity that Lord Ellenborough, with his knowledge, experience, activity, and cleverness, should be so entirely unable to submit to general rules of conduct. The Queen has been for some time much alarmed at his writing letters of his own to all the most important Indian Chiefs and Kings explaining his policy. All this renders the position of a Governor-General almost untenable, and that of the Government at home very hazardous.

---

[324] This was a later despatch of Lord Ellenborough's, also in reference to the pacification of Oudh, and not shown to the Cabinet before it was sent.

[325] See *ante*, p. 248, note 41.

Memorandum by Sir Charles Phipps.

LORD ABERDEEN CONSULTED

[*Undated.* ? *15th May 1858.*]

Upon being admitted to Lord Aberdeen, I informed him that the Queen and Prince were anxious to hear his opinion upon the present most unfortunate state of affairs, but that, knowing how easily every event was perverted in such times as the present, Her Majesty and His Royal Highness had thought that it might have been subject to misapprehension had he been known to have been at Buckingham Palace, and that I had been therefore directed to call upon him, with a view of obtaining his opinion and advice upon certain important points.

PREROGATIVE OF DISSOLUTION

The first was the question of a Dissolution of Parliament in the event of the Government being defeated upon the question which was at present pending. I told him that I was permitted to communicate to him in the strictest confidence, that in a late Audience which Lord Derby had with the Queen, he had asked her permission to be allowed to announce that, in the event of an adverse majority, he had Her Majesty's sanction to a Dissolution of Parliament.

That the Queen had declined to give such sanction, or even such a pledge, and equally guarded herself against being supposed to have made up her mind to refuse her sanction to a Dissolution, had told Lord Derby that she could not then make any prospective decision upon the subject. I told him that in point of fact Her Majesty was disinclined to grant to Lord Derby her authority for a Dissolution, but that the Queen had at once refused to grant to Lord Derby her sanction for making the announcement he wished, as she considered that it would be a very unconstitutional threat for him to hold over the head of the Parliament, with her authority, by way of biassing their decision.

Lord Aberdeen interrupted me by saying that the Queen had done quite right—that he never heard of such a request being made, or authority for such an announcement being sought—and he could not at all understand Lord Derby making such an application. He knew that the Government had threatened a Dissolution, that he thought that they had a perfect right to do so, but that they would have been quite wrong in joining the Queen's name with it.

He said that he had never entertained the slightest doubt that if the Minister advised the Queen to dissolve, she would, as a matter of course, do so. The Minister who advised the Dissolution took upon himself the heavy responsibility of doing so, but that the Sovereign was bound to suppose that the person whom she had appointed as a Minister was a gentleman and an honest man, and that he would not advise Her Majesty to take such a step unless he thought that it was for the good of the country. There was no doubt of the power and prerogative of the Sovereign to refuse a Dissolution—it was one of the very few acts which the Queen of England could do without responsible advice at the moment; but even in this case whoever was sent for to succeed, must, with his appointment, assume the responsibility of this act, and be prepared to defend it in Parliament.

He could not remember a single instance in which the undoubted power of the Sovereign had been exercised upon this point, and the advice of the Minister to dissolve Parliament had been rejected—for it was to be remembered that Lord Derby would be still at this time her Minister—and that the result of such refusal would be that the Queen would take upon herself the act of dismissing Lord Derby from office, instead of his resigning from being unable longer to carry on the Government.

The Queen had during her reign, and throughout the numerous changes of Government, maintained an unassailable position of constitutional impartiality, and he had no hesitation in saying that he thought it would be more right, and certainly more safe, for her to follow the usual course, than to take this dangerous time for exercising an unusual and, he believed he might say, an unprecedented, course, though the power to exercise the authority was undoubted.

He said that he did not conceive that any reasons of expediency as to public business, or the possible effects of frequent general elections, would be sufficient grounds for refusing a Dissolution (and reasons would have to be given by the new Minister in Parliament), and, as he conceived, the only possible ground that could be maintained as foundation for such an exercise of authority would be the fearful danger to the existence of our power in India, which might arise from the intemperate discussion upon every hustings of the proceedings of the Government with respect to that country—as the question proposed to the country would certainly be considered to be severity or mercy to the people of India.

Upon the second point, as to a successor to Lord Derby in the event of his resignation, he said that the Queen would, he thought, have no alternative but to send for Lord Palmerston. The only other person who could be suggested would be Lord John Russell, and he was neither the mover of the Resolutions which displaced the Government, nor the ostensible head of the Opposition, which the late meeting at Cambridge House pointed out Lord Palmerston to be. That he was not very fond of Lord Palmerston, though he had forgiven him all, and he had had *much* to forgive; and that in the last few days it had appeared that he had less following than Lord John; but the Queen could not act upon such daily changing circumstances, and it was evident that Lord Palmerston was the ostensible man for the Queen to send for.

STATE OF PARTIES

Lord Aberdeen seemed very low upon the state of public affairs. He said that the extreme Liberals were the only Party that appeared to gain strength. Not only was the Whig Party divided within itself, hated by the Radicals, and having a very doubtful support from the independent Liberals, but even the little band called the Peelites had entirely crumbled to pieces. In the House of Lords, whilst the Duke of Newcastle voted with the Opposition, he (Lord Aberdeen) had purposely abstained from voting, whilst, in the House of Commons, Cardwell moved the Resolution, and Mr Sidney Herbert would, he believed, vote for it; Gladstone would speak on the other side, and Sir J. Graham would also vote with the Government.

He concluded by saying that if the majority against the Government was a very large one, he thought that Lord Derby ought not to ask to dissolve; but that he knew that the members of the Government had said that the present Parliament was elected upon a momentary Palmerstonian cry, and was quite an exceptional case, and that they would not consent to be driven from office upon its verdict.

Memorandum by the Prince Albert.

THE QUEEN AND DISSOLUTION

Buckingham Palace, *16th May 1858.*

We saw Lord Derby after church. He brought interesting letters from Lord Canning to Lord Ellenborough, of which copies follow here. It is evident that Lord Canning thinks that he is taking a most merciful course, and expects pacification from his "Proclamation," attributing the slow coming in of the chiefs to the Proclamation not being yet sufficiently known.

Lord Ellenborough's, and indeed the Government's, hearts, must have had curious sensations in reading Lord Canning's frank declaration, that he did not mean to resign on hearing of the formation of the Tory Government unless told to do so, and he had no fears that he would be treated in a way implying want of confidence to make him resign, feeling safe as to that in Lord Ellenborough's hands!

Lord Derby spoke much of the Debate, which he expects to go on for another week. He expects to be beaten by from 15 to 35 votes under present circumstances, but thinks still that he could be saved if it were known that the Queen had not refused a Dissolution, which was stoutly maintained by Lord Palmerston's friends. He begged again to be empowered to contradict the assertion. The Queen maintained that it would be quite unconstitutional to threaten Parliament, and to use her name for that purpose. Lord Derby quite agreed, and disclaimed any such intention, but said there were modes of letting the fact be known without any risk. We agreed that we could not enter into such details. The Queen allowed him (Lord Derby) to know that a Dissolution would not be refused to him, and trusted that her honour would be safe in his hands as to the use he made of that knowledge. He seemed greatly relieved, and stated that had he had to resign, he would have withdrawn from public business, and the Conservative Party would have been entirely, and he feared for ever, broken up. On a Dissolution he felt certain of a large gain, as the country was in fact tired of the "Whig Family Clique"; the Radicals, like Mr Milner Gibson, Bright, etc., would willingly support a Conservative Government.

Albert.

Mr Disraeli to Queen Victoria.[326]

COLLAPSE OF THE ATTACK

---

[326] Lord Shaftesbury's Motion in the Lords had been lost by a majority of nine. In the Commons, Mr Cardwell was replied to in a brilliant speech by Sir Hugh Cairns, the Solicitor-General. The speeches of Sir James Graham, Mr Bright, and others, showed that the Opposition was disunited, and when it was understood that Mr Gladstone would support the Ministry, the Liberal attack collapsed. Mr Disraeli, deprived of the satisfaction of making an effective reply, subsequently compared the discomfiture of his opponents to an earthquake in Calabria or Peru. "There was," he said, in the course of a speech at Slough, "a rumbling murmur, a groan, a shriek, a sound of distant thunder. No one knew whether it came from the top or bottom of the House. There was a rent, a fissure in the ground, and then a village disappeared, then a tall tower toppled down, and the whole of the Opposition benches became one great dissolving view of anarchy."

House of Commons, *21st May 1858*.

The Chancellor of the Exchequer with his humble duty to your Majesty.

The fullest House; it is said 620 Members present; it was supposed we should have divided at three o'clock in the morning; Mr Gladstone was to have spoken for the Government at half-past ten—very great excitement—when there occurred a scene perhaps unprecedented in Parliament.

One after another, perhaps twenty Members, on the Opposition benches, rising and entreating Mr Cardwell to withdraw his Resolution. After some time, silence on the Government benches, Mr Cardwell went to Lord John Russell, then to Lord Palmerston, then to Lord John Russell again, then returned to Lord Palmerston, and retired with him.

What are called the interpellations continued, when suddenly Lord Palmerston reappeared; embarrassed, with a faint smile; addressed the House; and after various preluding, announced the withdrawal of the Motion of Censure.

A various Debate followed; the Chancellor of the Exchequer endeavouring, as far as regards Lord Canning, to fulfil your Majesty's wishes. It is impossible to estimate the importance of this unforeseen event to your Majesty's servants. It has strengthened them more than the most decided division in their favour, for it has revealed complete anarchy in the ranks of their opponents. With prudence and vigilance all must now go right.

The speech of Sir James Graham last night produced a very great effect. No report gives a fair idea of it. The great country gentleman, the broad views, the fine classical allusions, the happiest all omitted, the massy style, contrasted remarkably with Sir Richard Bethell.

The Earl of Derby to Queen Victoria.

CAUSES OF THE COLLAPSE

St James's Square, *23rd May 1858.*

(*Sunday night.*)

Lord Derby, with his humble duty, gratefully acknowledges your Majesty's gracious letter just received, and the telegraphic message with which he was honoured in answer to his on Friday night. Your Majesty can hardly be expected to estimate, at a distance from the immediate scene of action, the effect of the event of that evening. It was the utter explosion of a well-constructed mine, under the feet, not of the assailed, but of the assailants; and the effect has been the greater from the immense attendance in London of Members of the House of Commons. No effort had been spared. Lord Castlerosse, only just married, had been sent for from Italy—but Lord Derby hopes that he had not been induced to come—for nothing. It is said that of the 654 Members of whom the House is composed, 626 were actually in London. The Government could rely on 304 to 308, and the whole question turned on the absence, or the conversion, of a small number of "Liberal" Members. The result is to be attributed to two causes; first, and principally, to the fear of a Dissolution, and to the growing conviction that in case of necessity your Majesty would sanction such a course, which had been strenuously denied by Lord Palmerston—and in which Lord Derby hopes that your Majesty will have seen that your Majesty's name has never, for a moment, been brought in question; and secondly, to the effect produced by the correspondence between the Governor-General and Sir James Outram.[327] And here Lord Derby may perhaps be allowed the opportunity of removing a misconception from your Majesty's mind, as to any secret intelligence or underhand intrigue between Lord Ellenborough and Sir James Outram, to the detriment of Lord Canning. Lord Derby is in the position to know that if there is one person in the world to whom Lord Ellenborough has an utter aversion, and with whom he has no personal or private correspondence, it is Sir James Outram. Anything therefore in common in their opinions must be the result of circumstances wholly irrespective of private concert. Lord Derby has written fully to Lord Canning, privately, by the mail which will go out on Tuesday; and while he has not concealed from him the opinion of your Majesty's servants that the Proclamation, of which so much has been said, conveyed too sweeping an Edict of Confiscation against the landowners, great and small, of Oudh, he has not hesitated to express also his conviction that Lord Canning's real intentions, in execution, would not be found widely to differ from the views of your Majesty's servants. He has expressed to Lord Canning his regret at the premature *publication* of the Draft Proclamation, at the same time that he has pointed out the injustice done both to your Majesty's Government and to the Governor-General by the (Lord Derby will hardly call it fraudulent)

---

[327] Especially Outram's remonstrance against what he considered the excessive severity of the Proclamation.

suppression of the private letters addressed to the President of the Board of Control, and deprecating judgment on the text of the Proclamation, until explanation should be received. Lord Derby cannot but be of opinion that this suppression, of which Lord Palmerston was fully cognisant, was an act which no political or party interests were sufficient to justify.

OFFER TO MR GLADSTONE

The state of the Government, during the late crisis, was such as to render it impossible to make any arrangement for filling up Lord Ellenborough's place at the Board of Control. Application has since been made to Mr Gladstone,[328] with the offer of that post, or of that of the Colonial Department, which Lord Stanley would give up for the convenience of your Majesty's Government, though unwillingly, for India. Mr Gladstone demurred, on the ground of not wishing to leave his friends; but when pressed to name whom he would wish to bring with him, he could name none. Finally, he has written to ask advice as to his course of Sir James Graham, who has returned to Netherby, and of Lord Aberdeen; and by them he will probably be guided. Should he finally refuse, Lord Stanley *must* take India; and the Colonies must be offered in the first instance to Sir E. B. Lytton, who probably will refuse, as he wants a Peerage, and is doubtful of his re-election; and failing him, to Sir William Heathcote, the Member for the University of Oxford, who, without official experience, has great Parliamentary knowledge and influence, and, if he will accept, is quite equal to the duties of the office. Lord Derby trusts that your Majesty will forgive this long intrusion on your Majesty's patience. He has preferred the risk of it, to leaving your Majesty uninformed as to anything which was going on, or contemplated....

If Lord Dalhousie should be in a state to converse upon public affairs, there is no one with whom Lord Derby could confer more confidentially than with him; nor of whose judgment, though he regrets to differ with him as to the annexation of Oudh, he has a higher opinion. He will endeavour to ascertain what is his present state of health, which he fears is very unsatisfactory, and will see and converse with him, if possible.

---

[328] See Mr Disraeli's curious letter printed in Morley's *Gladstone*, vol. i. p. 587, asking Mr Gladstone whether the time had not come when he might deign to be magnanimous. Sir E. B. Lytton accepted the office.

Queen Victoria to the Earl of Derby.

Buckingham Palace, *4th June 1858.*

The Queen has to thank Lord Derby for his satisfactory letter received yesterday. She has heard from Mr Disraeli to-day relative to the answer given by him to the question asked yesterday in the House of Commons as to what the Government meant to do.[329] He says that he hears there are rumours of other Motions on the subject. These the Queen hopes there will be no difficulty in defeating.

The Duke of Cambridge seems rather uneasy altogether, but the Queen, though equally anxious about it, owns she cannot contemplate the possibility of any *real* attempt to divest the Crown of its prerogative in this instance. The Army will not, she feels sure, stand it for a moment, and the Queen feels sure, that if properly defined and explained, the House of Commons will not acquiesce in any such disloyal proceeding.

The Queen does not understand Lord John Russell's voting with the majority, for she never understood him to express any such opinion.

Mr Disraeli to Queen Victoria.

GOVERNMENT OF INDIA

House of Commons, *24th June 1858.*

The Chancellor of the Exchequer with his humble duty to your Majesty.

The India Bill was read a second time without a division.[330] Lord Stanley made a clear and vigorous exposition of its spirit and provi-

---

[329] A question was asked whether it was the intention of the Government to take any step in consequence of a resolution of the House in favour of placing the whole administration and control of the Army under the sole authority of a single Minister. Mr. Disraeli replied that "considering the great importance of the subject,... the comparatively small number of Members in the House when the division took pace, and the bare majority by which the decision was arrived at, Her Majesty's Government do not feel that it is their duty to recommend any measure in consequence of that resolution."

[330] This was the third Bill of the Session, and was founded on the Resolutions, *ante*, p. 279. The Government of India was transferred from the dual jurisdiction of the Company and the Board of Control, to the Secretary of State for India in Council, the members of the Council (after the provisions for representing vested interests should have lapsed) to be appointed by the Secretary

sions; Mr Bright delivered a powerful oration on the condition of India—its past government and future prospects; the rest of the discussion weak and desultory.

No serious opposition apprehended in Committee, which the Chancellor of the Exchequer has fixed for this day (Friday)[331] and almost hopes that he may conclude the Committee on Monday. He proposes to proceed with no other business until it is concluded.

When the Bill has passed, the temper of the House, and its sanitary state,[332] will assist him in passing the remaining estimates with rapidity; and he contemplates an early conclusion of the Session.

It will be a great thing to have carried the India Bill, which Mr Thomas Baring, to-night, spoke of in terms of eulogy, and as a great improvement on the project of the late Government. It is, the Chancellor of the Exchequer really thinks, a wise and well-digested measure, ripe with the experience of the last five months of discussion; but it is only the antechamber of an imperial palace; and your Majesty would do well to deign to consider the steps which are now necessary to influence the opinions and affect the imagination of the Indian populations. The name of your Majesty ought to be impressed upon their native life. Royal Proclamations, Courts of Appeal, in their own land, and other institutions, forms, and ceremonies, will tend to this great result.

Queen Victoria to the Earl of Derby.

INDIAN CIVIL SERVICE

Osborne, *8th July 1858.*

The Queen in reading in the papers yesterday, on her way here from the camp, the Debate in the House of Commons of the previous

---

of State. A certain term of residence in India was to be a necessary qualification, and the members were to be rendered incapable of sitting in Parliament, and with a tenure of office as assured as that of judges under the Act of Settlement.

[331] The letter is ante-dated. The 24th of June was a Thursday.

[332] In consequence of the polluted condition of the Thames, the Government carried a measure enabling the Metropolitan Board of Works, at a cost of £3,000,000, to purify "that noble river, the present state of which is little creditable to a great country, and seriously prejudicial to the health and comfort of the inhabitants of the Metropolis."—Extract from the Queen's Speech, at the close of the Session.

night, was shocked to find that in several important points her Government have surrendered the prerogativesTHE SOVEREIGN'S PREROGATIVES of the Crown. She will only refer to the clauses concerning the Indian Civil Service and the right of peace and war.

With respect to the first, the regulations under which servants of the Crown are to be admitted or examined have always been an undoubted right and duty of the Executive; by the clause introduced by Lord Stanley the system of "Competitive Examination" has been confirmed by Act of Parliament. That system may be right or wrong; it has since its introduction been carried on under the Orders in Council; now the Crown and Government are to be deprived of any authority in the matter, and the whole examinations, selection, and appointments, etc., etc., are to be vested in the Civil Commissioners under a Parliamentary title.

As to the right of the Crown to declare war and make peace, it requires not a word of remark; yet Lord Stanley agrees to Mr Gladstone's proposal to make over this prerogative with regard to Indian questions to Parliament under the auspices of the Queen's Government; she is thus placed in a position of less authority than the President of the American Republic.[333]

When a Bill has been introduced into Parliament, after having received the Sovereign's approval, she has the right to expect that her Ministers will not subsequently introduce important alterations without previously obtaining her sanction. In the first of the two instances referred to by the Queen, Lord Stanley introduced the alteration himself; in the second he agreed to it even without asking for a moment's delay; and the Opposition party, which attempted to guard the Queen's prerogative, was overborne by the Government Leader of the House.

The Queen must remind Lord Derby that it is to him as the head of the Government that she looks for the protection of those prerogatives which form an integral part of the Constitution.

The King of the Belgians to Queen Victoria.

Laeken, *16th July 1858.*

---

[333] An important amendment made at the instance of Mr Gladstone provided that, except for repelling actual invasion or upon urgent necessity, the Queen's Indian forces should not be employed in operations outside India, without Parliamentary sanction.

My truly beloved Victoria,—Nothing can be *kinder* or more *affectionate* than your dear letter of the 13th, and it would have done *your warm heart* good to have *seen how much I have been delighted and moved by it.* I can only say that I love you both more tenderly than I could love my own children. When your plans will be nearer maturity, you will have the great kindness to let me know what will be your Royal pleasure, to enable me *de m'y conformer bien exactement.*

The feeling which occasions some grumbling at the Cherbourg visit[334] is in fact a good feeling, but it is not over-wise. Two things are to be done—(1) To make every reasonable exertion to remain on personal good terms with the Emperor—which can be done. One party in England says it is with the French nation that you are to be on loving terms; this *cannot* be, as the French dislike the English as a nation, though they may be kind to you also personally. (2) The next is, instead of a good deal of unnecessary abuse, to have the Navy so organised that it can and must be superior to the French. All beyond these two points is sheer nonsense.

After talking of Chambord,[335] to my utter horror he is here, and asked yesterday to see me to-day. It is not fair to do so, as the legitimists affect to this hour to consider [us] here as rebels. I could not refuse to see him, as, though distantly, still he is a relation; but I mean to do as they did in Holland, to receive him, but to limit to his visit and my visit our whole intercourse. If he should speak to me of going to England, I certainly mean to tell him *que je considérais une visite comme tout à fait intempestive....* Your devoted Uncle,

Leopold R.

Queen Victoria to Sir E. Bulwer Lytton.

BRITISH COLUMBIA

Osborne, *24th July 1858.*

The Queen has received Sir E. Bulwer Lytton's letter.[336] If the name of New Caledonia is objected to as being already borne by an-

---

[334] On the 4th of August, the Queen and Prince, accompanied by the Prince of Wales, visited the Emperor and Empress at Cherbourg.

[335] See *ante*, p. 6.

[336] Stating that objections were being made in France to the name of New Caledonia being given to the proposed colony between the Pacific and the Rocky Mountains.

other colony or island claimed by the French, it may be better to give the new colony west of the Rocky Mountains another name. New Hanover, New Cornwall, and New Georgia appear from the maps to be the names of sub-divisions of that country, but do not appear on all maps. The only name which is given to the whole territory in every map the Queen has consulted is "Columbia," but as there exists also a Columbia in South America, and the citizens of the United States call their country also Columbia, at least in poetry, "British Columbia" might be, in the Queen's opinion, the best name.

Queen Victoria to the Earl of Derby.

ARMY COMMISSIONS

Osborne, *29th July 1858.*

The Queen has been placed in a most unpleasant dilemma by the last vote in the House of Commons;[337] she feels all the force of Lord Derby's objections to risking another defeat on the same question and converting the struggle into one against the Royal Prerogative; yet, on the other hand, she can hardly sit still, and from mere want of courage become a party to the most serious inroad which has yet been made upon it. It is the introduction of the principle into our legislation that the Sovereign is no longer the source of all appointments under the Crown, but that these appointments are the property of individuals under a Parliamentary title, which the Queen feels bound to resist. Lord John Russell's Motion and Sir James Graham's speech only went to the Civil appointments; but after their Motion had been carried on a division, Lord Stanley gave way to Sir De Lacy Evans also with regard to a *portion of the Army!* If this principle is recognised and sanctioned by the entire legislature, its future extension can no longer be resisted on constitutional grounds, and Lord John in fact reminded Lord Stanley that the latter had stated that he only refrained from making the application general from thinking it *premature*, himself being of opinion that it ought to be carried further, and yet its extension to the Army reduces the Sovereign to a mere signing machine, as, to carry the case to its extreme consequence, *Law* would *compel* her to sign the Commission for the officers, and they might have the right to sue at law for

[337] The Lords Amendments on the subject of competitive examination were rejected by a majority of thirteen in the Commons, and, in the circumstances, Lord Derby had advised abiding by the decision and not risking another defeat.

the recovery of their property vested in them by Act of Parliament (viz., their Commissions) if the Crown doubted for any reason the fitness of an appointment!! Have these consequences been considered and brought distinctly before Parliament? It strikes the Queen that all the Commons want is a Parliamentary security against the abolition of the Competitive System of Examinations by the Executive. Can this not be obtained by means less subversive of the whole character of our Constitution? The Queen cannot believe that Lord Derby could not find means to come to some agreement with the Opposition, and she trusts he will leave nothing undone to effect this.

Queen Victoria to the Earl of Derby.

NAVAL ESTIMATES

Osborne, *2nd August 1858.*

The Queen feels it her duty to address a few lines to Lord Derby on the subject of the reports made to Sir John Pakington on the subject of the French Naval preparations, to which she has already verbally adverted when she saw Lord Derby last. These reports reveal a state of things of the greatest moment to this country. It will be the first time in her history that she will find herself in an absolute minority of ships on the sea! and this inferiority will be much greater in reality than even apparent, as our fleet will have to defend possessions and commerce all over the world, and has even in Europe a strategical line to hold extending from Malta to Heligoland, whilst France keeps her fleet together and occupies the centre of that line in Europe.

The Queen thinks it irreconcilable with the duty which the Government owes to the country to be aware of this state of things without straining every nerve to remedy it. With regard to men in whom we are also totally deficient in case of an emergency, a Commission of Enquiry is sitting to devise a remedy; but with regard to our ships and dockyards we require action, and immediate action. The plan proposed by the Surveyor of the Navy appears to the Queen excessively moderate and judicious, and she trusts that the Cabinet will not hesitate to empower its execution, bearing in mind that £200,000 spent now will probably do more work during the six or nine months for working before us, than £2,000,000 would if voted in next year's estimate, letting our arrears in the dockyards, already admitted to be very great, accumulate in the interval. Time is most precious under these circumstances!

It is true that this sum of money would be in excess of the estimates of last Session, but the Queen feels sure that on the faith of the reports made by the Admiralty, the Government would find no difficulty in convincing Parliament that they have been good stewards of the public money, in taking courageously the responsibility upon themselves to spend judiciously what is necessary, and that the country will be deeply grateful for the honesty with which they will have served her.

The Queen wishes Lord Derby to communicate this letter to the Cabinet.

Queen Victoria to the Earl of Derby.

Babelsberg, *15th August 1858.*

The Queen has asked Lord Malmesbury to explain in detail to Lord Derby her objections to the draft of Proclamation for India. The Queen would be glad if Lord Derby would write it himself in his excellent language, bearing in mind that it is a female Sovereign who speaks to more than 100,000,000 of Eastern people on assuming the direct Government over them after a bloody civil war, giving them pledges which her future reign is to redeem, and explaining the principles of her Government. Such a document should breathe feelings of generosity, benevolence, and religious feeling, pointing out the privileges which the Indians will receive in being placed on an equality with the subjects of the British Crown, and the prosperity following in the train of civilisation.[338]

Queen Victoria to Lord Stanley.

PROCLAMATION FOR INDIA

Osborne, *4th September 1858.*

The Queen sends to Lord Stanley a Memorandum embodying her wishes with respect to the transaction of business between herself and the new Secretary of State. He will find that she has omitted any reference to Military appointments, as Lord Stanley seemed anxious to defer a settlement on this point; she expects, however, that in all cases in which her pleasure was taken by the Commander-in-Chief, even

[338] The draft Proclamation was accordingly altered so as to be in strict harmony with the Queen's wishes. See *post*, p. 304.

during the administration of the East India Company and Board of Control, the same practice will be continued unaltered.

The Queen has received Lord Stanley's letter of yesterday. He has given her no answer with respect to Sir James Melvill.[339]

Whenever the Proclamation is finally printed, the Queen would wish to have a copy sent her. A letter she has received from Lady Canning speaks of Lord Canning's supposed Amnesty in Oudh as a fabrication; she has sent the letter to Lord Derby.

Memorandum by Queen Victoria.

Osborne, *4th September 1858.*

The Queen wishes the practice of the Office[340] with reference to submissions to her to be as nearly as possible assimilated to that of the Foreign Office.

All despatches, when received and perused by the Secretary of State, to be sent to the Queen. They may be merely forwarded in boxes from the Office without being accompanied by any letter from the Secretary of State, unless he should think an explanation necessary. No draft of instructions or orders to be sent out without having been previously submitted to the Queen. The label on the boxes of the Office containing such drafts to be marked "For Approval."

In cases of Civil appointments the Secretary of State will himself take the Queen's pleasure before communicating with the gentlemen to be appointed.

Copies or a *précis* of the Minutes of the Council to be regularly transmitted to the Queen.

The Secretary of State to obtain the Queen's sanction to important measures previously to his bringing them before the Council for discussion.

Memorandum by the Prince Albert.

---

339 The Queen had asked how it was that Sir J. Melvill's name was not included among those submitted to her for appointments in connection with the new military organisation in India. Sir James had been Financial Secretary, and afterwards Chief Secretary, for the East India Company. He now became the Government Director of Indian railways, and a Member of the Council of India.

340 The India Office.

LORD PALMERSTON

Osborne, *4th September 1858.*

The most remarkable feature of the last Session of Parliament has been the extraordinary unpopularity of Lord Palmerston, for which nothing can account; the only direct reproach which is made to him, is to have appointed Lord Clanricarde Privy Seal, and to have been overbearing in his manner. Yet a House of Commons, having been elected solely for the object, and on the ground of supporting Lord Palmerston personally (an instance in our Parliamentary history without parallel), holds him suddenly in such abhorrence, that not satisfied with having upset his Government, which had been successful in all its policy, and thrown him out, it will hardly listen to him when he speaks. He is frequently received with hooting, and throughout the last Session it sufficed that [he] took up any cause for the whole House voting against it, even if contrary to the principles which they had themselves advocated, merely to have the satisfaction of putting him into a minority. How can this be accounted for? The man who was without rhyme or reason stamped the only *English* statesman, the champion of liberty, the man of the people, etc., etc., now, without his having changed in any one respect, having still the same virtues and the same faults that he always had, young and vigorous in his seventy-fifth year, and having succeeded in his policy, is now considered the head of a clique, the man of intrigue, past his work, etc., etc.—in fact hated! and this throughout the country. I cannot explain the enigma except by supposing that people had before joined in a cry which they thought was popular without themselves believing what they said and wrote, and that they now do the same; that the Radicals used his name to destroy other statesmen and politicians, and are destroying him now in his turn; that they hoped to govern through him, and that they see a better chance now of doing it through a weak and incapable Tory Government which has entered into a secret bargain for their support. Still the phenomenon remains most curious.[341]

Lord Palmerston himself remains, outwardly at least, quite cheerful, and seems to care very little about his reverses; he speaks on all subjects, bids for the Liberal support as before, even at the expense of his better conviction (as he used to do), and keeps as much as possible

[341] Charles Greville, in his Journal (16th June 1858), noted the same circumstance, and drew the inference that Palmerston's public career was drawing to a close.]

before the public; he made an official tour in Ireland, and is gone to visit the Emperor Napoleon at Paris; his Chinese policy upon which the general Dissolution had taken place in 1857 has just been crowned by the most complete success by the advantageous treaty signed at Pekin by Lord Elgin; and yet even for this the public will not allow him any credit. Lady Palmerston, on the contrary, is said to be very unhappy and very much hurt.

Albert.

Sir E. Bulwer Lytton to Queen Victoria.

THE IONIAN ISLANDS

Colonial Office, *1st November 1858.*

Sir E. B. Lytton, with his humble duty to the Queen, submits to your Majesty's pleasure the appointment of the Right Honourable W. E. Gladstone, as special High Commissioner to the Ionian Islands.

Differences of long standing between the Executive and Legislative branches of the Ionian Constitution, aggravated by recent dissensions between the Senate and Municipal Magistrature, render it very expedient to obtain the opinion of a statesman of eminence, formed upon the spot, as to any improvements in the workings and results of the Constitution which it might be in the power of the protecting Sovereign to effect. And Sir Edward thinks it fortunate for the public service that a person so distinguished and able as Mr Gladstone should be induced to undertake this mission.

Sir Edward ventures to add that, should Her Majesty be graciously pleased to approve this appointment, it is extremely desirable that Mr Gladstone should depart at the earliest possible day, and that Sir Edward may be enabled to make the requisite announcement to the Lord High Commissioner by the first mail.

Mr Disraeli to the Prince Albert.

LORD STANLEY AND MR DISRAELI

Grosvenor Gate, *18th November 1858.*

(*Wednesday night.*)

Sir,—After the Committee of the Cabinet on the Reform Bill, which sat this morning for five hours, Lord Stanley expressed a wish to have some private conversation with me.

Although I would willingly have deferred the interview till a moment when I was less exhausted, I did not think it wise, with a person of his temperament, to baulk an occasion, and therefore assented at once.

I give your Royal Highness faithfully, but feebly, and not completely, the results of our conversation.

1. With respect to the relations between his office and Her Majesty, he said he was conscious that they had been conducted with great deficiency of form, and, in many respects, in an unsatisfactory manner; but he attributed all this to the inexperience and "sheer ignorance" of a Department which had not been accustomed to direct communication with the Crown. Some portion of this, he said, he had already remedied, and he wished to remedy all, though he experienced difficulties, on some of which he consulted me.

He accepted, without reserve, and cordially, my position, that he must act always as the Minister of the Queen, and not of the Council, but he said I took an exaggerated view of his relations with that body; that he thoroughly knew their respective places, and should be vigilant that they did [? not] overstep their limits; that he had never been, of which he reminded me, an admirer of the East India Company, and had no intention of reviving their system; that the incident of submitting the legal case to the Council, etc., had originated in a demand on the part of the Commander-in-Chief, which involved, if complied with, a grant of money, and that, under these circumstances, an appeal to the Council was inevitable.

2. He agreed with me, that, on all military matters, he would habitually communicate with the Commander-in-Chief, and take His Royal Highness's advice on all such points; and that copies of all military papers, as I understood Lord Stanley, should be furnished to His Royal Highness.

3. Having arrived at this point, I laid before him the views respecting *military unity*, which formed the subject matter of recent conversations. Lord Stanley assented to the principles which I attempted to enforce; and in reply to my reminding him that the old military system of India had entirely broken down, he said he contemplated terminating the independent authority of the Commander-in-Chief at the inferior Presidencies, and of establishing the absolute and complete authority of Her Majesty's Commander-in-Chief in India. He did not seem to see his way to any further step at present, and I did not think it judicious on this occasion to press the subject further.

Throughout this interview, Lord Stanley's manner was candid, very conciliatory, and, for him, even soft. He was pleased to say that it was a source of great satisfaction to him that your Royal Highness had deigned to confer confidentially with me on the subject, and make me, as it were, a "Mediator" on matters which, he assured me with great emphasis, had occasioned him an amount of anxiety almost intolerable.

SUGGESTED RESIGNATION

He had recurred, in the course of this interview, to a suggestion which he had thrown out on Tuesday, viz. that the difficulties of the position might be removed, or greatly mitigated, by his retirement from the office, and accepting, if his continuance in the Government was desirable, another post. I therefore thought it best at once to point out to him that such a course of proceeding would only aggravate all the inconveniences and annoyances at present existing; that his retirement would be the signal for exaggerated rumours and factious machinations, and would have the most baneful effect on the discussion in Parliament generally of all those military topics with which we were threatened; that, far from being satisfactory to Her Majesty and your Royal Highness, I was convinced that the Queen and yourself would hear of such an intention with regret.

Lord Stanley ultimately adopted entirely this view of his position, and he parted from me with an earnest expression of his hope that the painful misconceptions which had prevailed might at once, or at least in due course, entirely disappear.

This, Sir, is a very imperfect report of an important interview, but, as I collected from Lord Stanley, that nothing was really settled in his conference on Tuesday with Lord Derby and the Lord Chancellor, I have thought it my duty, without loss of time, to forward it to your Royal Highness, and have the honour to remain, ever, Sir, your most obedient and sincerely obliged Servant,

B. Disraeli.

The Prince Albert to Mr Disraeli.

Windsor Castle, *18th November 1858.*

My dear Mr Disraeli,—I am very much obliged to you for your long letter after a Cabinet meeting of five hours, and subsequent interview with Lord Stanley, whom I am much pleased to hear you found so anxious to remedy the present state of things. I am glad that you made it clear to him that the Queen had never connected in her mind the objections which she felt bound to take with anything personal, which could be removed by Lord Stanley's relinquishing the Indian Secretaryship. The difficulty would still remain to be solved, only under additional complication and disadvantage. Lord Derby told me today that he was drawing up a Memorandum which, when seen by the Chancellor and Lord Stanley, was to be submitted to the Queen. Ever yours truly,

Albert.[342]

Queen Victoria to Lord Stanley.

THE INDIA OFFICE

Windsor Castle, *20th November 1858.*

The Queen has received Lord Stanley's letter entering into the subject of the difficulties which have arisen in the conduct of the new Indian Department. She had from the first foreseen that it would not be an easy matter to bring the establishments of the old Company's Government to fall into the practice and usages of the Constitutional Monarchy, and was therefore most anxious that distinct rules should be laid down before the installation of the new Government, which unfortunately was not done, but she trusts will now be devised and adopted.

The Queen most readily gives Lord Stanley credit for every intention to remove the obstacles in the way of the solution of these difficulties as far as he was able, but she cannot but fear that the particular form in which the opinion of the Law Officers has been asked, and the fact [that] the eighteen members of the Council (all naturally wedded to a system under which they were trained) were made parties to the discussion between herself and her Secretary of State on these difficulties—must increase instead of diminishing them.

The account given by Mr Temple, together with the last printed letters and Memoranda from the Punjab, give us serious cause of apprehension for the future, and show that the *British* Army is the only safeguard at present.

[342] On the same day Lord Stanley wrote a lengthy letter to the Queen justifying the course he had taken.

Queen Victoria to Viscount Canning.[343]

LORD CANNING'S PROCLAMATION

Windsor Castle, *2nd December 1858.*

The Queen acknowledges the receipt of Lord Canning's letter of the 19th October, which she received on the 29th November, which has given her great pleasure.

It is a source of great satisfaction and pride to her to feel herself in direct communication with that enormous Empire which is so bright a jewel of her Crown, and which she would wish to see happy, contented, and peaceful. May the publication of her Proclamation be the beginning of a new era, and may it draw a veil over the sad and bloody past!

The Queen rejoices to hear that her Viceroy approves this passage about Religion.[344] She strongly insisted on it. She trusts also that the certainty of the Amnesty remaining open till the 1st January may not be productive of serious evil.

The Queen must express our admiration of Lord Canning's own Proclamation, the wording of which is beautiful. The telegram received to-day brings continued good news, and announces her proclamation having been read, and having produced a good effect.

The Queen hopes to hear from Lord Canning, whenever he can spare time to write. She misses hearing from Lady Canning, not having heard from her since the 30th August; but the Queen fears that she is herself to blame, as she has not written to Lady Canning for a long time; she intends doing so by the next mail....

Both the Prince and herself hope that Lord Canning's health is now perfectly good, as well as dear Lady Canning's. We ask him to remember us to her, and also to Lord Clyde.

---

343 The Queen's Proclamation to her Indian subjects had been received by Lord Canning on the 17th of October, when he also learned that the title of Viceroy was in future to dignify the Governor-General's office.

344 "Firmly relying ourselves on the truth of Christianity, and acknowledging with gratitude the solace of religion, we disclaim alike the right and desire to impose our convictions on any of our subjects." The Proclamation proceeded to state that all the Queen's Indian subjects should be impartially protected by the law, and live unmolested in the observance of their several religions.

The Queen concludes with every wish for Lord Canning's success and prosperity, and with the assurance of her undiminished and entire confidence.

The Earl of Malmesbury to Queen Victoria.

FRANCE AND ITALY

London, *10th December 1858.*

The Earl of Malmesbury presents his humble duty to the Queen, and has already anticipated your Majesty's wishes respecting the Emperor Napoleon.[345] Lord Malmesbury has written to Lord Cowley a private letter, desiring him to show it to His Majesty. It is in the same sense as your Majesty's, and states that if he is anxious to improve the lot of the worst governed country, namely the Papal States, he should, instead of sulking with Austria, make an attempt with his Catholic brother to ameliorate the Papal Government. It is not for Protestant England to take the initiative, as her object would be misunderstood and attributed to sectarian motives; but England could give her moral support, and even her material aid *eventually*, if it were required to establish an improved Administration of the Roman States. Austria would gain by having a quiet frontier. The correspondence which took place in 1856 and 1857 between Lord Clarendon and Mr Lyons shows that this is the only effective way of ameliorating the condition of Italy without a war.

Lord Malmesbury thinks he can assure your Majesty that none is at present contemplated by the Emperor Napoleon (who has just contradicted the report officially), and Count Buol is of the same opinion. The latter is constantly hurting the vanity of the French Government by his irritable despatches, and neither party makes the slightest effort to command their temper; but it appears impossible that Napoleon can make a *casus belli* against Austria. Besides this, your Majesty may be assured that no warlike preparations are making in France, such as must precede such a plan as an Italian war.

---

[345] Viz. that the Emperor's mind should be diverted from his project of originating a war in Italy. On the previous day Lord Malmesbury had written to the Queen: "Lord Clarendon may have told your Majesty that the Emperor Napoleon was so ignorant of the locality of Villafranca that he looked for it on the map in the Adriatic, and was confounded when Lord Clarendon showed His Majesty that it was the Port of Nice and ten miles from his frontier!"

Lord Malmesbury entirely agrees with your Majesty that it is desirable that His Royal Highness the Prince of Wales should visit and remain at Rome incognito. It is also indispensable that when there His Royal Highness should receive no foreigner or stranger *alone*, so that no reports of pretended conversations with such persons could be circulated without immediate refutation by Colonel Bruce. Lord Malmesbury will instruct Mr Odo Russell to inform His Holiness of your Majesty's intentions in respect of the Prince.

Queen Victoria to the King of the Belgians.

Osborne, *17th December 1858.*

My Dearest Uncle,—I wrote in such a hurry on Wednesday that I wish to make amends by writing again to-day, and entering more properly into what *you* wrote about in your kind letter....

I really *hope* that there is no *real* desire for war in the Emperor's mind; we have also explained to him strongly how *entirely* he would *alienate* us from him if there was any *attempt* to *disturb standing and binding treaties*. The Empress-Dowager of Russia[346] is very ill, they say, with bronchitis and fever.

I did not tell you, that when we went on the 2nd to Claremont I was *not* pleased with the Queen's appearance. She had had a slight cold, and I thought her very *feeble*. They keep her rooms so fearfully [hot] that it must really be *very* weakening for her and predispose her to cold. I am ever, your devoted Niece,

Victoria R.

---

[346] The Empress Alexandra Feodorovna (formerly the Princess Louise Charlotte of Prussia, sister to King Frederick William IV.), widow of the Emperor Nicholas.

INTRODUCTORY NOTE
TO CHAPTER XXVIII

Parliamentary Reform was the question of the hour at the outset of the year 1859, and the Derby Government, though with difficulty able to maintain itself in power, took the courageous step of introducing a Reform Bill, the chief feature of which was the introduction of a franchise based on personal property. Mr Walpole and Mr Henley thereupon withdrew from the Ministry, and Lord John Russell, from below the gangway, proposed an Amendment, protesting against interference with the established freehold franchise, and calling for a larger extension of the suffrage in towns. Lord Palmerston and the Liberal Opposition supported the Amendment, while Mr Gladstone, who was opposed to most of the provisions of the Bill, supported it in preference to the Amendment, pleading, at the same time, for the retention of the small boroughs. The Ministry were defeated, and Parliament thereupon dissolved, but not until the civil functionaries and all ranks of the native and European army had received its thanks for the final suppression of the Indian Mutiny. The Ministry gained twenty-five seats at the polls, but were still in a minority, and as soon as it was known that Lord John Russell and Lord Palmerston were reconciled, the end was in sight. A hostile Amendment to the Address was carried by a majority of thirteen, but on Lord Derby's resignation, the Queen was placed in a dilemma by the competing claims of Lord Palmerston and Lord John Russell, who had each been Prime Minister and leader of the Liberal Party. Unwilling to be compelled to decide between them, she called upon Lord Granville to form a Ministry representative of all sections of the Liberal Party; but the difficulties proved insuperable, and Lord Palmerston eventually formed a Ministry in which the Whigs, the Peelites, and the Manchester School were all represented, though Mr Cobden declined to join the Government. Mr Gladstone, who had returned from the mission he had undertaken for the Derby Cabinet, and voted with them in the critical division, became Chancellor of the Exchequer, and kept his seat for Oxford University by a majority of nearly two hundred.

The continent of Europe was the scene of a contest between Austria on the one hand, who was struggling to maintain her position in Italy, and France with Sardinia on the other. Sardinia, under the guidance of Cavour, had joined the alliance of England and France against Russia; and in July 1858 an interview at Plombières, under rather mysterious circumstances, between Cavour and Louis Napoleon, led to effective confederacy; a marriage, arranged or suggested at the same time, between Princess Clothilde of Sardinia and a cousin of the Emperor, brought the two illustrious houses still closer together. In the spring of 1859, Sardinia prepared to take up arms to resist Austrian predominance, and the assistance of the guerilla leader, Garibaldi, was obtained. Count Cavour, in reply to interrogatories from the British Government, stated officially his grievances against Austria, while Lord Malmesbury despatched Lord Cowley on a special mission to Vienna to mediate between Austria and France. In April, however, after a curt summons to the Sardinians to disarm had been disregarded, Austria invaded Piedmont, and Victor Emmanuel placed himself at the head of his army. The first engagement took place, with unfavourable results to the Austrians, at Montebello, followed by French victories at Palestro and Magenta. A revolution had meanwhile taken place in Florence. The Grand Duke had fled, and a Commissioner to administer the affairs of the Grand Duchy had been appointed by the King of Sardinia with the assent of the Tuscans, who now joined the Franco-Sardinian alliance, while risings also took place in Parma and Modena. The Austrians were again defeated at Malegnano, and, on the 8th of June, the French Emperor and King Victor Emmanuel entered Milan amid great enthusiasm. The bloody action of Solferino was fought on the 24th of June, but on the 11th of July a treaty of peace was, somewhat unexpectedly, concluded between the French and Austrian Emperors at Villafranca, under which an Italian Confederation was to be erected, Lombardy substantially ceded to Sardinia, the Grand Duke of Tuscany and the Duke of Modena reinstated, and Venetia, though included in the Confederation, to remain subject to the Imperial Crown of Austria; these preliminaries were subsequently converted into a definite treaty at Zurich. Meanwhile, the newly constituted representative Assemblies in Tuscany, Romagna, and the Duchies, unanimously pronounced for incorporation in the kingdom of Victor Emmanuel.

At home, on the 14th of October, the Queen opened the Glasgow waterworks at the outflow of Loch Katrine, the construction of which had necessitated engineering operations at that time considered stupendous; a few days later an appalling shipping calamity occurred, in the wreck of the *Royal Charter* near Anglesey, and the loss of 459 lives.

CHAPTER XXVIII

1859

Queen Victoria to Sir Edward Bulwer Lytton.

Windsor Castle, *7th January 1859.*

The Queen returns Mr Gladstone's letters, and gladly accepts his patriotic offer.[347] He will have difficulty in solving a delicate question, affecting national feeling, against time, but his offer comes most opportunely.

Queen Victoria to the Earl of Derby.

NATIONAL DEFENCES

Windsor Castle, *13th January 1859.*

As the Cabinet are now meeting, and will probably come to a decision about the estimates for the year, the Queen thinks it her duty to urge upon them in the strongest manner her conviction that, under the present aspect of political affairs in Europe, there will be no safety to the honour, power, and peace of this country except in Naval and Military strength. The extraordinary exertions which France is making in her Naval Department oblige us to exercise the utmost vigour to keep up a superiority at sea, upon which our very existence may be said to depend, and which would be already lost at any moment that France were to be joined by any other country possessing a Navy.[348] The war

---

[347] See *ante*, p. 301. Mr Gladstone had been sent to enquire into the causes of the dissatisfaction of the inhabitants of the Ionian Islands with their High Commissioner, Sir John Young. He now offered to act himself for a limited time as High Commissioner, should it be decided to recall Sir John. He was succeeded in February by Sir Henry Storks.

[348] The French Emperor had signalised the opening of a new year by an ominous speech. To M. Hübner, the Austrian Ambassador at Paris, who had

in India has drained us of every available Battalion. We possess at this moment only fourteen old Battalions of the Line within the three kingdoms, and twelve Second Battalions newly raised, whilst our Mediterranean possessions are under-garrisoned, and Alderney has not as yet any garrison at all. Under these circumstances the Queen has heard it rumoured that the Government intend to propose a reduction on the estimates of 9,000 men for this year. She trusts that such an idea, if ever entertained, will upon reflection be given up as inconsistent with the duty which the Government owe to the country. Even if it were said that these 9,000 men have only existed on paper, and have not yet been raised, such an act at this moment would be indefensible; for it would require a proof that circumstances have arisen which make it desirable to ask for fewer troops than were considered requisite when the last estimates were passed, which really cannot be said to be the case! To be able to raise at any time an additional 9,000 men (in political danger) without having to go to Parliament for a supplementary vote and spreading alarm thereby, must be of the utmost value to the Government, and if not wanted, the vote will entail no additional expense.

England will not be listened to in Europe, and be powerless for the preservation of the general peace, which must be her first object under the present circumstances, if she is known to be despicably weak in her military resources, and no statesman will, the Queen apprehends, maintain that if a European war were to break out she could hope to remain long out of it. For peace and for war, therefore, an available Army is a necessity to her.

The Queen wishes Lord Derby to communicate this letter to the Cabinet.

Mr Odo Russell[349] to Mr Corbett.[350]

THE POPE

---

attended, with the other foreign representatives, to offer the usual congratulations on the 1st of January, he observed: "I regret that the relations between our two Governments are not more satisfactory; but I beg you to assure the Emperor that they in no respect alter my feelings of friendship to himself."

[349] Secretary of Legation at Florence, resident in Rome, afterwards Lord Ampthill.

[350] Secretary of Legation at Florence, afterwards successively Minister at Rio Janeiro and Stockholm.

(Submitted to Queen Victoria.)

Rome, *14th January 1859.*

Sir,—I had the honour of being received by the Pope at a private audience this morning at the Vatican. No one else was present.

His Holiness, whose manner towards me was most kind and benevolent, said: "You are appointed to succeed a very good man,[351] for whom I felt great affection, and I regret that he has left Rome. You may be as good as he was, and we shall become friends, but I do not know you yet, and Mr Lyons I had known for many years; he is going to America, I hear, and he will find the Americans far more difficult to deal with than with us.

"I am much gratified to hear that the Prince of Wales is likely to visit Rome, and Her Majesty, I feel sure, has done well to allow him to prosecute his studies here. It will be an honour to me to receive him at the Vatican, and I beg that you will confer with Cardinal Antonelli[352] as to the best means of making the Prince's visit here useful and pleasant. We are anxious that all his wishes should be attended to, that he may preserve a pleasant recollection of Rome in the future. Alas! so many erroneous impressions exist about this country that I hope you will not judge of us too rashly. We are advised to make reforms, and it is not understood that those very reforms, which would consist in giving this country a Government of laymen, would make it cease to exist. It is called 'States of the Church' (*États de l' Église*), and that is what it must remain. It is true I have lately appointed a layman to a post formerly held by an ecclesiastic, and I may do so again occasionally; but, however small we may be, we cannot yield to outer pressure, and this country must be administered by men of the Church. For my part, I shall fulfil my duties according to my conscience, and should Governments and events turn against me they cannot make me yield. I shall go with the faithful to the Catacombs, as did the Christians of the early centuries, and there await the will of the Supreme Being, for I dread no human Power upon earth and fear nothing but God."

"But, Holy Father," I said, "you speak as if some great danger threatened Rome—is there any [real?] cause for apprehension?"

---

[351] Richard Bickerton Pemell Lyons, who had just been transferred from Rome to Washington. He had recently succeeded his father, the Admiral, in the Barony of Lyons, and was himself subsequently promoted to an Earldom.
[352] Secretary of Foreign Affairs for the Papal States.

"Have you not heard," His Holiness answered, "that great excitement prevails throughout Italy?—the state of Lombardy is deplorable; evil spirits are at work even in my dominions, and the late speech of the King of Sardinia is calculated to inflame the minds of all the revolutionary men of Italy. It is true he says he will observe existing Treaties, but that will scarcely counter-balance the effect produced by other portions of his speech. News has also reached me of an extensive amnesty granted by the King of Naples—he did not yield to outer pressure, and he was right—but now, on the occasion of the marriage of his son, an act of clemency on his part is well advised."

"Is it true," I said, "that political prisoners are included in that Amnesty?"

"Yes," His Holiness answered; "I saw the name of Settembrini, and I think also of that other man in whom your Government took so much interest—his name begins with a 'P' if I remember rightly——"

"Poerio," I suggested.

"That is the name," the Pope continued; "and I fancy that all the other political prisoners will be released; they are to be sent to Cadiz at the expense of the King, they are to be clothed and receive some money, I believe, and after that arrangements have been made with the Minister of the United States to have them conveyed to that country; they are to be exiled for life. I hope this event may have the effect of making your Government and that of France renew diplomatic relations with Naples; I always regretted that rupture, but the King was right not to yield to outer pressure.

THE POPE AND LORD PALMERSTON

"It is lucky," the Pope ended with a smile, "that Lord Palmerston is not in office; he was too fond of interfering in the concerns of foreign countries, and the present crisis would just have suited him. *Addio, caro,*" the Pope then said, and dismissed me with his blessing.

I then, according to usage, called on Cardinal Antonelli, and recounted to him what had passed. He confirmed all the Pope had said, but denied that there was any very serious cause for immediate apprehension of any general disturbance of the peace of Italy. I have, etc.,

Odo Russell.

The Earl of Malmesbury to Queen Victoria.

London, *18th January 1859.*

The Earl of Malmesbury presents his humble duty to the Queen, and has the honour to inform your Majesty that he has seen the French Ambassador to-day, who came of his own accord to say that we need be in no apprehension, of a war *at present*, as the public opinion in France, especially in the large towns, had been so strongly pronounced against a war that it was impossible. Lord Malmesbury is also glad to inform your Majesty that the Cabinet has agreed to-day to make a great addition to the effective force of your Majesty's Navy.

Your Majesty's commands are obeyed respecting the telegram to Berlin.

The Earl of Malmesbury to Queen Victoria.

London, 25th *January 1859.*

The Earl of Malmesbury presents his humble duty to the Queen, and regrets to say that he shares your Majesty's apprehensions. The Emperor is extremely irritated at our not concurring in his views on Italy, and Lord Malmesbury believes that nothing will restrain him but the public opinion expressed against them, in France.[353] Austria has, against all our advice and common prudence, made a false move by sending troops into the Papal States *against* the wish of *the Pope*, and is now obliged to recall them. The speech of your Majesty is to be discussed in Cabinet to-day. Lord Derby intended to introduce a paragraph stating that your Majesty's Alliance with France remained "unimpaired," but it now appears to us that such a statement might provoke a question "*why*" it should be made a special one. Lord Malmesbury entirely agrees with your Majesty as to an allusion to Treaties.

---

[353] Yet the Emperor had just written to Queen Victoria on 20th January: "Le corps législatif va bientôt s'ouvrir, presque en même temps que le parlement; je tâcherai d'exprimer dans mon discours tout le désir que j'ai de vivre toujours en bonne et sincère intelligence avec votre Majesté et son gouvernement." Early in February the pamphlet *Napoléon et l'Italie*, nominally written by M. de la Guéronnière, but inspired by the Emperor, foreshadowed the war in Italy, and attempted to justify it.

Queen Victoria to Lord Stanley.

LORD CANNING

Windsor Castle, *25th January 1859.*

The Queen thinks that the time is come when the bestowal of some honour or reward on Lord Canning ought no longer to be delayed. He has now nearly arrived at the end of his tremendous task of quelling the Rebellion, and has triumphed over all his many difficulties. If any man deserves an acknowledgment of his services at the hands of the Crown, it is surely he, and the Queen would be sorry that the grace of it should be taken away from her by questions being asked in Parliament when it is assembled again, which will now be the case very soon.

A step in the Peerage and the G.C.B. appear to the Queen an appropriate reward. Perhaps a pension should be awarded to him? Lord Elphinstone also ought not to be left unrewarded, and a step in the Peerage with the G.C.B. does not appear too high an honour for him, for he also has greatly contributed to the saving to the Indian Empire.[354]

Queen Victoria to the King of the Belgians.

THE QUEEN'S FIRST GRANDCHILD

Buckingham Palace, *2nd February 1859.*

My dearest, kindest Uncle,—Accept my warmest thanks for your most kind letter of the 28th. I know how pleased you would be at the safety of our dear Vicky, and at the birth of our first grandson![355] Everything goes on so beautifully, Vicky recovering as fast and well as I did, and the dear little boy improving so much and thriving in every way.... The joy and interest taken *here* is as great almost as in Prussia, which is *very* gratifying.

I *think* that *the Speech* will do good, but it has not been easy to frame it, as the feeling *against* the *Emperor here* is *very strong*. I think *yet* that if *Austria* is *strong* and *well prepared,* and *Germany strong* and *well inclined* towards *us* (as *Prussia certainly* is), France will *not*

---

[354] Lord Canning was made an Earl and Lord Elphinstone (who had been Governor of Bombay during the Mutiny) a Peer of the United Kingdom, and both received the G.C.B.

[355] Frederick William Victor Albert, now German Emperor, born on the 27th of January.

be so eager to attempt what I *firmly* believe would *end* in the *Emperor's* downfall! Old Malakhoff *himself* said to the Duchess of Wellington that if the French had the *slightest defeat ce serait fini avec la Dynastie!* A pretty speech for an Ambassador, but a *very true one!*

Pray say everything most kind to your dear children and believe me ever, your devoted Niece,

Victoria R.

We are just arrived here, and go back to Windsor to-morrow *afternoon.*

Queen Victoria to the Earl of Malmesbury.

Buckingham Palace, *3rd February 1859.*

The Queen has this moment received Lord Malmesbury's letter. As she has not yet written (only telegraphed) to announce to the Emperor the birth of our grandson (we being in the habit since we know the Emperor and Empress personally to communicate to one another *reciprocally family events*), the Queen has an opportunity or a pretext for writing to the Emperor, and is therefore prepared to do so *tomorrow*. But as the terms to be used are of the most *vital* importance, she would wish Lord Malmesbury to consult forthwith with Lord Derby, and to let her have "the matter" to be put into the letter *before* the Queen *leaves town*, which we do at half-past four this afternoon.

The Earl of Derby to Queen Victoria.

LETTER TO THE EMPEROR NAPOLEON

St James's Square, *3rd February 1859.*

(*Thursday*,1 p.m.)

Lord Derby, with his humble duty, and in obedience to your Majesty's commands, received within this half hour through Lord Malmesbury, submits the accompanying very hastily drawn sketch of the language which, in his humble opinion, your Majesty might hold in a private and confidential letter to the Emperor of the French. Lord Derby is not sure that it is what your Majesty desired that he should submit; but he trusts that your Majesty will be pleased to receive it as an attempt to obey your Majesty's commands, and will excuse its many imperfections on account of the extreme haste in which it has unavoidably been written.

"I cannot refrain from taking this opportunity of expressing confidentially to your Imperial Majesty my deep anxiety for the preservation of the peace of Europe, nor can I conceal from myself how essentially that great object must depend upon the course which your Imperial Majesty may be advised to take. Your Majesty has now the opportunity, either by listening to the dictates of humanity and justice, and by demonstrating unmistakably your intention to adhere strictly to the faithful observance of Treaties, of calming the apprehensions of Europe, and restoring her confidence in your Majesty's pacific policy; or, by permitting yourself to be influenced by the ambitious or interested designs of others, of involving Europe in a war, the extent and termination of which can hardly be foreseen, and which, whatever glory it may add to the arms of France, cannot but interfere materially with her internal prosperity and financial credit. I am sure that your Majesty will not doubt the sincerity of the friendship which alone induces me to write thus unreservedly to your Majesty, and if anything could add to the sorrow with which I should view the renewal of war in Europe, it would be to see your Majesty entering upon a course with which it would be impossible for England to associate herself."[356]

The King of the Belgians to Queen Victoria.

Laeken, *4th February 1859.*

My dearest Victoria,— ... Heaven knows what dance our Emperor *Napoléon Troisième de nom* will lead us. In a few days he will have to make his speech. I fear he is determined on that Italian War. The discussions in Parliament may influence him; I fear party spirit in lieu of a good and right sense of what is the interest of Europe. It was praiseworthy that you said in your Speech that *treaties* must be respected, else indeed we return to the old *Faustrecht* we have been striving to get rid of. It is curious that your speech has made the funds fall again: I presume they hoped at Paris that you would have been able to say that you congratulated Parliament on the prospect of peace being preserved. For us poor people who find ourselves *aux premières loges*, these uncertainties are most unsatisfactory. Your devoted Uncle,

Leopold R.

---

[356] The Queen accordingly wrote a letter, which is printed in the *Life of the Prince Consort*, assuring the Emperor that rarely had any man had such an opportunity as was now his for exercising a personal influence for the peace of Europe, and that, by faithful observance of Treaty obligations, he might calm international anxieties.

Queen Victoria to the Earl of Derby.

THE INDIAN ARMY

Windsor Castle. *5th February 1859.*

With regard to a decision which will have to be taken when the report of the Indian Army Commission shall have been received, the Queen thinks it incumbent upon her not to leave Lord Derby in ignorance of her firm determination not to sanction, under any form, the creation of a British Army, distinct from that known at present as the Army of the Crown.

She would consider it dangerous to the maintenance of India, to the dependence of the Indian Empire on the mother country, and to her Throne in these realms.

Such an Army would be freed from the proper control of the constitutional monarchy. It would be removed from the direct command of the Crown, and entirely independent of Parliament. It would throw an unconstitutional amount of power and patronage into the hands of the Indian Council and Government; it would be raised and maintained in antagonism to the Regular Army of the Crown; and professional jealousy, and personal and private interests, would needs drive it into a position of permanent hostility towards that Army.

This hostility has been already strongly marked in the proceedings of the Commission itself.

Its detrimental effects would not be confined to India alone, but would form a most dangerous obstacle to the maintenance of the government of the Regular Army by the Queen. Already, during the Crimean War, most of the blows levelled at the Army and the prerogative of the Crown were directed by Indian officers, of whom, in future, a vast number would be at home, without employment or recognised position, in compact organisation, and moved by a unity of feeling.

There may be points of detail, admitting differences of opinion as to the relative advantages of a purely local or general Military Force for India; but these are mere trifles, which sink into insignificance in the Queen's estimation, when she has to consider the duty which she owes to her Crown and her Country.

THE QUEEN AND LORD STANLEY

The Queen hopes Lord Derby will not consider that she intends, by this letter, unduly to influence his free consideration and decision as to the advice he may think it his duty to offer, but merely to guard against his being taken by surprise, and to prevent, if possible, an unseemly public difference between herself and Lord Stanley. She is impelled to the apprehension that such may arise from the manner in which, since the first transfer of the Indian Government to the Crown, every act of Lord Stanley has uniformly tended to place the Queen in a position which would render her helpless and powerless in resisting a scheme which certain persons, imbued with the old Indian traditions, would appear to wish to force upon the Crown.

The Queen does not expect an answer to this letter from Lord Derby, and asks him to treat it as strictly confidential.

The Queen sees that Lord Stanley means to make a statement on Monday on the Indian Finances. She trusts that there will be nothing said in that statement to prejudge the Army Question.

Decipher from Lord Cowley.

Paris, *6th February 1859.*

(1 a.m. *Received* 4 a.m.)

A great change for the better. The Queen's letter has produced an excellent effect, as also the Debates in Parliament.[357] The Emperor has expressed himself ready to subscribe to every word of Lord Derby's speech.

The Earl of Derby to Queen Victoria.

THE INDIAN ARMY

St James's Square, *6th February 1859.*

Lord Derby, with his humble duty, submits to your Majesty his respectful acknowledgment of the explicitness with which the letter he had the honour of receiving last night conveys to him the intimation of your Majesty's views upon the important subject of the Indian Army. He cannot, however, disguise from your Majesty the deep pain which that communication has occasioned him; first, that your Majesty should think that Lord Stanley has so far mistaken his duty as system-

[357] Parliament was opened by the Queen in person on the 3rd; the ensuing debates, and especially the speeches of the Liberal leaders, showed that, however much the English nation, as a whole, might sympathise with Italian aspirations for the expulsion of the Austrians from Lombardy, they would regard unfavourably a war commenced in defiance of Treaty obligations.

atically to place your Majesty in a false position; and next because unless Lord Derby misconceives the purport of your Majesty's letter, he fears that it may leave him no alternative but that of humbly entreating to be relieved from a responsibility which nothing should have induced him to undertake but a sense of duty to your Majesty, and the conviction that he might rely with confidence upon your Majesty's continued support. It would ill become Lord Derby to attempt to argue a question on which your Majesty has expressed so strong a determination; he has studiously avoided taking any step which might prejudge a question so important as the organisation of your Majesty's Forces in India. He has awaited the report of the Commission appointed to enquire into the subject, and though aware of the wide difference of opinion which prevailed, has desired impartially to weigh and examine the arguments adduced on both sides, and he has in the meantime refused to give his sanction to a proposition, earnestly pressed upon the Government by Lord Canning, for immediately raising additional regiments for Indian Service. But the announcement of your Majesty's determination (if he rightly understands it), under no circumstances to continue an European Army in India, under terms of service different from those of the Line, paid out of Indian Revenues, and officered by men educated for that especial service, and looking to India for their whole career, places Lord Derby in a position of no little embarrassment; for notwithstanding the gracious intimation that your Majesty does not desire unduly to influence his judgment as to the advice which he may tender, it amounts to a distinct warning that if tendered in a particular direction it has no chance of being accepted by your Majesty. Nor, with that knowledge on his part not shared by his colleagues, can he freely discuss with them the course which they may consider it their duty to pursue.

Lord Derby humbly trusts, therefore, that your Majesty will be graciously pleased, so far as the members of the Government are concerned, to absolve him from the obligation of secrecy, and to allow him to place before them a state of things which may lead to the most serious results, so far as their power of serving your Majesty is concerned.

Lord Derby will give Lord Stanley a caution not to say anything in his statement of Indian Finance which may prejudge the question of a single or separate armies; but he hardly thinks the caution necessary, as European troops, whether in one Service or in two, will equally be chargeable to the revenues of India, which will only be affected by the proportion which the whole of the European may bear to the whole of the native forces.

Lord Derby hopes that he may be permitted to offer his humble congratulations to your Majesty on the very favourable reports received from Paris by telegraph, and upon the highly satisfactory effects produced by your Majesty's private letter to the Emperor.

The above is humbly submitted by your Majesty's most dutiful Servant and Subject,

Derby.

Queen Victoria to the Earl of Derby.

INDIVISIBILITY OF ARMY

Windsor Castle, *7th February 1859.*

The Queen is very sorry to learn from Lord Derby's letter, received last evening, that her communication to him on the Indian Army question had caused him deep pain. She had long hesitated whether she should write it, from a fear that its purport and motive might possibly be misunderstood; but feeling that there ought to exist nothing but the most unreserved and entire confidence between herself and her Prime Minister, she thought it incumbent upon her to let Lord Derby see exactly what was passing in her mind.

If, notwithstanding the Queen's expressed hope that Lord Derby might not consider the communication as intended unduly to influence his free consideration of the important subject, he should feel that its possession, without being at liberty to communicate it to his colleagues, does so in effect, she would ask him to return it to her, and to consider it as not having been written. If he should think, however, that a communication of the Queen's views to the Cabinet is due to them, she is quite prepared to make one. In that case it would naturally have to be differently worded, would omit every reference to Lord Stanley, and might go more into detail.

The Queen cannot close this letter without correcting some misapprehensions into which Lord Derby seems to have fallen. It was not the Queen's intention to impute any motives of systematic action to Lord Stanley; she referred simply to facts and steps, known as well to Lord Derby as to herself, which "uniformly tended" to place her in a powerless position with regard to the Army question.

The Queen protested against "the *creation* of a British Army distinct (in its existence and constitutional position) from that of the Crown," and not against the "*continuance* of an European Army, under terms of service different from the Line, paid out of Indian Revenues, and officered by men educated for that special service, and looking to India for their whole career." In fact, she does not understand what meaning Lord Derby attaches to the words "terms of service." Every force kept in India, however constituted, would be paid out of Indian Revenues. *This* would therefore not form the distinction, and Lord Derby cannot intend to convey that on these revenues one set of Englishmen can have a greater claim than another; nor does she see why English officers, commanding English soldiers and charged with the maintenance of *their* discipline and efficiency, should for that object require to be specially and differently educated, and be restricted to look to India for their whole career. Officers attached to native troops are in a different position.

H.R.H. The Prince of Wales.

From a drawing by F. Winterhalter, 1859

The Earl of Derby to Queen Victoria.

MISAPPREHENSION REMOVED

St James's Square, *7th February 1859.*

Lord Derby, with his humble duty, submits to your Majesty his grateful acknowledgments for your Majesty's most gracious note received this evening, the contents, and still more the tenor of which have relieved him from the painful apprehension that he might be called upon to choose between a strong sense of public duty, and, on the other side, his deep devotion to your Majesty's service, and his gratitude for the favourable consideration which his imperfect attempts to discharge his public duty had always received at your Majesty's hand. The explanation, with which he has now been honoured, of your Majesty's views has entirely dispelled those apprehensions, and he feels that he has only to thank your Majesty for the gracious explanation, with which he has been honoured, of your Majesty's motives in addressing to him the letter which certainly caused him "deep pain."...[358]

Queen Victoria to the Earl of Derby.

Windsor Castle, *8th February 1859.*

The Queen has received Lord Derby's letter of yesterday, and is pleased to find that he now appreciates the motives which dictated her first letter. It needs no assurance on her side that she never doubted those which actuate Lord Derby. The Queen will, in compliance with his request, defer any further notice of the subject until the Commissioners shall have made their report; it would not be fair, however, to Lord Derby, not to add that she fears from his explanation that he has not now correctly estimated the nature of the Queen's objection, which is not to a variety of forces, terms of service, local or general employment, etc., etc., etc., established in one Army, but to the principle of *two* British Armies.

---

[358] Lord Derby then proceeded to deal at some length with the status of the troops in India, concluding with the opinion that the local forces in India should never exceed those sent from home as part of the Regular Army, subject to the ordinary routine of service.

Queen Victoria to General Peel.[359]

13th February 1859.

The Queen relies with confidence that when the question of the Indian Army comes before the Cabinet, General Peel will stoutly defend the interests of the Crown and the British Army. On the opinion which he will give and maintain much of their decision must depend, and unless he speaks out boldly the Indian Secretary will have it all his own way.

Queen Victoria to the King of the Belgians.

THE EMPEROR'S SPEECH

Buckingham Palace, *15th February 1859.*

My dearest Uncle,—We came here to *settle* yesterday—and also here Spring seems *wonderfully forward!* It can't last—and frost is *sure* to *follow* and cut off everything. At Windsor and Frogmore everything is budding—willow I see is green—rose-leaves *out*, and birds singing like in May!

Accept my warmest thanks for your kind letter of the 11th. I *still* hope that matters *will cool* down—the Emperor *personally* expressed regret to Hübner for his words, disclaiming the construction put upon them, and saying that *no one could dispute* the right of Austria to her Italian possessions.[360] He has not written to me lately, but I wrote him ten days ago a long friendly letter, speaking out *plainly* our fears for the future, and urging him to aid us in averting the calamity of *War*....

Our Parliament is as quiet as possible as *yet*, but it will soon have more cause for *action* and excitement....

Bertie's interview with the Pope went off extremely well. He was extremely kind and gracious, and Colonel Bruce was present; it would never have done to have let Bertie go alone, as they might hereafter have pretended, God knows! what Bertie had said.... With Albert's love, ever your devoted Niece,

Victoria R.

---

[359] General Jonathan Peel, brother of Sir Robert Peel (the Premier), and Secretary of State for War.

[360] See *ante*, p. 310, note 2.

The Earl of Derby to Queen Victoria.

THE EMPEROR OF AUSTRIA

Downing Street, *21st February 1859.*

Lord Derby, with his humble duty, and in obedience to the commands which he had the honour of receiving from your Majesty last night, submits the following suggestions, as embodying the substance of what, in his humble judgment your Majesty might address with advantage in a private letter to the Emperor of Austria.

Your Majesty might say, that deeply penetrated with the conviction of the duty imposed upon your Majesty of acting on the principles enunciated in the speech from the Throne, of exercising whatever influence your Majesty could employ for the preservation of the general peace, your Majesty had looked with anxiety to the circumstances which threatened its continued existence. That your Majesty was unable to see in those circumstances, any which were beyond the reach of diplomatic skill, if there were only a mutual desire, on the part of the Chief Powers concerned, to give fair play to its exercise. That the only source of substantial danger was the present state of Italy; and that even in that there would be little danger of interruption to the general tranquillity, were it not for the antagonism excited by interests and engagements, real or supposed, of France and Austria.

That your Majesty believed that the supposed divergence of these interests and engagements might be capable of reconciliation if entered into with mutual frankness, and with a mutual disposition to avoid the calamities of war; but that, as it appeared to your Majesty, neither party would be willing to invite the other to a friendly discussion of the points of difference between them.

That in this state of affairs your Majesty, as a mutual friend of both Sovereigns, and having no individual interests to serve, entertained the hope that by the spontaneous offer of good offices, your Majesty might be the means of establishing certain bases, on which the Powers mainly interested might subsequently enter into amicable negotiations with regard to the questions chiefly in dispute, or threatening serious results.

Of these, the most pressing are those which relate to the Italian Peninsula.

That your Majesty, anxiously revolving in your mind the question how your Majesty's influence could best be brought to bear, had come to the conclusion that your Majesty's Ambassador at Paris, having the fullest knowledge of the views entertained by that Court, and possessing your Majesty's entire confidence, might usefully be intrusted with a highly confidential, but wholly unofficial mission, for the purpose of ascertaining whether there were any possibility consistently with the views of the two Courts of offering such suggestions as might be mutually acceptable as the basis of future arrangements; and, if such should happily be found to be the case, of offering them simultaneously to the two parties, as the suggestions of a mutual friend.

That your Majesty trusted His R.I.A.[361] Majesty would look upon this communication in the truly friendly light in which it was intended, and that Lord Cowley, in his unofficial and confidential character, might be permitted fully to develop the views which your Majesty entertained, and to meet with the most favourable consideration of his suggestions from His R.I.A. Majesty.

Lord Derby, before submitting the above to your Majesty, has thought it right to communicate it to Lord Malmesbury and Lord Cowley, and he is enabled to say that it meets with their entire concurrence.[362] He will be highly gratified if he is permitted to know that it is honoured by your Majesty's gracious approval. All which is humbly submitted by your Majesty's most dutiful Servant and Subject,

Derby.

Mr Disraeli to Queen Victoria.

CHURCH RATES

House of Commons, *21st February 1859.*

(*Monday.*)

The Chancellor of the Exchequer, with his humble duty to your Majesty, informs your Majesty that the Government measure on Church Rates was introduced to-night, in a very full House, and was received with so much favour that the Chancellor of the Exchequer has every belief that it will pass. This is very unexpected, and the satisfactory settlement of this long agitated and agitating question will be a

---

[361] Royal and Imperial Apostolic.

[362] The Queen acted on this advice, and wrote a letter on the 22nd to the Emperor of Austria, on the lines of Lord Derby's suggestions. The material parts of it are printed in the *Life of the Prince Consort*, vol. iv. chap. 92.

great relief to public life, and tend to restore and augment the good-humour of the country.[363]

It is generally rumoured that, on Friday next, Lord Palmerston is to move a vote of censure upon your Majesty's Government with respect to their Foreign Policy. The Chancellor of the Exchequer scarcely credits this, and would rather suppose that the formal censure will take the shape of a rattling critique, preceding some Motion for papers.

Queen Victoria to the King of the Belgians.

LORD COWLEY'S MISSION

Buckingham Palace, *1st March 1859.*

My Dearest Uncle,—Many thanks for your kind letter of the 25th. Matters remain much in the same state. Lord Cowley arrived on Sunday at Vienna, but we know nothing positive yet. I much fear the obstinacy of Austria.

It will indeed be a blessing if *we* could do something not only to avert the war for the present, but to prevent the *causes* of it, for the future. Nothing but improvement in the Italian Governments *can* bring about a *better state* of things. What is *really* the matter with the King of Naples[364]?

We found the poor Queen really very tolerably well at Claremont on Saturday. She is decidedly better than when we saw her at the end of November. Poor Joinville is suffering from an accident to his bad knee.

Here our Reform Bill has been brought in yesterday.[365] It is moderate, and ... [Lord John] has therefore allied himself with Mr Bright and Mr Roebuck against it! He has *no* other followers. The Debate on

---

[363] Since the Braintree case in 1853, no rate could legally be levied except by the majority of the rate-payers. The present Bill was designed to exempt Dissenters from payment, excluding them at the same time from voting on the subject in the vestry meeting. Sir John Trelawney, the leader of the Abolitionist party in the House, however, procured the rejection of the proposed measure, and a solution was not arrived at till 1868.

[364] Ferdinand II., known as Bomba, died on the 22nd of May in the same year.

[365] See Introductory Note, *ante*, p. 307.

Foreign Affairs on Friday was extremely moderate, and can only have done good.[366]

It is rumoured that you are going to Berlin to the Christening, but I doubt it! Oh! dearest Uncle, it *almost breaks* my heart *not* to witness our *first grandchild* christened! I don't think I *ever* felt so bitterly disappointed *about anything* as about this! And then it is an *occasion* so gratifying to both *Nations*, which brings them *so much* together, that it is *most* peculiarly mortifying! It is a *stupid law* in Prussia, I must say, to be so particular about having the child christened so soon. However, it is now no use lamenting; please God! we shall be more fortunate another time! With Albert's affectionate love, ever your devoted Niece,

Victoria R.

Affectionate love to your children. When does Philip go to Italy?

The Emperor of Austria to Queen Victoria.

THE EMPEROR'S REPLY

Vienne, *le 8 Mars 1859.*

Madame et Chère Sœur,—J'ai reçu des mains de Lord Cowley la lettre que votre Majesté a bien voulu lui confier et dont le contenu m'a offert un nouvel et précieux témoignage de l'amitié et de la confiance qu'elle m'a vouées, ainsi que des vues élevées qui dirigent sa politique. Lord Cowley a été auprès de moi le digne interprète des sentimens de votre Majesté, et je me plais à lui rendre la justice, qu'il s'est acquitté avec le zèle éclairé, dont il a déjà fourni tant de preuves, de la mission confidentielle dont il était chargé.

J'ai hautement apprécié les motifs qui vous ont inspiré la pensée de m'envoyer un organe de confiance pour échanger nos idées sur les dangers de la situation. Je m'associe à tous les désirs, que forme votre Majesté pour le maintien de la paix, et ce n'est pas sur moi que pèsera la responsabilité de ceux, qui évoquent des dangers de guerre sans pouvoir articuler une seule cause de guerre.

Lord Cowley connaît les points de vue auxquels j'envisage les questions qui forment l'objet ou le prétexte des divergences d'opinion

---

[366] In this debate Lord Palmerston urged the Ministry to mediate between Austria and France, in order to obtain their simultaneous withdrawal from Rome, and Mr Disraeli announced the confidential mission of Lord Cowley as "one of peace and conciliation."

qui subsistent entre nous et la France; il sait aussi que nous sommes disposés à contribuer à leur solution dans l'esprit le plus conciliant, en tant qu'on n'exige pas de nous des sacrifices que ne saurait porter aucune Puissance qui se respecte. Je forme des vœux pour que votre Majesté puisse tirer parti des élémens que Lui apportera son Ambassadeur, dans l'intérêt du maintien de la paix que nous avons également à cœur.

Mais quelles que soient les chances et les épreuves que l'avenir nous réserve, j'aime à me livrer à l'espoir que rien ne portera atteinte aux rapports d'amitié et d'union que je suis heureux de cultiver avec votre Majesté, et que Ses sympathies seront acquises à la cause que je soutiens et qui est celle de tous les États indépendans.

C'est dans ces sentimens que je renouvelle à votre Majesté l'assurance de l'amitié sincère et de l'inaltérable attachement avec lesquels je suis, Madame et chère Sœur, de votre Majesté, le bon et dévoué frère et ami,

François Joseph.

Queen Victoria to the Earl of Malmesbury.

A PROPOSED CONFERENCE

20th March 1859.

The Queen has received Lord Malmesbury's letter[367] written before the Cabinet yesterday. The Memorandum of Lord Cowley and the telegrams from Vienna give better hopes of the idea of Congress or Conference leading to a good result. Everything will now depend upon the Emperor Napoleon's acceptance of the conditions on which Austria is willing to agree to a Conference. The Queen would like to have a copy of Lord Cowley's memorandum.[368]

---

[367] Lord Cowley had returned from his mission to Vienna, and was now again at Paris. The complexion of affairs had been changed by a suggestion on the part of Russia (which may or may not have been ultimately prompted from Paris) for a Conference between England, France, Austria, Prussia and Russia, to settle the Italian Question. Cavour pressed for the admission of Piedmont to the Conference.

[368] Lord Malmesbury's letter to Lord Cowley, written immediately after the Cabinet, enjoined him to impress upon the Emperor that England would only address herself to the four points—evacuation of the Roman States by foreign troops, reform, security for Sardinia, and a substitute for the treaties of 1847 between Austria and the Duchies.

Queen Victoria to the Earl of Malmesbury.

Osborne, *22nd March 1859.*

The Queen thanks Lord Malmesbury for his communication of yesterday, which she received this morning. She quite approves the steps taken by the Government,[369] and concurs in Lord Malmesbury's views. If the understanding about a Conference first of the five Powers, and then of the Italian States with them, *could be* so far come to that France and Austria agree with us upon the conditions on which it is to take place, we need not wait for Russia's proposing it. She is evidently playing, as she always does, a double game, and from Sir John Crampton's[370] letter it appears that she never meant to propose a Congress, but merely to *accept* one, for ulterior objects.

Queen Victoria to the Earl of Malmesbury.

Osborne, *27th March 1859.*

The Queen trusts that Lord Malmesbury will act with the utmost circumspection in answering the many telegrams crossing each other from all directions respecting the proposed Congress. An understanding with Austria on every point ought, if possible, to precede our giving our opinion to France or Russia. If they can *once* get the Powers to agree upon a point upon which Austria disagrees, they have won the game, and the Emperor can proceed to his war, having a declaration of Europe against Austria as his basis.

Queen Victoria to the Earl of Malmesbury.

Buckingham Palace, *12th April 1859.*

The Queen has marked a passage in this draft, which she thinks it would be advisable to modify—so as not to *put* upon *record* (should the Austrians refuse to give way on this point) that we consider their

---

[369] An attempt to obtain the disarmament of Austria and Sardinia, and a proposal to obtain the co-operation of France, in guaranteeing to defend Sardinia against invasion by Austria for five years, unless Sardinia left her own territory. On the 23rd, Lord Malmesbury wrote that all the great Powers, except Austria, had agreed to a Congress upon the conditions laid down by the British Government.

[370] English Ambassador at St Petersburg, formerly Minister at Washington; see *ante*, p. 219. He had succeeded to the baronetcy in 1858.

conduct as "*reckless*." Should they persist, they would certainly not meet with as much sympathy as they would do if they yielded, and such a course on their part would be very much to be regretted, as we consider every sacrifice small, in comparison to the blessings of preserving peace; but still Austria would have a perfect right to stand out—and we originally supported her in this demand.

If something which *expressed* the *above* sentiments and opinions could therefore be substituted for the present passage, the Queen thinks it would be very desirable *for the future*, both as regards Austria and England.

The Earl of Derby to Queen Victoria.

ENGLAND AND AUSTRIA

Downing Street, *21st April 1859.*

Lord Derby, with his humble duty, submits to your Majesty that it has appeared to him, in consultation with his colleagues, with the exception of Lord Hardwicke and Sir John Pakington, who are out of Town, that the only step which can properly be taken at present is to protest strongly against the course which Austria is now taking, and to warn her that whatever may be the results to herself, she deprives herself of all claim to the support or countenance of England.[371] Your Majesty will see by another telegram, received a few minutes ago from Lord Cowley, that Hübner!! advises that England should threaten to come to the aid of Sardinia, if the contemplated invasion should take place! Your Majesty's servants are not, however, prepared to take so strong a step, which would commit them to measures to which they might be unable at the moment to give due effect; and which, if Austria were to disregard the measure, would involve them in War as the Allies of France. They have therefore limited themselves to a protest, the terms of which will require to be very carefully considered before it is embodied in a despatch. Lord Malmesbury will submit to your Majesty by this messenger the terms of his telegram.... To appeal at once to arms, when no question, except this of form, remained unsettled as to the meeting of Congress, and the subjects to be then discussed, had been unanimously agreed to, appears to Lord Derby to

[371] On the 19th, Count Buol despatched an emissary, Baron Kellersberg, to Turin, with a summons to Sardinia to disarm, under the threat of immediate hostilities if she declined. Sardinia indignantly refused, whereupon the Austrian troops crossed the Ticino.

indicate a reckless determination to go to war which it will be very difficult to justify in the eyes of Europe.

For the moment these events rather diminish than increase the probability of a rupture with France, while they will task her means to the uttermost, and not improbably overthrow her personal dynasty!

Queen Victoria to the King of the Belgians.

WAR IMMINENT

Windsor Castle, *26th April 1859.*

My Dearest Uncle,—I hardly know *what* to say, so confused and bewildered are we by the reports which come in three or four times a day! I have *no hope* of peace *left*. Though it is *originally* the wicked folly of Russia and France that have brought about this fearful crisis, it is the madness and blindness of Austria which have brought on the war *now!*[372] It has put *them* in the wrong, and entirely changed the feeling here, which was all that one could desire, into the most *vehement* sympathy for *Sardinia*, though we hope now again to be able to *throw* the blame of the war on France, who *now* won't hear of mediation, while Austria is again inclined to do so!

It is a melancholy, sad Easter; but what grieves me the most (indeed, distracts me)—for I have had nothing but disappointments in that quarter since November—is that in all probability Vicky will be unable to come in May! It quite *distracts me*. You also must be very anxious about dear Charlotte; I hope she will not remain at Trieste, but go to Vienna. Her being in Italy is really *not* safe.... Now with kind loves to your children, ever your affectionate and devoted Niece,

Victoria R.

The Earl of Derby to Queen Victoria.

Roehampton, *27th April 1859.*

... Lord Derby has thought it necessary, in consequence of the attitude assumed by Russia, notwithstanding her assurances that there is nothing hostile to England in her secret treaty with France, to call upon

---

[372] Referring to an understanding reported to have been arrived at between France and Russia, the suspicion of which created great indignation in England. Prince Gortschakoff and the French Emperor, in answer to enquiries, gave conflicting explanations.

Sir J. Pakington to say what addition could be made to the Channel Fleet within a period of two or three months, without weakening that in the Mediterranean. He has the honour of enclosing the answer, which he has just received by messenger. Lord Derby proposes to go up to Town to confer with Sir J. Pakington on this important subject to-morrow, and Lord Malmesbury has summoned a Cabinet for Friday to consider the general state of affairs.

France having absolutely refused the proffered mediation of England, and Austria having only accepted it under the condition of the disarmament of Sardinia, every effort to preserve the peace has been exhausted; and it only remains for this country to watch the course of events, to protect her own interests, and to look out for any opportunity which may offer to mediate between the contending parties. This policy, announced by Lord Derby in the City on Monday,[373] was received with unanimous approval. It will require a great deal to induce the country to be drawn into a war under any circumstances, and Lord Derby's anxious efforts will not be wanting to avoid it as long as possible.

Queen Victoria to the Earl of Derby.

LORD DERBY'S POLICY

Windsor Castle, *29th April 1859.*

The Queen has read the last telegrams with much pain, as they show that there is no chance left of stopping war. Indeed she thinks, considering the progress of revolution in the Duchies, and the daily increase of military strength of France and financial exhaustion of Austria, that it would not be morally defensible to try to restrain Austria from defending herself while she still can.

Count Buol's proposal to continue negotiations during the fight sounds strange, but ought not to be altogether put aside. The King of

[373] He had there described Austria's action as hasty, precipitate, and (because involving warfare) criminal, but the Government would still (he added) strive to avert war, by urging Austria, under the Treaty of Paris, to invoke the mediation of the Powers. The Derby Government, however, were supposed to be giving encouragement to Austria. See Lord Derby's letter of the 2nd of June, *post*, p. 336.

Sardinia's assumption of the Government of Tuscany[374] and military occupation of Massa-Carrara form gross infractions of the Treaties of 1815 and international law, and can hardly be left without a protest from us.

Has Lord Derby heard that a Russian Fleet is expected soon to appear in the Black Sea? The Queen has just heard it from Berlin, where it is supposed to be certain, and it would explain Lord Cowley's report of (the Queen believes) Prince Napoleon's[375] account of the Russian engagements, which are admitted to contemplate a junction of the French and Russian Fleets to defend the Treaty closing the Dardanelles.

The Earl of Derby to Queen Victoria.

FRANCE AND RUSSIA

Roehampton, *1st May 1859.*
(*Sunday night*, 12 P.M.)

... Lord Derby entirely concurs in your Majesty's opinion that no credit is to be attached to the denials of the French or Russian Governments in regard to the engagements subsisting between them.[376] It is very easy to convey denials in terms which are literally true, but practically and in spirit false; and Lord Derby has no doubt but that France is well assured that in any case she may rely upon the tacit assistance, if not the active co-operation, of Russia; and that both Powers are using their utmost endeavours to excite troubles in the East, as well as in Italy, as the result of which France may gratify her cherished designs of ambition in the latter, while Russia carries on her projects of aggrandisement in the former. This is a lamentable state of affairs; but it is Lord Derby's duty to assure your Majesty that no Government which could be formed in this country could hope to carry public opinion with it in taking an active part, as matters now stand, in opposition

---

[374] See Introductory Note, *ante*, p. 308. The Duchy of Modena and the Grand Duchy of Tuscany were in revolution, and the Duchy of Parma soon followed their example.

[375] See *post*, p. 331, note 30.

[376] Lord Cowley, in a letter of the 29th of April to Lord Malmesbury, described an interview with the Emperor of the French, when the latter denied in terms the existence of a signed Treaty between France and Russia. But, as Lord Cowley added, there might be moral engagements which might easily lead to a more specific alliance.

to France and Russia, if in truth they are acting in concert, as Lord Derby believes that they are. All that can be done is to maintain the principle of strict neutrality in regard to the affairs of Italy, and probably of Montenegro also, though there is not sufficient evidence of facts in that case to justify a positive conclusion. But in the meantime everything shows more conclusively the absolute necessity for the increase of your Majesty's Naval Force,[377] which was determined at the Council yesterday, and respecting which it will be necessary, on the very first day of the meeting of the new Parliament, to call for an explicit expression of opinion.

Your Majesty enquires as to a supposed pledge given by the Emperor of the French as to a denial of any Treaty with Sardinia. So far as Lord Derby can recollect at this moment, there never was more than an assurance that so long as Austria remained within her own limits, he would not interfere; and that he would not support Sardinia, unless she were herself invaded in any *unjustifiable* attack on Austria; and there was also a denial in the *Moniteur*, to which your Majesty probably refers, of there having been any engagement entered into *as a condition of the marriage*.[378] These are just the denials to which Lord Derby has already adverted, which appear at first sight satisfactory, but which may be afterwards explained away, so as to escape the charge of absolute falsehood.

Lord Derby trusts that your Majesty will have understood, and excused, his absence from the Council on Saturday, in consequence of the misunderstanding as to the time appointed.

Queen Victoria to the Earl of Malmesbury.

THE POSITION OF FRANCE

Windsor Castle, *3rd May 1859.*

---

[377] The Emperor had interrogated Lord Cowley as to this.

[378] In July 1858, the joint action of France and Sardinia had been concerted at the confidential interview at Plombières, between the Emperor and Cavour, the former undertaking to assist Sardinia, under certain contingencies, against Austria. On the same occasion the marriage was suggested of the Princess Clothilde of Sardinia to the Prince Napoleon Joseph Paul, son of Prince Jerome Napoleon Bonaparte. An interesting account of the events of this time, and of the character and aims of Cavour, will be found in De la Gorce's *Histoire du Second Empire*; see especially vol. ii. book 14.

The Queen has carefully read the enclosed draft. She thinks that, without saying anything offensive to France,[379] this important document would not place matters before that Power in the world in accordance with the facts, and would lead to erroneous inferences if it left out altogether, as it does, any reference to the responsibility which France has had in bringing about the present state of affairs.... Austria and Sardinia are spoken of as the offenders, and blamed, not without sufficient ground, for the parts which they have respectively acted, and France is treated as if standing on a line with us in fostering civilisation, liberty, and peace. The inference would be that *we* forsake her in her noble course, and deserve again the name of "*perfide Albion.*"

The Queen would ask Lord Malmesbury to consider this. For the sake of showing how she thinks the omissions dangerous to our position might be supplied, she has added some pencil remarks.

Queen Victoria to the King of the Belgians.

THE GENERAL ELECTION

Windsor Castle, *3rd May 1859.*

Dearest Uncle,—Many thanks for you dear, kind letter of the 30th. God knows we *are* in a sad mess. The rashness of the Austrians is indeed a *great* misfortune, for it has placed them in the wrong. Still there is *one* universal feeling of *anger* at the conduct of France, and of *great suspicion.* The Treaty with Russia is *denied*, but I am perfectly certain that there *are engagements....*

Here the Elections are not as satisfactory as could be wished, but the Government still think they will have a clear gain of 25 to 30 seats, which will make a difference of 50 or 60 votes on a Division. It gives unfortunately no majority; still, it must be remembered that the Opposition are very much divided, and not at all a compact body, which the supporters of the Government are.[380]

---

[379] *I.e.*, if the despatch were to abstain from reprobating the French policy.

[380] After their defeat on the 1st of April on the proposed Reform Bill, the Ministry had dissolved Parliament, and had gained in the elections twenty-five seats—not enough to counterbalance the Palmerstonian triumph of 1857. If, therefore, the various sections of the Liberal Party could unite, the displacement of the Derby Government was inevitable. Such a combination was, in fact, arranged at a meeting at Willis's Rooms organised by Lord Palmerston, Lord John Russell, Mr Bright and Mr Sidney Herbert.

Lord John has been holding moderate and prudent language on Foreign Affairs, whereas Lord Palmerston has made bad and mischievous speeches, but *not* at all in accordance with the feelings of the country. The country wishes for strict neutrality, but strong defences, and we are making our Navy as strong as we can.

You ask me if Louis Oporto[381] is grown? He is, and his figure much improved. He is a good, kind, amiable boy whom one must like. He has sailed this morning with the Bridegroom, and on the 16th or 17th we may expect them back with the dear young Bride.

I venture to send you a letter I received some days ago from dear Vicky, and the religious tone of which I think will please you. May I beg you to return it me, as her letters are very valuable to me?...

We are well fagged and worked and worried; we return to Town to-morrow afternoon.

With kindest love to your children, ever your devoted Niece,

Victoria R.

Queen Victoria to the King of the Belgians.

Buckingham Palace, *9th May 1859.*

My Dearest Uncle,—I write to-day instead of to-morrow to profit by the return of your messenger. Many, many thanks for your dear letter of the 6th. What *are* the Austrians about? They would *not* wait when they ought to have done so, and *now* that they should have long ago made a rush and an attack with their overwhelming force, they do *nothing!* nothing since the 30th! leaving the French to become stronger and more *fit* for the struggle every day!! It is indeed distracting, and most difficult to understand them or do anything for them. The Emperor leaves Paris for Genoa to-morrow. It is *not* true that the Empress was so warlike; Lord Cowley says, on the contrary, she is very unhappy about it, and that the Emperor himself is low and altered. Old Vaillant goes with him as General-Major.... Ever your devoted Niece,

Victoria R.

---

[381] Brother and successor of King Pedro V. of Portugal, and father of King Carlos. The King had married in May 1858 the Duchess Stéphanie (born 1837), daughter of Prince Antoine of Hohenzollern.

The Earl of Malmesbury to Queen Victoria.

POLICY OF THE EMPEROR NAPOLEON

15th May 1859.

The Earl of Malmesbury presents his humble duty to the Queen, and has the honour to inform your Majesty that Count de Persigny[382] called on him yesterday. He passed an hour in attempting to prove what it seems he really believes himself—that the Emperor had no plan or even intention to make war in Italy; that His Imperial Majesty was drawn into it step by step by M. de Cavour, who finally menaced to publish his most confidential correspondence, etc.; that his army was totally unprepared, and is now in a very imperfect state, and that he himself was overcome with surprise and fear when he learnt in the middle of last month that the Austrians had 120,000 men on the Ticino.[383] The Emperor, however, now believes that he will easily gain a *couple* of victories, and that when he has *rejeté les Autrichiens dans leur tanière* (by which he means their great fortresses), he will return to govern at Paris, and leave a Marshal to carry on the sieges and the war. M. de Persigny's letters of appointment are not yet signed, and must go to Italy to be so. He stated that a week ago he was named Minister of Foreign Affairs, and that Fould,[384] Walewski, and others were to be dismissed, but that two days before the Emperor's departure Madame Walewska[385] and the Empress had on their knees obtained a reprieve, and that M. de Persigny was ordered to come here *sans raisonner...*

---

[382] Who had been re-appointed to London, where Marshal Pélissier, Duc de Malakhoff, had replaced him in 1858. See *ante*, p. 276. Both Malakhoff and Walewski were out of sympathy with the Emperor's present policy.

[383] Sir James Hudson, in a letter written at Turin on the 28th of February, and shown to Queen Victoria, described an interview with Cavour, who, in answer to the direct question, "Do you mean to attack Austria?" replied that the Italian question was becoming so complex that it was impossible to say what might happen. Sir J. Hudson added that he had learned confidentially that the understanding on the same subject between Cavour and the Emperor Napoleon was complete, and that it had been expressed thus: "Non seulement nous prendrons la première occasion de faire la guerre à l'Autriche, mais nous chercherons un prétexte."

[384] Achille Fould, a Jewish banker, was a colleague of Walewski, though not a loyal one, in the French Government.

[385] Madame Walewska was a Florentine by birth, descended on her mother's side from the princely family of Poniatowski.

Queen Victoria to the Earl of Malmesbury.

ATTITUDE OF RUSSIA

Buckingham Palace, *20th May 1859.*

The Queen was much surprised to receive the enclosed telegram. An alliance with Russia to *localise* and *arrest* the war by joint interference, which is here proposed to Russia, is a policy to which the Queen has not given her sanction, and which would require very mature deliberation before it could ever be entertained. The Queen is much afraid of these telegraphic short messages on principles of policy, and would beg Lord Malmesbury to be most cautious as they may lead us into difficulties without the possibility of previous consideration. How can we propose to join Russia, whom we know to be pledged to France? The Queen hopes Lord Malmesbury will stop the communication of this message, to Prince Gortschakoff.[386]

Queen Victoria to the Earl of Derby.

Osborne, *22nd May 1859.*

In answer to Lord Derby's letter of yesterday referring to the importance of concerting with Russia the best modes of preventing the extension of the war, the Queen wishes merely to observe: That Russia has acknowledged her desire to see the Austrians defeated, and her indifference to the maintenance of the Treaties of 1815; France wages war to drive the Austrians out of Italy, wresting from them the Italian provinces secured to them by those treaties; and that the Queen has declared from the Throne her adhesion to these treaties to which Parliament unanimously responded. France and Russia may therefore have an interest, and indeed *must* have one, in not being disturbed in any way in the prosecution of their Italian scheme. England can have no such interest. If France prove successful, the territorial arrangements of Europe, in which England has found safety, and which she helped to establish in order to obtain safety against France after a war of twenty years' duration, will be subverted, and she herself may some

386 A telegram had been received from St Petersburg, saying that Prince Gortschakoff entirely coincided with Lord Malmesbury's views as to localising the war; and Lord Malmesbury had proposed to send a telegraphic reply containing the words: "We are anxious to unite with Russia, not only in localising the war, but in arresting it."

day (perhaps *soon*) have her own safety imperilled. The Saxon provinces of Prussia will be in much greater danger when France shall have destroyed Austria in Italy and ruined her at home, than while the latter remains a powerful member of the German Confederation. What the Queen is naturally anxious to guard against is our being drawn by degrees into playing the game of those who have produced the present disturbance, and whose ulterior views are very naturally and very wisely by them concealed from us. The Queen is glad to hear that the telegram in question was not sent, having been alarmed by its being marked as having been despatched "at noon" on the 20th. The Queen wishes Lord Derby to show this letter to Lord Malmesbury.

Queen Victoria to the King of the Belgians.

ILLNESS OF DUCHESS OF KENT

Osborne, *25th May 1859.*

Dearest Uncle,—Thousand thanks for your dear kind letter and good wishes for my old birthday, and for your other dear letter of the 21st. Albert, who writes to you, will tell you how dreadfully our *great, great* happiness to have dearest Vicky, flourishing and so well and gay with us, was on Monday and a good deal too yesterday, clouded over and spoilt by the *dreadful* anxiety we were in about dearest Mamma. Thank God! to-day I feel another being—for we know she is "in a satisfactory state," and improving in every respect, but I am thoroughly shaken and upset by this *awful* shock; for it came on *so suddenly*—that it came like a thunderbolt upon us, and I think I *never* suffered as I did those four dreadful hours till we heard she was better! I hardly myself *knew how* I loved her, or how *my whole* existence seems bound up with her—till I saw looming in the distance the fearful possibility of *what* I will *not* mention. She was actually packing up to start for here! *How* I missed her yesterday I cannot say, or how gloomy my poor birthday on first getting up appeared I *cannot* say. However, that is passed—and please God we shall see her, with care, restored to her usual health ere long. I trust, dearest Uncle, you are quite well now—and that affairs will not prevent you from coming to see us next month?

Dear Vicky is now a most dear, charming companion—and so *embellie!*

I must end, having so much to write. Ever your devoted Niece,

Victoria R.

I shall write again to-morrow or next day how dear Mamma is.

Queen Victoria to the Earl of Derby.

THE QUEEN'S SPEECH

Buckingham Palace, *1st June 1859.*

The Queen takes objection to the wording of the two paragraphs[387] about the war and our armaments. As it stands, it conveys the impression of a determination on the Queen's part of maintaining a neutrality—*à tout prix*—whatever circumstances may arise, which would do harm abroad, and be inconvenient at home.[388] What the Queen may express is her wish to remain neutral, and her hope that circumstances will allow her to do so. The paragraph about the Navy[389] as it stands makes our position still more humble, as it contains a public apology for arming, and yet betrays fear of our being attacked by France.

The Queen suggests two amended forms for these passages, in which she has taken pains to preserve Lord Derby's words as far as is possible, with an avoidance of the objections before stated.

"Those endeavours have unhappily failed, and war has been declared between France and Sardinia on one side, and Austria on the other. I continue to receive at the same time assurances of friendship from both contending parties. It being my anxious desire to preserve to my people the blessing of uninterrupted peace, I trust in God's assistance to enable me to maintain a strict and impartial neutrality."

"Considering, however, the present state of Europe, and the complications which a war, carried on by some of its great Powers, may produce, I have deemed it necessary, for the security of my dominions and the honour of my Crown, to increase my Naval Forces to an amount exceeding that which has been sanctioned by Parliament."

---

[387] In the Speech to be delivered by the Queen at the opening of Parliament on the 7th of June.

[388] The passage originally ran: "Receiving assurances of friendship from both the contending parties, I intend to maintain a strict and impartial neutrality, and I hope, with God's assistance, to preserve to my people the blessing of continued peace."

[389] The passage originally ran: "I have, however, deemed it necessary, in the present state of Europe, with no object of aggression, but for the security of my dominions, and for the honour of my Crown, to increase my Naval Forces to an amount exceeding that which has been sanctioned by Parliament."

The Earl of Derby to Queen Victoria.

THE QUESTION OF NEUTRALITY

Downing Street, *2nd June 1859.*

Lord Derby, with his humble duty, submits to your Majesty that he has most anxiously, and with every desire to meet your Majesty's wishes, reflected upon the effect of the alterations suggested by your Majesty in the proposed Speech from the Throne. He has considered the consequences involved so serious that he has thought it right to confer upon the subject with the Chancellor of the Exchequer, as Leader of the House of Commons; and it is a duty which he owes to your Majesty not to withhold the expression of their clear and unhesitating conviction. Lord Derby trusts that your Majesty will forgive the frankness with which, in the accompanying observations, he feels it necessary to submit to your Majesty the grounds for the view which they are compelled to take.

The first paragraph to which your Majesty takes exception is that which intimates your Majesty's "intention" to maintain a strict and impartial neutrality, and "hope" to be enabled to preserve peace. Your Majesty apprehends that this may be interpreted into a determination to preserve neutrality *à tout prix*; but Lord Derby would venture to observe that such an inference is negatived by the subsequent words, which only imply a "hope" of preserving peace. With the cessation of that hope, neutrality would necessarily terminate. But as matters stand at present, Lord Derby is warranted in assuring your Majesty that if there is one subject on which more than another the mind of the country is unanimous, it is that of an entire abstinence from participation in the struggle now going on in Italy. He collects this from the language of politicians of almost every class, from all the public papers, from Addresses and Memorials which he receives every day—some urging, and some congratulating him upon the adoption of a perfectly neutral policy. The sympathies of the country are neither with France nor with Austria, but were it not for the intervention of France, they would be general in favour of Italy. The charge now made against your Majesty's servants, by the opposition Press, as the *Morning Post* and *Daily News*, is that their neutrality covers such wishes and designs in favour of Austria; and any word in your Majesty's Speech which should imply a doubt of the continuance of strict impartiality, would, undoubtedly, provoke a hostile Amendment, which might very possibly be carried in the Sardinian sense, and which, if so carried, would place your Majesty in the painful position of having to select an Administration, pledged against the interests of Austria and of Germany. Lord Derby says nothing of the personal results to your Majesty's present servants, because, in such cases, personal considerations ought not to be allowed to prevail; and it is in the interest of the country only, and even of the very cause which your Majesty desires to uphold, that he earnestly trusts that your Majesty will not require any alteration in this part of the Speech. There is, at this moment, in the country, a great jealousy and suspicion of France, and of her ulterior designs—as indicated by the demand of means of defence, the formation of Volunteer Corps, etc.—but it is neutralised, partly by sympathy for Italy, partly by suspicions, industriously circulated, of the pro-Austrian tendencies of the present Government. It is very important that the language of the Speech should be so decided as to negative this impression, and Lord Derby cannot but feel that if neutrality be spoken of not as a thing decided upon, but which, it is hoped, may be maintained, such language will be taken to intimate the expectation of the Government that it may, at no distant time, be departed from. In Lord Derby's humble opinion Peace should be spoken of as subject to doubt, because, out of the present struggle, complications may arise which may necessarily involve us in war; but neutrality, as between the present belligerents, should be a matter open to no doubt or question. If there be no attempt made to run counter to public opinion, and Austria should sustain serious reverses, the jealousy of France will increase, and the feeling of the country will support your Majesty in a war, should such arise, against her aggression; but if the slightest pretext be afforded for doubting the *bonâ fide* character of British neutrality, or the firm determination to maintain it, an anti-German feeling will be excited, which will be fatal to the Administration, and seriously embarrassing to your Majesty.

THE NAVY

The same observations apply, with hardly less force, to part of the Amendment suggested by your Majesty to the paragraph regarding the Navy. With submission to your Majesty, Lord Derby can hardly look upon it as humiliating to a great country, in announcing a large increase of its Naval Force, to disclaim any object of aggression. These words, however, might, if your Majesty were so pleased, be omitted, though Lord Derby cannot go so far as to say that in his humble judgment the omission would be an improvement; but he trusts that your Majesty will be satisfied with a general reference to the "state of

Europe" without speaking of the "complications which a war carried on by some of the GreatLORD DERBY'S CRITICISMS Powers may produce." These words would infallibly lead to a demand for explanation, and for a statement of the nature of the "complications" which the Government foresaw as likely to lead to war. In humbly tendering to your Majesty his most earnest advice that your Majesty will not insist on the proposed Amendments in his Draft Speech, he believes that he may assure your Majesty that he is expressing the unanimous opinion of his Colleagues. Of their sentiments your Majesty may judge by the fact that in the original draft he had spoken of your Majesty's "intention" to preserve peace "as long as it might be possible"; but by universal concurrence these latter words were struck out, and the "hope" was, instead of them, substituted for the "intention." Should your Majesty, however, be pleased so to order, Lord Derby will immediately submit the question to the consideration of his Colleagues, in order that your Majesty may be put, in the most authentic form, in possession of their views. He assures your Majesty that nothing can be more repugnant to his feelings than to appear to offer objections to any suggestions emanating from your Majesty; and he has only been induced to do so upon the present occasion by the deep conviction which he entertains of the danger attending the course proposed, and the serious embarrassments which it would cause your Majesty. He regrets more especially having been compelled to take this step at a moment when your Majesty's thoughts are very differently engaged, and when it may be doubly irksome to have matters of public business pressed upon your Majesty's consideration.

The above is humbly submitted by your Majesty's most dutiful Servant and Subject,

Derby.

Queen Victoria to the Earl of Derby.

Buckingham Palace, *3rd June 1859.*

The Queen has received Lord Derby's answer to her observations on the proposed Speech. There is in fact no difference of opinion between her and Lord Derby; the latter only keeps in view the effect which certain words will have in Parliament and upon the country, whilst she looks to the effect they will produce upon the European conflict. If the Queen were not obliged to speak, both positions might be well reconciled; but if what she is going to declare from the Throne is to allay suspicions purposely raised by the Opposition against the Government that they intended to take part at some moment or other in the war, and is to give absolute security to the country against this contingency, this will be the very thing France would wish to bring about in order to ensure to her the fullest liberty in prosecuting her schemes for disturbing and altering the territorial state of Europe. How is this impression to be avoided? Lord Derby thinks that the expression of "hope" to be able to preserve peace to this country is a sufficient indication that this country reserves to herself still a certain liberty of action; but the Queen would have interpreted it rather as the expression of a hope, that we may not be attacked, particularly when followed by the sentence in which all intention of aggression is disclaimed, and that our armaments are merely meant for defence. The sense would then appear as this: "As the belligerents separately assure me of their friendship, I am determined to maintain a strict neutrality between them, and hope they may not change their minds, and attack me; I arm, but merely to defend myself if attacked." This would abdicate on the part of this country her position as one of the arbiters of Europe, declare her indifference to treaties or the balance of power (which are, in fact, of the greatest value to her), and would preclude her from any action to preserve them. The Queen fully enters into the Parliamentary difficulty, and would deprecate nothing more than to expose the Government to a defeat on an Amendment which would lead to the formation of a new Government on the principle of neutrality *à tout prix* imposed by Parliament on the Crown.

It will be for Lord Derby and his colleagues to consider how far they may be able to avoid this danger without exposing themselves to that pointed out by the Queen. She puts herself entirely in his hands, and had suggested the verbal amendments merely with a view to indicate the nature of the difficulty which had struck her. Whatever decision Lord Derby may on further reflection come to, the Queen is prepared to accept.[390]

---

[390] Ultimately the Cabinet recommended the modification of the declaration of neutrality by the insertion of the words "between them"; so as to run: "I intend to maintain *between them* a strict and impartial neutrality," etc.; and in the second paragraph proposed to omit the words "with no object of aggression, but"—and adopting the form of the Queen's paragraph, but omitting the words referring to possible complications, to leave it thus: "Considering, however, the present state of Europe, I have deemed it necessary for the security of my Dominions," etc.

Queen Victoria to the Earl of Malmesbury.

NEGOTIATIONS WITH RUSSIA

Buckingham Palace, *5th June 1859.*

The Queen has read Lord Cowley's letter with regret. Nothing could be more dangerous and unwise than at this moment to enter into negotiations with Russia on the best manner of disposing of the Emperor of Austria's dominions. The Queen cannot understand how Lord Cowley can propose anything so indefensible in a moral point of view.

Mr Disraeli to Queen Victoria.

DEBATE ON THE ADDRESS

House of Commons [? *7th June 1859.*]

(*Tuesday, quarter-past eight o'clock.*)

The Chancellor of the Exchequer with his humble duty to your Majesty.

Lord Hartington[391] spoke like a gentleman; was badly seconded.

Chancellor of Exchequer rose immediately at six o'clock, and is just down. The House very full, and very enthusiastic.

The Chancellor of Exchequer presumes to say he thinks he satisfied his friends.[392]

---

[391] Lord Hartington, afterwards eighth Duke of Devonshire, moved an Amendment to the Address, expressing a want of confidence in the Ministry.

[392] He flung his taunts right and left at the now united Opposition, and was especially bitter against Sir James Graham. Referring to the Liberal meeting on the 6th, Mr Disraeli reminded the House that Willis's Rooms had, as Almack's, formerly been maintained by fashionable patronesses. "The distinguished assemblies that met within those walls were controlled by a due admixture of dowagers and youthful beauties—young reputations and worn celebrities—and it was the object of all social ambition to enter there. Now Willis's Rooms are under the direction of patrons, and there are two of these patrons below the gangway" (indicating Lord John Russell and Mr Sidney Herbert). In regard to its Foreign Policy, he said the Government should not be condemned without direct documentary evidence. Lord Malmesbury has since deplored Mr Disraeli's neglect to produce the Blue Book with the correspondence relating to the affairs of Italy and Austria, and stated that, had he laid it on the table, the debate would have ended differently (*Memoirs of an Ex-Minister*, vol. ii. p. 188).

The Earl of Derby to Queen Victoria.

St James's Square, *10th June 1859.*

Lord Derby, with his humble duty, submits to your Majesty that the tone of the Government Agents in the House of Commons is less sanguine to-day than it was yesterday with regard to the issue of the Debate to-night. There are no actual changes announced of votes, but the tone of the Opposition is more confident; and when an opinion begins to prevail that the Government are likely to be in a minority, it often realises itself by the effect which it produces on waverers and lukewarm supporters. The Division will certainly take place to-night; and, without absolutely anticipating failure, Lord Derby cannot conceal from your Majesty that he considers the situation very critical. Mr Gladstone expressed privately his opinion last night that, even if successful on the present occasion, the Government could not possibly go on, which does not look like an intention, on the part of the Liberal Party, of considering the present division as decisive.[393]...

Mr Disraeli to Queen Victoria.

House of Commons, *11th June 1859.*
(*Saturday morning, half-past two o'clock.*)

The Chancellor of the Exchequer with his humble duty to your Majesty:

For the Amendment	323
For the Address	310
	——
Majority against your Majesty's servants	13
	——

Queen Victoria to the Earl of Derby.

THE MINISTRY DEFEATED

Buckingham Palace, *11th June 1859.*

[393] The rest of the letter relates to the distribution of honours to the outgoing Ministers.

The Queen was very much grieved to receive Mr Disraeli's report of the division of yesterday, although she was fully prepared for this event.

She did not answer Lord Derby's letter of yesterday in order not to anticipate it. Now that the fate of the Government is decided, she is prepared to grant those favours and acknowledgments of service for which Lord Derby asked in his letter. The Queen *could* not reconcile it with her own feelings, however, were she to omit this opportunity, when Lord Derby for the second time resigns the post of her Prime Minister, of giving to him personally a public mark of her approbation of his services. The Queen therefore asks him to accept the Garter from her hands.

As the Queen holds a Drawing-room to-day, and receives the City Address after it, Lord Derby will be aware how little time she has this morning (being naturally anxious to have some conversation with him with as little delay as possible); she would ask him to come here either at half-past eleven or half-past twelve o'clock.

The Earl of Derby to Queen Victoria.

St James's Square, *11th June 1859.*

Lord Derby, with his humble duty, submits to your Majesty the expression of his deep gratitude for your Majesty's most gracious note this moment received, and for the terms in which your Majesty has been pleased to speak of his very imperfect services. He gratefully accepts the honour which your Majesty has been pleased to confer upon him as a mark of your Majesty's personal favour. As a Minister, he could never have advised your Majesty to bestow it upon him, and he could not have accepted it on the recommendation of any Government to which he was politically opposed; but as a spontaneous act of your Majesty, it acquires in his eyes a value which nothing else could have given to it. Lord Derby is this moment going down to the Cabinet, as a matter of form, and will obey your Majesty's commands as soon as possible after half-past eleven, when he will have an opportunity of expressing in person his deep sense of your Majesty's goodness, and his entire devotedness, in whatever situation he may be placed, to your Majesty's service.

Memorandum by Earl Granville.

LORD GRANVILLE SUMMONED

[*Undated. 11th June 1859.*]

I waited at four o'clock this afternoon[394] upon the Queen by Her Majesty's gracious commands. The Queen was pleased to remark upon the importance of the present crisis. Her Majesty informed me that Lord Derby had resigned, and that she had sent for me to desire that I should attempt to form another Administration, which Her Majesty wished should be strong and comprehensive. I respectfully assured the Queen that Her Majesty's commands came upon me by surprise; that at any time I felt my own insufficiency for such a post, and that at this time there were special difficulties; that I believed the only two persons who could form a strong Liberal Government were either Lord Palmerston or Lord John Russell; and that, although it had sometimes happened that two statesmen of equal pretensions preferred having a nominal chief to serving under one another, I did not believe that this was the case now. I said that I had reason to believe that Lords Palmerston and John Russell were ready to co-operate with one another, while I doubted whether either would consent to serve under a younger man of such small pretensions as myself.

The Queen in reply informed me that her first thoughts had been turned to Lord Palmerston and Lord John Russell, that they had both served her long and faithfully, and that Her Majesty felt it to be an invidious task to select one of the two. Her Majesty was also of opinion that as different sections of the Liberal Party were more or less represented by each, it might be more easy for the Party to act together under a third person. Her Majesty added that she had selected me as the Leader of the Liberal Party in the House of Lords, and a person in whom both Lord Palmerston and Lord John Russell had been in the habit of placing confidence, and she expressed her confident hope that their attachment to herself would induce them to yield that assistance without which it would be difficult to form a strong and comprehensive Government.

I proceeded to state some of the most salient difficulties of the task, and asked Her Majesty's permission to ascertain by negotiation what it would be possible to do.

---

[394] The 11th of June.

Her Majesty informed me that Her Majesty's experience of former changes of administration had taught her that the construction of an administration had failed when the person entrusted with the task had acted merely as a negotiator, and that the success of other attempts had been owing to the acceptance of the charge by the person for whom she had sent. Her Majesty laid Her Majesty's commands upon me to make the attempt, and I had the honour of conveying two letters from Her Majesty to Lord Palmerston and Lord John Russell, stating that Her Majesty relied upon their assistance.

Queen Victoria to { **Viscount Palmerston.**
Lord John Russell.

THE RIVAL LEADERS

Buckingham Palace, *11th June 1859.*

The Queen gives these lines to Lord Granville, whom she has entrusted with the task of forming an administration on the resignation of Lord Derby. She has selected him as the Leader of the Liberal Party in the House of Lords. She feels that it is of the greatest importance that both Lord Palmerston and Lord John Russell should lend their services to the Crown and country in the present anxious circumstances, and thought at the same time that they might do so most agreeably to their own feelings by acting under a third person. They having both served the Queen long and faithfully as her First Minister, she must not conceal from Lord Palmerston (John Russell) that it is a great relief to her feelings not to have to make the choice of one of them, and she trusts that they will feel no difficulty to co-operate with one in whom they have both been in the habit of placing confidence. From the long experience the Queen has had of Lord Palmerston's (John Russell's) loyal attachment to her and the service of the Crown, she feels confident she may rely on Lord Palmerston's (John Russell's) hearty assistance.[395]

---

[395] In reply, Lord Palmerston (in a letter printed in Ashley's *Life of Lord Palmerston*, vol. ii. p. 155) accepted his responsibility for uniting with others to overthrow the Derby Ministry, and undertook to serve under either Lord John Russell or Lord Granville, but stipulated that any Government he joined must be an efficient and representative one.

Earl Granville to Queen Victoria.

LORD GRANVILLE UNSUCCESSFUL

Bruton Street, *12th June 1859.*

(2 a.m.)

Lord Granville presents his humble duty to your Majesty, and begs to submit that he saw Lord Palmerston immediately after he had left Buckingham Palace. Lord Granville stated what had passed there, omitting any reference to your Majesty's objection to the effect likely to be produced on the Continent by Lord Palmerston's name, if he had the direction of the Foreign Affairs. Nothing could be more frank and cordial than Lord Palmerston's manner. He agreed to lead the House of Commons; he said that he had certainly anticipated that your Majesty would have sent for either Lord John or himself, but having taken a part in the defeat of the present Government, he felt bound to put aside any personal objects, and co-operate with me; and that there was no person whom he should prefer or even like as much as myself. He added that his co-operation must depend upon my being able to form a strong Government. Lord Granville then saw Lord John Russell, and had a very long conversation with him. Lord John had no objection to serving under Lord Granville, but thought that he could not give effect to his political views unless he was either Prime Minister or Leader of the House of Commons, and he doubted whether he had confidence in any one but Lord Palmerston for the Foreign Office. Lord Granville again saw Lord Palmerston, who informed him that if he had been sent for, he should have objected to go to the House of Lords, and that he could not now give up the lead of the House of Commons (which Lord Granville had already proposed to him to retain) to Lord John. This answer rendered it unnecessary for Lord Granville to allude to the objections to his holding the Foreign Office. Lord Granville has seen Lord Clarendon, who acted up to the full spirit of your Majesty's letter, but deprecates strongly the attempt to form a Government without Lord John Russell. Sir George Grey is of the same opinion. Sir George Lewis, Mr Herbert, and Mr Gladstone think every effort should be made to secure Lord John, but that it would not be impossible to form a Government without him. Mr Milner Gibson, with whom Lord Granville had a more reserved conversation, considered it a *sine quâ non* condition of support from the Liberal Party below the gangway, that Lord John should be a member of the Government. Lord Granville thinks that in his third interview with Lord Palmerston he observed more dissatisfaction at not being sent for by your Majesty. Lord Palmerston suggested that Lord John's absence from the Government would make it more difficult for a Leader of the House, who was not Prime Minister, to hold his position.

Lord Granville has written to Lord John asking for a final answer before he informs your Majesty, whether he is able to attempt the task which your Majesty has with so much kindness and indulgence laid upon him.[396]

Queen Victoria to the Earl of Derby.

LORD PALMERSTON PREMIER

Buckingham Palace, *12th June 1859.*

The Queen writes to inform Lord Derby that after a fruitless attempt on the part of Lord Granville to form a Government comprising Lord Palmerston and Lord John Russell, she has now charged Lord Palmerston with the task, which she trusts may prove more successful....

---

[396] This letter, and Lord John's reply declining to occupy only the third office in the State, and expressing his anxiety for adequate security in the handling of Foreign Affairs and Reform, are printed in Walpole's *Life of Lord John Russell*, vol. ii. chap. xxvii.

Lord Granville then wrote to Lord John: "I am glad that I wrote to you yesterday evening, as your answer gave me information which I had not gathered from your conversation in the morning. I came away from Chesham Place with the impression that union between you and Palmerston with or without me was impossible. Your letter afforded a good opportunity of arrangement. As soon as I found by it that I was an obstacle instead of a facility towards the formation of a strong Government. I went to the Queen to ask her to excuse me from the task which she had so unexpectedly and so graciously imposed upon me. In answer to a question, I stated to Her Majesty that it was disagreeable to me to advise as to which of you and Palmerston she should send for, but that I was ready to do so if it was her wish.

"The Queen did not press me. It is a great relief to have finished this business. I have asked Palmerston to do whatever would strengthen the Government, and assist him the most as regards myself."

Viscount Palmerston to Queen Victoria.

94 Piccadilly, *12th June 1859.*

Viscount Palmerston presents his humble duty to your Majesty, and begs to report that he has been to Pembroke Lodge, and has had a satisfactory conversation with Lord John Russell, who has agreed to be a Member of the Government without any suggestion that Viscount Palmerston should leave the House of Commons; but Viscount Palmerston is sorry to say that Lord John Russell laid claim to the Foreign Office in a manner which rendered it impossible for Viscount Palmerston to decline to submit his name to your Majesty for that post when the List of the new Government shall be made out for your Majesty's consideration and approval....

Queen Victoria to Viscount Palmerston.

13th June 1859.

Lord Clarendon has just left the Queen. She had a long and full conversation with him. Nothing could be more friendly than his language, and he expressed himself ready to do anything for the Queen's service. But he positively declines entering the Cabinet or taking any *other office*. He says, as *Foreign* Secretary, he should be ready to join the Government should there be a vacancy; but that he has never directed his attention much to general politics, and his taking any other office, after having held the Foreign Seals during a long and important time, would be of no use to the Government, and would only injure himself. The Queen told him that he might have any office almost (naming several of those which Lord Palmerston discussed with her), but she could not urge nor press him to do what *he felt* would injure him, and indeed she found him quite determined in his purpose.

His absence from the Cabinet the Queen sincerely deplores, and she knows that Lord Palmerston will feel it a serious loss.

Queen Victoria to Earl Granville.

AN INDISCREET DISCLOSURE

Buckingham Palace, *13th June 1859.*

The Queen is much shocked to find her whole conversation with Lord Granville yesterday and the day before detailed in this morning's leading article of the *Times*.[397] What passes between her and a Minister in her own room in confidential intercourse ought to be sacred, and it will be evident to Lord Granville that if it were not so, the Queen would be precluded from treating her Ministers with that unreserved confidence which can alone render a thorough understanding possible; moreover, any Minister could state what he pleased, against which the Queen would have no protection, as she could not well insert contradictions or explanations in the newspapers herself.

Earl Granville to Queen Victoria.

London, *13th June 1859.*

Lord Granville presents his humble duty to your Majesty, and feels deeply your Majesty's reproof.

Lord Granville was extremely annoyed this morning at seeing the article in the *Times* of to-day, repeating with some accuracy, but in a vulgar, inflated manner, the account which Lord Granville gave yesterday afternoon to many of his political friends, and which he believed your Majesty had authorised him to do. Lord Granville in that account laid much stress on the reasons which your Majesty gave for sending for Lord Granville, as he found that attempts had been made to attribute every sort of motive which might render the Court unpopular.

Besides the gross impropriety of the appearance of reporting your Majesty's conversation, Lord Granville regrets the indirect attack upon Lord John Russell.

Lord Granville begs respectfully to express to your Majesty his vexation at the annoyance, which he has thus been the cause of inflicting on your Majesty, particularly at a moment when your Majesty had just given him an additional proof of the indulgent kindness and confidence which your Majesty has been pleased to place in him.

---

397 A circumstantial account of the Queen's conversation with Lord Granville had appeared in the *Times*, and Lord Derby drew attention to the matter in the House of Lords. Lord Granville in reply expressed his regret in not having used more complete reserve, and frankly attributed the disclosures to his non-observance of adequate discretion.

Viscount Palmerston to Queen Victoria.

MR COBDEN

94 Piccadilly, *1st July 1859.*

Viscount Palmerston presents his humble duty to your Majesty, and has been unable till within the last few minutes to make any Report about Mr Cobden, from whom he had received no communication till about an hour ago, when Mr Cobden came to him.[398] The result of a long conversation between them has been that Mr Cobden, against the advice of all his friends and of his constituents, has decided to decline taking office. He grounds his decision upon feelings personal to himself. He thinks that after having so often and so strongly disapproved of the Foreign Policy of Viscount Palmerston as tending too much to involve this country in war, it would be inconsistent for him to join the present Cabinet, and he also said that, at his time of life and with his general habits, he does not consider himself fit for administrative office.

Viscount Palmerston used every [means] in his power to induce him to change his decision, and showed that, with respect to present and future action, there is no apparent difference between his views and those of Mr Cobden, since both would desire that this country should remain neutral in the war now raging in Italy. All his arguments, however, were useless, and though Mr Cobden discussed the matter in the most friendly and good-humoured manner, and promised to give out of office all support to the Government, and said that he thought he could do so more effectually out of office than in office, he could not be persuaded to make any change in the answer which he came to give.

Viscount Palmerston will consider what arrangement he may have to propose to your Majesty in consequence of Mr Cobden's answer.

The Ministry as Formed by Viscount Palmerston.

in the month of June *1859.*

First Lord of the Treasury	Viscount Palmerston.
Lord Chancellor	Lord Campbell.

[398] Mr Cobden had been visiting the United States. On landing at Liverpool he learned that he had been elected at Rochdale, and at the same time he received an offer of the Board of Trade.

President of the Council	Earl Granville.
Lord Privy Seal	Duke of Argyll.
Home Secretary	Sir G. C. Lewis.
Foreign Secretary	Lord John (afterwards Earl) Russell.
Colonial Secretary	Duke of Newcastle.
Secretary for War	Mr Sidney Herbert (afterwards Lord Herbert of Lea).
Secretary for India	Sir Charles Wood (afterwards Viscount Halifax).
Chancellor of the Exchequer	Mr Gladstone.[399]
First Lord of the Admiralty	Duke of Somerset.
President of the Board of Trade	Mr Milner Gibson (appointed in July).
Postmaster-General	Earl of Elgin.
Chancellor of the Duchy of Lancaster	Sir George Grey.
Chief Secretary for Ireland	Mr (afterwards Viscount) Cardwell.

Viscount Palmerston to Queen Victoria.

MR BRIGHT

94 Piccadilly, *2nd July 1859.*

Viscount Palmerston presents his humble duty to your Majesty....

Viscount Palmerston has heard from several persons that Mr Bright would be highly flattered by being made a Privy Councillor; would your Majesty object to his being so made if it should turn out that he wishes it? There have been instances of persons made Privy

[399] Lord Aberdeen wrote, in a letter printed in Parker's *Sir James Graham*, vol. ii. p. 388, that the wish of Lord Palmerston, expressed in a speech at Tiverton, "to see the Germans turned out of Italy by the war, has secured Gladstone ... notwithstanding the three articles of the *Quarterly* and the thousand imprecations of late years."

Councillors without office, and if Mr Bright could be led by such an honour to turn his thoughts and feelings into better channels such a change could not fail to be advantageous to your Majesty's service....

Queen Victoria to Viscount Palmerston.

Buckingham Palace, *2nd July 1859.*

The Queen has received Lord Palmerston's letter of to-day. She is sorry not to be able to give her assent to his proposal with regard to Mr Bright.[400] Privy Councillors have sometimes exceptionally been made without office, yet this has been as rewards, even in such cases, for services rendered to the State. It would be impossible to allege any service Mr Bright has rendered, and if the honour were looked upon as a reward for his systematic attacks upon the institutions of the country, a very erroneous impression might be produced as to the feeling which the Queen or her Government entertain towards these institutions. It is moreover very problematical whether such an honour conferred upon Mr Bright would, as suggested, wean him from his present line of policy, whilst, if he continued in it, he would only have obtained additional weight in the country by his propounding his views as one of the Queen's Privy Councillors.

Earl Canning to Queen Victoria.

PACIFICATION OF INDIA

Calcutta, *4th July 1859.*

Lord Canning presents his humble duty to your Majesty, and begs permission to offer to your Majesty his respectful thanks for your Majesty's most gracious letter of the 18th of May.

Lord Canning ventures to believe that he is well able to figure to himself the feelings with which your Majesty will have welcomed the termination of the Mutiny and Rebellion in India, and of the chief miseries which these have brought in their train. He hopes that your Majesty will not have thought that there has been remissness in not marking this happy event by an earlier public acknowledgment and

---

[400] In 1859, Lord Palmerston, in offering Mr Cobden a seat in the Cabinet, rejected the idea of accepting Mr Bright as a colleague, on the ground that his public speeches made it impossible. Mr Bright, later in life, was a welcome guest at Windsor, and the Queen became warmly attached to him as one of her Ministers.

thanksgiving in India, as has already been done in England.[401] The truth is, that although this termination has long been steadily and surely approaching, it is but just now that it can be said to be complete in the eyes of those who are near to the scene of action. It is only within the last three weeks that the exertions of our Troops on the Oudh and Nepaulese frontier, and in some other parts, have been remitted, and almost every Gazette has recounted engagements with the rebels, which, although they have invariably had the same issue, would scarcely have consisted with a declaration that peace and tranquillity were restored. Now, however, military operations have fairly ceased, and the rains and the climate, which would make a continuance of those operations much to be regretted, will do their work amongst the rebels who are still in arms in the Nepaul jungles more terribly than any human avengers.

Lord Canning has used every exertion and device to bring these wretched men to submission; but many—it is difficult to say how many, but certainly some few thousands—still hold out. With some of them the reason no doubt is that they belong to the most guilty Regiments, and to those which murdered their officers; but this cannot apply to all; and it is to be feared that the prevailing cause is the bad influence of their leaders—the Nana, Bala Rao, and the Begum;[402] or rather the Begum's infamous advisers. It is certain that all of these, believing their own position to be desperate, have spared no pains to persuade their followers that the Government is seeking to entrap them, and that, if they submit, their lives will be taken....

Queen Victoria to Viscount Palmerston.

A MILITARY ENQUIRY

Buckingham Palace, *5th July 1859.*

The Queen is much shocked to see that the Government last night moved for a Committee of the House of Commons to enquire into the Military Departments, without having previously communicated with the Queen on the subject. She is the more surprised at this, as Lord Palmerston told her, when she saw him on the formation of the present Government, and she expressed her anxiety on the subject, that there would be no more trouble about it, and he thought it would drop. The

---

[401] There had been a Public Thanksgiving in England on the 1st of May.

[402] Bala Rao was a brother of Nana Sahib, chief instigator of the Sepoy Mutiny. See *ante*, p. 238, note 24.

Queen expects that the names of those who it is proposed should compose the Committee, and the wording of it, will be submitted to her.

Viscount Palmerston to Queen Victoria.

CONSTITUTIONAL QUESTION

Piccadilly, *5th July 1859.*

Viscount Palmerston presents his humble duty to your Majesty, and begs to state that the re-appointment of the Committee on the Organisation of the Military Departments was unavoidable. That Committee had been affirmed by the House of Commons and consented to by the late Government, and had begun its sittings; but when a Dissolution of Parliament was announced, it suspended its further sittings, with the understanding that it should be revived in the new Parliament; and to have departed from that understanding would have been impossible. That which Viscount Palmerston intended to convey in what he said to your Majesty on the subject was, that the evidence given by Lord Panmure might be deemed as having fully set aside the objection urged against the present organisation by persons unacquainted with the bearing upon it of the fundamental principles of the Constitution, namely, that the Crown acts in regard to Military matters without having any official adviser responsible for its acts. Such a condition of things, if it could exist, would be at variance with the fundamental principles of the British Constitution, and would be fraught with danger to the Crown, because then the Sovereign would be held personally answerable for administrative acts, and would be brought personally in conflict in possible cases with public opinion, a most dangerous condition for a Sovereign to be placed in.

The maxim of the British Constitution is that the Sovereign can do no wrong, but that does not mean that no wrong can be done by Royal authority; it means that if wrong be done, the public servant who advised the act, and not the Sovereign, must be held answerable for the wrongdoing.

But the Ministers of the Crown for the time being are the persons who are constitutionally held answerable for all administrative acts in the last resort, and that was the pith and substance of the evidence given by Lord Panmure. Those persons who want to make great changes in the existing arrangements were much vexed and disappointed by that evidence, and the attempt made yesterday to put off the Committee till next year on the ground that the evidence now to be taken would be one-sided only, and would tend to create erroneous impressions, was founded upon those feelings of disappointment.

Viscount Palmerston submits names of the persons whom Mr Sidney Herbert proposes to appoint on the Committee, and they seem to be well chosen.

Lord John Russell to Queen Victoria.

Pembroke Lodge, *10th July 1859.*

(7 p.m.)

Lord John Russell presents his humble duty to your Majesty. He has just received from Lord Palmerston, who is here, the paper, a copy of which is enclosed.[403]

Lord John Russell has to add that Lord Palmerston and he are humbly of opinion that your Majesty should give to the Emperor of the French the moral support which is asked. It is clearly understood that if the Emperor of Austria declines to accept the propositions, Great Britain will still maintain her neutral position.

But it is probable that her moral support will put an end to the war, and your Majesty's advisers cannot venture to make themselves responsible for its continuance by refusing to counsel your Majesty to accept the proposal of France.

Queen Victoria to Lord John Russell.

FRANCE AND AUSTRIA

Pavilion, Aldershot, *10th July 1859.*

The Queen has just received Lord John Russell's letter with the enclosure which she returns, and hastens to say in reply, that she does

---

[403] At the seat of war, a series of decisive French victories had culminated in the battle of Solferino, on Midsummer Day (see Introductory Note, *ante*, p. 308). But the French Emperor was beginning to think these successes too dearly purchased, at the expense of so many French lives, and, actuated either by this, or some similar motive, he attempted, on the 6th of July, to negotiate through the British Government with Austria. The attempt was a failure, but an armistice was signed on the 8th, and again the Emperor sought the moral support of England. The paper which Lord John Russell submitted was a rough memorandum of M. de Persigny's, proposing as a basis of negotiation the cession of Lombardy to Piedmont, the independence of Venetia, and the erection of an Italian Confederation.

not consider the Emperor of the French or his Ambassador justified in asking the support of England to proposals he means to make to his antagonist to-morrow. He made war on Austria in order to wrest her two Italian kingdoms from her, which were assured to her by the treaties of 1815, to which England is a party; England declared her neutrality in the war. The Emperor succeeded in driving the Austrians out of one of these kingdoms after several bloody battles. He means to drive her out of the second by diplomacy, and neutral England is to join him with her moral support in this endeavour.

The Queen having declared her neutrality, to which her Parliament and people have given their unanimous assent, feels bound to adhere to it. She conceives Lord John Russell and Lord Palmerston ought not to ask her to give her "moral support" to one of the belligerents. As for herself, she sees no distinction between moral and general support; the moral support of England *is* her support, and she ought to be prepared to follow it up.

The Queen wishes this letter to be communicated to the Cabinet.[404]

Queen Victoria to Lord John Russell.

END OF THE WAR

Osborne, *12th July 1859.*

The Queen has to acknowledge the receipt of Lord John Russell's letter reporting to her the result of the deliberations of the Cabinet, which has very much relieved her mind. Lord John does not say whether her letter was read to the Cabinet, but from his former letter she concludes it was. She is most anxious that there should exist no misapprehension on their part as to the Queen's views. Our position must be consistent and precisely defined. A negotiation to stop the effusion of blood, and to attain "a peace which would be for the interests of all belligerents," is a very vague term. Who is to judge of those interests? Is M. de Persigny or the Emperor Napoleon's opinion to be the guide, as they just now proposed to us? Austria must be considered the exponent of her own interests. Prussia has explained to us the interests of Germany in the maintenance of the line of the fortresses on the

---

[404] The Queen not having been informed whether this instruction had been complied with, a correspondence took place on the subject between the Prince and Lord Granville. See the *Life of Lord Granville*, vol. i. chap. xiii.

Mincio, and was answered; her views were entirely erroneous, and her apprehensions exaggerated. It will require the greatest caution on our part not to lose our neutral position, nor to be made the advocate of one side. Are the wishes of the Lombards, Tuscans, etc., really ascertainable, while their countries are occupied by French and Sardinian armies? The Queen encloses an extract of a letter from the first Napoleon to his son, Prince Eugène,[405] showing how the expression of a wish for annexation has already of old been used as a means for conquest.

Queen Victoria to Lord John Russell.

ASCENDANCY OF FRANCE

Osborne, *13th July 1859*.

The Queen has received the news of a concluded peace,[406] which Lord John Russell has sent to her yesterday, with as much surprise as it must have caused Lord John. It was a joyous intelligence, as far as the stopping of the further effusion of innocent blood and the security against further diplomatic complications is concerned, but it gives cause for serious reflection. The Emperor Napoleon, by his military successes, and great apparent moderation or prudence immediately after them, has created for himself a most formidable position of strength in Europe. It is remarkable that he has acted towards Austria now just as he did towards Russia after the fall of Sebastopol; and if it was our lot then to be left alone to act the part of the extortioner whilst he acted that of the generous victor, the Queen is doubly glad that we should not now have fallen into the trap, to ask Austria (as friends and neutrals) concessions which he was ready to waive. He will now probably omit no occasion to cajole Austria as he has done to Russia, and turn her spirit of revenge upon Prussia and Germany—the Emperor's probable next victims. Should he thus have rendered himself the master of the entire Continent, the time may come for us either to obey or to fight him with terrible odds against us. This has been the Queen's view from the beginning of this complication, and events have hitherto wonderfully supported them. How Italy is to prosper under the

[405] Eugène de Beauharnais, Duke of Leuchtenberg, son of the Empress Josephine by her first marriage, and adopted son of Napoleon I.

[406] The armistice had arranged that the Emperors should meet at Villafranca, where peace was concluded. See Introductory Note, *ante*, p. 308. The Italian Confederation was to be under the presidency of the Pope.

Pope's presidency, whose misgovernment of his own small portion of it was the ostensible cause of the war, the Queen is at a loss to conceive. But the Emperor will be able to do just as he pleases, being in military command of the country, and having Sardinia, the Pope, and Austria as his debtors.

The Queen would like this letter to be communicated to the Cabinet.

Lord John Russell to Queen Victoria.

Foreign Office, *13th July 1859.*

Lord John Russell presents his humble duty to your Majesty; he will read your Majesty's letter to the Cabinet to-morrow.

The Emperor Napoleon is left no doubt in a position of great power. That position has been made for him by allowing him to be the only champion of the cause of the people of Italy.

But that is no reason why we should seek a quarrel with France, and there is some reason to doubt whether the speeches made in the House of Lords, while they display our weakness and our alarm, are really patriotic in their purpose and tendency.

To be well armed, and to be just to all our neighbours, appears to Lord John Russell to be the most simple, the most safe, and the most honest policy.

Queen Victoria to Lord John Russell.

Osborne, *14th July 1859.*

The Queen acknowledges the receipt of Lord John Russell's communications of yesterday. She entirely agrees with him "that we have no reason to seek a quarrel with France," and that "the most simple and most safe and most honest" line of conduct for us will be "to be well armed, and to be just to all our neighbours."

She trusts that as the poor Duchess of Parma[407] appears to be overlooked in the Italian Peace merely because nobody thinks it his business to befriend her, we shall in the above spirit ask for justice and consideration for her.

---

[407] Louise Marie de Bourbon, daughter of the Duc de Berri, and widow of Charles III., Duke of Parma. She was at this time Regent for her son Robert, a minor (born 1848), the present Duke.

The Queen concurs with Lord John that it will now be useless to communicate to France the advice given to the Porte.

Mr Odo Russell to Lord John Russell.

*(***Submitted to the Queen.***)*

THE VIEWS OF THE POPE

Rome, *17th July 1859.*

My Lord,—Some days since a letter from the "Pontifical Ante-chamber," directed to "Signor Odoni Russell, Agente Officioso di Sua Maestà Britannica," informed me that His Holiness the Pope desired to see me.

In consequence I proceeded to the Vatican, and was ushered into the presence of His Holiness by Monsignore Talbot, the "Cameriere" in waiting, who immediately withdrew, and I remained alone with the Pope.

His Holiness welcomed me with his usual benevolence and good humour. He seemed very gay, and spoke with more than customary frankness, so much so indeed that I have felt some hesitation as to the propriety of submitting what passed between us to your Lordship. But after mature reflection, I think it best you should be in possession of an accurate and conscientious account of the sentiments of His Holiness in the present important juncture of affairs.

"Caro mio Russell," the Pope said, "you have been so long at Naples that I was already thinking of sending after you to bring you back; we do not like you to leave us, and the more so as I have heard you were attached to the Mission of Mr Elliot,[408] who is a son of Lord Minto; and if he entertains the same political views as his father, he is a dangerous man to the peace of Italy. Now I knew Lord Minto here, and although he may be a very good man, I do not think him a man of any capacity, and his doctrines were calculated to bring on the ruin of Italy."

I replied, "I cannot agree with your Holiness, for I consider Lord Minto to be a very clever man, whose honest, sound, and liberal views, had they been listened to, might have prevented the crisis which is now convulsing Italy."

---

[408] Mr (afterwards Sir) Henry Elliot, P.C., G.C.B., was Plenipotentiary to Naples. He was subsequently Ambassador at Vienna, and died in 1907.

The Pope said, "Well, of course you belong to his party, but, *Poveri noi!* what is to become of us with your uncle and Lord Palmerston at the head of affairs in England? They have always sympathised with the turbulent spirits of Italy, and their accession to power will greatly increase the hopes of the Piedmontese Party. Indeed, I well know what the English Government want: they want to see the Pope deprived of his temporal power."

I replied, "Again I regret to find your Holiness so entirely mistaken with respect to the policy of England. We derive great happiness from our free institutions, and we would be glad to see our neighbours in Europe as happy and as prosperous as we are, but we have no wish to interfere with the internal concerns of other nations, or to give advice without being asked for it; least of all as a Protestant Power would *we* think of interfering one way or the other with the Government of your Holiness."

THE POPE ON ENGLISH LIBERALISM

The Pope said, "I do not doubt the good intentions of England, but unfortunately you do not understand this country, and your example is dangerous to the Italian minds, your speeches in Parliament excite them, and you fancy because constitutional liberties and institutions suit you, that they must suit all the world. Now the Italians are a dissatisfied, interfering, turbulent and intriguing race; they can never learn to govern themselves, it is impossible; only see how they follow Sardinia in all she tells them to do, simply because they love intrigue and revolution, whilst in reality they do not know what they want; a hot-headed people like the Italians require a firm and just government to guide and take care of them, and Italy might have continued tranquil and contented, had not the ambition of Sardinia led her to revolutionise the whole country. The Grand Duke of Tuscany, for instance, is an excellent and just man, and nevertheless, at the instigation of Piedmont, he was turned out of the country, and for no earthly purpose. I suppose you have read Monsieur About's book about Rome[409]? well, all he says is untrue, pure calumny, and it would be easy for me to have it all refuted; but he is really not worthy of such an honour. His book, I see, has been translated into English, and I have no doubt it will be much read and believed in England. Such books and our refu-

[409] Edmond About, a French journalist (1828-1885), had published *La Question Romaine,* an attack on the Papacy. See De la Gorce, *Histoire du Second Empire*, vol. ii. p. 365.

gees mislead your countrymen, and I often wonder at the language your statesmen hold about us in the Houses of Parliament. I always read their speeches. Lord Palmerston, Lord John Russell, and Mr Gladstone do not know us; but when I think how kindly and hospitably Lord Granville was received at Rome last winter, and then read the extraordinary speech he made last February about us, I think the gout he suffered from here must have gone to his head when he reached England, and I wonder how Her Majesty the Queen could send for him to form a Government! Then again, Mr Gladstone, who allowed himself to be deceived about the Neapolitan prisoners—he does not know us and Italy—and Mr Cobden,—I knew him in 1847—he is always in favour of peace, and he must be very fond of animals, for when he came here from Spain he wanted me to write to that country and put a stop to bull-fights—a very good man, but I do not know his views about Italy. And Lord Stratford de Redcliffe, do you think he will be employed again? he seemed so anxious to get a place. Mr Disraeli was my friend; I regret him. But tell me, *caro mio Russell*, if you are a prophet, how all this war and fuss is to end?"

THE TEMPORAL POWER

I replied, "Your Holiness has better claims to being a prophet than I have, and I sincerely hope all this may end well for Italy; but as regards the present and the past, I must again say that I deeply regret to see your Holiness misconceive the honest views and sincere sympathies of the statesmen you have named, for the welfare of Italy; they would like to see Italy independent, prosperous, progressing and contented, and able to take care of herself without foreign troops. Your Holiness has done me the honour to speak freely and openly with me; permit me to do the same, and ask your Holiness what England must think when she sees the temporal power of your Holiness imposed upon three millions of people by the constant presence of French and Austrian bayonets, and when, after ten years of occupation, the Austrians withdraw suddenly, there is at once an insurrection throughout the country; and if the French were to leave Rome it is generally acknowledged that a revolution would compel your Holiness to seek refuge in some foreign country. At the same time, when the troops of your Holiness are employed as at Perugia,[410] the Government is too weak to

[410] An insurrection against the Pope at Perugia bad been put down with great cruelty on the 20th of June.

control them; they pillage and murder, and, instead of investigating their conduct, the excesses committed by them are publicly rewarded."

The Pope smiled, paused, took a pinch of snuff, and then said good-humouredly: "Although I am not a prophet, I know one thing; this war will be followed by an European Congress, and a Congress about Italian Affairs is even worse for us than war. There will be changes in Italy, but mark my words, whatever these changes are, the Pope will ever be the Pope, whether he dwells in the Vatican or lives concealed in the Catacombs.

"Lastly, I will give you some advice. Prepare and take care of yourselves in England, for I am quite certain the French Emperor intends sooner or later to attack you."

The Pope then beckoned to me to approach, and making the sign of the Cross, he gave me his blessing in Latin, then with both his hands, he took one of mine, pressed it, and said with great warmth, "Be our friend in the hour of need." I have the honour to be, etc., etc.,

Odo Russell.

Queen Victoria to Lord John Russell.

DISAPPOINTMENT OF CAVOUR

Osborne, *18th July 1859.*

The Queen returns these interesting letters to Lord John.[411]

---

[411] These were letters from Lord Cowley and Sir James Hudson in reference to the Peace of Villafranca. The former announced, as a result of his conversation with the Empress and other persons, that among the causes which induced the French Emperor to consent to peace were his horror at any further sacrifice of life and time, disgust at what he considered Italian apathy for the cause which the French were upholding, and distrust of the intentions of the King of Sardinia and Count Cavour. Sir James Hudson described the unanimous feeling at Turin that the Nationalist cause had been betrayed. Cavour, he wrote, could obtain no further response to his remonstrances with Napoleon than "Il fait bien chaud: il fait bien chaud." Moreover, Napoleon knew (continued Sir James) "that Mazzini had dogged his footsteps to Milan, for, the day before yesterday, sixty-six Orsini bombshells were discovered there by the chief of the Sardinian police, who arrested the man (a known follower of Mazzini) who had them. The story is that he brought them from England for the purpose of using them against the Austrians!!" Count Cavour, who resigned in disgust and was succeeded by Rattazzi, remained out of office till the following January.

The whole aspect of affairs gives cause for serious reflection and great anxiety for the future.

The conduct of France as regards Italy shows how little the Emperor Napoleon cared for, or thought of, its independence when he undertook this war, which (though in the last instance begun by Austria) *he* brought on, for purposes of his own.

The manifesto of the Emperor of Austria shows how unfortunate for her own interests the policy of Prussia has been.[412] She had made herself answerable for the issue of the war by restraining the minor states, and stands now humiliated and isolated. Her position in Germany is at present very painful, and may be for the future very dangerous.

The Queen feels strongly that we are not without considerable responsibility in having from the first urged her to take no part in the war, which certainly had great influence on her actions—and she will very naturally look to us not to desert her when the evil hour for her may come.[413]

---

[412] He stated that he believed he could obtain better terms direct from the French Emperor than those to which England, Russia, and Prussia were likely to give their moral support as a basis of mediation.

[413] Lord Cowley wrote to Lord John Russell on the 20th of July:—

"... The two Emperors met in the most cordial manner, shaking hands as if no difference had existed between them. As soon as they were alone, the Emperor of Austria took the initiative, and stated at once that he was ready to cede to the Emperor of the French, for the sake of the restoration of peace, the territory which the latter had conquered, but that he could not do more, giving the reasons which I have mentioned to your Lordship in former despatches. The Emperor of the French replied that his own position in France, and the public declarations which he had made, rendered something in addition necessary: that the war had been undertaken for the freedom of Italy, and that he could not justify to France a peace which did not ensure this object. The Emperor Francis Joseph rejoined that he had no objection to offer to the Confederation which formed part of the Emperor Napoleon's programme, and that he was ready to enter it with Venetia, and when the Emperor Napoleon remarked that such a result would be a derision, if the whole power and influence of Austria were to be brought to bear upon the Confederation, the Emperor Francis Joseph exclaimed against any such interpretation being given to his words, his idea being that Venetia should be placed on the same footing, in the Italian Confederation, as Luxemburg holds in the Germanic Confederation....

Queen Victoria to Sir Charles Wood.

INDIAN AFFAIRS

Osborne, *23rd July 1859.*

The Queen's attention has been attracted by No. 86 (Foreign Department) of the printed abstracts of letters received from India, relating to the affairs of Bussahir.[414] She would ask Sir C. Wood to consider, with his Council, whether means could not be found for making acts of confiscation, sequestration, spoliation, transfer of Government, or whatever they may be called, dependent upon some formal

---

"In the course of conversation between the two Imperial Sovereigns, the Emperor of Austria remarked to the Emperor of the French with many expressions of goodwill, and of a desire to see the dynasty of the latter firmly established on the throne of France, that His Majesty took an odd way to accomplish his end. 'Believe me,' said the Emperor Francis Joseph, 'dynasties are not established by having recourse to such bad company as you have chosen; revolutionists overturn, but do not construct.' The Emperor Napoleon appears to have taken the remark in very good part, and even to have excused himself to a certain degree, observing that it was a further reason that the Emperor Francis Joseph should aid him in putting an end to the war, and to the revolutionary spirit to which the war had given rise.

"The Emperors having separated in the same cordial manner in which they had met, the Emperor of the French himself drew up the preliminaries and sent them in the evening to Verona by his cousin, the Prince Napoleon. Being introduced to the Emperor of Austria, who received His Imperial Highness very courteously, His Majesty said, after reading the preliminaries, that he must beg the Prince to excuse him for a short time, as he had others to consult before signing them. He then went into an adjoining room where, according to Prince Napoleon's account, a loud and angry discussion ensued, in which the Prince distinguished the Emperor's voice broken by tears, as if His Majesty had been obliged to have recourse to persuasion, to silence the opposition made to the conditions, and it was not until some time had elapsed that His Majesty returned and signed the paper containing them, or rather I infer that he retained the paper signed by the Emperor Napoleon, and returned one of similar purport signed by himself; for among all the curious circumstances connected with this transaction, not the least curious is the fact that there does not exist any document recording the preliminaries with the double signature of both Emperors."

[414] Bussahir was a State in the upper course of the Sutlej. In January, the Punjab, including the Sutlej States, had been made a distinct presidency, but Bussahir was not finally included until 1862.

and judicial proceeding which should secure the Queen from acts being done in her name—which might not be entirely justifiable morally, as well as legally—which should relieve the Government agents from the fearful responsibility of being sole advisers on steps implying judicial condemnation without trial on their mere personal opinion, and from which they derive themselves additional personal advancement in power, position, possibly emolument, etc., etc., and lastly, which would give the people of India security that the Government only acts after impartial judicial investigation and the sifting of evidence.

The Queen would wish a report to be made to her upon this important subject.

Queen Victoria to Lord John Russell.[415]

NON-INTERVENTION

Osborne, *21st August 1859.*

The Queen sends the enclosed draft to Lord John Russell; she is very sorry that she cannot give her approval to it. There are many points in it to which she cannot but feel the gravest objections. It is unnecessary, however, for her to go into these details, as it is against the principle of England volunteering at this moment the intrusion of a scheme of her own for the redistribution of the territories and Governments of Northern Italy, that she must above all protest. Moreover, a step of such importance, reversing the principle of non-intervention, which the Queen's Government has hitherto publicly declared and upheld, should, in the Queen's opinion, not be brought before her without having received the fullest deliberation and concurrence of the assembled Cabinet.

Lord John Russell to Queen Victoria.

Pembroke Lodge, *23rd August 1859.*

Lord John Russell presents his humble duty to your Majesty; he begs to explain that with respect to reversing the principle of non-intervention, he has never proposed any such course. If intervention

[415] A month earlier, on his return from the war, the Emperor had tried to enlist British support in his scheme for a European congress. But the Cabinet decided (24th July), with the Queen's full concurrence, that no answer should be returned to this proposal, till a Treaty, embodying the preliminaries of Villafranca, should have been signed.

were to mean giving friendly advice, or even offering mediation, your Majesty's Government from January to May would have pursued a course of intervention, for they were all that time advising Austria, France, Sardinia, and Germany.

If by friendly and judicious advice we can prevent a bloody and causeless war in Italy we are bound to give such advice.

If we refrain from doing so, we may ultimately be obliged to have recourse to intervention; that is to say, we may have to interfere against the ruthless tyranny of Austria, or the unchained ambition of France. It is with a view to prevent the necessity of intervention that Lord John Russell advises friendly representations.

Queen Victoria to Lord John Russell.

NON-INTERVENTION

Aldershot, *23rd August 1859.*

... With regard to Lord John's letter of to-day, the Queen wishes merely to say that from the outbreak of the war our negotiations have ceased, and that the war is not over till the peace is concluded. Our interference before that period may be prompted by a desire to prevent a future war; but our first duty is not to interfere with the closing of the present. The desire to guard Italy against "the ruthless tyranny of Austria, and the unchained ambition of France" may produce a state of things in Italy, forcing both to make common cause against her, and backed by the rest of Europe to isolate England, and making her responsible for the issue. It will be little satisfaction then to reflect upon the fact that our interference has been merely *advice*.

Viscount Palmerston to Queen Victoria.

FOREIGN POLICY

94 Piccadilly, *23rd August 1859.*

Viscount Palmerston presents his humble duty to your Majesty, and begs to state that Lord John Russell has shown him your Majesty's communication, in which your Majesty objects to a proposed despatch to Lord Cowley, on the ground that it would be a departure from the principle of non-intervention which has been publicly proclaimed as the rule for Great Britain in the late events between France and Austria. But Viscount Palmerston would beg humbly to submit to your Majesty that the intervention which all parties agreed that this country ought to abstain from, was active interference by force of arms in the war then going on, but that neither of the great political parties meant or asserted that this country should not interfere by its advice and opinions in regard to the matters to which the war related. Viscount Palmerston can assert that neither he nor any of those who were acting with him out of office ever contemplated giving such a meaning to the doctrine of non-intervention; and that such a meaning never was attached to it by the Conservative Leaders while they were in office, is proved from one end of their Blue Book to the other.[416] The whole course of the Derby Government, in regard to the matters on which the war turned, was one uninterrupted series of interventions by advice, by opinions, and by censure now addressed to one party and now to another. Whatever may be thought of the judgment which was shown by them, or of the bias by which they were guided, the principle on which they acted was undoubtedly right and proper.

England is one of the greatest powers of the world, no event or series of events bearing on the balance of power, or on probabilities of peace or war can be matters of indifference to her, and her right to have and to express opinions on matters thus bearing on her interests is unquestionable; and she is equally entitled to give upon such matters any advice which she may think useful, or to suggest any arrangements which she may deem conducive to the general good.

It is no doubt true that the Conservative Party, since they have ceased to be responsible for the conduct of affairs, have held a different doctrine, and in their anxiety lest the influence of England should be exerted for the benefit of Italy, and to the disadvantage of Austria, have contended that any participation by Great Britain in the negotiations for the settlement of Italy would be a departure from the principle of non-intervention; but their own practice while in office refutes their newly adopted doctrine in opposition; and if that doctrine were to be admitted, Great Britain would, by her own act, reduce herself to the rank of a third-class European State.

Queen Victoria to Lord John Russell.

ITALIAN POLICY

Osborne, *24th August 1859.*

---

[416] This was the Blue Book, the production of which would, according to Lord Malmesbury, have saved the Derby Ministry.

The Queen is really placed in a position of much difficulty, giving her deep pain. She has been obliged to object to so many drafts sent to her from the Foreign Office on the Italian Question, and yet, no sooner is one withdrawn or altered, than others are submitted exactly of the same purport or tendency, if even couched in new words. The Queen has so often expressed her views that she is almost reluctant to reiterate them. She wishes, however, Lord John to re-peruse THE QUEEN AND LORD JOHN RUSSELL the two drafts enclosed, which just came to her. If they have any meaning or object, it must be to show to France that it would be to her interest to break in the Treaty of Zurich the leading conditions to which she pledged herself to Austria at Villafranca. Those preliminaries contained but three provisions affecting Austria: (1) That Austria was to cede Lombardy; (2) That an Italian Confederation should be encouraged, of which Venetia was to form part; (3) That the Dukes of Tuscany and Modena were to return to their Duchies. The two latter clauses must be considered as compensations for the losses inflicted in the first. Both the latter are now to be recommended by England, a neutral in the war, to be broken.

Now, either it is expected that our advice will not be listened to, in which case it would not be useful and hardly dignified to give it, or it is expected that France will follow it. If, on finding herself cheated, Austria were to feel herself obliged to take up arms again, we should be directly answerable for this fresh war. What would then be our alternative? Either to leave France in the lurch, to re-fight her own battle, which would entail lasting danger and disgrace on this country, or to join her in the fresh war against Austria—a misfortune from which the Queen feels herself equally bound to protect her country.

As this is a question of principle on which she clearly understood her Cabinet to have been unanimous, she must ask her correspondence to be circulated amongst its members, with a view to ascertain whether they also would be parties to its reversal, and in order to prevent the necessity of these frequent discussions, which, as the Queen has already said, are very painful to her.

Earl Granville to the Prince Albert.

MEDIATION OF LORD GRANVILLE

London, *29th August 1859.*

Sir,—In the middle of last week I received at Aldenham a letter from Mr Sidney Herbert,[417] in which he told me that he had just received a visit from Lord Palmerston, much perturbed and annoyed, saying that the Queen had objected to all Lord John's despatches, and appeared to think that it was objectionable for England to give any advice on the subject of Italian affairs. Mr Herbert gave some good advice to Lord Palmerston, but, from the tone of his letter, I gather that he thought the objections made at Osborne unreasonable. I answered that I entirely concurred with him in the interest of everybody, that no feelings of irritation should exist between the Sovereign and her leading Ministers; that it was possible that the Queen, forgetting how very sensitive Lord John was to criticism, had pulled him up more sharply than he liked, but that I was convinced the objections made were not exactly those mentioned by Lord Palmerston. I heard nothing more till I received on Saturday evening a telegram, summoning me to a Cabinet this day. I came to Town immediately, and saw Lord Palmerston yesterday. I enquired the reason of the sudden summons for a Cabinet. He told me that there had been a discussion between the Queen and Lord John; that the Queen had objected to his (Lord John's) proposal that the despatch of 25th July should be now communicated to the French Government. Lord John had informed him of the fact, and had requested him to communicate with the Queen on the subject. Lord Palmerston then read to me a well-written memorandum on the abstract question of giving advice, which he had sent to Her Majesty. He told me that he had been to Osborne; that the Queen had expressed a wish through Sir Charles Wood that he should not discuss the whole matter with her; that he had had a satisfactory conversation with your Royal Highness, of which he gave me an abstract, which, however, contained his own arguments at greater length than your Royal Highness's. He said that Lord John had made a mistake with respect to the end of the despatch, in which Lord Cowley is desired to withhold it till after the Peace of Zurich was concluded. Lord John gave a different interpretation to it from what appeared to be the case, as described by a previous letter of Lord John, in which he had said that the sentence was added at the suggestion of the Cabinet, and with his entire approval. Lord Palmerston states that the Queen did not feel herself authorised to sanction a departure from what had been decided by the Cabinet, without the concurrence of the Cabinet, and that she thought

[417] See Lord Fitzmaurice's *Life of Lord Granville*, vol. i. chap. xiii.

it desirable, if the Cabinet met, that they should agree on the future policy as regards Italy. Lord John also wished for a Cabinet.

I replied that there seemed to be a double question: first, a difference between the Queen and Lord John Russell and himself; and second, the whole question of our Italian Policy. On the first point I could not but remember the apprehension generally felt at the formation of his first Government; that the feeling between the Sovereign and himself might not be such as to give strength to the Government; that the result, however, was most satisfactory. I was not aware of either the Queen or himself having given way on any one point of principle, but the best understanding was kept up in the most honourable way to both, and that, at the end of his Ministry, I knew that the Queen had expressed to several persons how much she regretted to lose his services. That I most sincerely hoped that there was no chance of misunderstanding now arising; that would be most disadvantageous to the Sovereign, to the public service, to the Government, and, above all, to himself. He interrupted me by assuring me that there was not the slightest chance of this. He repeated to me flattering things said by the Queen at the close of his last Administration, and told me that it was impossible for the Queen to have been more kind and civil than at his visit last week at Osborne. I continued that in Italian matters I believed the Cabinet was agreed. Our language to Italian Governments ought to show sympathy with Italy, and let them know that we were anxious that they should be left free to act and decide for themselves; that it should inform them in the clearest manner that in no case were they to obtain active assistance from us, and it ought to avoid giving any advice as to their conduct, which might make us responsible for the evil or danger which might accrue from following such advice. That our language to France and Austria ought to press upon them in every *judicious* manner the expediency of doing that which was likely to secure the permanent happiness of Italy, and to persuade them to abstain from forcing upon the Italians, persons and forms of Government to which they objected; nothing like a menace or a promise to be used....

I then saw Sidney Herbert, who told me that Charles Wood's report had entirely changed the aspect of things; that it was clear that the Queen had come to the assistance of the Cabinet, instead of opposing them; that reason had been entirely on her side, and that Johnny had reduced the question now to the single point, which was not of much importance, whether the 25th July despatch should now be communicated or not. He told me that Lord John was in a state of great irritation, and ready to kick over the traces. I dined at Lord Palmerston's, and met Sir Charles Wood and Mr Gladstone. I had some guarded conversation with the latter, who seemed very reasonable. Sir Charles Wood gave me all the information which I required. It appears to me that the really important point is that the whole Cabinet should know the real question between the Queen and her Ministers, and that, if Lord John can find plausible reasons for changing the date of the communication of the despatch, it may be better for the Queen to consent to this. Some of us will take care to have a decided opinion about the future course of our policy.

I presume Sir George Grey will be at the Cabinet, and will be able to report to your Royal Highness what has passed. If he is not there, I will write again. I have the honour to be, Sir, with great respect, your Royal Highness's obedient, humble, and faithful Servant,

Granville.

Earl Granville to the Prince Albert.

THE QUEEN'S POSITION

Privy Council Office, *29th August 1859.*

Sir,—The Cabinet was very satisfactory. Lord John looked ill, and evidently ashamed of much of his case. Many of the Cabinet thought that the despatch of 25th July had not only been sent but communicated. Others attached a different meaning to the closing paragraph than what it appears to bear. Lord John produced a most objectionable draft of despatch in lieu of that of the 25th. It was universally condemned, and Lord Palmerston was empowered to tell the Queen that the Cabinet now thought that the despatch of the 25th might be communicated.

Lords Palmerston and John Russell asked for further powers during the Recess, and recommended that we should give an opinion in favour of annexation of duchies to Sardinia. This was decidedly objected to, and we all professed our readiness to meet again if necessary.[418]

[418] "Pam. asked for fuller powers to act during the recess, which was met by a general assurance of readiness to come up by night trains." Lord Granville to the Duke of Argyll. See the *Life of Lord Granville*, vol. i. p. 358.

The Cabinet thoroughly understood what had passed between the Queen and her two Ministers, although we could not get Lord John to show us all we required.

Gladstone took me aside after it was over to say that I must have thought him stupid yesterday evening, that now he knew the facts he thought Her Majesty had been put to most unnecessary annoyance. The Chancellor said something of the same sort. I never saw the Cabinet more united.

The Duke of Argyll, Lord Elgin, and Mr Cardwell were absent. I am, Sir, with great respect, your obedient, humble, and faithful Servant,

Granville.

Queen Victoria to Lord John Russell.

SARDINIA AND CENTRAL ITALY

Balmoral, *5th September 1859.*

Lord John Russell will not be surprised if the despatches of Lord Cowley and drafts by Lord John in answer to them, which the Queen returns to him, have given her much pain. Here we have the very interference with advice to which the Queen had objected when officially brought before her for her sanction, to which the Cabinet objected, and which Lord John Russell agreed to withdraw, carried on by direct communication of the Prime Minister through the French Ambassador with the Emperor; and we have the very effect produced which the Queen dreaded, viz. the French Minister insinuating that we called upon his master to do that which he would consider so dishonourable that he would rather resign than be a party to it! What is the use of the Queen's open and, she fears, sometimes wearisome correspondence, with her Ministers, what the use of long deliberations of the Cabinet, if the very policy can be carried out by indirect means which is set aside officially, and what protection has the Queen against this practice? Lord John Russell's distinction also between his own official and private opinion or advice given to a Foreign Minister is a most dangerous, and, the Queen thinks, untenable theory, open to the same objections, for what he states will have the weight of the official character of the Foreign Secretary, whether stated as his private or his public opinion. His advice to the Marquis d'Azeglio[419] is moreover quite open to the inference drawn by Count Walewski, that it is an encouragement to *Sardinia*, to Military intervention in and occupation of the Duchies, and Lord John Russell's answer hardly meets this point if left as it stands at present; for "the *name* of the King of Sardinia,... *the chief of a well-disciplined army*," will have little influence unless he is prepared to use that army.

The Queen must ask Lord John to instruct Lord Cowley to state to Count Walewski that no opinions expressed on Foreign Policy are those of "Her Majesty's Government" but those which are given in the official and regular way, and that Her Majesty's Government never thought of advising the French Government to break the solemn engagements into which the Emperor Napoleon entered towards the Emperor of Austria at Villafranca.

The Queen asks Lord John to communicate this letter to Lord Palmerston.

Queen Victoria to Lord John Russell.

ENGLAND INVOLVED

Balmoral, *6th September 1859.*

The Queen returns Lord Palmerston's letter, together with the other papers sent to her, to Lord John. She is glad to find that he thinks that no answer ought to be given to Count Persigny, but she thinks it important that it should be *stated to him that no answer can be given.* Unfortunately, here has been again the Prime Minister declaring that he *quite agrees* with the French Ambassador, but that the proposal should come officially from France to be placed before the Cabinet. The inference must be that the Cabinet and the Queen will, as a matter of course, agree also, when it is so submitted. Now what is it that Lord Palmerston has approved? A plan for an alliance of England with France for the purpose of *overruling* Austria, if the Duchies in which she is the heir, and to which the Archdukes were to return in accordance with the stipulations of Villafranca, were given to Sardinia and Austria should object. It is hoped indeed that this will not immediately lead to war with her, but France is to expect that she will not be left to

---

[419] Massimo d'Azeglio, Sardinian Commissioner in the Romagna. He had been Prime Minister of Sardinia from 1849 till 1852, when Cavour, who had been in his ministry, succeeded him.

fight single-handed for an object declared to be more English than French! Thus we are dragged step by step into the position of a party in the Italian strife. The Queen thinks it incumbent upon her not to leave Lord John Russell in ignorance of the fact that *she* could not approve such a policy reversing our whole position since the commencement of the War.

The Queen must leave it to Lord John to consider how far it would be fair to his colleagues in the Cabinet to leave them unacquainted with the various private steps lately taken, which must seriously affect their free consideration of the important question upon which they have hitherto pledged themselves to a distinct principle.

Queen Victoria to Viscount Palmerston.

Balmoral, *6th September 1859.*

The Queen returns to Lord Palmerston his correspondence with M. de Persigny. Lord John Russell will have sent him her letter to him on this subject. She has nothing to add, but to repeat her conviction of the great danger and inconvenience arising out of such private communications, and the apprehension she must naturally feel that the attempt to convince the Emperor Napoleon that it would be for his interest to break his word to the Emperor of Austria should reflect upon the honour of the Queen's Government. She must insist upon this being distinctly guarded against.

Lord John Russell to Queen Victoria.

LORD JOHN RUSSELL'S CRITICISMS

Abergeldie, *7th September 1859.*

Lord John Russell presents his humble duty to your Majesty; he cannot refrain from making some remarks on your Majesty's letter of yesterday.

Lord Palmerston appears to have answered M. de Persigny by saying that he personally agreed with him, but that the proposition he had sketched must come from the French Government; that it must come from them officially, and it would then have to be maturely considered by the Cabinet.

Lord John Russell sees nothing to object to in this language. It might be embarrassing to Lord Palmerston if such a proposition were to come from France, and were to be rejected by the Cabinet. But Lord

Palmerston could easily explain the matter to M. de Persigny. Lord Palmerston does not appear to have committed your Majesty, or Lord John Russell, or the Cabinet in any way.

On the other hand, your Majesty cannot mean that the Cabinet is to be precluded from maturely considering any proposition which may come officially from France.

Lord John Russell feels, on his own part, that he must offer to your Majesty such advice as he thinks best adapted to secure the interests and dignity of your Majesty and the country. He will be held by Parliament responsible for that advice. It will be always in your Majesty's power to reject it altogether.

Lord John Russell is of opinion that there never was a time when it was less expedient to fetter this country by prospective engagements. But it does not follow that the policy pursued last autumn and winter, and which ended in a war in Italy, would be the best course in any future contingency. Should another war arise it will be very difficult for Great Britain to remain neutral. For this reason it is desirable to prevent such a war, if possible. It was difficult last winter, and may be still more difficult this winter. For the present there is no better course than to keep this country free from engagements. After the peace of Zurich is made, or not made, we shall see our way better.

Lord John Russell has never concealed his opinions from his colleagues. He even warned them that France might make such a proposition as M. de Persigny now contemplates.

The enclosed letter from Lord Palmerston and Mr Fane's[420] despatch will show the feelings which exist between Austria and Prussia. The Emperor Napoleon does not appear to have satisfied Prince Metternich. His object evidently is to gain time.

Queen Victoria to Lord John Russell.

Balmoral, *7th September 1859.*

The Queen has received Lord John Russell's letter. She can ask for nothing better than "that we should be kept from any engagements," and she never could have intended to convey the impression that she wished to "see the Cabinet precluded from taking into consideration any proposal France might make." What she objects to is

[420] Julian Henry Fane, son of the eleventh Earl of Westmorland, and Secretary of Embassy at Vienna.

binding beforehand the Government by expressions of opinion of its leading members to the French Government, and thus *bringing about* those French proposals which it will be most embarrassing to the Cabinet either to reject or adopt. It is absolutely necessary, therefore, that the French Government should be told that the opinions given were private opinions not binding the Government. Lord John has not yet sent to the Queen drafts in conformity with her wishes expressed in her letter of the day before yesterday.

Viscount Palmerston to Queen Victoria.

LETTERS TO FOREIGN SOVEREIGNS

Broadlands, *9th September 1859.*

Viscount Palmerston presents his humble duty to your Majesty, and has had the honour to receive your Majesty's communication of the 6th of this month; and although he had the honour of addressing your Majesty yesterday afternoon, he deems it his duty to submit some observations upon this communication.

Your Majesty states that Viscount Palmerston in his letter to Count Persigny endeavoured to persuade the Emperor of the French to break his word to the Emperor of Austria, but Viscount Palmerston must beg very respectfully but entirely to deny that accusation....[421]

Your Majesty is pleased to observe upon the danger and inconvenience of private communications with Foreign Ministers, and to add that your Majesty must insist upon this being distinctly guarded against. Viscount [Palmerston] would be very desirous of knowing the precise meaning of those last words. If your Majesty means that what is to be guarded against is any attempt to induce a Foreign Sovereign to break his word, Viscount Palmerston cordially subscribes to that opinion, and maintains that he has not done so in the past, and declares that he has no intention of doing so in the future. But if your Majesty's meaning is that Viscount Palmerston is to be debarred from communicating with Foreign Ministers except for the purpose of informing them officially of formal decisions of the British Government, Viscount Palmerston would beg humbly and respectfully to represent to your Majesty that such a curtailment of the proper and constitutional functions of the office which he holds would render it impossible for

[421] Lord Palmerston then gives a very long and detailed account of his position.

him to serve your Majesty consistently with his own honour or with advantage to the public interest.

Queen Victoria to Viscount Palmerston.

THE QUEEN'S OPINION

Balmoral, *11th September 1859.*

Lord Palmerston has written (on the 8th) a long letter to the Queen, which, besides giving his private opinion on the politics of Italy, which were not disputed, purports to show that when a principle of policy had been adopted by the Cabinet and sanctioned by the Sovereign, the Foreign Secretary ought not to be impeded in carrying out the details, either by objections raised to them by the Sovereign, or by making them dependent on the meetings of Cabinets, difficult to obtain at this time of year. Now the question raised by the Queen was *just the reverse.* The principle adopted by the Cabinet and sanctioned by the Queen was: not to interfere by active advice with the peace to be made at Zurich; the Foreign Secretary had submitted a draft which had appeared to the Queen to be in contradiction to this principle, which, upon the Sovereign's objection, he withdrew; the Cabinet was summoned and rejected a similar draft submitted to them, and the Queen then complained that the very same advice should have been given by the Prime Minister in an indirect way to which the Sovereign and Cabinet could not agree openly. Lord Palmerston's letter was not communicated to the Queen until it had been alluded to in a public despatch, and Count Walewski had insinuated to our Ambassador that, rather than be a party to a line of conduct, which he would look upon as dishonourable for his master, he would resign office. What the Queen has asked for is: an intimation to the French Government that private communications like that of Lord Palmerston to M. de Persigny must not be looked upon as the official expression of the opinion of Her Majesty's Government, and that we disclaim ever having intended to induce the Emperor to break his engagements made at Villafranca, whatever they may have been. The Queen does not conceive that Lord Palmerston can object to this course, nor does he attempt to do so in his letter.

P.S.—Since writing the above the Queen has received Lord Palmerston's letter of the 9th. As she has just written at length, she does not conceive that it would be necessary to make any further observations in reply, except to a distinct question put by him in the latter part of his letter, viz. what the Queen wishes to have "distinctly guarded against."

It is the danger and inconvenience of private communications with Foreign Ministers, without a distinct understanding that they are strictly private, and not to be treated as conveying the opinions of Her Majesty's Government, where the sanction of the Crown and adhesion of the Cabinet have not been obtained. Lord John Russell has now expressed this in a paragraph in one of his drafts to Lord Cowley, which he will send to Lord Palmerston.

As a proof of the necessity of such caution, the Queen, has only to refer to the public use made of Lord Palmerston's private letter to Count Persigny, and the use made to our prejudice by the Emperor Napoleon at the time of the armistice at Villafranca of a private communication with Count Persigny, which was represented to imply assent to certain conditions of peace by England, with a desire of pressing them on Austria, when no opinion had been expressed by the Government to justify such an inference.

The Duke of Newcastle to Queen Victoria.

ST JUAN

Downing Street, *26th September 1859.*

The Duke of Newcastle presents his humble duty to your Majesty.

Your Majesty will receive from Sir George Lewis full information of the serious intelligence which has been received to-day from Washington and Vancouver Island respecting the Military occupation by United States troops of the island of St Juan,[422] and of the view taken of it by your Majesty's Government.

The Duke of Newcastle begs leave to receive your Majesty's instructions upon the acceptance of an offer made by Lord Clarendon whilst on a visit at Clumber last week. Lord Clarendon received not long ago a private letter from the President of the United States. He proposes that in answering this letter he should express his concern at these untoward events, and particularly at their occurrence at a time when, if not speedily settled, they would prevent the fulfilment of a

---

[422] A dispute had arisen out of the Oregon affair (see *ante*, vol. ii. pp. 30 and 72), concerning the rival claims of this country and the United States to the small island of St Juan, situated between Vancouver Island and the State of Washington, which is adjacent to the Canadian frontier.

project which he had reason to think had been in contemplation—a visit to Washington by the Prince of Wales on his return from Canada.

Lord Clarendon expresses his belief that nothing would so much gratify Mr Buchanan as a visit from His Royal Highness to the United States during his Presidency....

Lord Palmerston and Lord John Russell see no objection to such a letter from Lord Clarendon, which, whilst it would carry weight as coming from one occupying so high a position in this country, would bear no official character; but as the name of the Prince of Wales would be used, however hypothetically, such a letter would not be written by Lord Clarendon or accepted by the Government without your Majesty's sanction.

The Duke of Newcastle therefore requests to be favoured with your Majesty's commands that he may communicate them to Lord Clarendon.

Queen Victoria to Lord John Russell.[423]

Windsor Castle, *1st December 1859.*

The Queen returns Lord Cowley's interesting letter. She trusts that it will be made quite clear to the Emperor that he has no chance of getting us to join him in the war with Austria, which he may be tempted or driven to renew. This alternative constantly recurs to his mind....

Lord John Russell to Queen Victoria.

ENGLAND AND FRANCE

Foreign Office, *1st December 1859.*

Lord John Russell presents his humble duty to your Majesty; he has written to Lord Cowley, according to your Majesty's gracious permission. The question of supporting the Emperor of the French, if Austria should attempt force to impose a government in Italy against the popular will, must be judged of according to the circumstances, should they arise. Lord John Russell is certainly not prepared to say that a case may not arise when the interests of Great Britain might require that she should give material support to the Emperor of the

[423] On the 10th of November the Treaty of Zurich, embodying the terms arranged at Villafranca, had been signed, and a Congress was determined upon, to settle Italian affairs.

French. But he considers such a case as very improbable, and that the fear of such an alliance will prevent Austria from disturbing the peace of Europe.

Queen Victoria to Lord John Russell.

Windsor Castle, *2nd December 1859.*

The Queen was extremely sorry to find from Lord John Russell's letter of yesterday that he contemplates the possibility of our joining France in a fresh Italian war or demonstration of war against Austria, which the Queen had put entirely out of the question. If the Emperor of the French were allowed to believe in such a possibility, he would have it in his power to bring it about, or obtain a just cause of complaint against us, if we abandoned him. It would be just as dangerous and unfair towards the Emperor to mislead him in this respect as it would be for the Queen to conceal from Lord John that under no pretence will she depart from her position of neutrality in the Italian quarrel, and inflict upon her country and Europe the calamity of war on that account.

Queen Victoria to Lord John Russell.

SIR JAMES HUDSON

Windsor Castle, *6th December 1859.*

The Queen has received Lord John Russell's letter recommending Sir James Hudson[424] as the Second Representative at the Congress of Paris. The Queen must decline sanctioning this selection. Lord John Russell has in his last letters avowed his conviction that England cannot again remain neutral in an Italian war, and his opinion that she ought to support France and Sardinia by arms if Austria were to attempt to recover her supremacy by force. Lord Cowley wrote on the 29th ult. that Prince Metternich declared that Austria kept her Army ready because she could not permit either the military occupation of the Duchies by Sardinia or their annexation to that kingdom. Lord Palmerston sent to the Queen yesterday evening the copy of a letter he wrote to Count Persigny urging the Emperor Napoleon by every argument he can find to consent to this annexation, even to the length of

---

[424] Sir James Hudson, Minister at Turin, had been a sympathiser in the policy of Cavour, to an extent almost incompatible with his position as a British representative.

assuring him that such a state would always be obliged to lean on France.

The Queen cannot help drawing her conclusions from these facts, and feels more than ever the great responsibility resting on her, to preserve to her people the blessings of peace. She wishes this letter to be communicated to Lord Palmerston and to the Cabinet.

The Queen approves of Lord Cowley as her First Representative at the Congress.

Queen Victoria to Lord John Russell.

CENTRAL ITALY

Osborne, *7th December 1859.*

The Queen has received Lord John Russell's letter of yesterday. Although to avoid a long written discussion, she has not in her last letter stated any reason for her objecting to Sir James Hudson as Plenipotentiary at the Congress, she has no objection to state to Lord John that it is simply her want of confidence in him, being the result of her having watched his conduct at his post at Turin during these last years. The Queen's representative at Paris ought to be a person in whom she can have entire confidence, that *English* interests alone will sway his conduct. From Lord John Russell's letter it appears that many of his colleagues in Cabinet saw equal objections to the appointment.

The Queen repeats her wish that her letter of yesterday may be communicated to the Cabinet.

Lord Cowley's letter, which she returns, is not calculated to diminish the Queen's alarm as to the direction in which we are being systematically driven, viz. *War* to support the Emperor Napoleon, who almost claims such support already as his right! He has already shifted his ground further, and asks for it in case Austria should oppose "the armed interference of Sardinia in the affairs of Central Italy." Now Sardinia can have no more right to such interference than Austria; yet the Emperor says "he is quite determined to renew the war in case Austria resists." It is under these circumstances that the advice of the Prime Minister of England to the Emperor, to withdraw the only impediment which restrains the action of Sardinia, becomes a matter of such grave moment.

The Queen is determined to hold to her neutrality in the Italian intrigues, revolutions, and wars. It is true, Lord John says, "it becomes a great power like Great Britain to preserve the peace of Europe, by throwing her great weight into the scale which has justice on its side." But where justice lies, admits of every variety of opinion.

The Party placed in absolute power by a revolution and a foreign invasion is not necessarily the exponent of the real wishes of a people, and Lord Cowley reports Mr Layard "hot from Italy to confirm him in the opinion he has always held, that the annexation of Tuscany to Sardinia is not practicable." This, however, Lord Palmerston urges, and if it be agreed to by the Emperor and attempted by Sardinia, Lord John would probably wish England to fight for it as the cause of justice.

Has Lord John ever contemplated the probability of Austria not being abandoned a second time by Germany, when attacked by France? The Emperor is sure to have calculated upon this, and has not played his game badly, if he can get the Alliance of England to sanction and foster his attack upon the Rhine, which would inevitably follow. The Queen believes this to be a cherished object of France, and the success certain if we become her dupes. The Queen can hardly for a moment bring herself to think of the consequences.

She would wish this letter also to be shown to the Cabinet.

Earl Granville to the Prince Albert.

MEETING OF THE CABINET

London, *8th December 1859.*

Sir,—Lord John stated in what appeared to me a very fair way what had taken place between himself and Lord Palmerston in their communications with Her Majesty, and read Her Majesty's letters. At the end of his statement the Chancellor asked what was the question to be decided by the Cabinet. Lord John answered that he wished to know whether he was to inform Her Majesty that the Cabinet were of opinion that they were still respectfully of opinion that Sir James Hudson was the fittest person to be named Second Plenipotentiary, or whether he should acquiesce in Her Majesty's commands, reserving his own opinion as to the fitness of Sir James. The Chancellor answered: "Undoubtedly the second course will be the best." I then stated my reasons, or rather repeated them, for objecting to Sir James Hudson. Mr Gladstone made a hesitating remark. Sir G. Lewis and the Duke of Argyll, Sir Charles Wood, and Sir George Grey—the latter very strongly—supported the second course proposed by Lord John. Lord Palmerston spoke with some temper and dogmatically as to who were right and who were wrong, but advised Lord John to take the second course. The appointment of Lord Wodehouse[425] was proposed. Some of us do not think it a very good one, but there are no sufficient grounds for our opposing it. I am not sure that Gladstone would not go any lengths in supporting Lords Palmerston and John Russell on the Italian Question, although he is more cautious than they are. The feeling of the rest of the Cabinet, as far as I can judge, is perfectly sound about war, and on our taking an English and not a purely Sardinian attitude; but they are all inclined to sympathise with the national feeling in Italy, and averse to the restoration of the Dukes by force or by intrigue.

Lord John was sore and nervous, but talked of his letter to the Queen, and Lord Palmerston's to Persigny, as "unlucky." Lord Palmerston seems convinced that he is perfectly in the right, and everybody else in the wrong, and would, I am sure, take advantage of any step, taken without sufficient consideration by the Queen, to make a stand for his own policy....

I have the honour to be, Sir, with great respect, your Royal Highness's obedient and faithful Servant,

Granville.

Queen Victoria to the Lord Chancellor (Lord Campbell).

DIVORCE CASES

Windsor Castle, *26th December 1859.*

The Queen wishes to ask the Lord Chancellor whether no steps can be taken to prevent the present publicity of the proceedings before the new Divorce Court. These cases, which must necessarily increase when the new law becomes more and more known, fill now almost daily a large portion of the newspapers, and are of so scandalous a character that it makes it almost impossible for a paper to be trusted in the hands of a young lady or boy. None of the worst French novels from which careful parents would try to protect their children can be as bad as what is daily brought and laid upon the breakfast-table of

[425] Under Secretary of State for Foreign Affairs, and afterwards, as Earl of Kimberley, a member of successive Liberal Cabinets.

every educated family in England, and its effect must be most pernicious to the public morals of the country.[426]

Queen Victoria to the Emperor of the French.

Windsor Castle, *le 31 Décembre 1859.*

Sire et mon cher Frère,—Je viens comme de coutume offrir à votre Majesté nos félicitations bien sincères à l'occasion de la nouvelle année. Puisse-t-elle ne vous apporter que du bonheur et du contentement! L'année qui vient de s'écouler a été orageuse et pénible et a fait souffrir bien des cœrs. Je prie Dieu que celle dans laquelle nous entrons nous permette de voir s'accomplir l'œuvre de la pacification, avec tous ses bienfaits pour le repos et le progrès du monde. Il y aura encore à réconcilier bien des opinions divergentes et des intérêts apparemment opposés; mais avec l'aide du Ciel et une ferme résolution de ne vouloir que le bien de ceux dont nous avons à régler le sort, il ne faut pas en désespérer.

Nous avons eu le plaisir de posséder pendant quelques semaines notre chère fille et son mari, qu'il nous a été bien doux de revoir au sein de notre famille. Notre fils aîné passe ses vacances avec nous, mais retournera prochainement à Oxford pour reprendre ses études.

Lady Ely vient de nous dire qu'elle a trouvé votre Majesté ainsi que l'Impératrice et le petit Prince dans la meilleure santé ce qui nous a fait bien du plaisir d'entendre.

Le Prince me charge d'offrir ses hommages les plus affectueux à votre Majesté, et, en vous renouvelant les expressions de ma sincère amitié, je me dis, Sire et cher Frère, de V.M.I, la bonne et affectionnée Sœur et Amie,

Victoria R.

---

[426] Lord Campbell replied that having attempted in the last session to introduce a measure to give effect to the Queen's wish, and having been defeated, he was helpless to prevent the evil.

INTRODUCTORY NOTE
TO CHAPTER XXIX

At the end of 1859, Mr Cobden had offered his services to the Government to negotiate a commercial treaty with France, and had been warmly encouraged in the scheme by Mr Gladstone. In January 1860, he was officially appointed a Plenipotentiary, with Lord Cowley, for this purpose, and on the 23rd of that month the treaty was signed. It included mutual remissions and reductions of import duties, and was contingent on obtaining the assent of the British Parliament, but neither party was fettered by any engagement not to extend similar concessions to other countries. In February, on the introduction of the Budget, the treaty was brought before the House of Commons, and ratified by a great majority; at the same time Mr Gladstone abolished a large number of import duties, but increased the income-tax for incomes over £150, from ninepence to tenpence in the pound. His proposal to repeal the paper duties was rejected by the Peers, the majority in its favour in the Commons having sunk to nine. A Commons Committee was appointed to deal with this conflict between the Houses, and resolutions defining the powers of the Peers in money bills were passed by the Lower House, Lord Palmerston clearly showing himself in sympathy with the Lords. Mr Gladstone expressed a desire to resign, in consequence of his difference with his colleagues, while Lord Derby and Lord Malmesbury intimated privately that they would support Lord Palmerston in office against any Radical secession. A Reform Bill of Lord John Russell, reducing the Borough Franchise to £6, and making a moderate redistribution of seats, was received with indifference, and eventually dropped.

Italian affairs mainly absorbed the attention of the country. The intended international congress was abandoned, owing to the attitude adopted by the French Emperor towards the Pope, but the former now obtained the annexation of Savoy and Nice, not, as had been arranged in 1858 as a reward for assisting to set Italy free "from the Alps to the

Adriatic"—an ideal which had not been realised—but as a price for assisting Piedmont to incorporate the Central Italian Provinces. The annexation was strongly resented, and suspicions of French designs were aroused to such an extent as to give a substantial impetus to the Volunteer movement in this country. By the summer, 130,000 Volunteers had been enrolled, and, at a review in Hyde Park, 21,000 men marched past the Queen, while in August, in consequence of the same apprehensions, it was decided by a large vote to carry out the recommendations of the National Defence Commission.

The Swiss made an ineffectual protest against the annexation of that part of Savoy which had been neutralised by the treaty of Vienna, while, on the other hand, the Emperor Napoleon maintained that the people of Savoy and Nice had the same right to transfer their country to France, as Tuscany and the Æmilia (under which name the Duchies of Parma and Modena and the Romagna were now united) had to place themselves under the King of Sardinia. This they decided in March, by universal suffrage, to do; a few days later the treaty for the annexation of Savoy and Nice was signed, and in April it was ratified in the Piedmontese Parliament, Garibaldi, the deputy for Nice, his native town, voting against it. In the same month, a *plébiscite*, taken in the provinces affected, showed an immense majority in favour of annexation. Garibaldi himself was soon afterwards engaged in rendering assistance to the Sicilians in their insurrection against the despotic King Francis II. Assuming the title of "Dictator of Sicily, in the name of Victor Emmanuel," Garibaldi attacked and occupied Palermo, and having established his ascendency in the island, invaded the Neapolitan territory on the mainland. The Sardinian Government, for diplomatic reasons, disavowed the expedition, but gave a retrospective assent to it later in the year.

The French Emperor's policy in Syria added to the distrust with which he was regarded. The Maronites, a Christian tribe, had been attacked and massacred by the Druses, and the Emperor had proposed to send troops to restore order. This step was eventually taken, after a European conference had been held; but the Emperor's proposal was so severely criticised that he wrote a long letter to the French Ambassador in London, reviewing and justifying his policy in Italy and elsewhere, since the Peace of Villafranca.

Garibaldi had ignored the instructions of Victor Emmanuel to abstain from further operations against Naples, until the two Sicilies had voted for absorption into United Italy; King Francis fled to Gaëta, and

Garibaldi entered the capital. At the same time, Cavour, in spite of a French protest, determined upon the invasion of the Papal States, and acted so promptly that in three weeks all effective opposition to the Italian cause in that territory was put down, and Umbria and the Marches were conquered. In October, the Piedmontese Parliament voted for the annexation of such of the southern Italian provinces as should declare themselves in favour of it; the Two Sicilies having accepted the offer by overwhelming majorities, the King and Garibaldi joined hands at Teano, and finally defeated the Bourbon army, afterwards entering Naples. The Marches and Umbria also declared for incorporation in the new Kingdom.

In July, the Prince of Wales, accompanied by the Duke of Newcastle, left England for a tour in Canada, where he was welcomed with unbounded enthusiasm; he afterwards proceeded to the United States, visiting New York, Chicago, and other great cities, being received by President Buchanan at Washington. The Prince returned home in the course of November.

The Abolitionist troubles, which for some time had been acute in the States, came to a crisis in the last days of the year, South Carolina adopting autonomous ordinances, declaring her own independence and sovereignty as a State, and her secession from the Union.

The refusal of the Chinese Government to ratify the Treaty of Tien-tsin, and an unwarranted attack on certain British ships, led to a revival of hostilities. A desire being expressed by the Chinese to resume negotiations, some of the British representatives despatched for that purpose were treacherously captured, and treated with great cruelty. The allied troops of England and France thereupon, marched to Pekin, when reparation was made, and retribution, exacted for the outrages. A Convention was eventually signed on the 24th of October.

CHAPTER XXIX
1860

The King of the Belgians to Queen Victoria.

Laeken, *6th January 1860.*

My dearest Victoria,—I have to thank you for a *most affectionate* and gracious letter of the 3rd....

I will speak to my pianist about Wagner's *Lohengrin*; he plays with great taste and feeling, and I purchased a fine Parisian piano to enable him to go on satisfactorily.

Now I must speak a little of passing events. Louis Napoleon wished for a Congress because it would have placed a new authority between himself and the Italians, whom he fears evidently concerning their fondness of assassinating people. The pamphlet, "The Pope and the Congress," remains *incomprehensible*[427]; it will do him much harm, and will deprive him of the confidence of the Catholics who have been in France his most devoted supporters. Now the Congress is then postponed, but what is to be done with Italy? One notion is, that there would be some arrangement by which Piedmont would receive more, Savoy would go to France, and England would receive Sardinia. I am sure that England would by no means wish to have Sardinia. It will give me great pleasure to hear what Lord Cowley has reported on these subjects. I understand that Louis Napoleon is now much occupied with Germany, and studies its resources. This is somewhat alarming, as he had followed, it seems, the same course about Italy.

---

[427] This famous pamphlet, issued (like that of February 1859, *ante*, p. 313, note 7) under the nominal authorship of M. de la Guéronnière, expounded the Emperor's view that the Pope should be deprived of his temporal dominions, Rome excepted. Its publication brought about the resignation of Count Walewski (who was succeeded by M. de Thouvenel) and the abandonment of the proposed Congress.

Gare la bombe, the Prussians may say. One cannot understand why Louis Napoleon is using so many odd subterfuges when plain acting would from the month of September have settled everything. I must say that I found Walewski at that time very sensible and conservative. His retiring will give the impression that things are now to be carried on in a less conservative way, and people will be much alarmed. I know Thouvenel, and liked him, but that was in the poor King's time. In England his nomination will not give much pleasure, I should imagine, as he was in the situation to oppose English notions in the Orient.... Your devoted Uncle,

Leopold R.

Queen Victoria to Lord John Russell.

Windsor Castle, *11th January 1860.*

The Queen has received Lord John Russell's letter, written after the Cabinet yesterday evening. She was much relieved by finding a proposal to call upon France and Austria not to interfere in Italy substituted for the former one implying war on our part for the defence of the Provisional Governments of Central Italy. The Queen must consider this new proposal, however, as partial and incomplete as long as Sardinia is not asked as well to abstain from interference. Austria has reversionary rights in Tuscany and Modena, Sardinia has no rights at all, if a desire for acquisition is not to be considered as one. Austria will probably say she has no intention of interfering as long as Sardinia does not, but she cannot allow Sardinia to possess herself of her inheritance under her very eyes. It is also incorrect to place France and Austria entirely in the same line; Austria being an Italian power in virtue of Venetia, and France having nothing whatever to do in Italy.

Lord John Russell to Queen Victoria.

WHIG TRADITIONS

Pembroke Lodge, *11th January 1860.*

Lord John Russell presents his humble duty to your Majesty; he has just had the honour to receive your Majesty's letter of this date.

Lord John Russell has sent to Lord Palmerston the proposal he humbly submits to your Majesty.

He will therefore only venture to say that the doctrines of the Revolution of 1688, doctrines which were supported by Mr Fox, Mr

Pitt, the Duke of Wellington, Lord Castlereagh, Mr Canning, and Lord Grey, can hardly be abandoned in these days by your Majesty's present advisers. According to those doctrines, all power held by Sovereigns may be forfeited by misconduct, and each nation is the judge of its own internal government.[428]

Lord John Russell can hardly be expected to abjure those opinions, or to act in opposition to them.

Queen Victoria to Lord John Russell.

Windsor Castle, *11th January 1860.*

The Queen has received Lord John Russell's note of this day, in which she is not able to find any answer to her letter, or even an allusion to what she had written, viz. that Austria and France being asked to abstain from interference, such an arrangement would be partial and incomplete unless Sardinia was pledged also to non-interference. The Queen cannot make out what the doctrines of the Revolution of 1688 can have to do with this, or how it would necessitate Lord John to abjure them.

Queen Victoria to the King of the Belgians.

AFFAIRS OF ITALY

Windsor Castle, *17th January 1860.*

My beloved Uncle,—Your dear letter of the 13th reached me on Saturday, and I at once forwarded your letter to good and faithful Clark, who was for *two* months unable to attend us from a severe attack of illness, but who is, I am happy to say, much better, indeed his own good self again, and who is now *here*.[429] This good account you

---

[428] In a despatch of the 27th of October, Lord John took the same ground in the case of Naples. After quoting with approval the view taken by Vattel of the lawfulness of the assistance given by the United Provinces to the Prince of Orange, and his conclusion that it is justifiable to assist patriots revolting against an oppressor for "good reasons," he stated that the question was whether the people of Naples and of the Roman States took up arms against their Government for good reasons; and of this matter, he added, the people themselves were the best judges.

[429] The Queen, later in the year, lent Bagshot Park temporarily to Sir James Clark.

give us of your precious health makes us truly happy. It is such a blessing.

Affairs are in a sad and complicated state, and though we modify matters as much as we *can*, we can't entirely keep our Ministers (*the two*) from doing *something*. You will hear no doubt of the last proposal soon, viz. that France and Austria should *both* agree *not* to interfere in Italy—France withdrawing her troops from Rome, and Sardinia to be asked not to send any troops into the Duchies until there has been a *final vote* expressive of their wishes. We could *not prevent* this *proposal*, which I doubt being accepted—as the rest of the Cabinet thought it could *not* be opposed, and entailed *no* material *support*. This country *never* would consent to be entangled in a *war* for this Italian quarrel....

We have a large party again to-day for the *Play* which we have to-morrow. We had a very successful one last week. The Persignys come to-day.

Now I must end. With Albert's love, ever your devoted Niece,

Victoria R.

Queen Victoria to Lord John Russell.

ANNEXATION OF SAVOY

Windsor Castle, *21st January 1860.*

The Queen returns the enclosed important letter from Lord Cowley, and Lord John Russell's answers—documents which she trusts will be communicated to the Cabinet. The Emperor shows unwillingness to evacuate Rome and Lombardy, disinclination to admit of the annexation of the Duchies to Sardinia, a feeling that he could not do so without appearing dishonourable in the eyes of Austria, and a determination to rob Sardinia of Savoy in order to repay the French Nation for the rupture with the Pope, and the abandonment of a protective tariff by the reconquest of at least a portion of the "*frontières naturelles de la France*."[430] Lord Cowley's letter proves clearly that it is (as the

[430] The cession by King Victor Emmanuel of Savoy (the cradle of his race) and of Nice to France was the consideration offered at Plombières for obtaining French support to the movement for freeing Italy "from the Alps to the Adriatic"; that result not having been achieved, a like price was now offered for French assistance in effecting the annexation of the Central Italian provinces.

Queen all along felt and often said) most dangerous for us to offer to bind ourselves to a common action with the Emperor with regard to Italy, whilst he has entered into a variety of engagements with the different parties engaged in the dispute, of which we know nothing, and has objects in view which we can only guess at, and which have not the good of Italy in view, but his own aggrandisement to the serious detriment of Europe.

With regard to Lord John Russell's answer, the Queen will only say that our proposal having been made by us after serious reflection and the anxious discussion of the Cabinet and the Queen, no deviation from it ought to take place without affording them ample opportunity to consider the bearings and probable results of such alteration.

VICTOR EMMANUEL

Queen Victoria to Viscount Palmerston.

Windsor Castle, *22nd January 1860.*

The Queen has received Lord Palmerston's note and enclosures. She rather expects to be advised by her Ministers as to the course to be adopted in matters which may lead to angry debate in the House of Lords, than to give personal directions on a case so incompletely placed before her; Lord Willoughby's letter does not even name the persons in question nor the grounds upon which he assumes "they would not be received at Court."[431] The Queen does not know how far admission or non-admission trenches upon the privileges of the House; from the submitted printed regulation, however, she would gather that the Lord High Chamberlain has full power to admit or exclude. If Lord Palmerston were to see Lord Granville as Leader, and the Lord Chancellor as Speaker, of the House of Lords together with Lord Willoughby, they might so far discuss the question as to enable Lord Palmerston to submit a decision for the Queen's consideration to-morrow.

---

[431] Lord Willoughby's question had reference to a Peeress, who, he thought, would not be received at Court. The difference between a State Opening of Parliament and a Drawing-room was pointed out in Lord Palmerston's reply. Though it would be "unpleasant to the Peeresses to find themselves sitting next to a person with whom they do not associate," the Premier advised no interference with the lady in question, if she persisted in attending.

Queen Victoria to the King of the Belgians.

Windsor Castle, *31st January 1860.*

My dearest Uncle,—Accept my warmest thanks for your kind letter of the 27th, received on Saturday—by which I am delighted to see what sport you have had. I have *such* an aversion for hunting that I am *quite* pleased to hear of the destruction of the *fifty-one* foxes. I suppose it was not cold enough for *wolves*.

I think Parliament has had a wholesome effect upon certain people; and that they are *altogether frightened*. There has been a strong despatch written relative to Savoy—and altogether I think matters are taking a better turn. The feeling of *all* parties and this *whole* country is—to *let Italy settle its own affairs*—and *England to keep quite out of it....*

We shall see the good Aumales to-night, who are staying with the Van de Weyers at *New Lodge*,[432] which is *un vrai bijou*: you *must* see it when you come here again, for it is one of the nicest and most charming houses I know.

I must now end. With Albert's affectionate love, ever your devoted Niece,

Victoria R.

The King of the Belgians to Queen Victoria.

Laeken, *3rd February 1860.*

My dearest Victoria,—... New Lodge must be exceedingly pretty, and, God willing, I ought once to get sight of it. By all one can hear, the Italians certainly will attack the Austrians, if they are not told to leave it alone; Victor Emmanuel speaks openly of it, just as he did last year, when one also thought it was a mere bravado. Things look in most directions very gloomy; my neighbour is creating dangers for himself by the constitutional Government he gives to Italy. The French say, "Sommes-nous moins que les Italiens pour avoir un peu de liberté?" This may become more dangerous as things move on, not that I should regret it; we can never have any security as long as France remains without a constitutional Government. We have had slight beginnings of cold, but not much of it, but the glass was fearfully low. My ball of the 1st was rather pretty, and people were in great dancing

[432] On the borders of Windsor Forest.

mood. Princess Orloff, a Troubetzkoï, is a very pleasing young woman. There is also a pretty Princess Metchersky. We had some new English families *inconceivably ugly*; it is quite a calamity, they look as if they had been selected on purpose. Having still the happiness of being one of your Privy Council, I mean to propose some measure to obviate such a sad state of affairs. We have all of a sudden snow.... Your truly devoted Uncle,

Leopold R.

Queen Victoria to Sir Charles Wood.

INDIAN HONOURS

Windsor Castle, *9th February 1860.*

The Queen has attentively read Lord Canning's letter and enclosure. She quite agrees in his proposal as to the nature of the Order of Chivalry to be instituted, and the details which he recommends with regard to it. She also thinks that titles should be confined to those now known and borne in India, and to be given sparingly; but would object to the illimited power of the Governor-General and Viceroy in this respect. The highest dignities and titles ought to proceed directly from the Crown at the Viceroy's recommendation. The Queen concurs in the view that honours cannot well be made hereditary amongst Hindoos and Mussulmans, but where Princes (as we may hope will be the case sometimes hereafter) have become Christians, the hereditary nature of honours should not be withheld.[433] ...

Queen Victoria to Viscount Palmerston.

THE QUEEN AND HER MINISTERS

Windsor Castle, *10th February 1860.*

[433] Lord Canning had written that he thought it would be best to adhere to the precise titles already in use in India, and that they should be at the direct disposal of the Queen's Representative, without reference to the Crown. He did not recommend that titles should be hereditary (except in very special cases), in a country where primogeniture was not established. As to the proposed Order of Knighthood, Lord Canning thought that the institution of such an Order would be both expedient and opportune. He recommended that it should include both British-born and Native subjects.

The Queen sends a letter to Lord Palmerston which she has received yesterday evening from Lord John Russell.[434] She is induced to do so from a feeling that it is to Lord Palmerston, as head of the Government, that she has to look, when she may have reason to take exception to the tone of communications she may receive from members of his Cabinet. Lord Palmerston will not fail to perceive that the enclosed is not the kind of communication which the Foreign Secretary ought to make, when asked by his Sovereign to explain the views of the Cabinet upon a question so important and momentous as the annexation of Savoy to France, and the steps which they propose to take with regard to it. She need not remind Lord Palmerston that in her letter communicated to the Cabinet she had given no opinion whatever upon Italian liberation from a foreign yoke, nor need she protest against a covert insinuation, such as is contained in Lord John's letter, that she is no well-wisher of mankind and indifferent to its freedom and happiness. But she must refer to the constitutional position of her Ministers towards herself. They are responsible for the advice they gave her, but they are bound fully, respectfully, and openly to place before her the grounds and reasons upon which their advice may be founded, to enable her to judge whether she can give her assent to that advice or not. The Government must come to a standstill if the Minister meets a demand for explanation with an answer like the following: "I was asked by the Cabinet to give an answer, but as I do not agree with you, I think it useless to explain my views."

The Queen must demand that respect which is due from a Minister to his Sovereign. As the Queen must consider the enclosed letter as deficient in it, she thinks Lord John Russell might probably wish to reconsider it, and asks Lord Palmerston to return it to him with that view.

That Lord Palmerston may be acquainted with the course the correspondence has taken, the Queen encloses the two preceding letters.

---

[434] The letter ran:—"Lord John Russell unfortunately does not partake your Majesty's opinions in regard to Italy, and he is unwilling to obtrude on your Majesty unnecessary statements of his views.... Whatever may be the consequence, the liberation of the Italian people from a foreign yoke is, in the eyes of Lord Palmerston and Lord John Russell, an increase of freedom and happiness at which as well-wishers to mankind they cannot but rejoice."

Viscount Palmerston to Queen Victoria.

MR GLADSTONE'S BUDGET

94 Piccadilly, *10th February 1860.*

Viscount Palmerston presents his humble duty to your Majesty, and begs to state that Mr Gladstone made this afternoon his financial statement.[435] His speech lasted three hours, from five to eight, and was admirable, detailed, clear, comprehensive and eloquent; and he did not appear to be fatigued by the effort.[436] The statement was well received by the House, and though parts of the arrangement may, and no doubt will, be disputed and attacked as the various measures of which the arrangement is composed, pass through the House, there seems to be a fair probability that the Government will not sustain any serious defeat upon any part of the arrangement. The scheme is too extensive and complicated to admit of an abstract of it being given to your Majesty in this Report; but no doubt a condensed summary of it will be given in the newspapers of to-morrow.

Queen Victoria to Viscount Palmerston.

Windsor Castle, *11th February 1860.*

The Queen acknowledges the receipt of Lord Palmerston's two letters of yesterday evening. She willingly accepts Lord John Russell's expressions of regret, and certainly was led to read that one passage which Lord Palmerston explains in the sense which he supposed.

The Queen has received the draft to Lord Cowley, and has written her observations upon it to Lord John, who will communicate them to him. She thinks that the omissions which she has pointed out can be very well supplied consistently with that international courtesy which Lord Palmerston truly says ought to be observed.[437]

---

[435] The Budget of 1860 was contemporaneous with the commercial treaty with France negotiated by Mr Cobden, reducing *inter alia* the import duties on French wine and brandy, and English coal, flax, and pig-iron. Mr Gladstone abolished the duties on a large number of imports, and proposed to repeal that on paper (regarded not only as a means for the diffusion of knowledge, but a commodity in various industries).

[436] This was all the more remarkable, as the Budget had been postponed owing to his illness.

[437] In this despatch, Lord John wrote that the Government could not believe that a country in the circumstances of France could be endangered by the existence, "on the other side of the Alps, of a State of 11,000,000 of people

Earl Granville to the Prince Albert.

Brighton, *11th February 1860.*

Sir,—Lord John produced before the Cabinet his draft of despatch in answer to M. Thouvenel. He read, without allusion to the previous correspondence, the Queen's Memorandum on his draft.

Lord Palmerston supported Lord John, who was fidgety and nervous. We all criticised the draft. We thought it too much or too little. We recommended that he should either write shortly, saying that he did not acquiesce in M. Thouvenel's arguments, but as the French Government did not consider the question as now in existence, and promised that it should not be revised without the consent of Savoy, and consultation with the Great Powers, if the Government would reserve what they had to say on a question of such immense European importance—or going into the subject he should state the whole argument and objections of the Government to the scheme.

We thought the historical reminiscences offensive to France, while the language of the despatch was not sufficiently firm to satisfy what was expected from the Government. We warned him that in this case public opinion would be at least as critical as the Queen.

Lord John gave us to understand that he would alter his draft, but I do not feel any security that it will be done in a satisfactory manner.

I am, Sir, with the greatest respect, your Royal Highness's obedient, humble, and faithful servant,

Granville.

Earl Cowley to Lord John Russell.

(Submitted to the Queen.)

LORD COWLEY AND THE EMPEROR

Paris, *7th March 1860.*

My dear Lord John,—I send a messenger this evening, in order that you may not hear from any one else of the passage of arms which took place between the Emperor and myself yesterday evening. You will find the account of it in the enclosed despatch. The more I reflect on it, the less I think that I could pass over the Emperor's conduct and

---

lately joined by a cement not yet dry, threatened, on the side of Lombardy, by Austria, and not very certain of its own independence."

language without notice. His tone and manner were really offensive, and if I had let them pass unheeded might have been repeated on another occasion. I must say that nothing could have been more friendly than His Majesty's bearing after I had spoken to him. He was profuse in his excuses, and the Empress told me later in the evening that he was *désolé*—"qu'il s'était laissé entraîner par un mouvement d'humeur," etc. I, of course, said that I should think no more about it.

One good thing has been gained by it, that the Emperor has declared that he does not mean to act in defiance of the opinion of the Great Powers....

I wish that I had not this disagreeable history to trouble you with, but do not attach greater importance to it than it merits. I look upon it as at an end.

Cowley.

/Enclosure./

LORD COWLEY AND THE EMPEROR

Earl Cowley to Lord John Russell.

(Submitted to the Queen.)

Paris, *7th March 1860.*

My Lord,—It is with extreme regret that I call your Lordship's attention to the following occurrence.

There was a concert last night at the Tuileries, to which the Chiefs of the Diplomatic Body were invited. On these occasions seats are assigned to the Ambassadors according to their accidental rank, and I was placed between the Nuntio and the Russian Ambassador. It is customary for the Emperor, during the interval between the two parts of the concert, to say a few words to each of the Ambassadors individually, and it is obvious that what His Majesty says to one may easily be overheard by that one's immediate neighbours.

Yesterday evening the Emperor, after saying a few words of no importance to the Nuntio, addressed himself to me in a manner and tone very unusual with him, animadverting upon the hostile sentiments evinced towards him in the English Parliament and Press.[438] "Wishing

[438] The annexation of Savoy had been debated in the House of Commons, and Mr Bright had expressed his readiness that Savoy should rather perish than

to avoid a discussion, I merely observed that I regretted that matters should be in such a state, but that His Majesty must be aware that there was quite as great irritation on this side the water. The Emperor enquired sharply whether this was to be wondered at, considering the terms and imputations applied to himself, and to the French nation, in England? They were only defending themselves against unfair attacks, His Majesty said. It was really too bad, he continued; he had done all in his power to maintain a good understanding with England, but the conduct of England rendered it impossible. What had England to do with Savoy? And why was she not to be satisfied with the declaration that His Majesty had made to me, that he had no intention to annex Savoy to France without having previously obtained the consent of the Great Powers.

LORD COWLEY'S REMONSTRANCE

"Pardon me, Sire," I said, "for interrupting your Majesty, but it is just what you did not say. Had you permitted me to convey that assurance to Her Majesty's Government, I will answer for it that all those interpellations in Parliament would long since have ceased, and that Her Majesty's Government and the country would at all events have awaited the decision at which the Great Powers might have arrived."

"But I told you," continued the Emperor, "that I would consult the Great Powers."

"Yes, Sire," I replied, "but your Majesty did not add that you would abide by their decision."

This conversation had taken place, not only within the hearing of the Russian Ambassador, but the Emperor's remarks were addressed almost as much to my colleague as to myself. Turning then entirely towards General Kisseleff, the Emperor continued: "The conduct of England is inexplicable. I have done all in my power to keep on the best terms with her; but I am at my wits' end *(je n'en puis plus)*. What," His Majesty exclaimed again, "has England to do with Savoy? What would have been the consequence if, when she took possession of the Island of Perim[439] for the safety of her Eastern dominions, I had raised the same objections that she has now raised to the annexation of Savoy, which I want as much for the safety of France?"

---

that England should interfere in a matter in which she had no concern. He was sharply censured by Lord John Manners.

[439] Perim had been permanently taken possession of by Great Britain, in 1857.

His Majesty continued to speak for a few seconds in the same strain, and I felt my position to be most awkward. With the remembrance of His Majesty's intemperate words to M. de Hübner on New Year's Day, 1859,[440] in my mind, I did not like to leave unnoticed observations of the tendency I have mentioned. At the same time I had to bear in mind that I was not present on an official occasion, but that I was the Emperor's guest, and that it would not be right to continue a discussion in the presence of others. These thoughts passed rapidly through my mind, and I determined to be guided by a night's reflection in taking any further step in this matter. What that reflection might have produced I cannot say, but circumstances led to more immediate explanations.

As the Emperor moved on, the circle in which we were standing was not strictly kept, and after a few minutes I found myself standing a little in front, in the open space round which the circle was formed. The Emperor again accosted me, and was beginning in the same strain, when I ventured to interrupt His Majesty and to tell him that I considered myself justified in calling his attention to the unusual course he had adopted, in indulging, in presence of the Russian Ambassador, in his animadversions on the conduct of England. That His Majesty, if he had, or thought he had, any cause for remonstrance or blame with regard to England, should address himself to me, was not only natural, but would be a course which I should always beg him to take, because free discussion was the best remedy for pent-up feeling. I should answer as best I could, and endeavour to convince His Majesty when I thought him wrong. Or if His Majesty considered it right to complain of the conduct of England to the Russian Ambassador, I had no desire to interfere, provided it was not done in my presence; but what I could not approve, or consider compatible with my own dignity, or that of the Government which I represented, was that complaints respecting England should be addressed to me in the hearing of the Russian Ambassador, and to the Russian Ambassador in my hearing.

Leaving then this official tone, I added that, considering the long and intimate relations which His Majesty had been graciously pleased to permit should exist between himself and me, and knowing, as he did, the personal attachment which I bore him, and the anxiety which I had ever manifested to smooth difficulties and prevent misunderstandings between the two Governments, in doing which I had perhaps

[440] See *ante*, p. 310, note 2.

exposed myself to the suspicion of being more French than I ought to be, I had not expected to have been addressed, as I had been, in the presence of the Russian Ambassador, or to have heard words addressed to that Ambassador complaining of the sentiments of the English nation.

The Emperor frequently interrupted me, expressing his great regret at what had occurred. He could assure me, His Majesty said, that he had spoken without any bad intention—that he had just read what had occurred in Parliament the night before, and that he had been greatly hurt at the strictures passed upon his conduct; I must recollect further that he had not spoken of the Government, but of those who attacked him. Again, His Majesty begged me to think no more of the matter, repeating the assurance that he had spoken without intention.

In the course of this second conversation the Emperor again asked, but in a very different tone, why England had taken up the question of Savoy which so little regarded her. Had it been Prussia or one of the Continental Powers, His Majesty could have understood it, but not a word of remonstrance had proceeded from any one of them. I replied that I did not think the Emperor could rely on that silence as indicating approbation, but at all events, I said, the position of Her Majesty's Government was very different from that of the other powers. How was it possible, I asked, for Her Majesty's Government to remain silent in presence of the interpellations respecting Savoy which were, night after night, put to them? And if His Majesty enquired why these interpellations were put, I would answer him that, if my judgment was correct, it was not so much on account of the actual plan of annexing Savoy, as on account of the circumstances connected with the whole transaction. They were, in fact, interpellations of mistrust. And how, I asked, could it be otherwise? What could the English people think on its transpiring that in spite of His Majesty's declarations, both before and during the war, that in going to war he meditated no special advantages for France, overtures had positively been made months before, to Sardinia, for the eventual cession of Savoy; why had not His Majesty told us fairly, in commencing this war, that if, by the results of the war, the territory of Sardinia should be greatly augmented, he might be obliged, in deference to public opinion in France, to ask for some territorial advantage? Such a declaration, although it might have rendered the British Government still more anxious to prevent the war, would have hindered all the manifestation of public opinion which is now taking place.

THE EMPEROR'S *AMENDE*

The Emperor seemed to feel the weight of these observations, and he ended the conversation by saying, that if this question of Savoy should go further, he had pledged himself to consult the Great Powers, and that he need hardly add that if their opinion should be unfavourable to his wishes, it would have great weight with him. "It is not likely," said His Majesty, "that I should act against the advice of Europe."

I end, my Lord, as I commenced, in regretting this occurrence. I could have wished that the Emperor had not spoken to me a second time yesterday, and that I had had a little time for reflection. I feel that I spoke to His Majesty under considerable emotion, caused by the tone and manner which he had adopted; but I am certain that not a word escaped me which was not respectful to himself. To have passed the matter over, would, in my judgment, have been a fault, but on the whole I should have preferred conveying impressions to His Majesty through M. Thouvenel. I earnestly trust, however, that Her Majesty's Government will view my conduct in a favourable light.

It is but justice to my Russian colleague to state that nothing could have been in better taste than his remarks in answer to the Emperor's observations to him. I have told General Kisseleff this morning that having had an opportunity to do so, I had expressed to the Emperor the opinion that it would have been better had His Majesty avoided irritating topics concerning England in the presence of another foreign representative. It is not my intention to open my lips on the subject to any one else.

Cowley.

Lord John Russell to Queen Victoria.

Chesham Place, *9th March 1860.*

Lord John Russell presents his humble duty to your Majesty, and has the honour to submit a despatch which he received in a private letter from Lord Cowley.

The strange scene related in it will remind your Majesty of some scenes already famous in the history of Napoleon I. and Napoleon III.

Lord John Russell requests your Majesty's permission to write a secret despatch in answer, entirely approving the conduct and language of Lord Cowley.

Queen Victoria to Lord John Russell.

THE QUEEN'S APPROVAL

Osborne, *10th March 1860.*

The Queen, in returning Lord Cowley's private letter and secret despatch, agrees with Lord John Russell, that he has deserved praise for his mode of answering the Emperor's Napoleonic address.[441] ...

Queen Victoria to Sir Charles Wood.

Osborne, *12th March 1860.*

The Queen is sorry to find that Lord Canning does not approve of any of the modes suggested by Sir Charles Wood, for giving the Chiefs security of title and possession. The object appears to the Queen so important as a means of protection against the temptation of our own representatives to seize upon the possessions of these Chiefs at any convenient opportunity—and as a means of giving confidence to those Chiefs that the Queen's Government is not actuated by rapacity—that she must hope Lord Canning will indicate some mode, appearing less objectionable to him, for attaining the same object. The Queen would be glad to have a copy of Lord Canning's letter.

Queen Victoria to Lord John Russell.

SWISS CLAIMS

Buckingham Palace, *25th March 1860.*

The Queen has just seen the Swiss Note, and has returned it to the Foreign Office.[442] With reference to Lord John Russell's letter of this

---

[441] The ratification by the House of Commons of the Commercial Treaty, and Mr Gladstone's message to the Emperor, enclosing a copy of his Budget speech, gave the Emperor an opportunity of making amends to Lord Cowley for his hasty language.

[442] The Swiss Government claimed that the districts of Chablais and Faucigny (being parts of Savoy which had been handed over to Sardinia by the Treaty of Vienna under a guarantee for their neutrality) should be given to Switzerland for the protection of their frontier. The French Emperor maintained that it was sufficient for him to guarantee the neutrality of those districts. Speaking on the night of the 26th, Lord John Russell said: "The powers of Europe, if they wish to maintain peace, must respect each other's limits, and, above all, restore and not disturb that commercial confidence which is the result of

morning, she has only to express her anxiety that her Government should not look upon this question as one of an *optional* character to take up or not. We have no choice, and the consideration whether what we are doing may be pleasing or displeasing to France cannot be entertained for a moment, although the Queen is grieved to find from Lord Cowley's last letter that he considers the question from that point of view. We are parties to a treaty of guarantee together with other Powers, and have as such a clear and solemn *duty* to perform. We should therefore openly and avowedly call upon our partners in this treaty and guarantee to consider the note addressed by the Swiss Confederation to us.

The proper course would be to summon the Ministers of the Contracting Powers to the Foreign Office (not excluding the French Ambassador), and to go with them into the matter. This would take it out of the hands of the Emperor and M. de Thouvenel, and make (the Queen is certain of it) a deep impression upon them.

The Queen wishes this letter to be shown to Lord Palmerston and Lord John's other colleagues.

Queen Victoria to Lord John Russell.

Buckingham Palace, *2nd April 1860.*

The Queen has received Lord John Russell's letter and Memorandum.[443] In whatever Lord John might say in the House of Commons, care should be taken not to give the French a handle to make the other Powers believe that there exists an understanding between them and us. It is by making each of them believe in their turn that the others have agreed with France that the Emperor paralyses their action. If he will promise distinctly to give up the neutral territory to Switzerland, that would be an understanding which we might well avow, but the Queen fears Count Persigny with all his anxiety to smooth matters (as he says) will not be able to give this assurance, and consequently if Lord John sent the Commons home with a declaration that matters would be *satisfactorily* settled, and the Emperor intends to keep the

---

peace, which tends to peace, and which ultimately forms the happiness of nations."

[443] Describing a conversation between Lord Palmerston and Persigny, the former suggesting that a statement should be made by Lord John in the House, in reference to the securities to be given for the neutrality and independence of Switzerland, such as would pacify the Emperor.

neutral territory after all, it would unnecessarily make them dupes once more, as the Government have from time to time given assurances based on French promises, which were belied by subsequent acts.

Is the Memorandum for the Queen to keep?

The Conference should be here, and on *no* account at Paris.

Queen Victoria to the King of the Belgians.

DEATH OF PRINCE HOHENLOHE

Buckingham Palace, *25th April 1860.*

My dearest Uncle,—I write to you on this paper to-day, as it is our good Alice's birthday—her seventeenth! She is a good, dear, amiable child, and in very good looks just now. Her future is still undecided, she is quite free, and *all* we wish is a good, kind husband—*no* brilliant position (which there is not to be got), but a quiet, comfortable position.

Bertie returned last night delighted with his tour,[444] and with our beloved old Coburg, in *spite of snow*. I will tell him to give you an account of it. He made a very favourable impression there. He gives a good account of dear Stockmar too.

Many, many thanks for your dear kind letter of the 20th, with the enclosure from dear Charlotte, whose happy, contented disposition is a great blessing.

I was sure you would grieve for poor, dear, honest Ernest Hohenlohe[445]; Feodore feels it dreadfully, and writes beautifully about it. Thank God! she has every comfort in her second son, Hermann, who—by an arrangement made last year with the eldest and poor Ernest—has the entire management of everything; Charles has a certain income and Weikersheim[446]; while Hermann has Langenburg and the management of everything else; he naturally leaves the Austrian Service.

---

[444] The Prince of Wales had been spending a week at Coburg and Gotha, which he had not previously seen.

[445] Prince Ernest died on the 12th of April, and was succeeded by his second son Hermann.

[446] A small town in Würtemberg, and part of the estate of the Princes of Hohenlohe-Langenburg.

We are too delighted to hear that you are, D.V., ready to come by the 2nd of June; it will be so great a pleasure, and to dear Mamma too, who is *unberufen* wonderfully well. She is here again since yesterday, and will stay till the 2nd. Clém was quite astonished at her looks. The poor Queen will be seventy-eight to-morrow. She is very tolerably well.

How well do I remember that speech of Oscar's in the carriage. It certainly took us *all* in....

I fear I must end for to-day. With Albert's affectionate love, ever your devoted Niece,

Victoria R.

Bertie was much pleased with little Louise.[447]

Queen Victoria to Lord John Russell.

ENGLAND AND NAPLES

[*Undated. ? 26th April 1860.*]

The Queen has just received Lord John Russell's letter. She must say that she would consider it the *deepest* degradation to this country if she was compelled to appear at the Emperor's Congress summoned to Paris, in order to register and put her seal to the acts of spoliation of the Emperor!

Lord Cowley was very strong on the effect which our yielding that point would have on his position at the French Court.

Queen Victoria to Lord John Russell.

Buckingham Palace, *30th April 1860.*

The Queen thinks that the main argument is omitted in the draft, viz. that the attempts, such as Sardinia is suspected to contemplate, are morally bad and reprehensible in themselves, besides being politically inexpedient. The Queen would be sorry to see a despatch go forth on this subject, arguing on the ground of expediency alone. She trusts Lord John Russell will find it easy to introduce a passage which would place it on record, that we do attach importance to public justice and morality. When amended, the Queen would like to have a copy of the draft.

---

[447] Elder child of the Duke of Brabant (now King Leopold II.).

Lord John Russell to Queen Victoria.

THE DOCTRINES OF 1688

House of Commons, *30th April 1860.*

Lord John Russell presents his humble duty to your Majesty. He is sorry he cannot agree that there would be any moral wrong in assisting to overthrow the Government of the King of the Two Sicilies. The best writers on International Law consider it a merit to overthrow a tyrannical government, and there have been few governments so tyrannical as that of Naples. Of course the King of Sardinia has no right to assist the people of the Two Sicilies unless he was asked by them to do so, as the Prince of Orange was asked by the best men in England to overthrow the tyranny of James II.—an attempt which has received the applause of all our great public writers, and is the origin of our present form of government.[448]

Queen Victoria to Lord John Russell.

Buckingham Palace, *30th April 1860.*

The Queen has received Lord John Russell's letter, and trusts he will see, upon further reflection, that the case before us is not one in which the Revolution of 1688, and the advent of William III. called to the Throne, can be appealed to as a parallel. The draft warns the Government of Sardinia "*not to seek for new acquisitions*," as the new "*Provinces* annexed have hardly as yet been thoroughly amalgamated." Now, no public writer nor the International Law will call it morally right, that one state should abet revolution in another, not with the disinterested object of defending a suffering people against tyranny, but in order to extinguish that State and make it "an acquisition" of its own. If William III. had made England a Province of Holland, he would not have received the applause Lord John quotes. The Queen trusts that in appreciation of this distinction, he will introduce some amendment in the sense indicated in her former letter.

---

[448] See *ante*, p. 383.

Lord John Russell to Queen Victoria.

House of Commons, *30th April 1860.*

Lord John Russell presents his humble duty to your Majesty; he confesses he cannot see anything morally wrong in giving aid to an insurrection in the kingdoms of Naples and Sicily. But he admits that to do so for the sake of making new acquisitions would be criminal, and that he is not justified in imputing this motive to the King of Sardinia. Count Cavour would probably at once disclaim it.

He therefore proposes to alter these words. The despatch went this evening by the usual messenger; but, if your Majesty approves of the alteration, it can be made to-morrow morning by telegraph to Turin.

Sir Charles Wood to Queen Victoria.

INDIAN HONOURS

India Office, *3rd May 1860.*

Sir Charles Wood, with his humble duty, begs to submit for your Majesty's consideration, whether the letters of thanks to those Civil Servants who have not been thought deserving of the honour of C.B. should run in your Majesty's name, or in that of the Government.

Your Majesty desired that thanks for service should be in your Majesty's name, but there will be nearly two hundred of these letters to different officers, and Sir Charles Wood doubted whether it would be right to use your Majesty's name so profusely. He is inclined to think that it would be better to use your Majesty's name only when addressing higher officers. Sir Charles Wood encloses drafts of letters in both ways.

Sir Charles Wood also encloses an address on the occasion of the Thanksgiving in India, delivered by a Hindoo.

Queen Victoria to Sir Charles Wood.

Buckingham Palace, *4th May 1860.*

The Queen returns these papers. She wishes the thanks to Civil Servants to be given in all cases, where to be given by the Home Government, in her own name. The Bath or Knighthood comes directly from the Sovereign, and so should the thanks; the Civil Servants are the Queen's servants, and not the servants of the Government. The

Hindoo address is very striking and gratifying as a symptom.[449] Presuming that Sir Charles does not want the copy back again, the Queen has kept it.

Queen Victoria to the King of the Belgians.

Buckingham Palace, *8th May 1860.*

My dearest Uncle,—... Really it is too bad! *No* country, no human being would ever dream of *disturbing* or *attacking* France; every one would be glad to see her prosperous; but *she* must needs disturb every quarter of the Globe and try to make mischief and set every one by the ears; and, of course, it will end some day in a *regular crusade* against *the universal disturber* of *the world!* It is really monstrous!

Dear Mamma returned to Frogmore on Friday, and Alfred left us on Thursday, sailed from Portsmouth on Saturday, but had to stop at Plymouth for some derangement in the machinery till to-day. He was very low at going, though very happy to return to his ship. Now, with Albert's affectionate love, ever your devoted Niece,

Victoria R.

Queen Victoria to the King of the Belgians.

VISIT TO ALDERSHOT

Buckingham Palace, *15th May 1860.*

My dearest Uncle,—Many, many thanks for your very kind letter received on Saturday. We returned yesterday evening from Aldershot, where we spent two very pleasant days with very warm weather. Sunday was a beautiful day and we rode over to Farnham, the Bishop of Winchester's Palace, and it was quite beautiful, the country is so green and sweet—and enjoyable. The warm rain of last week has produced a burst of Spring which is quite beautiful. Yesterday morning it rained when we first went out, but it cleared and became a beautiful day, and we had a pretty field day. Your old Regiment looked extremely well. In the afternoon we saw some very interesting rifle-shooting. The whole Army practises this now most unremittingly, and we saw three different companies of the Guards fire at 300 yards, and so on to 900 yards, and *hit* the target! They fired in *volleys*. It is very satisfactory,

---

[449] The copy of this address does not seem to have been preserved.

as this precision would be very *telling* in action. I think you would be interested by it.

I *hope* you have forgiven my hurried note of Saturday—but I was *so* anxious at the time. We go to Osborne on the 19th, I am happy to say, till the 31st.

Affairs continue to be very threatening, and keep everybody in suspense.... Ever, dearest Uncle, your devoted Niece,

Victoria R.

Queen Victoria to the King of the Belgians.

Osborne, *22nd May 1860.*

My dearest Uncle,—I write to you from here, where it is wonderfully beautiful and unusually *hot* for May—it is *quite* like July, but the *late* Spring has brought out everything together in the most wonderful manner. The foliage of many trees is hardly out yet, but there are all the fruit-trees in fullest blossom—the lilacs and peonies out—the thorns only beginning and every wild flower in profusion—the grass splendidly green, and a fragrance about everything which is too delicious; and the birds singing *most* beautifully. The nightingales were last night singing all round the house....

Affairs are in a most bewildered state. Lord Palmerston is *very stout and right* about our neighbour. I am glad to be able to *refute most positively* the report of our *ships* having *prevented* the Neapolitans from firing; the *case* is *quite* clear, and the French and Neapolitan Governments themselves have spread this falsehood.

The House of Lords have thrown the Bill for the Abolition of the paper Duties[450] *out* by a very large majority, which is a *very good thing*. It will save us a large amount of revenue.

I must end for to-day. Hoping that these lines will find you quite well, ever your devoted *Daughter* (I *wrote* by mistake *but* will leave, as it *only* expresses what *my feelings* are) and Niece,

Victoria R.

---

[450] This part of Mr Gladstone's financial scheme had lost a good deal of its early popularity: it had only passed the third reading in the Commons by the small majority of nine, and the Premier had already told the Queen that the Peers would perform a public service by rejecting it. The majority against it in the House of Lords was 89.

We have quite a small party on the 1st, with some choral singing.

Viscount Palmerston to Queen Victoria.

THE HOUSE OF LORDS AND MONEY BILLS

94 Piccadilly, *22nd May 1860.*

Viscount Palmerston presents his humble duty to your Majesty, and begs to state that the Cabinet met to-day at half-past twelve to consider what (if anything) should be done in consequence of the vote of the House of Lords last night. Lord John Russell, Mr Gladstone, and Mr Milner Gibson were desirous of finding some means of visiting their displeasure upon the House of Lords, but it was shown to them that the only measures which could be adopted were far too violent for the occasion, and that the House of Commons itself is powerless in the matter. When the Lords do anything inconsistent with the asserted privileges of the House of Commons, as, for instance, inserting a taxing Clause in a Bill sent up to them, or making an alteration in a Money Bill sent up to them, the House of Commons is necessarily invited to do something afterwards in the matter, by assenting to what has been done by the Lords; and the Commons then assert their claimed rights by throwing out the Bill thus, improperly, as the Commons say, meddled with by the Lords; but when the Lords throw out a Bill there is nothing for the Commons to do, as the Bill has vanished, and the Commons are therefore furnished with no opportunity of asserting the right which they may claim. But, moreover, the Commons have always contended that the Lords cannot originate or alter a Money Bill, but it has never been contended that the Lords may not reject a Money Bill, though there are few instances of their having done so. These arguments at length prevailed, and by four o'clock it was agreed that Viscount Palmerston should give notice that he would on Thursday move that a Committee be appointed to examine COMMITTEE OF THE COMMONS the Journals of the House of Lords to ascertain the fate of the Bill thus lost like Sir John Franklin, and that on Friday he should move the appointment of a Committee to search for precedent applicable to the case. This course it was thought, while binding the Government to no particular course, would in some degree satisfy those who think some step necessary. The measures mentioned, though it is fair to say not actually proposed, were that Parliament should be prorogued, and reassembled either in the Autumn or Winter, that then the same Bill should be brought in, and be sent up to the Lords, and that if that Bill were again rejected, Parliament should be dissolved. It was objected to all this, that the case did not warrant such a course; that whether the Lords have or have not overstepped their proper functions, the opinion of the great majority of the public is that the Lords have done a right and useful thing (in confirmation of which it may be stated that the people in the gallery of the House of Lords are said to have joined in the cheers which broke out when the numbers of the division were announced).

Viscount Palmerston, at the meeting of the House, gave notice accordingly that he should on Thursday move for a Committee to search the Lords' Journals—a usual form of motion; and that he should on Friday move to appoint a Committee to search for precedents in order to ascertain facts; but he added that he did not take this course with any view of hostility towards the House of Lords. An attempt was made by Mr Whalley and Mr Digby Seymour to set up a complaint that this was not the sort of proceeding which the gravity of the occasion required, but this endeavour was put down by an unmistakable manifestation of a contrary opinion by the rest of the House....

Queen Victoria to the Duke of Somerset.

Buckingham Palace, *29th June 1860.*

Before sanctioning the proposed change in the Naval Uniform,[451] the Queen wishes to know what the State occasions are on which the full dress is to be worn. The officers generally wear an undress without epaulettes, which in consequence are of little inconvenience to them. She has always understood the Service to cling very much to its present uniform, and she would be sorry to shock their feelings.

Viscount Palmerston to Queen Victoria.

MR GLADSTONE SUGGESTS RESIGNATION

House of Commons, *2nd July 1860.*

(8.30 P.M.)

Viscount Palmerston has had the honour of receiving your Majesty's letter of this afternoon. Nothing of much importance as to Foreign Affairs was done at the Cabinet to-day.... The material question for discussion was the course to be pursued about the Tax Bill

---

[451] The principal change proposed was that full dress should cease to be obligatory at Courts-Martial.

Report. Lord John Russell had altered his opinion since Saturday, and had yesterday sent Viscount Palmerston a Draft of Resolution which he wished to be circulated to the members of the Cabinet before their meeting at twelve to-day....

After a long discussion, the draft, of which the enclosed is a copy, was agreed to by all except Mr Gladstone. This draft is a combination of parts of Lord John's, parts of Sir James Graham's, and parts of Viscount Palmerston's. No mention of course was made in Cabinet of Sir James Graham having made any suggestion.

When all the other members had left the room Mr Gladstone requested Viscount Palmerston to submit to your Majesty that he could no longer continue to carry on the business of his Department.[452] His opinion strongly was that action and not a Resolution was required, that one of three courses ought to be pursued: either that the Paper Duty Repeal Bill should again be sent up to the Lords; or that a Bill should be sent up for suspending the Paper Duties for a year; or that a Bill should be sent up reducing those duties gradually year by year; or fourthly that with the Repeal of the Paper Duties should be coupled the imposition of Spirit Duties. Viscount Palmerston said he really could not undertake the communication which Mr Gladstone wished to be submitted to your Majesty, and earnestly entreated Mr Gladstone to reconsider the matter; he urged in detail all the reasons which ought to dissuade such a step, and he thought that he had produced some impression on Mr Gladstone. It was agreed between them that Viscount Palmerston, instead of giving notice this afternoon of a Motion to-morrow, and laying the Resolution on the table this evening, should give notice this afternoon of a Motion for Thursday, and promise to lay the Resolution on the table to-morrow. This gives Mr Gladstone more time to think, and more room to turn round in. Mr Milner Gibson has no intention of going out, and has so told Mr Gladstone, strongly advising him to stay in; and Viscount Palmerston's impression is that Mr Gladstone, having failed to become master of the Cabinet by a threat of resignation, will in the end yield to the almost unanimous decision of his colleagues. The only person who supported Mr Gladstone's views, except Mr Milner Gibson, was the Duke of Argyll, who,

[452] This is said to have been an incident of frequent occurrence during the second administration of Lord Palmerston.

however, like Mr Gibson, had no intention whatever of accompanying Mr Gladstone in resignation.[453]...

Viscount Palmerston to Queen Victoria.

PRIVILEGE RESOLUTIONS

Piccadilly, *6th July 1860.*

Viscount Palmerston presents his humble duty to your Majesty, and begs to state that the House of Commons this night passed the three Privilege Resolutions after two divisions.[454]...

The Debate which did not begin till half-past eight, after questions on the adjournment to Monday, was commenced by Mr Digby Seymour, Member for Southampton, who went into an elaborate discussion of the precedents mentioned in the appendix to the Report of the Committee, arguing against the right of the Lords. He attacked Viscount Palmerston's speech, and highly praised that of Mr Gladstone, who, he said, if he lost his place in the Cabinet in consequence of that speech would be rewarded by a Throne in the affections of the Nation. Mr Horsman then made a very able, eloquent, and remarkable speech, well worth reading....

Mr Bright made an indignation speech in reply. He went over the same ground as the former speaker about the precedents, was astonished and shocked at Mr Horsman's speech, was displeased with the Resolutions, and with Viscount Palmerston's speech, was in admiration unbounded of Mr Gladstone, but all the time was so hoarse that his efforts to make himself heard gave to his utterance an appearance of passion even greater than that which he actually felt. After his speech the House began skirmishing as to the question of finishing the Debate or adjourning it, but the Resolutions were at last agreed to.

---

[453] The Queen wrote to King Leopold: "As I told you in my little note of Sunday, Lord John became *quite* reasonable, and is very moderate about this affair; on the other hand Mr Gladstone has threatened to resign—and it is still uncertain if he will not persist in his intention. He is terribly excited."

[454] The Resolutions, which the Committee recommended, and the House of Commons adopted, declared *inter alia* that the Commons had in their own hands the power "so to impose and remit taxes, and frame bills of supply, that their rights as to the matter, manner, measure, and time might be maintained inviolate."

The King of the Belgians to Queen Victoria.

Laeken, *13th July 1860.*

My beloved Victoria,—...Bertie has then set out on his interesting journey,[455] which though not without fatigue will be full of information and satisfaction for his young mind. I am glad to hear that dear Albert went with him,[456] he can have no equal to his good and distinguished father for kindness, and a wise guidance of his young life....

Queen Victoria to the King of the Belgians.

Osborne, *31st July 1860.*

My dearest Uncle,— ... I venture now to confide a *secret* to you—the details of which you shall hear verbally from us when we have the happiness of seeing you in October. It is that *our* surmises respecting Louis of Hesse[457] have turned out to be true, and that we have *reason* to *hope* that this *affair* will be in due time realised. The feelings are very reciprocal on both sides, though nothing definitive will be settled till the young people meet again, probably later this Autumn (*but not in Germany*). Please do not say anything about it to any one. Your very great kindness and affection for our children has induced me to mention this to *you*, who moreover *saw the first dawning of these prospects.*

Dear Mamma starts to-day for Edinburgh—sleeping to-night at York. With Albert's affectionate love, ever your devoted Niece,

Victoria R.

---

[455] In consequence of the loyal and patriotic assistance rendered by Canada during the Crimean War, and the expressed desire of the Canadians to be visited by the Queen in person and to welcome one of her sons as Governor-General, it was decided that the Prince of Wales should make a tour there. During the course of the visit, which was made in company with the Duke of Newcastle, the Prince opened the magnificent bridge over the St Lawrence; he subsequently availed himself of President Buchanan's invitation already referred to (*ante*, p. 373), and was received with the greatest enthusiasm at Washington. The Prince returned to England in November.

[456] Referring to a previous letter, in which the Queen had informed the King of the Belgians that Prince Albert had accompanied the Prince of Wales as far as Plymouth.

[457] Prince Louis of Hesse, afterwards Grand Duke Louis IV.

Queen Victoria to Earl Canning.

TRANQUILLITY OF INDIA

Osborne, *2nd August 1860.*

The Queen thanks Lord Canning very much for a most interesting letter of the 30th of May, giving a most comprehensive and gratifying account of his progress through her Indian dominions, and of his reception of the different Princes and Chiefs. Such reception and such kind considerate treatment of them is, as Lord Canning knows, entirely in unison with the Queen's *own* feelings, and both the Prince and herself have been peculiarly gratified at reading this account, and feel sure of the good effect it must have on these Princes, and on India in general.

We have just seen Lord Clyde looking wonderfully well; he speaks in high terms of Lord Canning, and enthusiastically of dear Lady Canning. Alas! another most valuable public servant and friend of ours, Lord Elphinstone,[458] only returned to die! Lord Canning will grieve much no doubt to hear this.

Both he and Lady Canning will have heard with interest of the birth of our second grandchild and first grand-daughter.[459] Nothing can go better than the Princess Royal does. Of the Prince of Wales's arrival in Canada we could not yet hear, but shall do so in a few days.

This country and Europe continue to be in a state of alarms, or rather more profound distrust in, the conduct and purposes of our neighbour. Fortunately the feeling of Germany is so unanimous upon this subject, and the Emperor's attempt to produce disaffection or division there has so signally failed and produced so diametrically a contrary effect, and Belgium has shown such an enthusiastic spirit of loyalty only equal to the public spirit which this country has shown in the Volunteer movement, that it is to be hoped these sinister designs are checked for a time at least.

With the Prince's kind remembrance to Lord Canning, the Queen concludes, hoping this letter will find him in good health, and Lady Canning safely returned from her expedition.

---

[458] See *ante*, p. 313.

[459] The Princess Charlotte of Prussia, now Hereditary Princess of Saxe-Meiningen, was born on the 24th of July.

Queen Victoria to the King of the Belgians.

VISIT TO SCOTLAND

Holyrood, *7th August 1860.*

My dearest Uncle,—I have *many* excuses for sending a few hurried lines from here, instead of my usual letter, but I was much hurried yesterday; the separation from baby quite upset me, as she too cried very much—but she is consoled again.

Many thanks for your dear letter of the 3rd, which I shall duly answer on Friday.

We came down here by *night* train, arriving at eight. We paid dear Mamma a visit at her really charming residence at Cramond,[460] quite near the sea, with beautiful trees, and very cheerful.

And this afternoon she was present the whole time at the splendid Volunteer Review, which lasted from half-past three till near six, in the open carriage with me, and enjoyed it so much; and I was so *happy* to have *her* with me on this memorable occasion, having had *you* with me on the previous occasion.[461] And it was magnificent—finer decidedly than in London—there were more (1,400 more), and then the scenery here is so splendid! That fine mountain of Arthur's Seat, crowded with thousands and thousands to the very top—and the Scotch are very noisy and demonstrative in their loyalty. Lord Breadalbane, at the head of his Highlanders, was the picture of a Highland chieftain. The dust was quite fearful! At nine we leave for Balmoral. Ever your devoted Niece,

Victoria R.

Queen Victoria to the King of the Belgians.

THE HIGHLANDS

Balmoral, *10th September 1860.*

My beloved Uncle,—I have no letter from you, but trust you are quite well. Here we have had a week of very fine weather, but since Saturday it has been extremely cold. We made a most delightful incognito expedition on Tuesday last, 4th, returning on Wednesday, 5th. We drove off from here quite early at eight, for twenty-one miles up to

[460] The Duchess of Kent was spending the summer at Cramond House, near Edinburgh.

[461] The Review in Hyde Park, which took place on the 23rd of June.

the *Geldie*, a small river—*rode* from here on ponies across the hills to Glen Fishie, a beautiful spot, where the old Duchess of Bedford used to live in a sort of encampment of wooden huts—on to Loch Inch, a beautiful but not wild lake (another twenty miles), crossed the Spey in a ferry, and posted in very rough vehicles to Grantown, again twenty miles, coming in there at nine. We passed close by Kinrara where you used to be, but, unfortunately, not by the house. *No* one knew us—anywhere or at the little inn. We went under the names of Lord and Lady Churchill, and Lady Churchill and General Grey who went with us, under the names of Miss Spencer and Dr Grey! Two maids *only* went with us (whom we had sent round with our things), and *no* servants but our two excellent Highlanders, viz. Albert's first stalker or head keeper, and *my own Highland servant* and factotum—*both* excellent, intelligent, devoted people. *Only* when we had *left* was it found out. We posted to Tomantoul, a wretched village—fourteen miles, *in four hours!!* with a pair of wretched tired horses—over a big hilly road. At Tomantoul we again took our ponies and rode by Avon Side and Glen Avon, also very fine; back to Loch Bulig—eight miles from here—whence we returned home in our carriage. It was a *most delightful* and enjoyable, as well as *beautiful*, expedition. I have been besides on many other ones for the day.

In Italy I fear the state of affairs is very distressing—but really the miserable, weak, and foolish conduct of the King of Naples[462] and the squabbles of the whole family takes away all one's sympathy! We leave here alas! on Saturday, stop till Monday evening at Edinburgh to see Mamma, and go on that night straight to Osborne, where we expect to arrive on Tuesday for breakfast. With Albert's affectionate love, ever your devoted Niece,

Victoria R.

Viscount Palmerston to Queen Victoria.

Broadlands, *18th September 1860.*

Viscount Palmerston presents his humble duty to your Majesty, and will have the honour of waiting upon your Majesty at Osborne tomorrow. Your Majesty must naturally feel regret at shortening so much your Majesty's agreeable holiday in the Highlands, though the happiness of meeting the Princess Royal must amply make amends for

---

[462] King Francis had just fled from Naples to Gaëta, and Garibaldi shortly afterwards arrived in Naples.

it; but the fact is that of all the gifts which good fairies were in the habit of bestowing on their favourites, that which would have been the most desirable would have been the power which the Irishman ascribed to a bird, of being in two places at one and the same time.

Viscount Palmerston to Queen Victoria.

AUSTRIAN PROPOSAL

Osborne, *20th September 1860.*

Viscount Palmerston presents his humble duty to your Majesty, and submits the accompanying letters which he has received from Lord John Russell, together with Lord John's letter to him; and he certainly agrees with Lord John in thinking that a meeting at present between your Majesty and the Emperor of Austria, though in many respects likely to be useful, would on the whole be so liable to misconstruction, and would prove such a fertile source of misrepresentation, that it would be better to avoid it. Such a meeting would undoubtedly be useful to the Emperor of Austria, by reason of the good advice which he would receive from your Majesty, and from His Royal Highness the Prince Consort; but your Majesty will probably be able to find some other way of conveying to the Emperor counsel calculated to save him from some of the dangers by which he appears to be beset.

Queen Victoria to Lord John Russell.

21st September 1860.

The Queen received these letters from Lord Palmerston, who likewise communicated to her Lord John Russell's letter, respecting the hint thrown out by Count Rechberg[463] of a meeting with the Emperor of Austria. The Queen agrees with Lord Palmerston, that while such an interview might for many reasons have been desirable, under present circumstances it might lead to much talk and to many rumours which might do harm, or at any rate give rise to useless conjectures. It would therefore be better to "nip this project in the bud" as Lord John suggests, but care should be taken to do this in such a manner as not to

---

[463] In a letter to Mr Julian Fane, Count Rechberg, the Austrian Foreign Minister, had said that he had desired to bring about an interview between the Queen and the Emperor of Austria, but that there would have been difficulties in the way. Lord John Russell was of opinion that the idea should be nipped in the bud, and in this Lord Palmerston fully concurred.

let it appear that there was any disinclination on the Queen's part to meet the Emperor of Austria.

The King of Naples to Queen Victoria.

APPEAL FROM KING OF NAPLES

Gaëta, *le 6 Octobre 1860.*

Madame ma Sœur,—Le mémorandum qu'à la date d'aujourd'hui mon Gouvernement adresse à celui de votre Majesté, les protestations que dans ces derniers temps je lui ai fait parvenir donneront à votre Majesté une idée claire des conflits par lesquels j'ai passé, et de la situation où je me trouve.

A la sagacité de votre Majesté ne peut échapper la transcendance des événements qui se passent dans le Royaume des Deux Siciles, et dans les États Pontificaux. J'étais, et je suis seul à lutter contre toutes les forces de la révolution Européenne. Cette révolution s'est présentée avec un pouvoir que jamais on ne lui avait connu, armes, parcs d'artillerie, munitions, vaisseaux, rien ne lui a manqué, pas même les ports d'une puissance pour se recruter, et son drapeau pour la couvrir.

Ces événements établissent un nouveau droit public, fondé sur la destruction des anciens traités et des principes reconnus du droit des gens. La cause que je défends seul à Naples n'est pas seulement ma propre cause; elle est la cause de tous les Souverains et de tous les États indépendants.

La question qui se débat dans le Royaume des Deux Siciles, est une question de vie ou de mort pour d'autres États d'Europe.

C'est à ce titre, et non par un intérêt personnel que j'ose m'adresser à la haute raison de votre Majesté, à Sa prévoyance et à Sa justice.

La grande position qu'occupe votre Majesté dans le monde, Sa sagesse, les relations amicales qui ont toujours existé entre nos deux familles, et la bienveillance particulière dont votre Majesté a daigné toujours m'honorer, me font espérer, que votre Majesté verra dans cet appel que je fais avec confiance à Sa politique et à Sa justice, une nouvelle preuve du respect que j'ai eu toujours pour Elle, de l'affection sincère, et des sentiments de haute considération avec lesquels j'ai l'honneur d'être, Madame ma Sœur, de votre Majesté, le bon Frère,

Francois.

The King of the Belgians to Queen Victoria.

TOUR OF PRINCE ALFRED

Laeken, *2nd November 1860.*

My beloved Victoria,— ... Bertie's visit seems to have gone off most splendidly; its effects will be useful. The enemies of England always flatter themselves that mischief may come from that part of the world. To see, therefore, friendly feelings arise, instead of war, will disappoint them much. Alfred's appearance at the Cape[464] has also been a most wise measure. South Africa has a great future to expect, it is a pity it is so far and I too old to go there; the plants alone are already a great temptation. I should like very much to hear what came to your knowledge of the Warsaw meeting.[465] Prince Gortschakoff tried hard to make it believe that it would bring *Russia nearer to France*. If this was to be the result of the meeting it would be a very sad one indeed....

SARDINIA AND NAPLES

The way in which the English Press misunderstands all these things is quite lamentable. The meeting of the Sovereigns had this time a better object than the oppression of the liberties of Nations; that this should not be seen by people who would be the first sufferers of the supremacy of a certain power is very lamentable, but they see everything only according to the colour of *their* spectacles. *Le Flibustive* movement at Naples is very shameful, but that poor King has been so calumniated that Garibaldi is the rage of the present moment; Colonel

---

[464] Prince Alfred, who, some time before, had been appointed to the *Euryalus*, in the course of the summer visited South Africa. After making a tour through Kaffraria, Natal, and the Orange Free State, he returned to Cape Town, where, in September, he laid the foundation stone of the breakwater in Table Bay. In a letter written by the Prince Consort a few weeks earlier to Baron Stockmar, he remarks upon the noteworthy coincidence that almost in the same week in which the elder brother would open the great bridge across the St Lawrence, the younger would lay the foundation stone of the breakwater for the Cape Town Harbour. "What a cheering picture is here," he wrote, "of the progress and expansion of the British race, and of the useful co-operation of the Royal Family in the civilisation which England has developed and advanced" (*Life of the Prince Consort*, vol. v. p. 88).

[465] The Emperors of Russia and Austria, and the Prince Regent of Prussia met at Warsaw on 20th October, and held a conference which extended over several days.

Walker[466] has been shot, and Garibaldi, who comes out of that self-same school, is divinised. But it is time I should end. With my best love to dear Albert, I remain ever, my beloved Victoria, your devoted old Uncle,

Leopold R.

Queen Victoria to Lord John Russell.

Windsor Castle, *3rd November 1860.*

The Queen returns the enclosed draft,[467] which she is afraid is not likely to produce the beneficial results which Lord John seems to anticipate.

The expression of our hope, that Rome and Venetia, from their Italian nationality, will soon share in the freedom and good government of the rest of Italy, can only be understood as a declaration on our part that we wish to see them share the annexation to Sardinia, after that of the Two Sicilies shall have been completed.

The declaration at the end after the quotations of the former protests, vague as it is, viz. "That if other Powers interfere England would do as she pleases," means either nothing at all (for England is free to do as she pleases) or it means a threat of war, either an empty threat, or one intended to be followed up when the occasion arises. The first would hardly be dignified for a great Power like England, and as to the second, the Queen for one is not prepared to decide to go to war to ensure the success of the Italian Revolution.

But is such a declaration at the present moment called for by anything that has happened? Another despatch has accepted as satisfactory the French explanation about the order given to the fleet before Gaëta, and Austria has renewed her assurances that she will not interfere; the only Power likely to continue to interfere and to produce war—

[466] Walker, in the course of one of the Nicaraguan revolutions, had seized the supreme power, and had been recognised as President by the U.S. Government; he was afterwards expelled, and, on venturing to return, was arrested, and shot on the 25th of September 1860.

[467] This draft despatch, prepared in order to be sent to all the Powers, expressed approval of the Italian Revolution. It concluded: "Her Majesty's Government deem it right to declare that if any other Power should attempt forcible interference, Her Majesty's Government will hold themselves free to act in such a manner as the rights of nations, the independence of Italy, and the interests of Europe may seem to them to require."

Sardinia—is held to have an exceptional right to it, as an "Italian" Power.

The Queen thinks this important despatch should not be laid before her again without its having received the deliberate consideration and assent of the whole Cabinet, and in case Lord John should bring it before them the Queen would wish him to communicate this letter also to them, as embodying her views on the subject.

Lord John Russell to Queen Victoria.

Pembroke Lodge, *3rd November 1860.*

Lord John Russell presents his humble duty to your Majesty....

With regard to the position of Great Britain, Lord John Russell is bound to advise that it shall not suffer by the change of circumstances.

From 1815 to 1859 Austria ruled Italy. If Italians had reason to complain, England had nothing to fear from the use of Austrian influence against British interests.

But if France were to sway the united Navies of Genoa and Naples, and Great Britain to look on from fear or apathy, or excessive love of peace, she might soon have to defend her possessions of Malta, Corfu, and Gibraltar.

Austria would hardly attempt any new aggression on Italy, unless she were assisted by France.

Italy as one Power would derive strength from the declaration of Great Britain, as a disinterested friend.

A letter of Lord Cowley will show your Majesty the suspicions and doubts which exist as to French policy in Italy.[468] All these projects will be scattered to the winds by the word of the British Government.

Queen Victoria to the King of Naples.

REPLY TO KING OF NAPLES

Windsor Castle, *3rd November 1860.*

---

[468] Lord Cowley wrote that he had heard through Count Metternich that the Emperor of the French would never consent to the annexation of Naples to Piedmont, that he wished the Pope to retain Umbria and the Marches, and that the Romagna should be an independent State.

Sir, my Brother,—The letter I have received from your Majesty, dated from Gaëta on the 6th of October, is altogether devoted to political considerations.

These considerations have for a long time occupied the thoughts of my confidential advisers, and I have directed them to convey to my Ministers abroad such instructions as occasion appeared to me to require.

I will therefore confine this letter to those topics which are not the immediate subjects of political controversy.

Upon your Majesty's accession to the Throne I lost no time in assuring your Majesty of my sincere wishes for the prosperity of your reign, and the permanence of your dynasty.

At the same time I was fully aware of the difficulties of the period at which your Majesty succeeded to the Crown. That these difficulties should not have been surmounted, and that they should now threaten to overwhelm the Monarchy, of which your Majesty is the heir, is to me a source of deep concern.

It only remains that I should ask your Majesty to express to the Queen my sincere sympathy in her misfortunes. I avail myself of this opportunity to renew to your Majesty the assurance of the invariable friendship and high consideration with which I am, Sir, my Brother, your Majesty's good Sister,

Victoria R.

Queen Victoria to the King of the Belgians.

RETURN OF PRINCE ALFRED

Windsor Castle, *13th November 1860.*

My beloved Uncle,—...Here we have the happiness of having our dear Alfred back since the 9th, who gives *very* interesting accounts of his expedition, and has brought back *many* most interesting trophies, splendid horns of *all* those wonderful animals, photographs, etc. He *is* grown, though very *short* for his age, but I think less so than his brother at the same age. Major Cowell[469] gives an *excellent* report of him in *every way*, which, as you will readily believe, makes us *very*

[469] Major (afterwards Sir John) Cowell was appointed as Tutor to Prince Alfred in 1856. He was then a Lieutenant of Engineers, and had been Adjutant to Sir Harry Jones at Bomarsund and before Sebastopol.

happy. He is really such a dear, gifted, handsome child, that it makes one doubly anxious he should have as few failings as mortal men can have. Our poor Bertie is still on the Atlantic, detained by very contrary winds, which those large vessels with only an auxiliary screw and only eight days' coal cannot make any way against. Two powerful steamers have now gone out to look for him and bring him in....

With Albert's affectionate love, ever your devoted Niece,

Victoria R.

Viscount Palmerston to Queen Victoria.

Piccadilly, *22nd November 1860.*

Viscount Palmerston presents his humble duty to your Majesty, and begs to submit that, as it appears from a despatch from Lord Cowley that the commercial negotiations at Paris have been brought to a conclusion, and that Mr Cobden has left Paris, the time has come for your Majesty to consider what substantial mark of your Majesty's approval your Majesty would be pleased to confer upon Mr Cobden. Mr Cobden has now for about twelve months been laboriously employed without salary or emolument in negotiating the complicated details of commercial arrangements between England and France, which cannot fail to tend to the material advantage of both countries, but more especially to the increased development of the industry and commerce of your Majesty's subjects. It would be an ungracious proceeding to leave the services of Mr Cobden with no other acknowledgment than the praises contained in a Foreign Office despatch, and Viscount Palmerston therefore with the concurrence of Lord John Russell would beg to submit for the gracious approval of your Majesty that Mr Cobden might be offered his choice of being created a Knight Grand Cross of the Civil Order of the Bath, or of being made a Member of your Majesty's Privy Council.

(*Note, in Queen's hand.*—Was agreed to offer him either to be made a P.C., or a Baronet.)[470]

[470] Mr Cobden declined both the Honours.

The King of the Belgians to Queen Victoria.

THE EMPRESS OF AUSTRIA

Laeken, *22nd November 1860.*

My beloved Victoria,—I have to thank you for a most kind letter of the 20th. I hope you will see the young and very nice Empress of Austria,[471] perhaps you made a little excursion to Plymouth. I had, and have still, some cold, and therefore I was apprehensive of waiting at the station on the 20th in the evening; I sent Marie and Philip to receive the Empress. Yesterday before daybreak I went myself to Antwerp. I first paid the Empress a visit, and then I took her to your beautiful ship. She was much struck with it, and it was *very kind* of you, and indeed, for an invalid, invaluable. It will show, besides, that even beyond Garibaldi, and that amiable, disinterested *Annex*ander, you can feel some interest. I saw the Empress already dressed for her departure, but I think there is something very peculiar about her, which is very pleasing. Poor soul, to see her go away under, I fear, not very safe circumstances, as she coughs a great deal, quite grieves one; though it certainly increased my stupid cold, still I should have been sorry not to have assisted at her going to sea. It was a beautiful day, but this night it has begun to blow from the West-south-west, which I fear will create a sea to the Westward.

That you had your sons about you must have been a great satisfaction to you. Bertie got well through his truly tremendous tour. I think that the effect on the Americans will last for some time. That the poor Duke of Newcastle got home without accident is surprising. Affy has something most winning, and is a dear little rogue. Eugénie's expedition[472] is most astonishing. She also coughs much, and I never heard Scotland recommended for Winter excursions. I believe that the death of her sister affected her a good deal. She seems to have been a good deal *choquée* that she had been dancing in Africa when that poor sister was dying. Next to this, there seems a difference of opinion with her master on the subject of the Pope. You will recollect that at the time of his elections the clergy rendered him undoubted good service; I even doubt that he would have been elected without their aid. Now he puts

---

[471] The Empress Elizabeth was on her way to Madeira, in a ship placed at her disposal by the Queen.

[472] The Empress of the French was making a tour in England and Scotland for the benefit of her health; she had sustained a bereavement by the death of her sister, the Duchess of Alba.

the axe to the root of the whole Catholic Church by destroying the Pope, and he does this *without the slightest provocation*, and for the benefit of the revolution *et des révolutionnaires....*

I remain ever, my beloved Victoria, your devoted Uncle,

Leopold R.

Queen Victoria to the King of the Belgians.

BETROTHAL OF PRINCESS ALICE

Windsor Castle, *1st December 1860.*

Dearest Uncle,—I hasten to announce to you that yesterday our dear young couple here were engaged, and that we *are all* very happy.[473] Louis was spoken to yesterday on our return from Aldershot by Albert,—who told him he would have an opportunity of speaking to Alice—and this opportunity he took last night after dinner when he was standing alone with her at the fire, and every one else was occupied in talking. They whispered it to me, and then, after we left the drawing-room, we sent for good Louis—and the young people met and confirmed in a very touching manner *what* they had merely been able to whisper to one another before. He was very much overcome. He is a dear, good, amiable, high-principled young man—who I am sure will make our dearest Alice *very* happy, and she will, I am sure, be a most devoted loving wife to him. She is *very, very* happy, and it is a pleasure to see their young, happy faces beaming with love for one another. Alice is so extremely reasonable and quiet. She wishes everything kind and affectionate to be said to you, and *hopes* for your *blessing!* I am very, very happy, so are we both, but I am still a good deal agitated and flurried by the whole event.

On Tuesday the Empress arrives, but only to luncheon. I must end now in haste. Ever your devoted Niece,

Victoria R.

Pray tell it to good Philip, and also to Leopold and Marie.

Queen Victoria to Viscount Palmerston.

THE SEE OF WORCESTER

Windsor Castle, *1st December 1860.*

---

473 See *ante*, p. 405.

The Queen has received Lord Palmerston's second letter respecting the Bishopric of Worcester,[474] just as she was going to answer the first. While not objecting to the nomination of Mr Bayley,[475] she wanted to point out the importance of, at a future vacancy, not to confine the selection to respectable parish priests, but to bear in mind that the Bench of Bishops should not be left devoid of some University men of acknowledged standing and theological learning; it would be seriously weakened if, in controversies on points of doctrine agitating the Church, no value were attached to the opinions at least of some of those who are to govern her. Lord Palmerston may now have an opportunity of selecting a stronger man of Liberal views from Cambridge.

Viscount Palmerston to Queen Victoria.

EPISCOPAL APPOINTMENTS

Piccadilly, *2nd December 1860.*

Viscount Palmerston presents his humble duty to your Majesty, and very sincerely congratulates your Majesty upon the arrangement of a marriage which bids so fair to secure for Her Royal Highness the Princess Alice that happiness to which her amiable and estimable qualities so justly entitle her.

With respect to bishops, Viscount Palmerston would beg to submit that the bishops are in the Church what generals of districts are in the Army: their chief duties consist in watching over the clergy of their diocese, seeing that they perform properly their parochial duties, and preserving harmony between the clergy and the laity, and softening the asperities between the Established Church and the Dissenters. For these purposes it is desirable that a bishop should have practical knowledge of parochial functions, and should not be of an overbearing and intolerant temperament. His diocesan duties are enough to occupy all his time, and the less he engages in theological disputes the better. Much mischief has been done by theological bishops, and if the Bench were filled with men like the Bishops of Oxford and Exeter there would be no religious peace in the land. Nor have men chosen merely

---

[474] Bishop Henry Pepys had died in November, and was succeeded in the following January by Canon Henry Philpott of Norwich, Master of St Catharine's College, Cambridge.

[475] Probably the Rev. Emilius Bayley, Rector of St George's, Bloomsbury; now the Rev. Sir Emilius Laurie.

for their learning succeeded better; Thirlwall, Bishop of St David's, and Blomfield, the late Bishop of London, were chosen on account of their learning; the former is acknowledged to be inefficient, the latter greatly mismanaged his diocese. The theological learning of the Bishop of Exeter[476] has caused much mischief to the Established Church. Viscount Palmerston would also beg to submit that the intolerant maxims of the High Church bishops have exasperated the Dissenters who form a large portion of the nation, and have given offence to many good Churchmen. The Bishop of Exeter, the late Bishop of Carlisle,[477] and the late Bishop of Rochester,[478] the two latter individuals kind-hearted and good-natured men, refused to consecrate burial grounds unless a wall of separation divided the portion allotted to Churchmen from the portion allotted to Dissenters—a demand which gave offence to both communities. Viscount Palmerston would beg to submit that several of the bishops whom he has had the honour of recommending to your Majesty had distinguished themselves by their classical and academical attainments, and he may mention in this respect the names of Baring, Longley, Tait, Wigram, and Waldegrave. Viscount Palmerston can assure your Majesty that although his selection of bishops has been much found fault with by the High Church, Puseyite, and semi-Catholic Party, they have given great satisfaction to the nation at large, and Viscount Palmerston has received communications to that effect, verbal and written, from persons of all classes, and political parties in all parts of the country. The people of this country are essentially Protestant, they feel the deepest aversion to Catholicism, and they see that the High Church, Tractarian, and Puseyite doctrines lead men to the Church of Rome. The disgraceful scenes last year at St George's in the East[479] were only an exaggerated outburst of a very general and deeply-rooted feeling. Viscount Palmerston believes that the clergy of the Established Church were never more exemplary in the performance of their duties, more respected by the Laity and, generally speaking, on better terms with the Nonconformist body than at the present time.

---

[476] Henry Phillpotts, who was Bishop from 1830 to 1869.

[477] The Hon. Henry Montagu Villiers, who was transferred to Durham.

[478] George Murray, who had died in the previous February.

[479] For a considerable period, during 1859, discreditable scenes of brawling took place at this Church as a protest against the High Church practices of the Rector, the Rev. Bryan King.

Queen Victoria to the King of the Belgians.

AFFAIRS OF NAPLES

Windsor Castle, *4th December 1860.*

My beloved Uncle,—I have to thank you for another dear letter of the 29th. I trust that you have received both mine now. We expect the Empress at half-past one, and I will certainly give her your message. She is very amiable, and one must like her. There seems to be no doubt that there were many scenes, partly about the Pope, and also on account of her sister's funeral; she was so angry with Fould about it that she insisted on his dismissal.[480] Then the Priests are said to try and work upon her, and say that her son will die if the Emperor continues *dans cette voie* against the Pope.

We saw Mr Elliot[481] from Naples yesterday, who has always been very fair. He says that *if*, when the King came to the Throne, he had *only* insisted on the laws of the country being properly carried out, *no* reforms or change in the Constitution would have been necessary—but from the want of energy, and also no strength of intellect and great indecision of character of the poor King, as well as an unfortunate *Pietät* for the memory of his father, nothing right was done; bad counsellors surrounded him, the Queen Mother had a bad influence, and finally everything was given up as lost—when it might yet have been prevented. They dislike extremely being annexed, but prefer it to having back the former state of things.

We have since ten or twelve days almost incessant rain, so that we shall soon be on an island. This is the more distressing as we can't go to Osborne at present—there being a sort of epidemic fever which the doctors declare is in the air and that it would be running too great a risk if we went. But we have perpetual sunshine in the house when we look at our dear young lovers, who are *so* happy, so devoted to each other, that it does one good to see it; he is so modest and unassuming that we feel as if he was one of our own children; and he is *so* good and amiable, has such an open honest character, such a warm heart, such high principles, and is withal so merry and *aufgeweckt* that I feel we have *gained* a son and shall *not* lose a daughter—for we shall be able to have them a good deal with us, Louis not having any duties to detain him much at home at present. I can't say what happiness and comfort it is to me. I feel my dear child will first of all have a peaceful,

---

[480] See *ante*, p. 333.
[481] See *ante*, p. 356.

quiet, happy home, without difficulties—and secondly, that she will not be entirely cut off from us and monopolised as our poor Vicky is.

I add a few lines since we have seen the Empress. She came at half-past one, and stayed till a little after three. She looked very pretty, but very sad—and in speaking of her health and of her return from Algiers began to cry. She seems to be much better, however, for her journey; before she could neither eat nor sleep, nor would she take notice of anything. She never mentioned the Emperor but once when she offered his compliments, and there was not the slightest allusion to politics. It is altogether very strange. She remains another week in England, and then goes back as she came. I gave her your message, and she enquired after you. Ever your devoted Niece,

Victoria R.

Queen Victoria to the King of the Belgians.

VISIT OF THE EMPRESS EUGENIE

Windsor Castle, 11th December 1860.

My beloved Uncle,—I have to thank you for two *most* kind letters of the 4th and 7th. Your kind interest in our dear child's happiness—your approval of this marriage of our dear Alice, which, I cannot deny, has been for *long* an ardent wish of mine, and just therefore I feared *so* much it *never* would come to pass, gives us the greatest pleasure. *Now*—that *all* has been so *happily* settled, and that I find the young man so very charming—my joy, and my *deep* gratitude to God are very great! He is so loveable, so very *young*, and like one of our own children—not the *least in the way*—but a dear, pleasant, *bright* companion, full of fun and spirits, and I am *sure* will be a *great* comfort to us, besides being an excellent husband to our dear, good Alice, who, though radiant with joy and much in love (which well she may be), is as quiet and sensible as possible.

The Empress is still here, and enjoys her liberty of *all* things. We went to town for the Smithfield Cattle Show yesterday, and visited her at Claridge's Hotel. She very civilly wanted us to avoid the trouble, but we felt that it would not be civil if we did not, and that hereafter even the French might say that she had not been treated with due respect. She looked very pretty, and was in very good spirits, but again carefully avoided any allusion to her husband and to politics, though she talked a great deal about all she was seeing!...

I must now wish you good-bye. Ever your devoted Niece,

Victoria R.

INTRODUCTORY NOTE
TO CHAPTER XXX

Early in 1861—a year destined to close in sorrow and desolation— Queen Victoria experienced a heavy grief in the death of her mother, the Duchess of Kent, at the age of seventy-four.

In January, fresh overtures were made to Lord Palmerston by the Conservative leaders, with a view of supporting him in office against the dissentients in his Ministry, especially Lord John Russell and Mr Gladstone, whose views on the questions of Reform and National Defence respectively were opposed to those of the Premier. Lord Palmerston was indifferent to the support of Mr Gladstone; but a unity of view on the Italian policy of the Government held the three Liberal statesmen together.

The attack on the Paper Duties was repeated by Mr Gladstone, who, on this occasion, combined all his fiscal proposals in a single Bill. The measure, after strong opposition, passed the Commons by a majority of fifteen, and the Peers subsequently accepted the Budget, which took a penny off the income tax, while maintaining the existing tea and sugar Duties. In July, Lord John Russell, who had entered Parliament in 1813, before he came of age and had been leader of the House of Commons at the time of the Queen's accession, was transferred to the House of Lords. In August, the Queen and the Prince Consort, with the Prince of Wales and Prince Alfred, paid a third visit to Ireland.

The affairs of Italy still continued to attract public attention. At the end of 1860, the French fleet had been despatched to Gaëta to protect the interests of King Francis; this protection, given in violation of the principle of non-intervention, was withdrawn in January, and the garrison surrendered to the Piedmontese Admiral. On the 18th of February, the new Parliament of Italy met at Turin, the debates emphasising the vital necessity of including both Rome and Venetia in a united nation; Victor Emmanuel was declared King of Italy, a title promptly recognised by Great Britain; but in June, to the profound grief of the Italian nation, Cavour, its Prime Minister, and the mainspring of the Piedmontese policy, died while still in the prime of life.

King Frederick William of Prussia had died in January, and was succeeded by his brother, William I., Prince of Prussia, who was crowned with Queen Augusta, at Königsberg, on the 18th of October, Lord Clarendon attending as British representative. In the following month, King Pedro of Portugal, son and successor of Donna Maria, and his brother Ferdinand, died of typhoid fever; another brother, Prince John, succumbed to the same malady before the close of the year.

Events of great importance took place in North America, where the secession of South Carolina was followed by that of other Southern States. The delegates of the latter assembled in February at Montgomery, Alabama, and nominated Jefferson Davis as their President, Abraham Lincoln having been previously elected as the new President of the United States. The first shot had been fired, on the 9th of January, in Charleston Harbour, where a Secessionist battery opened its guns on a vessel sent by the Federal Government to reinforce Fort Sumter. In April, the Confederate troops attacked the Fort, which was compelled to surrender, whereupon President Lincoln issued a proclamation calling for 75,000 volunteers; President Davis replied by issuing (in default of an official fleet) letters of marque to privately owned vessels, and Lincoln declared the Southern ports in a state of blockade. In May, Lord John Russell announced that the British Government would recognise the South as a belligerent power, and a proclamation of neutrality was issued. At Bull Run, on the 21st of July, the Federals were defeated, and fled in confusion to Washington. Hostilities continued during the year, and Great Britain was nearly involved in war, by the seizure, on the 8th of November, by the captain of a Federal vessel, the *San Jacinto*, of Messrs Slidell and Mason, the envoys accredited by the Confederate States to Great Britain and France. This high-handed action was taken while the envoys in question were passengers to Europe, by the British mail steamer *Trent*, between Havana and St Thomas, and the public mind of Great Britain was greatly excited in consequence; but eventually the envoys were transferred to a British ship-of-war, and arrived in Great Britain, not, however, until in view of a threatened aggression on British North America, troops had been despatched from England to strengthen the

Canadian garrisons on the frontier. The despatch of Lord Russell to the American Government, which led to a pacific result, had been revised by Prince Albert, in the direction of leaving open to that Government an honourable retreat from the aggressive attitude they had taken up; the Prince's action in this respect, the beneficial effect of which it would be difficult to exaggerate, was destined to be the last of a long series of political services rendered to this country.

It had become apparent in the autumn that Prince Albert's normal health was impaired, and in November he began to suffer from persistent insomnia; towards the end of the month the fever originated which was to prove fatal to him. He suffered at first from rheumatic pains and constant weakness, until, early in December, what was thought to be influenza developed, and the Prince was confined to his room. By the 11th his condition, though not hopeless, had become grave, and the serious nature of the illness was made public; and, although on the 12th the Queen could write hopefully to King Leopold, the malady continued to increase. On the evening of the 13th, a rally took place, and encouraging reports were brought hourly to the Queen through the night; but congestion of the lungs supervened on the following day, in the closing hours of which, to the inexpressible grief both of the Queen and her subjects, the Prince passed peacefully away. The letters of the Queen to King Leopold and Lord Canning express, in language to which nothing can be added, the intensity of her grief, and, no less, the noble and unselfish courage with which she resolved to devote her life to her children and country.

CHAPTER XXX

1861

Viscount Palmerston to Queen Victoria.

CONSERVATIVE OVERTURES

Broadlands, *1st January 1861.*

Viscount Palmerston presents his humble duty to your Majesty, and begs to be allowed to wish your Majesty and His Royal Highness the Prince Consort many prosperous returns of New Year's Day, with increasing happiness to your Majesty and the Royal Family, and progressive advantage to the Nation who have the good fortune to have your Majesty for their Sovereign; and to adopt the language of Pope, he would say,

"May day improve on day, and year on year,
Without a pain, a trouble, or a fear."

This Autumn and Winter, however, have been productive of events in three of the four quarters of the Globe, which future years are not likely to repeat. The capture of Pekin in Asia by British and French troops; the Union in Europe of nearly the whole of Italy into one Monarchy; and the approaching and virtually accomplished Dissolution in America of the great Northern Confederation, are events full of importance for the future, as well as being remarkable in time present.

Viscount Palmerston submits two letters which your Majesty may feel an interest in seeing. With regard to that from Lord John Russell stating a half-formed wish to go to the House of Lords, Viscount Palmerston does not expect that the desire will be repeated when the Session begins, although Lord John said last year that he felt attendance in the House of Commons in addition to the labour of his office, more than he could well get through. He would be a loss to Viscount Palmerston in the House of Commons, especially after the removal of

Mr Sidney Herbert to the House of Lords;[482] and speaking confidentially to your Majesty with regard to the future, Viscount Palmerston would think himself doing better service by recommending the House of Lords for Mr Gladstone, than for Lord John Russell.

Mr Herbert will take the title of Lord Herbert of Lea, the title of Herbert being that borne by his elder brother during the life of the late Lord Pembroke.

The other letter from Lord Malmesbury relates to a communication which he made to Viscount Palmerston last year from Lord Derby and Mr Disraeli at the beginning of the Session, to the effect that, if the Government were then to break up from internal dissensions, the Conservative Party would support during the then ensuing Session any administration which Viscount Palmerston might be able provisionally to make, to carry through the business of the Session.[483] Viscount Palmerston is not aware of any circumstances which can have led to the expectation that the present administration is likely to be broken up by internal divisions in the course of this next Session. There are no questions ahead so likely to produce discord as the Reform Bill of last year, and the differences between the two Houses about the Paper Duties, about which it was very difficult to prevent Lord John and Mr Gladstone from flying off, or the Fortification Question, upon which Mr Gladstone announced to his colleagues, nearly a dozen times, that he was firmly resolved to resign. Viscount Palmerston has asked Lord Malmesbury to come over to him to Broadlands at any time before the 21st or 22nd of this month, which is the probable time at which the Cabinet will have to meet in London.

Viscount Palmerston finds he has not got Lord John Russell's letter at hand, but the only thing of any interest in it was the intimation which Viscount Palmerston quoted.

---

[482] Mr Herbert had been latterly in bad health, and resigned office in the summer. He died on the 2nd of August.

[483] In his memoirs, Lord Malmesbury describes an interview with Lord and Lady Palmerston on the 1st of June 1860, apparently the one at which this communication was made. "It is evident," he writes, "he [Lord Palmerston] does not wish to lose Lord John, though he would be very glad if Gladstone resigned."

The Emperor of the French to Queen Victoria.

Paris, *le 31 Décembre 1860.*

Madame et très chère Sœur,—Je ne veux pas laisser cette année s'écouler sans venir porter à votre Majesté l'expression de mes souhaits pour son bonheur et celui du Prince et de sa famille. J'espère que l'année qui va commencer sera heureuse pour nos deux nations, et qu'elle verra encore nos liens se resserrer. L'Europe est bien agitée, mais tant que l'Angleterre et la France s'entendent, le mal pourra se localiser.

Je félicite votre Majesté du succès que nos deux armées ont obtenu en Chine; laissons toujours nos étendards unis; car Dieu semble les protéger.

J'ai bien envié l'Impératrice qui a pu vous faire une visite et revoir votre charmante famille: elle en a été bien heureuse.

Je saisis avec empressement cette occasion de renouveler à votre Majesté les sentiments de haute estime et de sincère amitié avec lesquels je suis, de votre Majesté le bon Frère,

Napoléon.

The Princess Royal to Queen Victoria and the Prince Albert.

DEATH OF KING OF PRUSSIA

Potsdam, *2nd January 1861.*

Beloved Parents,—At last I can find a moment for myself to sit down and collect my thoughts and to write to you an account of these two last dreadful days! My head is in such a state, I do not know where I am hardly—whether I am in a dream or awake, what is yesterday and what to-day! What we have so long expected is come at last! All the confusion, bustle, excitement, noise, etc., is all swallowed up in that one thought for me—I have seen death for the first time! It has made an impression upon me that I shall never, never forget as long as I live—and I feel so ill, so confused and upset by all that I have gone through in the last forty-eight hours, that you must forgive me if I write incoherently and unclearly. But to go back to Monday evening (it seems to me a year now). At a quarter to eight in the evening of Monday the 31st, I took dear darling Affie to the railway station, and took leave of him with a heavy heart. You know I love that dear boy distractedly, and that nothing could have given me more pleasure than his dear, long-wished-for visit. At nine o'clock Fritz and I went to tea at the Prince Regent's; we four were alone together. The Princess was rather low and unwell, the Prince low-spirited, and I thinking of nothing but Affie and of how dear he is. While we were sitting at tea we received bad news from Sans Souci,[484] but nothing to make us particularly uneasy. Fritz and I went home and to bed, not being in a humour to sit up till twelve.

About half-past one we heard a knock at the door and my wardrobe maid brought in a telegram saying the King was given up, and a note from the Prince Regent saying he was going up immediately. We got up in the greatest hurry and dressed—I hardly know how; I put on just what I found, and had not time to do my hair or anything. After we had hurried on our clothes we went downstairs and out—for there was no time to get a carriage or a footman or anything—it was a splendid night, but twelve degrees of cold (Réaumur). I thought I was in a dream finding myself alone in the street with Fritz at two o'clock at night. We went to the Prince Regent's, and then with them in their carriages to the railway station—we four all alone in the train. We arrived at Sans Souci and went directly into the room where the King lay—the stillness of death was in the room—only the light of the fire and of a dim lamp. We approached the bed and stood there at the foot of it, not daring to look at one another or to say a word. The Queen was sitting in an armchair at the head of the bed, her arm underneath the King's head, and her head on the same pillow on which he lay; with her other hand she continually wiped the perspiration from his forehead. You might have heard a pin drop; no sound was heard but the crackling of the fire and the *death-rattle*, that dreadful sound which goes to one's heart, and which tells plainly that life is ebbing. This rattling in the throat lasted about an hour longer, and then the King lay motionless. The doctors bent their heads low to hear whether he still breathed—and we stood, not even daring to sit down, watching the death-struggle; every now and then the King breathed very fast and loud, but never unclosed his eyes; he was very red in the face, and the cold perspiration pouring from his forehead. I never spent such an awful time! And to see the poor Queen sitting there quite rent my heart—three, four, five, six, seven struck, and we were still standing there—one member of the family came in after the other and remained motionless in the room, sobs only breaking the silence. Oh! it is dreadful to see a person die! All the thoughts and feelings that crowded on my mind in those hours I cannot describe, more than in my whole past lifetime.

---

[484] The palace at Potsdam, built by Frederick the Great, the usual residence of the King of Prussia.

The light of the morning dawned, and the lamps were taken away—oh, how sad for the first morning in the year! We all went into the next room, for I assure you, anxiety, watching, standing, and crying had worn us out. The Princess fell asleep on a chair, I on a sofa, and the rest walked up and down the room asking one another, How long will it last? Towards the middle of the day, Marianne and I went into the room alone, as we wished to stay there; we came up and kissed the Queen's hand and knelt down and kissed the King's; it was quite warm still. We stood about and waited till five o'clock and then had some dinner, and I felt so sick and faint and unwell, that Fritz sent me here to bed. At one o'clock this morning I got up and dressed, and heard that the King had not many minutes more to live, but by the time I had got the carriage I heard all was over. I drove to Sans Souci and saw the King and Queen. May God bless and preserve them, and may theirs be a long and happy and blessed reign. Then I went into the room where the King lay, and I could hardly bring myself to go away again. There was so much of comfort in looking at that quiet, peaceful form, at rest at last after all he had suffered—gone home at last from this world of suffering—so peaceful and quiet he looked, like a sleeping child. Every moment I expected to see him move or breathe—his mouth and eyes closed, and such a sweet and happy expression—both his hands were on the coverlid. I kissed them both for the last time; they were quite cold then. Fritz and I stood looking at him for some time. I could hardly bring myself to believe that this was really death, that which I had so often shuddered at and felt afraid of; there was nothing there dreadful or appalling, only a heavenly calm and peace. I felt it did me so much good, and was such a comfort. "Death, where is thy sting? Grave, where is thy victory?" He was a just and good man, and had a heart overflowing with love and kindness, and he has gone to his rest after a long trial which he bore with so much patience. I am not afraid of death now, and when I feel inclined to be so, I shall think of that solemn and comforting sight, and that death is only a change for the better. We went home and to bed and this morning went there at ten. I sat some time with the poor Queen, who is so calm and resigned and touching in her grief. She does not cry, but she looks heartbroken. She said to me: "I am not longer of any use in this world. I have no longer any vocation, any duties to perform. I only lived for him." Then she was so kind to me, kinder than she has ever been yet, and said I was like her own child and a comfort to her. I saw the corpse again this morning; he is unaltered, only changed in colour, and the hands are stiffened.

The funeral will be on Saturday; the King will lie in state till then. His wish was to be buried in Friedenskirche before the altar—and his heart at Charlottenburg in the Mausoleum. Of course all will be done that he wishes. His servants are in a dreadful state. They adored him, and nursed him day and night for three years with the most devoted attachment. The King and Queen stay at Sans Souci till after the funeral, and Fritz and I here at Potsdam.... Ever your most dutiful and devoted Daughter,

Victoria.

P.S.—The funeral will only take place on Monday, and the body will be embalmed to-morrow. To-morrow evening there will be prayers at the bedside, and the day after the lying in state.

Queen Victoria to the Emperor of the French.

LETTER TO THE EMPEROR NAPOLEON

Osborne, *le 3 Janvier 1861.*

Sire et cher Frère,—Les bons vœux que votre Majesté veut bien m'exprimer à l'occasion de la nouvelle année me sont bien chers, et je vous prie d'en accepter mes remercîments sincères, ainsi que l'expression des vœux que je forme pour le bonheur de votre Majesté, de l'Impératrice et de votre cher enfant; le Prince se joint à moi dans ces sentiments.

Votre Majesté a bien raison si elle regarde avec quelque inquiétude l'état agité de l'Europe, mais je partage aussi avec elle le ferme espoir, que le mal peut être beaucoup amoindri, tant que la France et l'Angleterre s'entendent, et j'y ajouterai, tant que cette entente a pour but désintéressé de préserver au monde la paix et à chaque nation ses droits et ses possessions, et d'adoucir des animosités, qui menacent de produire les plus graves calamités, des guerres civiles et des luttes de races. La bénédiction de Dieu ne manquera pas à l'accomplissement d'une tâche aussi grande et sacrée.

Je me réjouis avec votre Majesté des glorieux succès que nos armées alliées viennent d'obtenir en Chine, et de la belle paix que ces succès ont amenée. Elle sera féconde, je l'espère, en bienfaits pour nos deux pays aussi bien que pour ce peuple bizarre que nous avons forcé à entrer en relations avec le reste du monde.

Il nous a fait bien du plaisir de voir l'Impératrice et d'entendre depuis que son voyage en Angleterre lui a fait tant de bien.

Agréez l'assurance de la parfaite amitié avec laquelle je suis, Sire et mon Frère, de votre Majesté Impériale, la bonne Sœur,

Victoria R.

Viscount Palmerston to Queen Victoria.

ITALIAN AFFAIRS

Broadlands, *10th January 1861.*

Viscount Palmerston presents his humble duty to your Majesty, and has many apologies to make for not having sooner answered your Majesty's previous communications. He is glad to be able to say that Lady Jocelyn's youngest boy, whose illness has been the cause of very great anxiety, is now in the course of gradual, but favourable recovery.

Viscount Palmerston returns to your Majesty the letter of the Emperor of the French, and your Majesty's excellent answer; it is to be hoped that he will profit by the sound advice which that answer contains.

Upon the subject of Italy your Majesty reminds Viscount Palmerston that he stated last summer that it would be better for the interests of England that Southern Italy should be a separate Monarchy, rather than that it should form part of an united Italy. Viscount Palmerston still retains that opinion; because a separate kingdom of the Two Sicilies would be more likely, in the event of war between England and France, to side, at least by its neutrality, with the strongest Naval Power, and it is to be hoped that such Power would be England. But then it would be necessary that the Two Sicilies as an independent and separate State should be well governed, and should have an enlightened Sovereign. This unfortunately has become hopeless and impossible under the Bourbon Dynasty, and no Englishman could wish to see a Murat or a Prince Napoleon on the Throne of Naples.[485] The course of events since last summer seems to have finally decided the fate of Sicily and Naples, and there can be no doubt that for the interest of the people of Italy, and with a view to the general balance of Power in Europe, a united Italy is the best arrangement. The Italian Kingdom will never side with France from partiality to France, and the stronger that kingdom becomes the better able it will

[485] Prince Napoleon Murat, a son of Joachim Murat, King of Naples, 1808-1815, had returned to France from the United States in 1848; an attempt was now being made to form a Murat party in Southern Italy.

be to resist political coercion from France. The chief hold that France will have upon the policy of the Kingdom of Italy consists in the retention of Venetia by Austria.

Viscount Palmerston has heard no more from Lord John Russell about his wish eventually to go to the House of Lords, and it is probable that this wish often before expressed will, as upon former occasions, be allowed to sleep undisturbed....

Queen Victoria to Lord John Russell.

Windsor Castle, *19th January 1861.*

The Queen has received Lord John Russell's letter enclosing his correspondence with Lord Clarendon.[486] She has kept the latter in order to show it to Lord Palmerston this evening, not knowing whether he has seen it already. She must say that Lord Clarendon's arguments are very conclusive. Has it ever occurred to Lord John Russell that, if Lord Clarendon were to go to Berlin carrying the highest compliment the Queen has to bestow, viz. the Order of the Garter to the new King of Prussia, and from thence to Vienna empty-handed to the Emperor of Austria for the purpose of giving good advice, the Emperor might look upon it as an offensive public proceeding towards him?

Viscount Palmerston to Queen Victoria.

CONSERVATIVE OVERTURES

Piccadilly, *27th January 1861.*

Viscount Palmerston presents his humble duty to your Majesty....

Viscount Palmerston saw Lord Malmesbury on Friday before the Cabinet. They both came up in the same train though not in the same carriage, and Lord Malmesbury came to Viscount Palmerston's in Piccadilly at three o'clock.

He said that he was charged by Lord Derby and Mr Disraeli with a message similar to that which he had conveyed last year, namely, that if Mr Gladstone were to propose a democratic Budget making a great transfer of burthens from indirect to direct Taxation, and if, the Cabinet refusing its concurrence, Mr Gladstone were to retire, the Conservative Party would give the Government substantial support

---

[486] Lord Clarendon was appointed to represent the Queen at the Coronation of the King of Prussia.

except in the case of the Government wishing to take an active part in war against Austria. That this did not of course mean an abstinence from usual attacks and criticisms in debate, but that no step would in such case be taken to produce a change of Government. In fact, said Lord Malmesbury, neither the Conservative leaders nor the Party wish at present to come into office, and have no intention of taking any step to turn the present Government out. Mr Bright had indeed proposed to Mr Disraeli to join together with the Radical Party, the Conservatives, for the purpose of turning out the present Government; and especially to get rid of Viscount Palmerston and Lord John Russell. Mr Bright said he would in that case give the Conservative Government a two years' existence, and by the end of that time the country, it might be hoped, would be prepared for a good and real Reform Bill, and then a proper Government might be formed.

This proposal, which it must be owned was not very tempting, Lord Malmesbury said had been declined. He also said that Count Persigny, on returning from one of his trips to Paris, had brought a similar proposal from Mr Cobden for a co-operation of Radicals and Conservatives to overthrow the present Government; but that also had been declined. Viscount Palmerston requested Lord Malmesbury to convey his thanks to Lord Derby and Mr Disraeli for the handsome communication which they had thus made to him, and to assure them that he fully appreciated the honourable and patriotic motives by which it had been prompted....

Queen Victoria to the King of the Belgians.

Windsor Castle, *29th January 1861.*

My beloved Uncle,—I write to you on a sad anniversary — already *seventeen* years ago, that it pleased God to take dearest Papa away from us all! He, who *ought* to have lived for twenty years longer at least!...

We hear from Berlin that the poor King is much *angegriffen*, and very irritable, but that my letter announcing to him that I would give him the Garter had given him *so* much pleasure that he had been seen to smile for the *first* time since the 2nd of January.

I think you will be gratified by the little extract from a letter from our dear friend the Queen, about Vicky, which I venture to send you—as well as by the following extract from Vicky's own letter to me, written on her wedding day, in which she says:—"Every time our dear wedding day returns I feel so happy and thankful—and live every moment of that blessed and never-to-be-forgotten day over again in thought. I love to dwell on every minute of that day; not a hope has been disappointed, not an expectation that has not been realised, and much more—that few can say—and I *am* thankful as I ought to be."

These two extracts are very gratifying to our hearts.

I must now wish you good-bye. With Albert's affectionate love, ever your devoted Niece,

Victoria R.

Viscount Palmerston to Sir Charles Phipps.

THE PROVOSTSHIP OF ETON

94 Piccadilly, *10th February 1861.*

My dear Phipps,—In the box which I sent to the Queen on Friday morning, giving a short account of the Debate on Thursday, I placed a separate paper submitting for her approvalDR GOODFORD that Dr Goodford, Headmaster of Eton, might be recommended to the Fellows to be elected to the office of Provost now vacant; and I mentioned that the matter was rather pressing. I have had no answer as yet, and the election is fixed for to-morrow.

The election is on the same footing as that of a bishop who is nominally elected by the Chapter of the Diocese, but who is named for being so elected by the Crown. The Crown recommends the person to be named Provost, and the Fellows as a matter of course elect him. But the election must be made within a stated period—I believe fifteen days after the vacancy has happened; and if the Crown does not within that period recommend, the Fellows proceed to make their own choice.

The election is fixed for to-morrow, and it would not, I think, be desirable to let the Royal prerogative drop on this occasion. The persons who have been named as candidates are Dr Goodford, Headmaster, and with regard to him it is to be said that the office has generally been given to the Headmaster, and that, as far as the Provost has any function connected with improvements in the arrangement of the school, there is an advantage in his having been conversant with the details of the existing system. Dr Goodford is qualified for the office by his degree.

The next candidate is Mr Coleridge, once a master in the school, but he is not qualified by a sufficient degree, and there was a prejudice against him on account of his Puseyite tendencies.

The third is Dr Chapman, late Bishop of Colombo, qualified by his degree, but having no peculiar claims or other recommendations for the office.

The fourth is Mr Birch, formerly tutor to the Prince of Wales, scarcely of sufficient calibre for the office, and not qualified by a sufficient degree.

Between Dr Goodford and Dr Chapman I think the preference should be given to Dr Goodford, and the more especially because Dr Chapman is supposed to entertain theological opinions similar to those of Mr Coleridge, his brother-in-law.

If the Queen should approve of Dr Goodford being recommended, perhaps she would have the goodness to sign the document sent in the accompanying box, and if it is returned by the earliest opportunity it is just possible that I may be able to send it to Windsor in time for the election to-morrow.[487] Yours sincerely,

Palmerston.

Queen Victoria to Lord John Russell.

10th February 1861.

The Queen has received Lord John Russell's letter enclosing the draft of one to General Garibaldi, which she now returns. She had much doubt about its being altogether safe for the Government to get into correspondence, however unofficial, with the General, and thinks that it would be better for Lord John *not* to write to him. Lord Palmerston, who was here this afternoon on other business, has undertaken to explain the reasons in detail to Lord John—in which he fully concurs.

Lord John Russell to Queen Victoria.

GARIBALDI

Chesham Place, *11th February 1861.*

[487] Dr Goodford was elected, and remained Provost till his death in 1884.

Lord John Russell presents his humble duty to your Majesty; he earnestly entreats your Majesty to consider whether any step ought to be omitted by which the peace of Europe may be preserved.

General Garibaldi is generally esteemed by Italians; even Count Ludolf speaks of him in the highest terms of praise. General Garibaldi has lost his country, and is full of resentment at Count Cavour for selling it. He respects and admires England for her disinterested conduct.

But it is evident the French Emperor is again exciting the Hungarian party. The Garibaldian legion is told to hold itself in readiness, and the *Pays* and *Patrie* are instructed to praise the Legion. They are being assembled in Genoa and Piedmont.

There is little chance of Garibaldi's refusing to take part in this expedition, and if he does proceed to the Dalmatian or Istrian coast, his name will have an immense effect.

It does not seem reasonable to throw away any chance of saving the Austrian Empire and the peace of Europe.

Lord John Russell will wait till Monday next to learn definitively your Majesty's pleasure.

The proposed letter appears to him to give some hope of preventing great misfortunes. In this belief it is Lord John Russell's duty to endeavour to prevent the frightful war which is impending.

Kossuth is fabricating paper to the extent of from 140 to 300,000,000 of florins to furnish the sinews of insurrection. In the month of March Hungary will be in a blaze. But if Italy, Germany, and France keep away, the fire may burn out of itself.

Viscount Palmerston to Queen Victoria.

11th February 1861.

Viscount Palmerston presents his humble duty to your Majesty, and in returning Lord John's letter begs to submit, that as Lord John is so anxious to send it, and seems so strongly of opinion that it is an effort which might be successful in dissuading Garibaldi from attempting to create disturbances in the Austrian territory by going thither with a band of adventurers, it may be best to let the letter go, though it might perhaps be improved by pointing more directly to the nature of the expedition which it advises Garibaldi not to undertake.

There may be inconveniences which may arise from the letter, but they might be dealt with; on the other hand, if Garibaldi undertakes his expedition, it would be a matter of regret if it could be thought or said that a step which might have prevented the mischief had been omitted.

Queen Victoria to Lord John Russell.

Buckingham Palace, *12th February 1861.*

The Queen has received Lord John Russell's reiterated request for her sanction to his writing to General Garibaldi. She still entertains the same objections to the step, as implying a recognition of the General's position as a European Power as enabling him to allow the impression to prevail, that he is in communication with the British Government and acts under its inspiration, as possibly leading to a prolonged and embarrassing correspondence, and as implying for the future that when the disapprobation of the Government is not expressed (as in the present instance), it gives its consent to his aggressive schemes. The Queen will not prevent, however, Lord John from taking a step which he considers gives a chance of averting a great European calamity. Should Lord John therefore adhere to his opinion, she asks him to let her see the letter again, upon the precise wording of which so much depends.

Queen Victoria to the King of the Belgians.

A HAPPY ANNIVERSARY

Buckingham Palace, *12th February 1861.*

My dearest Uncle,—Many, many thanks for your dear letter of the 8th. Here we have cold again since the day before yesterday, and last night seven degrees of frost. On Sunday we celebrated, with feelings of *deep gratitude* and love, the *twenty-first* anniversary of our blessed marriage, a day which had brought us, and I may say the *world* at *large*, such incalculable blessings! *Very* few can say with me that their husband at the end of twenty-one years is *not* only full of the friendship, kindness, and affection which a truly happy marriage brings with it, but the same tender love of the *very first days of our marriage!*

We missed dear Mamma and *three* of our children,[488] but had *six* dear ones round us—and assembled in the evening those of our Household *still* remaining who were *with us then!...*

---

[488] The Duchess of Kent was at Frogmore; the Princess Royal, now Crown Princess of Prussia, was at Potsdam; the Prince of Wales had just entered

In Parliament things go on quietly enough, and every one *hopes* for a short session....

Hoping that these lines will find you well, believe me ever, your devoted Niece,

Victoria R.

Viscount Palmerston to Queen Victoria.

LORD JOHN RUSSELL AND GARIBALDI

Downing Street, *13th February 1861.*

Viscount Palmerston presents his humble duty to your Majesty, and begs to state that the Cabinet at its meeting this afternoon were of opinion that Lord John Russell's proposed letter to Garibaldi, as altered by Lord John, might do good, and could scarcely be attended with any material inconvenience, and that therefore it might go.[489]

---

upon his first term at Cambridge; and Prince Alfred had joined his ship, the *Euryalus*, at Plymouth.

[489] It accordingly was sent in the following form:—

General,—You did me the honour, some time ago, to write me a letter, thanking me for a speech I made in Parliament.

I was not insensible to the value of that compliment. My present purpose however is not compliment.

I wish you seriously to reconsider your declaration that you propose to begin a war in the Spring.

It seems to me that no individual, however distinguished, has a right to determine for his country the momentous question of peace or war with a foreign State.

Italy, represented by a free Parliament, is about to assemble and declare her own sentiments and wishes.

It is surely for the King and the Parliament together to decide on questions which may involve all Europe in bloodshed.

I cannot believe that you will be the man to give the signal of dissension in Italy. I remain, General, your obedient Servant,

John Russell.

The reply received was as follows:—

Caprera, *4th March 1861.*

Queen Victoria to Viscount Palmerston.

Buckingham Palace, *22nd February 1861.*

The Queen is very glad to see that the Government is seriously taking up the question of iron-sided ships, and looks forward to the result of Lord Palmerston's conference with the Duke of Somerset. The number wanted appears large, but the Queen must add that she does not consider one ship a sufficient preponderance over the French Navy for this country. Twenty-seven to twenty-six would give that number.

Queen Victoria to the King of the Belgians.

DEATH OF DUCHESS OF KENT

Frogmore, *16th March 1861.*

My dearly beloved Uncle,—On this, the most dreadful day of my life, does your poor broken-hearted child write one line of love and devotion. *She* is gone![490] That *precious, dearly beloved tender* Mother—whom I never was parted from but for a few months—without whom *I* can't *imagine life*—has been taken from us! It is *too*

Noble Lord,—Italy owes you much gratitude. You, however, judge me somewhat harshly; giving credence to rumours which attribute to me projects that are not known to any one.

I hope to make war again for my country. But I desire that you, deserving as you are of my esteem and attachment, should believe that I will not undertake anything which may injure or be in contradiction with the rights of the King and Parliament of Italy.

I do not love war, Minister, but, in the present condition of my country, it appears most difficult to constitute her in a normal manner, without war.

I am sure that Italy is able to make her war of liberation even this year. The person who directs does not feel the same certainty, and I leave it to you to weigh his motives. I, if I am not called upon by events, shall continue in my retreat, and I will, in every way, endeavour to gain your good-will, and that of the generous nation to whom my country owes so much, etc., etc., etc. I am your devoted Servant,

G. Garibaldi.

[490] The Duchess of Kent died on the 16th of March. She had had a surgical operation in the arm, on account of an abscess, a short time before, but till the 15th the medical reports had been encouraging. On that day the Queen went to Frogmore, and was with her mother at the time of her death.

dreadful! But she is at peace—at rest—her fearful sufferings at an end! It was quite painless—though there was very *distressing*, heartrending breathing to witness. I held her dear, dear hand in mine to the very last, which I am truly thankful for! But the watching that precious life going out was fearful! Alas! she never knew me! But she was spared the pang of parting! How this will *grieve* and *distress you! You* who are now doubly precious to us. Good Alice was with us all through, and *deeply* afflicted, and wishes to say everything kind to you. Bertie and Lenchen are now here—all much grieved, and have seen her *sleeping* peacefully and eternally! Dearest Albert is dreadfully overcome—and well he may, for *she* adored him! I feel so truly *verwaist*. God bless and protect you. Ever your devoted and truly unhappy Niece and Child,

Victoria R.

P.S.—The devotion of dearest Mamma's ladies and maids is not to be described. Their love and their devotion were *too touching*. There we all were round her—the poor, good, old Clark, who is so devoted to us all. Ever again, your devoted Child,

Victoria R.

Queen Victoria to the King of the Belgians.

BEREAVEMENT

Windsor Castle, *26th March 1861*.

My dearest Uncle,—Your sad little letter of the 21st reached me on Saturday. On Sunday I took leave of those dearly beloved remains—a dreadful moment; I had never been near a coffin before, but dreadful and heartrending as it was, it was so beautifully arranged that it would have pleased *her*, and most probably *she* looked down and blessed *us*—as we poor sorrowing mortals knelt around, overwhelmed with grief! It was covered with wreaths, and the carpet strewed with sweet, white flowers. *I* and our daughters did *not* go *yesterday*—it would have been *far* too much for *me*—and Albert when he returned, with tearful eyes told me it was well I did not go—so affecting had been the sight—so *universal* the sympathy.

Poor little Arthur went too. I and my girls prayed at home together, and dwelt on her happiness and peace.

But oh! dearest Uncle—the loss—the truth of it—which *I cannot, do not* realise even when I go (as I do *daily*) to Frogmore—the *blank* becomes *daily* worse!

The constant intercourse of *forty-one*, years cannot cease without the *total want* of *power* of *real enjoyment* of *anything*. A sort of cloud which hangs over you, and seems to *oppress* everything—and a positive *weakness* in the powers of reflection and mental exertion. The doctors *tell* me I *must not* attempt to *force* this. Long conversation, loud talking, the talking of many people together, I *can't* bear yet. It must come *very* gradually....

I try to be, and very often am, quite *resigned*—but dearest Uncle, this is a life sorrow. On *all* festive or mournful occasions, on *all* family events, *her love* and *sympathy* will be so *fearfully wanting*. Then again, except Albert (who I very often don't see but very little in the day), I have *no human* being except our children, and that is not the same *Verhältniss*, to *open* myself to; and besides, a *woman* requires *woman's* society and sympathy sometimes, as men do *men's*. All this, beloved Uncle, will show you that, without *dwelling* constantly upon it, or *moping* or becoming *morbid*, though the *blank* and the *loss to me*, in my isolated position especially, is *such* a *dreadful*, and such an *irreparable one*, the worst *trials* are *yet* to come. My poor birthday, I can hardly think of it! Strange it is how often *little trifles*, insignificant in themselves, upset one more even than greater things....

But the general sympathy for *me*, and approval of the manner in which I have shown my grief, as well as the affection and respect for dearest Mamma's memory in the country, is *quite wonderful and most touching*. Ever your devoted Niece,

Victoria R.

Queen Victoria to the King of the Belgians.

RENEWED GRIEF

Buckingham Palace, *30th March 1861*.

My dearly beloved Uncle,—It is a comfort for me to write to you, and I think you may like to hear from your poor motherless child. It is *to-day* a *fortnight* already, and it seems but yesterday—*all* is before me, and at the same time *all, all* seems *quite impossible*. The blank—the desolation—the fearful and awful *Sehnsucht und Wehmuth* come back with redoubled force, and the *weeping*, which day after day is my welcome friend, is my greatest relief.

We have an immense deal to do—and everything is in the greatest *order*; but to *open her* drawers and presses, and to look at all her dear jewels and trinkets in order to identify everything, and relieve her really excellent servants from all responsibility and anxiety, is like a sacrilege, and I feel as if my heart was being torn asunder! So many recollections of my childhood are brought back to me, and these dumb souvenirs which she wore and used, and which so painfully survive *what* we so *dearly* and *passionately* loved, touch chords in one's heart and soul, which are *most* painful and yet pleasing too. We have found many most interesting and valuable letters—the existence of which I was not aware of—and which, I *think*, must have come back with poor Papa's letters, viz. letters from *my* poor father asking for dearest Mamma's hand—and sending a letter from you, encouraging him to ask her. And many others—very precious letters—from dear Grand-mamma; Albert has also found at Clarence House, where he went to-day, many of dear Grandpapa's.[491] ...

Frogmore we mean to keep just as dear Mamma left it—and keep it cheerful and pretty as it still is. I go there constantly; I feel so accus-tomed to go down the hill, and *so* attracted to it, for I fancy *she* must be there.

Was poor dear Grandpapa's death-bed such a sad one? You speak of its distressing impressions.[492] ...

She watches *over us now*, you may be sure! Ever your devoted, sorrowing Child and Niece,

Victoria R.

Albert is so kind, and does all with such tenderness and feeling. Vicky goes on Tuesday, and we on Wednesday, to Osborne, where I think the air and quiet will do me good.

---

[491] Duke Francis Frederick of Saxe-Coburg-Saalfeld, and Duchess Augusta Caroline Sophia, the parents of the Duchess of Kent and King Leopold.

[492] In a recent letter King Leopold had said that he was not quite sixteen years old when his father died (1806), and the elder son, Ernest, being alarmingly ill at Königsberg, he was himself called upon to be the support of his mother. "The recollections of that death-bed," he adds, "are fresh in my memory, as if it had been yesterday. I thank God that your recollections of that terrible mo-ment are so peaceful, and that you may preserve an impression ... without any distressing addition."

The King of the Belgians to Queen Victoria.

FATHERLY ADVICE

Laeken, *1st April 1861.*

My beloved Victoria,—Your dear letter of the 30th *moved me very much.* I can see everything, and it makes me shed tears of the sincerest sorrow.

The bereavement, the impossibility, they are what one feels most deeply and painfully, that nothing will bring back the beloved object, that there is a rupture with everything earthly that nothing can remedy. Your good, dear Mamma was without ostentation, sincerely religious, a great blessing, and the only solid support we can find. Happy those whose faith cannot be shaken; they can bear the hardships of earthly life with fortitude.

True it is that if we compare the sorrows of our earthly life with the hope of an eternal existence, though painfully felt, still they shrink as it were in appreciation.

You feel so *truly*, so *affectionately*, that even in that you must gratify the dear being we lost. When I think of poor Aunt Julia,[493] she was so alone that I cannot help to pity her even in all the objects she valued and left behind; the affectionate care which is shown to everything connected with your dear Mamma could not have existed, and still she was a noble character, and with a warm, generous heart. In all your dear Mamma's letters there will everywhere be found traces of the affection which united us. From early childhood we were close allies; she recollected everything so well of that period which now, since the departure of the two sisters, is totally unknown to every one but me, which, you can imagine, is a most melancholy sensation. Time flies so fast that all dear recollections soon get isolated. Your stay at Osborne will do you good, though Spring, when fine, affects one very much, to think that the one that was beloved does not share in these pleasant sensations. You must try, however, not to shake your precious health too much. Your dear Mamma, who watched your looks so affectionately, would not approve of it.... Your devoted old Uncle,

Leopold R.

---

[493] Sister of King Leopold, and widow of the Grand Duke Constantine, who had lived in retirement at Geneva for many years, and died at Elfenau on the 15th of August 1860.

Queen Victoria to the King of the Belgians.

Osborne, *9th April 1861.*

My dearly beloved Uncle,—Your dear, *sad* letter of the 5th found a warm response in my poor heart, and I thank you with all my heart for it. I am *now most* anxiously waiting for an answer to my letter asking you to come to us *now*. You would, I think, find it soothing, and it would painfully interest you to look over her letters and papers, which make me *live* in times I heard her talk of when I was a child. It is touching to find how she treasured up every little flower, every bit of hair. I found some of dear Princess Charlotte's, and touching relics of my poor Father, in a little writing-desk of his I had never seen, with his last letters to her, and her notes *after* his death written in a little book, expressing such longing to be reunited to him! *Now* she *is!* And what a comfort it is to think *how many very dear ones* are gone on before her whom she will find! All these notes show how very, very much she and my beloved Father *loved* each other. *Such* love and affection! I hardly knew it was *to that extent*. Then her love for *me*—it is *too* touching! I have found little books with the accounts of my babyhood, and they show *such* unbounded tenderness! Oh! I am so wretched to think *how, for a time, two people most* wickedly estranged us!... To miss a mother's friendship—not to be able to have her to confide in—when a girl *most* needs it, was fearful! I *dare not* think of it—it drives me *wild* now! But thank God! that is all passed *long, long* ago, and she had forgotten it, and only thought of the last very happy years.

And all that was brought by my good angel, dearest Albert, whom *she* adored, and in whom she had such unbounded confidence....

On Sunday our dear little Beatrice was four years old. It upset me much, for she was the idol of that beloved Grandmamma, and the child so fond of her. She continually speaks of her—how she "is in Heaven," but hopes she will return! She is a most darling, engaging child.... Ever your devoted Niece,

Victoria R.

Queen Victoria to Lord John Russell.

THE DANISH QUESTION

Osborne, *27th May 1861.*

The Queen returns the proposed draft of answer to the observations of the Russian Government on Lord John Russell's proposals with regard to the Danish Question. She has to observe that this reverses the whole position taken by us hitherto. Prince Gortschakoff is quite right in reminding us that the engagements taken in 1852[494] did not contain a formal guarantee (*obliging* to take up arms for the defence of the object guaranteed) in deference to the opinion of the British Government which, on general principles, has always objected to such engagements. These principles are as important now as ever, and yet Lord John proposes "to renew the *guarantee* of the integrity of the Danish Monarchy contained in the Treaty of 8th May 1852," thereby giving those engagements the force of a guarantee, which was on principle objected to by us at the time. Both Russia and France in their answers object to such a guarantee now, even with regard to Schleswig alone, as involving the guaranteeing powers in future grave difficulties, and Lord John proposes to extend it to Holstein, a part of Germany and not of Denmark, by way of obviating the difficulty. The Queen cannot give her sanction to this proposal.

Lord John Russell to Queen Victoria.

WAR IN AMERICA

Foreign Office, *30th May 1861.*

Lord John Russell presents his humble duty to your Majesty; he has the honour to submit letters from the Emperor and Empress of Austria of a private nature. The Cabinet decided yesterday that the ports of your Majesty's Dominions ought to be closed to the ships of war and privateers of the Belligerents in America.[495] A letter for that object has been sent to the Law Officers of the Crown, and will be, when put into proper form, submitted for your Majesty's approbation.

---

[494] A Treaty was signed by the European Powers on the 8th of May 1852, by which the succession of the line of Sonderburg-Glücksburg to the Danish throne was settled, and the integrity of the kingdom guaranteed. See *ante*, vol. ii. p. 358.

[495] See Introductory Note, *ante*, p. 421.

Queen Victoria to Viscount Palmerston.

Osborne, *30th May 1861.*

The Queen returns these papers. She thinks it of great importance that we should be strong in Canada, and thinks an increase in Artillery as important as the sending of two more battalions, as that Arm cannot be supplied at all by the Colony. The Naval forces would, however, require strengthening even more. It is less likely that the remnant of the United States could send expeditions by land to the North while quarrelling with the South, than that they should commit acts of violence at sea.

Queen Victoria to Lord John Russell.

Buckingham Palace, *5th June 1861.*

The Queen has perused the accompanying draft to Sir James Hudson. She is of opinion that so important a step as proposals on our part for the solution of the Roman Question, with which we are not directly concerned, and for the solution of which we are for many obvious reasons perhaps the Power possessing the least favourable position, is a subject of such great importance, that it should not be undertaken without the most mature consideration. Has this draft been brought before the Cabinet? The Queen wishes to have their united advice before giving her decision. Her opinion at present is against our volunteering a scheme which will render us responsible for the result of grave complications, from which we have hitherto stood happily quite clear. The Queen wishes these lines to be communicated to the Cabinet.[496]

---

[496] Lord John Russell had written that the withdrawal of the French troops from Rome would probably be followed by tumults and bloodshed; and as both the Roman party and Garibaldi hated the Government of the Pope, and wished to put an end to his temporal power, he suggested that the Pope should be allowed to retain his sovereignty during his lifetime, in a restricted territory and with restricted powers; that Italian troops should occupy the towns and villages outside a limit of five miles from Rome; and that the King of Italy and the Emperor of the French should agree not to recognise the temporal power of any future Pope.

Lord John Russell to Queen Victoria.

DEATH OF CAVOUR

Pembroke Lodge, *6th June 1861.*

Lord John Russell presents his humble duty to your Majesty; the despatch relating to Rome had been sent, seeming to Lord John Russell quite unobjectionable. But your Majesty will see that it was instantly suspended, and that Count Cavour is dying.[497] The despatch was solely intended to save the poor old Pope from insult, and Rome from tumult, but beyond this it is of no consequence, and the death of Cavour may give a new complexion to the affairs of Italy.

Nothing will be done on the despatch at present.

Viscount Palmerston to Queen Victoria.

Piccadilly, *18th June 1861.*

Viscount Palmerston presents his humble duty to your Majesty....

Viscount Palmerston submits a note from Garter King at Arms, by which your Majesty will see that there are now three Garters vacant; and Viscount Palmerston would beg to suggest for your Majesty's consideration that those Garters might appropriately be conferred upon Lord Canning for his great services in India, upon Lord John Russell for his long political services under your Majesty, and upon the Duke of Somerset, senior Duke after the Duke of Norfolk, and the able administrator of an important branch of your Majesty's service.[498]

Viscount Palmerston is not aware whether by the regulations of the Order the Garter could be sent out to Lord Canning in India. If that were possible, it might have the double advantage of strengthening his hands during the remainder of his stay, by affording so public a mark of your Majesty's approval; and moreover of making sure that Lord Canning should receive this mark of your Majesty's royal favour, while the Government is in the hands of an administration similar to that at whose recommendation he was sent out, which perhaps might be more agreeable to his feelings than running the chance, always pos-

---

[497] Count Cavour died at Turin on the 6th of June. It is curious to note that the words of the Emperor Napoleon, on hearing of the death of Cavour, appear to have been "Le cocher est tombé du siège; il faut voir maintenant si les chevaux iront s'emporter, ou rentrer à l'écurie."

[498] The Duke was First Lord of the Admiralty. All the three Peers mentioned received the Garter early in 1862.

sible, though Viscount Palmerston hopes it may not be probable, that political combinations might, before his return in May or June 1862, have produced administrative changes.

Queen Victoria to Viscount Palmerston.

DEATH OF LORD CAMPBELL

24th June 1861.

The Queen approves of Sir R. Bethell[499] as Lord Campbell's successor. Lord Palmerston is aware of the Queen's objections to the appointment; they will have weighed with him as much as with her. If therefore he finally makes this recommendation, the Queen must assume that under all the circumstances he considers it the best solution of the difficulty, and that his Colleagues take the same view.

The Duchess of Sutherland to Queen Victoria.

THE DUCHESS OF SUTHERLAND

Stafford House, *26th June 1861.*

Madam,—I shall never forget your Majesty and the Prince's kindness.[500]

I am anxious to tell your Majesty as strongly as *it was*, what *his* feeling was of my service to your Majesty; he approved and delighted in it; dear as it was to me—it could not have been if this had not been so, nor those occasional absences, if he had not had devoted children when I was away; still, when the great parting comes one grudges every hour, and the yearning is terrible.

Even in his last illness he showed an anxious feeling, as if he feared I might resign, saying that I knew what an interest it had been to him, how he had liked hearing of the Queen and her family. He spoke very late in life of your Majesty's constant kindness. This feeling and early associations made him take a great interest in the Princess Royal's marriage, which did not leave him. If it ever crossed your Majesty—if your Majesty should ever feel that I might have been devoted, if I had had but one service, pray believe that he took the

[499] Lord Campbell died at the age of eighty-two; his successor was created Lord Westbury.

[500] The Duke of Sutherland had died in the preceding February.

greatest pleasure and pride in that other great service; and that therefore he really felt it best it should be so.

Since I have written this I have received your Majesty's most kind letter—and the precious gift of the photograph so wonderfully like, and rendering exactly that most kind and loving countenance. I shall like much sending one to your Majesty of my dearest husband.

I repeat to myself the precious word that I am dear to your Majesty again and again; and that my love to your Majesty was returned. How often I shall think of this in my altered life, in my solitude of heart! The admiration I have ever felt for the Prince has been one of the great pleasures of my life; that he should be your Majesty's husband, a constant thankfulness. I feel I owe him much, and that great approbation and admiration are not barren feelings. I have the honour to remain, Madam, your Majesty's devoted Subject,

Harriet Sutherland.

I fear I have written worse than usual—I can hardly see to do so—weak eyes and tears.

Viscount Palmerston to Queen Victoria.

MR LAYARD

Piccadilly, *8th July 1861.*

Viscount Palmerston presents his humble duty to your Majesty, and begs to state that Lord Elcho[501] this afternoon moved a Resolution that the new Foreign Office should not be built in the Palladian style. Mr Charles Buxton seconded the Motion. Mr Cowper[502] opposed it, stating reasons for preferring the Italian style to the Gothic. Mr Layard was for neither, but seemed to wish that somebody would invent a new style of architecture. Mr Tite,[503] the architect, was strongly for the Italian style; Lord John Manners, swayed by erroneous views in religion and taste, was enthusiastic for Gothic;[504] Mr Dudley Fortescue con-

[501] Now Earl of Wemyss.

[502] Mr William Cowper, at this time First Commissioner of Works.

[503] Mr (afterwards Sir) William Tite, was now Member for Bath; he had been the architect entrusted with the task of rebuilding the Royal Exchange.

[504] Mr Gilbert Scott had made his first designs for the new Foreign Office in the Gothic style; his appointment as architect for the building was made by the Derby Government, but the scheme which they favoured, for a Gothic

fided in a low voice to a limited range of hearers some weak arguments in favour of Gothic; Mr Osborne seemed to be against everything that anybody had ever proposed, and wanted to put off the building till some plan better suited to his own taste should have been invented. Viscount Palmerston answered the objections made to the Italian plan, and Lord Elcho's Motion was negatived by 188 to 75. The House then went into Committee of Supply, and the first estimate being that for the Foreign Office, some of the Gothic party who had not been able to deliver their speeches on Lord Elcho's Motion, let them off on this estimate....

Queen Victoria to Viscount Palmerston.

Osborne, *24th July 1861.*

The Queen is sorry that she cannot alter her determination about Mr Layard.[505] She fully recognises the importance of the Parliamentary exigencies; but the Queen cannot sacrifice to them the higher interests of the country. Neither Mr Layard nor Mr Osborne ought to be proposed as representatives of the Foreign Office in the House of Commons, and therefore of the Crown to foreign countries. If Lord Palmerston can bring Mr Layard into office in some other place, to get his assistance in the House of Commons, she will not object.

Viscount Palmerston to Queen Victoria.

MR LAYARD

94 Piccadilly, *24th July 1861.*

Viscount Palmerston presents his humble duty to your Majesty, and regrets very much to find that he has not succeeded in removing your Majesty's objections to Mr Layard as Under-Secretary of State for the Foreign Department; but he still hopes that he may be able to do so. If he rightly understands your Majesty's last communication on

---

building, was opposed by Lord Palmerston, and Scott adopted the Italian style in deference to his views.

505 In the course of July, Lord John Russell, who had entered Parliament for the first time in 1813, was raised to the Peerage as Earl Russell and Viscount Amberley. To supply the loss to the Government of two such powerful debaters as Lord Russell and Lord Herbert, Lord Palmerston had suggested Mr Layard as Under-Secretary for Foreign Affairs, mentioning also the claims of Mr Bernal Osborne.

this subject, he is led to infer that your Majesty's main objection is founded on a dislike that Mr Layard should be the representative and organ of the Foreign Policy of the Crown in the House of Commons.

With regard to his being a subordinate officer in the Foreign Office, your Majesty's sanction to that was obtained in 1851-52, when Mr Layard was Under-Secretary to Lord Granville. His tenure of office at that time was short; not from any fault of his, but because the Government of that day was overthrown by Viscount Palmerston's Motion in the House of Commons in February 1852 about the Militia; and Lord Granville speaks highly of Mr Layard's performance of his official duties at that time. There is no reason, but the reverse, for thinking him less competent now than then; and an Under-Secretary of State is only the instrument and mouthpiece of his principal to say what he is told, and to write what he is bid.

With regard to Mr Layard's position in the House of Commons, he would in no respect be the representative of the Foreign Policy of the country; that function will belong to Viscount Palmerston, now that the Secretary of State for Foreign Affairs will be removed to the House of Lords, and it will be Viscount Palmerston's duty and care to see that nobody infringes upon that function. Mr Layard would be useful to answer unimportant questions as to matters of fact, but all questions involving the Foreign Policy of the country will be answered by Viscount Palmerston as head of the Government, as was done when Lord Clarendon was Foreign Secretary and in the House of Lords. But there are not unfrequently great debates on Foreign Affairs in the House of Commons, and there are many members, some of them not perhaps of great weight, who join in attacks on such matters. It is of great importance to your Majesty's Government to have a sufficient number of speakers on such occasions. Lord John Russell and Lord Herbert were ready and powerful. Mr Gladstone is almost the only one on the Treasury Bench who follows up foreign questions close enough to take an active part; it would be of great advantage to Viscount Palmerston to have as assistant on such occasions a man like Mr Layard, knowing the details of matters discussed, able to make a good speech in reply to Mr Fitzgerald, or Mr Baillie Cochrane,[506] or Mr Hennessy,[507] or Sir G. Bowyer,[508] and who would shape his course in strict conformity with the line which might be chalked out for him by

[506] Afterwards Lord Lamington.

[507] Mr (afterwards Sir) John Pope Hennessy, M.P. for King's County.

[508] M.P. for Dundalk.

Viscount Palmerston. Your Majesty need therefore be under no apprehension that Mr Layard or anybody else, who might in the House of Commons hold the office of Under-Secretary of State for Foreign Affairs, would appear to the world as the organ or representative of the Foreign Policy of your Majesty's Government. With respect to giving Mr Layard any other office of the same kind, there is none other in which he could be placed without putting into the Foreign Office somebody far less fit for it, and putting Mr Layard into some office for which he is far less fit. His fitness is for the Foreign Department, and to use the illustration, which was a favourite one of the late Mr Drummond, it would be putting the wrong man into the wrong hole. Viscount Palmerston has, as charged with the conduct of the business of the Government in the House of Commons, sustained a severe loss by the removal of two most able and useful colleagues, Lord Herbert and Lord John Russell, and he earnestly hopes that your Majesty will be graciously pleased to assist him in his endeavours, not indeed to supply their place, but in some degree to lessen the detriment which their removal has occasioned.

Queen Victoria to Viscount Palmerston.

MR LAYARD

Osborne, *25th July 1861.*

The Prince has reported to the Queen all that Lord Palmerston said to him on the subject of Mr Layard; this has not had the effect of altering her opinion as to the disqualifications of that gentleman for the particular office for which Lord Palmerston proposes him. This appointment would, in the Queen's opinion, be a serious evil. If Lord Palmerston on sincere self-examination should consider that without it the difficulty of carrying on his Government was such as to endanger the continuance of its success, the Queen will, of course, have to admit an evil for the country in order to avert a greater. She still trusts, however, that knowing the nature of the Queen's objections, he will not place her in this dilemma.

Viscount Palmerston to Queen Victoria.

94 Piccadilly, *26th July 1861.*

Viscount Palmerston presents his humble duty to your Majesty, and begs to be allowed to make his grateful and respectful acknowledgments for your Majesty's gracious and condescending acquiescence in his recommendation of Mr Layard for the appointment of Under-Secretary of State for the Foreign Department. It is always a source of most sincere pain to Viscount Palmerston to find himself differing, on any point, in opinion with your Majesty, a respect for whose soundness of judgment, and clearness of understanding, must always lead him to distrust the value of his own conclusions when they differ from those to which your Majesty has arrived. But the question about Mr Layard turned mainly upon considerations connected with the conduct of public business of your Majesty's Government in the House of Commons.

Viscount Palmerston sits in that House four days in every week during the Session of Parliament, from half-past four in the afternoon to any hour however late after midnight at which the House may adjourn. It is his duty carefully to watch the proceedings of the House, and to observe and measure the fluctuating bearings of Party and of sectional associations on the present position of the Government, and on its chances for the future; and he is thus led to form conclusions as to persons and parties which may not equally strike, or with equal force, those who from without and from higher regions may see general results without being eye- and ear-witnesses of the many small and successive details out of which those results are built up.

It was thus that Viscount Palmerston was led to a strong conviction that the proposed appointment of Mr Layard would be a great advantage to your Majesty's Government as regards the conduct of business in the House of Commons, and the position of your Majesty's Government in that House; and he is satisfied that he will be able to prevent Mr Layard in any subsidiary part which he may have to take in any discussion on foreign questions, from departing from the line which may be traced out for him by Lord John Russell and Viscount Palmerston....

Queen Victoria to the King of the Belgians.

THE KING OF SWEDEN

Osborne, *13th August 1861.*

My beloved Uncle,—Since Saturday we have great heat. *Our* King of Sweden[509] arrived yesterday evening. We went out in the yacht to meet him, and did so; but his ship going slow, the *dress* of the

[509] Charles XV., who succeeded to the throne in 1859.

hohen Herrn only arrived at a quarter to nine, and we only sat down to dinner at a quarter past nine! The King and Prince Oscar[510] are very French, and very Italian! I think that there is a dream of a Scandinavian Kingdom floating before them. The King is a fine-looking man.... He is not at all difficult to get on with, and is very civil. Oscar is very amiable and mild, and very proud of his three little boys. They leave again quite early to-morrow.

Our *dear* children leave us, alas! on Friday quite early, for Antwerp.[511] It will again be a painful trial! Their stay has been very pleasant and *gemüthlich*, and we have seen more of and known dear Fritz more thoroughly than we ever did before, and really he is *very* excellent, and would, I am convinced, make an excellent King. The little children are *very great* darlings, and we shall miss them sadly.

On the 16th we go to poor, dear Frogmore, and on the 17th we shall visit that dear grave! Last year she was still so well, and so full of life; but it was a *very* sad birthday, two days after the loss of that dear beloved sister, whom she has joined so soon! Oh! the agony of *Wehmuth*, the bitterness of the blank, do *not* get better with time! Beloved Mamma, how hourly she is in my mind!

The King of Prussia will have great pleasure in visiting you at Wiesbaden; he will arrive at Ostend on the 16th....

Good-bye, and God bless you, dearest Uncle. Ever your devoted Niece,

Victoria R.

Viscount Palmerston to Queen Victoria.

SWEDISH POLITICS

Downing Street, *14th August 1861.*

Viscount Palmerston presents his humble duty to your Majesty, and hastens to answer the enquiry contained in your Majesty's note, which was delivered to him at Southampton. He must, in the first place, explain that much of what was said to him by the King of Sweden and by Prince Oscar was not clearly understood by him. They would both speak English—which they spoke with difficulty and in an

[510] Brother and heir to Charles XV., whom he succeeded, as Oscar II., in 1872; died 1907.

[511] The Crown Prince and Princess of Prussia, accompanied by their two children, were on a visit to the Queen.

indistinct utterance of voice—and he did not like to break the conversation into French, because to have done so would have looked like a condemnation of their English, of any imperfection of which they did not seem to be at all conscious.

The King was very guarded in all he said about France; the Prince spoke with more freedom and with less caution. The result of what Viscount Palmerston gathered from their conversation, and perhaps for this purpose they may be put together, because they probably both feel and think nearly alike, though the Prince lets his thoughts out more than the King, may be summed up as follows.

They were much pleased and flattered by the kind and friendly reception given them by the French Emperor, and both he and they seem to have had present to their minds that the existing Royal Family of Sweden is descended from General Bernadotte—a General in the Army of the First Napoleon. They think the French Emperor sincerely desirous of maintaining his alliance with England, believing it to be for his interest to do so. But they consider the French Nation essentially aggressive, and they think that the Emperor is obliged to humour that national feeling, and to follow, as far as the difference of circumstances will allow, the policy of his Uncle. They consider the principle of nationalities to be the deciding principle of the day, and accordingly Venetia ought to belong to Italy, Poland ought to be severed from Russia, and Finland ought to be restored to Sweden. Holstein should be purely German with its own Duke, Schleswig should be united to Denmark, and when the proper time comes, Denmark, so constituted, ought to form one Monarchy with Sweden and Norway. But they see that there are great if not insuperable obstacles to all these arrangements, and they do not admit that the Emperor of the French talked to them about these things, or about the map of Europe revised for 1860. They lamented the dangerous state of the Austrian Empire by reason of its financial embarrassments, and its differences between Vienna and Hungary. They admitted the difficulty of re-establishing a Polish State, seeing that Russia, Prussia, and Austria are all interested in preventing it; but they thought that Russia might make herself amends to the Eastward for giving up part of her Polish possessions.

They said the Swedes would be more adverse than the Danes to a Union of Denmark with Sweden. They said the Finns are writhing under the Russian yoke, and emigrate in considerable numbers to Sweden. They think Russia paralysed for ten years to come by her war against England and France, by her internal changes, and her money embarrassments. When the Prince asked Viscount Palmerston to sit down, it was for the purpose of urging in the strongest and most earnest manner that some British ships of war, or even one single gunboat, if more could not be spared, should every year visit the Baltic, and make a cruise in that sea. He said that the British Flag was never seen there, although Great Britain has great interests, commercial and political, in that sea. That especially for Sweden it would be a great support if a British man-of-war were every year to show itself in Swedish waters. He said that our Navy know little or nothing of the Baltic, and when a war comes, as happened in the late war with Russia, our ships are obliged, as it were, to feel their way about in the dark; that the Russians send ships of war into British ports—why should not England send ships of war into Russian ports? That we survey seas at the other side of the Globe, why should we not survey a sea so near to us as the Baltic; that as far as Sweden is concerned, British ships would be most cordially received. I said that this should receive due consideration; and in answer to a question he said the best time for a Baltic cruise would be from the middle of June to the latter end of August.

They both thought the Emperor of the French extremely popular in France—but, of course, they only saw outward demonstrations. They are very anxious for the maintenance of the Anglo-French Alliance; and they think the Emperor obliged to keep a large Army and to build a strong Navy in order to please and satisfy the French Nation. Such is the summary of the impression made upon Viscount Palmerston by the answers and observations drawn out by him in his conversations with the King and the Prince; most of these things were said as above reported, some few of the above statements are perhaps inferences and conclusions drawn from indirect answers and remarks.

Queen Victoria to Viscount Palmerston.

SWEDEN AND DENMARK

Osborne, *18th August 1861.*

The Queen is very much obliged to Lord Palmerston for his detailed account of his conversation with the King of Sweden, and sends both Memorandums back to him in accordance with his wishes, in the expectation of having them returned to her after they shall have been copied.

FRANCE AND SWEDEN

The King may have been embarrassed by the presence of the Crown Prince of Prussia here at Osborne, and have on that account postponed speaking openly to Lord Palmerston. His desire to acquire Denmark and Finland is not unnatural, and would not be very dangerous; but the important part of the matter is, that the Emperor Napoleon has evidently tried to bribe him for his schemes by such expectations. After having established a large kingdom, dependent upon him and possessing a fleet, in the South of Europe on his right flank, he evidently tries to establish by the same means a similar power on his left flank in the North. If then the Revolution of Poland and Hungary takes Germany also in the rear, he will be exactly in the all-powerful position which his Uncle held, and at which he himself aims, with that one difference: that, unlike his Uncle, who had to fight England all the time (who defended desperately her interests in Europe), he tries to effect his purposes in alliance with England, and uses for this end our own *free* Press and in our own free country!

The Polish and Hungarian Revolutions (perhaps the Russian) and the assistance which may be (nobly?) given to them by Sweden, can easily be made as popular in this country as the Italian has, and efforts to produce this result are fully visible already. The position and prospects of the Ally, when the Emperor shall have the whole Continent at his feet, and the command of the Mediterranean and the Baltic, will not be a very pleasant one. Moreover, the Ally will probably have irritated him and the French Nation all the time by abusing them, and by showing that, although we may have approved of her policy, we did not intend that France should reap any benefits from it. All this is probably not thought of by our journalists, but requires the serious attention of our statesmen.

Lord Palmerston will perhaps show this letter to Lord Russell when he sends him the copies of the Memoranda, which he will probably do.

Queen Victoria to the King of the Belgians.

FROGMORE

Osborne, *20th August 1861*.

My beloved Uncle,—Before I thank you for your dear letter of the 14th, or at least before I answer it, I wish to tell you *how soothed* I was by that visit to that *lovely* peaceful *Mausoleum at Frogmore*.

We parted from our dear children and grandchildren with heavy hearts at seven on the morning of the 16th, for their visit, excepting the *blank* which clouds over everything, has been most peaceful and satisfactory, and we have learnt to know and most highly appreciate the great *excellence* of dear Fritz's character; noble, high-principled, so anxious to do what is right, and to improve in every way, and so sweet-tempered and affectionate—so, beyond everything, devoted to Vicky.

I thought much of poor, dear Aunt Julia on the 15th; *that loss* was the *signal* for my irreparable one!

We went that afternoon (16th) to Frogmore, where we slept. The first evening was terribly trying, and I must say quite overpowered me for a short time; *all* looked *like life*, and yet *she* was not there! But I got calmer; the very fact of being surrounded by all she liked, and of seeing the dear pretty house inhabited again, was a satisfaction, and the next morning was beautiful, and we went after breakfast with wreaths up to the Mausoleum, and into the vault which is *à plain-pied*, and so pretty—so airy—*so* grand and simple, that, affecting as it is, there was no anguish or bitterness of grief, but calm repose! We placed the wreaths upon the splendid granite sarcophagus, and at its feet, and *felt* that *only* the *earthly robe* we loved so much was there. The pure, tender, loving spirit *which loved us* so tenderly, is above us—loving us, praying for us, and *free* from *all* suffering and woe—*yes*, that *is* a *comfort*, and that *first birthday* in *another* world must have been a *far* brighter one than *any* in this poor world below! I only grieve *now* that we should be going so far away from Frogmore, as I long to go there; only Alice and dear Augusta Bruce[512](who feels as a daughter of hers) went with us. The morning was so beautiful, and the garden *so* lovely!...

The news from Austria are very sad, and make one very anxious. The King of Sweden is full of wild notions put into his head by the Emperor Napoleon, for whom he has the greatest admiration!...

It is high time I should end my long letter. With Albert's affectionate love, ever your devoted Niece,

Victoria R.

---

[512] Lady Augusta Bruce, who bad been living with the Duchess of Kent at the time of her death, was appointed by the Queen to be her resident Bedchamber Woman.

Queen Victoria to the King of the Belgians.

VISIT TO IRELAND

Vice-Regal Lodge, Phoenix Park, *26th August 1861.*

My beloved Uncle,—*Not* to miss your messenger I write a few hurried lines to thank you for your two dear letters of the 16th and the 22nd, the last of which I received yesterday morning here.... Would to God that affairs in Hungary took a favourable turn—*mais j'en ai bien peur*. We had a very good passage on Wednesday night, since which it has blown very hard. We left Osborne on Wednesday morning (21st) at quarter to nine, and anchored in Kingstown Bay at half-past eleven that night. The next day (22nd) we landed at eleven and came here, and it rained the whole day. On Saturday we all went over to the camp, where there was a field-day. It is a fine *emplacement* with beautiful turf. We had two cooling showers. Bertie marched past with his company, and did not look at all so very small.

Yesterday was again a very bad day. I have felt weak and very nervous, and so low at times; I think *so* much of dearest mamma, and miss her love and interest and solicitude *dreadfully*; I feel as if we were no longer cared for, and miss writing to her and telling her everything, dreadfully. At the Review they played one of her marches, which entirely upset me.

Good Lord Carlisle[513] is most kind and amiable, and so much beloved. We start for Killarney at half-past twelve. This is the *dearest of days*, and one which fills my heart with love, gratitude, and emotion. God bless and protect for ever my beloved Albert—the purest and best of human beings! We miss our four little ones and baby sadly, but have our four eldest (except poor Vicky) with us.

Now good-bye, dearest Uncle. Ever your devoted Niece,

Victoria R.

Queen Victoria to Earl Canning.

Balmoral, *9th September 1861.*

The Queen has not heard of Lord Canning for some time, but is happy to hear indirectly that he is well, and that everything is going on well under his admirable administration.

---

[513] Lord Carlisle was Viceroy in both the administrations of Lord Palmerston; as Lord Morpeth he had been Chief Secretary in the Melbourne Government.

It is most gratifying to the Queen to see how peaceful her Indian Dominions are, and considering the very alarming state of affairs during the years 1857, '58, and even '59, it must be a source of unbounded satisfaction and pride to Lord Canning to witness this state of prosperity at the end of his Government.

As Lord Canning will now soon return to England, the Queen is anxious to offer him the Rangership of the Park at Blackheath, with the house which dear Lord Aberdeen had for some years, hoping that he might find it acceptable and agreeable from its vicinity to London.[514]

The King of the Belgians to Queen Victoria.

THE ORLEANS PRINCES

Laeken, *17th October 1861.*

My beloved Victoria,—Receive my sincerest thanks for your dear letter of the 14th, which arrived very exactly. I am so happy to see all the good which your stay in the Highlands has done you, and I am sure it will be *lasting*, though Windsor must have the effect of reviving strongly some feelings.... When one looks back on those times, one must say that they were full of difficulties, and one ought to feel very grateful that such a happy present has grown out of them. I regret much Paris and Robert[515] having joined the Federal Army, mixing in a civil war!! The object is to show courage, to be able to say: "*Ils se sont beaucoup distingués.*" They have a chance of being shot for Abraham Lincoln and the most rank Radicalism. I don't think that step will please in France, where Radicalism is at discount fortunately. The poor Queen is very unhappy about it, but now nothing can be done, only one may wish to see them well out of it. Poor Queen! constantly new events painful to her assail her. I had rather a kind letter from the Emperor Napoleon about the state of Mexico. I fear he will find his wishes to see there a stable Government not much liked in England, though his plans are *not* for any advantage France is to derive from it. To-morrow we go to Liège to be in readiness for the following day. The King William III.[516] will arrive for dinner, stay the night, and go very early on Sunday. He will be extremely well received here, his

---

[514] Lord Aberdeen had died on the 14th of December 1860.

[515] The Comte de Paris and the Duc de Chartres, sons of the Duc d'Orléans, eldest son of King Louis Philippe.

[516] The King of Holland.

procédé being duly appreciated. To be very civilly received in a country which one was heir to, is rather *un peu pénible*, and one feels a little awkward.... Your devoted and only Uncle,

Leopold R.

The Duchess of Manchester[517] to Queen Victoria.

THE COURT OF HANOVER

Hanover [*Undated. October 1861*].

Madam,—Though your Majesty has only very lately seen the Princess Royal, I cannot refrain from addressing your Majesty, as I am sure your Majesty will be pleased to hear how well Her Royal Highness was looking during the Manœuvres on the Rhine, and how much she seems to be beloved, not only by all those who know her, but also by those who have only seen and heard of her. The English could not help feeling proud of the way the Princess Royal was spoken of, and the high esteem she is held in. For one so young it is a most flattering position, and certainly as the Princess's charm of manner and her kind unaffected words had in that short time won her the hearts of all the officers and strangers present, one was not astonished at the praise the Prussians themselves bestow on Her Royal Highness. The Royal Family is so large, and their opinions politically and socially sometimes so different, that it must have been very difficult indeed at first for the Princess Royal, and people therefore cannot praise enough the high principles, great discretion, sound judgment, and cleverness Her Royal Highness has invariably displayed.

Your Majesty would have been amused to hear General Wrangel[518] tell at the top of his voice how delighted the soldiers were to see the Princess on horseback, and the interest she showed for them. What pleased them specially was to see Her Royal Highness ride without a veil—such an odd thing in soldiers to remark. The King of Prussia is looking very well, but the Queen I thought very much altered. Her Majesty looks very pale and tired, and has such a painful

---

[517] Louise Frederica Augusta, wife of the seventh Duke of Manchester, and Mistress of the Robes. She was daughter of the Count von Alten of Hanover, and is now Dowager Duchess of Devonshire.

[518] The Queen had met General von Wrangel at Babelsberg in August 1858. "He is seventy-six," she wrote, "and a great character." He had commanded a division in the Danish war of 1848, and it had fallen to him in the same year, as Commandant of the troops, to dissolve the Berlin Assembly by force.

drawn look about the mouth. How the Queen will be able to go through all the fatigues of the Coronation I do not know, as Her Majesty already complained of being tired, and knocked up by the manœvres and dinners, and had to go to Mentz for a few days to rest herself. Their Majesties' kindness was very great, and the Duke told me of the extreme hospitality with which they were entertained. Every one, high and low, were rivalling each other in civility and friendliness towards the strangers, especially the English, and one really felt quite ashamed of those wanton attacks the *Times* always makes on Prussia, and which are read and copied into all the Prussian papers. The last night all the officers dined together. General Forey put himself into the President's place and insisted, to the exclusion of Lord Clyde, who was by far the senior officer, and who was expected to do it, on proposing the health of the King, the Royal Family, the Army, and Nation. Not content with doing it in French, he drew out of his pocket a document written for him in German, for he did not know the language, and read it with the most extraordinary pronunciation. The English officers all admired the way the Germans kept their countenance notwithstanding the absurdity of the exhibition.

On the 21st they have had great doings here at Hanover. I hear that to the astonishment of everybody the Queen appeared at the *Enthüllung*, where all other people were *en grande tenue*, in a little small round hat with a lilac feather. Her Maids of Honour—she has only one now besides that English Miss Stewart—were ordered to wear hats to keep Her Majesty in countenance. I wonder if your Majesty has read the speech the King has addressed to his people on the occasion of the *Enthüllung* and the Crown Prince's birthday. It cannot fail to excite the greatest pity that such things, however well meant, should be written. Has your Majesty also heard of the pamphlet that has been published here called *Das Welfe*—that name Welfe is quite an *idée fixe* of the King now, and he brings it in on every occasion, and this pamphlet is written throwing the whole idea into ridicule, and beginning with the last years of the late King's reign. The Crown Prince[519] is very much liked, but, unfortunately, his new tutor will probably also leave very shortly—he has no authority over him, the Prince still regretting M. de Issendorf. Besides, he is not allowed to exercise his judgment in the smallest way—the King going on the principle that a King only can educate a King. The reason the other tutor left, or was dismissed, was partly on account of his remonstrating against the religious instruc-

[519] Prince Ernest Augustus, born 1845; the present Duke of Cumberland.

tions, which were carried so far that the Prince had hardly any time left to learn other things. Besides the Prince, who dislikes the clergyman, had drawn a caricature, to which the man very much gives himself, and the King thought M. de Issendorf had known of it, which turned out not to be the case.... I have the honour to remain, your Majesty's most obedient and devoted Servant and Subject,

Louise Manchester.

The Crown Princess of Prussia to Queen Victoria.

CORONATION OF KING OF PRUSSIA

Könisberg, *19th October 1861.*

My beloved Mamma,—Last night I could not write to you as I would have wished, because I felt so knocked up that I went to bed. I have got such a very bad cold on my chest, with a cough that leaves me no rest, and of course cannot take care of myself, and am obliged to stand and sit in every sort of draught with a low gown and without a cloak, so it is no wonder to have caught cold. I have not had a cough since I don't know when. I should like to be able to describe yesterday's ceremony to you, but I cannot find words to tell you how fine and how touching it was; it really was a magnificent sight! The King looked so very handsome and so noble with the crown on; it seemed to suit him so exactly. The Queen, too, looked beautiful, and did all she had to do with perfect grace, and looked so *vornehm*; I assure you the whole must have made a great impression on everybody present, and all those to whom I have talked on the subject quite share my feeling. The moment when the King put the crown on the Queen's head was very touching, I think there was hardly a dry eye in the church. The *Schlosshof* was the finest, I thought—five bands playing "God save the Queen," banners waving in all directions, cheers so loud that they quite drowned the sound of the music, and the procession moving slowly on, the sky without a cloud; and all the uniforms, and the ladies' diamonds glittering in the bright sunlight. I shall never forget it all, it was so very fine! Dearest Fritz's birthday being chosen for the day made me very happy; he was in a great state of emotion and excitement, as you can imagine, as we all were. Mr Thomas[520] was in the chapel. I hope he will have been able to take down some useful memo-

[520] George Housman Thomas, artist (1824-1868). The picture he produced on this occasion was entitled, *Homage of the Princess Royal at the Coronation of the King of Prussia.*

randa. The Grand Duke of Weimar,[521] the King and ourselves, have ordered drawings of him.

A BRILLIANT CEREMONY

The *coup d'œil* was really beautiful; the chapel is in itself lovely, with a great deal of gold about it, and all hung with red velvet and gold—the carpet, altar, thrones and canopies the same. The Knights of the Black Eagle with red velvet cloaks, the Queen's four young ladies all alike in white and gold, the two Palastdamen in crimson velvet and gold, and the Oberhofmeisterin in gold and white brocade with green velvet, Marianne and Addy in red and gold and red and silver; I, in gold with ermine and white satin, my ladies, one in blue velvet, the other in red velvet, and Countess Schulenberg, together with the two other Oberhofmeisterin of the other Princesses, in violet velvet and gold. All these colours together looked very beautiful, and the sun shone, or rather poured in at the high windows, and gave quite magic tinges.

The music was very fine, the chorales were sung so loud and strong that it really quite moved one. The King was immensely cheered, wherever he appeared—also the Queen, and even I.

There were illuminations last night, but I did not go to see them, as I was too tired and felt so unwell. There are five degrees of cold (Réaumur), and one is exposed to draughts every minute.

Sixteen hundred people dined in the Schloss last night! The King and Queen were most kind to me yesterday; the King gave me a charming little locket for his hair, and only think—what will sound most extraordinary, absurd, and incredible to your ears—made me Second *Chef* of the 2nd Regiment of Hussars! I laughed so much, because really I thought it was a joke—it seemed so strange for ladies; but the Regiments like particularly having ladies for their *Chefs!* The Queen and the Queen Dowager have Regiments, but I believe I am the first Princess on whom such an honour is conferred.

DISTINGUISHED GUESTS

The Archduke addressed the King yesterday, in the name of all the foreign Princes present, in a very pretty speech.

It is such a pleasure to see good Philip here, and the two Portuguese cousins. Juan[522] is very nice, but he does not talk much; he has a

---

[521] Charles Alexander, 1818-1901, grandfather of the present Grand Duke.

very fine, tall figure, and is nice-looking. I should think he must be like his father. Prince Hohenzollern [523] is become Royal Highness, and the title is to descend to his eldest son. Half Europe is here, and one sees the funniest combinations in the world. It is like a happy family shut up in a cage! The Italian Ambassador sat near Cardinal Geisel, and the French one opposite the Archduke. The Grand Duke Nicolas is here—he is so nice—also the Crown Prince of Würtemberg,[524] Crown Prince of Saxony,[525] Prince Luitpold of Bavaria,[526] Prince Charles of Hesse[527] (who nearly dies of fright and shyness amongst so many people), and Heinrich; Prince Elimar of Oldenburg,[528] Prince Frederic of the Netherlands,[529] and the Grand Duke and Duchess of Weimar, who wish to be most particularly remembered to you and Papa.

The King and Queen are most kind to Lord Clarendon, and make a marked difference between their marked cordiality to him and the stiff etiquette with which the other Ambassadors are received.

I think he is pleased with what he sees. The King has given the Queen the Order of the Black Eagle in diamonds. I write all these details, as you wish them, at the risk of their not interesting you, besides my being, as you know, a very bad hand at descriptions. I shall make a point of your having newspapers.

I am unable to appear at the *cour* this morning, as my cough is too violent: I hope to be able to be at the concert this evening, but I own it seems very doubtful. The state dinner looked very well; we were waited on by our *Kammerherren* and pages—the King being waited on by the *Oberhofchargen*—and our ladies stood behind our chairs. After the first two dishes are round, the King asks to drink, and that is the signal for the ladies and gentlemen to leave the room and go to dinner, while the Pages of Honour continue to serve the whole dinner really wonderfully well, poor boys, considering it is no easy task.

---

[522] Prince John, brother of King Pedro, was making a tour with his elder brother, Louis, the Duc d'Oporto.
[523] Prince Charles Anthony of Hohenzollern was the father of the young Queen Stéphanie of Portugal, who had died in 1859.
[524] Prince Charles Frederick, 1823-1891.
[525] Prince Albert, who became King in 1873.
[526] Brother of King Maximilian II.
[527] Son of the Elector Frederick William I.
[528] Brother of the reigning Grand Duke.
[529] Uncle of the King of Holland.

To-morrow we leave Königsberg for Dantzic—we have not had one day's bad weather here, nothing but sunshine and a bright blue sky. I was so glad that Heaven smiled upon us yesterday, it would have been so sad if it had poured; it looked a little threatening early in the morning and a few drops fell, but it cleared completely before nine o'clock.

Fritz would thank you for your dear letters himself, but he is at the University, where they have elected him *Rector Magnificus*, and where he has to make a speech. We have all got our servants and carriages and horses here *every* day—300 footmen in livery, together with other servants in livery, make 400. All the standards and colours of the whole Army are here, and all the Colonels. Altogether, you cannot imagine what a crush and what a scramble there is on every occasion; there was a man crushed to death in the crowd the other day, which is quite dreadful. I must say good-bye now, and send this scrawl by a messenger, whom Lord Clarendon means to expedite. Ever your most dutiful and affectionate Daughter,

Victoria.

The Earl of Clarendon to Queen Victoria.

THE PRINCESS ROYAL

Königsberg, *19th October 1861.*

Lord Clarendon presents his humble duty to your Majesty, and humbly hopes that your Majesty will not be displeased at his not having written sooner, but every moment has been occupied by *fêtes* and ceremonies here, and the visits to Royal Personages, who are in great numbers, and Lord Clarendon also wished to delay sending off the messenger until the Coronation was over.

That most interesting and imposing ceremony took place yesterday, and with the most complete and unalloyed success; everything was conducted with the most perfect order; the service not too long, the vocal music enchanting, but *the* great feature of the ceremony was the manner in which the Princess Royal did homage to the King. Lord Clarendon is at a loss for words to describe to your Majesty the exquisite grace and the intense emotion with which Her Royal Highness gave effect to her feelings on the occasion. Many an older as well as younger man than Lord Clarendon, who had not his interest in the Princess Royal, were quite as unable as himself to repress their emotion at that which was so touching, because so unaffected and sincere....

If His Majesty had the mind, the judgment, and the foresight of the Princess Royal, there would be nothing to fear, and the example and influence of Prussia would soon be marvellously developed. Lord Clarendon has had the honour to hold a very long conversation with Her Royal Highness, and has been more than ever astonished at the *statesmanlike* and comprehensive views which she takes of the policy of Prussia, both internal and foreign, and of the *duties* of a Constitutional King.

Lord Clarendon is not at all astonished, but very much pleased, to find how appreciated and beloved Her Royal Highness is by all classes. Every member of the Royal Family has spoken of her to Lord Clarendon in terms of admiration, and through various channels he has had opportunities of learning how strong the feeling of educated and enlightened people is towards Her Royal Highness. All persons say most truly that any one who saw Her Royal Highness yesterday can never forget her.

Lord Clarendon is sorry to say that the Princess Royal has a feverish cold to-day—nothing at all serious—and as Her Royal Highness stayed in bed this afternoon, did not attend the great concert at the Palace this evening, and, as Lord Clarendon hopes, will not go to Dantzic to-morrow, Her Royal Highness will probably be quite fit for the many fatiguing duties she will have to perform next week....

The Earl of Clarendon to Queen Victoria.

THE EMPEROR NAPOLEON'S AIMS

Berlin, *20th October 1861.*

Lord Clarendon presents his humble duty to your Majesty, and humbly begs to say that yesterday he had the honour of being sent for by the Queen, with whom he had a long and interesting conversation....

The Queen expressed her deep regret at the tone of the English newspapers, but admitted that the German Press repaid the English insults with large interest. Her Majesty said, however, that she and the King, and all sensible men with whom their Majesties hold communication, were determined to disregard the attacks, and by every possible means to draw nearer to England.

AUSTRIA AND PRUSSIA

Lord Clarendon took the opportunity of warning the Queen respecting the Emperor and his *idée fixe*, that his dynasty could only be secured by the territorial aggrandisement of France. Lord Clarendon expressed his conviction that if the King had resembled M. de Cavour, some strong proposals would already have been made to them, but that the Emperor's plans had been foiled by the honourable character of the King. There ought, nevertheless, to be no delusion here, but on the contrary, a careful avoidance of the traps which cajolery and flattery were setting for Prussia, because at any moment the Emperor might think it necessary for his own purposes in France to seize upon the left bank of the Rhine, and that all classes in France, no matter to what party belonging, would be delighted at his so doing, and his popularity and power in France would be enormously increased by it. The Queen agreed, but was under the notion, which Lord Clarendon was able effectually to dispel, that the dilapidated state of French finances would prevent the Emperor from undertaking a war upon a large scale.

Lord Clarendon thinks that he strengthened the Queen's opinion respecting "eventualities" and the necessity of making preparations and evoking a national spirit against foreign aggression, such as that recently manifested in England, and which had done so much in favour of peace as far as we ourselves were concerned. Her Majesty, however, said that Prussian policy towards Germany opened so large a chapter that she wished to reserve the discussion of it for our next conversation.

Lord Clarendon fears that Count Bernstorff is disposed to think that Austria's difficulty is Prussia's opportunity, and to be exigent as to the concessions upon which a better understanding between the two countries must be based. Lord Clarendon was confidentially informed yesterday that a Cabinet had just been held for the first time since Count Bernstorff became a member of it, and that with respect to internal affairs he had greatly alarmed and annoyed some of his colleagues by his retrograde opinions. Lord Clarendon had the honour of dining with the Crown Prince and Princess last night. The dinner was perfect, and everything conducted in the most admirable manner; there was afterwards a ball at "The Queen's" which was really a splendid fête. The festivities and the visitings are so uninterrupted that everybody is unwell and tired. The Duc de Magenta's grand fête takes place on the 29th. The Austrian Minister gives a ball to-morrow (*Sunday*), which day has unfortunately been fixed by the King, to the annoyance of all the English; but Lord Clarendon has determined that the Embassy shall attend, otherwise the King might consider that we wished to give him a public lesson upon the observance of the Sabbath. Lord Clarendon trusts that your Majesty will approve the decision. Lord Granville's visit appears to be highly appreciated by the Court.

Queen Victoria to the King of the Belgians.

Balmoral, *21st October 1861.*

My dearest Uncle,—You will excuse a long letter as this is our last day, alas! Many, many thanks for your dear letters of the 17th and 18th, which I received yesterday. I am glad to see that my account of our mountain expedition amused you, and that you remember all so well. If it could amuse you later, I would send you my *Reisebeschreibung* to read. I will have it copied and send it you later. We have had a most beautiful week, which we have thoroughly enjoyed—I going out every day about twelve or half-past, taking luncheon with us, carried in a basket on the back of a Highlander, and served by an *invaluable* Highland servant I have, who is *my factotum here*, and takes the most wonderful care of me, combining the offices of groom, footman, page, and *maid*, I might almost say, as he is so handy about cloaks and shawls, etc. He always leads my pony, and always attends me out of doors, and *such* a good, handy, *faithful*, attached servant I have nowhere; it is quite a sorrow for me to leave him behind. Now, with Albert's affectionate love, ever your devoted Niece,

Victoria R.

Queen Victoria to Viscount Palmerston.

THE *TIMES* AND PRUSSIA

Windsor Castle, *25th October 1861.*

The Queen has long seen with deep regret the persevering efforts made by the *Times*, which leads the rest of our Press, in attacking, vilifying, and abusing everything German, and particularly everything Prussian. That journal had since years shown the same bias, but it is since the Macdonald affair of last year,[530] that it has assumed that tone

[530] At Bonn, in September 1860, Captain Macdonald, a railway passenger, had been ejected from his seat in the train by the railway authorities, and committed to prison. The incident became the subject of considerable diplo-

of virulence, which could not fail to produce the deepest indignation amongst the people of Germany, and by degrees estrange the feelings of the people of this country from Germany. Lord Palmerston, probably not reading any German newspaper, nor having any personal intercourse with that country, can hardly be aware to what extent the mischief has already gone, though he will agree with the Queen that national hatred between these two peoples is a real political calamity for both. The Queen had often intended to write to Lord Palmerston on the subject, and to ask him whether he would not be acting in the spirit of public duty if he endeavoured, as far at least as might be in his power, to point out to the managers of the *Times* (which derives some of its power from the belief abroad that it represents more or less the feelings of the Government) how great the injury is which it inflicts upon the best interests of this country. She has, however, refrained from doing so, trusting in the chance of a change in tone, and feeling that Lord Palmerston might not like to enter into discussion with the Editors of the *Times*....

The Queen believes that Lord Palmerston is the only person who could exercise any influence over Mr Delane, and even if this should not be much, it will be important that that gentleman should know the mischief his writings are doing, and that the Government sincerely deplore it.

Mr Delane to Viscount Palmerston.[531]

THE ENGLISH PRESS

16 Serjeant's Inn, *28th October 1861.*

My dear Lord,—I shall be very glad to give the Prussians a respite from that most cruel of all inflictions—good advice.

Indeed, I would not have intruded anything so unwelcome during the splendid solemnities of the Coronation had not the King uttered those surprising anachronisms upon Divine Right.

Pray observe, too, in extenuation of my offence that I sent a faithful chronicler to Königsberg, who has described all the splendours in a proper and reverent spirit, and done what man can do to render such ceremonies intelligible, and the recital of them not too wearisome to

---

matic correspondence, as well as of some fierce attacks on Prussia in the *Times*.

[531] Enclosed in the following letter.

those who believe in Divine Right as little as your Lordship's very faithful Servant,

John T. Delane.

Viscount Palmerston to Queen Victoria.

THE *TIMES*

Windsor Castle, *30th October 1861.*

Viscount Palmerston presents his humble duty to your Majesty, and begs to state that when he received a few days ago from Lord Russell the Memorandum which your Majesty intended for him, and which he returned to Lord Russell, he wrote to Mr Delane in accordance with your Majesty's wishes, and he has this morning received the accompanying answer.

Viscount Palmerston would, however, beg to submit that an erroneous notion prevails on the Continent as to English newspapers.

The newspapers on the Continent are all more or less under a certain degree of control, and the most prominent among them are the organs of political parties, or of leading public men; and it is not unnatural that Governments and Parties on the Continent should think that English newspapers are published under similar conditions.

But in this country all thriving newspapers are commercial undertakings, and are conducted on commercial principles, and none others are able long to maintain an existence. Attempts have often been made to establish newspapers to be directed by political men, and to be guided by the same considerations by which those men would govern their own conduct, but such papers have seldom succeeded. The Peelite Party tried some years ago such an experiment with the *Morning Chronicle*, but after spending a very large sum of money on the undertaking they were obliged to give it up. The *Times* is carried on as a large commercial enterprise, though, of course, with certain political tendencies and bias, but mainly with a view to profit upon the large capital employed.

The actual price at which each copy of the newspaper is sold barely pays the expense of paper, printing, and establishment; it is indeed said that the price does not repay those expenses. The profit of the newspaper arises from the price paid for advertisements, and the greater the number of advertisements the greater the profit. But advertisements are sent by preference to the newspaper which has the greatest circulation; and that paper gets the widest circulation which is the most amusing, the most interesting, and the most instructive. A dull paper is soon left off. The proprietors and managers of the *Times* therefore go to great expense in sending correspondents to all parts of the world where interesting events are taking place, and they employ a great many able and clever men to write articles upon all subjects which from time to time engage public attention; and as mankind take more pleasure in reading criticism and fault-finding than praise, because it is soothing to individual vanity and conceit to fancy that the reader has become wiser than those about whom he reads, so the *Times*, in order to maintain its circulation, criticises freely everybody and everything; and especially events and persons, and Governments abroad, because such strictures are less likely to make enemies at home than violent attacks upon parties and persons in this country. Foreign Governments and Parties ought therefore to look upon English newspapers in the true point of view, and not to be too sensitive as to attacks which those papers may contain.

The Earl of Clarendon to Queen Victoria.

DEMOCRACY IN PRUSSIA

Berlin, *5th November 1861.*

Lord Clarendon presents his humble duty to your Majesty, and humbly begs to say that as he leaves Berlin to-morrow, the Princess Royal has most kindly just given him an Audience of leave, although Her Royal Highness was still suffering considerable pain in her ear, and was quite unfit for any exertion. Her Royal Highness's countenance bears traces of the severe illness of the last few days, but Lord Clarendon trusts that the worst is now over, and that care alone is necessary for her complete recovery. Her Royal Highness is still so weak that she was obliged to desist from writing, which she attempted this morning, and Lord Clarendon took the liberty of earnestly recommending that the journey to Breslau, upon which Her Royal Highness appeared to be bent, should be given up. Lord Clarendon intends to repeat the same advice to the Queen, whom he is to see this evening, as there are to be four days of rejoicings at Breslau, for the fatigue of which the Crown Princess must be utterly unfit.

Her Royal Highness is much alarmed at the state of things here, and Lord Clarendon thinks with great reason, for the King has quite made up his mind as to the course that he will pursue. He sees democracy and revolution in every symptom of opposition to his will. His Ministers are mere clerks, who are quite content to register the King's decrees, and there is no person from whom His Majesty seeks advice, or indeed who is capable or would have the moral courage to give it. The King will always religiously keep his word, and will never overturn the institutions he has sworn to maintain, but they are so distasteful to him, and so much at variance with his habit of thought and settled opinions as to the rights of the Crown, that His Majesty will never, if he can avoid it, accept the consequences of representative Government, or allow it to be a reality. This is generally known, and among the middle classes is producing an uneasy and resentful feeling, but as far as Lord Clarendon is able to judge, there is no fear of revolution—the Army is too strong, and the recollection of 1848 is too fresh to allow of acts of violence.

Lord Clarendon had the honour of an Audience of the King on Sunday. His Majesty was most friendly and kind, but evidently unwell and irritable. Lord Clarendon therefore thought that it would be neither prudent nor useful to say the many things that the Queen had wished that the King should hear from Lord Clarendon. He touched upon the subject of Constitutional Government, and His Majesty said: "I have sworn to maintain our Institutions, and I declare to you, and I wish you to inform your Government, that I will maintain them."

Lord Clarendon proposes to remain Friday at Brussels, and hopes to have the honour of seeing the King.

Queen Victoria to the King of the Belgians.

DEATH OF KING OF PORTUGAL

Windsor Castle, *12th November 1861.*

My beloved Uncle,—I hardly know *how* to *write*, for my head reels and swims, and my heart is very sore![532] *What* an awful misfortune this is! How the hand of death seems bent on pursuing that poor, dear family! once so prosperous. Poor Ferdinand so proud of his children—of his five sons—now the eldest and *most* distinguished, the head of the family, *gone*, and also another of fifteen, and the youngest *still* ill! The two others at sea, and will land to-morrow in utter igno-

[532] King Pedro of Portugal died of typhoid fever on the 11th of November; his brother Ferdinand had died on the 6th; and Prince John, Duke of Beja, succumbed in the following December.

rance of everything, and poor, dear, good Louis (whom I thought dreadfully low when we saw him and Jean for an hour on Friday) King! It is an almost incredible event! a terrible calamity for Portugal, and a *real* European loss! Dear Pedro was so good, so clever, so distinguished! He was so attached to my beloved Albert, and the characters and tastes suited so well, and he had such confidence in Albert! *All, all gone! He* is happy now, united again to dear Stéphanie,[533] whose loss he never recovered.... Ever your devoted Niece,

Victoria R.

Viscount Palmerston to Queen Victoria.

THE AFFAIR OF THE *TRENT*

Downing Street, *13th November 1861.*

... Viscount Palmerston met yesterday at dinner at Baron Brunnow's the Grand Duke Constantine and the Grand Duchess, and they were overflowing with thankfulness for the kind and gracious reception they had met with at Windsor Castle.

There was reason to suspect that an American federal steamer of war of eight guns, which had lately arrived at Falmouth, and from thence at Southampton, was intended to intercept the Mail Packet coming home with the West Indian Mail, in order to take out of her Messrs Mason and Slidell, the two Envoys from the Southern Confederacy, supposed to be coming in her.[534]

Viscount Palmerston had on Monday a meeting at the Treasury of the Chancellor, Doctor Lushington, the three Law Officers,[535] the Duke of Somerset, Sir George Grey, and Mr Hammond.[536] The result of their deliberation was that, according to the Law of Nations, as laid down by Lord Stowell, and practised and enforced by England in the war with France, the Northern Union being a belligerent is entitled by its ships of war to stop and search any neutral Merchantmen, and the West India Packet is such; to search her if there is reasonable suspicion that she is carrying enemy's despatches, and if such are found on

[533] The young Queen Stéphanie of Portugal had died in 1859.

[534] See Introductory Note, *ante*, p. 421.

[535] Sir William Atherton, Attorney-General, Sir Roundell Palmer, Solicitor-General, and Dr Phillimore, Counsel to the Admiralty.

[536] Permanent Under-Secretary of State for Foreign Affairs, afterwards Lord Hammond.

board to take her to a port of the belligerent, and there to proceed against her for condemnation. Such being ruled to be the law, the only thing that could be done was to order the *Phaeton* frigate to drop down to Yarmouth Roads from Portsmouth, and to watch the American steamer, and to see that she did not exercise this belligerent right within the three-mile limit of British jurisdiction, and this was done. But Viscount Palmerston sent yesterday for Mr Adams to ask him about this matter, and to represent to him how unwise it would be to create irritation in this country merely for the sake of preventing the landing of Mr Slidell, whose presence here would have no more effect on the policy of your Majesty with regard to America than the presence of the three other Southern Deputies who have been here for many months. Mr Adams assured Viscount Palmerston that the American steamer had orders not to meddle with any vessel under any foreign flag; that it came to intercept the *Nashville*, the Confederate ship in which it was thought the Southern Envoys might be coming; and not having met with her was going back to the American coast to watch some Merchantmen supposed to be taking arms to the Southern ports.

Viscount Palmerston heard from a source likely to be well informed that at the interview between the Emperor and the King of Prussia at Compiègne, the Emperor, among other things, said to the King that there were three systems of alliance between which France and Prussia might choose: an alliance of France with England, an alliance of Prussia with England, an alliance of France with Prussia. The first the Emperor said now to a certain degree exists, but is precarious and not likely to last long, because England is too exacting; the second would not be useful to Prussia, but might be dangerous, inasmuch as it would look like hostility to France, and England would not be likely to back Prussia effectually if a rupture took place between Prussia and France. The last was the system best for Prussia, and was calculated to promote her interests; at all events, the Emperor hoped that if at any time there should be a rupture between France and England, Prussia would remain neutral. The King of Prussia said he was not come to discuss matters of that kind with the Emperor, but only to pay him a visit of compliment. Your Majesty will be able to compare this statement with the accounts your Majesty may have received of what passed at that visit....

The Chancellor[537] told the Cabinet as he was going away that he would soon have to shut up the Court of Chancery in consequence of having disposed of all the suits before it; and that in future the progress of a Chancery suit will be the emblem of rapidity, and not as formerly synonymous with endless delay.

Queen Victoria to the King of the Belgians.

Windsor Castle, *26th November 1861.*

My beloved Uncle,— ... Albert is a little rheumatic, which is a plague—but it is very difficult not to have something or other of this kind in this season, with these rapid changes of temperature; *unberufen, unberufen*, he is much better this winter than he was the preceding years.[57] ...

Footnote 57: The Prince had been unwell, even before the receipt of the distressing news from Portugal, and began to suffer from a somewhat continuous insomnia. On the 22nd of November, he drove to Sandhurst to inspect the new buildings in progress there. The day was very wet, and, though he returned in the middle of the day to Windsor, the exertion proved too severe for him; on the 24th he complained of rheumatic pains, and of prolonged sleeplessness.

Viscount Palmerston to Queen Victoria.

REDRESS DEMANDED

Downing Street, *29th November 1861.*

Viscount Palmerston presents his humble duty to your Majesty, and begs to state that the Cabinet at its meeting this afternoon resumed the consideration of the forcible capture of the Southern Envoys from on board the *Trent* steamer upon which the law officers had yesterday given the opinion contained in the accompanying report. The law officers and Doctor Phillimore, Counsel to the Admiralty, were in attendance. The result was that it appeared to the Cabinet that a gross outrage and violation of international law has been committed, and that your Majesty should be advised to demand reparation and redress. The Cabinet is to meet again to-morrow at two, by which time Lord Russell will have prepared an instruction to Lord Lyons for the consideration of the Cabinet, and for submission afterwards to your

---

537 Lord Westbury.

Majesty. The general outline and tenor which appeared to meet the opinions of the Cabinet would be, that the Washington Government should be told that what has been done is a violation of international law, and of the rights of Great Britain, and that your Majesty's Government trust that the act will be disavowed and the prisoners set free and restored to British Protection; and that Lord Lyons should be instructed that if this demand is refused he should retire from the United States.

It is stated by Mrs and Miss Slidell, who are now in London, that the Northern officer who came on board the *Trent* said that they were acting on their own responsibility without instructions from Washington; that very possibly their act might be disavowed and the prisoners set free on their arrival at Washington. But it was known that the *San Jacinto*, though come from the African station, had arrived from thence several weeks before, and had been at St Thomas, and had there received communications from New York; and it is also said that General Scott, who has recently arrived in France, has said to Americans in Paris that he has come not on an excursion of pleasure, but on diplomatic business; that the seizure of these envoys was discussed in Cabinet at Washington, he being present, and was deliberately determined upon and ordered; that the Washington Cabinet fully foresaw it might lead to war with England; and that he was commissioned to propose to France in that case to join the Northern States in war against England, and to offer France in that case the restoration of the French Province of Canada.

General Scott will probably find himself much mistaken as to the success of his overtures; for the French Government is more disposed towards the South than the North, and is probably thinking more about Cotton than about Canada....

Earl Russell to Queen Victoria.

AN ULTIMATUM

Foreign Office, *29th November 1861.*

Lord Russell presents his humble duty to your Majesty; Mr Gladstone has undertaken to explain to your Majesty what has taken place at the Cabinet to-day.

Lord Russell proposes to frame a draft for to-morrow's Cabinet of a despatch to Lord Lyons, directing him to ask for the release of Messrs Mason and Slidell and their two companions, and an apology.

In case these requirements should be refused, Lord Lyons should ask for his passports.

The Lord Chancellor and the law officers of the Crown are clear upon the law of the case.

Lord Russell will be glad to have your Majesty's opinion on the draft which will go to your Majesty about four o'clock to-morrow, without loss of time, as the packet goes to-morrow evening.[538]

Queen Victoria to Earl Russell.

THE PRINCE'S LAST LETTER

Windsor Castle, *1st December 1861.*

Note in the Queen's handwriting.

[This draft was the last the beloved Prince ever wrote; he was very unwell at the time, and when he brought it in to the Queen, he said: "I could hardly hold my pen."

Victoria R.]

The Queen returns these important drafts, which upon the whole she approves, but she cannot help feeling that the main draft, that for communication to the American Government, is somewhat meagre. She should have liked to have seen the expression of a hope that the American captain did not act under instructions, or, if he did, that he misapprehended them—that the United States Government must be fully aware that the British Government could not allow its flag to be insulted, and the security of her mail communications to be placed to jeopardy, and Her Majesty's Government are unwilling to believe that the United States Government intended wantonly to put an insult upon this country, and to add to their many distressing complications by forcing a question of dispute upon us, and that we are therefore glad to

---

[538] The draft of the despatch to Lord Lyons reached Windsor on the evening of the 30th, and, in spite of his weak and suffering state, the Prince prepared the draft of the Queen's letter early the following morning. The letter has been printed in *facsimile* by Sir Theodore Martin, who adds that it has a special value as "representing the last political Memorandum written by the Prince, while it was at the same time inferior to none of them, as will presently be seen, in the importance of its results. It shows, like most of his Memorandums, by the corrections in the Queen's hand, how the minds of both were continually brought to bear upon the subjects with which they dealt."

believe that upon a full consideration of the circumstances, and of the undoubted breach of international law committed, they would spontaneously offer such redress as alone could satisfy this country, viz. the restoration of the unfortunate passengers and a suitable apology.

Queen Victoria to the King of the Belgians.

Windsor Castle, *4th December 1861.*

My dearest Uncle,—I have many excuses to make for not writing yesterday, but I had a good deal to do, as my poor dear Albert's rheumatism has turned out to be a regular influenza, which has pulled and lowered him very much. Since Monday he has been confined to his room. It affects his appetite and sleep, which is very disagreeable, and you know he is always *so* depressed when anything is the matter with him. However, he is decidedly better to-day, and I hope in two or three days he will be quite himself again. It is extremely vexatious, as he was so particularly well till he caught these colds, which came upon worries of various kinds.... Ever your devoted Niece,

Victoria R.

Queen Victoria to the King of the Belgians.

ILLNESS OF THE PRINCE

Windsor Castle, *6th December 1861.*

My beloved Uncle,—I am thankful to report decidedly better of my beloved Albert. He has had much more sleep, and has taken much more nourishment since yesterday evening. Altogether, this nasty, feverish sort of influenza and deranged stomach is *on* the mend, but it will be slow and tedious, and though there has *not* been one alarming symptom, there has been such restlessness, such sleeplessness, and such (till to-day) *total* refusal of all food, that it made one *very, very* anxious, and I can't describe the *anxiety* I have gone through! I feel today a good deal shaken, for for four nights I got only two or three hours' sleep. We have, however, every reason to hope the recovery, though it may be *somewhat* tedious, will not be *very* slow. You shall hear again to-morrow. Ever your devoted Niece,

Victoria R.

Queen Victoria to the King of the Belgians.

HOPE NOT ABANDONED

Windsor Castle, *9th December 1861.*

My beloved Uncle,—I enclose you Clark's report, which I think you may like to hear. Our beloved invalid goes on well—but it *must* be tedious, and I need not tell you *what* a trial it is to me. Every day, however, is bringing us nearer the end of this tiresome illness, which is much what I had at Ramsgate, only that I was much worse, and not at first well attended to. You shall hear daily.

You will, I know, feel for me! The night was excellent; the first good one he had. Ever your devoted Niece,

Victoria R.

The Americans *may* possibly get out of it.

The King of the Belgians to Queen Victoria.

Laeken, *11th December 1861.*

My beloved Victoria,—*How I do feel for you from the bottom of my heart*; that you should have this totally unexpected tribulation of having dear Albert unwell, when not long ago we rejoiced that he was bearing this time of the year so well. Now we must be very patient, as an indisposition of this description at this time of the year is generally mending slowly. The great object must be to arrange all the little details exactly as the patient may wish them; that everything of that description may move very smoothly is highly beneficial. Patients are very different in their likings; to the great horror of angelic Louise, the moment I am ill I become almost invisible, disliking to see anybody. Other people are fond of company, and wish to be surrounded. The medical advisors are, thank God! excellent, and Clark knows Albert so well. Albert will wish you not to interrupt your usual airings; you want air, and to be deprived of it would do you harm. The temperature here at least has been extremely mild—this ought to be favourable. I trust that every day will now show some small improvement, and it will be very kind of you to let me frequently know how dear Albert is going on. Believe me ever, my beloved Victoria, your devoted Uncle,

Leopold R.

H.R.H. The Prince Consort, 1861.
From the picture by Smith, after Corbould, at Buckingham Palace.

Queen Victoria to the King of the Belgians.

Windsor Castle, *11th December 1861.*

Dearest Uncle,—I can report another good night, and *no* loss of strength, and continued satisfactory symptoms. But more we dare *not* expect for some days; *not* losing ground is a *gain, now*, of *every* day.

It is very sad and trying for me, but I am well, and I think really *very* courageous; for it is the first time that *I* ever witnessed anything of this kind though *I* suffered from the same at Ramsgate, and was much worse. The trial in every way is so very trying, for I have lost my guide, my support, my all, *for a time*—as we can't ask or tell him anything. Many thanks for your kind letter received yesterday. We have been and are reading Von Ense's book[539] to Albert; but it is *not* worth much. He likes very much being read to as it soothes him. W. Scott is also read to him. You shall hear again to-morrow, dearest Uncle, and, please God! each day will be more cheering. Ever your devoted Niece,

Victoria R.

Queen Victoria to the King of the Belgians.

Windsor Castle, *12th December 1861.*

My beloved Uncle,—I can again report favourably of our *most* precious invalid. He maintains his ground well—had another very good night—takes plenty of nourishment, and shows surprising strength. I am constantly in and out of his room, but since the *first four dreadful* nights, *last* week, *before* they had declared it to be *gastric fever*—I do not sit up with him at night as I could be of no use; and there is nothing to cause alarm. I go out twice a day for about an hour. It is a very trying time, for a fever with its despondency, weakness, and occasional and *invariable* wandering, is most painful to witness—but we have *never* had *one unfavourable* symptom; to-morrow, reckoning from the 22nd, when dear Albert first fell ill—after going on a wet day to look at some buildings—having likewise been unusually depressed with worries of different kinds—is the *end* of the *third week*; we *may* hope for improvement *after* that, but the Doctors say they should *not* be *at all disappointed if* this did *not* take place till the *end* of the *fourth week.* I cannot sufficiently praise the skill, attention, and devotion of Dr Jenner,[540] who is the *first fever* Doctor in Europe, one may say—and good old Clark is here every day; good Brown is also *most* useful.... We have got Dr Watson[541] (who succeeded Dr Chambers[542]) and Sir H. Holland[543] has also been here. But I have kept

---

[539] The *Memoirs* of Varnhagen von Ense (1785-1858), who served for some years in the Austrian and the Russian Armies, and was later in the Prussian Diplomatic Service.

[540] Dr (afterwards Sir) William Jenner, K.C.B. (1815-1898), was at this time Physician-Extraordinary to the Queen.

[541] Afterwards Sir Thomas Watson (1792-1882), F.R.S.

[542] Dr. William Frederick Chambers (1786-1855) was well known as a consulting physician.

[543] Sir Henry Holland (1788-1873) was Physician-in-Ordinary to the Queen and the Prince Consort.

clear of these two. Albert sleeps a good deal in the day. He is moved every day into the next room on a sofa which is made up as a bed. He has only *kept* his bed entirely since Monday. Many, many thanks for your dear, kind letter of the 11th. I knew how *you* would *feel* for and think of me. I am very wonderfully supported, and, excepting on three occasions, have borne up very well. I am sure Clark will tell you so. Ever your most devoted Niece,

Victoria R.

General Grey to Sir Charles Wood.

Windsor Castle, *13th December 1861.*

My dear Wood,—The Queen desires me to acknowledge the receipt of your letter, and to say that she quite approves of the purport of your despatch to the Governor-General, understanding it to be, not that there is to be any reduction of the Artillery force which it had been determined to leave permanent in India as the proper establishment for that country, but simply that some batteries which it had been resolved to bring home, at all events, are to return somewhat sooner than had been intended, etc., etc., etc.,

Grey.

Queen Victoria to the King of the Belgians.

DEATH OF THE PRINCE

Osborne, *20th December 1861.*

My *own* dearest, kindest *Father*,—For as such have I *ever* loved you! The poor fatherless baby of eight months is now the utterly broken-hearted and crushed widow of forty-two! My *life* as a *happy* one is *ended!* the world is gone for *me!* If I *must live* on (and I will do nothing to make me worse than I am), it is henceforth for our poor fatherless children—for my unhappy country, which has lost *all* in losing him—and in *only* doing what I know and *feel* he would wish, for he *is* near me—his spirit will guide and inspire me! But oh! to be cut off in the prime of life—to see our pure, happy, quiet, domestic life, which *alone* enabled me to bear my *much* disliked position, cut off at forty-two—when I *had* hoped with such instinctive certainty that God never *would* part us, and would let us grow old together (though *he* always talked of the shortness of life)—is *too awful*, too cruel! And yet it *must* be for *his* good, his happiness! His purity was too great, his aspiration *too high* for this poor, *miserable* world! His great soul is *now only* enjoying *that* for which it *was* worthy! And I will *not* envy him—only pray that *mine* may be perfected by it and fit to be with him eternally, for which blessed moment I earnestly long. Dearest, dearest Uncle, *how* kind of you to come! It will be an unspeakable *comfort*, and you *can do* much to tell people to do what they ought to do. As for my *own good, personal* servants—poor Phipps in particular—nothing can be more devoted, heartbroken as they are, and anxious only to live as *he* wished!

Good Alice has been and is wonderful.[544]

The 26th will suit me perfectly. Ever your devoted, wretched Child,

Victoria R.

Sir Charles Wood to Queen Victoria.

DEATH OF LADY CANNING

22nd December 1861.

Sir Charles Wood, with his humble duty, begs to enclose to your Majesty two letters from India, one giving an account of Lord Canning's investing the Indian Chiefs with the Star of India; and the other an account of poor Lady Canning's illness and death, which, even at this sad moment, may not be without interest for your Majesty.

Sir Charles Wood hopes that he may be forgiven if, when having to address your Majesty, he ventures to lay before your Majesty the expression of his heartfelt sympathy in the sorrow under which your Majesty is now suffering, and his deep sense of the irreparable calamity which has befallen your Majesty and the country.

Though it cannot be any consolation, it must be gratifying to your Majesty to learn the deep and universal feeling of regret and sorrow which prevails amongst all classes of your Majesty's subjects, and in none so strongly as in those who have had the most opportunity of appreciating the inestimable value of those services, of which by this awful dispensation of Providence the country has been deprived.

[544] By a singular coincidence, the Princess was to pass away on the anniversary of the Prince's death. She died on the 14th of December 1878.

Earl Canning to Queen Victoria.

DEATH OF LADY CANNING

Barrackpore, *22nd November 1861.*[545]

Lord Canning presents his humble duty to your Majesty. Your Majesty will have heard by the last mail of the heavy blow which has fallen upon Lord Canning. The kindness of your Majesty to Lady Canning has been so invariable and so great that he feels it to be right that your Majesty should receive a sure account of her last illness with as little delay as possible.

The funeral is over. It took place quite privately at sunrise on the 19th. There is no burial-place for the Governor-General or his family, and the cemeteries at Calcutta are odious in many ways: Lord Canning has therefore set a portion of the garden at Barrackpore (fifteen miles from Calcutta) apart for the purpose. It is a beautiful spot—looking upon that reach of the grand river which she was so fond of drawing—shaded from the glare of the sun by high trees—and amongst the bright shrubs and flowers in which she had so much pleasure.

Your Majesty will be glad, but not surprised, to know of the deep respect which has been paid to her memory, not only by the familiar members of the household and intimate friends, who refused to let any hired hands perform the last offices, but by the Civil and Military bodies, and by the community at large. The coffin was conveyed to Barrackpore by the Artillery, and was borne through the Garden by English soldiers.

Lord Canning feels sure that your Majesty will not consider these details as an intrusion. He feels sure of your Majesty's kind sympathy. She loved your Majesty dearly, and Lord Canning is certain that he is doing what would have been her wish in thus venturing to write to your Majesty. In the last connected conversation which he had with her, just before the illness became really threatening, she said that she must write again to the Queen, "for I don't want her to think that it was out of laziness that I was not at Allahabad." The fact is, that she had always intended to be present at the Investiture, and had made all her arrangements to go from Darjeeling to Allahabad for the purpose; but Lord Canning, hearing of the bad state of the roads, owing to the heavy and unseasonable rains, and knowing how fatiguing an additional journey of nearly 900 miles would be, had entreated her to

[545] Received on the 22nd of December, or thereabouts.

abandon the intention, and to stay longer in the Hills, and then go straight to Calcutta. Whether all might have gone differently if the first plan had been held to, God alone knows. His will has been done.

Queen Victoria to the King of the Belgians.

A NOBLE RESOLVE

Osborne, *24th December 1861*.

My beloved Uncle,—Though, please God! I am to see you so soon, I must write these few lines to prepare you for the trying, sad existence you will find it with your poor forlorn, desolate child—who drags on a weary, pleasureless existence! I am also anxious to repeat *one* thing, and *that one* is *my firm* resolve, my *irrevocable decision*, viz. that *his* wishes—*his* plans—about everything, *his* views about *every* thing are to be *my law!* And *no human power* will make me swerve from *what he* decided and wished—and I look to *you* to *support* and *help* me in this. I apply this particularly as regards our children—Bertie, etc.—for whose future he had traced everything *so* carefully. I am *also determined* that *no one* person, may *he* be ever so good, ever so devoted among my servants—is to lead or guide or dictate *to me*. I know *how he* would disapprove it. And I live *on* with him, for him; in fact *I* am only *outwardly* separated from him, and *only* for *a time*.

No one can tell you more of my feelings, and can put you more in possession of many touching facts than our excellent Dr Jenner, who has been and is my great comfort, and whom I would *entreat* you to *see and hear* before you see *any one else*. Pray do this, for *I fear much* others trying to see you first and say things and wish for things which I *should not* consent to.

Though miserably weak and utterly shattered, my spirit rises when I think *any* wish or plan of his is to be touched or changed, or I am to be *made to do* anything. I know you will help me in my utter darkness. It is but for a short time, and *then* I go—*never, never* to part! Oh! that blessed, blessed thought! He seems so *near* to *me*, so *quite my own* now, my precious darling! God bless and preserve you. Ever your wretched but devoted Child,

Victoria R.

What a Xmas! I won't think of it.

Viscount Palmerston to Queen Victoria.

BUSINESS STILL TRANSACTED

Piccadilly, *30th December 1861.*

Viscount Palmerston presents his humble duty to your Majesty, and has read with deep emotion your Majesty's letter of the 26th, every word of which went straight to the heart. Viscount Palmerston would, however, humbly express a hope that the intensity of your Majesty's grief may not lead your Majesty to neglect your health, the preservation of which is so important for the welfare of your Majesty's children, and for that of your Majesty's devotedly attached and affectionate subjects; and which is so essentially necessary to enable your Majesty to perform those duties which it will be the object of your Majesty's life to fulfil.

Lord Granville has communicated to Viscount Palmerston your Majesty's wish that Mr Dilke[546] should be made a Baronet, and that Mr Bowring[547] should be made a Companion of the Bath, and both of these things will be done accordingly. But there are three other persons whose names Viscount Palmerston has for some time wished to submit to your Majesty for the dignity of Baronet, and if your Majesty should be graciously pleased to approve of them, the list would stand as follows:

Mr Dilke.

Mr William Brown,[548] of Liverpool, a very wealthy and distinguished merchant, who lately made a magnificent present of a public library to his fellow-citizens.

Mr Thomas Davies Lloyd, a rich and highly respectable gentleman of the county of Carnarvon.

Mr Rich, to whom the Government is under great obligation, for having of his own accord and without any condition vacated last year his seat for Richmond in Yorkshire, and having thus enabled the Government to obtain the valuable services of Mr Roundell Palmer as your Majesty's Solicitor-General.

---

[546] Sir Charles Wentworth Dilke was on the Executive Committee of the Exhibition of 1851, and on the Royal Commission for the Exhibition of 1862. He died in 1869.

[547] Mr Edgar Bowring's Companionship was conferred on him for services in connection with the earlier Exhibition. He was afterwards M.P. for Exeter, 1868-1874.

[548] Mr Brown became a baronet in 1863.

Viscount Palmerston has put into this box some private letters which Lord Russell thinks your Majesty might perhaps like to look at.

Queen Victoria to Earl Canning.

COMFORT AND HOPE

Osborne, *10th January 1862*.

Lord Canning little thought when he wrote his kind and touching letter of the 22nd November, that it would only reach the Queen when *she* was *smitten* and *bowed* down to the earth by an event similar to the one which he describes—and, strange to say, by a disease greatly analogous to the one which took from him *all* that he loved best. In the case of her adored, precious, perfect, and great husband, her dear lord and master, to whom this Nation owed more than it ever can truly know, however, the fever went on most favourably till the day previous to the awful calamity, and then it was congestion of the lungs and want of strength of circulation (the beloved Prince had always a weak and feeble pulse), which at the critical moment, indeed only two hours before God took him, caused this awful result. To lose one's partner in life is, as Lord Canning knows, like losing *half* of one's *body* and *soul*, torn forcibly away—and dear Lady Canning was such a dear, worthy, devoted wife! But to the Queen—to a poor helpless woman—it is not that only—it is the stay, support and comfort which is lost! To the Queen it is like *death* in life! Great and small—*nothing* was done without his loving advice and help—and she feels *alone* in the wide world, with many helpless children (except the Princess Royal) to look to her—and the whole nation to look to her—*now* when she can barely struggle with her wretched existence! Her misery—her utter despair—she *cannot* describe! Her *only* support—the *only* ray of comfort she gets for *a moment*, is in the *firm conviction* and certainty of his nearness, his undying love, and of their eternal reunion! Only she prays always, and pines for the latter with an anxiety she cannot describe. Like dear Lady Canning, the Queen's darling is to rest in a garden—at Frogmore, in a Mausoleum the Queen is going to build for him and herself.

Though ill, the Queen was able to tell her precious angel of Lord Canning's bereavement, and he was deeply grieved, recurring to it several times, and saying, "What a loss! She was such a distinguished person!"

May God comfort and support Lord Canning, and may he think in his sorrow of his widowed and broken-hearted Sovereign—bowed to the earth with the greatest of human sufferings and misfortunes! She lived but *for* her husband!

The sympathy of the many thousands of her subjects, but above all their sorrow and their admiration for him, are soothing to her bleeding, pierced heart!

The Queen's precious husband, though wandering occasionally, was conscious till nearly the last, and knew her and kissed her an hour before his pure spirit fled to its worthy and fit eternal Home!

Also from Benediction Books ...

Wandering Between Two Worlds: Essays on Faith and Art
Anita Mathias
Benediction Books, 2007
152 pages
ISBN: 0955373700

Available from www.amazon.com, www.amazon.co.uk

In these wide-ranging lyrical essays, Anita Mathias writes, in lush, lovely prose, of her naughty Catholic childhood in Jamshedpur, India; her large, eccentric family in Mangalore, a sea-coast town converted by the Portuguese in the sixteenth century; her rebellion and atheism as a teenager in her Himalayan boarding school, run by German missionary nuns, St. Mary's Convent, Nainital; and her abrupt religious conversion after which she entered Mother Teresa's convent in Calcutta as a novice. Later rich, elegant essays explore the dualities of her life as a writer, mother, and Christian in the United States-- Domesticity and Art, Writing and Prayer, and the experience of being "an alien and stranger" as an immigrant in America, sensing the need for roots.

About the Author

Anita Mathias is the author of *Wandering Between Two Worlds: Essays on Faith and Art.* She has a B.A. and M.A. in English from Somerville College, Oxford University, and an M.A. in Creative Writing from the Ohio State University, USA. Anita won a National Endowment of the Arts fellowship in Creative Nonfiction in 1997. She lives in Oxford, England with her husband, Roy, and her daughters, Zoe and Irene.

Visit Anita's website
http://www.anitamathias.com,
and Anita's blog
http://dreamingbeneaththespires.blogspot.com, (Dreaming Beneath the Spires).

The Church That Had Too Much
Anita Mathias
Benediction Books, 2010
52 pages
ISBN: 9781849026567

Available from www.amazon.com, www.amazon.co.uk

The Church That Had Too Much was very well-intentioned. She wanted to love God, she wanted to love people, but she was both hampered by her muchness and the abundance of her possessions, and beset by ambition, power struggles and snobbery. Read about the surprising way The Church That Had Too Much began to resolve her problems in this deceptively simple and enchanting fable.

About the Author

Anita Mathias is the author of *Wandering Between Two Worlds: Essays on Faith and Art.* She has a B.A. and M.A. in English from Somerville College, Oxford University, and an M.A. in Creative Writing from the Ohio State University, USA. Anita won a National Endowment of the Arts fellowship in Creative Nonfiction in 1997. She lives in Oxford, England with her husband, Roy, and her daughters, Zoe and Irene.

Visit Anita's website
http://www.anitamathias.com,
and Anita's blog
http://dreamingbeneaththespires.blogspot.com (Dreaming Beneath the Spires).

CPSIA information can be obtained
at www.ICGtesting.com
Printed in the USA
BVHW030047060521
606541BV00001B/7

9 781849 023795